W9-CCJ-844

EXPLORING LANGUAGE

EXPLORING LANGUAGE

EIGHTH EDITION

Edited by

Gary Goshgarian
Northeastern University

 LONGMAN

An imprint of Addison Wesley Longman, Inc.

New York • Reading, Massachusetts • Menlo Park, California • Harlow, England
Don Mills, Ontario • Sydney • Mexico City • Madrid • Amsterdam

Publishing Partner: Anne Elizabeth Smith

Developmental Editor: Lynn Walterick

Project Coordination and Text Design: Ruttle, Shaw & Wetherill, Inc.

Electronic Production Manager: Christine Pearson

Manufacturing Manager: Willie Lane

Electronic Page Makeup: Ruttle, Shaw & Wetherill, Inc.

Printer and Binder: Maple-Vail Book Manufacturing Group

Cover Printer: The Lehigh Press, Inc.

For permission to use copyrighted material, grateful acknowledgment is made to the copyright holders on pp. 573–577, which are hereby made part of this copyright page.

Library of Congress Cataloging-in-Publication Data

Exploring language/edited by Gary Goshgarian. –8th ed.
     p.   cm.
  ISBN 0-321-01219-4
   1. College readers.   2. English language–Rhetoric.   3. English
language. I. Goshgarian, Gary.
PE1417.E96   1997
808'.0427—dc21   96–45506
                                              CIP

Copyright © 1998 by Addison-Wesley Educational Publishers Inc.

All rights reserved. No part of this publication may be reproduced, stored in a retrieval system, or transmitted, in any form or by any means, electronic, mechanical, photocopying, recording, or otherwise, without the prior written permission of the publisher. Printed in the United States.

ISBN 0-321-01219-4

1 2 3 4 5 6 7 8 9 10–MA—00999897

For my sons, Nathan and David

CONTENTS

1   COMING TO LANGUAGE   1

LANGUAGE BASICS AND BEGINNINGS

Language and Thought   5
Susanne K. Langer
> "Language is the highest and most amazing achievement of the symbolistic human mind. The power it bestows is almost inestimable, for without it anything properly called 'thought' is impossible."

The Language Instinct   11
Steven Pinker
> "Language is not a cultural artifact that we learn the way we learn to tell time. . . . Instead, it is a distinct piece of the biological makeup of our brains."

A Brief History of English   19
Paul Roberts
> "In 1500 English was a minor language, spoken by a few people on a small island. Now it is perhaps the greatest language of the world. . . . "

SOME PERSONAL BEGINNINGS

Wordstruck   30
Eudora Welty
> "I live in gratitude to my parents for initiating me—and as early as I begged for it, without keeping me waiting—into knowledge of the word, into reading and spelling, by way of the alphabet."

Homemade Education   35
Malcolm X
> "In the street, I had been the most articulate hustler out there. . . . But now, trying to write simple English, I not only wasn't articulate, I wasn't even functional."

The Man That Spelt *Knife* Was a Fool   39
Johnny Connors
> Desperate to learn to read, a young Irish gypsy relates his struggles for "the little bit of knowledge" he gained.

The Language of Silence   43
Maxine Hong Kingston
> "When I went to kindergarten and had to speak English for the first time, I became silent. A dumbness—a shame—still cracks my voice in two. . . . "

Talking in the New Land   49
Edite Cunha Pedrosa
> "'Your name will be Mary Edith Cunha,' she [my teacher] declared. 'In America you only need two or three names. Mary Edith is a lovely name. And it will be easier to pronounce.' My name was . . . Maria Edite dos Anjos Cunha. I had no trouble pronouncing it."

7 LANGUAGE, GENDER, AND SEXISM   395

9   STANDARD AND NONSTANDARD ENGLISH   **519**

RHETORICAL CONTENTS

For your convenience, the following is an arrangement of the expository essays in this textbook. Because these classifications are not rigid, some essays fit more than one category.

CAUSE AND EFFECT: TELLING WHY

PERSUASION AND ARGUMENT: APPEALING TO REASON AND EMOTIONS

HUMOR AND SATIRE: MAKING US LAUGH WHILE WE THINK

Paired Essays

The essays in this text are arranged according to themes. However, several are closely related because they address similar experiences or take opposing sides on language issues. For your convenience, this table presents such paired selections.

5   LANGUAGE AND CULTURAL AND ETHNIC IDENTITY

6   SLURS, STEREOTYPES, SWEARS, AND FREE SPEECH

7   LANGUAGE, GENDER, AND SEXISM

8   DOUBLE TALK, EUPHEMISMS, AND PROFESSIONAL JARGON

9   STANDARD AND NONSTANDARD ENGLISH

PREFACE

The twentieth century draws to a close with a rumble of language controversies. Movies are under fire for celebrating dumb and dumber use of language; radio, for giving air to offensive shock-jock claims; the news media, for reporting stories in slanted prose; nighttime television, for increased use of profanity; and daytime talk shows, for rendering complex human issues in a sensational mixture of crude discourse and the latest psychobabble. Politicians are blasted for reducing intricate social issues to sound bites. Higher education is locked in First Amendment debates over what to do about incidents of hate speech—racist, sexist, and other forms of offensive discourse—on American campuses. The growing multiculturalism of American society has spawned a host of "politically correct" handbooks of nonbiased language, as well as a lot of critical backlash from conservatives. Crying cultural imperialism and racism, proponents of bilingual education go head-to-head with English-only advocates who are fighting to make English the official tongue of the nation. Advertisers have been threatened by the FCC over bloated claims for their products. And a sex-blind translation of the Bible has brought down some unholy thunder. To our north, Canada is still threatening to pull itself apart over French Quebec's insistence on independence. The former Soviet Union continues to pull itself apart in Chechnya and the Caucasus where ethnocentric forces spill blood in part over the official tongue. And in Bosnia-Herzegovinia, Rwanda, and Burundi, political euphemisms have reached an obscene new low in "ethnic cleansing."

But language news isn't all negative or fraught with conflict. There have, in fact, been some positive langauge developments, especially at home. Since the early 1990s, verbal SAT scores have been on the rise—a trend that continues in spite of television, telephones, CDs, and video games. Also, on the music scene, there's been a surprising outbreak or civility. Gangsta rap, which had plagued the airwaves with language as nasty as it wanted to be, was pronounced dead in 1996 by Dr. Dre and other original gangstas. Attesting to the vitality of American English and the inventiveness of its users, our language continues to grow. According to language historian Bill Bryson, some 20,000 new words are added to English each year. Since the last edition of this book (1995), wordsmiths have provided us with such items as *dream team*, *downsize*, *mosh pit*, *dumbing down*, and *deadbeat dad* which, for better or worse, may be with us well into the next century.

But all such language activity is not just about American English. It's about American society; it's about you and me. For language is both the prime medium of our culture and a mirror. How we express ourselves as individuals and as a society says much about us. Just as your own choice of language reflects something about your personal style, education, cultural background, origin, and values, so does the language that makes up the media, the arts, and the political and social scenes. In short, language and culture are as inextricable as the dancer and the dance.

As did its seven forerunners, this eighth edition of *Exploring Language* brings together some very readable pieces that explore the various ways in which language and American society are interconnected. Once again, the book aims to lead students to a keener understanding of how language works: how it reconstructs the real world for us, how it can be used to lead, mislead, and manipulate us. Organized by nine major langauge areas, these selections demonstrate the subtle complexities and richness of English. They also invite students to debate current social and cultural issues that are inseparable from langauge. And they serve as models for composition, representing a diversity of expository techniques: narration, illustration, definition, process analysis, argumentation, persuasion, comparison, and contrast.

NEW TO THE EIGHTH EDITION

Over a third of the material in this book is new, most of it written since 1995. Pieces that were dated or no longer useful to students and instructors were dropped. And more essays by woman and minorities were included—in fact, these pieces comprise nearly 50 percent of the book.

New Topics, New Essays　　Each of the nine sections has been updated and strengthened. Many new topics were added to the already broad spectrum covered—essays that treat English in its present relation to race and ethnic identity, debates about "politically correct" bias-free language, political propaganda, bureaucratic doublespeak, advertising, journalism, insult humor, ethnic prejudice, obscenity, slang, and other matters that suggest language's endless potential to be used and abused.

Literary Selections　　At the suggestion of instructors and their students, select poems and short fiction have been added to some of the chapters. Such selections demonstrate that language issues can be addressed in nonexpository contexts and that literature is ultimately about language. They also show how the dramatic forms can enhance understanding of complex issues. The inclusion of fiction and poetry broadens the cultural slant of the prose pieces and the students' reactions to them. And working with these pieces can help students become better readers and writers through literature.

Case Studies　　Five of the nine chapters include a "Case Study" that focuses on a particular language issue, such as black English, freedom of speech, and sexism in the Bible. In each case are clustered two or more pieces that not only take opposing views of the particular issue but that broaden understanding of the topic.

Improved Apparatus　　Almost all of the apparatus in the book has been improved and updated with great effort to create penetrating thought and stimulating assignments. Specifically, more research questions have been added to the Writing Assignments following each essay in the book.

Paired Essays and Debates A key feature of *Exploring Language* since its first edition was published in 1976 has been the debate format. Essays on emotional or controversial topics are paired with others presenting opposing views. Each of the nine chapters includes paired pieces. Some might be juxtaposed on a common obsession. For instance, in the first chapter, "Coming to Language," three people from diverse backgrounds—Eudora Welty, Malcolm X, and Irish gypsy Johnny Connors—give inspiring accounts of their discovery of the written word. Some juxtaposed pieces might be indirect debates such as adman Charles O'Neill's defense of his craft ("The Language of Advertising") and William Lutz's condemnation of the weasel language of advertisers ("With These Words I Can Sell You Anything"). Or, the debates might run head-on as in S. I. Hayakawa's "Bilingualism in America: English Should Be the *Only* Language" and James Fallow's "Viva Bilingualism," which undercuts the English-only movement's anxiety that our national tongue and unity is doomed. Or, Michiko Kakutani whose "The Word Police" directly attacks the efforts of Rosalie Maggio, author of "Bias-Free Language." Or, former President Spiro Agnew who in "English Anyone?" takes on feminists such as Alleen Pace Nilsen ("Sexism in English: A 1990s Update"). Or, Jim Quinn who in "Simonspeak" takes on language guardian John Simon ("Why Good English Is Good for You") for all his carping about slang, jargon and bad usage. Or, Nat Nentoff who goes head to head with Charles R. Lawrence over free speech versus censorship on college campuses.

Humor There is no reason why discussion of language should not be fun; nor is there any reason why writing models cannot be entertaining. Thus, many of the selections in the eighth edition of *Exploring Language* are funny. Nearly every section contains some humorous selections—pieces by well-known columnists George Will and Diane White; famous language watchers such as William Lutz, Bill Bryson, and Jim Quinn; and Pulitzer Award–winning humorists such as Dave Barry and Russell Baker. And, as always, there are more priceless headline gaffes in "Two-Headed Monsters."

Apparatus This book is not just a collection of interesting thoughts on language. The selections offer varied and solid assistance to composition students trying to develop their own writing skills. First, the essays serve as models of many different expository techniques and patterns. Second, each selection is preceded by a headnote containing useful thematic and biographical information, as well as clues to writing strategies. Third, each essay is followed by a series of "user-friendly" review questions convering both topical and rhetorical strategies. These have been designed to help students think analytically about the content and forms of the essays. In addition, there are abundant suggestions for class discussion and writing assignments aimed at helping students relate particular essays to others in the book and to their own experience.

ACKNOWLEDGMENTS

Many people behind the scenes are at the very least deserving of thanks and acknowledgment for their help with this eighth edition. It is impossible to thank all of them, but there are some for whose help I am particularly grateful. I would like, first, to thank those instructors who answered lengthy questionnaires on the effectiveness of the essays and supplied many helpful comments and suggestions: Cynthia Bates, University of California, Davis; Jim Karasiewicz, Maple Woods Community College; John Ruden, Sacramento City College; Otto Schlumpf, Clark College; Linda Toonan, University of Wisconsin, Green Bay.

A special thanks goes out to colleagues P. Carey Reid, Francis Blessington, Maryemma Graham, Anthony Triglio, and Staurt Peterfreund whose suggestions are reflected in this book. A very special thanks to Pamela B. Farrell for her continued support and to Jeanne Phoenix Laurel and Joyce Tesar of Niagara College, and Patricia Gantt of Dickinson University for their assistance in preparing some of the study apparatus.

I am also very grateful to Charles O'Neill for updating his essay, "The Language of Advertising," as he has in every edition since the first where it originally appeared. Thanks also to Edward S. Herman for updating his provocative criticism on the media in "Terrorism: Civilized and Barbaric"; and to Eugene R. August for revising his fine piece, "Real Men Don't: Anti-Male Bias in English."

To all the instructors and students who have used *Exploring Language* over the years I am enormously grateful.

To the people at Longman, especially my editor, Anne Smith, and development editor, Lynn Walterick, my warm appreciation.

Finally, to my wife Kathleen for her keen insight, her many hours of assistance, and her encouragement, once again—my loving appreciation.

GARY GOSHGARIAN

EXPLORING LANGUAGE

1 COMING TO LANGUAGE

JOHANNES KEPLER'S UPHILL BATTLE

All animals communicate—some by chemicals, some by sight, some by sound. But only humans have language. All animals behave according to genetical programs—to nest, to burrow, to spawn. But only humans are predisposed to use symbolic language. In fact, it is language that separates us from the rest of the animal kingdom. Without language humans would not be human in any important ways.

Language is the basis of all thought and the highest intellectual activity we practice. It is also the way we define ourselves—who we are as a species, as individuals, as a society, and a culture. How you use language—your word choice, your style of expression—says much about you and your value system. Even the most casual statement, whether spoken or written, could pinpoint your age group, socioeconomic class, ethnic background, education, birthplace, cultural interests, prejudices, worldliness (or lack thereof), and much more. Likewise, the success of communication between individuals tells much about the health of a society and its culture. In short, we are our language.

Language is such an intricate part of our culture that we can no more separate the two than we can a dancer from a dance. Consequently, we all too often lose sight of just how powerful the social impact of language is—how language can lead and mislead us, how it can be used to distort reality, to hurt others, to shape our perception of the world. As noted in the Preface, the goal of this book is to foster your appreciation and understanding of the many powers of language, while sharpening your own skills of expression.

LANGUAGE BASICS AND BEGINNINGS

Chapter 1 begins with a look at some fundamental aspects of language that may open your eyes to truths about it and yourself. In her essay, "Language and Thought," Susanne K. Langer examines the uniquely human phenomenon of language: symbolism. That is, the relationship between word and thought, and the difference between symbols and signs—differences that separate human from beast.

But where does our language-making ability come from? Traditionally, linguists have maintained that language is a cultural invention, the result of our responses to social situations; that we think in terms of our vocabulary, and that children must be taught new words and grammatical rules to enhance their sophistication as language users. But recent advances in language science have produced new insights as outlined in the next piece, "Language Instinct," by Steven Pinker. Taken from his popular recent book, *The Language Instinct*, the MIT professor elaborates on Darwin's claim that we produce language by instinct. He argues that children are born with a sophisticated universal grammar the way birds are born to sing songs. What is revolutionary is Pinker's claim that we do not think in terms of words as is popularly believed—that confused language is not the result of sloppy thinking, nor does the twisted language of propaganda distort our view of reality. Instead, says Pinker, we see through the words to the meaning automatically.

The next essay, "A Brief History of English," by Paul Roberts, is a captivating look at the evolution of our native language from the tongue of obscure Germanic tribes that invaded England in the sixth century A.D. to contemporary English spoken by over 350 million people around the world. Perhaps in this context we can better appreciate the historic forces of change and diversity that continue to shape American English.

SOME PERSONAL BEGINNINGS

The chapter moves from explorations of some fundamental realities about language in general and English in particular to some personal narratives. As individuals we come to language in different ways, yet we share in the magic that opens the world to us and us to it. The five essays in this section explore the ways in which people of diverse backgrounds discovered the power of the word in shaping the world and the self within it. The first is by Eudora Welty, one of America's most honored fiction writers. In "Wordstruck," the author nostalgically describes how she first came to love words, lost in the magic of books on her mother's lap.

Like Eudora Welty, Malcolm X was possessed by words. But he did not discover their power on his mother's lap or in the cozy confines of his bedroom. He came to language in a prison cell where he spent seven years of his young life. "Homemade Education," the second essay, is an inspiring account of how the one-time fiery orator and powerful black leader taught himself how to read and write, thereby liberating his mind while his body was behind bars.

The next narrative centers on a man once obsessed with seeking out the written word. In "The Man That Spelt *Knife* Was a Fool," Johnny Connors tells of the difficulties he endured as an itinerant gypsy child in England who wanted to read—difficulties that led him from night school to corner shops to the local dump.

In "The Language of Silence," bestselling author Maxine Hong Kingston describes a traumatizing debut with English. At home and in Chinese school, this daughter of immigrants came alive in the family tongue. But in American kindergarten, confused and frightened, she found no natural voice in English. Like the other Chinese girls, she instead took refuge in silence, which even today, she says, still stifles her voice.

Finally, in "Talking in the New Land," Edite Cunha Pedrosa gives an equally moving account of her struggle in a new world and language. Just seven years old and a week out of her Portuguese village, Pedrosa was told by her teacher that in

America Maria Edite dos Anjos Cunha would simply not do, that her new name was Mary Edith. With little left to lose, Pedrosa began suffering a kind of linguistic schizophrenia having to find identity in the new language and culture while holding on to that of her non–English-speaking parents. Pedrosa did not cope well with American assimilation. She found herself in limbo, at once resenting the English she had to learn and hating the Portuguese that held her back.

The final selection in the chapter is a poem by the former American poet laureate, Richard Wilbur. In his lovely piece, "The Writer," Wilbur captures some of the agony and triumph of the writing process.

LANGUAGE AND THOUGHT

Susanne K. Langer

Language is the highest achievement of the human mind. It is what separates us from the animal kingdom. It is the basis of thought because it contains the symbols of thought. How are thought and language related to each other? How do signs, which animals respond to, differ from the symbols that constitute language? This essay answers these and many more questions about language and thought. It was written by one of this century's most influential writers and philosophers, Susanne K. Langer, author of *Philosophy in a New Key* (1942), *Feeling and Form* (1953), and *Mind: An Essay in Human Feeling* (1967).

1   A symbol is not the same thing as a sign; that is a fact that psychologists and philosophers often overlook. All intelligent animals use signs; so do we. To them as well as to us sounds and smells and motions are signs of food, danger, the presence of other beings, or of rain or storm. Furthermore, some animals not only attend to signs but produce them for the benefit of others. Dogs bark at the door to be let in; rabbits thump to call each other; the cooing of doves and the growl of a wolf defending his kill are unequivocal signs of feelings and intentions to be reckoned with by other creatures.

2   We use signs just as animals do, though with considerably more elaboration. We stop at red lights and go on green; we answer calls and bells, watch the sky for coming storms, read trouble or promise or anger in each other's eyes. That is animal intelligence raised to the human level. Those of us who are dog lovers can probably all tell wonderful stories of how high our dogs have sometimes risen in the scale of clever sign interpretation and sign using.

3   A sign is anything that announces the existence or the imminence of some event, the presence of a thing or a person, or a change in the state of affairs. There are signs of the weather, signs of danger, signs of future good or evil, signs of what the past has been. In every case a sign is closely bound up with something to be noted or expected in experience. It is always a part of the situation to which it refers, though the reference may be remote in space and

time. Insofar as we are led to note or expect the signified event we are making correct use of a sign. This is the essence of rational behavior, which animals show in varying degrees. It is entirely realistic, being closely bound up with the actual objective course of history—learned by experience, and cashed in or voided by further experience.

4   If man had kept to the straight and narrow path of sign using, he would be like the other animals, though perhaps a little brighter. He would not talk, but grunt and gesticulate the point. He would make his wishes known, give warnings, perhaps develop a social system like that of bees and ants, with such a wonderful efficiency of communal enterprise that all men would have plenty to eat, warm apartments—all exactly alike and perfectly convenient—to live in, and everybody could and would sit in the sun or by the fire, as the climate demanded, not talking but just basking, with every want satisfied, most of his life. The young would romp and make love, the old would sleep, the middle-aged would do the routine work almost unconsciously and eat a great deal. But that would be the life of a social, superintelligent, purely sign-using animal.

5   To us who are human, it does not sound very glorious. We want to go places and do things, own all sorts of gadgets that we do not absolutely need, and when we sit down to take it easy we want to talk. Rights and property, social position, special talents and virtues, and above all our ideas, are what we live for. We have gone off on a tangent that takes us far away from the mere biological cycle that animal generations accomplish; and that is because we can use not only signs but symbols.

6   A symbol differs from a sign in that it does not announce the presence of the object, the being, condition, or whatnot, which is its meaning, but merely *brings this thing to mind*. It is not a mere "substitute sign" to which we react as though it were the object itself. The fact is that our reaction to hearing a person's name is quite different from our reaction to the person himself. There are certain rare cases where a symbol stands directly for its meaning: in religious experience, for instance, the Host is not only a symbol but a Presence. But symbols in the ordinary sense are not mystic. They are the same sort of thing that ordinary signs are; only they do not call our attention to something necessarily present or to be physically dealt with—they call up merely a conception of the thing they "mean."

7   The difference between a sign and a symbol is, in brief, that a sign causes us to think or act *in the face* of the thing signified, whereas a symbol causes us to think *about* the thing symbolized. Therein lies the great importance of symbolism for human life, its power to make this life so different from any other animal biography that generations of men have found it incredible to suppose that they were of purely zoological origin. A sign is always embedded in reality, in a present that emerges from the actual past and stretches to the future; but a symbol may be divorced from reality altogether. It may refer to what is not the case, to a mere idea, a figment, a dream. It serves, therefore, to liber-

ate thought from the immediate stimuli of a physically present world; and that liberation marks the essential difference between human and nonhuman mentality. Animals think, but they think *of* and *at* things; men think primarily *about* things. Words, pictures, and memory images are symbols that may be combined and varied in a thousand ways. The result is a symbolic structure whose meaning is a complex of all their respective meanings, and this kaleidoscope of *ideas* is the typical product of the human brain that we call the "stream of thought."

8   The process of transforming all direct experience into imagery or into that supreme mode of symbolic expression, language, has so completely taken possession of the human mind that it is not only a special talent but a dominant, organic need. All our sense impressions leave their traces in our memory not only as signs disposing our practical reactions in the future but also as symbols, images representing our *ideas* of things; and the tendency to manipulate ideas, to combine and abstract, mix and extend them by playing with symbols, is man's outstanding characteristic. It seems to be what his brain most naturally and spontaneously does. Therefore his primitive mental function is not judging reality, but *dreaming his desires.*

9   Dreaming is apparently a basic function of human brains, for it is free and unexhausting like our metabolism, heartbeat, and breath. It is easier to dream than not to dream, as it is easier to breathe than to refrain from breathing. The symbolic character of dreams is fairly well established. Symbol mongering, on this ineffectual, uncritical level, seems to be instinctive, the fulfillment of an elementary need rather than the purposeful exercise of a high and difficult talent.

10   The special power of man's mind rests on the evolution of this special activity, not on any transcendently high development of animal intelligence. We are not immeasurably higher than other animals; we are different. We have a biological need and with it a biological gift that they do not share.

11   Because man has not only the ability but the constant need of *conceiving* what has happened to him, what surrounds him, what is demanded of him—in short, of symbolizing nature, himself, and his hopes and fears—he has a constant and crying need of *expression.* What he cannot express, he cannot conceive; what he cannot conceive is chaos, and fills him with terror.

12   If we bear in mind this all-important craving for expression, we get a new picture of man's behavior; for from this trait spring his powers and his weaknesses. The process of symbolic transformation that all our experiences undergo is nothing more nor less than the process of *conception,* underlying the human faculties of abstraction and imagination.

13   When we are faced with a strange or difficult situation, we cannot react directly, as other creatures do, with flight, aggression, or any such simple instinctive pattern. Our whole reaction depends on how we manage to conceive the situation—whether we cast it in a definite dramatic form, whether we see it as a disaster, a challenge, a fulfillment of doom, or a fiat of the Divine Will. In

words or dreamlike images, in artistic or religious or even in cynical form, we must *construe* the events of life. There is great virtue in the figure of speech, "I can *make* nothing of it," to express a failure to understand something. Thought and memory are processes of *making* the thought content and the memory image; the pattern of our ideas is given by the symbols through which we express them. And in the course of manipulating those symbols we inevitably distort the original experience, as we abstract certain features of it, embroider and reinforce those features with other ideas, until the conception we project on the screen of memory is quite different from anything in our real history.

14   Conception is a necessary and elementary process; what we do with our conceptions is another story. That is the entire history of human culture—of intelligence and morality, folly and superstition, ritual, language, and the arts—all the phenomena that set man apart from, and above, the rest of the animal kingdom. As the religious mind has to make all human history a drama of sin and salvation in order to define its own moral attitudes, so a scientist wrestles with the mere presentation of "the facts" before he can reason about them. The process of *envisaging* facts, values, hopes, and fears underlies our whole behavior pattern; and this process is reflected in the evolution of an extraordinary phenomenon found always, and only, in human societies—the phenomenon of language.

15   Language is the highest and most amazing achievement of the symbolistic human mind. The power it bestows is almost inestimable, for without it anything properly called "thought" is impossible. The birth of language is the dawn of humanity. The line between man and beast—between the highest ape and the lowest savage—is the language line. Whether the primitive Neanderthal man was anthropoid or human depends less on his cranial capacity, his upright posture, or even his use of tools and fire, than on one issue we shall probably never be able to settle—whether or not he spoke.

16   In all physical traits and practical responses, such as skills and visual judgments, we can find a certain continuity between animal and human mentality. Sign using is an ever evolving, ever improving function throughout the whole animal kingdom, from the lowly worm that shrinks into his hole at the sound of an approaching foot, to the dog obeying his master's command, and even to the learned scientist who watches the movements of an index needle.

17   This continuity of the sign-using talent has led psychologists to the belief that language is evolved from the vocal expressions, grunts and coos and cries, whereby animals vent their feelings or signal their fellows; that man has elaborated this sort of communion to the point where it makes a perfect exchange of ideas possible.

18   I do not believe that this doctrine of the origin of language is correct. The essence of language is symbolic, not signific; we use it first and most vitally to formulate and hold ideas in our own minds. Conception, not social control, is its first and foremost benefit.

19   Watch a young child that is just learning to speak play with a toy; he says the name of the object, e.g.: "Horsey! horsey! horsey!" over and over again, looks at the object, moves it, always saying the name to himself or to the world at large. It's quite a time before he talks to anyone in particular; he talks first of all to himself. This is his way of forming and fixing the *conception* of the object in his mind, and around this conception all his knowledge of it grows. *Names* are the essence of language; for the *name* is what abstracts the conception of the horse from the horse itself, and lets the mere idea recur at the speaking of the name. This permits the conception gathered from one horse experience to be exemplified again by another instance of a horse, so that the notion embodied in the name is a general notion.

20   To this end, the baby uses a word long before he *asks* for the object; when he wants his horsey he is likely to cry and fret, because he is reacting to an actual environment, not forming ideas. He uses the animal language of *signs* for his wants; talking is still a purely symbolic process—its practical value has not really impressed him yet.

21   Language need not be vocal; it may be purely visual, like written language, or even tactual, like the deaf-mute system of speech; but it *must be denotative.* The sounds, intended or unintended, whereby animals communicate do not constitute a language because they are signs, not names. They never fall into an organic pattern, a meaningful syntax of even the most rudimentary sort, as all language seems to do with a sort of driving necessity. That is because signs refer to actual situations, in which things have obvious relations to each other that require only to be noted; but symbols refer to ideas, which are not physically there for inspection, so their connections and features have to be represented. This gives all true language a natural tendency toward growth and development, which seems almost like a life of its own. Languages are not invented; they grow with our need for expression.

22   In contrast, animal "speech" never has a structure. It is merely an emotional response. Apes may greet their ration of yams with a shout of "Nga!" But they do not say "Nga" between meals. If they could *talk about* their yams instead of just saluting them, they would be the most primitive men instead of the most anthropoid of beasts. They would have ideas, and tell each other things true or false, rational or irrational; they would make plans and invent laws and sing their own praises, as men do.

TOPICAL CONSIDERATIONS

1. Langer's opening statement is "A symbol is not the same thing as a sign." In your own words, what is the difference between signs and symbols? Give examples from your own experience.

2. What would human beings be like if they used only signs? What would be the state of human communications?

3. Langer says that animals communicate in signs alone, but recent scientific studies have shown that dolphins use sonar to relay messages. Does that mean that Langer's hypothesis is invalid, or does it mean it needs modification?

4. Which do we depend more on, signs of symbols? Which are we most apt to misconstrue? Give some examples to explain your answer. Can you think of any words that function as both signs and symbols?

5. According to Langer, how did language develop?

6. Langer says that symbols cause us to think about the thing symbolized. What do the following symbols make us think about, or what messages are communicated by them? Clothes with alligator trademarks on them; a dorm windowsill stacked with beer cans; a shark-tooth pendant; a peace sign window decal; a large black motorcycle; a swastika; a happy-face lapel button.

RHETORICAL CONSIDERATIONS

1. What is Langer's thesis? Where does she state it?

2. In the opening paragraphs, Langer uses comparison to clarify the difference between signs and symbols. What comparisons does she specifically use? How effective are they in helping the reader understand her points?

3. In paragraph 2, Langer gives some examples of signs, yet she waits until paragraph 3 to define *sign*. Why do you think she uses this strategy? Is it effective for her purposes?

4. How many examples of symbols does Langer give in the first six paragraphs? Do you think she should have given more? Why, or why not?

WRITING ASSIGNMENTS

1. Write a paper entitled "A Sign of the Times" in which you choose and discuss an appropriate sign of the state of today's world.

2. Write a paper entitled "A Symbol of the Times" in which you choose and discuss an appropriate symbol of the state of today's world.

3. Write an essay describing all the different symbols and signs you responded to in getting to class today.

4. The very clothes we wear convey symbolic messages of some sort—socioeconomic status, awareness, worldiness, imperviousness, sometimes even political statements. Describe some of the messages you like to project through your choice of clothing, boots, shoes, jewelry, and so on.

THE LANGUAGE INSTINCT

Steven Pinker

As Susanne K. Langer explained, language is the quintessential example of humankind's capacity to use symbols—and what, among other
things, distinguishes us from other animals. But is language a cultural
invention of our species as is commonly believed? Not so, says linguist
and author Steven Pinker. In this essay, Pinker takes issue with the
popular wisdom that language is an artifact of our ancient culture—an
invention. Instead he makes the claim that we produce language as spiders spin webs—as the result of an instinct. He believes that we are
born with the ability to communicate, not that we learn to do so as the
result of imitation or instruction.

Steven Pinker is a professor of linguistics at the Massachusetts Institute of Technology. This essay is excerpted from his popular book *The
Language Instinct* (1994).

1   As you are reading these words, you are taking part in one of the wonders of
the natural world. For you and I belong to a species with a remarkable ability:
we can shape events in each other's brains with exquisite precision. I am not
referring to telepathy or mind control or the other obsessions of fringe science; even in the depictions of believers these are blunt instruments compared to an ability that is uncontroversially present in every one of us. That
ability is language. Simply by making noises with our mouths, we can reliably
cause precise new combinations of ideas to arise in each other's minds. The
ability comes so naturally that we are apt to forget what a miracle it is. So let
me remind you with some simple demonstrations. Asking you only to surrender your imagination to my words for a few moments, I can cause you to think
some very specific thoughts:

> When a male octopus spots a female, his normally grayish body suddenly becomes
> striped. He swims above the female and begins caressing her with seven of his
> arms. If she allows this, he will quickly reach toward her and slip his eighth arm into
> her breathing tube. A series of sperm packets moves slowly through a groove in his
> arm, finally to slip into the mantle cavity of the female.

> Cherries jubilee on a white suit? Wine on an altar cloth? Apply club soda immedi-
> ately. It works beautifully to remove the stains from fabrics.

When Dixie opens the door to Tad, she is stunned, because she thought he was dead. She slams it in his face and then tries to escape. However, when Tad says, "I love you," she lets him in. Tad comforts her, and they become passionate. When Brian interrupts, Dixie tells a stunned Tad that she and Brian were married earlier that day. With much difficulty, Dixie informs Brian that things are nowhere near finished between her and Tad. Then she spills the news that Jamie is Tad's son. "My what?" says a shocked Tad.

2   Think about what these words have done. I did not simply remind you of octopuses; in the unlikely event that you ever see one develop stripes, you now know what will happen next. Perhaps the next time you are in a supermarket you will look for club soda, one out of the tens of thousands of items available, and then not touch it until months later when a particular substance and a particular object accidentally come together. You now share with millions of other people the secrets of protagonists in a world that is the product of some stranger's imagination, the daytime drama *All My Children*. True, my demonstrations depended on our ability to read and write, and this makes our communication even more impressive by bridging gaps of time, space, and acquaintanceship. But writing is clearly an optional accessory; the real engine of verbal communication is the spoken language we acquired as children.

3   In any natural history of the human species, language would stand out as the preeminent trait. To be sure, a solitary human is an impressive problem-solver and engineer. But a race of Robinson Crusoes would not give an extraterrestrial observer all that much to remark on. What is truly arresting about our kind is better captured in the story of the Tower of Babel, in which humanity, speaking a single language, came so close to reaching heaven that God himself felt threatened. A common language connects the members of a community into an information-sharing network with formidable collective powers. Anyone can benefit from the strokes of genius, lucky accidents, and trial-and-error wisdom accumulated by anyone else, present or past. And people can work in teams, their efforts coordinated by negotiated agreements. As a result, *Homo sapiens* is a species, like blue-green algae and earthworms, that has wrought far-reaching changes on the planet. Archeologists have discovered the bones of ten thousand wild horses at the bottom of a cliff in France, the remains of herds stampeded over the clifftop by groups of paleolithic hunters seventeen thousand years ago. These fossils of ancient cooperation and shared ingenuity may shed light on why saber-tooth tigers, mastodons, giant woolly rhinoceroses, and dozens of other large mammals went extinct around the time that modern humans arrived in their habitats. Our ancestors, apparently, killed them off.

4   Language is so tightly woven into human experience that it is scarcely possible to imagine life without it. Chances are that if you find two or more people together anywhere on earth, they will soon be exchanging words. When there is no one to talk with, people talk to themselves, to their dogs, even to their plants. In our social relations, the race is not to the swift but to the

verbal—the spellbinding orator, the silver-tongued seducer, the persuasive child who wins the battle of wills against a brawnier parent. Aphasia, the loss of language following brain injury, is devastating, and in severe cases family members may feel that the whole person is lost forever.

5 . . . Language is not a cultural artifact that we learn the way we learn to tell time or how the federal government works. Instead, it is a distinct piece of the biological makeup of our brains. Language is a complex, specialized skill, which develops in the child spontaneously, without conscious effort or formal instruction, is deployed without awareness of its underlying logic, is qualitatively the same in every individual, and is distinct from more general abilities to process information or behave intelligently. For these reasons some cognitive scientists have described language as a psychological faculty, a mental organ, a neutral system, and a computational module. But I prefer the admittedly quaint term "instinct." It conveys the idea that people know how to talk in more or less the sense that spiders know how to spin webs. Web-spinning was not invented by some unsung spider genius and does not depend on having had the right education or on having an aptitude for architecture or the construction trades. Rather, spiders spin spider webs because they have spider brains, which give them the urge to spin and the competence to succeed. Although there are differences between webs and words, I will encourage you to see language in this way, for it helps to make sense of the phenomena we will explore.

6 Thinking of language as an instinct inverts the popular wisdom, especially as it has been passed down in the canon of the humanities and social sciences. Language is no more a cultural invention than is upright posture. It is not a manifestation of a general capacity to use symbols: a three-year-old . . . is a grammatical genius, but is quite incompetent at the visual arts, religious iconography, traffic signs, and the other staples of the semiotics curriculum. Though language is a magnificent ability unique to *Homo sapiens* among living species, it does not call for sequestering the study of humans from the domain of biology, for a magnificent ability unique to a particular living species is far from unique in the animal kingdom. Some kinds of bats home in on flying insects using Doppler sonar. Some kinds of migratory birds navigate thousands of miles by calibrating the positions of the constellations against the time of day and year. In nature's talent show we are simply a species of primate with our own act, a knack for communicating information about who did what to whom by modulating the sounds we make when we exhale.

7 Once you begin to look at language not as the ineffable essence of human uniqueness but as a biological adaptation to communicate information, it is no longer as tempting to see language as an insidious shaper of thought, and, . . . it is not. Moreover, seeing language as one of nature's engineering marvels—an organ with "that perfection of structure and co-adaptation which justly excites our admiration," in Darwin's words—gives us a new respect for your ordinary Joe and the much-maligned English language (or any language). The

complexity of language, from the scientist's point of view, is part of our biological birthright; it is not something that parents teach their children or something that must be elaborated in school—as Oscar Wilde said, "Education is an admirable thing, but it is well to remember from time to time that nothing that is worth knowing can be taught." A preschooler's tacit knowledge of grammar is more sophisticated than the thickest style manual or the most state-of-the-art computer language system, and the same applies to all healthy human beings, even the notorious syntax-fracturing professional athlete and the, you know, like, inarticulate teenage skateboarder. . . .

8   The conception of language as a kind of instinct was first articulated in 1871 by Darwin himself. In *The Descent of Man* he had to contend with language because its confinement to humans seemed to present a challenge to his theory. As in all matters, his observations are uncannily modern:

> As . . . one of the founders of the noble science of philology observes, language is an art, like brewing or baking; but writing would have been a better simile. It certainly is not a true instinct, for every language has to be learned. It differs, however, widely from all ordinary arts, for man has an instinctive tendency to speak, as we see in the babble of our young children; while no child has an instinctive tendency to brew, bake, or write. Moreover, no philologist now supposes that any language has been deliberately invented; it has been slowly and unconsciously developed by many steps.

Darwin concluded that language ability is "an instinctive tendency to acquire an art," a design that is not peculiar to humans but seen in other species such as song-learning birds.

9   A language instinct may seem jarring to those who think of language as the zenith of the human intellect and who think of instincts as brute impulses that compel furry or feathered zombies to build a dam or up and fly south. But one of Darwin's followers, William James, noted that an instinct possessor need not act as a "fatal automaton." He argued that we have all the instincts that animals do, and many more besides; our flexible intelligence comes from the interplay of many instincts competing. Indeed, the instinctive nature of human thought is just what makes it so hard for us to see that it is an instinct:

> It takes . . . a mind debauched by learning to carry the process of making the natural seem strange, so far as to ask for the *why* of any instinctive human act. To the metaphysician alone can such questions occur as: Why do we smile, when pleased, and now scowl? Why are we unable to talk to a crowd as we talk to a single friend? Why does a particular maiden turn our wits so upside-down? The common man can only say, "*Of course* we smile, *of course* our heart palpitates at the sight of the crowd, *of course* we love the maiden, that beautiful soul clad in that perfect form, so palpably and flagrantly made for all eternity to be loved!"
>
> And so, probably, does each animal feel about the particular things it tends to do in presence of particular objects. . . . To the lion it is the lioness which is made to be loved; to the bear, the she-bear. To the broody hen the notion would probably seem monstrous that there should be a creature in the world to whom a nestful of

eggs was not the utterly fascinating and precious and never-to-be-too-much-sat-upon object which it is to her.

Thus we may be sure that, however mysterious some animals' instincts may appear to us, our instincts will appear no less mysterious to them. And we may conclude that, to the animal which obeys it, every impulse and every step of every instinct shines with its own sufficient light, and seems at the moment the only eternally right and proper thing to do. What voluptuous thrill may not shake a fly, when she at last discovers the one particular leaf, or carrion, or bit of dung, that out of all the world can stimulate her ovipositor to its discharge? Does not the discharge then seem to her the only fitting thing? And need she care or know anything about the future maggot and its food?

10   I can think of no better statement of my main goal. The workings of language are as far from our awareness as the rationale for egg-laying is from the fly's. Our thoughts come out of our mouths so effortlessly that they often embarrass us, having eluded our mental censors. When we are comprehending sentences, the stream of words is transparent; we see through to the meaning so automatically that we can forget that a movie is in a foreign language and subtitled. We think children pick up their mother tongue by imitating their mothers, but when a child says *Don't giggle me!* or *We holded the baby rabbits,* it cannot be an act of imitation. I want to debauch your mind with learning, to make these natural gifts seem strange, to get you to ask the "why" and "how" of these seemingly homely abilities. Watch an immigrant struggling with a second language or a stroke patient with a first one, or deconstruct a snatch of baby talk, or try to program a computer to understand English, and ordinary speech begins to look different. The effortlessness, the transparency, the automaticity are illusions, masking a system of great richness and beauty.

11   In this century, the most famous argument that language is like an instinct comes from Noam Chomsky, the linguist who first unmasked the intricacy of the system and perhaps the person most responsible for the modern revolution in language and cognitive science. . . . Chomsky called attention to two fundamental facts about language. First, virtually every sentence that a person utters or understands is a brand-new combination of words, appearing for the first time in the history of the universe. Therefore a language cannot be a repertoire of responses; the brain must contain a recipe or program that can build an unlimited set of sentences out of a finite list of words. That program may be called a mental grammar (not to be confused with pedagogical or stylistic "grammars," which are just guides to the etiquette of written prose). The second fundamental fact is that children develop these complex grammars rapidly and without formal instruction and grow up to give consistent interpretations to novel sentence constructions that they have never before encountered. Therefore, he argued, children must innately be equipped with a plan common to the grammars of all languages, a Universal Grammar, that tells them how to distill the syntactic patterns out of the speech of their parents. Chomsky put it as follows:

It is a curious fact about the intellectual history of the past few centuries that physical and mental development have been approached in quite different ways. No one would take seriously the proposal that the human organism learns through experience to have arms rather than wings, or that the basic structure of particular organs results from accidental experience. Rather, it is taken for granted that the physical structure of the organism is genetically determined, though of course variation along such dimensions as size, rate of development, and so forth will depend in part on external factors. . . .

The development of personality, behavior patterns, and cognitive structures in higher organisms has often been approached in a very different way. It is generally assumed that in these domains, social environment is the dominant factor. The structures of mind that develop over time are taken to be arbitrary and accidental; there is no "human nature" apart from what develops as a specific historical product. . . .

But human cognitive systems, when seriously investigated, prove to be no less marvelous and intricate than the physical structures that develop in the life of the organism. Why, then, should we not study the acquisition of a cognitive structure such as language more or less as we study some complex bodily organ?

At first glance, the proposal may seem absurd, if only because of the great variety of human languages. But a closer consideration dispels these doubts. Even knowing very little of substance about linguistic universals, we can be quite sure that the possible variety of language is sharply limited. . . . The language each person acquires is a rich and complex construction hopelessly underdetermined by the fragmentary evidence available [to the child]. Nevertheless individuals in a speech community have developed essentially the same language. This fact can be explained only on the assumption that these individuals employ highly restrictive principles that guide the construction of grammar.

12   By performing painstaking technical analyses of the sentences ordinary people accept as part of their mother tongue, Chomsky and other linguists developed theories of the mental grammars underlying people's knowledge of particular languages and of the Universal Grammar underlying the particular grammars. . . .

TOPICAL CONSIDERATIONS

1. In paragraphs 1 and 2, Pinker describes language as verbal (oral) noise that transmits precise combinations of ideas into other people's minds. Do you agree or disagree with this description? How could language not be verbal noise? How could it fail to transmit ideas to other people's minds?

2. In paragraph 5, Pinker claims that language "develops in the child spontaneously, without conscious effort or formal instruction." Do you agree with this claim? If you lock this hypothetical child in a room alone, will he or she develop language? If not, what is missing?

3. In paragraphs 5–7, why does Pinker say that language is not a cultural invention, or a cultural artifact? If it is not a cultural invention, then what is it? What evidence does Pinker supply for the argument that language is an instinct, rather than an invention? What analogies to other animals does he use?

4. According to Pinker (paragraph 9), why do we find the idea of language as instinct difficult to swallow? How could admitting that human language is instinct make us seem like robots (automatons)? What evidence does Pinker use to show that human beings need not perceive themselves as predetermined to act in a certain way?

5. According to Noam Chomsky, what two important facts of language help to show that language is an instinct, or that a "plan common to the grammars of all languages, a Universal Grammar" is biologically programmed into all human brains?

6. What is Pinker describing when he uses the term "language"? Is he talking about a specific language, such as English, or Japanese, or American Sign Language? Or is he using the word in a different way? Can you write a clear definition of what he means by "language"?

RHETORICAL CONSIDERATIONS

1. What is the purpose of the first passage of indented quoted material? What is the source for this passage? How does the style of each paragraph differ—what kinds of writing does each illustrate? How does this indented passage differ from the three long quoted passages Pinker uses later?

2. Why does Pinker provide examples in paragraphs 3 and 4 of the ways that human beings have used language? What kinds of activities does language make possible? How does this information help make his discussion seem important to readers who have never considered language as an instinct?

3. Describe how the style of the intended quotations in paragraph 8 differs from Pinker's own writing. How effective is each quoted passage? Do you think that Pinker is justified in quoting so extensively? If not, can you think of effective ways to paraphrase or edit these using ellipses?

4. Does the William James quote in paragraph 9 help to allay readers' fears that calling language an instinct makes us behave in a robotlike fashion? If not, what is unsatisfying about Pinker's placement of this quote?

5. What is Pinker's tone in this article, and his sense of reader expectations? Does he write for scientists, general readers, or some other audience? How does he want to make his readers feel about the subject matter he discusses? How can you tell? Select evidence to justify your answer.

WRITING ASSIGNMENTS

1. How do Pinker's ideas differ from Susanne K. Langer's in her essay, "Language and Thought"? Specifically, what does each author believe about language's ability to refer to a reality "out there," rather than a symbolic reality? What does each author say about children's development of language? In your opinion, which author offers a more convincing argument, and why?

2. Using your library's resources, examine scientific or journalistic literature on the efforts human beings have made to communicate in language with animals, such as gorillas or porpoises—or to figure out whether animals such as whales are communicating with each other in language. How would Pinker need to account for

these efforts and possible successes? Would such examples change anything about his argument? Why or why not?

3. Using your school's library, research the origins and development of American Sign Language. How does this system of communication qualify as "a language" according to Pinker's discussion? How would Pinker have to change his assumptions about language and its development in children if he were to consider this example of a language that does not involve communicating through voice?

A BRIEF HISTORY OF ENGLISH

Paul Roberts

Nobody knows exactly how languages began, but as Paul Roberts explains in this famous essay, language development is best understood if we examine historical change. With an engaging storytelling flair, Roberts makes accessible a long and complicated evolution, tracing fourteen hundred turbulent years as English rose from its Anglo-Saxon roots to become a literary standard spoken by 350 million people around the world today. As Roberts's brief history makes clear, some of the same forces of change continue to operate. Everyday English picks up new words, redefines old ones, and grows in dialectal diversity.

Paul Roberts was a well-known linguist and the author of several books on English history and grammar, including *Patterns of English* (1956) and *Understanding English* (1958), from which this essay is taken.

1 No understanding of the English language can be very satisfactory without a notion of the history of the language. But we shall have to make do with just a notion. The history of English is long and complicated, and we can only hit the high spots.

2 The history of our language begins a little after A.D. 600. Everything before that is pre-history, which means that we can guess at it but can't prove much. For a thousand years or so before the birth of Christ our linguistic ancestors were savages wandering through the forests of northern Europe. Their language was a part of the Germanic branch of the Indo-European family.

3 At the time of the Roman Empire—say, from the beginning of the Christian Era to around A.D. 400—the speakers of what was to become English were scattered along the northern coast of Europe. They spoke a dialect of Low German. More exactly, they spoke several different dialects, since they were several different tribes. The names given to the tribes who got to England are *Angles, Saxons,* and *Jutes.* For convenience, we can refer to them all as Anglo-Saxons.

4 Their first contact with civilization was a rather thin acquaintance with the Roman Empire on whose borders they lived. Probably some of the Anglo-Saxons wandered into the Empire occasionally, and certainly Roman mer-

chants and traders traveled among the tribes. At any rate, this period saw the first of our many borrowings from Latin. Such words as *kettle, wine, cheese, butter, cheap, plum, gem, bishop, church* were borrowed at this time. They show something of the relationship of the Anglo-Saxons with the Romans. The Anglo-Saxons were learning, getting their first taste of civilization.

5   They still had a long way to go, however, and their first step was to help smash the civilization they were learning from. In the fourth century the Roman power weakened badly. While the Goths were pounding away at the Romans in the Mediterranean countries, their relatives, the Anglo-Saxons, began to attack Britain.

6   The Romans had been the ruling power in Britain since A.D. 43. They had subjugated the Celts whom they found living there and had succeeded in setting up a Roman administration. The Roman influence did not extend to the outlying parts of the British Isles. In Scotland, Wales, and Ireland the Celts remained free and wild, and they made periodic forays against the Romans in England. Among other defense measures, the Romans built the famous Roman Wall to ward off the tribes in the north.

7   Even in England the Roman power was thin. Latin did not become the language of the country as it did in Gaul and Spain. The mass of people continued to speak Celtic, with Latin and the Roman civilization it contained in use as a top dressing.

8   In the fourth century, troubles multiplied for the Romans in Britain. Not only did the untamed tribes of Scotland and Wales grow more and more restive, but the Anglo-Saxons began to make pirate raids on the eastern coast. Furthermore, there was growing difficulty everywhere in the Empire, and the legions in Britain were siphoned off to fight elsewhere. Finally, in A.D. 410, the last Roman ruler in England, bent on becoming emperor, left the islands and took the last of the legions with him. The Celts were left in possession of Britain but almost defenseless against the impending Anglo-Saxon attack.

9   Not much is surely known about the arrival of the Anglo-Saxons in England. According to the best early source, the eighth-century historian Bede, the Jutes came in 449 in response to a plea from the Celtic king, Vortigern, who wanted their help against the Picts attacking from the north. The Jutes subdued the Picts but then quarreled and fought with Vortigern, and, with reinforcements from the Continent, settled permanently in Kent. Somewhat later the Angles established themselves in eastern England and the Saxons in the south and west. Bede's account is plausible enough, and these were probably the main lines of the invasion.

10   We do know, however, that the Angles, Saxons, and Jutes were a long time securing themselves in England. Fighting went on for as long as a hundred years before the Celts in England were all killed, driven into Wales, or reduced to slavery. This is the period of King Arthur, who was not entirely mythological. He was a Romanized Celt, a general, though probably not a king. He had some success against the Anglo-Saxons, but it was only tempo-

rary. By 550 or so the Anglo-Saxons were firmly established. English was in England.

11   All this is pre-history, so far as the language is concerned. We have no record of the English language until after 600, when the Anglo-Saxons were converted to Christianity and learned the Latin alphabet. The conversion began, to be precise, in the year 597 and was accomplished within thirty or forty years. The conversion was a great advance for the Anglo-Saxons, not only because of the spiritual benefits but because it reestablished contact with what remained of Roman civilization. This civilization didn't amount to much in the year 600, but it was certainly superior to anything in England up to that time.

12   It is customary to divide the history of the English language into three periods: Old English, Middle English, and Modern English. Old English runs from the earliest records—i.e., seventh century—to about 1100; Middle English from 1100 to 1450 or 1500; Modern English from 1500 to the present day. Sometimes Modern English is further divided into Early Modern, 1500–1700, and Late Modern, 1700 to the present.

13   When England came into history, it was divided into several more or less autonomous kingdoms, some of which at times exercised a certain amount of control over the others. In the century after the conversion the most advanced kingdom was Northumbria, the area between the Humber River and the Scottish border. By A.D. 700 the Northumbrians had developed a respectable civilization, the finest in Europe. It is sometimes called the Northumbrian Renaissance, and it was the first of the several renaissances through which Europe struggled upward out of the ruins of the Roman Empire. It was in this period that the best of the Old English literature was written, including the epic poem *Beowulf*.

14   In the eighth century, Northumbrian power declined, and the center of influence moved southward to Mercia, the kingdom of the Midlands. A century later the center shifted again, and Wessex, the country of the West Saxons, became the leading power. The most famous king of the West Saxons was Alfred the Great, who reigned in the second half of the ninth century, dying in 901. He was famous not only as a military man and administrator but also as a champion of learning. He founded and supported schools and translated or caused to be translated many books from Latin into English. At this time also much of the Northumbrian literature of two centuries earlier was copied in West Saxon. Indeed, the great bulk of Old English writing which has come down to us is in the West Saxon dialect of 900 or later.

15   In the military sphere, Alfred's great accomplishment was his successful opposition to the Viking invasions. In the ninth and tenth centuries, the Norsemen emerged in their ships from their homelands in Denmark and the Scandinavian peninsula. They traveled far and attacked and plundered at will and almost with impunity. They ravaged Italy and Greece, settled in France, Russia, and Ireland, colonized Iceland and Greenland, and discovered America several centuries before Columbus. Nor did they overlook England.

16   After many years of hit-and-run raids, the Norsemen landed an army on the east coast of England in the year 866. There was nothing much to oppose them except the Wessex power led by Alfred. The long struggle ended in 877 with a treaty by which a line was drawn roughly from the northwest of England to the southeast. On the eastern side of the line Norse rule was to prevail. This was called the Danelaw. The western side was to be governed by Wessex.

17   The linguistic result of all this was a considerable injection of Norse into the English language. Norse was at this time not so different from English as Norwegian or Danish is now. Probably speakers of English could understand, more or less, the language of the newcomers who had moved into eastern England. At any rate, there was considerable interchange and word borrowing. Examples of Norse words in the English language are *sky, give, law, egg, outlaw, leg, ugly, scant, sly, crawl, scowl, take, thrust*. There are hundreds more. We have even borrowed some pronouns from Norse—*they, their,* and *them.* These words were borrowed first by the eastern and northern dialects and then in the course of hundreds of years made their way into English generally.

18   It is supposed also—indeed, it must be true—that the Norsemen influenced the sound structure and the grammar of English. But this is hard to demonstrate in detail.

19   We may now have an example of Old English. The favorite illustration is the Lord's Prayer, since it needs no translation. This has come to us in several different versions. Here is one:

> Fæder ure [thorn]u[eth]e eart on heofonum si [thorn]in nama gehalgod. Tobecume [thorn]in rice. Gewur[eth]e [thorn]in willa on eor[eth]an swa swa on heofonum. Urne gedæghwamlican hlaf syle us to dæg. And forgyf us ure gyltas swa swa we forgyfa[thorn] urum glytendum. And ne gelæd [thorn]u us on costnunge ac alys us of yfele. So[eth]lice.

20   Some of the differences between this and Modern English are merely differences in orthography. For instance, the sign æ is what Old English writers used for a vowel sound like that in modern *hat* or *and.* The *th* sounds of modern *thin* or *then* are represented in Old English by [thorn] or [eth]. But of course there are many differences in sound too. *Ure* is the ancestor of modern *our,* but the first vowel was like that in *too* or *ooze. Hlaf* is modern *loaf;* we have dropped the *h* sound and changed the vowel, which in *hlaf* was pronounced something like the vowel in *father.* Old English had some sounds which we do not have. The sound represented by *y* does not occur in Modern English. If you pronounce the vowel in *bit* with your lips rounded, you may approach it.

21   In grammar, Old English was much more highly inflected than Modern English is. That is, there were more case endings for nouns, more person and number endings for verbs, a more complicated pronoun system, various endings for adjectives, and so on. Old English nouns had four cases—nominative, genitive, dative, accusative. Adjectives had five—all these and an instrumental

case besides. Present-day English has only two cases for nouns—common case and possessive case. Adjectives now have no case system at all. On the other hand, we now use a more rigid word order and more structure words (prepositions, auxiliaries, and the like) to express relationships than Old English did.

22   Some of this grammar we can see in the Lord's Prayer. *Heofonum,* for instance, is a dative plural; the nominative singular was *heofon. Urne* is an accusative singular; the nominative is *ure.* In *urum gyltendum* both words are dative plural. *Forgyfaþ* is the third person plural form of the verb. Word order is different: "urne gedæghwamlican hlaf syle us" in place of "Give us our daily bread." And so on.

23   In vocabulary Old English is quite different from Modern English. Most of the Old English words are what we may call native English: that is, words which have not been borrowed from other languages but which have been a part of English ever since English was a part of Indo-European. Old English did certainly contain borrowed words. We have seen that many borrowings were coming in from Norse. Rather large numbers had been borrowed from Latin, too. Some of these were taken while the Anglo-Saxons were still on the Continent (*cheese, butter, bishop, kettle,* etc.); a large number came into English after Conversion (*angel, candle, priest, martyr, radish, oyster, purple, school, spend,* etc.). But the great majority of Old English words were native English.

24   Now, on the contrary, the majority of words in English are borrowed, taken mostly from Latin and French. Of the words in *The American College Dictionary* only about 14 percent are native. Most of these, to be sure, are common, high-frequency words—*the, of, I, and, because, man, mother, road,* etc.; of the thousand most common words in English, some 62 percent are native English. Even so, the modern vocabulary is very much Latinized and Frenchified. The Old English vocabulary was not.

25   Sometime between the year 1000 and 1200 various important changes took place in the structure of English, and Old English became Middle English. The political event which facilitated these changes was the Norman Conquest. The Normans, as the name shows, came originally from Scandinavia. In the early tenth century they established themselves in northern France, adopted the French language, and developed a vigorous kingdom and a very passable civilization. In the year 1066, led by Duke William, they crossed the Channel and made themselves masters of England. For the next several hundred years, England was ruled by kings whose first language was French.

26   One might wonder why, after the Norman Conquest, French did not become the national language, replacing English entirely. The reason is that the Conquest was not a national migration, as the earlier Anglo-Saxon invasion had been. Great numbers of Normans came to England, but they came as rulers and landlords. French became the language of the court, the language of the nobility, the language of polite society, the language of literature. But it

did not replace English as the language of the people. There must always have been hundreds of towns and villages in which French was never heard except when visitors of high station passed through.

27   But English, though it survived as the national language, was profoundly changed after the Norman Conquest. Some of the changes—in sound structure and grammar—would no doubt have taken place whether there had been a Conquest or not. Even before 1066 the case system of English nouns and adjectives was becoming simplified; people came to rely more on word order and prepositions than on inflectional endings to communicate their meanings. The process was speeded up by sound changes which caused many of the endings to sound alike. But no doubt the Conquest facilitated the change. German, which didn't experience a Normal Conquest, is today rather highly inflected compared to its cousin English.

28   But it is in vocabulary that the effects of the Conquest are most obvious. French ceased, after a hundred years or so, to be the native language of very many people in England, but it continued—and continues still—to be a zealously cultivated second language, the mirror of elegance and civilization. When one spoke English, one introduced not only French ideas and French things but also their French names. This was not only easy but socially useful. To pepper one's conversation with French expressions was to show that one was well-bred, elegant, *au courant.* The last sentence shows that the process is not yet dead. By using *au courant* instead of, say, *abreast of things,* the writer indicates that he is no dull clod who knows only English but an elegant person aware of how things are done in *le haut monde.*

29   Thus French words came into English, all sorts of them. There were words to do with government: *parliament, majesty, treaty, alliance, tax, government;* church words: *parson, sermon, baptism, incense, crucifix, religion;* words for foods: *veal, beef, mutton, bacon, jelly, peach, lemon, cream, biscuit;* colors: *blue, scarlet, vermilion;* household words: *curtain, chair, lamp, towel, blanket, parlor;* play words: *dance, chess, music, leisure, conversation;* literary words: *story, romance, poet, literary;* learned words: *study, logic, grammar, noun, surgeon, anatomy, stomach;* just ordinary words of all sorts: *nice, second, very, age, bucket, gentle, final, fault, flower, cry, count, sure, move, surprise, plain.*

30   All these and thousands more poured into the English vocabulary between 1100 and 1500, until at the end of that time many people must have had more French words than English at their command. This is not to say that English became French. English remained English in sound structure and in grammar, though these also felt the ripples of French influence. The very heart of the vocabulary, too, remained English. Most of the high-frequency words— the pronouns, the prepositions, the conjunctions, the auxiliaries, as well as a great many ordinary nouns and verbs and adjectives—were not replaced by borrowings.

31   Middle English, then, was still a Germanic language, but it differed from Old English in many ways. The sound system and the grammar changed a good deal. Speakers made less use of case systems and other inflectional de-

vices and relied more on word order and structure words to express their meanings. This is often said to be a simplification, but it isn't really. Languages don't become simpler; they merely exchange one kind of complexity for another. Modern English is not a simple language, as any foreign speaker who tries to learn it will hasten to tell you.

32   For us Middle English is simpler than Old English just because it is closer to Modern English. It takes three or four months at least to learn to read Old English prose and more than that for poetry. But a week of good study should put one in touch with the Middle English poet Chaucer. Indeed, you may be able to make some sense of Chaucer straight off, though you would need instruction in pronunciation to make it sound like poetry. Here is a famous passage from the *General Prologue to the Canterbury Tales,* fourteenth century:

>   Ther was also a nonne, a Prioresse.
>   That of hir smyling was ful symple and coy,
>   Hir gretteste oath was but by Seinte Loy,
>   And she was cleped Madam Eglentyne.
>   Ful wel she song the service dyvyne,
>   Entuned in hir nose ful semely.
>   And Frenshe she spak ful faire and fetisly,
>   After the scole of Stratford-atte-Bowe,
>   For Frenshe of Parys was to hir unknowe.

33   Sometime between 1400 and 1600 English underwent a couple of sound changes which made the language of Shakespeare quite different from that of Chaucer. Incidentally, these changes contributed much to the chaos in which English spelling now finds itself.

34   One change was the elimination of a vowel sound in certain unstressed positions at the end of words. For instance, the words *name, stone, wine, dance* were pronounced as two syllables by Chaucer but as just one by Shakespeare. The *e* in these words became, as we say, "silent." But it wasn't silent for Chaucer; it represented a vowel sound. So also the words *laughed, seemed, stored* would have been pronounced by Chaucer as two-syllable words. The change was an important one because it affected thousands of words and gave a different aspect to the whole language.

35   The other change is what is called the Great Vowel Shift. This was a systematic shifting of half a dozen vowels and diphthongs in stressed syllables. For instance, the word *name* had in Middle English a vowel something like that in the modern word *father; wine* had the vowel of modern *mean; he* was pronounced something like modern *hey; mouse* sounded like *moose; moon* had the vowel of *moan.* Again the shift was thoroughgoing and affected all the words in which these vowel sounds occurred. Since we still keep the Middle English system of spelling these words, the differences between Modern English and Middle English are often more real than apparent.

36   The vowel shift has meant also that we have come to use an entirely different set of symbols for representing vowel sounds than is used by writers of

such languages as French, Italian, or Spanish, in which no such vowel shift occurred. If you come across a strange word—say, *bine*—in an English book, you will pronounce it according to the English system, with the vowel of *wine* or *dine*. But if you read *bine* in a French, Italian, or Spanish book, you will pronounce it with the vowel of *mean* or *seen*.

37   These two changes, then, produced the basic differences between Middle English and Modern English. But there were several other developments that had an effect upon the language. One was the invention of printing, an invention introduced into England by William Caxton in the year 1475. Where before books had been rare and costly, they suddenly became cheap and common. More and more people learned to read and write. This was the first of many advances in communication which have worked to unify languages and to arrest the development of dialect differences, though of course printing affects writing principally rather than speech. Among other things it hastened the standardization of spelling.

38   The period of Early Modern English—that is, the sixteenth and seventeenth centuries—was also the period of the English Renaissance, when people developed, on the one hand, a keen interest in the past and, on the other, a more daring and imaginative view of the future. New ideas multiplied, and new ideas meant new language. Englishmen had grown accustomed to borrowing words from French as a result of the Norman Conquest; now they borrowed from Latin and Greek. As we have seen, English had been raiding Latin from Old English times and before, but now the floodgates really opened, and thousands of words from the classical languages poured in. *Pedestrian, bonus, anatomy, contradict, climax, dictionary, benefit, multiply, exist, paragraph, initiate, scene, inspire* are random examples. Probably the average educated American today has more words from French in his vocabulary than from native English sources, and more from Latin than from French.

39   The greatest writer of the Early Modern English period is of course Shakespeare, and the best-known book is the King James Version of the Bible, published in 1611. The Bible (if not Shakespeare) has made many features of Early Modern English perfectly familiar to many people down to present times, even though we do not use these features in present-day speech and writing. For instance, the old pronouns *thou* and *thee* have dropped out of use now, together with their verb forms, but they are still familiar to us in prayer and in Biblical quotation: "Whither thou goest, I will go." Such forms as *hath* and *doth* have been replaced by *has* and *does;* "Goes he hence tonight?" would now be "Is he going away tonight?"; Shakespeare's "Fie on't, sirrah" would be "Nuts to that, Mac." Still, all these expressions linger with us because of the power of the works in which they occur.

40   It is not always realized, however, that considerable sound changes have taken place between Early Modern English and the English of the present day. Shakespearean actors putting on a play speak the words, properly enough, in their modern pronunciation. But it is very doubtful that this pronunciation would be understood at all by Shakespeare. In Shakespeare's time, the word *reason* was pronounced like modern *raisin; face* had the sound of modern

glass; the *l* in *would, should, palm* was pronounced. In these points and a great many others the English language has moved a long way from what it was in 1600.

41   The history of English since 1700 is filled with many movements and countermovements, of which we can notice only a couple. One of these is the vigorous attempt made in the eighteenth century, and the rather halfhearted attempts made since, to regulate and control the English language. Many people of the eighteenth century, not understanding very well the forces which govern language, proposed to polish and prune and restrict English, which they felt was proliferating too wildly. There was much talk of an academy which would rule on what people could and could not say and write. The academy never came into being, but the eighteenth century did succeed in establishing certain attitudes which, though they haven't had much effect on the development of the language itself, have certainly changed the native speaker's feeling about the language.

42   In part a product of the wish to fix and establish the language was the development of the dictionary. The first English dictionary was published in 1603; it was a list of 2500 words briefly defined. Many others were published with gradual improvements until Samuel Johnson published his *English Dictionary* in 1755. This, steadily revised, dominated the field in England for nearly a hundred years. Meanwhile in America, Noah Webster published his dictionary in 1828, and before long dictionary publishing was a big business in this country. The last century has seen the publication of one great dictionary: the twelve-volume *Oxford English Dictionary*, compiled in the course of seventy-five years through the labors of many scholars. We have also, of course, numerous commercial dictionaries which are as good as the public wants them to be if not, indeed, rather better.

43   Another product of the eighteenth century was the invention of "English grammar." As English came to replace Latin as the language of scholarship it was felt that one should also be able to control and dissect it, parse and analyze it, as one could Latin. What happened in practice was that the grammatical description that applied to Latin was removed and superimposed on English. This was silly, because English is an entirely different kind of language, with its own forms and signals and ways of producing meaning. Nevertheless, English grammars on the Latin model were worked out and taught in the schools. In many schools they are still being taught. This activity is not often popular with school children, but it is sometimes an interesting and instructive exercise in logic. The principal harm in it is that it has tended to keep people from being interested in English and has obscured the real features of English structure.

44   But probably the most important force in the development of English in the modern period has been the tremendous expansion of English-speaking peoples. In 1500 English was a minor language, spoken by a few people on a small island. Now it is perhaps the greatest language of the world, spoken natively by over a quarter of a billion people and as a second language by many millions more. When we speak of English now, we must specify whether we

mean American English, British English, Australian English, Indian English, or what, since the differences are considerable. The American cannot go to England or the Englishman to America confident that he will always understand and be understood. The Alabaman in Iowa or the Iowan in Alabama shows himself a foreigner every time he speaks. It is only because communication has become fast and easy that English in this period of its expansion has not broken into a dozen mutually unintelligible languages.

TOPICAL CONSIDERATIONS

1. Roberts states in the opening of his essay that there can be no real understanding of the English language without an understanding of its history. Discuss some of the ways, as outlined by Roberts, in which history has had a bearing on the development of the English language since the time of the Roman Empire.

2. In paragraph 4, Roberts lists English words borrowed from Latin, noting that in their nature these words "show something of the relationship of the Anglo-Saxons with the Romans." What kind of relationship do you suppose these two peoples had, based on the list of words given by Roberts?

3. According to Roberts, what are the three major periods in the history of the English language? How are they differentiated from one another?

4. In terms of grammar, Roberts says that Old English was much more highly inflected than Modern English is (paragraph 21). What does he mean by this?

5. What political event facilitated the change from Old to Middle English? How did this change occur? Do you think that political events still play a part in language development? Explain your answer.

6. What was the position of the French language after the Norman Conquest? Can you think of any contemporary societies where there is a class split along language lines—that is, one language spoken by "polite society," another by "the people"? What kind of effect does this split in language have on those countries?

7. In his conclusion, Roberts notes the many different English-speaking people around the world. Have you ever been to an English-speaking place where you had difficulty being understood? Explain your experience. What exactly were the sources of the difficulties, if any?

RHETORICAL CONSIDERATIONS

1. How does Roberts organize the material in his essay? Is his organizational method effective in terms of the content of the piece? Why or why not?

2. Characterize the style and tone of this essay. To what audience do you suppose Roberts is aiming this piece? Explain your answer.

3. Is Roberts successful in demonstrating the connection between history and language development? Locate one or two passages in which you find that connection to be especially strong.

4. Roberts gives many examples of words borrowed from such languages as Latin, French, and Norse. Do you find such examples helpful in understanding the article? Why or why not?

WRITING ASSIGNMENTS

1. Roberts's piece is based on the idea that English has been affected by historical events. Choose a more recent event—say, the advent of computers, mass media advertising, feminism, current sporting events, the Persian Gulf War, or the Vietnam War—and write a paper exploring how English has been influenced by it. You might consult a dictionary for a listing of current additions to the English language, among other sources.

2. Choose a short passage of modern prose. Using a dictionary, look up a dozen of the words in the passage, paying special attention to the origins of the words. Write a paragraph in which you detail your findings, noting whether or not they reflect Roberts's claims about the historical development of the English language.

3. Write a paper describing how your own dialect of English differs from that of other English speakers. This might be a personal narrative, outlining an experience you have had with dialect differences, or an informative essay regarding regional or national differences in English.

WORDSTRUCK*

Eudora Welty

She begged to be read to. She begged to hear the written word aloud. And when, at last, she learned to read on her own, she spent hours with her books—lost in language and the language of the imagination. In this selection, we learn how one of America's most gifted and honored writers came to language as a young girl.

Eudora Welty was born in 1909 in Jackson, Mississippi, where she still lives in her father's house. Throughout her life, she devoted her stories and novels to a depiction of life in the South, recreating the interplay of blacks and whites, town and country folk, family and society—all with subtlety, insight, and a remarkable eye for telling detail. Those talents can be found in all of her stories, as well as in the following recollection taken from her autobiographical memoirs, *One Writer's Beginnings* (1984), which describes how her propensity for listening closely to the talk of her family and friends and her voracious reading formed the seeds of her creativity. Among her major novels are *Delta Wedding* (1946) and *The Optimist's Daughter* (1972), which won a Pulitzer Prize. Many of her short stories appear in *The Wide Net* (1943) and *The Bride of Innisfallen* (1955).

1   I learned from the age of two or three that any room in our house, at any time of day, was there to read in, or to be read to. My mother read to me. She'd read to me in the big bedroom in the mornings, when we were in her rocker together, which ticked in rhythm as we rocked, as though we had a cricket accompanying the story. She'd read to me in the dining room on winter afternoons in front of the coal fire, with our cuckoo clock ending the story with "Cuckoo," and at night when I'd got in my own bed. I must have given her no peace. Sometimes she read to me in the kitchen while she sat churning, and the churning sobbed along with *any* story. It was my ambition to have her read

---

*Editor's title.

to me while *I* churned; once she granted my wish, but she read off my story before I brought her butter. She was an expressive reader. When she was reading "Puss in Boots," for instance, it was impossible not to know that she distrusted *all* cats.

2   It had been startling and disappointing to me to find out that story books had been written by *people,* that books were not natural wonders, coming up of themselves like grass. Yet regardless of where they came from, I cannot remember a time when I was not in love with them—with the books themselves, cover and binding and the paper they were printed on, with their smell and their weight and with their possession in my arms, captured and carried off to myself. Still illiterate, I was ready for them, committed to all the reading I could give them.

3   Neither of my parents had come from homes that could afford to buy many books, but though it must have been something of a strain on his salary, as the youngest officer in a young insurance company, my father was all the while carefully selecting and ordering away for what he and Mother thought we children should grow up with. They bought first for the future.

4   Besides the bookcase in the livingroom, which was always called "the library," there were the encyclopedia tables and dictionary stand under windows in our diningroom. Here to help us grow up arguing around the diningroom table were the Unabridged Webster, the Columbia Encyclopedia, Compton's Pictured Encyclopedia, the Lincoln Library of Information, and later the Book of Knowledge. And the year we moved into our new house, there was room to celebrate it with the new 1925 edition of the Britannica, which my father, his face always deliberately turned toward the future, was of course disposed to think better than any previous edition. . . .

5   I was presented, from as early as I can remember, with books of my own, which appeared on my birthday and Christmas morning. Indeed, my parents could not give me books enough. They must have sacrificed to give me on my sixth or seventh birthday—it was after I became a reader for myself—the ten-volume set of *Our Wonder World.* These were beautifully made, heavy books I would lie down with on the floor in front of the diningroom hearth, and more often than the rest volume 5, *Every Child's Story Book,* was under my eyes. There were the fairy tales—Grimm, Andersen, the English, the French, "Ali Baba and the Forty Thieves"; and there was Aesop and Reynard the Fox; there were they myths and legends, Robin Hood, King Arthur, and St. George and the Dragon, even the history of Joan of Arc; a whack of *Pilgrim's Progress* and a long piece of *Gulliver.* They all carried their classic illustrations. I located myself in these pages and could go straight to the stories and pictures I loved; very often "The Yellow Dwarf" was first choice, with Walter Crane's Yellow Dwarf in full color making his terrifying appearance flanked by turkeys. Now that volume is as worn and backless and hanging apart as my father's poor *Sanford and Merton.* The precious page with Edward Lear's "Jumblies" on it has been in danger of slipping out for all these years. One measure of my love for Our Wonder World was that for a long time I wondered if I

would go through fire and water for it as my mother had done for Charles Dickens; and the only comfort was to think I could ask my mother to do it for me.

6   I believe I'm the only child I know of who grew up with this treasure in the house. I used to ask others, "Did you have Our Wonder World?" I'd have to tell them The Book of Knowledge could not hold a candle to it.

7   I live in gratitude to my parents for initiating me—and as early as I begged for it, without keeping me waiting—into knowledge of the word, into reading and spelling, by way of the alphabet. They taught it to me at home in time for me to begin to read before starting to school. I believe the alphabet is no longer considered an essential piece of equipment for traveling through life. In my day it was the keystone to knowledge. You learned the alphabet as you learned to count to ten, as you learned "Now I lay me" and the Lord's Prayer and your father's and mother's name and address and telephone number, all in case you were lost.

8   My love for the alphabet, which endures, grew out of reciting it but, before that, out of seeing the letters on the page. In my own story books, before I could read them for myself, I fell in love with various winding, enchanted-looking initials drawn by Walter Crane at the heads of fairy tales. In "Once upon a time," an "O" had a rabbit running it as a treadmill, his feet upon flowers. When the day came, years later, for me to see the Book of Kells, all the wizardry of letter, initial, and word swept over me a thousand times over, and the illumination, the gold, seemed a part of the word's beauty and holiness that had been there from the start.

9   Learning stamps you with its moments. Childhood's learning is made up of moments. It isn't steady. It's a pulse.

10   In a children's art class, we sat in a ring on kindergarten chairs and drew three daffodils that had just been picked out of the yard; and while I was drawing, my sharpened yellow pencil and the cup of the yellow daffodil gave off whiffs just alike. That the pencil doing the drawing should give off the same smell as the flower it drew seemed part of the art lesson—as shouldn't it be? Children, like animals, use all their senses to discover the world. Then artists come along and discover it the same way, all over again. Here and there, it's the same world. Or now and then we'll hear from an artist who's never lost it.

11   In my sensory education I include my physical awareness of the *word*. Of a certain word, that is; the connection it has with what it stands for. At around age six, perhaps, I was standing by myself in our front yard waiting for supper, just at that hour in a late summer day when the sun is already below the horizon and the risen full moon in the visible sky stops being chalky and begins to take on light. There comes the moment, and I saw it then, when the moon goes from flat to round. For the first time it met my eyes as a globe. The word "moon" came into my mouth as though fed to me out of a silver spoon. Held in my mouth the moon became a word. It had the roundness of a Concord grape Grandpa took off his vine and gave me to suck out of its skin and swallow whole, in Ohio. . . .

12   My mother always sang to her children. Her voice came out just a little bit in the minor key. "Wee Willie Winkie"'s song was wonderfully sad when she sang the lullabies.

13   "Oh, but now there's a record. She could have her own record to listen to," my father would have said. For there came a Victrola record of "Bobby Shafftoe" and "Rock-a-Bye Baby," all of Mother's lullabies, which could be played to take her place. Soon I was able to play her my own lullabies all day long.

14   Our Victrola stood in the diningroom. I was allowed to climb onto the seat of a diningroom chair to wind it, start the record turning, and set the needle playing. In a second I'd jumped to the floor, to spin or march around the table as the music called for—now there were all the other records I could play too. I skinned back onto the chair just in time to lift the needle at the end, stop the record and turn it over, then change the needle. That brass receptacle with a hole in the lid gave off a metallic smell like a human sweat, from all the hot needles that were fed it. Winding up, dancing, being cocked to start and stop the record, was of course all in one the act of *listening*—to "Overture to *Daughter of the Regiment*," "Selections from *The Fortune Teller*," "Kiss Me Again," "Gypsy Dance from *Carmen*," "Stars and Stripes Forever," "When the Midnight Choo-Choo Leaves for Alabam," or whatever came next. Movement must be at the very heart of listening.

15   Ever since I was first read to, then started reading to myself, there has never been a line read that I didn't *hear*. As my eyes followed the sentence, a voice was saying it silently to me. It isn't my mother's voice, or the voice of any person I can identify, certainly not my own. It is human, but inward, and it is inwardly that I listen to it. It is to me the voice of the story or the poem itself. The cadence, whatever it is that asks you to believe, the feeling that resides in the printed word, reaches me through the reader-voice. I have supposed, but never found out, that this is the case with all readers—to read as listeners— and with all writers, to write as listeners. It may be part of the desire to write. The sound of what falls on the page begins the process of testing it for truth, for me. Whether I am right to trust so far I don't know. By now I don't know whether I could do either one, reading or writing, without the other.

16   My own words, when I am at work on a story, I hear too as they go, in the same voice that I hear when I read in books. When I write and the sound of it comes back to my ears, then I act to make my changes. I have always trusted this voice.

TOPICAL CONSIDERATIONS

1. Are there similarities between your recollections and those of Eudora Welty? Are there particular books you enjoyed as a child that you remember vividly? What books, and what do you remember best about them?

2. According to Welty, what is the value of being read to? From your own experience, can you identify with her observations? Can you think of other values she has not mentioned?

3. What value is implied in Welty's statement that she was disappointed to learn that "story books had been written by people"?

4. What does the author mean by "Learning stamps you with its moments"? What two examples does she give? Can you give two examples from your own life?

5. Had there been a television set in Eudora Welty's home, how might it have affected her development?

6. Is Welty's view of childhood and reading one you can identify with, or is it too rarified a view? Explain.

RHETORICAL CONSIDERATIONS

1. Would you classify this writing as subjective or objective?

2. Think over this essay. What do you remember best about it? What part was most interesting? Where was it least interesting? What are the differences between the two parts?

3. How does the first-person point of view affect your response to the essay?

4. Take another look at paragraph 3. How is the use of a long sentence followed by a very short one effective here?

5. In your own words, try to define Welty's attitude toward her childhood. How does the tone of the essay reinforce this? Is the tone consistent throughout?

6. Do you think this essay is sentimental? Why or why not?

7. Is there anything in this essay suggesting that Eudora Welty is, in fact, a highly accomplished writer? Using details, explain your answer.

WRITING ASSIGNMENTS

1. Using the first-person narrative voice, write a recollection of your earliest experiences with words, reading, and books. Try to employ Welty's use of details to make the memory vivid.

2. Was there a particular person who was influential in your appreciation for language and books? If so, write a paper explaining how he or she helped you develop your language skills and appreciation for books.

3. If reading was a painful rather than enjoyable experience for you as a child, write an essay describing conflicts this caused. You may want to make the tone humorous and ironic.

4. Is it fair to expect or even hope that every child be an avid reader? Does such exclusive focus on what is "worthwhile" ignore the merits of other childhood activities? Explain yourself in a paper.

5. Welty lists various children's books to which she traces her love for writing and reading—fairy tales by the brothers Grimm and Hans Christian Andersen, fables by Aesop, and the myths of Robin Hood and King Arthur. Visit the children's section of your local library. Choose one of the above books and read it, considering as you go along why this story would or would not be a positive learning experience for someone just "coming to language." Support your ideas with specific attention to plot, style, and especially language.

HOMEMADE EDUCATION*

Malcolm X

It was said that he was the only man in America who could start a race riot—or stop one. A one-time street hustler, Malcolm X, born Malcolm Little in 1925, rose to become one of the most articulate, fiery, and powerful leaders of black America during the 1960s. His writings and lectures taught African Americans that by acting they could take control over their own destiny. Becoming an orthodox Muslim in 1964, Malcolm X began to distance himself from the teachings of black Muslims. The next year, while addressing a rally in Harlem, he was gunned down by rival members of the Black Muslim movement.

In 1946, Malcolm X was arrested for robbery. During the seven years he spent in prison, he discovered not only the religion of Islam, but also the world of language. Like Eudora Welty, he became obsessed with the written word and gravitated toward books, which he called "intellectual vitamins." The piece below is his account of coming to language—an inspiring glimpse of one man's struggle to find self-expression and the power of words. This excerpt comes from *The Autobiography of Malcolm X* (1965), an absorbing personal narrative written with the assistance of novelist Alex Haley, author of the bestselling novel *Roots* (1976). In 1992, Spike Lee directed the popular movie, *Malcolm X,* based on the autobiography.

1   I've never been one for inaction. Everything I've ever felt strongly about, I've done something about. I guess that's why, unable to do anything else, I soon began writing to people I had known in the hustling world, such as Sammy the Pimp, John Hughes, the gambling house owner, the thief Jumpsteady, and several dope peddlers. I wrote them all about Allah and Islam and Mr. Elijah Muhammad. I had no idea where most of them lived. I addressed their letters in care of the Harlem or Roxbury bars and clubs where I'd known them.

2   I never got a single reply. The average hustler and criminal was too uneducated to write a letter. I have known many slick sharp-looking hustlers, who would have you think they had an interest in Wall Street; privately, they would get someone else to read a letter if they received one. Besides, neither would I have replied to anyone writing me something as wild as "the white man is the devil."

---

*Editor's title.

3   What certainly went on the Harlem and Roxbury wires was that Detroit Red was going crazy in stir, or else he was trying some hype to shake up the warden's office.

4   During the years that I stayed in the Norfolk Prison Colony, never did any official directly say anything to me about those letters, although, of course, they all passed through the prison censorship. I'm sure, however, they monitored what I wrote to add to the files which every state and federal prison keeps on the conversation of Negro inmates by the teachings of Mr. Elijah Muhammed.

5   But at that time, I felt that the real reason was that the white man knew that he was the devil.

6   Later on, I even wrote to the Mayor of Boston, to the Governor of Massachusetts, and to Harry S. Truman. They never answered; they probably never even saw my letters. I handscratched to them how the white man's society was responsible for the black man's condition in this wilderness of North America.

7   It was because of my letters that I happened to stumble upon starting to acquire some kind of a homemade education.

8   I became increasingly frustrated at not being able to express what I wanted to convey in letters that I wrote, especially those to Mr. Elijah Muhammed. In the street, I had been the most articulate hustler out there—I had commanded attention when I said something. But now, trying to write simple English, I not only wasn't articulate, I wasn't even functional. How would I sound writing in slang, the way I would *say* it, something such as, "Look, daddy, let me pull your coat about a cat. Elijah Muhammad—"

9   Many who today hear me somewhere in person, or on television, or those who read something I've said, will think I went to school far beyond the eighth grade. This impression is due entirely to my prison studies.

10   It had really begun back in the Charlestown Prison, when Bimbi first made me feel envy of his stock of knowledge. Bimbi had always taken charge of any conversation he was in, and I had tried to emulate him. But every book I picked up had few sentences which didn't contain anywhere from one to nearly all of the words that might as well have been in Chinese. When I just skipped those words, of course, I really ended up with little idea of what the book said. So I had come to the Norfolk Prison Colony still going through only book-reading motions. Pretty soon, I would have quit even these motions, unless I had received the motivation that I did.

11   I saw that the best thing I could do was get hold of a dictionary—to study, to learn some words. I was lucky enough to reason also that I should try to improve my penmanship. It was sad. I couldn't even write in a straight line. It was both ideas together that moved me to request a dictionary along with some tablets and pencils from the Norfolk Prison Colony school.

12   I spent two days just riffling uncertainly through the dictionary's pages. I'd never realized so many words existed! I didn't know *which* words I needed to learn. Finally, just to start some kind of action, I began copying.

13   In my slow, painstaking, ragged handwriting, I copied into my tablet every-thing printed on that first page, down to the punctuation marks.

14   I believe it took me a day. Then, aloud, I read back, to myself, everything I'd written on the tablet. Over and over, aloud, to myself, I read my own hand-writing.

15   I woke up the next morning, thinking about those words—immensely proud to realize that not only had I written so much at one time, but I'd writ-ten words that I never knew were in the world. Moreover, with a little effort, I also could remember what many of these words meant. I reviewed the words whose meanings I didn't remember. Funny thing, from the dictionary's first page right now, that "aardvark" springs to my mind. The dictionary had a pic-ture of it, a long-tailed, long-eared, burrowing African mammal, which lives off termites caught by sticking out its tongue as an anteater does for ants.

16   I was so fascinated that I went on—I copied the dictionary's next page. And the same experience came when I studied that. With every succeeding page, I also learned of people and places and events from history. Actually the dictio-nary is like a miniature encyclopedia. Finally the dictionary's A section had filled a whole tablet—and I went on into the B's. That was the way I started copying what eventually became the entire dictionary. It went a lot faster after so much practice helped me pick up handwriting speed. Between what I wrote in my tablet, and writing letters, during the rest of my time in prison I would guess I wrote a million words.

17   I suppose it was inevitable that as my word-base broadened, I could for the first time pick up a book and read and now begin to understand what the book was saying. Anyone who has read a great deal can imagine the new world that opened. Let me tell you something: from then until I left that prison, in every free moment I had, if I was not reading in the library, I was reading on my bunk. You couldn't have gotten me out of books with a wedge. Between Mr. Muhammad's teachings, my correspondence, my visitors . . . and my reading of books, months passed without my even thinking about being imprisoned. In fact, up to then, I never had been so truly free in my life.

TOPICAL CONSIDERATIONS

1. What exactly motivates Malcolm X to "get hold of a dictionary—to study, to learn some words"?

2. Explain how Malcolm X could be the "most articulate hustler" on the street yet be unable to write simple English that was articulate and functional.

3. Why does the author compare the dictionary to a miniature encyclopedia?

4. In your own words, summarize what Malcolm X means when he says, "In fact, up to then, I never had been so truly free in my life." Can you in any way relate to his sense of freedom here? Have you ever had a similarly intense learning experi-ence? If so, what was it like?

5. Would this essay be likely to inspire an illiterate person to learn to read? Why or why not?

6. How are Malcolm X's and Eudora Welty's attitudes toward books, language, and learning similar? How are they different?

7. Having read this essay, do you feel that studying a dictionary is or is not an effective way to improve language skills?

8. What do you think Malcolm X hoped his readers would learn from this essay? How do you think he wanted them to respond?

RHETORICAL CONSIDERATIONS

1. What is the point of view in this selection? Is it consistent throughout? Is it effective? Why or why not?

2. Consider the introductory paragraph. What would you say is its function? Does it establish the thesis and controlling idea of the essay? Did it capture your attention? Did it make you want to read on? Explain.

3. What is your reaction to the example of slang at the end of paragraph 8? Is it effective? What does it add to the essay? What does it illustrate? What would be the effect of eliminating it?

4. What do you remember best about this piece? Explain why.

WRITING ASSIGNMENTS

1. Think of a situation in which you lacked the language skills you needed to communicate effectively. It may have been a college interview, writing a letter to a friend, or expressing your ideas in class. Write an essay explaining the circumstance—how it made you feel and how you solved or coped with the problem. The tone of the piece could be serious, or dramatic, or even humorous.

2. Most students probably take literacy for granted. But imagine that you were illiterate—that is, you could not read or write. Brainstorm and make an extensive list of all the things you could not do. Selecting one or more of those items, write a personal essay on what it is like to be illiterate. You might try adopting the point of view of an illiterate young parent or successful salesperson who had kept his or her illiteracy a secret.

3. Do a little research to find out what kinds of services your community offers to adults who want to learn to read. You might start by contacting Town Hall, the Department of Education, and reading clinics. After gathering information, write an essay outlining what is available and whether or not you feel these services are adequate.

4. Read *The Autobiography of Malcolm X* as the basis for a research paper on his literacy experience. In particular, describe how Malcolm X's determination to read led him to become a powerful writer and orator.

THE MAN THAT SPELT *KNIFE* WAS A FOOL

Johnny Connors

Unlike Eudora Welty, Johnny Connors had no home full of books; nor was he fortunate enough to have a dictionary like Malcolm X. But what Connors shared with them was a determination to educate himself using whatever the environment could offer. What follows is an intriguing account of one young man's desperate struggle to learn to read and write—a struggle that would lead from the classroom to the rubbish dumps.

Johnny Connors grew up an Irish gypsy, one of the thousands who still move about the outskirts of European society in covered wagons. A dark-skinned Caucasian people believed to have originated in India, gypsies are nomads who have preserved some of their old Romany language. In England and Ireland they have been regarded with suspicion and are often forced to keep on the move, which explains why gypsy children such as Connors do not attend schools for very long. Of course, Connors—like Eudora Welty, and Malcolm X—not only learned to read, but he grew up to write his story, which appeared in the book *Gypsies* by Jeremy Sanford (1972), from which this excerpt is taken.

1   About four weeks had passed and I could write my name JOHN.
2   And nearly every minute during the day I would be saying,
3   "ZABQAZXOUWZ. ACB792Y14MN2Q," and so on.
4   I would sing it all day, "ABCDEFGHIJKLMNOPQRSTUVWXYZ."
5   Six weeks had passed and I could tell the time of the clock myself.
6   That was six weeks at night school. Then the Nun asked me, would I like to go to a real classroom with little girls, because it was a girls' school. I said I would, so the next day for the first time in my life I was in a classroom. When the girls of the class saw me I could hear them whispering to one another, "He is a gyppo."
7   I was nearly mad. I shouted, "Ah, shut up your big mouths." I know it was wrong of me to treat young ladies that way, but they had started it.
8   After a while that day I got settled down to the class. And then I asked the teacher, "Could I go to the toilet?"

9   "Yes, John, go right ahead out to the yard."

10   I went into the toilet and I bolted one of the doors, and two girls came in.

11   It was a girls' toilet I was in.

12   "Hurry on, Mary, and pull your bloomers up when you leave."

13   I made a burst for the door and my trousers tripped me up. I ran out the gate of the school. As I was going out I met the Reverend Mother.

14   "What's wrong, John?" said the Reverend Mother.

15   "Those girls followed me into the toilet, the dirty things. They should be ashamed of themselves."

16   I could see a smile on the Reverend Mother's face.

17   "You go back to your class, John, and I will sort it all out."

18   I was ashamed of my life. Then it was playtime and the girls came to like me. I would skip with them, play ball with them. They became great pals of mine. The big bully girls were afraid of me, because when the big bully girls would bully the little girls I would stop them.

19   There was one big girl: I christened her Young Elephant. She was a very fat girl and she would bump into the little girls and the little girls would fall flat on their faces. So one day she was bullying all the other little girls. "Hold on there, you overgrown young elephant, don't be pushing any of the little girls." So from that day onwards she never pushed any of the little girls, and if she tried to the little girls would say, "I will get John to call you more names."

20   I really enjoyed being at school. But the police and corporation gave my Daddy three days' notice and I had to leave school.

21   That night when I came back to the wagon, my Daddy said, "Johnny, to-morrow is your last day at school."

22   "What?" I said, "I am not going to stop going to school."

23   "Well, if you don't you will have to follow the wagons a very long road."

24   "Why?" I said.

25   "Because we are being shifted on Saturday."

26   I could not sleep that night, I was fed up.

27   The next morning I went to school, and I told the teacher that this was my last day at school. She was very upset.

28   "Why must you stop going to school, John?" said the teacher.

29   "Because we are getting shifted."

30   "Oh, I am sorry to hear that, John."

31   At playtime all the girls gathered round me, "Please don't leave, John." Some of them was crying.

32   That evening I was forced to say good luck to all.

33   I was a very happy little boy and I wanted to go to school and I would not be able to go to school. So I said to myself, "I will learn myself how to read proper." Every sweet-paper with writing on it I would collect them all day. Tea bags, sugar bags and butter wrappers. I would stay at shop windows reading everything that was in the windows. And big words like "Palmolive," I would

split them up, Pal-mo-live. And "Corporation," Cor-por-ation. The only words that had me beat were medical words. "Physician" was a killer. I did really lose my temper with that word PHYSICIAN. What really was making me angry was that words like PHYSICIAN, LAMB or KNIFE had silent letter words, and I would say to myself, the man that spelt KNIFE was a fool.

34   When I would be sent to the shops on errands, I would be hours reading everything in the shop. My Mammy often told me to get Lyons' tea. Instead I would get some other strange brand of tea so as I could read the strange words on the packet. Because I knew every word on the Lyons' tea packet.

35   The same way when my Daddy would send me for cigarettes. He would say to me, "Make sure you get Woodbines," and I would say, "Maybe they have no Woodbines, what kind will I get if they have no Woodbines?" My Daddy would say, "Get any kind." I would get the strangest packet of cigarettes the shop had in stock so as I could read the writing on the packet. And if I was beaten at a word, I would go back into the shop and ask the person in the shop what the word meant. There were times people got angry with me over me asking so many questions. And they would simply say, "Buzz off, you are a nuisance."

36   Sweets with strange wrappings was the sweets I liked very much, even if they were horrible sweets. I don't think I ever enjoyed a sweet in them times, because I was not interested in the sweets, the wrapping was what I got more enjoyment out of. In other words, strange things were more helpful to me.

37   Also milestones, finger-posts, and most of all the rubbish-dumps were my teacher. When I would see a dump I would rather collect the old newspapers, comics and books out of the dump than go to the movies. Furthermore, I had been locked up on many occasions by the police and convicted for taking old books and papers and educational articles of my own choosing from dumps. So you could say I paid the hard way for the little bit of knowledge I have.

TOPICAL CONSIDERATIONS

1. What language skills did Connors acquire at school? Do you think it odd that it took him four weeks to learn to write his name?

2. How did Connors begin to master social skills at school? What does this suggest about his oral language skills?

3. Johnny Connors is forced to leave school. Does he remind you of Eudora Welty or Malcolm X in his determination to learn to read? What are the similarities?

4. What examples of Connors's persistence were particularly impressive to you? Is it difficult for you to imagine an environment in which one must struggle, as Connors did, to find material to read? Where might you find such an environment?

5. What do you think was Connors's intention in writing this selection? What do you think he wanted you to get out of it? What did you get out of it? What do you remember best about it?

RHETORICAL CONSIDERATIONS

1. What do you make of the opening sentence of this piece? Is it an effective lead? Did it capture your attention? Did it make you want to read on? How well did it forecast what the essay was about? Explain your answers.

2. Find the occasional lapses from standard English in Connors's discussion. Do they detract from it? Do they contribute to it? Explain your answers.

3. In general, the conclusion of an essay is supposed to be a culmination of preceding points. Its function is to wrap things up into a neat package, to complete the unity of the discussion. Evaluate the effectiveness of the concluding paragraph here. Does it tie the essay together? How well does it function as a culmination of preceding points? Do you see any reflections of the opening paragraph? Explain.

4. Do you think Johnny Connors is a good writer? Using details from the essay, explain why or why not.

5. Take any section of this essay and eliminate specific details. What does this demonstrate about Connors's style? Would the essay be stronger if he made more general statements?

6. Do you think the title of this piece is a good one? Why or why not? What title might you have chosen, and why?

WRITING ASSIGNMENTS

1. Connors concludes the essay saying: "So you could say I paid the hard way for the little bit of knowledge I have." Consider your own language learning background. Did you struggle? Did you pay a price for what you learned? Or was language learning a part of your environment and upbringing? Write an essay exploring the way you acquired reading and writing skills.

2. Having read essays on coming to language by Welty, Malcolm X, Connors, and Kingston, which follows, select the writer you feel you have the most in common with and write an essay explaining the similarities in language experience.

3. Make a list of 15 or 20 words, such as "knife," that typify some of the difficulty in making sense of English spelling and pronunciation. Then write a paper in which you try to describe the illogic and the inconsistencies you have found. What advice can you offer to somebody interested in learning to read and write English? (In preparation, you might first want to read the essay by Bill Bryson on pages 522–531.)

4. Contact a literacy agency in your community or at your school. Write an essay that discusses the demographics of illiteracy in your community. That is, examine the kinds of people who make up the majority of those who cannot read. According to the agency, what are the most common reasons for illiteracy in your area? What are some strategies for combating the problem? What is your sense of the effectiveness of those strategies?

THE LANGUAGE OF SILENCE*

Maxine Hong Kingston

Maxine Hong Kingston, born in 1940, was raised in a Chinese immigrant community in Stockton, California. As a first-generation American, she found herself having to adjust to two distinctly contrasting cultures. For a young girl this was confusing and difficult, as she recalls in this selection from her highly praised and popular autobiography, *The Woman Warrior: Memoirs of a Girlhood Among Ghosts* (1976). To the Chinese immigrant, white Americans are "ghosts"—pale, threatening, and, at times, comical spectres who speak an incomprehensible tongue. As we see, becoming American means adopting new values, defining a new self, and finding a new voice.

Ms. Kingston taught in several high schools and business schools before the publication of her award-winning autobiography. Since then, she has published *China Men* (1980) and her first novel, *Tripmaster Monkey: His Fake Book* (1989). Her latest book is *Hawaii One Summer* (1997).

1 Long ago in China, knot-makers tied string into buttons and frogs, and rope into bell pulls. There was one knot so complicated that it blinded the knot-maker. Finally an emperor outlawed this cruel knot, and the nobles could not order it anymore. If I had lived in China, I would have been an outlaw knot-maker.

2 Maybe that's why my mother cut my tongue. She pushed my tongue up and sliced the frenum. Or maybe she snipped it with a pair of nail scissors. I don't remember her doing it, only her telling me about it, but all during childhood I felt sorry for the baby whose mother waited with scissors or knife in hand for it to cry—and then, when its mouth was wide open like a baby bird's, cut. The Chinese say "a ready tongue is an evil."

3 I used to curl up my tongue in front of the mirror and tauten my frenum into a white line, itself as thin as a razor blade. I saw no scars in my mouth. I

---

*Editor's title.

thought perhaps I had had two frena, and she had cut one. I made other children open their mouths so I could compare theirs to mine. I saw perfect pink membranes stretching into precise edges that looked easy enough to cut. Sometimes I felt very proud that my mother committed such a powerful act upon me. At other times I was terrified—the first thing my mother did when she saw me was to cut my tongue.

4   "Why did you do that to me, Mother?"

5   "I told you."

6   "Tell me again."

7   "I cut it so that you would not be tongue-tied. Your tongue would be able to move in any language. You'll be able to speak languages that are completely different from one another. You'll be able to pronounce anything. Your frenum looked too tight to do those things, so I cut it."

8   "But isn't 'a ready tongue an evil'?"

9   "Things are different in this ghost country."

10   "Did it hurt me? Did I cry and bleed?"

11   "I don't remember. Probably."

12   She didn't cut the other children's. When I asked cousins and other Chinese children whether their mothers had cut their tongues loose, they said, "What?"

13   "Why didn't you cut my brothers' and sisters' tongues?"

14   "They didn't need it."

15   "Why not? Were theirs longer than mine?"

16   "Why don't you quit blabbering and get to work?"

17   If my mother was not lying she should have cut more, scraped away the rest of the frenum skin, because I have a terrible time talking. Or she should not have cut at all, tampering with my speech. When I went to kindergarten and had to speak English for the first time, I became silent. A dumbness—a shame—still cracks my voice in two, even when I want to say "hello" casually, or ask an easy question in front of the check-out counter, or ask directions of a bus driver. I stand frozen, or I hold up the line with the complete, grammatical sentence that comes squeaking out at impossible length. "What did you say?" says the cab driver, or "Speak up," so I have to perform again, only weaker the second time. A telephone call makes my throat bleed and takes up that day's courage. It spoils my day with self-disgust when I hear my broken voice come skittering out into the open. It makes people wince to hear it. I'm getting better, though. Recently I asked the postman for special-issue stamps; I've waited since childhood for postmen to give me some of their own accord. I am making progress, a little every day.

18   My silence was thickest—total—during the three years that I covered my school paintings with black paint. I painted layers of black over houses and flowers and suns, and when I drew on the background, I put a layer of chalk on top. I was making a stage curtain, and it was the moment before the curtain parted or rose. The teachers called my parents to school, and I saw they had been saving my pictures, curling and cracking, all alike and black. The teach-

ers pointed to the pictures and looked serious, talked seriously too, but my parents did not understand English. ("The parents and teachers of criminals were executed," said my father.) My parents took the pictures home. I spread them out (so black and full of possibilities) and pretended the curtains were swinging open, flying up, one after another, sunlight underneath, mighty operas.

19   During the first silent year I spoke to no one at school, did not ask before going to the lavatory, and flunked kindergarten. My sister also said nothing for three years, silent in the playground and silent at lunch. There were other quiet Chinese girls not of our family, but most of them got over it sooner than we did. I enjoyed the silence. At first it did not occur to me I was supposed to talk or to pass kindergarten. I talked at home and to one or two of the Chinese kids in class. I made motions and even made some jokes. I drank out of a toy saucer when the water spilled out of the cup, and everybody laughed, pointing at me, so I did it some more. I didn't know that Americans don't drink out of saucers.

20   I liked the Negro students (Black Ghosts) best because they laughed the loudest and talked to me as if I were a daring talker too. One of the Negro girls had her mother coil braids over her ears Shanghai-style like mine; we were Shanghai twins except that she was covered with black like my paintings. Two Negro kids enrolled in Chinese school, and the teachers gave them Chinese names. Some Negro kids walked me to school and home, protecting me from the Japanese kids, who hit me and chased me and stuck gum in my ears. The Japanese kids were noisy and tough. They appeared one day in kindergarten, released from concentration camp,[1] which was a tic-tac-toe mark, like barbed wire, on the map.

21   It was when I found out I had to talk that school became a misery, that the silence became a misery. I did not speak and felt bad each time that I did not speak. I read aloud in first grade, though, and heard the barest whisper with little squeaks come out of my throat. "Louder," said the teacher, who scared the voice away again. The other Chinese girls did not talk either, so I knew the silence had to do with being a Chinese girl.

22   Reading out loud was easier than speaking because we did not have to make up what to say, but I stopped often, and the teacher would think I'd gone quiet again. I could not understand "I." The Chinese "I" has seven strokes, intricacies. How could the American "I," assuredly wearing a hat like the Chinese, have only three strokes, the middle so straight? Was it out of politeness that this writer left off strokes the way a Chinese has to write her own name small and crooked? No, it was not politeness; "I" is a capital and "you" is a lower-case. I stared at that middle line and waited so long for its black center to resolve into tight strokes and dots that I forgot to pronounce it. The other

---

[1]*Concentration camp*: refers to one of the U.S. camps where Japanese Americans were imprisoned during World War II.

troublesome word was "here," no strong consonant to hang on to, and so flat, when "here" is two mountainous ideographs.[2] The teacher, who had already told me every day how to read "I" and "here," put me in the low corner under the stairs again, where the noisy boys usually sat.

23   When my second grade class did a play, the whole class went to the auditorium except the Chinese girls. The teacher, lovely and Hawaiian, should have understood about us, but instead left us behind in the classroom. Our voices were too soft or nonexistent, and our parents never signed the permission slips anyway. They never signed anything unnecessary. We opened the door a crack and peeked out, but closed it again quickly. One of us (not me) won every spelling bee, though.

24   I remember telling the Hawaiian teacher, "We Chinese can't sing 'Land where our fathers died.'" She argued with me about politics, while I meant because of curses. But how can I have that memory when I couldn't talk? My mother says that we, like ghosts, have no memories.

25   After American school, we picked up our cigar boxes, in which we had arranged books, brushes, and an inkbox neatly, and went to Chinese school, from 5:00 to 7:30 P.M. There we chanted together, voices rising and falling, loud and soft, some boys shouting, everybody reading together, reciting together and not alone with one voice. When we had a memorization test, the teacher let each of us come to his desk and say the lesson to him privately, while the rest of the class practiced copying or tracing. Most of the teachers were men. The boys who were so well behaved in the American school played tricks on them and talked back to them. The girls were not mute. They screamed and yelled during recess, when there were no rules; they had fist-fights. Nobody was afraid of children hurting themselves or of children hurting school property. The glass doors to the red and green balconies with the gold joy symbols were left wide open so that we could run out and climb the fire escapes. We played capture-the-flag in the auditorium, where Sun Yat-sen and Chiang Kai-shek's pictures hung at the back of the stage, the Chinese flag on their left and the American flag on their right. We climbed the teak ceremonial chairs and made flying leaps off the stage. One flag headquarters was behind the glass door and the other on stage right. Our feet drummed on the hollow stage. During recess the teachers locked themselves up in their office with the shelves of books, copybooks, inks from China. They drank tea and warmed their hands at a stove. There was no play supervision. At recess we had the school to ourselves, and also we could roam as far as we could go— downtown, Chinatown stores, home—as long as we returned before the bell rang.

26   At exactly 7:30 the teacher again picked up the brass bell that sat on his desk and swung it over our heads, while we charged down the stairs, our cheering magnified in the stairwell. Nobody had to line up.

---

[2]*Ideographs*: composite characters in Chinese writing made by combining two or more other characters.

27   Not all of the children who were silent at American school found voice at Chinese school. One new teacher said each of us had to get up and recite in front of the class, who was to listen. My sister and I had memorized the lesson perfectly. We said it to each other at home, one chanting, one listening. The teacher called on my sister to recite first. It was the first time a teacher had called on the second-born to go first. My sister was scared. She glanced at me and looked away; I looked down at my desk. I hoped that she could do it because if she could, then I would have to. She opened her mouth and a voice came out that wasn't a whisper, but it wasn't a proper voice either. I hoped that she would not cry, fear breaking up her voice like twigs underfoot. She sounded as if she were trying to sing through weeping and strangling. She did not pause or stop to end the embarrassment. She kept going until she said the last word, and then she sat down. When it was my turn, the same voice came out, a crippled animal running on broken legs. You could hear splinters in my voice, bones rubbing jagged against one another. I was loud, though. I was glad I didn't whisper. There was one little girl who whispered. . . .

28   How strange that the emigrant villagers are shouters, hollering face to face. My father asks, "Why is it I can hear Chinese from blocks away? Is it that I understand the language? Or is it they talk loud?" They turn the radio up full blast to hear the operas, which do not seem to hurt their ears. And they yell over the singers that wail over the drums, everybody talking at once, big arm gestures, spit flying. You can see the disgust on American faces looking at women like that. It isn't just the loudness. It is the way Chinese sounds, ching-chong ugly, to American ears, not beautiful like Japanese sayonara words with the consonants and vowels as regular as Italian. We make guttural peasant noise and have Ton Duc Thang names you can't remember. And the Chinese can't hear Americans at all; the language is too soft and western music unhearable. I've watched a Chinese audience laugh, visit, talk-story, and holler during a piano recital, as if the musician could not hear them. A Chinese-American, somebody's son, was playing Chopin, which has no punctuation, no cymbals, no gongs. Chinese piano music is five black keys. Normal Chinese women's voices are strong and bossy. We American-Chinese girls had to whisper to make ourselves American-feminine. Apparently we whispered even more softly than the Americans. Once a year the teachers referred my sister and me to speech therapy, but our voices would straighten out, unpredictably normal, for the therapists. Some of us gave up, shook our heads, and said nothing, not one word. Some of us could not even shake our heads. At times shaking my head no is more self-assertion than I can manage. Most of us eventually found some voice, however faltering. We invented an American-feminine speaking personality. . . .

TOPICAL CONSIDERATIONS

1. Kingston employed silence rather than language in the early grades. What accounts for the difference in attitude between kindergarten where she "enjoyed the silence" and first grade where "silence became a misery"?

2. Kingston's teacher punished her for failing to read "I" and "here." How does this episode demonstrate the clash of Chinese and American culture? Are there other episodes in the essay that also demonstrate it?

3. How did Kingston's Chinese school differ from the American one? What impact did the former have on her language development?

4. What do you make of Kingston's paintings? How do they relate to her "language of silence"?

5. According to Kingston, why do Americans not like the sound of Chinese? Do you think her observation is accurate, or an exaggeration? Explain.

6. Look over this essay again. What are some of the specific details by which the author characterizes Chinese women? Do you think her portrayal reinforces stereotypes of Chinese women? Explain your answer.

7. Examine the conclusion of the essay. Would you say this is a moment of triumph or defeat for Kingston? Explain.

RHETORICAL CONSIDERATIONS

1. Take another look at Kingston's story about her mother cutting her tongue. Do you take this to be literally true or not? Find specific details from the telling to support your conclusion. How does this episode, true or not, serve the author's purpose in the essay? How does it prefigure her attitude toward her own speech and language?

2. At what point in the essay do you know Kingston's focus? What are the cues to her purpose? Does this lead capture your attention?

3. Consider the author's voice in this essay. What sense do you get of her as an individual? Use some specific details to support your answer.

WRITING ASSIGNMENTS

1. Assume that you are a teacher with Kingston as a pupil. How would you handle her? What different tactics would it take to get her to come out of herself? Write a paper in which you describe your role.

2. Did you have difficulties "coming to language" as a child? Do you remember resorting to protective silence because of your accent, a different primary language, or a different cultural identity? Did you feel fear and/or embarrassment? If so, write a paper describing your experience. Have these experiences in any way left their mark on you? If so, in what way?

3. Kingston admits that even as an adult she has "a terrible time talking." She says that she still freezes with shame, that she can hardly be heard, that her voice is broken and squeaky. What about her writing style? Do you see any reflection of her lack of self-assertiveness, any signs of hesitation or uncertainty? In a paper, consider these questions as you try to describe her style as it relates to her experience as a young girl.

TALKING IN THE NEW LAND

Edite Cunha Pedrosa

At the age of seven, Maria Edite dos Anjos Cunha was taken from her little house in Sobreira, Portugal, to Peabody, Massachusetts. A week later, on her first day of school, her teacher announced that her name would now be Mary Edith Cunha. Not only could she not pronounce the new name, but from that moment on she never quite knew who she was. The narrative that follows is a thoughtful and moving account of what it was like to lose her language and name. "What else was left?" asks the author, who recounts her struggle to establish her identity in a new land where, for her, bilingualism became a crushing burden.

"Talking in the New Land" was written while Edite Cunha Pedrosa was an Ada Comstock Scholar at Smith College. She graduated in 1991. This article first appeared in *New England Monthly* magazine, in August 1990.

1   Before I started school in America I was Edite. Maria Edite dos Anjos Cunha. Maria, in honor of the Virgin Mary. In Portugal it was customary to use Maria as a religious and legal prefix to every girl's name. Virtually every girl was so named. It had something to do with the apparition of the Virgin to three shepherd children at Fatima. In naming their daughters Maria, my people were expressing their love and reverence for their Lady of Fatima.

2   Edite came from my godmother, Dona Edite Baetas Ruivo. The parish priest argued that I could not be named Edite because in Portugal the name was not considered Christian. But Dona Edite defended my right to bear her name. No one had argued with her family when they had christened her Edite. Her family had power and wealth. The priest considered privileges endangered by his stand, and I became Maria Edite.

3   The dos Anjos was for my mother's side of the family. Like her mother before her, she had been named Maria dos Anjos. And Cunha was for my father's side. Carlos dos Santos Cunha, son of Abilio dos Santos Cunha, the tailor from Saíl.

4   I loved my name. "Maria Edite dos Anjos Cunha," I'd recite at the least provocation. It was melodious and beautiful. And through it I knew exactly who I was.

5   At the age of seven I was taken from our little house in Sobreira, São Martinho da Cortiça, Portugal, and brought to Peabody, Massachusetts. We moved

into the house of Senhor João, who was our sponsor in the big land. I was in America for about a week when someone took me to school one morning and handed me over to the teacher, Mrs. Donahue.

6   Mrs. Donahue spoke Portuguese, a wondrous thing for a woman with a funny, unpronounceable name.

7   *"Como é que te chamas?"* she asked as she led me to a desk by big windows.

8   "Maria Edite dos Anjos Cunha," I recited, all the while scanning Mrs. Donahue for clues. How could a woman with such a name speak my language?

9   In fact, Mrs. Donahue was Portuguese. She was a Silva. But she had married an Irishman and changed her name. She changed my name, too, on the first day of school.

10   "Your name will be Mary Edith Cunha," she declared. "In America you only need two or three names. Mary Edith is a lovely name. And it will be easier to pronounce."

11   My name was Edite. Maria Edite. Maria Edite dos Anjos Cunha. I had no trouble pronouncing it.

12   "Mary Edith, Edithhh, Mary Edithhh," Mrs. Donahue exaggerated it. She wrinkled up her nose and raised her upper lip to show me the proper positioning of the tongue for the *th* sound. She looked hideous. There was a big pain in my head. I wanted to scream out my name. But you could never argue with a teacher.

13   At home I cried and cried. *Mãe* and *Pai* wanted to know about the day. I couldn't pronounce the new name for them. Senhor João's red face wrinkled in laughter.

14   Day after day Mrs. Donahue made me practice pronouncing that name that wasn't mine. Mary Edithhhhh. Mary Edithhh. Mary Edithhh. But weeks later I still wouldn't respond when she called it out in class. Mrs. Donahue became cross when I didn't answer. Later my other teachers shortened it to Mary. And I never knew quite who I was. . . .

15 Mrs. Donahue was a small woman, not much bigger than my seven-year-old self. Her graying hair was cut into a neat, curly bob. There was a smile that she wore almost every day. Not broad. Barely perceptible. But it was there, in her eyes, and at the corners of her mouth. She often wore gray suits with jackets neatly fitted about the waist. On her feet she wore matching black leather shoes, tightly laced. Matching, but not identical. One of them had an extra-thick sole, because like all of her pupils, Mrs. Donahue had an oddity. We, the children, were odd because we were of different colors and sizes, and did not speak in the accepted tongue. Mrs. Donahue was odd because she had legs of different lengths.

16   I grew to love Mrs. Donahue. She danced with us. She was the only teacher in all of Carroll School who thought it important to dance. Every day after recess she took us all to the big open space at the back of the room. We stood in a circle and joined hands. Mrs. Donahue would blow a quivering note from

the little round pitch pipe she kept in her pocket, and we became a twirling, singing wheel. Mrs. Donahue hobbled on her short leg and sang in a high trembly voice, "Here we go, loop-de-loop." We took three steps, then a pause. Her last "loop" was always very high. It seemed to squeak above our heads, bouncing on the ceiling. "Here we go, loop-de-lie." Three more steps, another pause, and on we whirled. "Here we go, loop-de-loop." Pause. "All on a Saturday night." To anyone looking in from the corridor we were surely an irregular sight, a circle of children of odd sizes and colors singing and twirling with our tiny hobbling teacher.

17   I'd been in Room Three with Mrs. Donahue for over a year when she decided that I could join the children in the regular elementary classes at Thomas Carroll School. I embraced the news with some ambivalence. By then the oddity of Mrs. Donahue's classroom had draped itself over me like a warm safe cloak. Now I was to join the second-grade class of Miss Laitinen. In preparation, Mrs. Donahue began a phase of relentless drilling. She talked to me about what I could expect in second grade. Miss Laitinen's class was well on its way with cursive writing, so we practiced that every day. We intensified our efforts with multiplication. And we practiced pronouncing the new teacher's name.

18   "Lay-te-nun." Mrs. Donahue spewed the *t* out with excessive force to demonstrate its importance. I had a tendency to forget it.

19   "Lay-nun."

20   "Mary Edith, don't be lazy. Use that tongue. It's Lay-te"—she bared her teeth for the *t* part—"nun."

21   One morning, with no warning, Mrs. Donahue walked me to the end of the hall and knocked on the door to Room Six. Miss Laitinen opened the door. She looked severe, carrying a long rubber-tipped pointer which she held horizontally before her with both hands. Miss Laitinen was a big, masculine woman. Her light, coarse hair was straight and cut short. She wore dark cardigans and very long, pleated plaid kilts that looked big enough to cover my bed.

22   "This is Mary Edith," Mrs. Donahue said. Meanwhile I looked at their shoes. Miss Laitinen wore flat, brown leather shoes that laced up and squeaked on the wooden floor when she walked. They matched each other perfectly, but they were twice as big as Mrs. Donahue's.

23   "Mary Edith, say hello to Miss Laitinen." Mrs. Donahue stressed the *t*—a last-minute reminder.

24   "Hello, Miss Lay-te-nun," I said, leaning my head back to see her face. Miss Laitinen was tall. Mrs. Donahue's head came just to her chest. They both nodded approvingly before I was led to my seat.

25 Peabody, Massachusetts. "The Leather City." It is stamped on the city seal, along with the image of a tanned animal hide. And Peabody, an industrial city of less than fifty thousand people, has the smokestacks to prove it. They rise up all over town from sprawling, dilapidated factories. Ugly, leaning, wooden buildings that often stretch over a city block. Strauss Tanning Co. A. C.

Lawrence Leather Co. Gnecco & Grilk Tanning Corp. In the early sixties, the tanneries were in full swing. The jobs were arduous and health-threatening, but it was the best-paying work around for unskilled laborers who spoke no English. The huge, firetrap factories were filled with men and women from Greece, Portugal, Ireland, and Poland.

26   In one of these factories, João Nunes, who lived on the floor above us, fed animal skins into a ravenous metal monster all day, every day. The pace was fast. One day the monster got his right arm and wouldn't let go. When the machine was turned off João had a little bit of arm left below his elbow. His daughter Teresa and I were friends. She didn't come out of her house for many days. When she returned to school, she was very quiet and cried a lot.

27   *"Rosa Veludo's been hurt."* News of such tragedies spread through the community fast and often. People would tell what they had seen, or what they had heard from those who had seen. *"She was taken to the hospital by ambulance. Someone wrapped her fingers in a paper bag. The doctors may be able to sew them back on."*

28   A few days after our arrival in the United States, my father went to work at the Gnecco & Grilk leather tannery, on the corner of Howley and Walnut streets. Senhor João had worked there for many years. He helped *Pai* get the job. Gnecco & Grilk was a long, rambling, four-story factory that stretched from the corner halfway down the street to the railroad tracks. The roof was flat and slouched in the middle like the back of an old workhorse. There were hundreds of windows. The ones on the ground floor were covered with a thick wire mesh.

29   *Pai* worked there for many months. He was stationed on the ground floor, where workers often had to stand ankle-deep in water laden with chemicals. One day he had a disagreement with his foreman. He left his machine and went home vowing never to return. . . .

30   *Pai* and I stood on a sidewalk in Salem facing a clear glass doorway. The words on the door were big. DIVISION OF EMPLOYMENT SECURITY. There was a growing coldness deep inside me. At Thomas Carroll School, Miss Laitinen was probably standing at the side blackboard, writing perfect alphabet letters on straight chalk lines. My seat was empty. I was on a sidewalk with *Pai* trying to understand a baffling string of words. DIVISION had something to do with math, which I didn't particularly like. EMPLOYMENT I had never seen or heard before. SECURITY I knew. But not at that moment.

31   *Pai* reached for the door. It swung open into a little square of tiled floor. We stepped in to be confronted by the highest, steepest staircase I had ever seen. At the top, we emerged into a huge, fluorescently lit room. It was too bright and open after the dim, narrow stairs. *Pai* took off his hat. We stood together in a vast empty space. The light, polished tiles reflected the fluorescent glow. There were no windows.

32   Far across the room, a row of metal desks lined the wall. Each had a green vinyl-covered chair beside it. Off to our left, facing the empty space before us, was a very high green metal desk. It was easily twice as high as a normal-size

desk. Its odd size and placement in the middle of the room gave it the appearance of a kind of altar that divided the room in half. There were many people working at desks or walking about, but the room was so big that it still seemed empty.

33   The head and shoulders of a white-haired woman appeared to rest on the big desk like a sculptured bust. She sat very still. Above her head the word CLAIMS dangled from two pieces of chain attached to the ceiling. As I watched the woman she beckoned to us. *Pai* and I walked toward her.

34   The desk was so high that *Pai's* shoulders barely cleared the top. Even when I stood on tiptoe I couldn't see over it. I had to stretch and lean my head way back to see the woman's round face. I thought that she must have very long legs to need a desk that high. The coldness in me grew. My neck hurt.

35   "My father can't speak English. He has no work and we need money."

36   She reached for some papers from a wire basket. One of her fingers was encased in a piece of orange rubber.

37   "Come around over here so I can see you." She motioned to the side of the desk. I went reluctantly. Rounding the desk I saw with relief that she was a small woman perched on a stool so high it seemed she would need a ladder to get up there.

38   "How old are you?" She leaned down toward me.

39   "Eight."

40   "My, aren't you a brave girl. Only eight years old and helping daddy like that. And what lovely earrings you have."

41   She liked my earrings. I went a little closer to let her touch them. Maybe she would give us money.

42   "What language does your father speak?" She was straightening up, reaching for a pencil.

43   "Portuguese."

44   *"What is she saying?" Pai* wanted to know.

45   *"Wait,"* I told him. The lady hadn't yet said anything about money.

46   "Why isn't your father working?"

47   "His factory burned down."

48   *"What is she saying?" Pai* repeated.

49   *"She wants to know why you aren't working."*

50   *"Tell her the factory burned down."*

51   *"I know, I did."* The lady was looking at me. I hoped she wouldn't ask me what my father had just said.

52   "What is your father's name?"

53   "Carlos S. Cunha. C-u-n-h-a." No one could ever spell *Cunha.* Pai nodded at the woman when he heard his name.

54   "Where do you live?"

55   "Thirty-three Tracey Street, Peabody, Massachusetts." Pai nodded again when he heard the address.

56   "When was your father born?"

57   *"Quando é que tu naçestes?"*

58   "When was the last day your father worked?"

59   *"Qual foi o último dia que trabalhastes?"*

60   "What was the name of the factory?"

61   *"Qual éra o nome da fábrica?"*

62   "How long did he work there?"

63   *"Quanto tempo trabalhastes lá?"*

64   "What is his Social Security number?"

65   I looked at her blankly, not knowing what to say. What was a Social Security number?

66   *"What did she say?"* *Pai* prompted me out of silence.

67   *"I don't know. She wants a kind of number."* I was feeling very tired and worried. But *Pai* took a small card from his wallet and gave it to the lady. She copied something from it onto her papers and returned it to him. I felt a great sense of relief. She wrote silently for a while as we stood and waited. Then she handed some papers to *Pai* and looked at me.

68   "Tell your father that he must have these forms filled out by his employer before he can receive unemployment benefits."

69   I stared at her. What was she saying? Employer? Unemployment benefits? I was afraid she was saying we couldn't have any money. Maybe not, though. Maybe we could have money if I could understand her words.

70   *"What did she say? Can we have some money?"*

71   *"I don't know. I can't understand the words."*

72   *"Ask her again if we can have money,"* *Pai* insisted. *"Tell her we have to pay the rent."*

73   "We need money for the rent," I told the lady, trying to hold back tears.

74   "You can't have money today. You must take the forms to your father's employer and bring them back completed next week. Then your father must sign another form which we will keep here to process his claim. When he comes back in two weeks there may be a check for him." The cold in me was so big now. I was trying not to shiver.

75   "Do you understand?" The lady was looking at me.

76   I wanted to say, "No, I don't," but I was afraid we would never get money and *Pai* would be angry.

77   "Tell your father to take the papers to his boss and come back next week."

78   Boss. I could understand boss.

79   *"She said you have to take these papers to your 'bossa' and come back next week."*

80   *"We can't have money today?"*

81   *"No. She said maybe we can have money in two weeks."*

82   *"Did you tell her we have to pay the rent?"*

83   *"Yes, but she said we can't have money yet."*

84   The lady was saying good-bye and beckoning the next person from the line that had formed behind us.

85   I was relieved to move on, but I think *Pai* wanted to stay and argue with her. I knew that if he could speak English, he would have. I knew that he thought it was my fault we couldn't have money. And I myself wasn't so sure that wasn't true.

86   That night I sat at the kitchen table with a fat pencil and a piece of paper. In my second-grade scrawl I wrote: Dear Miss Laitinen, Mary Edith was sick.

87   I gave the paper to *Pai* and told him to sign his name.

88   *"What does it say?"*

89   *"It says that I was sick today. I need to give it to my teacher."*

90   *"You weren't sick today."*

91   *"Ya, but it would take too many words to tell her the truth."*

92   *Pai* signed the paper. The next morning in school, Miss Laitinen read it and said that she hoped I was feeling better.

93 When I was nine, *Pai* went to an auction and bought a big house on Tremont Street. We moved in the spring. The yard at the side of the house dipped downward in a gentle slope that was covered with a dense row of tall lilac bushes. I soon discovered that I could crawl in among the twisted trunks to hide from my brothers in the fragrant shade. It was paradise. . . .

94 I was mostly wild and joyful on Tremont Street. But there was a shadow that fell across my days now and again.

95   *"Ó Ediiiite."* *Pai* would call me without the least bit of warning, to be his voice. He expected me to drop whatever I was doing to attend him. Of late, I'd had to struggle on the telephone with the voice of a woman who wanted some old dishes. The dishes, along with lots of old furniture and junk, had been in the house when we moved in. They were in the cellar, stacked in cardboard boxes and covered with dust. The woman called many times wanting to speak with *Pai*.

96   "My father can't speak English," I would say. "He says to tell you that the dishes are in our house and they belong to us." But she did not seem to understand. Every few days she would call.

97   *"Ó Ediiiite."* *Pai's* voice echoed through the empty rooms. Hearing it brought on a chill. It had that tone. As always, my first impulse was to pretend I had not heard, but there was no escape. I couldn't disappear into thin air as I wished to do at such calls. We were up in the third-floor apartment of our new house. *Pai* was working in the kitchen. Carlos and I had made a cavern of old cushions and were sitting together deep in its bowels when he called. It was so dark and comfortable there I decided not to answer until the third call, though that risked *Pai's* wrath.

98   *"Ó Ediiite."* Yes, that tone was certainly there. *Pai* was calling me to do something only I could do. Something that always awakened a cold beast deep in my gut. He wanted me to be his bridge. What was it now? Did he have to talk to someone at City Hall again? Or was it the insurance company? They were always using words I couldn't understand: liability, and premium, and dividend. It made me frustrated and scared.

99   "You wait. My dotta come." *Pai* was talking to someone. Who could it be? That was some relief. At least I didn't have to call someone on the phone. It was always harder to understand when I couldn't see people's mouths.

100   *"Ó Ediiiiite."* I hated Carlos. *Pai* never called his name like that. He never had to do anything but play.

101   *"Que éééé?"*

102   *"Come over here and talk to this lady."*

103   Reluctantly I crawled out from the soft darkness and walked through the empty rooms toward the kitchen. Through the kitchen door I could see a slim lady dressed in brown standing at the top of the stairs in the windowed porch. She had on very skinny high-heeled shoes and a brown purse to match. As soon as *Pai* saw me he said to the lady, "Dis my dotta." To me he said, "See what she wants."

104   The lady had dark hair that was very smooth and puffed away from her head. The ends of it flipped up in a way that I liked.

105   "Hello. I'm the lady who called about the dishes."

106   I stared at her without a word. My stomach lurched.

107   *"What did she say?"* Pai wanted to know.

108   *"She says she's the lady who wants the dishes."*

109   *Pai's* face hardened some.

110   *"Tell her she's wasting her time. We're not giving them to her. Didn't you already tell her that on the telephone?"*

111   I nodded, standing helplessly between them.

112   *"Well, tell her again." Pai* was getting angry. I wanted to disappear.

113   "My father says he can't give you the dishes," I said to the lady. She clutched her purse and leaned a little forward.

114   "Yes, you told me that on the phone. But I wanted to come in person and speak with your father because it's very important to me that—"

115   "My father can't speak English," I interrupted her. Why didn't she just go away? She was still standing in the doorway with her back to the stairwell. I wanted to push her down.

116   "Yes, I understand that. But I wanted to see him." She looked at *Pai*, who was standing in the doorway to the kitchen holding his hammer. The kitchen was up one step from the porch. *Pai* was a small man, but he looked kind of scary staring down at us like that.

117   *"What is she saying?"*

118   *"She says she wanted to talk to you about getting her dishes."*

119   *"Tell her the dishes are ours. They were in the house. We bought the house and everything in it. Tell her the lawyer said so."*

120   The brown lady was looking at me expectantly.

121   "My father says the dishes are ours because we bought the house and the lawyer said everything in the house is ours now."

122   "Yes, I know that, but I was away when the house was being sold. I didn't know . . . "

123   *"Eeii."* There were footsteps on the stairs behind her. It was *Mãe* coming up from the second floor to find out what was going on. The lady moved away from the door to let *Mãe* in.

124   "Dis my wife," *Pai* said to the lady. The lady said hello to *Mãe*, who smiled and nodded her head. She looked at me, then at *Pai* in a questioning way.

125   *"It's the lady who wants our dishes," Pai* explained.

126   *"Ó." Mãe* looked at her again and smiled, but I could tell she was a little worried.

127   We stood there in kind of a funny circle; the lady looked at each of us in turn and took a deep breath.

128   "I didn't know," she continued, "that the dishes were in the house. I was away. They are very important to me. They belonged to my grandmother. I'd really like to get them back." She spoke this while looking back and forth between *Mãe* and *Pai*. Then she looked down at me, leaning forward again. "Will you tell your parents, please?"

129   The cold beast inside me had begun to rise up toward my throat as the lady spoke. I knew that soon it would try to choke out my words. I spoke in a hurry to get them out.

130   *"She said she didn't know the dishes were in the house she was away they were her grandmother's dishes she wants them back."* I felt a deep sadness at the thought of the lady returning home to find her grandmother's dishes sold.

131   *"We don't need all those dishes. Let's give them to her," Mãe* said in her calm way. I felt relieved. We could give the lady the dishes and she would go away. But *Pai* got angry.

132   *"I already said what I had to say. The dishes are ours. That is all."*

133   *"Pai, she said she didn't know. They were her grandmother's dishes. She needs to have them."* I was speaking wildly and loud now. The lady looked at me questioningly, but I didn't want to speak to her again.

134   *"She's only saying that to trick us. If she wanted those dishes she should have taken them out before the house was sold. Tell her we are not fools. Tell her to forget it. She can go away. Tell her not to call or come here again."*

135   "What is he saying?" The lady was looking at me again.

136   I ignored her. I felt sorry for *Pai* for always feeling that people were trying to trick him. I wanted him to trust people. I wanted the lady to have her grandmother's dishes. I closed my eyes and willed myself away.

137   *"Tell her what I said!" Pai* yelled.

138   *"Pai, just give her the dishes! They were her grandmother's dishes!"* My voice cracked as I yelled back at him. Tears were rising.

139   I hated *Pai* for being so stubborn. I hated the lady for not taking the dishes before the house was sold. I hated myself for having learned to speak English.

TOPICAL CONSIDERATIONS

1. Why was the author's name, Maria Edite dos Anjos Cunha, so powerful to her? What were the associations? Does your own name have special significance, special associations? Are these associations a source of pride and identity to you?

2. What values and assumptions underscored Mrs. Donahue's immediate response to Pedrosa's name? Explain the irony of that. What is your own reaction to her changing the author's name? How might you have felt if you were young Edite Pedrosa?

3. Pedrosa's father did not speak English. How was this deficiency an economic and social handicap for the Cunha family?

4. Why was it so painful for Pedrosa to serve as her father's translator? What was the "coldness" she felt when she attempted to translate for her father?

5. Try to explain why the author wanted to give the woman the dishes. Explain her father's resistance to parting with them. How did language figure into their diverse reactions?

6. What do you remember best about this essay? Is there anything here that might change your attitude toward non–English-speaking people? Explain your answer.

RHETORICAL CONSIDERATIONS

1. How does the episode with the priest prefigure the difficulties Pedrosa will face in keeping her name? How effective did you find this episode?

2. Select one scene and examine the techniques the author uses to depict the world from a child's point of view. In your answer, consider such things as spacial relations, scale, posture, physical details, and so on. Do you think she does an effective job here? Why or why not? Would you have done things differently?

3. Evaluate the concluding paragraph of this essay, particularly the last sentence. What technique was used here?

WRITING ASSIGNMENTS

1. Do you like your own name? Would you want to change it for any reason? Would you like to alter its ethnic, racial, or religious identity? Write a paper in which you talk about your name: what you like or don't like about it; what significance and identity it has for you; what sense of power or handicap you associate with it.

2. How were name choices made in your family? Write a paper explaining how names were selected for you and other family members. To do this, you might want to question your parents, grandparents, and other relatives. Do you discover family-tree patterns? Are there strong naming traditions in your heritage?

3. If you are bilingual, write a paper exploring what communication problems you had as a child. Did you, like Pedrosa, have to translate for your parents or grandparents? Was this emotionally difficult for you? Explain how you felt, recalling, if possible, any particularly telling experiences.

4. Did your parents or grandparents come to America from another country? If not, are you acquainted with anyone who did or whose family members did? Conduct an interview with this person about his or her language choices. What is his or her view of the importance of language? What about the relationship of language to ethnicity and identity? Did he or she retain the original language after moving to America? Was it passed on to any children? If not, why not? Transcribe your interview, writing an introduction to the person you worked with.

2 | SOME WORDS ON WRITING

"GOT IDEA. TALK BETTER. COMBINE WORDS. MAKE SENTENCES."

Common to each of the essays in this text is the exploration of how language constructs reality for us: how it can be used to lead, mislead, and manipulate us. While several pieces celebrate the joys of language, some lament its woes—that literacy in America is on the decline, that politicians and bureaucrats talk gobbledygook, that advertisers shamelessly torture the language to sell their goods, and that the ability of students to write clear, well-organized English is deteriorating. In short, you will hear a lot about bad writing.

But before you are exposed to all that, this chapter offers you some solid advice about good writing since, ultimately, that is what you are hoping to achieve in this course. Also, from a practical point of view, the essays in this chapter are intended to prepare you for writing projects assigned by your instructor or suggested by the Writing Assignments following each selection in this text. By the time you move into subsequent chapters, you should be familiar with some basic rhetorical principles and strategies so that you can enter with confidence the lively and fascinating debates about language.

Nearly every piece of writing you will do in college will be an exercise in persuasion—an attempt to influence your readers' attitude toward your subject matter. This is true whether you're discussing tragic irony in *Oedipus Rex*, analyzing the cause of World War I, writing a lab report on the solubility of salt, protesting next year's tuition increase, or explaining the joys of bungy jumping. How successful you are at persuading your readers will have a lot to do with the words you choose.

GETTING STARTED

The opening piece is for anyone who has ever sat in front of a blank piece of paper, unable to think of what to put on it. Just about everyone, of course. In "Freewriting," author and teacher Peter Elbow gives some useful techniques on getting started—that is, generating words and ideas even when you've drawn a blank.

FINDING THE RIGHT WORDS

The next three pieces address a fundamental principle of all communication—that language mirrors the user—and each offers solid advice on choosing your words. In the first, "Simplicity," William Zinsser says the first step in writing well is to ask yourself, "What am I trying to say?" and then to try to find the simplest, clearest way of saying it. Too many times writers opt for cluttered expression, empty jargon, and convoluted constructions to make what they're saying sound smarter than it is. But, as Zinsser points out, that is what makes bad writing. Next is some advice from one of America's most popular contemporary novelists, Kurt Vonnegut. In "How to Write with Style," Vonnegut gives eight friendly tips about the process of writing—among them, choosing a subject, saying what you mean, and writing in a voice that is all your own.

Writers don't always say what they mean. Sometimes language is like a funhouse mirror, reflecting distorted images instead of the truth. In "Selection, Slanting, and Charged Language," authors Newman P. Birk and Genevieve B. Birk demonstrate how words can warp reality while bending minds to certain ends. Their insights will help you to sharpen your own verbal strategies while making you alert to the linguistic manipulations of others.

REVISING THE PRODUCT

The key to good writing is rewriting. That fact is the thrust of the next essay in this chapter, "The Maker's Eye: Revising Your Own Manuscript." As Donald Murray explains, many student writers consider their first draft the final product. But to most professional writers, the first draft is just the beginning of the writing process. A professional novelist, short story writer, poet, and newspaper columnist, Murray stresses the importance of revision, which involves much more than simply proofreading, and offers some valuable advice on how to do it.

The chapter closes with a poem by former poet laureate, Richard Wilbur. Although "The Writer" is a meditation by the speaker on his daughter's struggle to write a story, the poem beautifully captures some of the predicament and promise we all face when engaged in the act of writing.

FREEWRITING

Peter Elbow

Anyone who has ever written knows the miserable experience of sitting down before a notebook or computer screen and not being able to come up with anything clever to say—maybe not being able to come up with anything at all. It happens to the best of writers. For students who have papers due regularly, the experience can be maddening. So here is some advice from a man who has taught and written on the subject long enough to appreciate the heartache.

Peter Elbow has taught writing at many colleges and universities including MIT, Franconia College, Evergreen State College, Wesleyan University and, currently, at the University of Massachusetts at Amherst. He is author of many articles and three books on writing including *Writing with Power* (1981) and *Embracing Contraries* (1986). This article first appeared as a chapter in *Writing without Teachers* (1975).

1   The most effective way I know to improve your writing is to do freewriting exercises regularly. At least three times a week. They are sometimes called "automatic writing," "babbling," or "jabbering" exercises. The idea is simply to write for ten minutes (later on, perhaps fifteen or twenty). Don't stop for anything. Go quickly without rushing. Never stop to look back, to cross something out, to wonder how to spell something, to wonder what word or thought to use, or to think about what you are doing. If you can't think of a word or a spelling, just use a squiggle or else write, "I can't think of it." Just put down something. The easiest thing is just to put down whatever is in your mind. If you get stuck it's fine to write "I can't think what to say, I can't think what to say" as many times as you want; or repeat the last word you wrote over and over again; or anything else. The only requirement is that you *never* stop.

2   What happens to a freewriting exercise is important. It must be a piece of writing which, even if someone reads it, doesn't send any ripples back to you. It is like writing something and putting it in a bottle in the sea. The teacherless class helps your writing by providing maximum feedback. Freewriting helps you by providing no feedback at all. When I assign one, I invite the writer to

let me read it, but also tell him to keep it if he prefers. I read it quickly and make no comments at all and I do not speak with him about it. The main thing is that a freewriting must never be evaluated in any way; in fact there must be no discussion or comment at all.

3   Here is an example of a fairly coherent exercise (sometimes they are very coherent, which is fine):

> I think I'll write what's on my mind, but the only thing on my mind right now is what to write for ten minutes. I've never done this before and I'm not prepared in any way—the sky is cloudy today, how's that? now I'm afraid I won't be able to think of what to write when I get to the end of the sentence—well, here I am at the end of the sentence—here I am again, again, again, again, at least I'm still writing— Now I ask is there some reason to be happy that I'm still writing—ah yes! Here comes the question again—What am I getting out of this? What point is there in it? It's almost obscene to always ask it but I seem to question everything that way and I was gonna say something else pertaining to that but I got so busy writing down the first part that I forgot what I was leading into. This is kind of fun oh don't stop writing—cars and trucks speeding by somewhere out the window, pens clittering across peoples' papers. The sky is still cloudy—is it symbolic that I should be mentioning it? Huh? I dunno. Maybe I should try colors, blue, red, dirty words—wait a minute—no can't do that, orange, yellow, arm tired, green pink violet magenta lavender red brown black green—now that I can't think of any more colors—just about done—relief? maybe.

4   Freewriting may seem crazy but actually it makes simple sense. Think of the difference between speaking and writing. Writing has the advantage of permitting more editing. But that's its downfall too. Almost everybody interposes a massive and complicated series of editings between the time words start to be born into consciousness and when they finally come off the end of the pencil or typewriter onto the page. This is partly because schooling makes us obsessed with the "mistakes" we make in writing. Many people are constantly thinking about spelling and grammar as they try to write. I am always thinking about the awkwardness, wordiness, and general mushiness of my natural verbal product as I try to write down words.

5   But it's not just "mistakes" or "bad writing" we edit as we write. We also edit unacceptable thoughts and feelings, as we do in speaking. In writing there is more time to do it so the editing is heavier: when speaking, there's someone right there waiting for a reply and he'll get bored or think we're crazy if we don't come out with *something*. Most of the time in speaking, we settle for the catch-as-catch-can way in which the words tumble out. In writing, however, there's a chance to try to get them right. But the opportunity to get them right is a terrible burden: you can work for two hours trying to get a paragraph "right" and discover it's not right at all. And then give up.

6   Editing, *in itself*, is not the problem. Editing is usually necessary if we want to end up with something satisfactory. The problem is that editing goes on *at the same time* as producing. The editor is, as it were, constantly looking over the shoulder of the producer and constantly fiddling with what he's doing

while he's in the middle of trying to do it. No wonder the producer gets nervous, jumpy, inhibited, and finally can't be coherent. It's an unnecessary burden to try to think of words and also worry at the same time whether they're the right words.

7   The main thing about freewriting is that it is *nonediting*. It is an exercise in bringing together the process of producing words and putting them down on the page. Practiced regularly, it undoes the ingrained habit of editing at the same time you are trying to produce. It will make writing less blocked because words will come more easily. You will use up more paper, but chew up fewer pencils.

8   Next time you write, notice how often you stop yourself from writing down something you were going to write down. Or else cross it out after it's written. "Naturally," you say, "it wasn't any good." But think for a moment about the occasions when you spoke well. Seldom was it because you first got the beginning just right. Usually it was a matter of a halting or even garbled beginning, but you kept going and your speech finally became coherent and even powerful. There is a lesson here for writing: trying to get the beginning just right is a formula for failure—and probably a secret tactic to make yourself give up writing. Make some words, whatever they are, and then grab hold of that line and reel in as hard as you can. Afterwards you can throw away lousy beginnings and make new ones. This is the quickest way to get into good writing.

9   The habit of compulsive, premature editing doesn't just make writing hard. It also makes writing dead. Your voice is damped out by all the interruptions, changes, and hesitations between the consciousness and the page. In your natural way of producing words there is a sound, a texture, a rhythm—a voice—which is the main source of power in your writing. I don't know how it works, but this voice is the force that will make a reader listen to you, the energy that drives the meanings through his thick skull. Maybe you don't *like* your voice; maybe people have made fun of it. But it's the only voice you've got. It's your only source of power. You better get back into it, no matter what you think of it. If you keep writing in it, it may change into something you like better. But if you abandon it, you'll likely never have a voice and never be heard.

TOPICAL CONSIDERATION

1. Elbow says that perhaps the most important characteristic of freewriting is its freedom from feedback. Explain what he means by this.

2. According to the author, how should writing be more like speaking? Explain the advantages he sees. Do you agree with him?

3. What is the role of editing in freewriting? When should it take place?

4. What is the "formula for failure" Elbow refers to in paragraph 8? Is this a formula you're familiar with? Is the "lesson" here something you can take to heart? Might it affect your writing at all?

5. Did this small article make you feel differently about your own writing? Did you find it encouraging? If so, explain what you got out of it. If you got nothing out of Elbow's advice, explain why.

RHETORICAL CONSIDERATIONS

1. At what point in this essay do you know the author's focus? What devices does he use to support his purpose?

2. How helpful was Elbow's example of freewriting in paragraph 3? How did it reflect his different tips in the first two paragraphs? Do you think this was a legitimate piece of freewriting, or one that had been edited? Explain your answer.

3. What audience do you think Elbow is writing for? Citing evidence from the piece, explain your answer.

WRITING ASSIGNMENTS

1. Look around your room. Find a particular feature or object at random and try freewriting about it for ten minutes. When you are through, edit it with a mind to creating a finished product.

2. Freewrite for ten or twenty minutes on how you cannot think of anything to say. When you've finished, go back and rework your material until you've got something you're satisfied with.

3. Freewrite for ten or twenty minutes using one of these words as a lead: car, professor, shoes, fat, easy, happy, first, never.

4. Freewrite for ten or twenty minutes using one of these topics as a starting point: capital punishment, dieting, racism, sexism, obscene language, religion, ecology, abortion.

5. Freewrite for at least a page. Then go back and note instances of selection, slanting, or charged language. Write a short paper explaining why you used such language and how it affected the paper. Now try rewriting your paper in neutral terms. How do the results compare?

SIMPLICITY

William Zinsser

William Zinsser has been writing well for years, and he is more than qualified to offer advice on how to do it. For thirteen years he served as writer, editor, and critic with the *New York Herald Tribune*. He also worked as a columnist for the *New York Times* and *Life*. He taught writing for nearly a decade at Yale and is the author of *On Writing Well*, fifth edition (1994), from which this essay is taken. Here Zinsser offers advice on keeping your writing simple. As he says, "the secret of good writing is to strip every sentence to its cleanest components." To illustrate how good tight prose needs to be worked at, he includes two pages from the actual manuscript of the first edition of his book that were rewritten for the fourth.

1   Clutter is the disease of American writing. We are a society strangling in unnecessary words, circular constructions, pompous frills and meaningless jargon.

2   Who can understand the viscous language of everyday American commerce and enterprise: the business letter, the interoffice memo, the corporation report, the notice from the bank explaining its latest "simplified" statement? What member of an insurance or medical plan can decipher the brochure that describes what the costs and benefits are? What father or mother can put together a child's toy—on Christmas Eve or any other eve—from the instructions on the box? Our national tendency is to inflate and thereby sound important. The airline pilot who announces that he is presently anticipating experiencing considerable precipitation wouldn't dream of saying that it may rain. The sentence is too simple—there must be something wrong with it.

3   But the secret of good writing is to strip every sentence to its cleanest components. Every word that serves no function, every long word that could be a short word, every adverb that carries the same meaning that's already in the verb, every passive construction that leaves the reader unsure of who is doing what—these are the thousand and one adulterants that weaken the strength of a sentence. And they usually occur, ironically, in proportion to education and rank.

is too dumb or too lazy to keep pace with the ~~writer's~~ train of

thought. My sympathics are ~~entirely~~ with him.)~~He's not so dumb.~~

If the reader is lost, it is generally because the writer ~~of the~~

~~article~~ has not been careful enough to keep him on the ~~proper~~

path.

This carelessness can take any number of ~~different~~ forms.

Perhaps a sentence is so excessively ~~long and~~ cluttered that the

reader, hacking his way through ~~all~~ the verbiage, simply doesn't

know what *it* ~~the writer~~ means. Perhaps a sentence has been so

shoddily constructed that the reader could read it in any of *several* ~~two~~

~~or three differ~~ent ways. ~~He thinks he knows what the writer is~~

~~trying to say, but he's not sure~~. Perhaps the writer has

switched pronouns in mid-sentence, or ~~perhaps he~~ has switched

tenses, so the reader loses track of who is talking t~~o whom~~, or

~~exactly~~ when the action took place. Perhaps Sentence B is not a

logical sequel to Sentence A — the writer, in whose head the

connection is ~~perfectly~~ clear, has not *bothered to provide* ~~given enough thought to~~

~~providing~~ the missing link. Perhaps the writer has used an

important word incorrectly by not taking the trouble to look it

up~~, and make sure~~. He may think that "sanguine" and "sanguinary"

mean the same thing, but ~~I can assure you that~~ the difference is

a bloody big one, ~~to the reader~~. *The reader* ~~He~~ can only ~~try to~~ infer ~~what~~

(speaking of big differences) what the writer is trying to imply.

these / Faced with ~~such a variety of~~ obstacles, the reader is at

first a remarkably tenacious bird. He ~~tends to~~ blame~~s~~ himself. ~~.~~

~~He~~ obviously missed something, ~~he thinks,~~ and he goes back

over the mystifying sentence, or over the whole paragraph,

Two pages of the final manuscript of this chapter from the first edition of *On Writing Well*. Although they look like a first draft, they had already been rewritten and retyped—like almost every other page—four or five times. With each rewrite I try to make what I have written tighter, stronger and more precise, eliminating every element that is not doing useful work. Then I go over it once more, reading it aloud, and am always amazed at how much clutter can still be cut. (In a later edition of this book I eliminated the sexist pronoun "he" to denote "the writer" and "the reader.")

6 —   ON WRITING WELL

piecing it out like an ancient rune, making guesses and moving

on. But he won't do this for long. ~~He will soon run out of patience.~~ The writer is making him work too hard, ~~harder than he should have to work~~ and the reader will look for ~~a writer~~ one who

is better at his craft.

The writer must therefore constantly ask himself: What am I

trying to say ~~in this sentence?~~ (Surprisingly often, he doesn't

know.) ~~And~~ Then he must look at what he has ~~just~~ written and ask:

Have I said it? Is it clear to someone encountering ~~who is coming upon~~ the

subject for the first time? If it's not, ~~clear,~~ it is because some

fuzz has worked its way into the machinery. The clear writer is a

person ~~who is~~ clear-headed enough to see this stuff for what it

is: fuzz.

I don't mean ~~to suggest~~ that some people are born

clear-headed and are therefore natural writers, whereas others ~~other people~~ are naturally fuzzy and will ~~therefore~~ never write well.

Thinking clearly is a ~~an entirely~~ conscious act that the writer

must force ~~keep forcing~~ upon himself, just as if he were embarking ~~starting~~

~~out~~ on any other ~~kind of~~ project that requires ~~calls for~~ logic: adding

up a laundry list or doing an algebra problem ~~or playing chess~~.

Good writing doesn't ~~just~~ come naturally, though most people

obviously think it does ~~it's as easy as walking~~. The professional

4   During the late 1960s the president of a major university wrote a letter to mollify the alumni after a spell of campus unrest. "You are probably aware," he began, "that we have been experiencing very considerable potentially explosive expressions of dissatisfaction on issues only partially related." He meant that the students had been hassling them about different things. I was far more upset by the president's English than by the student's potentially explosive expressions of dissatisfaction. I would have preferred the presidential

approach taken by Franklin D. Roosevelt when he tried to convert into English his own government's memos, such as this blackout order of 1942:

> Such preparations shall be made as will completely obscure all Federal buildings and non-Federal buildings occupied by the Federal government during an air raid for any period of time from visibility by reason of internal or external illumination.

5   "Tell them," Roosevelt said, "that in buildings where they have to keep the work going to put something across the windows."

6   Simplify, simplify. Thoreau said it, as we are so often reminded, and no American writer more consistently practiced what he preached. Open *Walden* to any page and you will find a man saying in a plain and orderly way what is on his mind:

> I went to the woods because I wished to live deliberately, to front only the essential facts of life, and see if I could not learn what it had to teach, and not, when I came to die, discover that I had not lived. I did not wish to live what was not life, living is so dear; nor did I wish to practice resignation, unless it was quite necessary. I wanted to live deep and suck out all the marrow of life, to live so sturdily and Spartan-like as to put to rout all that was not life, to cut a broad swath and shave close, to drive life into a corner, and reduce it to its lowest terms, and, if it proved to be mean, why then to get the whole and genuine meanness of it, and publish its meanness to the world; or if it were sublime, to know it by experience, and be able to give a true account of it.

7   How can the rest of us achieve such enviable freedom from clutter? The answer is to clear our heads of clutter. Clear thinking becomes clear writing; one can't exist without the other. It's impossible for a muddy thinker to write good English. You may get away with it for a paragraph or two, but soon the reader will be lost, and there's no sin so grave, for the reader will not easily be lured back.

8   Who is this elusive creature, the reader? The reader is someone with an attention span of about sixty seconds—a person assailed by forces competing for the minutes that might otherwise be spent on a magazine or a book. At one time these forces weren't so numerous or so possessive: newspapers, radio, spouse, home, children. Today they also include a "home entertainment center" (TV, VCR, video camera, tapes and CDs), pets, a fitness program, a lawn and a garden and all the gadgets that have been bought to keep them spruce, and that most potent of competitors, sleep. The person snoozing in a chair, holding a magazine or a book, is a person who was being given too much unnecessary trouble by the writer.

9   It won't do to say that the reader is too dumb or too lazy to keep pace with the train of thought. If the reader is lost, it's usually because the writer hasn't been careful enough. The carelessness can take any number of forms. Perhaps a sentence is so excessively cluttered that the reader, hacking through the verbiage, simply doesn't know what it means. Perhaps a sentence has been so shoddily constructed that the reader could read it in any of several ways. Perhaps the writer has switched pronouns in midsentence, or has

switched tenses, so the reader loses track of who is talking or when the action took place. Perhaps Sentence B is not a logical sequel to Sentence A—the writer, in whose head the connection is clear, hasn't bothered to provide the missing link. Perhaps the writer has used an important word incorrectly by not taking the trouble to look it up. The writer may think that "sanguine" and "sanguinary" mean the same thing, but the difference is a bloody big one. The reader can only infer (speaking of big differences) what the writer is trying to imply.

10   Faced with such obstacles, readers are at first remarkably tenacious. They blame themselves—they obviously missed something, and they go back over the mystifying sentence, or over the whole paragraph, piecing it out like an ancient rune, making guesses and moving on. But they won't do this for long. The writer is making them work too hard, and they will look for one who is better at the craft.

11   Writers must therefore constantly ask: What am I trying to say? Surprisingly often they don't know. Then they must look at what they have written and ask: Have I said it? Is it clear to someone encountering the subject for the first time? If it's not, that's because some fuzz has worked its way into the machinery. The clear writer is someone clearheaded enough to see this stuff for what it is: fuzz.

12   I don't mean that some people are born clearheaded and are therefore natural writers, whereas others are naturally fuzzy and will never write well. Thinking clearly is a conscious act that writers must force upon themselves, just as if they were embarking on any other project that requires logic: adding up a laundry list or doing an algebra problem. Good writing doesn't come naturally, though most people obviously think it does. The professional writer is constantly being bearded by strangers who say they'd like to "try a little writing sometime"—meaning when they retire from their real profession, like insurance or real estate. Or they say, "I could write a book about that." I doubt it.

13   Writing is hard work. A clear sentence is no accident. Very few sentences come out right the first time, or even the third time. Remember this as a consolation in moments of despair. If you find that writing is hard, it's because it *is* hard. It's one of the hardest things that people do.

TOPICAL CONSIDERATIONS

1. According to Zinsser, what is the major problem with modern-day writing? Do you agree with him? Why or why not?

2. In paragraph 3, Zinsser states that the "adulterants that weaken the strength of a sentence" usually occur in proportion to education and rank. What do you suppose he means by this? In your experience, do you find this to be true?

3. Why does Zinsser admire Thoreau's writing? How does Thoreau's description of ideal life echo Zinsser's ideas regarding ideal writing?

4. In paragraph 8, Zinsser says that "the reader is someone with an attention span of about sixty seconds." What evidence does he give for this statement? Do you agree with his portrayal of the average reader? Why or why not?

5. Zinsser reinforces the idea that clear writing is a result of clear thinking. Think about your own writing process. How do you perceive the connection between your own thought process and your writing?

RHETORICAL CONSIDERATIONS

1. Has Zinsser chosen an effective title for this piece? Why or why not?

2. Reread Zinsser's article, looking for places where he employs slanted or charged language. How does such language function in his article? Is this technique effective?

3. Does Zinsser's writing style appeal to you? What might be the opposing view to his argument for simple writing?

4. Zinsser has inserted a draft page of this essay in the final product, illustrating his revisions. Does this page help support his argument? If so, how? Is this an effective rhetorical strategy?

WRITING ASSIGNMENTS

1. Find an old piece of writing and revise it using Zinsser's rule of "simplicity." (See paragraph 3 for specific revision guidelines.) Then write a paragraph reflecting on your revisions and whether they are an improvement.

2. Reread Zinsser's paragraphs on typical readers (8–10). Choose three articles, each from a different publication, and write a paper analyzing them in terms of audience. Who is the targeted audience of each piece? Could any of these pieces be rewritten to hold reader attention better? How would you revise each piece if you were the editor?

3. Examine Zinsser's revisions on his draft page. Write a paragraph explaining why the revisions are or are not effective. Would you do anything differently? Do you agree with Zinsser's emphasis on simplicity?

4. Write a paper in which you reflect on your own writing and revision process. How does your process differ from the one Zinsser advocates in his article? What do you value most in a piece of good writing?

How to Write with Style

Kurt Vonnegut

Kurt Vonnegut is one of America's most popular contemporary humorists and novelists. The author of such favorites as *Cat's Cradle* (1963), *Slaughterhouse Five* (1969), *Sirens of Titan* (1971), *Breakfast of Champions* (1973), *Deadeye Dick* (1982), *Jailbird* (1987), *Hocus Pocus* (1990), and *Timequake* (1993), Vonnegut has also written short stories for periodicals ranging from *Ladies Home Journal* to *Playboy*. The enormous success of his writing can be attributed to his zany imagination and his style, which employs a popular idiom. Many consider him the Mark Twain of our day. What follows is his own practical advice on writing well.

1 Newspaper reporters and technical writers are trained to reveal almost nothing about themselves in their writings. This makes them freaks in the world of writers, since almost all of the other ink-stained wretches in that world reveal a lot about themselves to readers. We call these revelations, accidental and intentional, elements of style.

2 These revelations tell us as readers what sort of person it is with whom we are spending time. Does the writer sound ignorant or informed, stupid or bright, crooked or honest, humorless or playful—? And on and on.

3 Why should you examine your writing style with the idea of improving it? Do so as a mark of respect for your readers, whatever you're writing. If you scribble your thoughts any which way, your readers will surely feel that you care nothing about them. They will mark you down as an egomaniac or a chowderhead—or worse, they will stop reading you.

4 The most damning revelation you can make about yourself is that you do not know what is interesting and what is not. Don't you yourself like or dislike writers mainly for what they choose to show you or make you think about? Did you ever admire an empty-headed writer for his or her mastery of the language? No.

5 So your own winning style must begin with ideas in your head.

1. FIND A SUBJECT YOU CARE ABOUT

6   Find a subject you care about and which you in your heart feel others should care about. It is this genuine caring, and not your games with language, which will be the most compelling and seductive element in your style.

7   I am not urging you to write a novel, by the way—although I would not be sorry if you wrote one, provided you genuinely cared about something. A petition to the mayor about a pothole in front of your house or a love letter to the girl next door will do.

2. DO NOT RAMBLE, THOUGH

8   I won't ramble on about that.

3. KEEP IT SIMPLE

9   As for your use of language: Remember that two great masters of language, William Shakespeare and James Joyce, wrote sentences which were almost childlike when their subjects were most profound. "To be or not to be?" asks Shakespeare's Hamlet. The longest word is three letters long. Joyce, when he was frisky, could put together a sentence as intricate and as glittering as a necklace for Cleopatra, but my favorite sentence in his short story "Eveline" is this one: "She was tired." At that point in the story, no other words could break the heart of a reader as those three words do.

10   Simplicity of language is not only reputable, but perhaps even sacred. The *Bible* opens with a sentence well within the writing skills of a lively fourteen-year-old: "In the beginning God created the heaven and the earth."

4. HAVE THE GUTS TO CUT

11   It may be that you, too, are capable of making necklaces for Cleopatra, so to speak. But your eloquence should be the servant of the ideas in your head. Your rule might be this: If a sentence, no matter how excellent, does not illuminate your subject in some new and useful way, scratch it out.

5. SOUND LIKE YOURSELF

12   The writing style which is most natural for you is bound to echo the speech you heard when a child. English was the novelist Joseph Conrad's third language, and much that seems piquant in his use of English was no doubt colored by his first language, which was Polish. And lucky indeed is the writer

who has grown up in Ireland, for the English spoken there is so amusing and musical. I myself grew up in Indianapolis, where common speech sounds like a band saw cutting galvanized tin, and employs a vocabulary as unornamental as a monkey wrench.

13   In some of the more remote hollows of Appalachia, children still grow up hearing songs and locutions of Elizabethan times. Yes, and many Americans grow up hearing a language other than English, or an English dialect a majority of Americans cannot understand.

14   All these varieties of speech are beautiful, just as the varieties of butterflies are beautiful. No matter what your first language, you should treasure it all your life. If it happens not to be standard English, and if it shows itself when you write standard English, the result is usually delightful, like a very pretty girl with one eye that is green and one that is blue.

15   I myself find that I trust my own writing most, and others seem to trust it most, too, when I sound most like a person from Indianapolis, which is what I am. What alternatives do I have? The one most vehemently recommended by teachers has no doubt been pressed on you, as well: to write like cultivated Englishmen of a century or more ago.

6. SAY WHAT YOU MEAN TO SAY

16   I used to be exasperated by such teachers, but am no more. I understand now that all those antique essays and stories with which I was to compare my own work were not magnificent for their datedness or foreignness, but for saying precisely what their authors meant them to say. My teachers wished me to write accurately, always selecting the most effective words, and relating the words to one another unambiguously, rigidly, like parts of a machine. The teachers did not want to turn me into an Englishman after all. They hoped that I would become understandable—and therefore understood. And there went my dream of doing with words what Pablo Picasso did with paint or what any number of jazz idols did with music. If I broke all the rules of punctuation, had words mean whatever I wanted them to mean, and strung them together higgledy-piggledy, I would simply not be understood. So you, too, had better avoid Picasso-style or jazz-style writing, if you have something worth saying and wish to be understood.

17   Readers want our pages to look very much like pages they have seen before. Why? This is because they themselves have a tough job to do, and they need all the help they can get from us.

7. PITY THE READERS

18   They have to identify thousands of little marks on paper, and make sense of them immediately. They have to *read,* an art so difficult that most people don't

really master it even after having studied it all through grade school and high school—twelve long years.

19   So this discussion must finally acknowledge that our stylistic options as writers are neither numerous nor glamorous, since our readers are bound to be such imperfect artists. Our audience requires us to be sympathetic and patient teachers, even willing to simplify and clarify—whereas we would rather soar high above the crowd, singing like nightingales.

20   That is the bad news. The good news is that we Americans are governed under a unique Constitution, which allows us to write whatever we please without fear of punishment. So the most meaningful aspect of our styles, which is what we choose to write about, is utterly unlimited.

8. FOR REALLY DETAILED ADVICE

21   For a discussion of literary style in a narrower sense, in a more technical sense, I commend to your attention *The Elements of Style,* by William Strunk, Jr., and E. B. White (Macmillan, 1979). E. B. White is, of course, one of the most admirable literary stylists this country has so far produced.

22   You should realize, too, that no one would care how well or badly Mr. White expressed himself, if he did not have perfectly enchanting things to say.

TOPICAL CONSIDERATIONS

1. Examine one of your essays that was recently corrected by your English instructor. On the basis of the corrections, do you think your instructor agrees or disagrees with Vonnegut's advice?

2. According to Vonnegut, what is the advantage of reading "all those antique essays and stories" (paragraph 16)?

3. This article was originally published as an advertisement sponsored by the International Paper Company. Do you feel the average reader would enjoy and profit from the essay?

RHETORICAL CONSIDERATIONS

1. Why do you think Vonnegut chose Shakespeare and Joyce from the hundreds of great writers of the past to demonstrate the value of simplicity?

2. A key piece of advice Vonnegut gives is, "Sound like yourself." Do you think he follows his own advice? Give examples to support your answer.

3. Occasionally Vonnegut uses a simile or metaphor to make a point. Cite some examples from the essay. How do they contribute to the piece?

WRITING ASSIGNMENTS

1. Select an essay you have studied in this book—one that is considerably more formal than Vonnegut's. Rewrite a paragraph the way you think Vonnegut would have written it. Which style do you prefer, and why?

2. Write an essay showing how Vonnegut's essay embodies his own advice.

3. If you have read any of Vonnegut's novels, write a paper in which you try to demonstrate how Vonnegut the essayist sounds like Vonnegut the novelist.

4. If you are a fan of Vonnegut's novels, write him a letter telling why you enjoy his fiction. In it, employ the writing advice he gives in this essay.

SELECTION, SLANTING, AND CHARGED LANGUAGE

Newman P. Birk and Genevieve B. Birk

Nearly every essay in this book projects the same message (sometimes a warning): Language shapes our perception of reality. The way we use words—the exact language we select and the emphasis we give it— has the power of shaping another's judgment on a subject. What follows is a clear and revealing discussion of this fundamental principle that underlies all verbal communication. This piece is included for two simple reasons. First, as a writer, it is important to understand that the words you choose reflect your personal feelings, values, and attitudes toward a subject. Second, as a reader, you should be alert to the subtle powers of charged language to avoid being susceptible to those who control the words—be they propagandists, politicians, advertisers, or the editors of your local newspaper.

Newman Birk and Genevieve Birk are the authors of *Understanding and Using Language* (1972), from which this essay is taken.

A. THE PRINCIPLE OF SELECTION

1   *Before* it is expressed in words, our knowledge, both inside and outside, is influenced by the principle of selection. What we know or observe depends on what we notice; that is, what we select, consciously or unconsciously, as worthy of notice or attention. As we observe, the principle of selection determines which facts we take in.

2   Suppose, for example, that three people, a lumberjack, an artist, and a tree surgeon, are examining a large tree in a forest. Since the tree itself is a complicated object, the number of particulars or facts about it that one could observe would be very great indeed. Which of these facts a particular observer will notice will be a matter of selection, a selection that is determined by his interests and purposes. A lumberjack might be interested in the best way to cut the tree down, cut it up, and transport it to the lumber mill. His interest would then determine his principle of selection in observing and thinking about the tree. The artist might consider painting a picture of the tree, and his purpose would furnish his principle of selection. The tree surgeon's professional interest in

the physical health of the tree might establish a principle of selection for him. If each man were now required to write an exhaustive, detailed report on everything he observed about the tree, the facts supplied by each would differ, for each would report those facts that his particular principle of selection led him to notice.[1]

3 The principle of selection holds not only for the specific facts that people observe but also for the facts they remember. A student suddenly embarrassed may remember nothing of the next ten minutes of class discussion but may have a vivid recollection of the sensation of the blood mounting, as he blushed, up his face and into his ears. In both noticing and remembering, the principle of selection applies, and it is influenced not only by our special interest and point of view but by our whole mental state of the moment.

4 The principle of selection then serves as a kind of sieve or screen through which our knowledge passes before it becomes our knowledge. Since we can't notice everything about a complicated object or situation or action or state of our own consciousness, what we do notice is determined by whatever principle of selection is operating for us at the time we gain the knowledge.

5 It is important to remember that what is true of the way the principle of selection works for us is true also of the way it works for others. Even before we or other people put knowledge into words to express meaning, that knowledge has been screened or selected. Before an historian or an economist writes a book, or before a reporter writes a news article, the facts that each is to present have been sifted through the screen of a principle of selection. Before one person passes on knowledge to another, that knowledge has already been selected and shaped, intentionally or unintentionally, by the mind of the communicator.

B. THE PRINCIPLE OF SLANTING

6 When we put our knowledge into words, a second process of selection, the process of slanting, takes place. Just as there is something, a rather mysterious principle of selection, which chooses for us what we will notice, and what will then become our knowledge, there is also a principle which operates, with or without our awareness, to select certain facts and feelings from our store of knowledge, and to choose the words and the emphasis that we shall use to communicate our meaning.[2] Slanting may be defined as the process of selecting (1) knowledge—factual and attitudinal; (2) words; and (3) emphasis, to

---

[1] Of course, all three observers would probably report a good many facts in common—the height of the tree, for example, and the size of the trunk. The point we wish to make is that each observer would give us a different impression of the tree because of the different principle of selection that guided his observation.

[2] Notice that the "principle of selection" is at work as *we take in* knowledge, and that slanting occurs as *we express* our knowledge in words.

achieve the intention of the communicator. Slanting is present in some degree in all communication: one may *slant for* (favorable slanting), *slant against* (unfavorable slanting), or *slant both ways* (balanced slanting). . . .

C. SLANTING BY USE OF EMPHASIS

7   Slanting by use of the devices of emphasis is unavoidable,[3] for emphasis is simply the giving of stress to subject matter, and so indicating what is important and what is less important. In speech, for example, if we say that Socrates was a *wise old man,* we can give several slightly different meanings, one by stressing *wise,* another by stressing *old,* another by giving equal stress to *wise* and *old,* and still another by giving chief stress to *man.* Each different stress gives a different slant (favorable or unfavorable or balanced) to the statement because it conveys a different attitude toward Socrates or a different judgment of him. Connectives and word order also slant by the emphasis they give: consider the difference in slanting or emphasis produced by *old but wise, old and wise, wise but old.* In writing, we cannot indicate subtle stresses on words as clearly as in speech, but we can achieve our emphasis and so can slant by the use of more complex patterns of word order, by choice of connectives, by underlining heavily stressed words, and by marks of punctuation that indicate short or long pauses and so give light or heavy emphasis. Question marks, quotation marks, and exclamation points can also contribute to slanting.[4] It is impossible either in speech or in writing to put two facts together without giving some slight emphasis or slant. For example, if we have in mind only two facts about a man, his awkwardness and his strength, we subtly slant those facts favorably or unfavorably in whatever way we may choose to join them:

More Favorable Slanting	**Less Favorable Slanting**
He is awkward and strong.	He is strong and awkward.
He is awkward but strong.	He is strong but awkward.
Although he is somewhat awkard, he is very strong.	He may be strong, but he's very awkward.

With more facts and in longer passages it is possible to maintain a delicate balance by alternating favorable emphasis and so producing a balanced effect.

---

[3]When emphasis is present—and we can think of no instance in the use of language in which it is not—it necessarily influences the meaning by playing a part in the favorable, unfavorable, or balanced slant of the communicator. We are likely to emphasize by voice stress, even when we answer *yes* or *no* to simple questions.

[4]Consider the slanting achieved by punctuation in the following sentences: He called the Senator an honest man? *He* called the Senator an honest man? He called the Senator an honest man! He said one more such "honest" senator would corrupt the state.

8   All communication, then, is in some degree slanted by the *emphasis* of the communicator.

D. SLANTING BY SELECTION OF FACTS

9 To illustrate the technique of slanting by selection of facts, we shall examine three passages of informative writing which achieve different effects simply by the selection and emphasis of material. Each passage is made up of true statements or facts about a dog, yet the reader is given three different impressions. The first passage is an example of objective writing or balanced slanting, the second is slanted unfavorably, and third is slanted favorably.

1. Balanced Presentation

Our dog, Toddy, sold to us a cocker, produces various reactions in various people. Those who come to the back door, she usually growls and barks at (a milkman has said that he is afraid of her); those who come to the front door, she whines at and paws; also she tries to lick people's faces unless we have forestalled her by putting a newspaper in her mouth. (Some of our friends encourage these actions; others discourage them. Mrs. Firmly, one friend, slaps the dog with a newspaper and says, "I know how hard dogs are to train.") Toddy knows and responds to a number of words and phrases, and guests sometimes remark that she is a "very intelligent dog." She has fleas in the summer, and she sheds, at times copiously, the year round. Her blond hairs are conspicuous when they are on people's clothing or on rugs or furniture. Her color and her large brown eyes frequently produce favorable comment. An expert on cockers would say that her ears are too short and set too high and that she is at least six pounds too heavy.

10   The passage above is made up of facts, verifiable facts,[5] deliberately selected and emphasized to produce a *balanced* impression. Of course not all the facts about the dog have been given—to supply *all* the facts on any subject, even such a comparatively simple one, would be an almost impossible task. Both favorable and unfavorable facts are used, however, and an effort has been made to alternate favorable and unfavorable details so that neither will receive greater emphasis by position, proportion, or grammatical structure.

2. Facts Slanted Against

That dog put her paws on my white dress as soon as I came in the door, and she made so much noise that it was two minutes before she had quieted down enough

---

[5]*Verifiable facts* are facts that can be checked and agreed upon and proved to be true by people who wish to verify them. That a particular theme received a failing grade is a verifiable fact; one needs merely to see the theme with the grade on it. That the instructor should have failed the theme is not, strictly speaking, a verifiable fact, but a matter of opinion. That women on the average live longer than men is a verifiable fact; that they live better is a matter of opinion, a *value judgment*.

for us to talk and hear each other. Then the gas man came and she did a great deal of barking. And her hairs are on the rug and on the furniture. If you wear a dark dress they stick to it like lint. When Mrs. Firmly came in, she actually hit the dog with a newspaper to make it stay down, and she made some remark about training dogs. I wish the Birks would take the hint or get rid of that noisy, short-eared, overweight "cocker" of theirs.

11   This unfavorably slanted version is based on the same facts, but now these facts have been selected and given a new emphasis. The speaker, using her selected facts to give her impression of the dog, is quite possibly unaware of her negative slanting.

12   Now for a favorably slanted version:

3. Facts Slanted For

What a lively and responsive dog! When I walked in the door, there she was with a newspaper in her mouth, whining and standing on her hind legs and wagging her tail all at the same time. And what an intelligent dog. If you suggest going for a walk, she will get her collar from the kitchen and hand it to you, and she brings Mrs. Birk's slippers whenever Mrs. Birk says she is "tired" or mentions slippers. At a command she catches balls, rolls over, "speaks," or stands on her hind feet and twirls around. She sits up and balances a piece of bread on her nose until she is told to take it; then she tosses it up and catches it. If you are eating something, she sits up in front of you and "begs" with those big dark brown eyes set in that light, buff-colored face of hers. When I got up to go and told her I was leaving, she rolled her eyes at me and sat up like a squirrel. She certainly is a lively and intelligent dog.

13   Speaker 3, like Speaker 2, is selecting from the "facts" summarized in balanced version 1, and is emphasizing his facts to communicate his impression.

14   All three passages are examples of *reporting* (i.e., consist only of verifiable facts), yet they give three very different impressions of the same dog because of the different ways the speakers slanted the facts. Some people say that figures don't lie, and many people believe that if they have the "facts," they have the "truth." Yet if we carefully examine the ways of thought and language, we see that any knowledge that comes to us through words has been subjected to the double screening of the principle of selection and the slanting of language. . . .

15   Wise listeners and readers realize that the double screening that is produced by the principle of selection and by slanting takes place even when people honestly try to report the facts as they know them. (Speakers 2 and 3, for instance, probably thought of themselves as simply giving information about a dog and were not deliberately trying to mislead.) Wise listeners and readers know too that deliberate manipulators of language, by mere selection and emphasis, can make their slanted facts appear to support almost any cause.

16   In arriving at opinions and values we cannot always be sure that the facts that sift into our minds through language are representative and relevant and true. We need to remember that much of our information about politics, gov-

ernmental activities, business conditions, and foreign affairs comes to us selected and slanted. More than we realize, our opinions on these matters may depend on what newspaper we read or what news commentator we listen to. Worthwhile opinions call for knowledge of reliable facts and reasonable arguments for and against—and such opinions include beliefs about morality and truth and religion as well as about public affairs. Because complex subjects involve knowing and dealing with many facts on both sides, reliable judgments are at best difficult to arrive at. If we want to be fairminded, we must be willing to subject our opinions to continual testing by new knowledge, and must realize that after all they *are* opinions, more or less trustworthy. Their trustworthiness will depend on the representativeness of our facts, on the quality of our reasoning, and on the standard of values that we choose to apply.

17   We shall not give here a passage illustrating the unscrupulous slanting of facts. Such a passage would also include irrelevant facts and false statements presented as facts, along with various subtle distortions of fact. Yet to the uninformed reader the passage would be indistinguishable from a passage intended to give a fair account. If two passages (2 and 3) of casual and unintentional slanting of facts about a dog can give such contradictory impressions of a simple subject, the reader can imagine what a skilled and designing manipulation of facts and statistics could do to mislead an uninformed reader about a really complex subject. An example of such manipulation might be the account of the United States that Soviet propaganda has supplied to the average Russian. Such propaganda, however, would go beyond the mere slanting of the facts: it would clothe the selected facts in charged words and would make use of the many other devices of slanting that appear in charged language.

E. SLANTING BY USE OF CHARGED WORDS

18 In the passages describing the dog Toddy, we were illustrating the technique of slanting by the selection and emphasis of facts. Though the facts selected had to be expressed in words, the words chosen were as factual as possible, and it was the selection and emphasis of facts and not of words that was mainly responsible for the two distinctly different impressions of the dog. In the passages below we are demonstrating another way of slanting—by the use of charged words. This time the accounts are very similar in the facts they contain; the different impressions of the subject, Corlyn, are produced not by different facts but by the subtle selection of charged words.

19   The passages were written by a clever student who was told to choose as his subject a person in action, and to write two descriptions, each using the "same facts." The instructions required that one description be slanted positively and the other negatively, so that the first would make the reader favorably inclined toward the person and the action, and the second would make him unfavorably inclined.

20   Here is the favorably charged description. Read it carefully and form your opinion of the person before you go on to read the second description.

Corlyn

Corlyn paused at the entrance to the room and glanced about. A well-cut black dress draped subtly about her slender form. Her long blonde hair gave her chiseled features the simple frame they required. She smiled an engaging smile as she accepted a cigarette from her escort. As he lit it for her she looked over the flame and into his eyes. Corlyn had that rare talent of making every male feel that he was the one man in the world.

She took his arm and they descended the steps into the room. She walked with an effortless grace and spoke with equal ease. They each took a cup of coffee and joined a group of friends near the fire. The flickering light danced across her face and lent an ethereal quality to her beauty. The good conversation, the crackling logs, and the stimulating coffee gave her a feeling of internal warmth. Her eyes danced with each leap of the flames.

21   Taken by itself this passage might seem just a description of an attractive girl. The favorable slanting by use of charged words has been done so skillfully that it is inconspicuous. Now we turn to the unfavorably slanted description of the "same" girl in the "same" actions:

Corlyn

Corlyn halted at the entrance to the room and looked around. A plain black dress hung on her thin frame. Her stringy bleached hair accentuated her harsh features. She smiled an inane smile as she took a cigarette from her escort. As he lit it for her she stared over the lighter and into his eyes. Corlyn had a habit of making every male feel that he was the last man on earth.

She grasped his arm and they walked down the steps and into the room. Her pace was fast and ungainly, as was her speech. They each reached for some coffee and broke into a group of acquaintances near the fire. The flickering light played across her face and revealed every flaw. The loud talk, the fire, and the coffee she had gulped down made her feel hot. Her eyes grew more red with each leap of the flames.

22   When the reader compares these two descriptions, he can see how charged words influence the reader's attitude. One needs to read the two descriptions several times to appreciate all the subtle differences between them. Words, some rather heavily charged, others innocent-looking but lightly charged, work together to carry to the reader a judgment of a person and a situation. If the reader had seen only the first description of Corlyn, he might well have thought that he had formed his "own judgment on the basis of the facts." And the examples just given only begin to suggest the techniques that may be used in heavily charged language. For one thing, the two descriptions of Corlyn

contain no really good example of the use of charged abstractions; for another, the writer was obliged by the assignment to use the same set of facts and so could not slant by selecting his material.

F. SLANTING AND CHARGED LANGUAGE

23 . . . When slanting of facts, or words, or emphasis, or any combination of the three *significantly influences* feelings toward, or judgments about, a subject, the language used is charged language. . . .

24   Of course communications vary in the amount of charge they carry and in their effect on different people; what is very favorably charged for one person may have little or no charge, or may even be adversely charged, for others. It is sometimes hard to distinguish between charged and uncharged expression. But it is safe to say that whenever we wish to convey any kind of inner knowledge—feelings, attitudes, judgments, values—we are obliged to convey that attitudinal meaning through the medium of charged language; and when we wish to understand the inside knowledge of others, we have to interpret the charged language that they choose, or are obliged, to use. Charged language, then, is the natural and necessary medium for the communication of charged or attitudinal meaning. At times we have difficulty in living with it, but we should have even greater difficulty in living without it.

25   Some of the difficulties in living with charged language are caused by its use in dishonest propaganda, in some editorials, in many political speeches, in most advertising, in certain kinds of effusive salesmanship, and in blatantly insincere, or exaggerated, or sentimental expressions of emotion. Other difficulties are caused by the misunderstandings and misinterpretations that charged language produces. A charged phrase misinterpreted in a love letter; a charged word spoken in haste or in anger; an acrimonious argument about religion or politics or athletics or fraternities; the frustrating uncertainty produced by the effort to understand the complex attitudinal meaning in a poem or play or a short story—these troubles, all growing out of the use of charged language, may give us the feeling that Robert Louis Stevenson expressed when he said, "The battle goes sore against us to the going down of the sun."

26   But however charged language is abused and whatever misunderstandings it may cause, we still have to live with it—and even by it. It shapes out attitudes and values even without our conscious knowledge; it gives purpose to, and guides, our actions; through it we establish and maintain relations with other people and by means of it we exert our greatest influence on them. Without charged language, life would be but half life. The relatively uncharged language of bare factual statement, though it serves its informative purpose well and is much less open to abuse and to misunderstanding, can describe only the bare land of factual knowledge; to communicate knowledge of the turbulencies and the calms and the deep currents of the sea of inner experience we must use charged language.

TOPICAL CONSIDERATIONS

1. The authors say that slanting is the process of selecting knowledge, words, and emphasis. Is it possible to communicate something without slanting it one way or another? Can you think of any kind of writing that is unslanted?

2. One of the best places to find charged and slanted language is on the editorial pages of a newspaper. Look through the various editorials, political columns, and letters to the editor. How many examples of slanted and charged language can you find? How deliberately were the verifiable facts selected? Were some facts given more emphasis than others?

3. How can we determine whether a report is charged?

4. Some of the most slanted writing we are exposed to comes in the form of advertising. Select some ads from magazines or newspapers (or television commercials) and consider the charged and slanted language used to sell the products.

5. What do the authors mean in paragraph 24 when they say that we have difficulty living with charged language and difficulty living without it?

RHETORICAL CONSIDERATIONS

1. How well organized is this essay? Do the headings help structure it?

2. Many of the paragraphs in this essay have a similar pattern of organization. Using examples, explain how they are organized. Where are the topic sentences?

3. Select a paragraph from the essay and try to find examples of slanted or charged language in the discussion.

WRITING ASSIGNMENTS

1. Reread the two descriptions of Corlyn in this essay. Try to determine exactly how the writing influenced your judgments of her.

2. The authors use the example of Toddy to illustrate how slanted reporting can bend judgment for or against something. Do the same. Select some innocuous item— article of clothing, a toothbrush, your right shoe—and describe it, first slanting the language toward a favorable judgment, then toward an unfavorable judgment.

3. Write an essay using the authors' notion that "without charged language, life would be but half life" (paragraph 26).

4. Find two magazines or newspapers covering the same event or person—maybe a movie star or political figure or athlete. Then discuss the degree of slanting and chargedness in each. How did they differ? How did they use facts? How did they charge the language?

5. Write three descriptions of the outfit you are wearing: as it might be seen by an artist, a tailor, and a nudist.

6. Reread this essay, noting the major charges made by the Birks regarding slanted writing. Conduct interviews with three or four instructors or students in the journalism or communications departments of your school, asking them whether they agree with the claims made by the Birks. How do slanting, selection, and charged language function in their own work? Write a paper analyzing your findings in terms of the Birks' article.

THE MAKER'S EYE: REVISING YOUR OWN MANUSCRIPT

Donald M. Murray

The secret of good writing is rewriting. Every line of copy in this book has undergone the process—a process that many people underestimate. Because they see only the finished product, they aren't aware of the amount of cutting, rewording, reorganizing, and rewriting that goes into a piece to make it sound smooth and effortless. It is that process of revision—and the importance of it—that Donald M. Murray talks about here. Murray has made the art of writing well his business for decades. In 1954 he won the Pulitzer Prize for his editorials in the *Boston Globe*. He has also been an editor of *Time* magazine. Although he has published novels, short stories, and poetry, he is perhaps best known for his writings on writing. His *Write to Learn* is a popular college composition text. A basic message in Murray's essay is that the revising process is never ending. So, it is interesting to note that this essay is a rewrite of the original, which appeared in *The Writer* magazine.

1   When students complete a first draft, they consider the job of writing done—and their teachers too often agree. When professional writers complete a first draft, they usually feel that they are at the start of the writing process. When a draft is completed, the job of writing can begin.

2   That difference in attitude is the difference between amateur and professional, inexperience and experience, journeyman and craftsman. Peter F. Drucker, the prolific business writer, calls his first draft "the zero draft"—after that he can start counting. Most writers share the feeling that the first draft, and all of those which follow, are opportunities to discover what they have to say and how best they can say it.

3   To produce a progression of drafts, each of which says more and says it more clearly, the writer has to develop a special kind of reading skill. In school

we are taught to decode what appears on the page as finished writing. Writers, however, face a different category of possibility and responsibility when they read their own drafts. To them the words on the page are never finished. Each can be changed and rearranged, can set off a chain reaction of confusion or clarified meaning. This is a different kind of reading which is possibly more difficult and certainly more exciting.

4   Writers must learn to be their own best enemy. They must accept the criticism of others and be suspicious of it; they must accept the praise of others and be even more suspicious of it. Writers cannot depend on others. They must detach themselves from their own pages so that they can apply both their caring and their craft to their own work.

5   Such detachment is not easy. Science fiction writer Ray Bradbury supposedly puts each manuscript away for a year to the day and then rereads it as a stranger. Not many writers have the discipline or the time to do this. We must read when our judgment may be at its worst, when we are close to the euphoric moment of creation.

6   Then the writer, counsels novelist Nancy Hale, "should be critical of everything that seems to him most delightful in his style. He should excise what he most admires, because he wouldn't thus admire it if he weren't . . . in a sense protecting it from criticism." John Ciardi, the poet, adds, "The last act of the writing must be to become one's own reader. It is, I suppose, a schizophrenic process, to begin passionately and to end critically, to begin hot and to end cold; and, more important, to be passion-hot and critic-cold at the same time."

7   Most people think that the principal problem is that writers are too proud of what they have written. Actually, a greater problem for most professional writers is one shared by the majority of students. They are overly critical, think everything is dreadful, tear up page after page, never complete a draft, see the task as hopeless.

8   The writer must learn to read critically but constructively, to cut what is bad, to reveal what is good. Eleanor Estes, the children's book author, explains: "The writer must survey his work critically, coolly, as though he were a stranger to it. He must be willing to prune, expertly and hard-heartedly. At the end of each revision, a manuscript may look . . . worked over, torn apart, pinned together, added to, deleted from, words changed and words changed back. Yet the book must maintain its original freshness and spontaneity."

9   Most readers underestimate the amount of rewriting it usually takes to produce spontaneous reading. This is a great disadvantage to the student writer, who sees only a finished product and never watches the craftsman who takes the necessary step back, studies the work carefully, returns to the task, steps back, returns, steps back, again and again. Anthony Burgess, one of the most prolific writers in the English-speaking world, admits, "I might revise a page twenty times." Roald Dahl, the popular children's writer, states, "By the time I'm nearing the end of a story, the first part will have been reread and altered and corrected at least 150 times. . . . Good writing is essentially rewriting. I am positive of this."

10   Rewriting isn't virtuous. It isn't something that ought to be done. It is simply something that most writers find they have to do to discover what they have to say and how to say it. It is a condition of the writer's life.

11   There are, however, a few writers who do little formal rewriting, primarily because they have the capacity and experience to create and review a large number of invisible drafts in their minds before they approach the page. And some writers slowly produce finished pages, performing all the tasks of revision simultaneously, page by page, rather than draft by draft. But it is still possible to see the sequence followed by most writers most of the time in rereading their own work.

12   Most writers scan their drafts first, reading as quickly as possible to catch the larger problems of subject and form, then move in closer and closer as they read and write, reread and rewrite.

13   The first thing writers look for in their drafts is *information*. They know that a good piece of writing is built from specific, accurate, and interesting information. The writer must have an abundance of information from which to construct a readable piece of writing.

14   Next writers look for *meaning* in the information. The specifics must build to a pattern of significance. Each piece of specific information must carry the reader toward meaning.

15   Writers reading their own drafts are aware of *audience*. They put themselves in the reader's situation and make sure that they deliver information which a reader wants to know or needs to know in a manner which is easily digested. Writers try to be sure that they anticipate and answer the questions a critical reader will ask when reading the piece of writing.

16   Writers make sure that the *form* is appropriate to the subject and the audience. Form, or genre, is the vehicle which carries meaning to the reader, but form cannot be selected until the writer has adequate information to discover its significance and an audience which needs or wants that meaning.

17   Once writers are sure the form is appropriate, they must then look at the *structure*, the order of what they have written. Good writing is built on a solid framework of logic, argument, narrative, or motivation which runs through the entire piece of writing and holds it together. This is the time when many writers find it most effective to outline as a way of visualizing the hidden spine on which the piece of writing is supported.

18   The element on which writers may spend a majority of their time is *development*. Each section of a piece of writing must be adequately developed. It must give readers enough information so that they are satisfied. How much information is enough? That's as difficult as asking how much garlic belongs in a salad. It must be done to taste, but most beginning writers underdevelop, underestimating the reader's hunger for information.

19   As writers solve development problems, they often have to consider questions of *dimension*. There must be a pleasing and effective proportion among all the parts of the piece of writing. There is a continual process of subtracting and adding to keep the piece of writing in balance.

20   Finally, writers have to listen to their own voices. *Voice* is the force which drives a piece of writing forward. It is an expression of the writer's authority and concern. It is what is between the words on the page, what glues the piece of writing together. A good piece of writing is always marked by a consistent, individual voice.

21   As writers read and reread, write and rewrite, they move closer and closer to the page until they are doing line-by-line editing. Writers read their own pages with infinite care. Each sentence, each line, each clause, each phrase, each word, each mark of punctuation, each section of white space between the type has to contribute to the clarification of meaning.

22   Slowly the writer moves from word to word, looking through language to see the subject. As a word is changed, cut, or added, as a construction is re-arranged, all the words used before that moment and all those that follow that moment must be considered and reconsidered.

23   Writers often read aloud at this stage of the editing process muttering or whispering to themselves, calling on the ear's experience with language. Does this sound right—or that? Writers edit, shifting back and forth from eye to page to ear to page. I find I must do this careful editing in short runs, no more than fifteen or twenty minutes at a stretch, or I become too kind with myself. I begin to see what I hope is on the page, not what actually is on the page.

24   This sounds tedious if you haven't done it, but actually it is fun. Making something right is immensely satisfying, for writers begin to learn what they are writing about by writing. Language leads them to meaning, and there is the joy of discovery, of understanding, of making meaning clear as the writer employs the technical skills of language.

25   Words have double meanings, even triple and quadruple meanings. Each word has its own potential for connotation and denotation. And when writers rub one word against the other, they are often rewarded with a sudden insight, an unexpected clarification.

26   The maker's eye moves back and forth from word to phrase to sentence to paragraph to sentence to phrase to word. The maker's eye sees the need for variety and balance, for a firmer structure, for a more appropriate form. It peers into the interior of the paragraph, looking for coherence, unity, and em-phasis, which make meaning clear.

27   I learned something about this process when my first bifocals were pre-scribed. I had ordered a larger section of the reading portion of the glass be-cause of my work, but even so, I could not contain my eyes within this new limit of vision. And I still find myself taking off my glasses and bending my nose towards the page, for my eyes unconsciously flick back and forth across the page, back to another page, forward to still another, as I try to see each evolving line in relation to every other line.

28   When does this process end? Most writers agree with the great Russian writer Tolstoy, who said, "I scarcely ever reread my published writing. If by chance I come across a page, it always strikes me: all this must be rewritten; this is how I should have written it."

29   The maker's eye is never satisfied, for each word has the potential to ignite new meaning. This article has been twice written all the way through the writing process, and it was published four years ago. Now it is to be republished in a book. The editors made a few small suggestions, and then I read it with my maker's eye. Now it has been re-edited, revised, re-read, re-re-edited, for each piece of writing is to the writer full of potential and alternatives.

30   A piece of writing is never finished. It is delivered to a deadline, torn out of the typewriter on demand, sent off with a sense of accomplishment and shame and pride and frustration. If only there were a couple more days, time for just another run at it, perhaps then. . . .

TOPICAL CONSIDERATIONS

1. In what ways do amateur writers differ from professional writers according to Murray?

2. How must writers "learn to be their own best enemy"?

3. In paragraph 12, Murray says that most professional writers go over the drafts of their writing looking for the "larger problems of subject and form" before closing in on the rewrites. Does it surprise you that so many professional writers go through so much revision of their work? Do you follow such procedures when you write? If not, do you think you can?

4. Murray names eight things that writers must consider in the process of revising their own manuscripts. What are they?

5. What does Murray mean by the statement, "A piece of writing is never finished"?

RHETORICAL CONSIDERATIONS

1. In paragraph 9, Murray quotes Roald Dahl: "Good writing is essentially rewriting." How well does Murray illustrate this fundamental thesis in his essay?

2. How does Murray use his own essay to illustrate the statement at the end, "A piece of writing is never finished"?

WRITING ASSIGNMENTS

1. Write an essay in which you describe the process you go through in writing a paper. Consider what difficulties you have in coming up with an idea or slant or opening. Do you make the same eight considerations Murray lists when revising? Is it ever fun? Do you ever feel "immensely satisfied" when you think you've got it right?

2. Using Murray's list of eight considerations for revising, rework an essay recently returned to you by your instructor.

THE WRITER

Richard Wilbur

In a sense, all writing is about writing. But only on occasion does literature actually address the writing process. In this poem, Richard Wilbur
catches sight of his daughter writing a story and ruminates on the "life
and death" struggles inherent in the writing act.

Richard Wilbur was born in 1921 in New York City and was educated at
Amherst College. After serving in the army in World War II, he filled a
variety of teaching posts at Harvard, Wesleyan, Smith, and Wellesley.
He is the author of several books including collections of poetry, literary
criticism, and children's stories. He has received two Pulitzer Prizes and
a National Book Award. In 1987 he was named United States Poet Laureate by the Library of Congress. This poem is from his collection *The
Mind Reader* (1971).

In her room at the prow of the house
Where light breaks, and the windows are tossed
   with linden,
My daughter is writing a story.

I pause in the stairwell, hearing
5 From her shut door a commotion of typewriter-keys
Like a chain hauled over a gunwale.

Young as she is, the stuff
Of her life is a great cargo, and some of it heavy:
I wish her a lucky passage.

10 But now it is she who pauses,
As if to reject my thought and its easy figure.
A stillness greatens, in which

The whole house seems to be thinking,
And then she is at it again with a bunched clamor
15 Of strokes, and again is silent.

I remember the dazed starling
Which was trapped in that very room, two years ago;
How we stole in, lifted a sash

And retreated, not to affright it;
20 And how for a helpless hour, through the crack of
      the door,
    We watched the sleek, wild, dark

    And iridescent creature
    Batter against the brilliance, drop like a glove
    To the hard floor, or the desk-top,

25 And wait then, humped and bloody,
    For the wits to try it again; and how our spirits
    Rose when, suddenly sure,

    It lifted off from a chair-back,
    Beating a smooth course for the right window
30 And clearing the sill of the world.

    It is always a matter, my darling.
    Of life or death, as I had forgotten. I wish
    What I wished you before, but harder.

QUESTIONS FOR DISCUSSION

1. Who is speaking? How do you know? What gender, age, and class do you imagine this speaker to be?

2. In the first three stanzas, what images of ships and sailing does the speaker use? How do these images reflect the daughter's struggle to find her place in the world?

3. What memory does the speaker recall about a bird trapped in the house (stanzas 16–30)? How do these images reflect the daughter's struggle to write?

4. What is similar and what is different about the sailing images and the bird images? Which set of images is more effective in conveying the speaker's feelings about his daughter? Why?

5. To whom does the title of the poem refer? How do you know?

6. While it is not clear what the daughter is writing about, why might it be so difficult for her to write? Can you identify with her plight? Explain.

7. In the poem, neither the speaker nor the daughter is identified by name. How does this literary device help to show the speaker's mixed feelings about the daughter's struggle for autonomy, and the speaker's own separation anxiety?

WRITING ASSIGNMENTS

1. What difficulties do you encounter when you write? How do you resolve them? Do you show your work to anyone? Why or why not?

2. Have you ever tried to do something that your parents do (or did) well? How did they respond to your efforts? How did you feel about the responses (or about their lack of response)? Did you feel that they had been completely honest with

you about their responses? In either case, did you appreciate that honesty or did it create problems between you?

3. If you are a parent, how did you feel watching your child struggle with the tasks of growing up? Did you try to offer encouragement? Or did you find it wiser to remain silent?

4. If you are a parent, has your child ever surpassed you in some skill that you have struggled to master? How did you feel about this? How did you react to your child's accomplishment?

3 | MEDIA AND ADVERTISING

CLASSIFIEDS

PARKING SPOT for sale West 78th Street, Manhattan. Must vacate this Sat. A.M. Box 927

MIDTOWN REAL ESTATE – for building or farming. Box 561.

GREAT VIEW – My apartment, your view. Come up as often as you like and look out window. By week or month. Box 934.

R. Chast

Two of the most influential forces in our society are the news media and advertising. Much of what we know about the world comes from what the media tells us through newspapers, magazines, radio, and television; similarly, how we perceive that environment is influenced by the media's presentation of it. Underwriting most of that media is advertising. About $140 billion is spent every year on commercials and print ads—more than the gross national product of many countries in the world—accounting for a quarter of each television hour and the bulk of most newspapers and magazines. It goes without saying that tremendous power lies in the hands of those who write the news and the ads. This chapter examines both the media and advertising and how each uses and abuses the power of words.

Ours is a culture that has moved from the written word to the spoken. More and more we have come to rely on talking—face to face, on telephones, on radio and television, on talk shows. But what's being said is neither graceful nor memorable, claim social critics. Our culture doesn't seem to value eloquence as it once did. Political campaigns are reduced to sound bites, movie scripts are increasingly inane, television has slipped to the level of sixth-grade English, and broadcast news consists of little more than headlines. Not only are Americans growing less articulate, they don't seem to care. According to some, much of the blame rests with the media, especially broadcast news, which has become so competitive for audience (and revenue) that it has become another form of entertainment complete with high-power visuals and low-power English.

MAKING THE NEWS: JOURNALISM OR ENTERTAINMENT?

One sure sign of the crisis in eloquence is the growing stock of clichés that fill the newspapers and airwaves—those phrases on tap that substitute for original expressions. In the first piece, "Journalese as a Second Tongue," John Leo reviews some familiar catch phrases, euphemisms, descriptives, qualifiers, and other choice chestnuts of reporters. While professional jargon may not seem problematic in and of itself, in news reporting such tired codes often substitute for objective truth. The second piece examines broadcast news and how the entertainment values have corrupted our knowledge and views of world affairs. In "TV News: All the World in Pictures," Neil Postman and Steve Powers eloquently argue that TV news, with its heavy reliance on dramatic and dynamic images, has been packaged to suit the requirements of show biz rather than those of journalism. The next piece, "In Depth, but Shallowly," is a parody of those very "entertainment values." As former reporter and popular humorist Dave Barry says, " . . . *news* means *anything that you can take a picture of, especially if a local TV News Personality can stand in front of it.*" The trend toward making broadcast news a no-brain form of entertainment is nowhere more apparent than on TV talk shows. So says Tom Shachtman, author of the next piece. In "Dumbing Down: TV Talk-Show Talk," he reviews eight current talk shows on which hosts and guests alike hold forth on highly charged issues in lowly charged English.

REMAKING THE NEWS: JOURNALISM OR BIAS?

The next three essays raise some legitimate questions about journalists' objectivity. Since most news stories don't take place with reporters present, accounts are secondhand. Thus, for the sake of objectivity, reporters rely on attributions to other authorities (i.e., "according to police . . . ," or "the Supreme Court said today . . . ," or "Congress had mandated. . . . " But like the stock formulas John Leo examines, these "language collectives" tend to take on unwarranted authority and, thus, distort the news. Such is the claim of Charles C. Russell and Paul Many, two communications professors and authors of the piece, "Collective Bias." The chapter moves from collective references to collective myths. In "Read All About It! (But Don't Believe It)," journalist Caryl Rivers criticizes the media for employing language that draws from deeply rooted cultural legends about women. She argues that ever since Eve, women have gotten bad press for being either too strong or too weak; and the result is that women—especially working women—are suffering undeserved anxiety and guilt.

Is what we read and hear an accurate rendering of world events, or is the language politically slanted in favor of the status quo or government attitudes? Concerning the subject of terrorism, Edward S. Herman strongly believes that the Western press lacks a balanced perspective. In "Terrorism: Civilized and Barbaric," he attacks major American newspapers for disseminating more propaganda than hard news by promoting terrorist stereotypes. Analyzing reports of recent incidents, Herman argues that the media simply mirror the government's biases: Terrorism is what is done by them, not us.

The final selection speaks for itself. "Two-Headed Monsters" consists of some choice newspaper headlines compiled by the *Columbia Journalism Review*—headlines that, in the words of the trade, suffer the plague of "devil's print." Such headlines contain much more than was intended—misprints, double entendres, grammatical grotesqueries—and deliver more laughs than news.

MAKING CONSUMERS: ADVERTISING—MANIPULATION OR ART?

Advertising is everywhere—television, newspapers, magazines, billboards; it's printed on T-shirts, hot dogs, postage stamps, buses, and even license plates. It's everywhere people are, and its appeal goes right to the quick of our fantasies: happiness, material wealth, eternal youth, social acceptance, sexual fulfillment, and power. And it does so with carefully selected images and words. It is the most pervasive form of persuasion in America.

By nature, advertising language is a special language—one that combines words cleverly and methodically for the sole purpose of separating consumers from their money. All five authors in this section agree on that. But beyond that, their views diverge widely.

In the first piece, "With These Words I Can Sell You Anything," language-watcher William Lutz argues that advertisers tyrannically twist simple English words so that they appear to promise what the consumer desires. Taking a defensive posture in "The Language of Advertising," Charles A. O'Neill, a professional advertiser, admits that the language of ads can be very appealing. With reference to some recent ads, he nonetheless makes a persuasive argument that no ad can force consumers to part with their money.

ADVERTISING CASE STUDIES

The first two case studies are by professional writers who are outside the world of advertising and are critical of it. In "Printed Noise," George Will, *Newsweek* columnist, author, and ABC commentator, takes a humorous look at some weasel-worded concoctions that plague the all-American menu. "Egg McMuffin," "Fishamigig," "Liver with smothered onions," "Hot Fudge Nutty Buddy"—we've heard them all, and so often that we have probably missed the nonsense for the noise. The next essay, by *Boston Globe* columnist Diane White, also lodges a pointed complaint against the practices of ad writers. It's one thing to make the truth fascinating, as Charles O'Neill observes; it's another to distort reality with inflated language—or what White calls "Euphemisms for the Fat of the Land."

The final essay, "A Word from Our Sponsor," is the confession of a professional copywriter, Patricia Volk. Talking frankly about the craft of charging language to sell, she admits that there is only one rule: "There are no rules."

JOURNALESE AS A SECOND TONGUE

John Leo

Jargon is the special language of a trade; and nearly every trade has one to shortcut communication. Journalism is no exception. We hear reportage codes and formulas so frequently that we may have missed what's actually being communicated—and what's not. In the article below, John Leo explains where meaning and phrasing depart in reporting the news. As catchy as journalese might be, it can be "as misleading as olive sizes."

John Leo is a New York writer who served as New York City's Assistant Commissioner of the Environmental Protection Agency during the John Lindsay mayoral administration. He has been a reporter and editor for the *New York Times* and *Discover* magazine and a columnist in the *Village Voice*. This article first appeared in *Time* magazine in 1984.

1   As a cub reporter, Columnist Richard Cohen of the *Washington Post* rushed out one day to interview a lawyer described in many newspaper reports as "ruddy-faced." The man was woozily abusive and lurched about with such abandon that young Cohen instantly realized that the real meaning of ruddy-faced is drunk. This was his introduction to journalese, the fascinating second tongue acquired by most reporters as effortlessly as an Iranian toddler learns Farsi or a Marin County child learns psychobabble.

2   Fluency in journalese means knowing all about "the right stuff," "gender gap," "life in the fast lane" and the vexing dilemma of being caught "between a rock and a hard place," the current Scylla-Charybdis image. The Middle East is "strife-torn," except during those inexplicable moments when peace breaks out. Then it is always "much troubled." Kuwait is located just east of the adjective "oil-rich," and the Irish Republican Army always lurks right behind the

word "outlawed." The hyphenated modifier is the meat and potatoes of journalese. Who can forget "the break-away province of Biafra," "the mop-top quartet" (the mandatory second reference to the Beatles) and the "ill-fated Korean jetliner," not to be confused with the "ill-fitting red wig" of Watergate fame. Murderers on death row are often saved by "eleventh-hour" reprieves, which would be somewhere between 10 and 11 P.M. in English but shortly before midnight in journalese.

3   Much of the difficulty in mastering journalese comes from its slight overlap with English. "Imposing," for instance, when used to describe a male, retains its customary English meaning, but when used in reference to a female, it always means battle-ax. "Feisty" refers to a person whom the journalist deems too short and too easily enraged, though many in the journalese-speaking fraternity believe it is simply the adjective of choice for any male under 5 ft. 6 in. who is not legally dead. This usage reflects the continual surprise among tall journalists that short people have any energy at all. Women are not often feisty, though they are usually short enough to qualify. No journalist in America has ever referred to a 6-ft. male as feisty. At that height, men are simply "outspoken" (*i.e.,* abusive).

4   In general, adjectives in journalese are as misleading as olive sizes. Most news consumers know enough to translate "developing nations" and "disadvantaged nations" back into English, but far smaller numbers know that "militant" means fanatic, and "steadfast" means pigheaded. "Controversial" introduces someone or something the writer finds appalling, as in "the controversial Miss Fonda," and "prestigious" heralds the imminent arrival of a noun nobody cares about, as in "the prestigious Jean Hersholt Humanitarian Award."

5   Television anchorpersons add interest to their monologues by accenting a few syllables chosen at random. Since print journalists cannot do this, except when reading aloud to spouse and children, they strive for a similar effect by using words like crisis and revolution. Crisis means any kind of trouble at all, and revolution means any kind of change at all, as in "the revolution in meat packing." "Street value" lends excitement to any drug-bust story, without bearing any financial relationship to the actual value of drugs being busted. Many meaningless adjectives, preferably hyphenated for proper rhythm, are permanently welded to certain nouns: blue-ribbon panel, fact-finding mission, devout Catholic, and rock-ribbed Republican. In journalese there are no devout Protestants or Jews, and no Democrats with strong or stony ribs.

6   Historians of journalese will agree that the first flowering of the language occurred in the sexist descriptions of women by splashy tabloids during the '30s and '40s. In contrast to Pentagonese, which favors oxymorons (Peace-keeper missiles, build-down), the tabloids relied on synecdoche (leggy brunette, bosomy blonde, full-figured redhead). Full-figured, of course, meant fat, and "well-endowed" did not refer to Ford Foundation funding. "Statuesque" (too large, mooselike) and "petite" (too small, mouselike) were adjectives of last resort, meaning that the woman under discussion had no bodily parts that interested the writer. A plain, short woman was invariably "pert." For years, masters

of this prose cast about for a nonlibelous euphemism for "mistress." The winning entry, "great and good friend," used to describe Marion Davies' relationship to William Randolph Hearst, was pioneered, as it happens, by a non-Hearst publication, TIME magazine. "Constant companion" evolved later, and gave way to such clunking modernisms as "roommate" and "live-in lover." Nowadays, the only sexuality about which journalese is coy tends to be homosexuality, and that is adequately covered by "he has no close female friends" or "he is not about to settle down."

7   In political campaigns, underdogs fight uphill battles and hope for shifts of momentum and coattail effects, all leading to rising tides that will enable the favorite to snatch defeat from the jaws of victory. A politician who has no idea about what is going on can be described as one who prefers "to leave details to subordinates." A gangster who runs a foreign country will be referred to as "strongman" until his death, and dictator thereafter. Strongman, like many terms in journalese, has no true correlative. "Nicaraguan Strongman Somoza" is not balanced with "Cambodian Weakman Prince Sihanouk."

8   What to say about a public figure who is clearly bonkers? Since it is unsporting and possibly libelous to write: "Representative Forbush, the well-known raving psychopath," journalese has evolved the code words difficult, intense and driven. If an article says, "like many of us, Forbush has his ups and downs," the writer is wigwagging a manic-depressive.

9   Political journalese, of course, requires a knowledge of sources. An unnamed analyst or observer can often be presumed to be the writer of the article. The popular plural "observers," or "analysts," refers to the writer and his cronies. Insiders, unlike observer-analysts, sometimes exist in the real world outside the newsroom. This, however, is never true of quotable chestnut vendors in Paris, Greenwich Village bartenders and other colorful folk conjured up on deadline to lend dash to a story.

10   Almost all sources, like most trial balloonists, live in or around Washington. In order of ascending rectitude, they are: informants, usually reliable sources, informed sources, authoritative sources, sources in high places and unimpeachable sources. Informants are low-level operatives, whose beans are normally spilled to police rather than to reporters. Informed sources, because of their informed nature, are consulted most often by savvy journalists. An unimpeachable source is almost always the President, with the obvious exception of Richard Nixon, who was not unimpeachable.

11   Journalese is controversial but prestigious, and observers are steadfast in averring that it has the right stuff.

TOPICAL CONSIDERATIONS

1. In your own words, define what *journalese* is. How is journalese used? Before reading this article, had you taken notice of it? Have you used journalese in your own speech or writing? If so, give some examples.

2. Look over the article again. What do you think about journalism that uses euphemistic or indirect phrases such as "constant companion" to describe a mistress

or "has his ups and downs" to describe a mentally unstable public figure? Why are such journalese expressions enlisted? In general, would you prefer more explicit language by the media?

3. Consider Leo's interpretations of journalese terms *militant* and *steadfast* in paragraph 4. What do you make of these translations? Did you read the words with the same interpretations in mind? Why or why not?

4. Do you think journalese affects the credibility of reporting? Where and how? Which of Leo's examples do you condone and which would you disapprove of? What principle governs your decisions? Explain your answer.

5. Review some of the articles in Chapter 7, Language, Gender, and Sexism (pages 395–482). Now consider what Leo says about gender stereotyping in journalese. How has the press helped perpetuate sexual prejudice? Consider the values operating when certain males are called *feisty* and certain females are called *imposing*.

6. What do you think the author's purpose was in writing this piece? What did you learn from it? What most impressed you about the article? Do you think your response to media reporting has been altered any? Explain your answers.

RHETORICAL CONSIDERATIONS

1. Did you find this article funny? If so, in what ways did the humor contribute to your understanding of the subject matter? Explain with examples.

2. What would you say is the author's opinion of journalese? In what ways does he project this opinion?

3. Explain the effectiveness of the title Leo chose for his article. What are the implications of "a second tongue"?

WRITING ASSIGNMENTS

1. Go through a newspaper and locate as many examples of journalese as you can. Now edit out these terms so the stories read without them. How does the original language affect your perception of what you've read? How does your editing change the reporting? Does the tone of the articles change? Is the reporting less clever and colorful? less exciting? What about the clarity and credibility of the writing? Write your findings and observations in an essay.

2. For humorous effect, the closing line in Leo's article is rendered completely in journalese. Have some fun of your own by writing a news article completely in journalese formulas. Or, select a current news story low in journalese and rewrite it so that it's thick with the lingo.

TV NEWS: ALL THE WORLD IN PICTURES

Neil Postman and Steve Powers

Ideally, the news media should be concerned exclusively with facts, logic, and objective analysis. For the most part, most major American newspapers and wire services strive to fulfill those ideals. But what about television news? How can a medium whose fast-paced and dynamic images are intended for viewing pleasure deliver unbiased news? According to Neil Postman and Steve Powers, it can't. In this essay, the authors argue that nightly news is a visual entertainment package that creates the illusion of keeping the public informed. They argue that broadcast news shows are, on the contrary, "re-creations" that reveal the world as a series of incoherent and meaningless fragments.

Neil Postman is a critic, writer, communication theorist, and chairman of the Department of Communication Arts at New York University. He is the author of nineteen books, including *Amusing Ourselves to Death* (1985) and *Conscientious Objections* (1992). Steve Powers is an award-winning journalist with more than 30 years' experience in broadcast news, including serving as a correspondent for Fox Television News and the ABC Information Radio Network. They are coauthors of the book, *How to Watch TV News* (1992), from which this essay is excerpted.

1   When a television news show distorts the truth by altering or manufacturing facts (through re-creations), a television viewer is defenseless even if a re-creation is properly labeled. Viewers are still vulnerable to misinformation since they will not know (at least in the case of docudramas) what parts are fiction and what parts are not. But the problems of verisimilitude posed by re-creations pale to insignificance when compared to the problems viewers face when encountering a straight (no-monkey-business) show. All news shows, in a sense, are re-creations in that what we hear and see on them are attempts to represent actual events, and are not the events themselves. Perhaps, to avoid ambiguity, we might call all news shows "re-presentations" instead of "re-creations." These re-presentations come to us in two forms: language and pictures. The question then arises: what do viewers have to know about language and pictures in order to be properly armed to defend themselves against the seductions of eloquence (to use Bertrand Russell's apt phrase)? . . .

2   [Let us look at] the problem of pictures. It is often said that a picture is worth a thousand words. Maybe so. But it is probably equally true that one word is worth a thousand pictures, at least sometimes—for example, when it comes to understanding the world we live in. Indeed, the whole problem with news on television comes down to this: all the words uttered in an hour of news coverage could be printed on one page of a newspaper. And the world cannot be understood in one page. Of course, there is a compensation: television offers pictures, and the pictures move. Moving pictures are a kind of language in themselves, but the language of pictures differs radically from oral and written language, and the differences are crucial for understanding television news.

3   To begin with, pictures, especially single pictures, speak only in particularities. Their vocabulary is limited to concrete representation. Unlike words and sentences, a picture does not present to us an idea or concept about the world, except as we use language itself to convert the image to idea. By itself, a picture cannot deal with the unseen, the remote, the internal, the abstract. It does not speak of "man," only of *a* man; not of "tree," only of *a* tree. You cannot produce an image of "nature," any more than an image of "the sea." You can only show a particular fragment of the here-and-now—a cliff of a certain terrain, in a certain condition of light; a wave at a moment in time, from a particular point of view. And just as "nature" and "the sea" cannot be photographed, such larger abstractions as truth, honor, love, and falsehood cannot be talked about in the lexicon of individual pictures. For "showing of" and "talking about" are two very different kinds of processes: individual pictures give us the world as object; language, the world as idea. There is no such thing in nature as "man" or "tree." The universe offers no such categories or simplifications; only flux and infinite variety. The picture documents and celebrates the particularities of the universe's infinite variety. Language makes them comprehensible.

4   Of course, moving pictures, video with sound, may bridge the gap by juxtaposing images, symbols, sound, and music. Such images can present emotions and rudimentary ideas. They can suggest the panorama of nature and the joys and miseries of humankind.

5   Picture—smoke pouring from the window, cut to people coughing, an ambulance racing to a hospital, a tombstone in a cemetery.

6   Picture—jet planes firing rockets, explosions, lines of foreign soldiers surrendering, the American flag waving in the wind.

7   Nonetheless, keep in mind that when terrorists want to prove to the world that their kidnap victims are still alive, they photograph them holding a copy of a recent newspaper. The dateline on the newspaper provides the proof that the photograph was taken on or after that date. Without the help of the written word, film and videotape cannot portray temporal dimensions with any precision. Consider a film clip showing an aircraft carrier at sea. One might be able to identify the ship as Soviet or American, but there would be no way of telling where in the world the carrier was, where it was headed, or when the pictures were taken. It is only through language—words spoken over the pic-

tures or reproduced in them—that the image of the aircraft carrier takes on specific meaning.

8   Still, it is possible to enjoy the image of the carrier for its own sake. One might find the hugeness of the vessel interesting; it signifies military power on the move. There is a certain drama in watching the planes come in at high speeds and skid to a stop on the deck. Suppose the ship were burning: that would be even more interesting. This leads to an important point about the language of pictures. Moving pictures favor images that change. That is why violence and dynamic destruction find their way onto television so often. When something is destroyed violently it is altered in a highly visible way; hence the entrancing power of fire. Fire gives visual form to the ideas of consumption, disappearance, death—the thing that burned is actually taken away by fire. It is at this very basic level that fires make a good subject for television news. Something was here, now it's gone, and the change is recorded on film.

9   Earthquakes and typhoons have the same power. Before the viewer's eyes the world is taken apart. If a television viewer has relatives in Mexico City and an earthquake occurs there, then he or she may take a special interest in the images of destruction as a report from a specific place and time; that is, one may look at television pictures for information about an important event. But film of an earthquake can be interesting even if the viewer cares nothing about the event itself. Which is only to say, as we noted earlier, that there is another way of participating in the news—as a spectator who desires to be entertained. Actually to see buildings topple is exciting, no matter where the buildings are. The world turns to dust before our eyes.

10   Those who produce television news in America know that their medium favors images that move. That is why they are wary of "talking heads," people who simply appear in front of a camera and speak. When talking heads appear on television, there is nothing to record or document, no change in process. In the cinema the situation is somewhat different. On a movie screen, closeups of a good actor speaking dramatically can sometimes be interesting to watch. When Clint Eastwood narrows his eyes and challenges his rival to shoot first, the spectator sees the cool rage of the Eastwood character take visual form, and the narrowing of the eyes is dramatic. But much of the effect of this small movement depends on the size of the movie screen and the darkness of the theater, which make Eastwood and his every action "larger than life."

11   The television screen is smaller than life. It occupies about 15 percent of the viewer's visual field (compared to about 70 percent for the movie screen). It is not set in a darkened theater closed off from the world but in the viewer's ordinary living space. This means that visual changes must be more extreme and more dramatic to be interesting on television. A narrowing of the eyes will not do. A car crash, an earthquake, a burning factory are much better.

12   With these principles in mind, let us examine more closely the structure of a typical newscast, and here we will include in the discussion not only the pictures but all the nonlinguistic symbols that make up a television news show. For example, in America, almost all news shows begin with music, the tone of which suggests important events about to unfold. The music is very important,

for it equates the news with various forms of drama and ritual—the opera, for example, or a wedding procession—in which musical themes underscore the meaning of the event. Music takes us immediately into the realm of the symbolic, a world that is not to be taken literally. After all, when events unfold in the real world, they do so without musical accompaniment. More symbolism follows. The sound of teletype machines can be heard in the studio, not because it is impossible to screen this noise out, but because the sound is a kind of music in itself. It tells us that data are pouring in from all corners of the globe, a sensation reinforced by the world map in the background (or clocks noting the time on different continents). The fact is that teletype machines are rarely used in TV news rooms, having been replaced by silent computer terminals. When seen, they have only a symbolic function.

13   Already, then, before a single news item is introduced, a great deal has been communicated. We know that we are in the presence of a symbolic event, a form of theater in which the day's events are to be dramatized. This theater takes the entire globe as its subject, although it may look at the world from the perspective of a single nation. A certain tension is present, like the atmosphere in a theater just before the curtain goes up. The tension is represented by the music, the staccato beat of the teletype machines, and often the sight of news workers scurrying around typing reports and answering phones. As a technical matter, it would be no problem to build a set in which the newsroom staff remained off camera, invisible to the viewer, but an important theatrical effect would be lost. By being busy on camera, the workers help communicate urgency about the events at hand, which suggests that situations are changing so rapidly that constant revision of the news is necessary.

14   The staff in the background also helps signal the importance of the person in the center, the anchor, "in command" of both the staff and the news. The anchor plays the role of host. He or she welcomes us to the newscast and welcomes us back from the different locations we visit during the filmed reports.

15   Many features of the newscast help the anchor to establish the impression of control. These are usually equated with production values in broadcasting. They include such things as graphics that tell the viewer what is being shown, or maps and charts that suddenly appear on the screen and disappear on cue, or the orderly progression from story to story. They also include the absence of gaps, or "dead time," during the broadcast, even the simple fact that the news starts and ends at a certain hour. These common features are thought of as purely technical matters, which a professional crew handles as a matter of course. But they are also symbols of a dominant theme of television news: the imposition of an orderly world—called "the news"—upon the disorderly flow of events.

16   While the form of a news broadcast emphasizes tidiness and control, its content can best be described as fragmented. Because time is so precious on television, because the nature of the medium favors dynamic visual images, and because the pressures of a commercial structure require the news to hold its audience above all else, there is rarely any attempt to explain issues in depth or place events in their proper context. The news moves nervously from

a warehouse fire to a court decision, from a guerrilla war to a World Cup match, the quality of the film most often determining the length of the story. Certain stories show up only because they offer dramatic pictures. Bleachers collapse in South America: hundreds of people are crushed—a perfect television news story, for the cameras can record the face of disaster in all its anguish. Back in Washington, a new budget is approved by Congress. Here there is nothing to photograph because a budget is not a physical event; it is a document full of language and numbers. So the producers of the news will show a photo of the document itself, focusing on the cover where it says "Budget of the United States of America." Or sometimes they will send a camera crew to the government printing plant where copies of the budget are produced. That evening, while the contents of the budget are summarized by a voice-over, the viewer sees stacks of documents being loaded into boxes at the government printing plant. Then a few of the budget's more important provisions will be flashed on the screen in written form, but this is such a time-consuming process—using television as a printed page—that the producers keep it to a minimum. In short, the budget is not televisable, and for that reason its time on the news must be brief. The bleacher collapse will get more time that evening.

17   While appearing somewhat chaotic, these disparate stories are not just dropped in the news program helter-skelter. The appearance of a scattershot story order is really orchestrated to draw the audience from one story to the next—from one section to the next—through the commercial breaks to the end of the show. The story order is constructed to hold and build the viewership rather than place events in context or explain issues in depth.

18   Of course, it is a tendency of journalism in general to concentrate on the surface of events rather than underlying conditions; this is as true for the newspaper as it is for the newscast. But several features of television undermine whatever efforts journalists may make to give sense to the world. One is that a television broadcast is a series of events that occur in sequence, and the sequence is the same for all viewers. This is not true for a newspaper page, which displays many items simultaneously, allowing readers to choose the order in which they read them. If newspaper readers want only a summary of the latest tax bill, they can read the headline and the first paragraph of an article, and if they want more, they can keep reading. In a sense, then, everyone reads a different newspaper, for no two readers will read (or ignore) the same items.

19   But all television viewers see the same broadcast. They have no choices. A report is either in the broadcast or out, which means that anything which is of narrow interest is unlikely to be included. As NBC News executive Reuven Frank once explained:

> A newspaper, for example, can easily afford to print an item of conceivable interest to only a fraction of its readers. A television news program must be put together with the assumption that each item will be of some interest to everyone that watches. Every time a newspaper includes a feature which will attract a specialized group it can assume it is adding at least a little bit to its circulation. To the degree a

television news program includes an item of this sort . . . it must assume that its audience will diminish.

20   The need to "include everyone," an identifying feature of commercial television in all its forms, prevents journalists from offering lengthy or complex explanations, or from tracing the sequence of events leading up to today's headlines. One of the ironies of political life in modern democracies is that many problems which concern the "general welfare" are of interest only to specialized groups. Arms control, for example, is an issue that literally concerns everyone in the world, and yet the language of arms control and the complexity of the subject are so daunting that only a minority of people can actually follow the issue from week to week and month to month. If it wants to act responsibly, a newspaper can at least make available more information about arms control than most people want. Commercial television cannot afford to do so.

21   But even if commercial television could afford to do so, it wouldn't. The fact that television news is principally made up of moving pictures prevents it from offering lengthy, coherent explanations of events. A television news show reveals the world as a series of unrelated, fragmentary moments. It does not—and cannot be expected to—offer a sense of coherence or meaning. What does this suggest to a TV viewer? That the viewer must come with a prepared mind—information, opinions, a sense of proportion, an articulate value system. To the TV viewer lacking such mental equipment, a news program is only a kind of rousing light show. Here a falling building, there a five-alarm fire, everywhere the world as an object, much without meaning, connections, or continuity.

TOPICAL CONSIDERATIONS

1. According to Postman and Powers, how are still pictures like language? How are they different?

2. How do juxtapositions with other images, symbols, sound, music, or printed or verbal language help present the meaning of moving images (paragraph 4)? For each example in paragraphs 5–7, describe how these juxtapositions supply meaning to the moving images.

3. According to the authors, why are violence and destruction so often part of TV news stories? How are violence and destruction better suited for TV than other stories? How do TV screens make such stories more suited than other stories?

4. Why are music, machine sounds, and news workers routinely included in TV news broadcasts? How do these nonessential cues help make news broadcasts seem interesting and important?

5. What devices do news broadcasters use to make them seem in control of "the disorderly flow of events"? Why are stories placed in a particular sequence? How might such a sequence affect audience viewing habits?

6. Why do TV news stories concentrate on "the surface of events rather than underlying conditions"? Why do broadcasters sometimes omit stories that are important but that would interest (or be understood by) only a minority of viewers?

RHETORICAL CONSIDERATIONS

1. What attitude do Postman and Powers convey in their first paragraph about television news shows? What kind of judgments about TV news did you expect to find throughout the rest of the article? What analogies and phrases help you identify the authors' attitude?

2. What attitude is conveyed in comparing TV news to theater? Beyond the aspect of spectacle, what additional denotations or connotations are implicit in the term *theater*? How do these suggest the authors' distrust of TV as a reliable, accurate source of news information? (See paragraph 13.)

3. What kinds of "important" news events are overwhelmed or lost by TV's visual reportage? How significant are such stories to the purpose(s) of news reporting? Do the authors convince you of the urgency of such stories? Would their point seem less urgent if they had focused on sports and weather reporting, for example?

4. Do Postman and Powers offer a direct statement of what they would like to see changed? Or is it only implied? Explain your answer.

5. Do the authors suggest that news show producers are exercising a subtle form of censorship? If so, why do the authors never use this word or some other pejorative terms? What effect would such language have on readers involved in TV news production? on readers not involved in TV news?

WRITING ASSIGNMENTS

1. Using a family photograph, or a photo of friends, describe how this still picture conveys only a limited idea of what it shows. Did anything happen before or after the photo was snapped to make it especially important to you? Was anyone in the picture faking pleasure or caught in an uncharacteristic posture? In short, what might a stranger miss in this photo?

2. How do you think Postman and Powers would analyze the effect of closed captioning on television? Do you think they would include closed captioning as a visual element? Justify your answer.

3. Videotape a network or local television newscast. First, watch the newscast with the sound (and/or closed captioning) turned off; then, watch the whole newscast with the sound (and/or closed captioning) turned on. Select three stories near the beginning of the broadcast and record your impressions about how important each was. Did you have different impressions when the sound (or closed captioning) accompanied the pictures? Why or why not?

4. Discuss the impact and role of TV news reporting on the Vietnam War, the Civil Rights Movement, the Gulf War, the 1995 Oklahoma City bombing, the so-called Rodney King riots, the O. J. Simpson trial, or some other highly visible current event. How does television news, particularly the images it uses, help to create news rather than just retelling it?

IN DEPTH, BUT SHALLOWLY

Dave Barry

In the last piece, Neil Postman and Steve Powers criticize broadcast news for being little more than slickly packaged entertainment. They argue that what viewers hear and see on the news comes to them in bits and flashes with no coherence or depth of understanding. It seems that Dave Barry agrees. As its title suggests, this essay is a parody of the local On-the-Spot Action Eyewitness News show. As in all satire, here reality is viewed in a funny mirror to exaggerate a point and get a few laughs.

Dave Barry has been described as "America's most preposterous newspaper columnist," a man "incapable of not being funny." He is the author of ten books and is a Pulitzer Prize–winning humorist whose *Miami Herald* column is syndicated in more than 200 publications. His books include *Babies and Other Hazards of Sex* (1984), *Dave Barry's Greatest Hits* (1989), and, most recently, *Dave Barry Is Not Making This Up* (1994). This essay is from another of his collections, *Bad Habits* (1987).

1   If you want to take your mind off the troubles of the real world, you should watch local TV news shows. I know of no better way to escape reality, except perhaps heavy drinking.

2   Local TV news programs have given a whole new definition to the word *news*. To most people, *news* means *information about events that affect a lot of people*. On local TV news shows, *news* means *anything that you can take a picture of, especially if a local TV News Personality can stand in front of it*. This is why they are so fond of car accidents, burning buildings, and crowds: these are good for standing in front of. On the other hand, local TV news shows tend to avoid stories about things that local TV News Personalities cannot stand in front of, such as budgets and taxes and the economy. If you want to get a local TV news show to do a story on the budget, your best bet is to involve it in a car crash.

3   I travel around the country a lot, and as far as I can tell, virtually all local TV news shows follow the same format. First you hear some exciting music, the kind you hear in space movies, while the screen shows local TV News Person-

alities standing in front of various News Events. Then you hear the announcer:

4   ANNOUNCER: From the On-the-Spot Action Eyewitness News Studios, this is the On-the-Spot Action Eyewitness News, featuring Anchorman Wilson Westbrook, Co-Anchorperson Stella Snape, Minority-Group Member James Edwards, Genial Sports Personality Jim Johnson, Humorous Weatherperson Dr. Reed Stevens, and Norm Perkins on drums. And now, here's Wilson Westbrook.

5   WESTBROOK: Good evening. Tonight from the On-the-Spot Action Eyewitness News Studios we have actual color film of a burning building, actual color film of two cars after they ran into each other, actual color film of the front of a building in which one person shot another person, actual color film of another burning building, and special reports on roller-skating and child abuse. But for the big story tonight, we go to City Hall, where On-the-Spot reporter Reese Kernel is standing live.

6   KERNEL: I am standing here live in front of City Hall being televised by the On-the-Spot Action Eyewitness News minicam with Mayor Bryce Hallbread.

7   MAYOR: That's "Hallwood."

8   KERNEL: What?

9   MAYOR: MY NAME IS "HALLWOOD." YOU SAID "HALLBREAD."

10   KERNEL: Look, Hallbread, do you want to be on the news or don't you?

11   MAYOR: Yes, of course, it's just that my name is————

12   KERNEL: Listen, this is the top-rated news show in the three-county area, and if you think I have time to memorize every stupid detail, you'd better think again.

13   MAYOR: I'm sorry. "Hallbread" is fine, really.

14   KERNEL: Thank you, Mayor Hallbread. And now back to Wilson Westbrook in the On-the-Spot Action Eyewitness News Studios.

15   WESTBROOK: Thank you, Reese; keep us posted if anything further develops on that important story. And now, as I promised earlier, we have actual color film of various objects that either burned or crashed, which we will project on the screen behind me while I talk about them. Here is a building on fire. Here is another building on fire. Here is a car crash. This film was shot years ago, but you can safely assume that objects just like these crashed or burned in the three-county area today. And now we go to my Co-Anchorperson, Stella Snape, for a Special Report on her exhaustive three-week investigation into the problem of child abuse in the three-county area. Well, Stella, what did you find?

16   SNAPE: Wilson, I found that child abuse is very sad. What happens is that people abuse children. It's just awful. Here you see some actual color film of me standing in front of a house. Most of your child abuse occurs in houses. Note that I am wearing subdued colors.

17   WESTBROOK (*reading from a script*): Are any efforts under way here in the three-county area to combat child abuse?

18   SNAPE: Yes.

19   WESTBROOK: Thank you, Stella, for that informative report. On the lighter side, On-the-Spot Action Eyewitness Reporter Terri Tompkins has prepared a three-part series on roller-skating in the three-county area.

20   TOMPKINS: Roller-skating has become a major craze in California and the three-county area, as you can see by this actual color film of me on roller skates outside the On-the-Spot Action Eyewitness News Studio. This certainly is a fun craze. Tomorrow, in Part Two of this series, we'll see actual color film of me falling down. On Wednesday we'll see me getting up.

21   WESTBROOK: We'll look forward to those reports. Our next story is from Minority-Group Reporter James Edwards, who, as he has for the last 324 consecutive broadcasts, spent the day in the minority-group sector of the three-county area finding out what minorities think.

22   EDWARDS: Wilson, I'm standing in front of a crowd of minority-group members, and as you can see, their mood is troubled. (*The crowd smiles and waves at the camera.*)

23   WESTBROOK: Good report, James, Well, we certainly had a sunny day here in the three-county area, didn't we, Humorous Weatherperson Dr. Reed Stevens?

24   STEVENS: Ha ha. We sure did, though I'm certainly troubled by that very troubling report Stella did on child abuse. But we should see continued warm weather through Wednesday. Here are a bunch of charts showing the relative humidity and stuff like that. Ha ha.

25   WESTBROOK: Ha ha. Well, things weren't nearly as bright on the sports scene, were they, Genial Sports Personality Jim Johnson?

26   JOHNSON: No, Wilson, they certainly weren't. The Three-County Community College Cutlasses lost their fourth consecutive game today. Here you see actual color footage of me watching the game from the sidelines. The disgust is evident on my face. I intended to have actual color film of me interviewing the coach after the game, but the team bus crashed and everyone was killed.

27   WESTBROOK: Thank you, Jim. And now, here is Basil Holp, the General Manager of KUSP-TV, to present an Editorial Viewpoint:

28 HOLP: The management of KUSP-TV firmly believes that something ought to be done about earthquakes. From time to time we read in the papers that an earthquake has hit some wretched little country and knocked houses down and killed people. This should not be allowed to continue. Maybe we should have a tax or something. What the heck, we can afford it. The management of KUSP-TV is rolling in money.

29 ANNOUNCER: The preceding was the opinion of the management of KUSP-TV. People with opposing points of view are probably in the vast majority.

30 WESTBROOK: Well, that wraps up tonight's version of the On-the-Spot Action Eyewitness News. Tune in tonight to see essentially the same stories.

TOPICAL CONSIDERATIONS

1. Parody gets its humorous effect from exaggeration. However, there must be enough realism for the satire to work. How close does Barry get to capturing the local TV news show in your community? Consider the language—the vocabulary, usage, style, jargon, and so on—of the reporters. What about the personality types and the exchanges between personalities? Explain.

2. What aspects of this piece did you find the funniest? If possible, explain why. What, if any, comic efforts fell flat for you? Explain why.

3. What do you make of the names Barry gave his news people?

4. What is implied in the exchange between Reese Kernel and the Mayor over his name? What's the significance of the Mayor's concession, "I'm sorry. 'Hallbread' is fine, really."?

5. What do you make of Stella Snape's report on her "three-week exhaustive investigation" of child abuse? How does her report reflect such in-depth local coverage of provocative stories?

6. At the end, Barry gives us KUSP-TV's Editorial Viewpoint on earthquakes. What is he poking fun at here?

7. How might Neil Postman and Steve Powers ("TV News: All the World in Pictures") react to Barry's piece?

8. Did this essay affect your attitude toward local TV news shows? Will you regard them differently from now on? Why or why not?

RHETORICAL CONSIDERATIONS

1. Take another look at Barry's lead paragraph. Did it capture your attention? Did it make you want to read on? How well did it establish the tone and attitude of the piece? In your own words, how does it characterize local TV news shows? How well did the rest of the essay substantiate that claim?

2. Writers employ several strategies for creating humorous effects. Look over this piece again and try to find examples of humor created by stereotypes, repetition, surprise, irony, witty observations, understatement, overstatement, absurdities.

Can you find other comic devices? What struck you as some of the funniest aspects of the piece?

3. What's the message behind "and Norm Perkins on drums"?

4. What is Barry's message in the repetition of "actual color film" in paragraph 5?

5. Do you consider Westbrook's closing statement a satisfying ending to the essay? If so, why? If not, how would you have ended it?

WRITING ASSIGNMENTS

1. The major thrust of Barry's humor here is parody. Try some parody of your own by writing a TV news story, or sports, weather, or financial report. Try to capture the language, style, and personality of media people with enough comic twists and exaggeration to make it funny?

2. The next time you watch your local news show, take note of some of the features Barry satirizes here. Try to determine just how much is news and how much is fluff, mindless entertainment, idle chit-chat, self-promotion, and the like. Try to distinguish between real news and sensationalism while taking note of the proportion of time spent on different stories. Also try to determine if the personalities fit the stereotypes in Barry's piece. In an essay, write up your findings.

DUMBING DOWN: TV TALK-SHOW TALK

Tom Schachtman

The talk show is a phenomenon of contemporary television. Every day from dawn to midnight, some 80 million people tune their television sets to hear hosts and guests go head-to-head on a variety of provocative topics. With a major percentage of American society held captive, it goes without saying that such shows have measurable impact on the minds and language of viewers. Unfortunately, according to some critics, including Tom Schachtman, that impact is pathetic. Not only is incivility encouraged, but the language is made up of limited vocabulary, misused terms, and bad grammar, all spiced with the latest psychobabble. If talk shows are any measure, Americans are failing to communicate.

Tom Schachtman is the author of several works of fiction and nonfiction and has taught writing at New York University and Harvard's Extension School. His latest book is *The Inarticulate Society* (1996) from which this selection is excerpted.

1   On an Oprah Winfrey broadcast, when a young doctor confessed that he was something of a romantic, he reportedly received 40,000 letters from women wishing to share his life. While not every talk program can generate that amount of attention, collectively talk shows have an enormous audience, as many as 80 million viewers daily, and as the doctor's story makes clear, it is an audience that pays close attention to what is being said on the programs. To learn more about how language is being modeled for us on talk shows, on November 9, 1993, I spent the day watching and listening to snippets of eight mainstream syndicated talk shows.

2   At nine in the morning in New York, while NBC and some other channels carry game shows and cartoons, and while Mr. Rogers holds forth on public television, there are three talk shows in head-to-head competition: Jane Whitney on CBS, Montel Williams on the Fox network, and Regis Philbin and Kathie Lee Gifford on ABC.

3   Jane Whitney features a man whose problem is that he has two girlfriends. Tina and Jim are the guests in the first segment. She is angry about the situa-

tion, while he seems as contented as the cat who swallowed the cream. We later learn that Jim called the program and offered to appear with his two girl-friends, ostensibly to resolve their predicament. Jane Whitney's questioning demonstrates that she knows the terms "psychobabble," "avoiding commit-ment," "relationship," and "monogamous," but most of her queries are mono-syllabic: "Some people, like, sleep with only one person at a time."

4   Jim's two lovers have never met. Now, to applause, the second young woman emerges from behind a curtain, and then, under Jane's questioning, the two comment on how they are and are not alike.

> JANE: Do you feel you have anything in common with her?
> SECOND: Him.
> TINA: How do you know he loves you? He loves me!
> JANE: You're playing, like, seniority here. Like, bookends.

5   Montel Williams's guests are six couples made up of older women and younger men. Each woman introduces her young man, using such terms as "hunk," "sex appeal," and "perfect specimen of humanity," and making sure to announce his birth date, for the men are a decade or two younger than the women. The couples behave as though they are in the first flushes of affairs. We learn that the Montel Williams show arranged and taped a party at which these people were first introduced to one another, in exchange for promises to appear on the program. The basic subject of the program is sex. Queried by the host, one young man speaks of "not having to work for it" and another con-fides about older women, "they tell you what they want," which prompts an admission from one that "we want a little pleasure for ourselves." Titles over the screen inform us the "JOHN/Likes women of all ages" and "NICK/Loves older women." The snickering quotient of the program is high. At the transi-tion to commercials, footage of the mixer party is followed by a snippet from tomorrow's show, "Two sisters, one man. . . . You'd be surprised at how often this happens." At least one set of sisters are twins. During a later segment of the broadcast, a ponytailed male therapist comments on the couples, using such phrases as "comfort . . . not expected to last . . . emotional ties are sus-pended." The therapist is then questioned by the panel, which induces Mon-tel to tell about his own experiences with older women. A billboard asks us at home, "Are You a Mom Who Wishes Her Son Would Stop Dating Tramps?" Those who can answer "yes" are to call the show.

6   "Born to Be Unfaithful," Jane Whitney's next program, will feature people who have been unfaithful and are the offspring of unfaithful parents. The sub-ject after that is "Mothers who allow their teenage daughters to have sex in the house"; on videotape, one such mother says she prefers her daughter and the daughter's boyfriend to have sex at home "where I know that they're safe."

7   Barbara Walters visits Regis and Kathie Lee to impart backstage chatter about the celebrities she has interviewed for her latest special, to be broadcast that evening. In a clip, Barbara tries to learn from Julia Roberts whether the movie star thinks her husband of a few months is ugly or just differently hand-

some. Julia opts for handsome. In the studio Barbara and Kathie Lee brush cheeks and make hand motions to convey that they must phone one another for a lunch date very soon.

8   Fred Rogers visits a pretzel bakery. In an apron and baker's hat, he observes the various processes of the assembly line and kneads some dough with his own hands. His conversation with the bakers, aimed at an audience of preschool children, employs almost as large a vocabulary as that of the nine o'clock talk shows.

9   Not yet ready to make conclusions from such a small sample, later that day I watch segments of five more talk shows: Joan Rivers on CBS and, on NBC, Jerry Springer, Maury Povich, Sally Jessy Raphael, and Phil Donahue.

10   "How going back to the trauma of birth will help you clear up present problems" is the way Joan Rivers touts the subject of her program, but before discussing that she chats with a gossip columnist about the recent birth of Marla Maples's child, in which "aroma therapy" was used, and welcomes a pair of married guests to talk about "past-life therapy." The couple maintains that they were actually married in a previous life. The wife says that through reliving and understanding an incident in Roman times, she has been cured:

GUEST: All that anger drained away. . . . My heart got tender. I got compassionate.
JOAN: All this in one session?

11   . . . Then we are finally introduced to a female "prenatal psychologist." To investigate "early traumas . . . impressed on the psyche," this woman helps patients to go back to the moment of birth, even to the moment of conception. She has brought along some patients, whom Joan Rivers introduces: "My next guests have all been reborn, not through religion." These guests include another ponytailed male psychologist, who has been rescued by regression therapy from suicidal impulses, and a mother-and-daughter pair, similarly rescued from allergies. We shortly see a videotape of a volunteer who has gone through the therapy backstage. After the tape is shown, the volunteer comes onto the set and comments on reliving the attempt to get out of the birth canal: "I was engaged in some sort of battle."

12   From Boston, Jerry Springer features several trios, each consisting of a grandmother, her teenage daughter, and the daughter's infant. The infants have been born out of wedlock, one to a girl who became pregnant at twelve, the others to girls who were thirteen and fourteen. The teenagers had all considered abortion but had decided against it. Jerry asks about birth control. . . . A new grandmother allows that in retrospect she does "feel guilty" at not having given her daughter birth control instruction. "At thirteen, I didn't think she was going to be —you know—actively having sex with her boyfriend," who was nineteen; "I was in denial." Jerry Springer nods, and in general his treatment of an important subject, the epidemic of teenage pregnancies, is evenhanded. He questions the women sympathetically and with dignity, although he never refers to them by their names but says "Mom" and "Grandmom." He

asks a woman in the latter category if the sensation of becoming a grand-mother could have been a proud one, given the circumstances. She says, "I don't know; it's like, I was in the delivery room with her, and it's like—'Memo-ries.' " Audience members express their belief that the fathers should be ar-raigned on charges of statutory rape, but the new mothers and grandmothers all agree that would not help anyone . . .

13   Maury Povich has gone to Texas for "Return to Waco: Answers in the Ashes." In front of an audience of former cult members and Waco residents, Povich questions Mark Breault, who left the Branch Davidians in 1989; Breault's complaints to the authorities have been blamed by some survivors for instigating the raids . . .

14   The government's lead pathologist then summarizes his team's findings about the thirty-two people who died in the bunker. In the most literate lan-guage I have heard all day, language that is compassionate, direct, and precise, he details the manner and cause of death: So many had gunshot wounds, so many died of asphyxiation; a gunshot wound in the mouth may have been self-inflicted, but a wound in the back of the head almost certainly was not. His findings, being made public for the first time, devastate the people in the audi-ence and on the set whose relatives died in that bunker—as we at home are forced to learn because the cameras focus on their faces so that we become privy to their emotions. While the pathologist tells the story, Maury Povich ap-proaches one panel member whose face fills the screen and asks, "Is this what you think, Stan, happened to your family?"

15   "Could your sex life use a pick-me-up?" asks the announcer of the Phil Donahue show. Then voice and tape display aphrodisiacs, love potions, and an acupuncturist at work, and a panelist comments that "I'm getting turned on just by watching."

16   That, of course, is just what was intended.

17   Sally Jessy Raphael's program on November 9, 1993, deals with two 1986 cyanide poisoning deaths in the Seattle area, for which the wife of one of the victims was convicted and imprisoned. Of all the programs of this day, it is the worst exemplar in terms of use of language. First, Sally encapsulates the story for us in emotional kindergarten language: "Some family members say Stella was railroaded. 'She's innocent. Poor Stella.' Some say her daughter Cynthia was really the mastermind behind the deaths." A journalist has written a book about the case. He has corralled the guest panelists, but during the course of the program he must frequently interpret and augment what these guests say, for the guests prove remarkably unable to present their thoughts coherently or even clothed in words that aptly convey their meaning.

> STELLA'S NIECE: I didn't think that—there wasn't enough problems that would institute her to kill my uncle . . .
>
> STELLA'S FRIEND: She was somebody that would've taken a gun and shot him point-blank, instead of being sneaky and committed murder in the way that she was convicted.

18   When one guest is entirely unable to convey her meaning, Sally is forced to correct her in order that the audience can understand the story:

> FORMER HOUSEMATE: She used me as a scapegoat.
> SALLY: As a screen.
> AUDIENCE MEMBER: Maybe Cynthia was child-abused.

19   As with my student's use of "emitted" for "admitted," these poor grammatical, vocabulary and word usages are evidence of the sort of misperception of language that can only come from learning language in a secondarily oral way. Pop psychology terms aside, the discourse of the moderators, the guests, the experts, and most of the studio audience members of all these programs mixes grade-school vocabulary and grammar with a leavening of naughty language. Granted, there is no pretense of trying to be articulate, but neither are there many accidental instances of felicitous phrasing. Vocabulary levels are depressingly low, more in line with the spoken-word corpus than might be presumed, since parts of the programs are scripted, and since the guests and stars of these programs are not speaking in private but in rather public circumstances, in front of viewing audiences numbered in the tens of millions.

20   Talk show language has become almost completely detached from the literate base of English. It is as though the program-makers have concluded that literate English has nothing to do with the emotive, real-life concerns of human beings, and therefore cannot be used to describe or analyze them. As a result, talk shows exist in the realm of vocabularies limited to the few hundred most commonly used words in the spoken language, augmented by a few terms pirated from the sublanguage of therapy. To talk of "Mothers who allow their teenage daughters to have sex in the house," or to inquire "Are You a Mom Who Wishes Her Son Would Stop Dating Tramps?" is to speak down to the audience, not even to address the audience on its own level. These lines employ a vocabulary not much beyond that of a nine- or ten-year-old; the facts show that the daytime viewing audience is chronologically older and better educated than that. . . . But the programming elites seem to have nothing but contempt for their audiences composed of average Americans—for "the people we fly over," as one executive called them. Rather, the programmers embrace the fuzzy McLuhanesque belief that a world dominated by new electronic media will wholeheartedly share tribal emotions.

21   Walter Ong asserts that the culture of secondary orality may mean a return to the primacy of the unconscious for those within it.[1] That culture's gestation period is being shortened by the practices of today's news programs and talk shows, which encourage the audience to acquire information principally through images, and through a lexicon that mimics the oral rather than the literate language. The limited vocabulary, constrained syntax, unknowing or deliberate misuses of language, affectation of minor wit, constant reference to

---

[1]Walter J. Ong, *Rhetoric, Romance and Technology*, 1971.

base emotions, and chronic citation of pop cultural icons in attempts to bond with the audience—these characteristic elements of news and talk programs constitute an enfeebled discourse.

22   The antidote is well known, since most of the people who create news programs and talk shows are themselves literate and fully capable of using the literate-based language. That antidote is to use the power of words to haul these programs back up to a literate level they once attained. Purveyors of talk shows currently reject such a goal as not commensurate with their objective of gaining the largest audience. However, there is no evidence of which I am aware that demonstrates any inverse relationship between the shows' popularity and the vocabulary and articulateness levels of talk show hosts and hostesses (and that of their carefully screened guests). Precisely the opposite may be true: Articulate behavior is part of the hosts' and hostesses' attractiveness. Phil Donahue and Oprah Winfrey are articulate as well as charismatic people. Rush Limbaugh's ability to deflate liberal icons and to create telling puns—"femi-nazis" for strident feminists—have attracted him a wide following. All three, and many others among the talk-show stars, possess good vocabularies, but they have yet to employ them to best use. All too often, they reach for the simple instead of using their tremendous abilities to make complicated matters exciting and understandable. Given these stars' large talents and capacities to enthrall, audiences would undoubtedly follow them up the scale of literacy as gladly (and in just as large numbers) as they have followed them down the scale.

23   As for news broadcasts, the transformation could be even simpler. News broadcasts need to take a pledge to not only convey information but to set aside time in the broadcast to have that information illuminated by the minds and vocabularies of the reporters. Permit reporters once again to do the tasks of synthesis and analysis of information, as well as the job of being on the spot to collect it. Utilize television's fabulous educative ability. Employ vocabularies that may once in a while send an audience member scurrying to a dictionary—or, better yet, set a goal of encouraging the audience to incorporate interesting words into their own vocabularies. During the Gulf War, millions of Americans learned a new word when Peter Jennings of ABC News spoke of oil as a "fungible" commodity, which he explained meant that a unit of it from one source was essentially the same as a unit of it from another source. Network news divisions could improve the articulateness levels of their viewers by raising the vocabulary and sentence-structure levels of their own broadcasts and by taking the pledge to use "fungible" and other such marvelous if unfamiliar words when they are clearly appropriate. How about one new word a day? Such a practice would be unlikely to provoke viewers to turn away from their favorite newscasters and to the competition.

24   We need for our broadcasters once again to champion and employ the power of words as well as the power of images. This is not only in the public interest, but in their own. Informative broadcasting relies, in the end, on an audience that places some premium on the value of ideas. If its discourse is in-

creasingly impoverished, then the audience will retreat from information-based programs into the wholly pictorial realm of video games and interactive fictional programming, where the audience has the illusion of deciding what happens. Then there will be no more market for television news or talk shows. What the informative shows are doing by embracing images and diminished language is the equivalent of a restaurant slowly poisoning all of its customers.

TOPICAL CONSIDERATIONS

1. In paragraph 5, what does each of the following mean: "hunk"; "two sisters, one man"; "tramps"? How does each term gain audience interest? How is each an example of dumbing down the language of television?

2. According to Shachtman, what is wrong with talk show guests' descriptions of their emotional responses? What is wrong with the hosts' and producers' presentation of the complex problems of their guests? How do these examples show the dumbing down of TV language?

3. Why does Shachtman call coverage of the Branch Davidian raid in Waco, Texas "the most literate language I have heard all day" (paragraph 14)? What is different about the language here? What is different about the show's subject?

4. What is the culture of secondary orality, as Shachtman uses the term in paragraph 21? What does the word "secondary" mean? How does television present language in a way that can be described as secondary and oral? According to Shachtman, why is the culture created by secondary orality through TV becoming dumber and dumber?

5. Why does Shachtman believe that talk show producers allow illiterate language to be used? What evidence does he supply to prove that producers' assumptions are wrong? In your opinion, what would happen if talk shows used more sophisticated, accurate language?

6. Why does Shachtman praise newscaster Peter Jennings for introducing most audience members to a new word (paragraph 23)? Define "fungible" and use it in a new sentence of your own creation. How is this an example of the antidote that Shachtman recommends for dumbed-down television language?

RHETORICAL CONSIDERATIONS

1. Why does Shachtman provide several statistics: that he has watched 8 talk shows; that talk shows have 80 million viewers; that one guest's offhand comment generated 40,000 letters; and that Fred Rogers uses as large a vocabulary as that on adult programs? Are these figures effective? Why didn't Shachtman explain the significance of these details?

2. What is Shachtman's attitude toward aroma therapy, past-life therapy, and prenatal psychology? How can you tell? Does he assume that readers agree with his attitude, or does he try to persuade them?

3. Since Shachtman limits his sample of TV talk shows to one average day's fare, why do you think he cites promotional spots for upcoming shows, and calls for audience participation? What is the same and what is different about these teasers? What is the effect of juxtaposing these two kinds of samples?

4. At three points Shachtman uses indented quotes set up in script format to repro-
   duce the language from talk shows. Why do you think he uses this device, rather
   than reproducing the words within his own paragraphs? How would the effect
   have been different?

5. How and why does Shachtman's own language change in paragraph 19, where he
   begins analyzing his examples? Identify specific changes such as vocabulary, sentence structure, tone or attitude, pacing, paragraph length, references to authoritative sources, and so on. How does Shachtman's shift illustrate the kinds of
   change he is calling for in television language?

WRITING ASSIGNMENTS

1. In your opinion, why do people watch television talk shows? Do you think such
   shows function mostly as journalism, providing audiences new information and
   perspectives? Or are they mostly entertainment, keeping audiences interested by
   the bizarreness or foolishness of guests' problems and views?

2. Select one popular TV talk show for further study. Watch (or tape) a week's worth
   of the show. Gather comments and critiques on the show from editorials. Is the
   show better or worse than Shachtman indicates? What recommendations, if any,
   would you make to the show's producers to improve its intellectual quality?

COLLECTIVE BIAS

Charles G. Russell and Paul Many

The fundamental principle of good journalism is objectivity. Without it, the news loses credibility and fails in its reason for being. But as Newman and Genevieve Birk point out in Chapter 2, maintaining objectivity is difficult since language—the tool of the journalist—is inherently biased by culture and experience. As Russell and Many explain in the following essay, one common journalistic practice that illustrates this is the use of standard "collective terms"—for example, "the U.S. Senate," "the Supreme Court," "the White House," "the state legislature." Such collective references, say the authors, give the impression of rigid single-mindedness of large numbers of independent and separate individuals. But such institutions, of course, are made up of many people with different and changeable views—a fact that makes such reporting misleading and compromises journalistic integrity.

Charles G. Russell is professor of Communication at the University of Toledo and a management/communication consultant. Paul Many is associate professor of Communication at the University of Toledo. He has worked for newspapers in and around New York City. This essay first appeared in the Spring 1994 issue of *Et Cetera*.

1   Journalists, despite their cherished notions of objectivity, still find themselves constrained to using language. And if general semanticists agree on anything, they agree that language intertwines with the culture and experience of its users and become inherently biased by that culture and experience.

2   This bias of language becomes most apparent when journalists use such collective formations as *"the Supreme Court* said today," or *"the state legislature* has decided to. . . . "* We refer to such formations in this article as *language collectives*. We view language collectives as concepts which exist mainly in their encryption as language terms and not as symbols of truly tangible entities. . . .

3   Journalists use attribution to tell us *who* said what. Izard et al. in a widely used textbook in the field call it "an essential ingredient of almost every news story" (Izard, 1990, p. 81). It occupies this central role in journalistic writing for at least three reasons: First, the majority of news stories represents secondhand accounts since reporters rarely witness bank robberies or car accidents. Reporters therefore have to rely on outside sources for much of their information. Second, journalistic practice requires that reporters must not comment or give the appearance of commenting on news events, but, instead, must act as a conduit for others who do. Journalists use attribution to help news consumers accurately determine on *whose* authority they say something. Third, *who* says something may amount to an important story element in and of itself. The fact that a prosecutor running for office says something about a defendant becomes important because *he* has said it.

4   However, when journalists attribute to *language collectives* they attempt to walk on semantic water. Terms such as "the Supreme Court" and "the International Society for General Semantics" refer to entities that do not exist in the same way as a pumpkin or you. Language enters here to work its magic. As such terms enter the language, they begin to gain the same status as other terms similarly used that refer to more tangible, unitary entities. Along the way they also pick up other qualities and attributes that generalize from the contexts in which they usually appear. Language collectives result when such rolling snowball terms reach the bottom of the cultural hill and find their way into print.

PROBLEMS WITH LANGUAGE COLLECTIVES

5   Attribution used in this way becomes a Trojan Horse for connotations that compromise journalistic objectivity. When reporters attribute decisions to *the Supreme Court,* or state that *Congress* has mandated a particular action, undiscerning readers may perceive these entities as omnipotent, immutable, immortal, and/or monolithic. Such an attribution as omnipotence, for example, may attach itself to *the Supreme Court* when federal troops appear in the streets because of a decision the Court's *members* have made. Likewise, a reader may perceive the justices as immortal when a newspaper reporter cites a decision of *the Supreme Court* from a century ago.

6   Anyone who has served on even as lofty a body as a faculty committee, knows that human collectives more typically include a changeable roster of singular and all too fallible human beings, with annoyingly short memories.

7   At the simplest level of analysis, we violate logic by writing that "the university plans to," "police said," or "the city has condemned." How can a university, a charter on file in some governmental office and a collection of buildings, perform any action? *People* make up universities and usually some subset of them do the planning. As early as 1927 Fowler warned against such usages, calling them "ill-advised personification" (Fowler, 1927, pp. 432–434).

USE OF LANGUAGE COLLECTIVES IN JOURNALISM

8   In general, journalists use entities such as "Congress," "the Supreme Court," "the CIA," "the White House," etc. as a kind of metaphorical shorthand. Such metaphors may prove useful for quickly conveying complex information. A reporter may write that "Marcy Kaptur was elected to congress," for example, or that "decisions of the Supreme Court are compiled in a certain part of the library." Such metaphorical uses include *personification,* where a reporter attributes person qualities to a non-person ("The *Times* yesterday explained the theory of relativity.") and *metonymy,* in which the collective refers to an individual in a particular context ("The *Times* is late for the interview."). We might consider uses such as these appropriate in casual speech and in forms of literary discourse such as fiction and poetry (Lakoff et al., 1980, pp. 33–40). But in the referential discourse of front page news, we argue that such a shorthand use may mislead.

9   Journalism scholars over the last decade have focused on such aspects of attribution as source anonymity (Wulfemeyer, 1985 and Wulfemeyer et al. 1986), "veiled" attribution (Culbertson, 1975 and 1978), and unnamed news sources (Hale, 1984). Scholars seldom examine the practice of attribution to collectives and the effect this practice may have on readers' perceptions of the news. A close reading of several widely used journalism texts and stylebooks shows some authors make only oblique mentions of the problem (Metz, 1991, p. 241 and Brooks et al., 1992, p. 135). A few seem to condone the practice by omission, using examples of such attribution without comment (Mencher, 1991, p. 33). Others seem to condone it outright (Hough, 1968, p. 167). Many made no significant mention of the practice (Bernstein, 1958; Holley, 1981; Izard et al., 1990; Lippman, 1989; Stone, 1992).

FREQUENCY OF MISUSE OF LANGUAGE COLLECTIVES

10   A non-scientific sampling of the front pages of one local and three national newspapers of varying editorial philosophies and writing styles indicates the frequency of the practice of using *language collectives.*

Frequency of *Language Collective* Usage		
Newspaper	7 Day Headline Average	7 Day Article Average
Blade	3.1	17.7
New York Times	4.0	23.7
USA Today	5.25	17.0
Washington Post	4.1	13.1

Front pages were those of May 25–31, 1993.

11   On front pages, journalists cite *Congress* as responsible for legislation and actions more accurately identified as "247 members of Congress who voted for the legislation." The *CIA* receives credit for actions and interpretations of news more accurately attributable to specific individuals who acted or made the information available. The "White House" receives credit for actions and comments more accurately attributed to an individual spokesperson. The "Administration" allegedly acts when perhaps a more accurate attribution would show the specific individual(s) who acted.

CONCLUSIONS AND SUGGESTIONS FOR CHANGE

12   Attributing to such collectives saves words, of course, and some may use this device as a compromise that increases efficiency of expression. Accurately and precisely specifying the "whos" in a story remains one of a reporter's most important obligations to readers, however—one least open to such a compromise.

13   Beyond accuracy, the use of language collectives may unwittingly show bias toward the status quo. Readers, for example, may mistake the metaphor for the thing and think of *the Supreme Court* in the immutable, monolithic way noted earlier. Readers then might perceive this entity as larger and more powerful than the individuals who made a decision or took an action. Would readers be less likely to question a decision made by *the White House* than to question a particular, named inhabitant of it?

14   Readers might feel frustrated in identifying the individuals responsible for certain actions attributed to a source such as "City Council." The ambiguity in such an attribution could contribute to citizen uncertainty about exactly whom to blame (or perhaps, praise). A citizen might hesitate to fight "City Hall," but might participate in a campaign to unseat a particular, named councilperson.

15   We can find even greater ambiguity in the use of a language collective in such a construction as "Ohio policy prohibits. . . ." Whom do readers hold responsible when reporters attribute a policy or law to a state? Will readers demonstrate enough astuteness to find out the names of the specific individuals who instituted this policy, or begin to learn whom to hold responsible for applying it?

16   When journalists cite African-Americans, Hispanics, and other minority groups as sources, readers may infer that members of a group all think, act, believe, and view things alike. According to Hoffmann (1991), the use of collectives contributes to this erroneous inference.

17   Ultimately such indiscriminate usage could point readers away from such democratic ideals as equality. Reduced participation in government may occur from such use of collectives.

18   We offer a simple thesis: journalistic attributions that lack specificity when specificity could exist, that cite a group as responsible for the actions of some of its members, and that make the prejudicial claim that everyone in a group

shares common characteristics, do not meet the usual standards of journalistic accuracy and fairness.

19   We believe that general semanticists and others particularly concerned with vague and deceptive language should encourage journalists to avoid language collectives, replacing sources like "Congress," "CIA," "Ohio," etc., with specific, named individuals in the absence of promised confidentiality, and with a "veiled attribution" suggesting specific individuals when promised. In addition, journalists should name individuals responsible for reported actions. Thus journalists could more accurately report "Congress" as "235 members of congress," replace the "CIA" with "Susan Smith, spokesperson for the director of the CIA," and replace "Ohio" with "87 members of the Ohio House and 26 members of the Ohio Senate."

20   We may sacrifice economy of language to some degree, of course. The first of the journalistic "ABC's," however, requires *accuracy* and we would argue that if journalists need extra length to attain accuracy, let them use it.

21   Bringing the ideas of general semantics into the house of journalism may cause some journalists to agree with Harrison Salisbury who recognized after many years of reporting:

> [The war in Vietnam] was the first of the separating images which, as time went on, showed me that in war as in the simplest things in life, truth is multifaceted, a crystal that refracts light in many forms and many shapes, the quicksilver of the mind. (Salisbury, 1988, p. 123)

22   If journalists hold up a flawed truth to their readers, the forms and shapes it refracts will distort the reality that readers need to see to make them effective participants in the decision-making process of their government.

TOPICAL CONSIDERATIONS

1. What is a "language collective," according to the authors? When do journalists use language collectives? How are they different from "symbols of truly tangible entities"?

2. What is "attribution"? For what three reasons do journalists use attribution? Have you ever used attribution when you were writing a paper, or talking to a friend?

3. In the section "Problems with Language Collectives," what kinds of mistakes do the authors suggest readers could make when journalists use language collectives—even fairly and accurately? What kinds of sloppy thinking can language collectives lead to?

4. In the section "Use of Language Collectives in Journalism," why do the authors say that personification and metonymy are dangerous forms of language collectives? How can these two forms help hide the responsibility for a statement?

5. How could the continuing use of language collectives help "point readers away from . . . democratic ideals" (paragraphs 12–17)? How do language collectives make individual readers feel intimidated and frustrated? How do they unfairly represent minorities?

6. According to Russell and Many, what is a good solution to the problem that language collectives create? Do they think journalists should avoid all use of language collectives? Why or why not? Are they completely satisfied with their recommendations?

RHETORICAL CONSIDERATIONS

1. Who is the intended audience for this essay? How can you tell? Discuss the formality of language, citation apparatus, kinds of sources used, and the recommended solutions as you respond.

2. Why do the authors present a chart entitled "Frequency of Language Collective Usage"? Does this chart help you to understand the problem? Is it effectively organized? Why or why not?

3. How do the authors feel about journalists' ability to practice their craft ethically and fairly? Do they believe journalists are basically good people? Why is the integrity of journalists so important, according to the authors? Do you agree?

4. Throughout this article, Russell and Many use the term "journalists." Is this word a language collective, in the way that the authors have defined it? Is it a fair use of a language collective? Why or why not? Justify your answer.

WRITING ASSIGNMENTS

1. Have you ever used language collectives to veil your sources, as the authors describe in paragraph 9? For instance, have you ever told your parents, "But everybody's doing it"; or have you ever written in a college paper "everybody knows that . . ."? (Or have you used implied language collectives in such phrases as "it is common knowledge that . . . "?) How did your parent, reader, or listener respond? Was your strategy successful—and if not, why? Were you conscious of your strategy at the time you used it?

2. Find a piece of news reporting in your local paper that is relatively free of language collective use—one that identifies individual speakers, number of members voting, or other features in line with Russell and Many's recommendations. Then rewrite the article using as many language collective phrases as you can. How does the article change in tone? Do you find any implications that the collective seems immortal or omnipotent? Does the rewrite seem more or less interesting than the original piece?

3. In paragraph 16, Russell and Many discuss the problems that language collectives create for minority groups, inferring that such usage may contribute to prejudice. Locate news reporting by and about a minority group's members—African Americans, Chicanos, gays and lesbians, people with disabilities, and so on. Do these sources use language collectives? If so, do the uses you are able to identify create negative stereotypes, or positive ones? Are positive stereotypes misleading?

READ ALL ABOUT IT! (BUT DON'T BELIEVE IT)

Caryl Rivers

The previous essay shows how the media's practice of employing collective phrases can misrepresent the facts and, thus, slant the news. In the piece below, journalist Caryl Rivers examines another collective practice of the media: perpetuating the myths of womanhood that make up all too many headlines. "Is Superwoman Shedding Her Cape?" "Feminists Are Poor Role Models for U.S. Women," "Do Women Lack a Math Gene?"—these are only a few examples of the distorted notions that fill the news but that have no basis for reality, says Rivers.

Caryl Rivers is a professor of journalism at Boston University and the author of several books, including *Slick Spins and Fractured Facts: How Cultural Myths Distort the News* (1996). This piece first appeared in the *Boston Globe* in May 1996.

1   The headlines, it seems, are everywhere. "PMS Affects Millions!," declares one. "Do Women Lack A Math Gene?," asks another. Then there's "Supermom Gives Up!,"—not to mention "Women Over 35—Old Maids Forever?"

2   Such headlines, examples printed in mainstream newspapers and magazines, can be found in the American press nearly any day of the week. If your only source of information about women was the media, you'd expect to find the psych wards crammed with stressed-out working women, the streets littered with the bodies of victims of terminal PMS, desperate women over 30 rushing to the altar with the nearest available male and women leaving the work force in droves, eager to emulate June Cleaver in that '60s sitcom "Leave It to Beaver."

3   The American press greatly exaggerates the problems of women—especially working women. The result is that women may be experiencing undeserved guilt and worry.

4   An examination of hundreds of articles reveals two myths about women—myths that are polar opposites and that exist simultaneously in what might be called Mediaspace: the Myth of Female Weakness and the Myth of Female Strength.

5   Both fictions have deep roots in culture and mythology. The Myth of Female Weakness dates to Eve, who, the Bible says, couldn't resist eating the apple and so got humans kicked out of paradise. In the Middle Ages, sages wondered if woman had a soul. In the 19th century, it was accepted medical dogma that a woman's brain and her reproductive system could not develop at the same time.

6   The Myth of Female Strength shows up in the Bible and in Greek mythology: One glimpse of Medusa and a man was turned to stone; the sirens lured sailors to watery graves with their songs; and, of course, Delilah stole Samson's strength by cutting his hair.

7   The modern counterparts of these legends keep popping up in the press. Premenstrual syndrome, for example, got 1,810 mentions in the press during 1994 and '95, while pneumonia got 20. We all know that PMS kills more people than pneumonia, right?

8   If a woman's hormones aren't the problem, maybe it's her brain. The "math gene" story that suggested women were simply not biologically fit for doing mathematics was a big seller in the 1980s. It lingers still, despite critics' complaints that there is no evidence for a purely male "math gene." In fact, when you filter out a handful of geniuses, men and women perform very much alike on tests of mathematical ability.

9   What you don't see very often, however, is a headline such as this: "Do Caucasian males lack a math gene?" The same test that provoked the headline about women's math problems also showed that Asian males scored far better than Caucasians on the Scholastic Assessment Test. There was barely a whisper of this, however, in the media.

10 Politicians keep dredging up old ideas about female weakness. House Speaker Newt Gingrich suggested that women aren't suited for combat because men are programmed to hunt giraffe, and GOP presidential hopeful Pat Buchanan wrote that women aren't aggressive enough for modern competitive capitalism. (Fortunately, that isn't stopping women from applying to West Point or the MBA program at Harvard.) The hunting argument is still being used against women, even though historians say that the all-male, big-game hunt emerged fairly late in human history. It was gathering by males and females that took us across the line into humanhood. But a bunch of gals and guys carrying salad choppers for pulverizing roots doesn't quite have the sex appeal of the guy with the spear.

11 If women aren't too weak, then just maybe they are too strong. The images of women with power are tinged with dread—from Glenn Close, the nutty woman in "Fatal Attraction," to Demi Moore in "Disclosure" to Hillary Rodham Clinton.

12 Consider the language used in the media about Clinton. There were more than 50 references to her as Lady Macbeth. Who has she murdered lately? She's also been called a witch, a liar and a harridan, and there were several

comparisons of her to Lorena Bobbitt. As I remember, Mrs. Clinton stood by her man through bad times, while Mrs. Bobbitt took a sharp-edged instrument to her husband's anatomy. Why the comparison?

13 Such dark images are not often applied to males in politics. Gingrich's unfavorable rating may be sky-high, but nobody's calling him a warlock. Nobody is calling him Macbeth.

14   It wasn't only Hillary Clinton, of course, who got labeled. Nancy Reagan was vilified as being "meddlesome," Rosalynn Carter was called the "steel magnolia" and Kitty Dukakis was called a "dragon lady." When Texas Gov. Ann Richards gave a very sensible speech to young women graduates about standing on their own two feet and not waiting for Mr. Right to support them, she was called a "man-basher." It's going to be interesting to see how the coverage of Elizabeth Dole (who heads the American Red Cross and who has been more successful, in fact, than Hillary Clinton) shapes up as her husband's campaign goes on. Will she be able to escape the suspicion that she is too powerful?

15 Some women get hit with both mythologies at the same time. Anita Hill, for example, was portrayed as either a poor, weak, besotted woman desperately in love and so naive that she was used by Democrats as a tool to attack Supreme Court nominee Clarence Thomas—or as a steely feminist Joan of Arc who spent her weekends reading obscenity cases so she could discover Long Dong Silver. Take your choice.

16 There's another myth that influences the media's presentation of women: the notion that when women leave home and hearth, chaos descends upon us. That notion—which shaped news coverage as far back as the days of women's suffrage—still plays like elevator music in the background of today's coverage of women. Working women are pictured as stress-ridden candidates for heart attacks—despite the fact that for two decades, nearly all the studies show working women as healthier than homemakers, and there has been no rise in coronary symptoms among working women.

17 The suspicion that if women are too ambitious they will be damaged in some way was the strong undercurrent of a news story that reported that women over age 35 have a greater chance of getting killed by a terrorist than of getting married. There was absolutely no truth to the story—but it ended up on the covers of *Newsweek* and *People* magazines anyway.

18 Here's the story: Demographers say there is a general tendency for women to marry men two years their senior. It's also true that during the baby boom, each year brought an increasing number of babies; the baby crop in 1955 was larger than that in 1953, for example. So a 35-year-old woman who refused to marry anyone but a man two years her senior would find fewer such men. But if she married a man her own age, or a younger man, there was no shortage at all. This is a cover story? No.

19 Then there are the "trend stories" about women returning to hearth and home. One analyst noted that, in 1994, there was a dip among young women

entering the labor force; at the same time, mortgage rates dipped, prompting the analyst to suggest that women were leaving their jobs and, with their husbands, buying homes where they could start families. This "news" garnered these headlines around the U.S.:

- The Return of the Single Breadwinner
- Number of Stay-At-Home Moms on the Rise
- Mothers Jilt Jobs for Homes, Families
- More Women Choose to Stay Home

20   But as it turned out, there was no such trend. If the analyst had looked at the figures for men entering the labor force, he would have found that there was an even bigger dip among men. Were they running off to have babies? Or did the figure simply reflect a lousy job market?

21   And while there actually were lower mortgage rates, a story in the *New York Times* noted that young couples were carrying a much larger debt than in past years. Indeed, women may have been buying houses with their mates, but the debt on those houses would have tended to keep them in the job market. Once again, a phony story that leapt into the headlines.

22   Will it ever change? Don't hold your breath. The first woman started out with lousy press, and the daughters of Eve seem to have inherited her public relations problem. As long as old myths continue to play in our heads, as long as we accept a distorted view of women through history as passive, intellectually inferior and weak (except when they are snipping off men's private parts), we will keep on seeing exaggerated headlines about women and their problems.

23   So the next time you see a story about how women hate their jobs and want to go home, or how women with good jobs are miserable wrecks, or how some brain or body part makes women unfit to be chief executive officers, take it with a grain of salt. You may not be hearing the cool, "objective" voice of journalism, but the old, endlessly replaying tapes of myth.

TOPICAL CONSIDERATIONS

1. What role does women's biological difference from men play in the first two headlines that Rivers cites in paragraph 1? What role do women's social expectations and emotional makeup play in the second two headlines here? What does Rivers think about these assumptions? How can you tell from what she says throughout the article?

2. Do you think that such alleged differences make women less competent in the workforce? Can you turn the tables and identify differences that make men seem less able to compete in the workforce? How, for instance, might men's biological aggression foul up business deals?

3. What does Rivers say about the myth that women are too strong? What examples does she give? Can you think of any examples from your own experience?

4. What does Rivers say about the myth that women are too weak? What examples does she give? Can you think of any examples from your own experience?

5. How are the myths of women's strength and weakness contradictory? How is it possible for a woman to display too much strength and too much weakness at the same time? Can you show both strength and weakness in some of the figures that Rivers analyzes as "too strong"?

6. What is the third myth? How does it serve to explain what (according to the mainstream press) is wrong about women's participation in the workforce?

RHETORICAL CONSIDERATIONS

1. Rivers announces in paragraph 4 that there are two myths about women; then in paragraph 16 she adds a third myth—that women working outside of the home creates social chaos. What is the relationship of the third myth to the other two? Do you think this structure to her article is confusing, or does it make sense? Justify your answer.

2. Examine the two sentences that make up paragraph 3. Taken together, do these two sentences make a good thesis statement? Why or why not? How well does this thesis account for the material in the article? How well does it account for the relative amounts of space that Rivers devotes to each item in turn?

3. Where does Rivers provide citation to sources? What effect does her use of sources have on your willingness as a reader to trust her judgment? How do your expectations about the form and tone of this essay influence your answer?

4. Rivers cites sources for the myths of female strength and weakness that include the Bible, Greek mythology, the SATs, Shakespeare, and current popular films (in addition to news reporting). Why do you think she chooses these references? What kind of assumptions is she making about her readership's culture background? Do you think that these are sufficient references, or can you think of others?

5. In paragraph 19, Rivers cites faulty reasoning by a trends analyst: that because fewer women were entering the workforce, and mortgage rates dipped simultaneously, the two were related by cause and effect. What does she offer as another possible explanation in the following paragraph? Can you think of other possible explanations for these two trends?

6. In paragraph 15, the author talks about some women getting hit with both mythologies at the same time and offers the example of Anita Hill. How effective is this example? Can you offer others?

7. How successfully does Rivers use irony and humor—saying one thing and meaning another? For instance, consider the last sentence of paragraphs 7, 9, and 10. Do you think these references are effective, or should she have made her point more directly?

WRITING ASSIGNMENTS

1. Do you think the myths Rivers discusses are gender-specific? That is, can a man be both too strong and too weak at the same time? Can an individual, regardless of gender, be a target for these myths because of some other distinguishing feature such as age, race, class, sexual orientation, disability, weight, or other features? If you are (or know about) someone who has experienced these problems

with similar myths, write a paper comparing and contrasting the way the myths are applied in both cases.

2. What is the difference between a myth, a stereotype, and a cultural norm? Where do these three terms overlap? What are the differences in connotation of each term? Can you provide an example of one commonly accepted belief that could function as myth, as stereotype, and as cultural norm under different circumstances?

3. Think back to a time when you were judged by someone to be unacceptable in a certain situation. For example, you might think about a job that you interviewed for but you did not get; an unfair accusation by a teacher that you cheated or plagiarized; or a time you were denied housing because of discrimination based on disability, race, gender, or some other irrelevant feature. What myths were you judged by? Were some parts of the myth contradictory? What did you do about this incident? Write a letter to the person or organization that might have judged you unfairly explaining your views.

4. Find an example of a culture in which these myths about women do not exist, or are articulated differently from the mainstream American press version that Rivers describes. You will probably need to consult journal articles in feminism and gender studies, sociology, psychology, anthropology, and related disciplines. Discuss the differences that you find in your chosen culture, and compare and contrast these to American mainstream culture.

Terrorism: Civilized and Barbaric

Edward S. Herman

The familiar phrase "journalistic objectivity" underscores the belief that news reporting in our democracy is free of bias, that what we read and hear are simply the bald facts. But, of course, it is almost impossible to communicate without some bias, as Newman and Genevieve Birk explain ("Selection, Slanting, and Charged Language"). And, as the essays by John Leo ("Journalese as a Second Tongue") and Charles G. Russell and Paul Many ("Collective Bias") illustrate, the media will slant the news even when their intentions are to report objectively. In what follows, Edward S. Herman takes the criticism even further, arguing that the news reflects official political views of the government—views, he says, that have become largely internalized. In this pointed attack on the American press, Herman offers examples of major news organs, including the *New York Times*, operating on a "double standard." When reporting acts of violence by enemies of America, the language is highly charged; but similar acts of violence by the United States or our allies are either covered in euphemisms or not at all, he argues.

Edward S. Herman is a professor of finance at the University of Pennsylvania. He is the author of several books on information and terrorism including *The "Terrorism" Industry: The Experts and Institutions That Shape Our View of Terror* (1989), with Gerry O'Sullivan, *Beyond Hypocrisy: Decoding the News in an Age of Propaganda* (1992), and most recently *Triumph of the Market: Essays on Economics, Politics and the Media* (1995). Herman also writes a column for *Z Magazine*, an independent political journal, in which the following article originally appeared in June 1989. Herman has updated the article for this book.

1   The Western media's usage of *barbarism* and *civilization* rests not only on transference and a refusal to look honestly at history, but also on a mind-boggling double standard. This is dramatically illustrated in the consistently dichotomous Western handling of the shooting down of civilian airliners. When the Soviets shot down Korean airliner 007, the Reagan administration took advantage of the event to orchestrate a huge propaganda campaign of vilification. It is now clearly established that the administration knew that the So-

viets *did not know* that 007 was a civilian aircraft, but the Reaganites nevertheless built their campaign on the lie that a civilian plane was deliberately destroyed. The press went along with the Reaganite propaganda claims, raising an indignant outcry over "cold-blooded murder" and barbarism. Much was made of the messages relayed by the Soviet pilot and ground control honing in on 007 and matter-of-factly asserting that the target had been destroyed. The inhumanity of the act was dramatized by great attention paid to the grieving families of the victims. In the words of Leslie Gelb: "The point, if it needed reaffirmation, was that the leadership of the Soviet Union is different—call it tougher, more brutal or even uncivilized—than most of the rest of the world. President Reagan said the incident was 'horrifying' and cause for 'revulsion,' whatever the exact or possibly extenuating circumstances" (*NYT*, Sept. 4, 1983). The "savage" act of the Soviet Union, as James Reston pointed out, garnered it "the hatred of the civilized world" (Sept. 4, 1983). The *Times* editorialized on September 2 that "There is no conceivable excuse for any nation shooting down a harmless airliner."

2   In a more recent case of barbarism, on February 24, 1996, the Cuban airforce shot down two Miami-based Cessna aircraft piloted by members of the anti-Castro group, Brothers to the Rescue, which had entered Cuban airspace; four of the brothers were killed. The same group had overflown Havana in January, dropping political leaflets, and the State Department had warned the group that Cuba could justifiably retaliate against the overflight, but did nothing further to prevent it. When Cuba did retaliate, U.S. officials reacted strongly, calling it "a blatant violation of international law and the norms of a civilized country" (Secretary of State Christopher), quickly brought the matter to the UN Security Council, and tightened the embargo against Cuba. Once again the *New York Times* claimed that "There can be no justification for deliberately killing four civilians . . . [in a] murderously disproportionate reaction" (ed., Feb. 27, 1996). The paper ran on its front page transcripts of aerial conversations by Cuban pilots showing their cold-bloodedness as they were downing the planes.

3   Back on October 6, 1976, a bomb placed in a Cuban airliner exploded, killing 73 passengers. Venezuelan authorities charged Orlando Bosch and three other members of the Cuban exile community in Miami with the bombing. Two of the Cubans admitted to the bombing and named the others. Bosch had engaged in many other terrorist acts, had served in prison for a bazooka attack on a Polish freighter in Miami harbor, and was described by both the CIA and FBI as a dangerous terrorist. Bosch was released from a Venezuelan prison when his collaborators' confessions were declared inadmissible evidence, after which he came to Miami, where he lives comfortably; U.S. authorities have refused to prosecute him or return him to Cuba for trial. On August 1, 1990, the *New York Times* ran a sympathetic profile of Bosch ("Grizzled Castro Fighter With a Mission"), never calling him a terrorist, and twelve times referring to his opposition to Castro, without mentioning that it often took the form of indiscriminate bombings and assassinations. In contrast with

its sharp condemnation of Cuba for its retaliatory action of February 1996, the *New York Times* never editorialized on the 1976 bombing, and neither it nor U.S. officials ever attacked those responsible for that major terrorist attack in the language of condemnation used against Cuba for its downing of the Brothers to the Rescue planes.

4   When the United States shot down Iran airliner 655, killing 290 people in July 1988, Leslie Gelb said nothing about the implications of this act for the quality of the leadership of the responsible country (and Gelb has never said anything in retrospect about the significance for civilization and barbarism of the fact that the original claims by his government on 007 were outright lies). The U.S. media did not relay to the U.S. public the cold-blooded messages of those in the act of pulling the trigger on 290 civilians, nor did they focus on the grieving families of the victims, choosing instead to tap the feelings of the U.S. personnel obligated by their duties to kill. And the *New York Times* editorialists found that there is a conceivable excuse for shooting down a civilian airliner, namely a "tragic error."

5   In another instance of a civilized attack on a civilian airliner, the Israeli military shot down a Libyan plane that had gotten lost over the Sinai desert in February 1973, with 109 killed. In this case, the Israelis admitted knowing that it was a civilian airliner, but the U.S. press did not find this of any interest, and the words "cold-blooded," "murder," "savage," or "barbaric" were not used. The Soviet-Israeli contrast provides the ultimate double standard as the Soviets were declared barbarous on the basis of a Western lie, whereas the deliberate Israeli shooting down of a civilian plane aroused not the slightest indignation on the part of U.S. officials, Reston, and the *New York Times* editorial board.

6   A *New York Times* article by Robert Reinhold, entitled "Crew of Cruiser That Downed Iranian Airliner Gets a Warm Homecoming" (Oct. 25, 1988), describes the hero's welcome given the naval personnel who shot down the Iranian airliner when they returned to the United States. The captain is shown smiling, with a wreath around his neck and his happy wife looking on. This was a civilized response to the tragic error. The naval personnel had made it to national TV and become celebrities, and in civilized society celebrities receive suitable honors. It is possible that similar treatment accorded Soviet military personnel involved in the death of 269 people on 007 in the Soviet Union would have been considered by the Western press to be in bad taste, but then the Soviet act was an act of barbarism, not a tragic error.

THE CIVILIZED RETALIATE, BARBARIANS TERRORIZE

7   A close examination of mainstream media reporting will also disclose that only groups and countries deemed hostile to the United States terrorize; our own and our allies' assaults on others are regularly described as "retaliation" or "counterterror." Those designated terrorists almost always have grievances

and see themselves as retaliating, but as they are outsiders their claims are usually ignored, brushed aside, and disallowed. This designation is not based on an evaluation of factual claims, it reflects power, self-interest, and a self-righteous capacity to rationalize.

8   Thus, for example, Libya was declared a terrorist state in the 1980s for giving aid to the PLO and other groups that carried out armed attacks in Europe and the Middle East; Libya's and the PLO's claims that they were responding to prior Israeli and other state terror were disallowed. On the other hand, the U.S. sponsorship of the *contras* in Honduras to attack targets in Nicaragua never made us a terrorist state in the U.S. media, even though there wasn't even a pretense that the *contras* were organized in response to prior Nicaraguan attacks. U.S. allies are similarly exempt from the terrorist label. For example, South Africa in the 1980s not only engaged in severe repression of the black majority in its own country and illegally occupied Namibia, it carried out numerous cross-border attacks and sponsored terrorist organizations in Angola and Mozambique (among other countries) that resulted in a human toll vastly greater than that attributable to Libya. But it was never officially named a terrorist state, and was not so described in the media. It was even allowed to be engaged in "counterterrorism" against the black resistance, which was allegedly terrorizing. Even the National Police, National Guard, and Treasury Police of El Salvador, who were implicated in thousands of cases of rape, torture, and murder of civilians in the 1980s, received funds and training under an Antiterrorism Assistance Act passed by congress in 1983; so their victims were the "terrorists," not the killers and torturers given U.S. assistance.

9   On June 27, 1993, President Clinton ordered the bombing of Baghdad, as "retaliation" for a plot allegedly organized by the government of Iraq to assassinate former U.S. president George Bush on a visit to Kuwait. An excellent case can be made, however, that the bombing attack on Baghdad, which killed eight civilians and wounded many others, was an act of terrorism. It had no basis in international law, which under UN authority called for diplomatic processes except where force was necessary to repel an armed attack; and the United States had appealed to UN authority as a basis for the 1991 Persian Gulf War allegedly in order to protect the rule of law. The case against Iraq justifying the attack on Baghdad was circumstantial and was still being tried in a Kuwaiti court when the bombs were dropped, thus further underscoring its legal fragility. United States officials repeatedly stated that the purpose of the attack was to "teach Saddam Hussein a lesson," a rationale that has no status in international law. There were numerous U.S. press reports of political pressures on President Clinton to attack Iraq as he had been accused of being too "soft" in Bosnia and elsewhere, and had to prove his mettle. Iraq, whose leader Saddam Hussein had been effectively demonized, was a ready target for demonstrating toughness. But again, such a rationale not only has no legal status, it justifies the designation of the attack as "terrorist" because Iraqi citizens were being sacrificed to help bolster a politician's political status at home. It should also be noted that the attack on Bush never materialized, so the bombing and killing of civilians in Iraq was not in response to an *act* but to an alleged plot still not confirmed by a judicial process.

10   Additionally, Defense Secretary Les Aspin and former Bush national security adviser General Brent Scowcroft both acknowledged in public that during the Persian Gulf War the United States had deliberately tried to kill Saddam Hussein in its targeting strategies. They said this apologetically, but they were apologetic not for their assassination effort but for their lack of success. If this was so, however, wasn't the purported Iraqi assassination attempt against Bush "retaliation"? It is revealing that the question doesn't arise in the mainstream media. We have a natural right to assassinate; somebody else's response to this is terrorism, not retaliation, by rule of biased word usage.

TOPICAL CONSIDERATIONS

1. How would you define the political stand of the author? What supporting evidence can you offer?

2. Look up *terrorism* in the dictionary. Generally, in the media, who are the victims, who are the perpetrators, and what are the reasons for these designations? In reporting stories of terrorism, how, according to Herman, does the media operate under a "double standard"? Before reading this piece, were you aware of this? Has he opened your eyes to such practices? Do you agree with him? What recent double-standard examples can you come up with?

3. What are Herman's arguments against President Clinton's retaliatory bombing of Baghdad in 1993? What are your own views of the bombing? Do you agree with Herman, or do you think the president was justified?

4. Look this essay over again. Do you think that Herman is suggesting collusion between the media and the government in reporting stories of international barbarism? Why or why not? To what political end would the media maintain such double standards?

5. As Haig Bosmajian points out ("Dehumanizing People and Euphemizing War") in Chapter 4, Ronald Reagan once referred to the Soviet Union as an "evil empire." Now that the Cold War is over, have you seen a shift in the voice of the media? Have references to Russians been framed in less charged language than in the past? If you can find recent examples of more neutral reporting, what does this say about past practices? About continuing media practices with other nations and people not friendly to the United States?

6. What are the implications in the failure of the *New York Times* to use condemnatory language in reporting the Israeli downing of the Libyan plane in 1973?

7. In his essay earlier in this chapter, John Leo cites several journalistic formulas for nouns and adjectives. So does Herman in this article. How do their underlying assumptions compare? What political or ideological motivations does Leo find behind journalese?

RHETORICAL CONSIDERATIONS

1. How would you characterize the tone of this essay? Give some evidence to support your answer. How does the essay's tone contribute to the overall impact of the piece?

2. Find examples of the author's use of irony. Do you find his use of irony effective in making his argument and in convincing you to share his view?

3. What kinds of evidence does Herman use to support his points? How convincing do you think it is?

4. Do you think Herman's own report here uses charged, slanted language? Do you see any evidence of a double standard operating here? Explain your answers.

WRITING ASSIGNMENTS

1. Unfortunately, terrorism seems to be a predictable feature of contemporary world history. Look up a recent terrorist incident and examine how the media reported it. You might consider different newspapers, magazines, and television coverage. Make a note of charged and slanted language. How is that language used to color the incident? to prejudice readers for or against parties involved? If there is clearly a double standard operating, how do you interpret it? Write your analysis as an essay.

2. Herman complains that the press has traditionally been slanted against the PLO and in favor of Israel. Do some research on this claim as in the above assignment, but in this case examine the way the media has covered Middle East incidents since the fall of 1993, when the Prime Minister of Israel, Yitzhak Rabin, and PLO Chairman Yassir Arafat signed an accord officially agreeing to recognize each other and put an end to the ancient hostilities. Do you see any changes in the way the media characterizes incidents and parties of the Middle East today—in particular, Israel and the Israeli government and people? Palestinians? The PLO? PLO leaders?

3. Herman refers to three specific incidents of non-military airplanes being shot out of the sky—the Soviets' downing of the Korean Air 007 in September of 1983, the United States' downing of the Iranian airliner in July of 1988 and the Cubans' downing of the Brothers to the Rescue aircraft in 1996. Look up different reports of these incidents and write down your own analysis of the language of the reports. Do you see a double standard operating? Or is the coverage less biased than Herman claims?

4. Try doing the same in analyzing the language of Ronald Reagan's official statement about each airline incident. Transcripts of the president's speech were published in most major newspapers following the incidents.

5. Who are the current enemies of America? Selecting appropriate news stories, try to determine how the media portrays such enemies. Examine the kind of language used. Do you see evidence of Herman's "civilized and barbaric" dichotomy operating?

6. Using your library, find samples from different newspapers of the coverage of the Persian Gulf War (or the retaliatory bombing of Baghdad in 1993). Examine the language to determine how the enemy was characterized. Consider, for example, the portrayal of the Iraqi military. What about the Iraqi people? Iraqi politicians? Saddam Hussein? Those Arabic people who sympathized with Iraq? Those Arabic people who were opposed to Iraq? Iraqi Kurds? Do you see evidence of Herman's double standard working here? Write a paper with your findings, and try to determine where reporting ends and propaganda begins.

TWO-HEADED MONSTERS

From the *Columbia Journalism Review*

Words are the business of journalism, and accuracy of usage is undoubt-edly the pride of any newspaper. Occasionally, however, words may turn against the meaning intended, as is the case when printer's devils plague the presses. The result is news gone askew. Such was the case in the real headlines that follow, in which unforeseen misprints, double enten-dres, and grammatical goofs turned into news that did not fit the print. The *Columbia Journalism Review,* a watchdog magazine of the media, has a department called "The Lower Case" that gathers such gaffes; these examples were originally reprinted there.

MASSACRE WIDOW IN HOUSE RACE

New York Post 5/29/96

Culver police: Shooting victims unhelpful

The Independent (Los Angeles) 4/25/96

Dad wants 3 charged for sex with daughter

The Dallas Morning News 2/29/96

Former Car Dealer Dies In Mid-Sentence

The Caledonian-Record (St. Johnsbury, Vt.) 2/20/96

Police officer wrestles lurching patrol car away from baby

The Oakland Tribune 3/10/96

GOP hopeful on welfare

The Atlanta Journal 9/20/95

British cook Fanny Cradock

The Arizona Republic 1/2/95

Experts Increase Probability Of a Big Quake in California

The New York Times 1/21/95

Woman relishes passing out as holiday approaches

The Pantagraph (Bloomington, Ill.) 11/30/94

Starving Angolans eating dogs, bark

The Pretoria (South Africa) *News* 9/10/94

ISU revokes doctorate in plagiarism

The Des Moines Register 12/14/95

Lay position proposed by bishop for women

Danville (Va.) *Register & Bee* 10/11/94

City council takes up masturbation

Cambridge (Mass.) *Chronicle* 12/22/94

Disney keeps touching kids

Springfield (Ma.) *News-Leader* 10/28/94

Woman Saves Abenaki Tongue In Dictionary

The Times Argus (Barre-Montpelier, Vt.) 5/2/94

October is national breast awareness month

Madigan Mountaineer (Fort Louis, Wash.) 9/94

Dead couple 'overjoyed' at birth of their first child

The Ottawa (Canada) *Citizen* 10/15/94

Adults think teens having more sex than they are

Tonawanda (N.Y.) *News* 6/7/94

Prosecutors say Simpson had an hour to kill

The Frederick (Md.) *Post* 7/6/94

Spot Searches Dog Bus Riders

Isthmus (Madison, WI) 4/28/95

Parking lot floods when man bursts

Herald Sun (Durham, N.C.) 2/4/94

Clinton visits hurt soldiers

Sun-Sentinel (Broward County, Fla.) 3/26/94

Chinese claim to have dinosaur genes

San Luis Obispo County (Calif.) *Telegram-Tribune* 3/17/95

GOP freshmen turn on Gingrich

The Capital Times (Madison, Wisc.) 12/4/95

Murder suspect gets appointed attorney

Independent Journal (Marin County, Calif.) 11/10/95

Bad coupling cause of fire

Gaylord (Mich.) *Herald Times* 4/27/95

Council wants planners shrunk slowly

Auburn (Calif.) *Journal* 5/2/95

Are young Americans be getting stupider?

Corvallis (Oreg.) *Gazette-Times* 2/2/95

School superintendent candidate stood on principal in Michigan

Times Chronicle (Jenkintown, Pa.) 6/8/94

Dredging and finger grounding begin in riverboat pointing

The Evening Press (Muncie, Ind.) 6/21/95

Animal patent goes to Ohio mouse

Anchorage Daily News 12/24/92

Cherry Hill man enters 741-pound shark

Courier-Post (Cherry Hill, N.J.) 12/9/92

Many who moved to Florida leave after death

The Orlando Sentinel 9/19/94

Police awake, arrest suspect

Tahlequah (Okla.) *Daily Press* 4/17/94

Association for the Blind to run buses

Maple Register 5/17/94

Free vaccinations sought for every child by Clinton

The News-Herald (Willoughby, Ohio) 4/2/93

Suggest sex acts in office

The Oak Ridger (Oak Ridge, Tenn.) 8/22/94

Club Hears Trees Talk At Meeting

The Pilot (Southern Pines, N.C.) 5/27/93

Colon target of probe

New York Daily News 5/24/93

Shops sell chicken soup to nuts

The Miami Herald 7/6/93

Study: Dead patients usually not saved

The Miami Herald 3/7/93

Prince Charles backs bicycles over cars as he opens world talks

Daily News (Ludington, Mich.) 11/7/94

WITH THESE WORDS I CAN SELL YOU ANYTHING

William Lutz

In "Politics and the English Language," George Orwell writes that the "great enemy of clear language is insincerity." To fill the gap "between one's real and one's declared aims," he explains, one simply resorts to inflated language to give importance to the insignificant. Of course, Orwell is talking about the irresponsible habit of government officials who use language to exploit and manipulate. But he could just as well have been talking about the language of advertisers. At least that's the opinion of William Lutz, who assails the linguistic habits of hucksters. In his essay below, he alerts readers to the special power of "weasel words"—those familiar and sneaky critters that "appear to say one thing when in fact they say the opposite, or nothing at all."

William Lutz has been called the George Orwell of the 1990s. Chair of the Committee on Public Doublespeak of the National Council of Teachers of English, Mr. Lutz edits the *Quarterly Review of Doublespeak,* a magazine dedicated to the eradication of misleading official statements. He also teaches in the English department at Rutgers University. He is the author of *Beyond Nineteen Eighty-Four* (1989) and *Doublespeak* (1989), from which this essay is taken.

1   One problem advertisers have when they try to convince you that the product they are pushing is really different from other, similar products is that their claims are subject to some laws. Not a lot of laws, but there are some designed to prevent fraudulent or untruthful claims in advertising. Even during the happy years of nonregulation under President Ronald Reagan, the FTC did crack down on the more blatant abuses in advertising claims. Generally speaking, advertisers have to be careful in what they say in their ads, in the claims they make for the products they advertise. Parity claims are safe because they

are legal and supported by a number of court decisions. But beyond parity claims there are weasel words.

2   Advertisers use weasel words to appear to be making a claim for a product when in fact they are making no claim at all. Weasel words get their name from the way weasels eat the eggs they find in the nests of other animals. A weasel will make a small hole in the egg, suck out the insides, then place the egg back in the nest. Only when the egg is examined closely is it found to be hollow. That's the way it is with weasel words in advertising: Examine weasel words closely and you'll find that they're as hollow as any egg sucked by a weasel. Weasel words appear to say one thing when in fact they say the opposite, or nothing at all.

"HELP"—THE NUMBER ONE WEASEL WORD

3   The biggest weasel word used in advertising doublespeak is "help." Now "help" only means to aid or assist, nothing more. It does not mean to conquer, stop, eliminate, end, solve, heal, cure, or anything else. But once the ad says "help," it can say just about anything after that because "help" qualifies everything coming after it. The trick is that the claim that comes after the weasel word is usually so strong and so dramatic that you forget the word "help" and concentrate only on the dramatic claim. You read into the ad a message that the ad does not contain. More importantly, the advertiser is not responsible for the claim that you read into the ad, even though the advertiser wrote the ad so you would read that claim into it.

4   The next time you see an ad for a cold medicine that promises that it "helps relieve cold symptoms fast," don't rush out to buy it. Ask yourself what this claim is really saying. Remember, "helps" means only that the medicine will aid or assist. What will it aid or assist in doing? Why, "relieve" your cold "symptoms." "Relieve" only means to ease, alleviate, or mitigate, not to stop, end, or cure. Nor does the claim say how much relieving this medicine will do. Nowhere does this ad claim it will cure anything. In fact, the ad doesn't even claim it will *do* anything at all. The ad only claims that it will aid in relieving (not curing) your cold symptoms, which are probably a runny nose, watery eyes, and a headache. In other words, this medicine probably contains a standard decongestant and some aspirin. By the way, what does "fast" mean? Ten minutes, one hour, one day? What is fast to one person can be very slow to another. Fast is another weasel word.

5   Ad claims using "help" are among the most popular ads. One says, "Helps keep you young looking," but then a lot of things will help keep you young looking, including exercise, rest, good nutrition, and a facelift. More importantly, this ad doesn't say the product will keep you young, only "young *looking.*" Someone may look young to one person and old to another.

6   A toothpaste ad says, "Helps prevent cavities," but it doesn't say it will actually prevent cavities. Brushing your teeth regularly, avoiding sugars in foods,

and flossing daily will also help prevent cavities. A liquid cleaner ad says, "Helps keep your home germ free," but it doesn't say it actually kills germs, nor does it even specify which germs it might kill.

7   "Help" is such a useful weasel word that it is often combined with other action-verb weasel words such as "fight" and "control." Consider the claim, "Helps control dandruff symptoms with regular use." What does it really say? It will assist in controlling (not eliminating, stopping, ending, or curing) the *symptoms* of dandruff, not the cause of dandruff nor the dandruff itself. What are the symptoms of dandruff? The ad deliberately leaves that undefined, but assume that the symptoms referred to in the ad are the flaking and itching commonly associated with dandruff. But just shampooing with *any* shampoo will temporarily eliminate these symptoms, so this shampoo isn't any different from any other. Finally, in order to benefit from this product, you must use it regularly. What is "regular use"—daily, weekly, hourly? Using another shampoo "regularly" will have the same effect. Nowhere does this advertising claim say this particular shampoo stops, eliminates, or cures dandruff. In fact, this claim says nothing at all, thanks to all the weasel words.

8   Look at ads in magazines and newspapers, listen to ads on radio and television, and you'll find the word "help" in ads for all kinds of products. How often do you read or hear such phrases as "helps stop . . . ," "helps overcome . . . ," "helps eliminate . . . ," "helps you feel . . . ," or "helps you look . . . "? If you start looking for this weasel word in advertising, you'll be amazed at how often it occurs. Analyze the claims in the ads using "help," and you will discover that these ads are really saying nothing.

9   There are plenty of other weasel words used in advertising. In fact, there are so many that to list them all would fill the rest of this book. But, in order to identify the doublespeak of advertising and understand the real meaning of an ad, you have to be aware of the most popular weasel words in advertising today.

VIRTUALLY SPOTLESS

10 One of the most powerful weasel words is "virtually," a word so innocent that most people don't pay any attention to it when it is used in an advertising claim. But watch out. "Virtually" is used in advertising claims that appear to make specific, definite promises when there is no promise. After all, what does "virtually" mean? It means "in essence of effect, although not in fact." Look at that definition again. "Virtually" means *not in fact.* It does *not* mean "almost" or "just about the same as," or anything else. And before you dismiss all this concern over such a small word, remember that small words can have big consequences.

11   In 1971 a federal court rendered its decision on a case brought by a woman who became pregnant while taking birth control pills. She sued the manufacturer, Eli Lilly and Company, for breach of warranty. The woman lost her case.

Basing its ruling on a statement in the pamphlet accompanying the pills, which stated that, "When taken as directed, the tablets offer virtually 100% protection," the court ruled that there was no warranty, expressed or implied, that the pills were absolutely effective. In its ruling, the court pointed out that, according the *Webster's Third New International Dictionary,* "virtually" means "almost entirely" and clearly does not mean "absolute" (*Whittington* v. *Eli Lilly and Company,* 333 F. Supp. 98). In other words, the Eli Lilly company was really saying that its birth control pill, even when taken as directed, *did not in fact* provide 100 percent protection against pregnancy. But Eli Lilly didn't want to put it that way because then many women might not have bought Lilly's birth control pills.

12   The next time you see the ad that says that this dishwasher detergent "leaves dishes virtually spotless," just remember how advertisers twist the meaning of the weasel word "virtually." You can have lots of spots on your dishes after using this detergent and the ad claim will still be true, because what this claim really means is that this detergent does not *in fact* leave your dishes spotless. Whenever you see or hear an ad claim that uses the word "virtually," just translate that claim into its real meaning. So the television set that is "virtually trouble free" becomes the television set that is not in fact trouble free, the "virtually foolproof operation" of any appliance becomes an operation that is in fact not foolproof, and the product that "virtually never needs service" becomes the product that is not in fact service free.

NEW AND IMPROVED

13 If "new" is the most frequently used word on a product package, "improved" is the second most frequent. In fact, the two words are almost always used together. It seems just about everything sold these days is "new and improved." The next time you're in the supermarket, try counting the number of times you see these words on products. But you'd better do it while you're walking down just one aisle, otherwise you'll need a calculator to keep track of your counting.

14   Just what do these words mean? The use of the word "new" is restricted by regulations, so an advertiser can't just use the word on a product or in an ad without meeting certain requirements. For example, a product is considered new for about six months during a national advertising campaign. If the product is being advertised only in a limited test market area, the word can be used longer, and in some instances has been used for as long as two years.

15   What makes a product "new"? Some products have been around for a long time, yet every once in a while you discover that they are being advertised as "new." Well, an advertiser can call a product new if there has been "a material functional change" in the product. What is "a material functional change," you ask? Good question. In fact it's such a good question it's being asked all the time. It's up to the manufacturer to prove that the product has undergone

such a change. And if the manufacturer isn't challenged on the claim, then there's no one to stop it. Moreover, the change does not have to be an improvement in the product. One manufacturer added an artificial lemon scent to a cleaning product and called it "new and improved," even though the product did not clean any better than without the lemon scent. The manufacturer defended the use of the word "new" on the grounds that the artificial scent changed the chemical formula of the product and therefore constituted "a material functional change."

16   Which brings up the word "improved." When used in advertising, "improved" does not mean "made better." It only means "changed" or "different from before." So, if the detergent maker puts a plastic pour spout on the box of detergent, the product has been "improved," and away we go with a whole new advertising campaign. Or, if the cereal maker adds more fruit or a different kind of fruit to the cereal, there's an improved product. Now you know why manufacturers are constantly making little changes in their products. Whole new advertising campaigns, designed to convince you that the product has been changed for the better, are based on small changes in superficial aspects of a product. The next time you see an ad for an "improved" product, ask yourself what was wrong with the old one. Ask yourself just how "improved" the product is. Finally, you might check to see whether the "improved" version costs more than the unimproved one. After all, someone has to pay for the millions of dollars spent advertising the improved product.

17   Of course, advertisers really like to run ads that claim a product is "new and improved." While what constitutes a "new" product may be subject to some regulation, "improved" is a subjective judgment. A manufacturer changes the shape of its stick deodorant, but the shape doesn't improve the function of the deodorant. That is, changing the shape doesn't affect the deodorizing ability of the deodorant, so the manufacturer calls it "improved." Another manufacturer adds ammonia to its liquid cleaner and calls it "new and improved." Since adding ammonia does affect the cleaning ability of the product, there has been a "material functional change" in the product, and the manufacturer can now call its cleaner "new," and "improved" as well. Now the weasel words "new and improved" are plastered all over the package and are the basis for a multimillion-dollar ad campaign. But after six months the word "new" will have to go, until someone can dream up another change in the product. Perhaps it will be adding color to the liquid, or changing the shape of the package, or maybe adding a new dripless pour spout, or perhaps a————. The "improvements" are endless, and so are the new advertising claims and campaigns.

18   "New" is just too useful and powerful a word in advertising for advertisers to pass it up easily. So they use weasel words that say "new" without really saying it. One of their favorites is "introducing," as in, "Introducing improved Tide," or "Introducing the stain remover." The first is simply saying, here's our improved soap; the second, here's our new advertising campaign for our detergent. Another favorite is "now," as in, "Now there's Sinex," which simply means that Sinex is available. Then there are phrases like "Today's Chevrolet,"

"Presenting Dristan," and "A fresh way to start the day." The list is really end-less because advertisers are always finding new ways to say "new" without re-ally saying it. If there is a second edition of this book, I'll just call it the "new and improved" edition. Wouldn't you really rather have a "new and improved" edition of this book rather than a "second" edition?

ACTS FAST

19 "Acts" and "works" are two popular weasel words in advertising because they bring action to the product and to the advertising claim. When you see the ad for the cough syrup that "Acts on the cough control center," ask yourself what this cough syrup is claiming to do. Well, it's just claiming to "act," to do some-thing, to perform an action. What is it that the cough syrup does? The ad doesn't say. It only claims to perform an action or do something on your "cough control center." By the way, what and where is your "cough control center"? I don't remember learning about that part of the body in human biol-ogy class.

20   Ads that use such phrases as "acts fast," "acts against," "acts to prevent," and the like are saying essentially nothing, because "act" is a word empty of any specific meaning. The ads are always careful not to specify exactly what "act" the product performs. Just because a brand of aspirin claims to "act fast" for headache relief doesn't mean this aspirin is any better than any other as-pirin. What is the "act" that this aspirin performs? You're never told. Maybe it just dissolves quickly. Since aspirin is a parity product, all aspirin is the same and therefore functions the same.

WORKS LIKE ANYTHING ELSE

21 If you don't find the word "acts" in an ad, you will probably find the weasel word "works." In fact, the two words are almost interchangeable in advertis-ing. Watch out for ads that say a product "works against," "works like," "works for," or "works longer." As with "acts," "works" is the same meaningless verb used to make you think that this product really does something, and maybe even something special or unique. But "works," like "acts," is basically a word empty of any specific meaning.

LIKE MAGIC

22 Whenever advertisers want you to stop thinking about the product and to start thinking about something bigger, better, or more attractive than the product, they use that very popular weasel word, "like." The word "like" is the adver-tiser's equivalent of a magician's use of misdirection. "Like" gets you to ignore the product and concentrate on the claim the advertiser is making about it.

"For skin like peaches and cream" claims the ad for a skin cream. What is this ad really claiming? It doesn't say this cream will give you peaches-and-cream skin. There is no verb in this claim, so it doesn't even mention using the product. How is skin ever like "peaches and cream"? Remember, ads must be read literally and exactly, according to the dictionary definition of words. (Remember "virtually" in the Eli Lilly case.) The ad is making absolutely no promise or claim whatsoever for this skin cream. If you think this cream will give you soft, smooth, youthful-looking skin, you are the one who has read that meaning into the ad.

23   The wine that claims "It's like taking a trip to France" wants you to think about a romantic evening in Paris as you walk along the boulevard after a wonderful meal in an intimate little bistro. Of course, you don't really believe that a wine can take you to France, but the goal of the ad is to get you to think pleasant, romantic thoughts about France and not about how the wine tastes or how expensive it may be. That little word "like" has taken you away from crushed grapes into a world of your own imaginative making. Who knows, maybe the next time you buy wine, you'll think those pleasant thoughts when you see this brand of wine, and you'll buy it. Or, maybe you weren't even thinking about buying wine at all, but now you just might pick up a bottle the next time you're shopping. Ah, the power of "like" in advertising.

24   How about the most famous "like" claim of all, "Winston tastes good like a cigarette should"? Ignoring the grammatical error here, you might want to know what this claim is saying. Whether a cigarette tastes good or bad is a subjective judgment because what tastes good to one person may well taste horrible to another. Not everyone likes fried snails, even if they are called escargot. (*De gustibus non est disputandum*, which was probably the Roman rule for advertising as well as for defending the games in the Colosseum.) There are many people who say all cigarettes taste terrible, other people who say only some cigarettes taste all right, and still others who say all cigarettes taste good. Who's right? Everyone, because taste is a matter of personal judgment.

25   Moreover, note the use of the conditional, "should." The complete claim is, "Winston tastes good like a cigarette should taste." But should cigarettes taste good? Again, this is a matter of personal judgment and probably depends most on one's experiences with smoking. So, the Winston ad is simply saying that Winston cigarettes are just like any other cigarette: Some people like them and some people don't. On that statement R. J. Reynolds conducted a very successful multimillion-dollar advertising campaign that helped keep Winston the number-two-selling cigarette in the United States, close behind number one, Marlboro.

CAN IT BE UP TO THE CLAIM?

26 Analyzing ads for doublespeak requires that you pay attention to every word in the ad and determine what each word really means. Advertisers try to wrap their claims in language that sounds concrete, specific, and objective,

when in fact the language of advertising is anything but. Your job is to read carefully and listen critically so that when the announcer says that "Crest can be of significant value . . . ," you know immediately that this claim says absolutely nothing. Where is the doublespeak in this ad? Start with the second word.

27   Once again, you have to look at what words really mean, not what you think they mean or what the advertiser wants you to think they mean. The ad for Crest only says that using Crest "can be" of "significant value." What really throws you off in this ad is the brilliant use of "significant." It draws your attention to the word "value" and makes you forget that the ad only claims that Crest "can be." The ad doesn't say that Crest *is* of value, only that it is "able" or "possible" to be of value, because that's all that "can" means.

28   It's so easy to miss the importance of those little words, "can be." Almost as easy as missing the importance of the words "up to" in an ad. These words are very popular in sale ads. You know, the ones that say, "Up to 50% Off!" Now, what does that claim mean? Not much, because the store or manufacturer has to reduce the price of only a few items by 50 percent. Everything else can be reduced a lot less, or not even reduced. Moreover, don't you want to know 50 percent off of what? Is it 50 percent off the "manufacturer's suggested list price," which is the highest possible price? Was the price artificially inflated and then reduced? In other ads, "up to" expresses an ideal situation. The medicine that works "up to ten times faster," the battery that lasts "up to twice as long," and the soap that gets you "up to twice as clean" all are based on ideal situations for using those products, situations in which you can be sure you will never find yourself.

UNFINISHED WORDS

29 Unfinished words are a kind of "up to" claim in advertising. The claim that a battery lasts "up to twice as long" usually doesn't finish the comparison—twice as long as what? A birthday candle? A tank of gas? A cheap battery made in a country not noted for its technological achievements? The implication is that the battery lasts twice as long as batteries made by other battery makers, or twice as long as earlier model batteries made by the advertiser, but the ad doesn't really make these claims. You read these claims into the ad, aided by the visual images the advertiser so carefully provides.

30   Unfinished words depend on you to finish them, to provide the words the advertisers so thoughtfully left out of the ad. Pall Mall cigarettes were once advertised as "A longer finer and milder smoke." The question is, longer, finer, and milder than what? The aspirin that claims it contains "Twice as much of the pain reliever doctors recommend most" doesn't tell you what pain reliever it contains twice as much of. (By the way, it's aspirin. That's right; it just contains twice the amount of aspirin. And how much is twice the amount? Twice of what amount?) Panadol boasts that "nobody reduces fever faster," but, since Panadol is a parity product, this claim simply means that Panadol isn't

any better than any other product in its parity class. "You can be sure if it's Westinghouse," you're told, but just exactly what it is you can be sure of is never mentioned. "Magnavox gives you more" doesn't tell you what you get more of. More value? More television? More than they gave you before? It sounds nice, but it means nothing, until you fill in the claim with your own words, the words the advertisers didn't use. Since each of us fills in the claim differently, the ad and the product can become all things to all people, and not promise a single thing.

31   Unfinished words abound in advertising because they appear to promise so much. More importantly, they can be joined with powerful visual images on television to appear to be making significant promises about a product's effectiveness without really making any promises. In a television ad, the aspirin product that claims fast relief can show a person with a headache taking the product and then, in what appears to be a matter of minutes, claiming complete relief. This visual image is far more powerful than any claim made in unfinished words. Indeed, the visual image completes the unfinished words for you, filling in with pictures what the words leave out. And you thought that ads didn't affect you. What brand of aspirin do you use?

32   Some years ago, Ford's advertisements proclaimed "Ford LTD—700% quieter." Now, what do you think Ford was claiming with these unfinished words? What was the Ford LTD quieter than? A Cadillac? A Mercedes Benz? A BMW? Well, when the FTC asked Ford to substantiate this unfinished claim, Ford replied that it meant that the inside of the LTD was 700% quieter than the outside. How did you finish those unfinished words when you first read them? Did you even come close to Ford's meaning?

COMBINING WEASEL WORDS

33 A lot of ads don't fall neatly into one category or another because they use a variety of different devices and words. Different weasel words are often combined to make an ad claim. The claim, "Coffee-Mate gives coffee more body, more flavor," uses Unfinished Words ("more" than what?) and also uses words that have no specific meaning ("body" and "flavor"). Along with "taste" (remember the Winston ad and its claim to taste good), "body" and "flavor" mean nothing because their meaning is entirely subjective. To you, "body" in coffee might mean thick, black, almost bitter coffee, while I might take it to mean a light brown, delicate coffee. Now, if you think you understood that last sentence, read it again, because it said nothing of objective value; it was filled with weasel words of no specific meaning: "thick," "black," "bitter," "light brown," and "delicate." Each of those words has no specific, objective meaning, because each of us can interpret them differently.

34   Try this slogan: "Looks, smells, tastes like ground-roast coffee." So, are you now going to buy Taster's Choice instant coffee because of this ad? "Looks," "smells," and "tastes" are all words with no specific meaning and depend on your interpretation of them for any meaning. Then there's that great weasel

word "like," which simply suggests a comparison but does not make the actual connection between the product and the quality. Besides, do you know what "ground-roast" coffee is? I don't, but it sure sounds good. So, out of seven words in this ad, four are definite weasel words, two are quite meaningless, and only one has any clear meaning.

35   Remember the Anacin ad—"Twice as much of the pain reliever doctors recommend most"? There's a whole lot of weaseling going on in this ad. First, what's the pain reliever they're talking about in this ad? Aspirin, of course. In fact, any time you see or hear an ad using those words "pain reliever," you can automatically substitute the word "aspirin" for them. (Makers of acetaminophen and ibuprofen pain relievers are careful in their advertising to identify their products as nonaspirin products.) So, now we know that Anacin has aspirin in it. Moreover, we know that Anacin has twice as much aspirin in it, but we don't know twice as much as what. Does it have twice as much aspirin as an ordinary aspirin tablet? If so, what is an ordinary aspirin tablet, and how much aspirin does it contain? Twice as much as Excedrin or Bufferin? Twice as much as a chocolate chip cookie? Remember those Unfinished Words and how they lead you on without saying anything.

36   Finally, what about those doctors who are doing all that recommending? Who are they? How many of them are there? What kind of doctors are they? What are their qualifications? Who asked them about recommending pain relievers? What other pain relievers did they recommend? And there are a whole lot more questions about this "poll" of doctors to which I'd like to know the answers, but you get the point. Sometimes, when I call my doctor, she tells me to take two aspirin and call her office in the morning. Is that where Anacin got this ad?

READ THE LABEL, OR THE BROCHURE

37 Weasel words aren't just found on television, on the radio, or in newspaper and magazine ads. Just about any language associated with a product will contain the doublespeak of advertising. Remember the Eli Lilly case and the doublespeak on the information sheet that came with the birth control pills. Here's another example.

38   In 1983, the Estée Lauder cosmetics company announced a new product called "Night Repair." A small brochure distributed with the product stated that "Night Repair was scientifically formulated in Estée Lauder's U.S. laboratories as part of the Swiss Age-Controlling Skincare Program. Although only nature controls the aging process, this program helps control the signs of aging and encourages skin to look and feel younger." You might want to read these two sentences again, because they sound great but say nothing.

39   First, note that the product was "scientifically formulated" in the company's laboratories. What does that mean? What constitutes a scientific formulation? You wouldn't expect the company to say that the product was casually, mechanically, or carelessly formulated, or just thrown together one day when the

people in the white coats didn't have anything better to do. But the word "scientifically" lends an air of precision and promise that just isn't there.

40   It is the second sentence, however, that's really weasely, both syntactically and semantically. The only factual part of this sentence is the introductory dependent clause—"only nature controls the aging process." Thus, the only fact in the ad is relegated to a dependent clause, a clause dependent on the main clause, which contains no factual or definite information at all and indeed purports to contradict the independent clause. The new "skincare program" (notice it's not a skin cream but a "program") does not claim to stop or even retard the aging process. What, then, does Night Repair, at a price of over $35 (in 1983 dollars) for a .87-ounce bottle do? According to this brochure, nothing. It only "helps," and the brochure does not say how much it helps. Moreover, it only "helps control," and then it only helps control the "*signs* of aging," not the aging itself. Also, it "encourages" skin not to *be* younger but only to "look and feel" younger. The brochure does not say younger than what. Of the sixteen words in the main clause of this second sentence, nine are weasel words. So, before you spend all that money for Night Repair, or any other cosmetic product, read the words carefully, and then decide if you're getting what you think you're paying for.

OTHER TRICKS OF THE TRADE

41 Advertisers' use of doublespeak is endless. The best way advertisers can make something out of nothing is through words. Although there are a lot of visual images used on television and in magazines and newspapers, every advertiser wants to create that memorable line that will stick in the public consciousness. I am sure pure joy reigned in one advertising agency when a study found that children who were asked to spell the word "relief" promptly and proudly responded "r-o-l-a-i-d-s."

42   The variations, combinations, and permutations of doublespeak used in advertising go on and on, running from the use of rhetorical questions ("Wouldn't you really rather have a Buick?" "If you can't trust Prestone, who can you trust?") to flattering you with compliments ("The lady has taste." "We think a cigar smoker is someone special." "You've come a long way baby."). You know, of course, how you're *supposed* to answer those questions, and you know that those compliments are just leading up to the sales pitches for the products. Before you dismiss such tricks of the trade as obvious, however, just remember that all of these statements and questions were part of very successful advertising campaigns.

43   A more subtle approach is the ad that proclaims a supposedly unique quality for a product, a quality that really isn't unique. "If it doesn't say Goodyear, it can't be polyglas." Sounds good, doesn't it? Polyglas is available only from Goodyear because Goodyear copyrighted that trade name. Any other tire manufacturer could make exactly the same tire but could not call it "polyglas,"

because that would be copyright infringement. "Polyglas" is simply Goodyear's name for its fiberglass-reinforced tire.

44   Since we like to think of ourselves as living in a technologically advanced country, science and technology have a great appeal in selling products. Advertisers are quick to use scientific doublespeak to push their products. There are all kinds of elixirs, additives, scientific potions, and mysterious mixtures added to all kinds of products. Gasoline contains "HTA," "F–130," "Platformate," and other chemical-sounding additives, but nowhere does an advertisement give any real information about the additive.

45   Shampoo, deodorant, mouthwash, cold medicine, sleeping pills, and any number of other products all seem to contain some special chemical ingredient that allows them to work wonders. "Certs contains a sparkling drop of Retsyn." So what? What's "Retsyn"? What's it do? What's so special about it? When they don't have a secret ingredient in their product, advertisers still find a way to claim scientific validity. There's "Sinarest. Created by a research scientist who actually gets sinus headaches." Sounds nice, but what kind of research does this scientist do? How do you know if she is any kind of expert on sinus medicine? Besides, this ad doesn't tell you a thing about the medicine itself and what it does.

ADVERTISING DOUBLESPEAK QUICK QUIZ

46 Now it's time to test your awareness of advertising doublespeak. (You didn't think I would just let you read this and forget it, did you?) The following is a list of statements from some recent ads. Your job is to figure out what each of these ads really says.

DOMINO'S PIZZA: "Because nobody delivers better."
SINUTAB: "It can stop the pain."
TUMS: "The stronger acid neutralizer."
MAXIMUM STRENGTH DRISTAN: "Strong medicine for tough sinus colds."
LISTERMINT: "Making your mouth a cleaner place."
CASCADE: "For virtually spotless dishes nothing beats Cascade."
NUPRIN: "Little. Yellow. Different. Better."
ANACIN: "Better relief."
SUDAFED: "Fast sinus relief that won't put you fast asleep."
ADVIL: "Advanced medicine for pain."
PONDS COLD CREAM: "Ponds cleans like no soap can."
MILLER LITE BEER: "Tastes great. Less filling."
PHILIPS MILK OF MAGNESIA: "Nobody treats you better than MOM (Philips Milk of Magnesia)."
BAYER: "The wonder drug that works wonders."
CRACKER BARREL: "Judged to be the best."
KNORR: "Where taste is everything."
ANUSOL: "Anusol is the word to remember for relief."

DIMETAPP: "It relieves kids as well as colds."
LIQUID DRĀNO: "The liquid strong enough to be called Drāno."
JOHNSON & JOHNSON BABY POWDER: "Like magic for your skin."
PURITAN: "Make it your oil for life."
PAM: "Pam, because how you cook is as important as what you cook."
IVORY SHAMPOO AND CONDITIONER: "Leave your hair feeling Ivory clean."
TYLENOL GEL-CAPS: "It's not a capsule. It's better."
ALKA-SELTZER PLUS: "Fast, effective relief for winter colds."

THE WORLD OF ADVERTISING

47 In the world of advertising, people wear "dentures," not false teeth; they suffer from "occasional irregularity," not constipation; they need deodorants for their "nervous wetness," not for sweat; they use "bathroom tissue," not toilet paper; and they don't dye their hair, they "tint" or "rinse" it. Advertisements offer "real counterfeit diamonds" without the slightest hint of embarrassment, or boast of goods made out of "genuine imitation leather" or "virgin vinyl."

48   In the world of advertising, the girdle becomes a "body shaper," "form persuader," "control garment," "controller," "outerwear enhancer," "body garment," or "anti-gravity panties," and is sold with such trade names as "The Instead," "The Free Spirit," and "The Body Briefer."

49   A study some years ago found the following words to be among the most popular used in U.S. television advertisements: "new," "improved," "better," "extra," "fresh," "clean," "beautiful," "free," "good," "great," and "light." At the same time, the following words were found to be among the most frequent on British television: "new," "good-better-best," "free," "fresh," "delicious," "full," "sure," "clean," "wonderful," and "special." While these words may occur most frequently in ads, and while ads may be filled with weasel words, you have to watch out for all the words used in advertising, not just the words mentioned here.

50   Every word in an ad is there for a reason; no word is wasted. Your job is to figure out exactly what each word is doing in an ad—what each word really means, not what the advertiser wants you to think it means. Remember, the ad is trying to get you to buy a product, so it will put the product in the best possible light, using any device, trick, or means legally allowed. Your only defense against advertising (besides taking up permanent residence on the moon) is to develop and use a strong critical reading, listening, and looking ability. Always ask yourself what the ad is *really* saying. When you see ads on television, don't be misled by the pictures, the visual images. What does the ad *say* about the product? What does the ad *not* say? What information is missing from the ad? Only by becoming an active, critical consumer of the doublespeak of advertising will you ever be able to cut through the doublespeak and discover what the ad is really saying.

51   Professor Del Kehl of Arizona State University has updated the Twenty-third Psalm to reflect the power of advertising to meet our needs and solve our problems. It seems fitting that this chapter close with this new Psalm.

The Adman's 23rd

The Adman is my shepherd;
I shall ever want.
He maketh me to walk a mile for a Camel;
He leadeth me beside Crystal Waters
    In the High Country of Coors;
He restoreth my soul with Perrier.
He guideth me in Marlboro Country
For Mammon's sake.
Yea, though I walk through the Valley of the
    Jolly Green Giant,
In the shadow of B.O., halitosis, indigestion,
    headache pain, and hemorrhoidal tissue,
I will fear no evil,
For I am in Good Hands with Allstate;
Thy Arid, Scope, Tums, Tylenol, and Preparation H—
They comfort me.
Stouffer's preparest a table before the TV
In the presence of all my appetites;
Thou anointest my head with Brylcream;
My Decaffeinated Cup runneth over.
Surely surfeit and security shall follow me
All the days of Metropolitan Life,
And I shall dwell in a Continental Home
With a mortgage forever and ever.

Amen.

TOPICAL CONSIDERATIONS

1. How did weasel words get their name? Does it sound like an appropriate label? Why, according to Lutz, do advertisers use them?

2. What regulations restrict the use of the word "new"? How can these regulations be sidestepped according to the author? In your opinion, do these regulations serve the interests of the advertiser or the consumer?

3. Do you think that most people fail to comprehend how advertising works on them? When you read or watch ads, do you see through the gimmicks and weasel words?

4. Take a look at Lutz's Doublespeak Quick Quiz. Select five items and write a language analysis explaining what the ad really says.

5. According to the author, how can consumers protect themselves against weasel words?

RHETORICAL CONSIDERATIONS

1. The author uses "you" throughout the article. Do you find the use of the second person stylistically satisfying? Do you think it is appropriate for the article?

2. What do you think of Lutz's writing style? Is it humorous? informal? academic? What strategies does he use to involve the reader in the piece?

3. Evaluate the conclusion of this piece. Did you think Lutz's choice of the updated version of the Twenty-third Psalm was appropriate? Did you find it funny? Did it suit the theme of the essay?

4. What did you like most about this essay? What aspects of it are most memorable?

WRITING ASSIGNMENTS

1. The essays in this section deal with advertising language and its effects on consumers and their value systems. Describe how understanding the linguistic strategies of advertisers—as exemplified here by Lutz—will or will not change your reaction to advertising.

2. As Lutz suggests, look at some ads in a magazine and newspaper (or television and radio commercials). Then make a list of all uses of "help" you find over a twenty-four hour period. Examine the ads to determine exactly what is said and what the unwary consumer thinks is being said. Write up your report.

3. Invent a product and have some fun writing an ad for it. Use as many weasel words as you can to make your product shine.

4. Undertake a research project on theories of advertising: Find books by professional advertisers or texts for courses in advertising and marketing. Then go through them trying to determine how they might view Lutz's interpretation of advertising techniques. How would the authors view Lutz's claim that advertising language is loaded with "weasel words"?

THE LANGUAGE OF ADVERTISING

Charles A. O'Neill

Taking the minority opinion is advertising executive Charles A. O'Neill, who disputes the criticism of advertising language by William Lutz, and other critics of advertising. While admitting to some of the craftiness of his profession, O'Neill defends the huckster's language—both verbal and visual—against claims that it distorts reality. Examining some familiar television commercials and print ads, he explains why the language may be seductive but far from brainwashing.

This essay, originally written for the first edition of this text, has been updated for this edition. Charles O'Neill is a marketing executive for a mutual funds company.

1   The figure on the billboard looks like a rock singer, perhaps photographed in a music video taping session. He is poised, confident, as he leans against a railing, a view of the night-time city behind him; the personal geometry is just right. He wears a white suit, dark shirt, no tie. He sports a small red flower in his lapel. He holds a cigarette in his left hand. His attitude is distinctly confident, urban. His wry smile and full lips are vaguely familiar.

2   Think. You've seen him before, posed on the pages of magazines, on posters and matchbooks, sitting astride a motorcycle or playing in a band. Mick Jagger? Bill Wyman? No. He is truly a different sort of animal; in fact, he is a camel, a cartoon camel, and his name is Old Joe. Next to him on the billboard is one sentence: "Smoke New Camel Lights."

3   At first glance, this combination of artwork and text does not appear to be unusual. What is different about Camel's ad campaign is that it has spawned debates on newspaper editorial pages and has triggered organized protest. Old Joe, imported to these shores in the late 1980s, after a successful test run in Europe, has been declared by some an unwelcome visitor—an intruder whose very charm and decidedly cool style is seducing the nation's youth into a deadly habit that results in 400,000 deaths by lung cancer every year. Those who want to eliminate Joe—send him back to obscurity amid the pyramids, as it were—have a simple argument: "Everyone knows smoking is bad for the

health. You're using a cartoon to sell cigarettes to our children. The public interest is more important than your right to free speech. And it's in the public interest for us to protect our children from your unhealthy, dangerous product." Those who support Old Joe—principally his "colleagues" at R. J. Reynolds—argue that their constitutionally affirmed right to free speech extends to advertisements about their product. Given the opportunity, they would likely add: "People should make their own decisions about smoking. We've chosen to use a cartoon character in our ads only because it is noticeable and effective."

4   The obvious topic of the debate is cigarette advertising, but beneath the surface it signals something more interesting and broad based: the rather uncomfortable, tentative acceptance of advertising in our society. We recognize the legitimacy—even the value—of advertising, but on some level we can't quite fully embrace it as a "normal" part of our experience. At best, we view it as distracting. At worst, we view it as dangerous to our health and a pernicious threat to our social values. Not long ago, *Advertising Age* reported that a Pontifical Council—a group whose views may shape Catholic Church policy—initiated a study to review such topics as truth in advertising, ads as a creator of needs and whether advertising excludes people who should receive messages.

5   How does advertising work? Why is it so powerful? Why does it raise such concern? What case can be made for and against the advertising business? In order to understand advertising, you must accept that it is not about truth, virtue, love, or positive social values. It is about money. Ads play a role in moving customers through the sales process. This process begins with an effort to build awareness of a product, typically achieved by tactics designed to break through the clutter of competitive messages. By presenting a description of product benefits, ads convince the customer to buy the product. Once prospects have become purchasers, advertising is used to sustain brand loyalty, reminding customers of all the good reasons for their original decision to buy.

6   But this does not sufficiently explain the ultimate, unique power of advertising. Whatever the product or creative strategy, advertisements derive their power from a purposeful, directed combination of images. Images can take the form of words, sounds, or visuals, used individually or together. The combination of images is the language of advertising, a language unlike any other.

7   Everyone who grows up in the Western World soon learns that advertising language is different from other languages. Most children would be unable to explain how such lines as "With Nice 'n Easy, it's color so natural, the closer he gets the better you look!" (the famous ad for Clairol's Nice 'n Easy hair coloring) differed from ordinary language, but they would say, "It sounds like an ad." Whether printed on a page, blended with music on the radio, or whispered on the sound track of a television commercial, advertising language is "different."

8   Over the years, the texture of advertising language has frequently changed. Styles and creative concepts come and go. But there are at least four distinct,

general characteristics of the language of advertising that make it different from other languages. They lend advertising its persuasive power:

1. The language of advertising is edited and purposeful.

2. The language of advertising is rich and arresting; it is specifically intended to attract and hold our attention.

3. The language of advertising involves us; in effect, *we* complete the message.

4. The language of advertising is a simple language; it holds no secrets from us.

EDITED AND PURPOSEFUL

9 In his book, *Future Shock,* Alvin Toffler describes various types of messages we receive from the world around us each day. As he sees it, there is a difference between normal "coded" messages and "engineered" messages. Much of normal, human experience is "uncoded"; it is merely sensory. For example, Toffler describes a man walking down a street. Toffler notes that the man's sensory perceptions of this experience may form a mental image, but the message is not "designed by anyone to communicate anything, and the man's understanding of it does not depend directly on a social code—a set of agreed-upon signs and definitions."[1] In contrast, Toffler describes a talk show conversation as "coded"; the speakers' ability to exchange information with their host, and our ability to understand it, depend upon social conventions.

10   The language of advertising is coded. It is also a language of carefully engineered, ruthlessly purposeful messages. By Toffler's calculation, the average adult American is assaulted by at least 560 advertising messages a day. Not one of these messages would reach us, to attract and hold our attention, if it were completely unstructured. Advertising messages have a clear purpose; they are intended to trigger a specific response.

RICH AND ARRESTING

11 Advertisements—no matter how carefully "engineered"—cannot succeed unless they capture our attention. Of the hundreds of advertising messages in store for us each day, very few will actually command our conscious attention. The rest are screened out. The people who design and write ads know about this screening process; they anticipate and accept it as a premise of their business.

12   The classic, all-time favorite device used to breach the barrier is sex. The desire to be sexually attractive to others is an ancient instinct, and few drives are more powerful. A magazine ad for Ultima II, a line of cosmetics, invites readers to "find everything you need for the sexxxiest look around. . . . " The ad goes on to offer other "Sexxxy goodies," including "Lipsexxxxy lip color, naked eye color . . . Sunsexxxy liquid bronzer." No one will accuse Ultima's

marketing tacticians of subtlety. In fact, this ad is merely a current example of an approach that is as old as advertising. After countless years of using images of women in various stages of undress to sell products, ads are now displaying men's bodies as well. A magazine ad for Brut, a men's cologne, declares in bold letters, "MEN ARE BACK"; in the background, a photograph shows a muscular, shirtless young man preparing to enter the boxing ring—a "manly" image indeed; an image of man as breeding stock.

13   Every successful advertisement uses a creative strategy based on an idea that will attract and hold the attention of the targeted consumer audience. The strategy may include strong creative execution or a straightforward presentation of product features and customer benefits. Many ads use humor or simply a play on words:

> "Reeboks let U B U" (Reebok)
>
> "My chickens eat better than you do." (Perdue Chickens)
>
> "Look deep into our ryes." (Wigler's bakery products)
>
> "Me. 4 U." (The State of Maine)
>
> "We're the biggest jock school in New England. And we don't have any teams. There's no better place for VJs and DJs." (Northeast College of Broadcasting)

Even if the text contains no incongruity and does not rely on a pun for its impact, ads typically use a creative strategy based on some striking concept or idea. In fact, the concept and execution are often so good that many successful ads entertain while they sell.

14   Consider, for example, the campaigns created for Federal Express. A campaign was developed to position Federal Express as the company that would deliver packages, not just "overnight," but "by 10:30 A.M." the next day. The plight of the junior executive in "Presentation," one TV ad in the campaign, is stretched for dramatic purposes, but it is, nonetheless, all too real: The young executive, who is presumably trying to climb his way up the corporate ladder, is shown calling another parcel delivery service and all but begging for assurance that he will have his slides in hand by 10:30 the next morning. "No slides, no presentation," he pleads. Only a viewer with a heart of stone can watch without feeling sympathetic as the next morning our junior executives struggles to make his presentation *sans* slides. He is so lost without them that he is reduced to using his hands to perform imitations of birds and animals in shadows on the movie screen. What does the junior executive *viewer* think when he or she sees the ad?

1. Federal Express guarantees to deliver packages "absolutely, positively overnight."

2. Federal Express packages arrive early in the day.

3. What happened to that fellow in the commercial will absolutely not happen to me, now that I know what package delivery service to call.

15   A sound, creative strategy supporting an innovative service idea sold Federal Express. But the quality and objective "value" of execution doesn't matter. A magazine ad for Merit Ultra Lights made use of one word in its headline: "Yo!" This was, one hopes, not the single most powerful idea generated by the agency's creative team that particular month—but it probably sold cigarettes.

16   Soft-drink and fast-food companies often take another approach. "Slice of life" ads (so-called because they purport to show people in "real-life" situations) created to sell Coke or Pepsi have often placed their characters in Fourth-of-July parades or other family events. The archetypical version of this approach is filled-to-overflowing with babies frolicking with puppies in the sunlit foreground while their youthful parents play touch football. On the porch, Grandma and Pops are seen quietly smiling as they wait for all of this affection to transform itself into a climax of warmth, harmony, and joy. Beneath the veneer, these ads work through repetition: How-many-times-can-you-spot-the-logo-in-this-commercial?

17   More subtly, these ads seduce us into feeling that if we drink the right combination of sugar, preservatives, caramel coloring, and a few secret ingredients, we'll fulfill our yearning for a world where young folks and old folks live together in perfect bliss.

18   If you don't buy this version of the American Dream, search long enough and you are sure to find an ad designed to sell you what it takes to gain prestige within whatever posse you do happen to run with. As reported by the *Boston Globe*, "the malt liquor industry relies heavily on rap stars in delivering its message to inner-city youths, while Black Death Vodka, which features a top-hatted skull and a coffin on its label, has been using Guns N' Roses guitarist Slash to endorse the product in magazine advertising." A malt liquor company reportedly promotes its 40-ounce size with rapper King T singing, "I usually drink it when I'm just out clowning, me and the home boys, you know, be like downing it . . . I grab me a 40 when I want to act a fool." A recent ad for Sasson jeans is a long way from Black Death in execution, but a second cousin in spirit. A photograph of a young, blonde (they do have more fun, right?) actress appears with this text: "Baywatch actress Gena Lee Nolin Puts On Sasson. OO-LA-LA. Sasson. Don't put it on unless it's Sasson."

19   Ads do not often emerge like Botticelli's Venus from the sea, flawless and fully grown. Most often, the creative strategy is developed only after extensive research. "Who will be interested in our product? How old are they? Where do they live? How much money do they earn? What problem will our product solve?" Answers to these questions provide the foundation on which the creative strategy is built.

INVOLVING

20 We have seen that the language of advertising is carefully engineered; we have discovered a few of the devices it uses to get our attention. R. J. Reynolds has

us identifying with Old Joe in one of his many uptown poses. Coke and Pepsi have caught our eye with visions of peace and love. An actress offers a winsome smile. Now that they have our attention, advertisers present information intended to show us that their product fills a need and differs from the competition. It is the copywriter's responsibility to express, exploit, and intensify such product differences.

21   When product differences do not exist, the writer must glamorize the superficial differences—for example, differences in packaging. As long as the ad is trying to get our attention, the "action" is mostly in the ad itself, in the words and visual images. But as we read an ad or watch it on television, we become more deeply involved. The action starts to take place in us. Our imagination is set in motion, and our individual fears and aspirations, quirks and insecurities, superimpose themselves on that tightly engineered, attractively packaged message.

22   Consider, once again, the running battle among the low-calorie soft drinks. The cola wars have spawned many "look-alike" advertisements, because the product features and consumer benefits are generic, applying to all products in the category. Substitute one cola brand name for another, and the messages are often identical, right down to the way the cans are photographed in the closing sequence. This strategy relies upon mass saturation and exposure for impact.

23   Some companies have set themselves apart from their competitors by making use of bold, even disturbing, themes and images. In its controversial ad campaign, Benetton has tried to draw attention to its clothing line in unusual ways. One magazine ad displays a photograph of a father comforting his son, who is dying of AIDS, while other family members huddle nearby. The company's clothing may or may not be truly different from competitor's products, but the image surely is different—that of a company that focuses on social issues.

24   Is Benetton committing an outrageously immoral act by exploiting people who suffer from a horrible disease? Or is this company brilliantly drawing attention to itself while reminding a largely complacent consumer population that the scourge of AIDS need to be arrested? Benetton is far from the first company whose marketing efforts have been subject to the charge of exploitation. In fact, on one level, all advertising is about exploitation: the systematic, deliberate identification of our needs and wants, followed by the delivery of a carefully constructed promise that we will find fulfillment or satisfaction by purchasing Brand X.

25   Symbols offer an important tool for involving consumers in advertisements. Symbols have become important elements in the language of advertising, not so much because they carry meanings of their own, but because we bring meaning to them. One example is provided by the campaign begun in 1978 by Somerset Importers for Johnnie Walker Red Scotch. Sales of Johnnie Walker Red had been trailing sales of Johnnie Walker Black, and Somerset Importers needed to position Red as a fine product in its own right. Their agency produced ads that made heavy use of the color red. One magazine ad, often

printed as a two-page spread, is dominated by a close-up photo of red autumn leaves. At lower right, the copy reads, "When their work is done, even the leaves turn to Red." Another ad—also suitably dominated by a photograph in the appropriate color—reads: "When it's time to quiet down at the end of the day, even a fire turns to Red." Red. Warm. Experienced. Seductive.

26   As we have seen, advertisers make use of a great variety of techniques and devices to engage us in the delivery of their messages. Some are subtle, making use of warm, entertaining, or comforting images or symbols. Others, like Black Death Vodka and Ultima II, are about as subtle as MTV's "Beavis and Butt-head." Another common device used to engage our attention is old but still effective: the use of famous or notorious personalities as product spokespeople or models. Advertising writers did not invent the human tendency to admire or otherwise identify ourselves with famous people. Once we have seen a famous person in an ad, we associate the product with the person: "Joe DiMaggio is a good guy. He likes Mr. Coffee. If I buy a Mr. Coffee coffee maker and I use it when I have the boss over for dinner, then maybe she'll think I'm a good guy, too." "Guns 'N Roses rule my world, so I will definitely make the scene with a bottle of Black Death stuck into the waistband of my sweat pants." "Gena Lee Nolin is totally sexy. She wears Sasson. If I wear Sasson, I'll be sexy, too." The logic is faulty, but we fall under the spell just the same. Advertising works, not because Joe DiMaggio is a coffee expert, Slash has discriminating taste, or Gena knows her jeans, but because we participate in it. In fact, we charge ads with most of their power.

A SIMPLE LANGUAGE

27 Advertising language differs from other types of language in another important respect; it is a simple language. To determine how the copy of a typical advertisement rates on a "simplicity index" in comparison with text in a magazine article, for example, try this exercise: Clip a typical story from the publication you read most frequently. Calculate the number of words in an average sentence. Count the number of words of three or more syllables in a typical 100-word passage, omitting words that are capitalized, combinations of two simple words, or verb forms made into three-syllable words by the addition of -*ed* or -*es*. Add the two figures (the average number of words per sentence and the number of three-syllable words per 100 words), then multiply the result by .4. According to Robert Gunning, if the resulting number is seven, there is a good chance that you are reading *True Confessions*.[2] He developed this formula, the "Fog Index," to determine the comparative ease with which any given piece of written communication can be read. Here is the complex text of a typical cigarette endorsement:

> I demand two things from my cigarette. I want a cigarette with low tar and nicotine. But, I also want taste. That's why I smoke Winston Lights. I get a lighter cigarette, but I still get a real taste. And real pleasure. Only one cigarette gives me that: Winston Lights.

The average sentence in this ad runs seven words. *Cigarette* and *nicotine* are three-syllable words, with *cigarette* appearing four times; *nicotine*, once. Considering *that's* as two words, the ad is exactly fifty words long, so the average number of three-syllable words per 100 is ten.

$$
\begin{array}{rl}
7 & \text{words per sentence} \\
+\ 10 & \text{three-syllable words/100} \\
\hline
17 & \\
\times\ .4 & \\
\hline
6.8 & \text{Fog Index}
\end{array}
$$

28   According to Gunning's scale, this particular ad is written at about the seventh grade level, comparable to most of the ads found in mass circulation magazines. It's about as sophisticated as *True Confessions;* that is, harder to read than a comic book, but easier than *Ladies Home Journal.* Of course, the Fog Index cannot evaluate the visual aspect of an ad—another component of advertising language. The headline, "I demand two things from my cigarette," works with the picture (that of an attractive woman) to arouse consumer interest. The text reinforces the image. Old Joe's simple plea, "Try New Camel Lights," is too short to move the needle on the Fog Index meter, but in every respect it represents perhaps the simplest language possible, a not-distant cousin of Merit Ultra Lights' groundbreaking and succinct utterance, "Yo!"

29   Why do advertisers generally favor simple language? The answer lies with the consumer: Consider Toffler's speculation that the average American adult is subject to some 560 advertising or commercial messages each day. As a practical matter, we would not notice many of these messages if length or eloquence were counted among their virtues. Today's consumer cannot take the time to focus on anything for long, much less blatant advertising messages. With the advent of full-motion-video CD-ROMS, the proliferation of corporate-sponsored web sites, and an accelerating volume of product offerings, the message count today must be many times greater than it was in 1970 when Toffler published the first edition of his seminal book. In effect, Toffler's "future" is here now, and it is perhaps more "shocking" than he could have foreseen at the time. Every aspect of modern life runs at an accelerated pace. Overnight mail has moved in less than ten years from a novelty to a common business necessity. Voice mail, pagers, cellular phones, E-mail, the Internet—the world is always awake, always switched on, and hungry for more information, now. Time generally, and TV-commercial time in particular, is now dissected into increasingly smaller segments. Fifteen-second commercials are no longer unusual.

30   Toffler views the evolution toward shorter language as a natural progression: three-syllable words are simply harder to read than one- or two-syllable words. Simple ideas are more readily transferred from one person to another than complex ideas. Therefore, advertising copy uses increasingly simple language, as does society at large. In *Future Shock,* Toffler speculates:

> If the [English] language had the same number of words in Shakespeare's time as it does today, at least 200,000 words—perhaps several times that many—have dropped out and been replaced in the intervening four centuries. The high turnover rate reflects changes in things, processes, and qualities in the environment from the world of consumer products and technology.

It is no accident that the first terms Toffler uses to illustrate his point ("fast-back," "wash-and-wear," and "flashcube") were invented not by engineers, or journalists, but by advertising copywriters.

31   Advertising language is simple language; in the ad's engineering process, difficult words or images—which in other forms of communication may be used to lend color or fine shades of meaning—are edited out and replaced by simple words or images not open to misinterpretation. You don't have to ask whether Old Joe likes his Camels or whether King T likes to "grab a 40" when he wants to "act a fool."

WHO IS RESPONSIBLE?

32 Some critics view the advertising business as a cranky, unwelcomed child of the free enterprise system—a noisy, whining, brash kid who must somehow be kept in line, but can't just yet be thrown out of the house. In reality, advertising mirrors the fears, quirks, and aspirations of the society that creates it (and is, in turn, sold by it). This factor alone exposes advertising to parody and ridicule. The overall level of acceptance and respect for advertising is also influenced by the varied quality of the ads themselves. Some ads, including a few of the examples cited here, seem deliberately designed to provoke controversy. For example, it is easy—as some critics have charged—to conclude that Benetton's focus on social issues is merely a cynical effort to attract attention. But critics miss the point. If an ad stimulates controversy, so what? This is smart marketing—a successful effort to make the advertising dollar work harder.

33   In his book, *Strictly Speaking,* journalist Edwin Newman poses the question, "Will America be the death of English?" Newman's "mature, well thought out judgment" is that it will. As evidence, he cites a number of examples of fuzzy thinking and careless use of the language, not just by advertisers, but by many people in public life, including politicians and journalists.

> The federal government has adopted the comic strip character Snoopy as a symbol and showed us Snoopy on top of his doghouse, flat on his back, with a balloon coming out of his mouth, containing the words, "I believe in conserving energy," while below there was this exhortation: savEnergy. An entire letter e at the end was saved. In addition, an entire space was saved.
> . . . Spelling has been assaulted by Duz, E-Z Off, Fantastik, Kool, Kleen . . . and by products that make you briter, so that you will not be left hi and dri at a parti, but made welkom. . . . Under this pressure, adjectives become adverbs; nouns become adjectives; prepositions disappear, compounds abound.[3]

In this passage, Newman represents three of the charges most often levied against advertising:

1. Advertising debases English.

2. Advertising downgrades the intelligence of the public.

3. Advertising warps our vision of reality, implanting in us groundless fears and insecurities. (He cites, as examples of these groundless fears, "tattletale gray," "denture breath," "morning mouth," "unsightly bulge," and "ring around the collar.")

Other charges have been made from time to time. They include:

1. Advertising sells daydreams—distracting, purposeless visions of lifestyles beyond the reach of most of the people who are most exposed to advertising.

2. Advertising feeds on human weaknesses and exaggerates the importance of material things, encouraging "impure" emotions and vanities.

3. Advertising encourages unhealthy habits.

4. Advertising perpetuates racial and sexual stereotypes.

34   What can be said in advertising's defense? Advertising is only a reflection of society; slaying the messenger would not alter the fact—if it is a fact—that "America will be the death of English." A case can be made for the concept that advertising language is an acceptable stimulus for the natural evolution of language. Is "proper English" the language most Americans actually speak and write, or is it the language we are told we should speak and write?

35   What about the charge that advertising debases the intelligence of the public? Those who support this particular criticism would do well to ask themselves another question: Exactly how intelligent is the public? Sadly, evidence abounds that "the public" at large is not particularly intelligent, after all. Johnny can't read. Susie can't write. And the entire family spends the night in front of the television, channel surfing for the latest scandal—hopefully, one involving a sports hero or political figure said to be a killer or a frequent participant in perverse sexual acts.

36   Ads are effective because they sell products. They would not succeed if they did not reflect the values and motivations of the real world. Advertising both reflects and shapes our perception of reality. Consider several brand names and the impressions they create: Ivory Snow is pure; Edsel was a failure; Federal Express won't let you down. These attributes may well be correct, but our sense of what these brand names mean has as much to do with marketing communications as it does with objective "fact."

37   Advertising shapes our perception of the world as surely as architecture shapes our impression of a city. Good, responsible advertising can serve as a positive influence for change, while generating profits. Of course, the problem is that the obverse is also true: Advertising, like any form of mass communication, can be a force for both "good" and "bad." It can just as readily reinforce or encourage irresponsible behavior, ageism, sexism, ethnocentrism, racism, homophobia, heterophobia—you name it—as it can encourage support for di-

versity and social progress. People living in society create advertising. Society isn't perfect. In the end, advertising simply attempts to change behavior. Do advertisements sell distracting, purposeless visions? Occasionally. But perhaps such visions are necessary components of the process through which our society changes and improves.

38   Old Joe's days as Camel's spokesman appear to be numbered. His very success in reaching new smokers may prove to be the source of his undoing. But standing nearby and waiting to take his place is another campaign; another character, real or imagined; another product for sale. Perhaps, by learning how advertising works, we can become better equipped to sort out content from hype, product values from emotions, and salesmanship from propaganda.

NOTES

1. Alvin Toffler, *Future Shock* (New York: Random House, 1970), p. 146.
2. Curtis D. MacDougall, *Interpretive Reporting* (New York: Macmillan, 1968), p. 94.
3. Edwin Newman, *Strictly Speaking* (Indianapolis: Bobs-Merrill, 1974), p. 13.

TOPICAL CONSIDERATIONS

1. O'Neill opens his essay with a discussion of the controversial figure of Joe Camel. What are your views on the Joe Camel controversy? Do you think such ads target young people and, thus, should be outlawed? Why or why not?

2. Are you familiar with the Benetton AIDS patient ad O'Neill mentions here? If so, do you view it as an attempt to raise social awareness or as simple exploitation?

3. Do you think it is ethical for advertisers to create a sense of product difference when there really isn't any? Consider ads for gasoline, beer, and instant coffee.

4. In the last section of the essay, O'Neill anticipates potential objections to his defense of advertising. What are some of these objections? What does he say in defense of advertising? Which set of arguments do you find stronger?

5. O'Neill describes several ways in which the language of advertising differs from other kinds of language. Briefly list the ways he mentions. Can you think of any other characteristics of advertising language that set it apart?

6. What is "proper English," as contrasted with colloquial or substandard English? Do you use proper English in your written course work and in your own correspondence? What do you think about using proper English in advertising?

7. O'Neill asserts in paragraph 25 that "[symbols] have become important elements in the language of advertising." Can you think of some specific symbols from the advertising world that you associate with your own life? Are they effective symbols for selling? Explain your answer.

8. In paragraph 26, O'Neill claims that celebrity endorsement of a product leads to the "faulty" logic of associating the person with the product. Explain what he means. Why do people buy products sold by famous people?

RHETORICAL CONSIDERATIONS

1. How effective do you think O'Neill's introductory paragraphs are? How well does he hook the reader? What particular audience might he be appealing to early on? What attitude toward advertising is established in the introduction?

2. O'Neill is an advertising professional. Does his writing style reflect the advertising techniques he describes? Cite examples to support your answer.

3. Describe the author's point of view about advertising. Does he ever tell us how he feels? Does his style indicate his attitude?

WRITING ASSIGNMENTS

1. Obtain a current issue of each of the following publications: the *New Yorker, Time, GQ, Vogue,* and *People.* Choose one article from each periodical and calculate its Fog Index according to the technique described in paragraph 27. Choose one ad from each periodical and figure out its Fog Index. What different reading levels do you find among the publications? What do you know about the readers of these periodicals from your survey of the reading difficulty of the articles? Write a paper based on your findings.

2. Clip three ads that use sex as a selling device for products that have no sexual connotations whatever. Explain how sex helps sell the products. Do you consider these ads demeaning?

3. The author believes that advertising language mirrors the fears, quirks, and aspirations of the society that creates it. Do you agree or disagree with this statement? Explain in a brief essay.

4. Choose a brand-name product you use regularly and one of its competitors—one whose differences are negligible, if they exist at all. Examine some advertisements for each brand. Write a short paper explaining what really makes you prefer your brand.

Printed Noise

George F. Will

Most of us are so accustomed to the incessant roar of commerce that we hear it without listening. If we stopped and thought about some of the names advertisers have given their products, we might recognize a peculiarly American form of language pollution. In this amusing essay, George Will takes a look at some of the fanciful and familiar names given to menu items such as "Egg McMuffin," "Fishamagig," and "Hot Fudge Nutty Buddy." He concludes that all the asphyxiating cuteness amounts to a lot of verbal litter. Will, a former philosophy professor, is a nationally syndicated Pulitzer Prize–winning columnist for the *Washington Post* and *Newsweek* magazine, and TV news commentator for ABC. He is the author of several books including *Restoration* (1994).

1 The flavor list at the local Baskin-Robbins ice cream shop is an anarchy of names like "Peanut Butter 'N Chocolate" and "Strawberry Rhubard Sherbert." These are not the names of things that reasonable people consider consuming, but the names are admirably businesslike, briskly descriptive.

2 Unfortunately, my favorite delight (chocolate-coated vanilla ice cream flecked with nuts) bears the unutterable name "Hot Fudge Nutty Buddy," an example of the plague of cuteness in commerce. There are some things a gentleman simply will not do, and one is announce in public a desire for a "Nutty Buddy." So I usually settle for a plain vanilla cone.

3 I am not the only person suffering for immutable standards of propriety. The May [1978] issue of *Atlantic* contains an absorbing tale of lonely heroism at a Burger King. A gentleman requested a ham and cheese sandwich that the Burger King calls a Yumbo. The girl taking orders was bewildered.

4 "Oh," she eventually exclaimed, "you mean a Yumbo."

5 Gentleman: "The ham and cheese. Yes."

6 Girl, nettled: "It's called a Yumbo. Now, do you want a Yumbo or not?"

7 Gentleman, teeth clenched: "Yes, thank you, the ham and cheese."

8   Girl: "Look, I've got to have an order here. You're holding up the line. You want a Yumbo, don't you? You want a Yumbo!"

9   Whereupon the gentleman chose the straight and narrow path of virtue. He walked out rather than call a ham and cheese a Yumbo. His principles are anachronisms but his prejudices are impeccable, and he is on my short list of civilization's friends.

10   That list includes the Cambridge don who would not appear outdoors without a top hat, not even when routed by fire at 3 A.M., and who refused to read another line of Tennyson after he saw the poet put water in fine port. The list includes another don who, although devoutly Tory, voted Liberal during Gladstone's day because the duties of prime minister kept Gladstone too busy to declaim on Holy Scripture. And high on the list is the grammarian whose last words were: "I am about to—or I am going to—die: either expression is correct."

11   Gentle reader, can you imagine any of these magnificent persons asking a teenage girl for a "Yumbo"? Or uttering "Fishamagig" or "Egg McMuffin" or "Fribble" (that's a milk shake, sort of)?

12   At one point in the evolution of American taste, restaurants that were relentlessly fun, fun, fun were built to look like lemons or bananas. I am told that in Los Angeles there was the Toed Inn, a strange spelling for a strange place shaped like a giant toad. Customers entered through the mouth, like flies being swallowed.

13   But the mature nation has put away such childish things in favor of menus that are fun, fun, fun. Seafood is "From Neptune's Pantry" or "Denizens of the Briny Deep." And "Surf 'N Turf," which you might think is fish and horsemeat, actually is lobster and beef.

14   To be fair, there are practical considerations behind the asphyxiatingly cute names given hamburgers. Many hamburgers are made from portions of the cow that the cow had no reason to boast about. So sellers invent distracting names to give hamburgers cachet. Hence "Whoppers" and "Heroburgers."

15   But there is no excuse for Howard Johnson's menu. In a just society it would be a flogging offense to speak of "steerburgers," clams "fried to order" (which probably means they don't fry clams for you unless you order fried clams), a "natural cut" (what is an "unnatural" cut?) of sirloin, "oven-baked" meat loaf, chicken pot pie with "flaky crust," "golden croquettes," "grilled-in-butter Frankforts [sic]," "liver with smothered onions" (smothered by onions?), and a "hearty" Reuben sandwich.

16   America is marred by scores of Dew Drop Inns serving "crispy green" salads, "garden fresh" vegetables, "succulent" lamb, "savory" pork, "sizzling" steaks, and "creamy" or "tangy" coleslaw. I've nothing against Homeric adjectives ("wine-dark sea," "wing-footed Achilles") but isn't coleslaw just coleslaw? Americans hear the incessant roar of commerce without listening to it, and read the written roar without really noticing it. Who would notice if a menu proclaimed "creamy" steaks and "sizzling" coleslaw? Such verbal litter is to

language as Muzak is to music. As advertising blather becomes the nation's normal idiom, language becomes printed noise.

TOPICAL CONSIDERATIONS

1. What is George F. Will's major assertion here regarding the language of American menus? Is he concerned that some items have been given fanciful names to disguise inferior food? Or is he more concerned with the way advertising hype reduces language?

2. Are you so used to fast-food menu names such as "Fishamagig," "Egg McMuffin," or "Yumbo" that you never questioned them? Or have they ever seemed silly and offensive to you? Can you think of other similar names?

3. In paragraph 15, Will attacks the language of Howard Johnson menus. What is wrong with "steerburgers"? "oven-baked" meat loaf? clams "fried to order"? "liver with smothered onions"? And what's wrong with a "hearty" Reuben sandwich?

4. Will makes the point in the last paragraph that menus make us adjective-blind (or deaf). But just how effective would a menu be if it were stripped of all the empty adjectives? Is a "crispy green" salad more attractive than "salad"? Is "sizzling" steak more tantalizing than just plain "steak," or "tangy" coleslaw more appetizing than "coleslaw"? Are we so accustomed to the adjectives that we need their assurance?

RHETORICAL CONSIDERATIONS

1. How does Will use examples here? In other words, does he use examples to convince us of his position, or just to inform us?

2. How effective is the example of the *Atlantic* anecdote about the gentleman ordering a Yumbo? Did you find that example funny? Did it sufficiently dramatize Will's point?

3. How would you characterize Will's sense of humor? In what ways does he establish it? What humorous word choices can you find?

4. In the last paragraph Will makes an analogy: "Such verbal litter is to language as Muzak is to music." What is Muzak, and how effective is the comparison?

WRITING ASSIGNMENTS

1. Write your own essay on printed noise. Go through newspapers and magazines and find examples of advertisers' names for products to draw from.

2. Construct a menu of your own using some of the advertising principles Will attacks here. Use silly, childish names, overblown adjectives, and euphemisms to make ordinary fast food sound tantalizing.

EUPHEMISMS FOR THE FAT OF THE LAND

Diane White

> Tell the truth but make the truth fascinating. Such is the advertising philosophy of Charles O'Neill. But have you ever discovered an advertising pitch that made truth a lot more distorted than fascinating? Sure you have, and so has *Boston Globe* columnist Diane White, whose humorous complaint below is aimed at those copywriters whose strategy is to euphemize both the product and the consumer. It's selling by inflation—and, as Ms. White admits, that's a problem she doesn't need camouflaged by lingo.

1 Each time I buy pantyhose I wonder about the identity of the advertising genius who coined the term Queen Size.

2 For a while I thought this person might be a woman, perhaps someone who is herself Queen Size. Lately, though, I have come to think it is a man, someone along the lines of Frederick of Hollywood, who gave a grateful world the padded girdle. The term Queen Size is just about as essential as the false bum, and just as misleading.

3 Queen Size, let's face it, is a euphemism for fat, at least as it applies to pantyhose. Does Queen Size occur in the language to describe anything other than pantyhose, beds and bedding?

4 Its counterpart is not, as one might think, King Size, but Husky. Husky men are the equivalent of Queen Size women, that is, they are fat.

5 The term Queen Size, used to describe pantyhose, is deliberately evasive.

6 King Size, on the other hand, has a positive connotation. Often it indicates a bargain. Almost everybody knows Queen Size is no bargain. You can, for example, buy King Size boxes of detergent, but not Queen Size. Manufacturers tried to market Queen Size boxes of soap powder but only fat women would buy them.

7 I'm not sure which queen the perpetrator had in mind when he coined the term. Maybe the Hawaiian, Liliuokalani, a Queen Size woman if there ever was one. Or maybe Queen Elizabeth, the ocean-going one, that is.

8 There is a school of thought that holds that body image is all in the mind. I have tried to train my mind to think of myself as Queen Size. I have failed. The package of pantyhose may say Queen Size; my mirror says fat.

0   But I am insulting myself. The word fat, used as an adjective, is rapidly going the way of racial and ethnic slurs. Not only is it considered unfashionable to be fat, it is considered unconscionable to use the word fat to describe anybody, with the possible exception of 500-pound rapists.

10   For example, the magazine "Big Beautiful Woman" insists that I am not fat, merely Big. And not just Big, but Big and Beautiful.

11   I'm all in favor of positive thinking, but this is too much. The editors of BBW would probably say I've been brainwashed by the fashion industry into thinking that only thin is attractive.

12   I would like to be able to swallow the Big-is-Beautiful line, but somehow it won't go down. I know Big can indeed be Beautiful, but, more often than not, less big is a lot more beautiful.

13   But I'm a fan of BBW. Looking at its fashion layouts makes me feel as good as looking through the pages of Vogue makes me feel bad. I mean, I may be fat, but I'm not *that* fat. Yet.

14   My mind runs its brainwashed course when I study its Queen Size models. I can't help thinking how pretty they'd be if only they'd lose a few pounds.

15   This is one of the curses of journalism. Journalists are supposed to be realists, people willing and able to face the facts, no matter how ugly they may be. Therefore I know I am not Queen Size, but merely fat.

16   I might have a whole different way of looking at things if I were in advertising. Copywriters are paid not to tell the whole truth, to make the unpalatable palatable. If I were a copywriter I might be Big, or even Queen Size.

17   But I am not a copywriter. And I am not, of course, forced to buy Queen Size pantyhose. I have a choice.

18   For only $1.50 more I can purchase another brand and be Stately. Stately pantyhose are about the same dimensions as Queen Size, but even more dignified.

19   If I buy yet another brand I can be Statuesque. (This pantyhose has been personally endorsed by the Venus de Milo.)

20   Still another manufacturer offers a size called Goddess, apparently for those who are larger than life. I'm not sure for which goddess they named their product. Perhaps they mean to honor Juno, who lends her name to Junoesque, a charmingly classical euphemism for fat.

21   Why don't the people who make pantyhose face facts and call their giant size Huge or Humongous or Jumbo?

22   We all know why. Even I can't imagine stepping up to the hosiery counter and saying, "I'd like three pairs of Jumbo, please."

23   I can, though, imagine ordering a few pairs of Extra Large. But in a world where Queen Size is king, such simplicity is probably too much to ask for.

TOPICAL CONSIDERATIONS

1. Why did White decide that the person who coined the term *Queen Size* was a man instead of a woman?

2. According to White how is *King Size* a "positive" term and *Queen Size* not? Do you agree? Can you think of any uses of the term *Queen Size* that are positive?

3. What is White's argument against the publishers of *Big Beautiful Woman?*

4. How has White's training as a journalist worked against her acceptance of advertising language?

5. In the final paragraph, White says that "Extra Large" is preferable to "Queen Size." However, she adds, such "simplicity" would be too much to ask of advertisers—the implication being that advertising language complicates reality. How do her examples of fat euphemisms other than *Queen Size* complicate or even distort reality?

RHETORICAL CONSIDERATIONS

1. Can you single out a basic thesis statement in this essay?

2. Characterize the tone of the essay. Find examples of White's use of allusions, irony, and hyperbole. Where does the author display her sense of humor?

WRITING ASSIGNMENTS

1. Several of the essays in this section talk about how advertising language affects consumers and their value systems. How has Diane White's discussion of the transparent euphemizing strategies of advertisers affected your reaction to certain ads?

2. Invent a product and write an ad using the kind of euphemizing language White discusses.

3. Write an essay in which you examine media-based stereotypes of female beauty. Look through current fashion magazines or catalogs, noting the dominant images of beauty. How does American society perceive and deal with women who are overweight. Are they represented? Are they euphemized? Are they scorned? Are they treated as aberrations? What effects do American beauty standards have on "normal" women? (One noted research source for this paper is Naomi Wolf's book, *The Beauty Myth.*)

A WORD FROM OUR SPONSOR

Patricia Volk

The following piece, which originally appeared in the "On Language" column of the *New York Times Magazine*, was written by a professional advertising copywriter. However, Patricia Volk is anything but defensive of the practices of her profession. While demonstrating some of the jargon of the trade, Volk confesses that the language of advertising is a language "without rules," a language with "little to protect it." Ad people, she explains, will stop at nothing to make a product that the world neither wants nor needs sound wonderful. Besides being a copywriter, Patricia Volk is author of the award-winning short-story collection *The Yellow Banana and Other Stories* (1985) and the novel *White Light* (1987).

1   Linguistically speaking (and that's still the preferred way), there is only one rule in advertising: There are no rules. "We try harder," lacks parallelism. "Nobody doesn't like Sara Lee," is a double negative. And "Modess. Because. . . . " Because . . . why? My friends didn't know. My mother wouldn't tell. My sister said, like Mount Everest, because it was there. The word "creme" on a product means there's no cream in it. "Virtually," as in "Virtually all our cars are tested," means in essence, not in fact. Even a casual "Let's have lunch," said in passing on Mad Ave. means "Definitely, let's not."

2   Language without rules has little to protect it. Some of the most familiar lines would disappear like ring-around-the-collar if you put a mere "Says who?" after them. "Coke is it." Says who? "Sony. The one and only." Oh, yeah?

3   Still, one word in advertising has virtually limitless power. It gives "permission to believe." It inspires hope. It is probably (disclaimer) the oldest word in advertising.

4   What "new" lacks in newness, it makes up for in motivation. Unfortunately, new gets old fast. Legally, it's usable for only six months after a product is introduced. As in, say, "Introducing New Grippies. The candy that sticks to 'the woof of your mouf.' "

5   Once Grippies are six months old, unlike newlyweds, who get a year, and the New Testament which has gotten away with it for who knows how long, Grippies are reduced to just plain Grippies. That's when you improve them

and say "Introducing New Improved Grippies." Now they weally stick like cwazy to that woof.

6   Had you named your product "New" to start with, as in "New Soap. The soap that cleans like new," you'd never have to worry about your product sounding old. Introduced as "New New Soap," six months down the road it segues into "New Improved New Soap." Or you could avoid the six-month thing entirely and just call it "The Revolutionary New Soap" from day one.

PITCHING GLUE

7   How do you get the Grippies account in the first place? You "pitch" it in a flurry of work called a "push." A creative team works weekends and sleeps in the office. It's intense.

8   A successful pitch winds up in a "win," and you've "landed" the account. By the end of the week, everyone in the agency has a free box of Grippies and work begins. This is the "honeymoon period."

9   Everybody loves everybody else. You take the factory tour. You eat Grippies till your molars roll. And you attend "focus groups," i.e., meetings between researchers and preselected members of your "target audience," the people you hope will love Grippies.

10   You sit behind a two-way mirror and watch people eat Grippies. You take notes. You start hating the man who scratches the exposed area of his leg between the top of his sock and the bottom of his pants. "Look! He's doing it! He's doing it *again*!" And what you learn in the focus group, you use to build "share," which is the percentage of the population using your *kind* of product that buys yours in particular.

11   It gives you some idea of how large this country is when you realize that if you can raise Forever Glue's .01 share of market (one person per thousand) to .03, Forever Glue will be a dazzling success. So you do the "Nothing lasts like Forever" campaign, complete with "The Big Idea." You find a small town in a depressed area upstate and glue it back together. Brick by brick, clapboard by clapboard, you actually (favorite ad word) glue a town together and restore it in a classic "demo" with "product as hero." You get a corner office and a Tizio lamp.

12   Forever is stickier. Grippies are grippier. But what if your product is "parity," a "me-tooer"? What if it has no "unique selling point" or "exclusivity"? What if the world is not waiting for Mega-Bran, the cereal that tastes like Styrofoam pellets and gets soggy in the bowl?

13   Some folks "make it sing." It's what everybody thinks people in advertising do anyway, as in, "Oh, you're in advertising! You must write jingles!" So you write new words to Bon Jovi's "Never Say Good-bye," only the client doesn't want to spend $2 million for the rights. So you check out the P.D.'s, public domain songs, songs with lapsed copyrights that are at least 75 years old. You just have to hope the Mega-Bran lyrics work to the tune of "Ach, the Moon Climbs High," "Jim Crack Corn," or "Whoopee Ti Yi Yo—Git Along Little Dogies."

14   At last the new Mega-Bran campaign is ready to crawl through all the "loops" in the "approval cycle," from your client's kids to the network's lawyers. Everybody "signs off" on it.

15   In "pretest," you get "rich verbatims"— a lot of people who remember everything about your commercial. You go for it. You shoot a finished "spot." You spend $250,000 on production, "net net," and $3 million on network and uh-oh, nobody buys the bran. Your commercial has failed to generate "trial" and "brand awareness." It's the Edsel of brans.

16   Quick, you do another "execution," a celebrity endorsement using someone with a high "Q" (familiarity and popularity) score. (Bill Cosby has the highest.) You try "image advertising," which says almost nothing, but leaves the viewer feeling good about your product. (Soft drinks do it all the time.)

17   Still, no one remembers Mega-Bran. It's a case of "vampire video"—what people saw in your ad was so strong that it sucked the blood out of your message. The account becomes "shaky." "Doomers and gloomers" worry all over your carpet. They "bail." Bailers are people in a room who sniff out with whom the power lies; whatever that person says, the bailer agrees. The fastest bailer I ever knew was an account man who told me every time he was asked his opinion, he saw his mortgage float in front of his eyes.

18   The account goes from shaky to the ICU. Then it's "out the door." There is no funeral, no period of mourning because every loss presents an opportunity, a chance to roll up your sleeves, grease up your elbow and pitch again.

BODY PARTS

19 Clients like to find "niches" for their products. A niche is a special place no other product can fit. Sometimes you find the niche before you find the product and then you have to find a product to fill the niche you found.

20   Body parts are always good, though by now almost everything has been spoken for. There are still the navel and the philtrum. If you can do "exploratories" and with a little prodding make consumers aware that their philtrums sweat too much, smell funny or have unwanted hair, you're in business. You create a new form of consumer anxiety and cure it in a single stroke. You launch "Creme de Philtrum," with no cream in it, and have "preemptiveness." You're hot.

21   You don't have to go to school to write great copy. The best writers I know wrap fish in *The Elements of Style*. Schools say they can teach it, but you either have it or you don't. It's like perfect pitch, good gums, or being able to sit on the floor with your ankles around your neck. They use language to convince, persuade, and, at its best, educate. They twist and twiddle words and understand their power. They make people do things they hadn't thought of doing before. They make them change.

22   One of the best writers ever had a great line: "The only thing we have to fear is fear itself." It led a whole country out of Depression. Imagine what he could have done with detergent.

TOPICAL CONSIDERATIONS

1. How is the language of advertising a language "without rules"? Can you think of some current ads that illustrate this claim? What rules of grammar or meaning are being broken?

2. According to Volk, the advertiser's word "inspires hope." Do you agree? How do claims of "newness" appeal to the consumer? Have you ever been seduced into buying a product because it was "new" or "improved"? Can you think of any other potent "hope" words?

3. How does the author, who is an advertising copywriter, characterize her profession? Would you want to be an ad writer? Why or why not?

4. What strategies do ad writers resort to if their "product" is 'parity,' " if it has no 'unique selling point'?

5. What special power of advertising does Volk's hypothetical "Creme de Philtrum" illustrate? Can you think of any real products that this might describe?

6. Why does Volk say, "You don't have to go to school to write great copy"?

RHETORICAL CONSIDERATIONS

1. Volk says that the language of advertising has no rules. How well does she illustrate this assertion in her essay? Can you think of other examples?

2. How would you characterize Volk's attitude toward advertising claims?

3. Throughout the essay, Volk resorts to ad-industry jargon highlighted in quotation marks. What would you say her purpose is here? How do you evaluate her attitude toward the jargon? What do you think of some of the expressions? Do any strike you as particularly amusing?

4. Explain the effectiveness of the final paragraph. What point is being made? How does the paragraph summarize the theme of the essay? How consistent is her tone here with the rest of the piece?

WRITING ASSIGNMENTS

1. Can you think of any ads whose claims particularly irritate you? What bothers you about them?

2. Volk says that there is "limitless power" in the words of advertising because what is being sold is hope. Select a familiar ad and write a paper analyzing how its language—verbal and visual—inspires hope.

3. Has this essay in any way changed your attitude toward advertising? Has it sensitized you to the power of advertising language? Has it made you more wary of the claims in ads? Discuss the article's effect on you in an essay.

4. Would you like to be a professional copywriter? In an essay, explain why you would or would not want to write ad copy for a living.

5. Volk provides an inside look at the business of copywriting. Write an essay in which you examine her essay in terms of Lutz's "With These Words I Can Sell You Anything" and George Will's "Printed Noise." Do you suppose Volk agrees with the attitudes toward advertising as presented by Lutz and Will? How does her piece either reinforce or refute them?

4 | THE LANGUAGE OF POLITICS

"I have a brief statement, a clarification, and two denials."

Political language is power. Language that gets things done, influences governmental policy and action, identifies the dominant values of the moment, wins votes. Language that is capable of making war, peace, and presidents. But political language also reflects the political needs of its users at particular times. Thus, it has a reputation for being flexible and ambiguous. Or worse, evasive and irresponsible, often shifting to guarantee some policy's or policymaker's survival. That shiftiness is what has created Americans' traditional distrust of politicians. The essays in this chapter explore the various ways in which political language persuades while it undermines values.

PROPAGANDA: HOW IT BENDS LANGUAGE

The first selection, "How to Detect Propaganda," is a famous piece of language analysis. It was composed in 1937 by members of the former Institute for Propaganda Analysis, which monitored the various kinds of political propaganda that circulated before and during World War II. With its objective examination of the particular rhetorical devices that constitute propaganda, this selection acts as an introduction to the rest of the pieces in this chapter and a tool to understanding any language of manipulation.

POLITICAL DOUBLE TALK: HOW IT BENDS MINDS

The next three essays pick up where the IPA leaves off—they examine how political language can bend minds. The essay "Politics and the English Language" is the classic reminder that those who control language hold the power. This is George Orwell's famous attack on the rhetoric of politicians, what he called "the defense of the indefensible"—the double talk, pious platitudes, and hollow words of those who twist the native tongue to political advantage. In "Words Matter," Anthony Lewis worries about the social dangers of angry political rhetoric. While defending the constitutional right of free speech, Lewis says that Americans cannot be indifferent to the right-wing rhetoric of leaders who play on fear and hatred. On the lighter side, "Everyspeech," by former presidential speech writer Robert Yoakum is a parody of typical campaign rhetoric. It embodies many of the devices and formulas flagged by the IPA and George Orwell. And rounding out this cluster is the poem "next to of course god america i," by e. e. cummings. While not a typical campaign speech like Yoakum's, cummings' satirical sonnet might be seen as the everyspeech of chauvinistic windbags.

CASE STUDY: WARSPEAK

The case studies in this section focus on "warspeak"—that is, the highly charged language of war. The discussions move historically from examination of the rhetoric that fed the fires of Nazi Germany, to the Cold War, the Vietnam War, and finally the Persian Gulf War. In "Dehumanizing People and Euphemizing War," Haig Bosmajian reminds us that the Nazi efforts to exterminate the Jews began with language. Labels of "parasites" and "vermin" made it easier to justify mass slaughter. Applying Orwell's litmus to the rhetoric of Ronald Reagan's administration, Bosmajian demonstrates how the language that cast nuclear warheads as "peacemakers" and Russia as an "evil empire" invited hostility and aggression, not compromise and peace. Today Mr. Reagan and his Soviet counterparts are out of office; and thankfully, East–West threats are at last behind us. But the hostilities of the world persist. So do the warnings from history: Find the right metaphors, and any moral obstacle can be overcome.

While Ronald Reagan was president, and the threat of a nuclear war with the "evil Empire" was still real, Carol Cohn spent a year in a nuclear defense industry environment, made up exclusively of men who intellectualized about nuclear deterrence and the feasibility of fighting a nuclear war. There she learned the sexy, playful lingo that helped the users forget they were talking about mass murder. As she explains in "Wars, Wimps and Women: Talking Gender," she also learned how gender assumptions—that is, assumptions about how men and women are supposed to behave—embedded in contemporary English had long structured national security discourse. These assumptions, she explains, also dictated battle policy in the Persian Gulf War.

Although the Persian Gulf War lasted only six weeks in 1991, it contributed many expressions to our lexicon. In "When Words Go to War," columnist Bella English examines some of the choice examples of what might be called *Gulfspeak*—those "marvels of militarisms, euphemisms and acronyms" that came out of the Pentagon as well as Baghdad. Although it has been over seven years since the Gulf War was fought, analysts are still trying to make sense of such a complex achievement. And one way is through the language of metaphors. In his essay "Eleven Ways of Looking at the Gulf War," Arthur Asa Berger reviews the many schemas people have used to comprehend this edited-for-television war in the Gulf.

How to detect propaganda

Institute for Propaganda Analysis

During the late 1930s, as today, political propaganda was rife, both in the United States and abroad. In 1937, Clyde R. Miller of Columbia University founded the Institute for Propaganda Analysis to expose propaganda circulating at the time. With the backing of several prominent businesspeople, the Institute continued its mission for nearly five years, publishing various pamphlets and monthly bulletins to reveal its findings. The following essay is a chapter from one of its pamphlets. It presents a specific definition of propaganda, with an analysis of seven common devices necessary to bend the truth—and minds—to political causes.

1   If American citizens are to have clear understanding of present-day conditions and what to do about them, they must be able to recognize propaganda, to analyze it, and to appraise it.

2   But what is propaganda?

3   As generally understood, *propaganda is expression of opinion or action by individuals or groups deliberately designed to influence opinions or actions of other individuals or groups with reference to predetermined ends.* Thus propaganda differs from scientific analysis. The propagandist is trying to "put something across," good or bad, whereas the scientist is trying to discover truth and fact. Often the propagandist does not want careful scrutiny and criticism; he wants to bring about a specific action. Because the action may be socially beneficial or socially harmful to millions of people, it is necessary to focus upon the propagandist and his activities the searchlight of scientific scrutiny. Socially desirable propaganda will not suffer from such examination, but the opposite type will be detected and revealed for what it is.

4   We are fooled by propaganda chiefly because we don't recognize it when we see it. It may be fun to be fooled but, as the cigarette ads used to say, it is

more fun to know. We can more easily recognize propaganda when we see it if we are familiar with the seven common propaganda devices. These are:

1. The Name Calling Device
2. The Glittering Generalities Device
3. The Transfer Device
4. The Testimonial Device
5. The Plain Folks Device
6. The Card Stacking Device
7. The Band Wagon Device

5   Why are we fooled by these devices? Because they appeal to our emotions rather than to our reason. They make us believe and do something we would not believe or do if we thought about it calmly, dispassionately. In examining these devices, note that they work most effectively at those times when we are too lazy to think for ourselves; also, they tie into emotions which sway us to be "for" or "against" nations, races, religions, ideals, economic and political policies and practices, and so on through automobiles, cigarettes, radios, toothpastes, presidents, and wars. With our emotions stirred, it may be fun to be fooled by these propaganda devices, but it is more fun and infinitely more to our own interests to know how they work.

6   Lincoln must have had in mind citizens who could balance their emotions with intelligence when he made this remark " . . . but you can't fool all of the people all of the time."

NAME CALLING

7   "Name Calling" is a device to make us form a judgment without examining the evidence on which it should be based. Here the propagandist appeals to our hate and fear. He does this by giving "bad names" to those individuals, groups, nations, races, policies, practices, beliefs, and ideals which he would have us condemn and reject. For centuries the name "heretic" was bad. Thousands were oppressed, tortured, or put to death as heretics. Anybody who dissented from popular or group belief or practice was in danger of being called a heretic. In the light of today's knowledge, some heresies were bad and some were good. Many of the pioneers of modern science were called heretics; witness the cases of Copernicus, Galileo, Bruno. Today's bad names include: Facist, demagogue, dictator, Red, financial oligarchy, Communist, muckraker, alien, outside agitator, economic royalist, Utopian, rabble-rouser, troublemaker, Tory, Constitution-wrecker.

8   "Al" Smith called Roosevelt a Communist by implication when he said in his Liberty League speech, "There can be only one capital, Washington or Moscow." When "Al" Smith was running for the presidency many called him a tool of the Pope, saying in effect, "We must choose between Washington and

Rome." That implied that Mr. Smith, if elected President, would take his orders from the Pope. Likewise Mr. Justice Hugo Black has been associated with a bad name, Ku Klux Klan. In these cases some propagandists have tried to make us form judgments without examining essential evidence and implications. "Al Smith is a Catholic. He must never be President." "Roosevelt is a Red. Defeat his program." "Hugo Black is or was a Klansman. Take him out of the Supreme Court."

9   Use of "bad names" without presentation of their essential meaning, without all their pertinent implications, comprises perhaps the most common of all propaganda devices. Those who want to *maintain the status quo* apply bad names to those who would change it. . . . Those who want to *change the status quo* apply bad names to those who would maintain it. For example, the *Daily Worker* and the *American Guardian* apply bad names to conservative Republicans and Democrats.

GLITTERING GENERALITIES

10   "Glittering Generalities" is a device by which the propagandist identifies his program with virtue by use of "virtue words." Here he appeals to our emotions of love, generosity, and brotherhood. He uses words like truth, freedom, honor, liberty, social justice, public service, the right to work, loyalty, progress, democracy, the American way, Constitution-defender. These words suggest shining ideals. All persons of good will believe in these ideals. Hence the propagandist, by identifying his individual group, nation, race, policy, practice, or belief with such ideals, seeks to win us to his cause. As Name Calling is a device to make us form a judgment to *reject and condemn* without examining the evidence, Glittering Generalities is a device to make us *accept and approve* without examining the evidence.

11   For example, use of the phrases, "the right to work" and "social justice," may be a device to make us accept programs for meeting labor-capital problems which, if we examined them critically, we would not accept at all.

12   In the Name Calling and Glittering Generalities devices, words are used to stir up our emotions and to befog our thinking. In one device "bad words" are used to make us mad; in the other "good words" are used to make us glad.

13   The propagandist is most effective in the use of these devices when his words make us create devils to fight or gods to adore. By his use of the "bad words," we personify as a "devil" some nation, race, group, individual, policy, practice, or ideal; we are made fighting mad to destroy it. By use of "good words," we personify as a godlike idol some nation, race, group, etc. Words which are "bad" to some are "good" to others, or may be made so. Thus, to some the New Deal is "a prophecy of social salvation" while to others it is "an omen of social disaster."

14   From consideration of names, "bad" and "good," we pass to institutions and symbols, also "bad" and "good." We see these in the next device.

TRANSFER

15 "Transfer" is a device by which the propagandist carries over the authority, sanction, and prestige of something we respect and revere to something he would have us accept. For example, most of us respect and revere our church and our nation. If the propagandist succeeds in getting church or nation to approve a campaign in behalf of some program, he thereby transfers its authority, sanction, and prestige to that program. Thus we may accept something which otherwise we might reject.

16   In the Transfer device, symbols are constantly used. The cross represents the Christian Church. The flag represents the nation. Cartoons like Uncle Sam represent a consensus of public opinion. Those symbols stir emotions. At their very sight, with the speed of light, is aroused the whole complex of feelings we have with respect to church or nation. A cartoonist by having Uncle Sam disapprove a budget for unemployment relief would have us feel that the whole United States disapproves relief costs. By drawing an Uncle Sam who approves the same budget, the cartoonist would have us feel that the American people approve it. Thus the Transfer device is used both for and against causes and ideas.

TESTIMONIAL

17 The "Testimonial" is a device to make us accept anything from a patent medicine or a cigarette to a program of national policy. In this device the propagandist makes use of testimonials. "When I feel tired, I smoke a Camel and get the grandest 'lift.' " "We believe the John L. Lewis plan of labor organization is splendid; C.I.O. should be supported." This device works in reverse also; counter-testimonials may be employed. Seldom are these used against commercial products like patent medicines and cigarettes, but they are constantly employed in social, economic, and political issues. "We believe that the John L. Lewis plan of labor organization is bad; C.I.O. should not be supported."

PLAIN FOLKS

18 "Plain Folks" is a device used by politicians, labor leaders, businessmen, and even by ministers and educators to win our confidence by appearing to be people like ourselves—"just plain folks among the neighbors." In election years especially do candidates show their devotion to little children and the common, homey things of life. They have front porch campaigns. For the newspaper men they raid the kitchen cupboard, finding there some of the good wife's apple pie. They go to country picnics; they attend service at the old frame church, they pitch hay and go fishing; they show their belief in home

and mother. In short, they would win our votes by showing that they're just as common as the rest of us—"just plain folks"—and, therefore, wise and good. Businessmen often are "plain folks" with the factory hands. Even distillers use the device. "It's our family's whiskey, neighbor; and neighbor, it's your price."

CARD STACKING

19 "Card Stacking" is a device in which the propagandist employs all the arts of deception to win our support for himself, his group, nation, race, policy, practice, belief, or ideal. He stacks the cards against the truth. He uses under-emphasis and over-emphasis to dodge issues and evade facts. He resorts to lies, censorship, and distortion. He omits facts. He offers false testimony. He creates a smoke screen of clamor by raising a new issue when he wants an embarrassing matter forgotten. He draws a red herring across the trail to confuse and divert those in quest of facts he does not want revealed. He makes the unreal appear real and the real appear unreal. He lets half-truth masquerade as truth. By the Card Stacking device, a mediocre candidate, through the "build-up," is made to appear an intellectual titan; an ordinary prize fighter, a probable world champion; a worthless patent medicine, a beneficent cure. By means of this device propagandists would convince us that a ruthless war of aggression is a crusade for righteousness. Some member nations of the Non-Intervention Committee send their troops to intervene in Spain. Card Stacking employs sham, hypocrisy, effrontery.

THE BAND WAGON

20 The "Band Wagon" is a device to make us follow the crowd, to accept the propagandist's program en masse. Here his theme is: "Everybody's doing it." His techniques range from those of medicine show to dramatic spectacle. He hires a hall, fills a great stadium, marches a million men in parade. He employs symbols, colors, music, movement, all the dramatic arts. He appeals to the desire, common to most of us, to "follow the crowd." Because he wants us to "follow the crowd" in masses, he directs his appeal to groups held together by common ties of nationality, religion, race, environment, sex, vocation. Thus propagandists campaigning for or against a program will appeal to us as Catholics, Protestants, or Jews; as members of the Nordic race or as Negroes; as farmers or as school teachers; as housewives or as miners. All the artifices of flattery are used to harness the fears and hatreds, prejudices, and biases, convictions and ideals common to the group; thus emotion is made to push and pull the group on to the Band Wagon. In newspaper article and in the spoken word this device is also found. "Don't throw your vote away. Vote for our candidate. He's sure to win." Nearly every candidate wins in every election—before the votes are in.

PROPAGANDA AND EMOTION

21 Observe that in all these devices our emotion is the stuff with which propagandists work. Without it they are helpless; with it, harnessing it to their purposes, they can make us glow with pride or burn with hatred, they can make us zealots in behalf of the program they espouse. As we said at the beginning, propaganda as generally understood is expression of opinion or action by individuals or groups with reference to predetermined ends. Without the appeal to our emotion—to our fears and to our courage, to our selfishness and unselfishness, to our loves and to our hates—propagandists would influence few opinions and few actions.

22   To say this is not to condemn emotion, an essential part of life, or to assert that all predetermined ends of propagandists are "bad." What we mean is that the intelligent citizen does not want propagandists to utilize his emotions, even to the attainment of "good" ends, without knowing what is going on. He does not want to be "used" in the attainment of ends he may later consider "bad." He does not want to be gullible. He does not want to be fooled. He does not want to be duped, even in a "good" cause. He wants to know the facts and among these is included the fact of the utilization [of] his emotions.

23   Keeping in mind the seven common propaganda devices, turn to today's newspapers and almost immediately you can spot examples of them all. At election time or during any campaign, Plain Folks and Band Wagon are common. Card Stacking is hardest to detect because it is adroitly executed or because we lack the information necessary to nail the lie. A little practice with the daily newspapers in detecting these propaganda devices soon enables us to detect them elsewhere—in radio, news-reel, books, magazines, and in expression[s] of labor unions, business groups, churches, schools, political parties.

TOPICAL CONSIDERATIONS

1. Look at the definition of the word *propaganda* in paragraph 3. How many sets of people are involved—how many parties does it take to make propaganda? What are the roles or functions of each set of people?

2. What do the authors think is the best way to make sense of the world: through reason or emotion? What words in paragraphs 5 and 6 prompt you to select one way over the other?

3. Supply an example of the way emotion overrides reason for each of the seven common propaganda devices the authors identify.

4. Can you supply "bad names" from your own experience as a student? Some examples to get you started might include "geek," "nerd," and "teacher's pet" to refer to students; you can probably think of some generic terms for teachers as well. Compare these terms to the definition for propaganda. Do you think these terms qualify as propaganda?

5. How are name calling and glittering generalities similar devices? How are they different? What do the authors of the document say? What additional features can you find?

6. How do transfer, testimonial, and plain folks devices all make use of power or prestige to influence our thinking? Can you think of something or someone you respect that could be used as a propaganda device—for example, a major sports event such as the Superbowl or a football hero?

7. What is a countertestimonial? (Look up the word *testimonial* in your dictionary if this term is not clear to you.) How does use of John L. Lewis's name function as both testimonial and countertestimonial?

8. Give examples of times in your life when you have used the card stacking or band wagon devices to try to get something you wanted—such as permission from a parent, or an excused absence from a teacher.

RHETORICAL CONSIDERATIONS

1. Take another look at the definition of the word *propaganda*. Do you think it's a good definition? Are any important principles of definition violated?

2. What is the difference between "the propagandist" and "the scientist" in paragraph 3? What is their relationship to "truth and fact"? What is their relationship to each other? What is their relationship to the language they use?

3. What is "socially desirable propaganda"? Can you give examples from your own experience? Do you think that socially desirable propaganda uses the same devices that the authors of this article identify? Consider the "safe-sex" campaigns you've been exposed to.

4. What is the difference between a "bad name," as the authors describe it in the section "Name Calling," and a racial, ethnic, gender-based, or other kind of slur? For example, what is the difference between calling someone a Communist and calling someone a nigger? between calling someone an atheist and a queer?

5. Why do you think the authors use the stilted device of placing the sentence subject *after* the verb, instead of before, in the following two cases? "At their very sight, with the speed of light, is aroused the whole complex of feelings . . . " (paragraph 16), and "In election years especially do candidates show their devotion to little children . . . " (paragraph 18).

6. In the section "Propaganda and Emotion," do you find any places where the authors of this article might be criticized for using propaganda devices? Do you think this article itself functions as propaganda?

7. Who do you think the audience for this pamphlet was? What kinds of people was it written for—scientists? propagandists? professors? What did the authors assume about readers' lifestyles, reading skills, and values?

WRITING ASSIGNMENTS

1. Based on your understanding of the whole article, and on class discussion, develop your own definition of "propaganda." Make sure you define each key term that you use.

2. Following the suggestions set down in the final paragraph of this essay, collect examples of propaganda from at least five different sources. Examine them; then, describe in a paper what devices they use. How do the creators of each kind of

propaganda show that they are aware of their audience's emotions? What emotions do they appeal to? How much "truth and fact" do they seem to rely on?

3. Research and collect newspaper articles on an election—a race for student government on your campus, a recent town or state proposition, or even a national election. Be sure to collect a handful of articles from at least two major candidates, or from two sides of the issue. What propaganda devices did each side use? Which side won? How much of a role do you think propaganda played in deciding the outcome?

4. Do you think the authors of this article would advocate getting rid of all propaganda? Why, or why not? Be sure to include a discussion of what propaganda is, and what function or role it serves.

5. Compare this article to those by William Lutz ("With These Words, I Can Sell You Anything") and by Charles O'Neill ("The Language of Advertising") in Chapter 3. How are Lutz's "weasel words" similar to the propagandist's attempts to appeal to emotion that the Institute's authors identify? Do you think the Institute's authors would agree with O'Neill that the propaganda of advertising uses language in a way that is special or different from everyday language?

POLITICS AND THE ENGLISH LANGUAGE

George Orwell

George Orwell was a novelist, an essayist, and one of the most important social critics of the century. In 1945, he wrote a brilliant political satire, *Animal Farm;* and in 1949, his famous nightmare vision of a totalitarian state, *1984,* first appeared. This essay parallels the basic themes in Orwell's bitter attacks against the social forces that endanger free thought and truth. But this time he warns of a different kind of repression—that of language. Political rhetoric, he explains, is the enemy of truth and the cause of linguistic degeneration. Although the essay was written in 1945, the targets still exist, and the criticism is still valid.

1   Most people who bother with the matter at all would admit that the English language is in a bad way, but it is generally assumed that we cannot by conscious action do anything about it. Our civilization is decadent and our language—so the argument runs—must inevitably share in the general collapse. It follows that any struggle against the abuse of language is a sentimental archaism, like preferring candles to electric light or hansom cabs to aeroplanes. Underneath this lies the half-conscious belief that language is a natural growth and not an instrument which we shape for our own purposes.

2   Now, it is clear that the decline of a language must ultimately have political and economic causes: it is not due simply to the bad influence of this or that individual writer. But an effect can become a cause, reinforcing the original cause and producing the same effect in an intensified form, and so on indefinitely. A man may take to drink because he feels himself to be a failure, and then fail all the more completely because he drinks. It is rather the same thing that is happening to the English language. It becomes ugly and inaccurate because our thoughts are foolish, but the slovenliness of our language makes it easier for us to have foolish thoughts. The point is that the process is reversible. Modern English, especially written English, is full of bad habits which spread by imitation and which can be avoided if one is willing to take

the necessary trouble. If one gets rid of these habits one can think more clearly, and to think clearly is a necessary first step towards political regeneration: so that the fight against bad English is not frivolous and is not the exclusive concern of professional writers. I will come back to this presently, and I hope that by that time the meaning of what I have said here will have become clearer. Meanwhile, here are five specimens of the English language as it is now habitually written.

3   These five passages have not been picked out because they are especially bad—I could have quoted far worse if I had chosen—but because they illustrate various of the mental vices from which we now suffer. They are a little below the average, but are fairly representative samples. I number them so that I can refer back to them when necessary:

> 1. I am not, indeed, sure whether it is not true to say that the Milton who once seemed not unlike a seventeenth-century Shelley had not become, out of an experience ever more bitter in each year, more alien [sic] to the founder of that Jesuit sect which nothing could induce him to tolerate.
>
> PROFESSOR HAROLD LASKI (ESSAY IN FREEDOM OF EXPRESSION)

> 2. Above all, we cannot play ducks and drakes with a native battery of idioms which prescribes such egregious collocations of vocables as the Basic *put up with* for *tolerate* or *put at a loss* for *bewilder.*
>
> PROFESSOR LANCELOT HOGBEN (INTERGLOSSA)

> 3. On the one side we have the free personality: by definition it is not neurotic, for it has neither conflict nor dream. Its desires, such as they are, are transparent, for they are just what institutional approval keeps in the forefront of consciousness; another institutional pattern would alter their number and intensity, there is little in them that is natural, irreducible, or culturally dangerous. But *on the other side,* the social bond itself is nothing but the mutual reflection of these self-secure integrities. Recall the definition of love. Is not this the very picture of a small academic? Where is there a place in this hall of mirrors for either personality or fraternity?
>
> ESSAY ON PSYCHOLOGY IN POLITICS (NEW YORK)

> 4. All the "best people" from the gentlemen's clubs, and all the frantic fascist captains, united in common hatred of Socialism and bestial horror of the rising tide of the mass revolutionary movement, have turned to acts of provocation, to foul incendiarism, to medieval legends of poisoned wells, to legalize their own destruction of proletarian organizations, and rouse the agitated petty-bourgeoisie to chauvinistic fervor on behalf of the fight against the revolutionary way out of the crisis.
>
> COMMUNIST PAMPHLET

> 5. If a new spirit is to be infused into this old country, there is one thorny and contentious reform which must be tackled, and that is the humanization and galvanization of the B.B.C. Timidity here will bespeak canker and atrophy of the soul. The heart of Britain may be sound and of strong beat, for instance, but the British lion's roar at present is like that of Bottom in Shakespeare's *Midsummer Night's Dream*—as gentle as any sucking dove. A virile new Britain cannot continue indefinitely to be traduced in the eyes, or rather ears, of the world by the effete languors of Langham Place, brazenly masquerading as "standard English." When the Voice of Britain is heard at nine o'clock, better far and infinitely less ludicrous to hear

aitches honestly dropped than the present priggish, inflated, inhibited, school-ma'amish arch braying of blameless bashful mewing maidens!

LETTER IN TRIBUNE

4   Each of these passages has faults of its own, but, quite apart from avoidable ugliness, two qualities are common to all of them. The first is staleness of imagery; the other is lack of precision. The writer either has a meaning and cannot express it, or he inadvertently says something else, or he is almost indifferent as to whether his words mean anything or not. This mixture of vagueness and sheer incompetence is the most marked characteristic of modern English prose, and especially of any kind of political writing. As soon as certain topics are raised, the concrete melts into the abstract and no one seems able to think of turns of speech that are not hackneyed: prose consists less and less of *words* chosen for the sake of their meaning, and more and more of *phrases* tacked together like the sections of a prefabricated hen-house. I list below, with notes and examples, various of the tricks by means of which the work of prose-construction is habitually dodged:

DYING METAPHORS

5   A newly invented metaphor assists thought by evoking a visual image, while on the other hand a metaphor which is technically "dead" (e.g., *iron resolution*) has in effect reverted to being an ordinary word and can generally be used without loss of vividness. But in between these two classes there is a huge dump of worn-out metaphors which have lost all evocative power and are merely used because they save people the trouble of inventing phrases for themselves. Examples are: *Ring the changes on, take up the cudgels for, toe the line, ride roughshod over, stand shoulder to shoulder with, play into the hands of, no axe to grind, grist to the mill, fishing in troubled waters, on the order of the day, Achilles' heel, swan song, hotbed.* Many of these are used without knowledge of their meaning (what is a "rift," for instance?), and incompatible metaphors are frequently mixed, a sure sign that the writer is not interested in what he is saying. Some metaphors now current have been twisted out of their original meaning without those who use them even being aware of the fact. For example, *toe the line* is sometimes written *tow the line.* Another example is *the hammer and the anvil,* now always used with the implication that the anvil gets the worst of it. In real life it is always the anvil that breaks the hammer, never the other way about: a writer who stopped to think what he was saying would be aware of this, and would avoid perverting the original phrase.

OPERATORS OR VERBAL FALSE LIMBS

6   These save the trouble of picking out appropriate verbs and nouns, and at the same time pad each sentence with extra syllables which give it an appearance of symmetry. Characteristic phrases are *render inoperative, militate against,*

make contact with, be subjected to, give rise to, give grounds for, have the effect of, play a leading part (role) in, making itself felt, take effect, exhibit a tendency to, serve the purpose of, etc., etc. The keynote is the elimination of simple verbs. Instead of being a single word, such as *break, stop, spoil, mend, kill,* a verb becomes a *phrase,* made up of a noun or adjective tacked on to some general-purpose verb such as *prove, serve, form, play, render.* In addition, the passive voice is wherever possible used in preference to the active, and noun constructions are used instead of gerunds (*by examination of* instead of *by examining*). The range of verbs is further cut down by means of the *-ize* and *de-* formations, and the banal statements are given an appearance of profundity by means of the *not un-* formation. Simple conjunctions and prepositions are replaced by such phrases as *with respect to, having regard to, the fact that, by dint of, in view of, in the interests of, on the hypothesis that;* and the ends of sentences are saved from anticlimax by such resounding common places as *greatly to be desired, cannot be left out of account, a development to be expected in the near future, deserving of serious consideration, brought to a satisfactory conclusion,* and so on and so forth.

PRETENTIOUS DICTION

7   Words like *phenomenon, element, individual* (as noun), *objective, categorical, effective, virtual, basic, primary, promote, constitute, exhibit, exploit, utilize, eliminate, liquidate,* are used to dress up simple statements and give an air of scientific impartiality to biased judgments. Adjectives like *epoch-making, epic, historic, unforgettable, triumphant, age-old, inevitable, inexorable, veritable,* are used to dignify the sordid processes of international politics, while writing that aims at glorifying war usually takes on an archaic color, its characteristic words being: *realm, throne, chariot, mailed fist, trident, sword, shield, buckler, banner, jackboot, clarion.* Foreign words and expressions such as *cul de sac, ancien régime, deus ex machina, mutatis mutandis, status quo, gleichschaltung, weltanschauung,* are used to give an air of culture and elegance. Except for the useful abbreviations *i.e., e.g.,* and *etc.,* there is no real need for any of the hundreds of foreign phrases now current in English. Bad writers, and especially scientific, political and sociological writers, are nearly always haunted by the notion that Latin or Greek words are grander than Saxon ones, and unnecessary words like *expedite, ameliorate, predict, extraneous, deracinated, clandestine, subaqueous* and hundreds of others constantly gain ground from their Anglo-Saxon opposite numbers.[1] The jargon peculiar to Marxist writing

---

[1]An interesting illustration of this is the way in which the English flower names which were in use till very recently are being ousted by Greek ones, *snapdragon* becoming *antirrhinum, forget-me-not* becoming *myosotis,* etc. It is hard to see any practical reason for this change of fashion; it is probably due to an instinctive turning-away from the more homely word and a vague feeling that the Greek is scientific.

(hyena, hangman, cannibal, petty bourgeois, these gentry, lacquey, flunkey, mad dog, White Guard, etc.) consists largely of words and phrases translated from Russian, German, or French; but the normal way of coining a new word is to use a Latin or Greek root with the appropriate affix and, where necessary, the *-ize* formation. It is often easier to make up words of this kind (*deregionalize, impermissible, extramarital, non-fragmentary* and so forth) than to think up the English words that will cover one's meaning. The result, in general, is an increase in slovenliness and vagueness.

MEANINGLESS WORDS

8   In certain kinds of writing, particularly in art criticism and literary criticism, it is normal to come across long passages which are almost completely lacking in meaning.[2] Words *like romantic, plastic, values, human, dead, sentimental, natural, vitality,* as used in art criticism, are strictly meaningless, in the sense that they not only do not point to any discoverable object, but are hardly ever expected to do so by the reader. When one critic writes, "The outstanding feature of Mr. X's work is its living quality," while another writes, "The immediately striking thing about Mr. X's work is its peculiar deadness," the reader accepts this as a simple difference of opinion. If words like *black* and *white* were involved, instead of the jargon words *dead* and *living,* he would see at once that language was being used in an improper way. Many political words are similarly abused. The word *Fascism* has now no meaning except in so far as it signifies "something not desirable." The words *democracy, socialism, freedom, patriotic, realistic, justice,* have each of them several different meanings which cannot be reconciled with one another. In the case of a word like *democracy,* not only is there no agreed definition, but the attempt to make one is resisted from all sides. It is almost universally felt that when we call a country democratic we are praising it: consequently the defenders of every kind of regime claim that it is a democracy, and fear that they might have to stop using the word if it were tied down to any one meaning. Words of this kind are often used in a consciously dishonest way. That is, the person who used them has his own private definition, but allows his hearer to think he means something quite different. Statements like *Marshal Pétain was a true patriot, The Soviet Press is the freest in the world, The Catholic Church is opposed to persecution,* are almost always made with intent to deceive. Other

---

[2]Example: "Comfort's catholicity of perception and image, strangely Whitmanesque in range, almost the exact opposite in aesthetic compulsion, continues to evoke that trembling atmospheric accumulative hinting at a cruel, an inexorably serene timelessness. . . . Wrey Gardiner scores by aiming at simple bull's-eyes with precision. Only they are not so simple, and through this contented sadness runs more than the surface bittersweet of resignation." (*Poetry Quarterly*)

words used in variable meanings, in most cases more or less dishonestly, are: *class, totalitarian, science, progressive, reactionary, bourgeois, equality.*

9   Now that I have made this catalogue of swindles and perversions, let me give another example of the kind of writing that they lead to. This time it must of its nature be an imaginary one. I am going to translate a passage of good English into modern English of the worst sort. Here is a well-known verse from *Ecclesiastes:*

> I returned and saw under the sun, that the race is not to the swift, nor the battle to the strong, neither yet bread to the wise, nor yet riches to men of understanding, nor yet favour to men of skill; but time and chance happeneth to them all.

Here it is in modern English:

> Objective consideration of contemporary phenomena compels the conclusion that success or failure in competitive activities exhibits no tendency to be commensurate with innate capacity, but that a considerable element of the unpredictable must invariably be taken into account.

10   This is a parody, but not a very gross one. Exhibit (3), above, for instance, contains several patches of the same kind of English. It will be seen that I have not made a full translation. The beginning and ending of the sentence follow the original meaning fairly closely, but in the middle the concrete illustrations—race, battle, bread—dissolve into the vague phrase "success or failure in competitive activities." This had to be so, because no modern writer of the kind I am discussing—no one capable of using phrases like "objective consideration of contemporary phenomena"—would ever tabulate his thoughts in that precise and detailed way. The whole tendency of modern prose is away from concreteness. Now analyse these two sentences a little more closely. The first contains forty-nine words but only sixty syllables, and all its words are those of everyday life. The second contains thirty-eight words of ninety syllables; eighteen of its words are from Latin roots, and one from Greek. The first sentence contains six vivid images, and only one phrase ("time and chance") that could be called vague. The second contains not a single fresh, arresting phrase, and in spite of its ninety syllables it gives only a shortened version of the meaning contained in the first. Yet without a doubt it is the second kind of sentence that is gaining ground in modern English. I do not want to exaggerate. This kind of writing is not yet universal, and outcrops of simplicity will occur here and there in the worst-written page. Still, if you or I were told to write a few lines on the uncertainty of human fortunes, we should probably come much nearer to my imaginary sentence than to the one from *Ecclesiastes.*

11   As I have tried to show, modern writing at its worst does not consist in picking out words for the sake of their meaning and inventing images in order to make the meaning clearer. It consists in gumming together long strips of words which have already been set in order by someone else, and making the

results presentable by sheer humbug. The attraction of this way of writing is that it is easy. It is easier—even quicker, once you have the habit—to say *In my opinion it is not an unjustifiable assumption that* than to say *I think.* If you use ready-made phrases, you not only don't have to hunt about for words; you also don't have to bother with the rhythms of your sentences, since these phrases are generally so arranged as to be more or less euphonious. When you are composing in a hurry—when you are dictating to a stenographer, for instance, or making a public speech—it is natural to fall into a pretentious, Latinized style. Tags like *a consideration which we should do well to bear in mind* or *a conclusion to which all of us would readily assent* will save many a sentence from coming down with a bump. By using stale metaphors, similes and idioms, you save much mental effort, at the cost of leaving your meaning vague, not only for your reader but for yourself. This is the significance of mixed metaphors. The sole aim of a metaphor is to call up a visual image. When these images clash—as in *The Fascist octopus has sung its swan song, the jackboot is thrown into the melting pot*—it can be taken as certain that the writer is not seeing a mental image of the objects he is naming; in other words he is not really thinking. Look again at the examples I gave at the beginning of this essay: Professor Laski (1) uses five negatives in fifty-three words. One of these is superfluous, making nonsense of the whole passage, and in addition there is the slip *alien* for *akin,* making further nonsense, and several avoidable pieces of clumsiness which increase the general vagueness. Professor Hogben (2) plays ducks and drakes with a battery which is able to write prescriptions, and, while disapproving of the everyday phrase *put up with,* is unwilling to look *egregious* up in the dictionary and see what it means; (3), if one takes an uncharitable attitude towards it, is simply meaningless; probably one could work out its intended meaning by reading the whole of the article in which it occurs. In (4), the writer knows more or less what he wants to say, but an accumulation of stale phrases chokes him, like tea leaves blocking a sink. In (5), words and meaning have almost parted company. People who write in this manner usually have a general emotional meaning—they dislike one thing and want to express solidarity with another—but they are not interested in the detail of what they are saying. A scrupulous writer, in every sentence that he writes, will ask himself at least four questions, thus: What am I trying to say? What words will express it? What image or idiom will make it clearer? Is this image fresh enough to have an effect? And he will probably ask himself two more: Could I put it more shortly? Have I said anything that is avoidably ugly? But you are not obliged to go to all this trouble. You can shirk it by simply throwing your mind open and letting the ready-made phrases come crowding in. They will construct your sentences for you—even think your thoughts for you, to a certain extent—and at need they will perform the important service of partially concealing your meaning even from yourself. It is at this point that the special connection between politics and the debasement of language becomes clear.

12   In our time it is broadly true that political writing is bad writing. Where it is not true, it will generally be found that the writer is some kind of rebel, expressing his private opinions and not a "party line." Orthodoxy, of whatever color, seems to demand a lifeless, imitative style. The political dialects to be found in pamphlets, leading articles, manifestos, White Papers and the speeches of undersecretaries do, of course, vary from party to party, but they are all alike in that one almost never finds in them a fresh, vivid, home-made turn of speech. When one watches some tired hack on the platform mechanically repeating the familiar phrases—*bestial atrocities, iron heel, blood-stained tyranny, free peoples of the world, stand shoulder to shoulder*—one often has a curious feeling that one is not watching a live human being but some kind of dummy: a feeling which suddenly becomes stronger at moments when the light catches the speaker's spectacles and turns them into blank discs which seem to have no eyes behind them. And this is not altogether fanciful. A speaker who uses that kind of phraseology has gone some distance towards turning himself into a machine. The appropriate noises are coming out of his larynx, but his brain is not involved as it would be if he were choosing his words for himself. If the speech he is making is one that he is accustomed to make over and over again, he may be almost unconscious of what he is saying, as one is when one utters the responses in church. And this reduced state of consciousness, if not indispensable, is at any rate favorable to political conformity.

13   In our time, political speech and writing are largely the defence of the indefensible. Things like the continuance of British rule in India, the Russian purges and deportations, the dropping of the atom bombs on Japan, can indeed be defended, but only by arguments which are too brutal for most people to face, and which do not square with the professed aims of political parties. Thus political language has to consist largely of euphemism, question-begging and sheer cloudy vagueness. Defenceless villages are bombarded from the air, the inhabitants driven out into the countryside, the cattle machine-gunned, the huts set on fire with incendiary bullets: this is called *pacification*. Millions of peasants are robbed of their farms and sent trudging along the roads with no more than they can carry: this is called *transfer of population* or *rectification of frontiers*. People are imprisoned for years without trial, or shot in the back of the neck or sent to die of scurvy in Arctic lumber camps; this is called *elimination of unreliable elements*. Such phraseology is needed if one wants to name things without calling up mental pictures of them. Consider for instance some comfortable English professor defending Russian totalitarianism. He cannot say outright, "I believe in killing off your opponents when you can get good results by doing so." Probably, therefore, he will say something like this:

14   "While freely conceding that the Soviet régime exhibits certain features which the humanitarian may be inclined to deplore, we must, I think, agree that a certain curtailment of the right to political opposition is an unavoidable

concomitant of transitional periods, and that the rigors which the Russian people have been called upon to undergo have been amply justified in the sphere
of concrete achievement."

15   The inflated style is itself a kind of euphemism. A mass of Latin words falls
upon the facts like soft snow, blurring the outlines and covering up all the details. The great enemy of clear language is insincerity. When there is a gap between one's real and one's declared aims, one turns as it were instinctively to
long words and exhausted idioms, like a cuttlefish squirting out ink. In our age
there is no such thing as "keeping out of politics." All issues are political issues, and politics itself is a mass of lies, evasions, folly, hatred and schizophrenia. When the general atmosphere is bad, language must suffer. I should expect to find—this is a guess which I have not sufficient knowledge to
verify—that the German, Russian and Italian languages have all deteriorated
in the last ten or fifteen years, as a result of dictatorship.

16   But if thought corrupts language, language can also corrupt thought. A bad
usage can spread by tradition and imitation, even among people who should
and do know better. The deposed language that I have been discussing is in
some ways very convenient. Phrases like *a not unjustifiable assumption, leaves
much to be desired, would serve no good purpose, a consideration which we
should do well to bear in mind,* are a continuous temptation, a packet of as-
pirins always at one's elbow. Look back through this essay, and for certain you
will find that I have again and again committed the very faults I am protesting
against. By this morning's post I have received a pamphlet dealing with conditions in Germany. The author tells me that he "felt impelled" to write it. I
open it at random and here is almost the first sentence that I see: "[The Allies]
have an opportunity not only of achieving a radical transformation of Germany's social and political structure in such a way as to avoid a nationalistic reaction in Germany itself, but at the same time of laying the foundations of a
co-operative and unified Europe." You see, he "feels impelled" to write—
feels, presumably, that he has something new to say—and yet his words, like
cavalry horses answering the bugle, group themselves automatically into the
familiar dreary pattern. This invasion of one's mind by ready-made phrases
(*lay the foundations, achieve a radical transformation*) can only be prevented
if one is constantly on guard against them, and every such phrase anaes-
thetizes a portion of one's brain.

17   I said earlier that the decadence of our language is probably curable.
Those who deny this would argue, if they produced an argument at all, that
language merely reflects existing social conditions, and that we cannot influence its development by any direct tinkering with words and constructions. So far as the general tone or spirit of a language goes, this may be
true, but it is not true in detail. Silly words and expressions have often disappeared, not through any evolutionary process but owing to the conscious
action of a minority. Two recent examples were *explore every avenue* and
leave no stone unturned, which were killed by the jeers of a few journalists.

There is a long list of flyblown metaphors which could similarly be got rid of if enough people would interest themselves in the job, and it should also be possible to laugh the *not un-* formation out of existence,[3] to reduce the amount of Latin and Greek in the average sentence, to drive out foreign phrases and strayed scientific words, and, in general, to make pretentiousness unfashionable. But all these are minor points. The defence of the English language implies more than this, and perhaps it is best to start by saying what it does *not* imply.

18   To begin with it has nothing to do with archaism, with the salvaging of obsolete words and turns of speech, or with the setting up of a "standard English" which must never be departed from. On the contrary, it is especially concerned with the scrapping of every word or idiom which has outworn its usefulness. It has nothing to do with correct grammar and syntax, which are of no importance so long as one makes one's meaning clear, or with the avoidance of Americanisms, or with having what is called a "good prose style." On the other hand it is not concerned with fake simplicity and the attempt to make written English colloquial. Nor does it even imply in every case preferring the Saxon word to the Latin one, though it does imply using the fewest and shortest words that will cover one's meaning. What is above all needed is to let the meaning choose the word, and not the other way about. In prose, the worst thing one can do with words is to surrender to them. When you think of a concrete object, you think wordlessly, and then, if you want to describe the thing you have been visualizing you probably hunt about till you find the exact words that seem to fit it. When you think of something abstract you are more inclined to use words from the start, and unless you make a conscious effort to prevent it, the existing dialect will come rushing in and do the job for you, at the expense of blurring or even changing your meaning. Probably it is better to put off using words as long as possible and get one's meaning as clear as one can through pictures or sensations. Afterwards one can choose—not simply *accept*—the phrases that will best cover the meaning, and then switch round and decide what impression one's words are likely to make on another person. This last effort of the mind cuts out all stale or mixed images, all prefabricated phrases, needless repetitions, and humbug and vagueness generally. But one can often be in doubt about the effect of a word or a phrase, and one needs rules that one can rely on when instinct fails. I think the following rules will cover most cases:

1. Never use a metaphor, simile or other figure of speech which you are used to seeing in print.

2. Never use a long word where a short one will do.

3. If it is possible to cut a word out, always cut it out.

---

[3]One can cure oneself of the *not un-* formation by memorizing this sentence: *A not unblack dog was chasing a not unsmall rabbit across a not ungreen field.*

4. Never use the passive where you can use the active.

5. Never use a foreign phrase, a scientific word or a jargon word if you can think of an everyday English equivalent.

6. Break any of these rules sooner than say anything outright barbarous.

These rules sound elementary, and so they are, but they demand a deep change of attitude in anyone who has grown used to writing in the style now fashionable. One could keep all of them and still write bad English, but one could not write the kind of stuff that I quoted in those five specimens at the beginning of this article.

19   I have not here been considering the literary use of language, but merely language as an instrument for expressing and not for concealing or preventing thought. Stuart Chase and others have come near to claiming that all abstract words are meaningless, and have used this as a pretext for advocating a kind of political quietism. Since you don't know what Fascism is, how can you struggle against Fascism? One need not swallow such absurdities as this, but one ought to recognize that the present political chaos is connected with the decay of language, and that one can probably bring about some improvement by starting at the verbal end. If you simplify your English, you are freed from the worst follies of orthodoxy. You cannot speak any of the necessary dialects, and when you make a stupid remark its stupidity will be obvious, even to yourself. Political language—and with variations this is true of all political parties, from Conservatives to Anarchists—is designed to make lies sound truthful and murder respectable, and to give an appearance of solidity to pure wind. One cannot change this all in a moment, but one can at least change one's own habits, and from time to time one can even, if one jeers loudly enough, send some worn-out and useless phrase—some *jackboot, Achilles' heel, hotbed, melting pot, acid test, veritable inferno* or other lump of verbal refuse—into the dustbin where it belongs.

TOPICAL CONSIDERATIONS

1. Orwell argues that modern writers are destroying the English language. Explain some of the ways in which they are doing so.

2. What is a *euphemism?* Orwell cites "pacification" as an example from World War II (paragraph 14). Try to find some euphemisms that came out of the Persian Gulf War. Name and explain some of the euphemisms common in business today.

3. Orwell lists six rules at the end of the essay (paragraph 18). What does he mean by the last rule?

4. Toward the end of the essay, Orwell writes, "Look back through this essay, and for certain you will find that I have again and again committed the very faults I am protesting against" (paragraph 16). Where in the essay has he broken his own rules?

5. Does Orwell seem to criticize one end of the political spectrum more than the other? Support your answer.

RHETORICAL CONSIDERATIONS

1. Reread the first four paragraphs. What kind of personality does Orwell project— reasonable, honest, condescending, cynical? Explain your answer.

2. Orwell begins his arguments by citing five writers. How does he use these references throughout the essay?

3. Is there any emotional appeal in this essay? If so, what is it and how is it created?

4. Exactly where in the essay does Orwell begin to talk about politics and the English language? Why does he start his discussion there?

WRITING ASSIGNMENTS

1. Orwell gives five examples of bad writing from his own day. Have things changed much since then? Compile your own list from current newspapers, magazines, and books. How do your findings compare with Orwell's?

2. Orwell takes a passage from *Ecclesiastes* and "translates" it to illustrate bad writing by his contemporaries. Do the same with a different passage from the Bible or an excerpt from a poem or novel. Use some of the same techniques the author does.

3. Some of the most stunning examples of bloated political language come from campaign speeches. And we seem to hear them all the time, since in the United States we are never far from an election year, major or minor. Find a campaign speech from either a local or national figure and go through it trying to detect examples of the kinds of political double talk Orwell discusses. How does the speech sound without them? Write up your findings in an essay.

4. Have you ever been the victim of political propaganda? Have you ever voted for something or someone (or would have were you not under age) because of a campaigner's persuasive political language, or given to a cause for the same reason? Write an account of your experience, and try to explain how the language influenced you.

5. Try creating some political gobbledygook of your own. Imagine you're running for office—president, senator, mayor, school committee members, dog catcher, president of your class, or whatever. Using some of the features and tricks of political language Orwell discusses, write a campaign speech outlining why you, and not your opponent, should be elected.

6. Using at least three different kinds of biographical sources (such as a biographical dictionary, an encyclopedia, and a literary biography), prepare a report on the personal experiences and the political events that seem to have shaped Orwell's views on the English language. What ideals or attitudes about language prompted him to write this article? What kinds of political consequences did he attach to language use?

7. Read (or reread) one of the political satires mentioned in the headnote to this article: either *Animal Farm* or *1984*. How does language create power for the rulers in the novel? What kinds of power does Orwell think language can have? Examine what literary critics have said, by researching articles about the novel with reference tools such as the Modern Language Association bibliography, *Contemporary Literary Criticism*, or the *Dictionary of Literary Biography*.

WORDS MATTER

Anthony Lewis

Is there a connection between political language and acts of political violence? Specifically, was there a connection between the rhetoric of hate propagated by talk-radio personalities and the Oklahoma City bombing? or between the angry outbursts of fanatic antiabortionists and recent deadly attacks on abortion clinics? If such links exist, asks Anthony Lewis, how do we as a nation justify granting freedom of speech to the vocal proponents of hate-mongering and violence? His answer challenges us not to resort to the suppression of speech but rather to respond to it.

Anthony Lewis is a columnist for the *New York Times* where this essay first appeared in May 1995, a month after the bombing of the Murrah Federal Building in Oklahoma City.

1   When the courts held that American Nazis had a constitutional right to march through the streets of Skokie, Illinois, freedom of speech was the more secure for all of us. But it did not follow that we should be indifferent to the hateful message of the Nazis. To the contrary.

2   The First Amendment gives us responsibility along with freedom: the responsibility to answer propagators of hate. As Justice Brandeis put it, arguing against the suppression of bad speech, "The fitting remedy for evil counsels is good ones."

3   The Oklahoma City bombing has made us think again about hateful speech and how to deal with it. The country has learned a good deal about the paranoid ravings of "militia" groups and such radio spokesmen as Mark Koernke of Michigan. ("Death to the new world order!") G. Gordon Liddy has defended as perfectly reasonable his radio advice on how to kill Federal agents if they come at you. ("Shoot twice to the body, center of mass.")

4   Few other societies, even the most democratic, would permit such murderous talk. We do, and we should not change, but we ought to worry about it.

5   The more interesting question is the responsibility not of the crazies but of major leaders of opinion for the consequences of their angry words. Newt Gingrich and Rush Limbaugh bristled at the suggestion that their rhetoric had something to do with Oklahoma City, and of course it did not in any direct sense. But what about the climate that their words helped to create?

6   Over many years now right-wing politicians have demonized their opponents as un-American, treasonous, peculiar. The tactic was invented by

Richard Nixon and Joseph McCarthy. An example of its recent use was Mr. Gingrich's statement just before the election last fall that Democrats are "the enemy of normal Americans."

7   Anyone who thinks such words have had no effect is ignorant of political history. Even more significant lately has been the demonization of the Federal Government. The drumbeat of right-wing rhetoric in the last few years has been Washington as the enemy, the inhuman monster. Has that no connection with the rise of groups that claim Federal agents are about to descend on them in black helicopters? (A new member of the House, Helen Chenoweth of Idaho, has actually parroted those lunatic claims.)

8   Or think about the anti-abortion fanatics. They preach that every abortion is murder. Yet when some enthusiast for that view actually executes a doctor as a murderer, the preachers disavow responsibility.

9   Abortion is not some trivial issue. Attacks on clinics and doctors are a dangerous phenomenon in this country—and in no other. The Christian Coalition and other extreme opponents of abortion have such a strangehold on the Republican Party that Senator Bob Dole feels he has to please them by keeping the nomination of Dr. Henry Foster as Surgeon General off the floor of the Senate.

10   Pat Robertson, leader of the Christian Coalition, is very likely the country's most effective demagogue. He tells his followers that a satanic conspiracy started centuries ago by European bankers (with Jewish names) was behind Lincoln's assassination and is now trying to crush Americans under a "new world order." Do those words have no consequences?

11   Rush Limbaugh thinks it is cute to refer to people with whose views he disagrees as "feminazis." In a climate of calculated hate for The Other, how can we expect to have the civil discourse that is the mechanism of Madisonian democracy?

12   In France, Jean-Marie Le Pen is a figure of the extreme right: the political opponent of conservatives. In the United States today, many who call themselves conservatives are indistinguishable from Le Pen.

13   The underlying premise of so much right-wing rhetoric here, as of Le Pen in France, is that America has been undermined, subverted, ruined. And people believe it. When Richard L. Berke of the *New York Times* talked to voters last fall, many said things were terrible here; some said they couldn't stand it and were going to emigrate. What country were they talking about?

14   We cherish freedom of speech. But we can defend that freedom and still hold accountable leaders who play on fear and hatred. Words matter.

TOPICAL CONSIDERATIONS

1. In Lewis's opinion, was the U.S. Supreme Court's decision that Nazis should be permitted to march, and thereby to broadcast their hateful messages about racial exclusivity, a good one? Why or why not? What does he say the effect was for all Americans, including those who do not feel strongly about the Nazis or their opponents?

2. What does Justice Brandeis's statement mean, that "The fitting remedy for evil counsels is good ones"? What is a "counsel"? Try to translate this aphorism into a more contemporary sentence.

3. Does Lewis agree or disagree that people had the right to bomb the federal building in Oklahoma City (paragraphs 3 and 4)? Does he agree or disagree that people had the right to speak about murdering federal agents? Where does he draw the line between what is permissible and what is not? How can you tell what his views are?

4. What kinds of actions does Lewis say hateful speech can lead to (paragraphs 5–7)? How does he say hateful speech can lead to actions—that is, when and how does permissible free speech become impermissible action? How does Lewis believe that hateful speech should be dealt with?

5. Why does Lewis find "the anti-abortion fanatics" irresponsible when they claim that abortion is murder (paragraphs 8 and 9)? How does this claim help to create a climate in which the murder of a doctor who performs abortions seems justified? Do you agree with Lewis's claims about people who oppose abortion? Why or why not? Justify your answer.

6. Although Lewis disagrees with the views of Pat Robertson, Rush Limbaugh, and others, why does he believe that the American system of democracy that permits them to speak freely is preferable to any other government? What does he warn Americans that they must do if they wish to maintain this superior system of government?

RHETORICAL CONSIDERATIONS

1. Lewis uses loaded words to indicate the ideas and speakers with which he disagrees: for example, he calls the words of paramilitary group members "paranoid ravings." How many other examples of biased language can you find? Which words or phrases do you think are appropriate descriptions? Which ones do you think are unfairly prejudiced?

2. Why do you think Lewis refers to so many public figures and events? How effective is his assumption that readers will understand all his references? How reliable would his opinions sound if they were based on personal stories?

3. How convincing do you find Lewis's claim that hateful speech creates a "climate" in which disastrously harmful actions are more likely to take place? If you do not find this cause-and-effect sequence convincing, what additional evidence would you need to agree with Lewis's ideas?

4. Lewis uses four rhetorical questions in this essay (in paragraphs 5, 7, 11, and 13). What effect do these rhetorical questions have? What do they prompt readers to think about? Do you think this is an effective device for Lewis to use, or would you rather have seen more discussion about the issues he is referring to in these places?

5. What is the tone of this article? List specific examples of words and phrases that help you identify tone. How does Lewis use the tone of this essay to provide an example of the kinds of "good counsels" that he believes are an appropriate remedy for "evil counsels"?

WRITING ASSIGNMENTS

1. Have there been instances on your high school or college campus, or in your place of employment, when you think that free speech has been unfairly restricted? If so, write a letter to the editor of a school newspaper, an in-house newsletter, or a local paper that expresses your views about why such speech should not be restricted.

2. If you are unfamiliar with the names and events that Lewis cites, look up the details of each reference. Prepare a set of footnotes or a glossary that other students could use to familiarize themselves with the issues raised by each reference. Make sure that you use paraphrase, quote, and citation appropriately to set down the main ideas from your sources without committing unintentional plagiarism.

3. Look up the national newspaper reports and editorials that were prompted by the Supreme Court decision on the Nazis' right to march in Skokie, Illinois. (You might want to examine Chicago papers first to obtain specific dates and local commentary.) What were the arguments against allowing this march? What were the arguments for allowing it? In your opinion, which side presents the stronger case? Do you think that either allowing or forbidding the march was the best choice— or can you think of or locate a compromise that you believe would have been preferable?

EVERYSPEECH

Robert Yoakum

In this piece, writer Robert Yoakum serves up an amusing parody of political speech. The familiar phrases, the barbs of sarcasm, the idle promises, and more, are prominent in campaigns whether candidates seek the office of town selectman or the American presidency. As you read, try to identify obvious attempts to demonize the opponent and generalizations that oversimplify complex issues. Find examples of speech that flatters or inflames the audience. And consider, how this speech differs from any you have heard during recent political campaigns.

Robert Yoakum wrote speeches for John F. Kennedy's 1960 campaign. His essay below first appeared in the *New York Times* in November 1994.

1   Ladies and gentlemen. I am delighted to see so many friends from the Third Congressional District. And what better site for some straight talk than at this greatest of all state fairs, where ribbons reward American individual enterprise, whether for the biggest beets or the best bull?

2   Speaking of bull, my opponent has said some mighty dishonest things about me. But what can you expect from a typical politician? I want to address some fundamental issues that set me apart from my opponent and his failed party— the party of gutlessness and gridlock.

3   The American people are ready for straight talk, although don't count on the press to report it straight. The press, like my opponent, has no respect for the public.

4   This democracy must return to its roots or it will perish, and its roots are you—the honest, hard-working, God-fearing people who made this the greatest nation on earth. Yes, we have problems. But what problems would not be solved if the press and politicians had faith in the people?

5   Take crime, for example. Rampant, brutal crime. My rival in this race believes that redemption and rehabilitation are the answer to the lawlessness that is tearing our society apart.

6   Well, if R and R is what you want for those robbers and rapists, don't vote for me. If pampering the punks is what you want, vote for my opponent.

7   Do I believe in the death penalty? You bet! Do I believe in three strikes and you're out? No, I believe in *two* strikes and you're out! I believe in three strikes and you're *dead!*

8   You can count on me to crack down on crime, but I won't ignore the other

big C word: character. Character made our nation great. Character, and re-spect for family values. A belief in children and parents. In brothers and sis-ters and grandparents.

9   Oh, sure, that sounds corny. Those cynical inside-the-Beltway journalists will ridicule me tomorrow, but I would rather be guilty of a corny defense of family values than of coddling criminals.

10   While I'm making myself unpopular with the press and a lot of politicians, I might as well alienate even more Washington wimps by telling you frankly how I feel about taxes. I'm against them! Not just in an election year, like my adversary, but every year!

11   I'm in favor of slashing wasteful welfare, which is where a lot of your hard-earned tax dollars go. The American people have said "enough!" to welfare, but inside the Beltway they don't give a hoot about the industrious folks I see before me today. They're too busy with their cocktail parties, diplomatic func-tions and society balls.

12   My opponent loves those affairs, but I'd rather be with my good friends here than with those fork-tongued lawyers, cookie-pushing State Department fops and high-priced lobbyists. I promise that when elected, my main office will be right here in the Third District. My branch office will be in D.C. And I promise you this: I shall serve only two terms and then return to live with the folks I love.

13   So on Nov. 8, if you want someone with an independent mind and the courage to change—*to change back to good old American values*—if you've had enough and want someone tough, vote for me. Thank you, and God bless America.

TOPICAL CONSIDERATIONS

1. What is the event at which this speech is given? Why is it a fitting venue? What state might it be? What is special about the time of year at which the speech is presented?

2. The speaker says that he will "address some fundamental issues." Does the speaker do what he says he will do in addressing issues? (What does it mean to "address issues"?) What does he say about the two biggest issues, crime and taxes? How do you feel about his stance on these issues? What might be the au-thor's intention here?

3. How well does the speaker define the term "character" in paragraph 8? How well does he define the term "family values"? What exactly has he said about these two qualities?

4. Could this be a real speech? Why or why not? Explain your answer. What phrases, claims, promises, and accusations from this speech have you heard before?

RHETORICAL CONSIDERATIONS

1. How does the speaker try to make his opponent in this political race look like a poor choice for voters? What kinds of events does he say the opponent prefers?

What kinds of underhanded things does he accuse his opponent of doing? What attitude does he imply his opponent holds about politics? How does the speaker use these implications to make himself look like a good choice for voters?

2. Why does the discussion of character and family values fall between the speaker's discussion of crime and taxes? How does it work to defuse possible objections that listeners might have to some of the specific comments the speaker has made? For instance, if you don't believe in the death penalty, how might you feel as you read the material in paragraph 7? How would you feel after paragraph 8?

3. What kind of language does this speaker use to describe politicians and those associated with them (e.g., lobbyists and people who work for the State Department)? Why is he so harsh in condemning people he works and associates with every day? Does he create a convincing amount of distance between himself and the other Washington, D.C., Beltway insiders? Why or why not? Justify your answer.

4. What does the abbreviation "R and R" refer to, in the context of the speech? (Look at paragraph 5.) How does the speaker use the similarity to the conventional abbreviation "rest and relaxation" to help build his case? Do you think this is a fair and appropriate use of the allusion? Why or why not?

5. This speaker makes great use of alliteration, repetition of beginning consonant sounds (e.g., "the biggest beets or the best bull"). Identify at least five instances of alliteration from different parts of this speech. What is the effect of this device? Why do you think the speaker uses it so much?

WRITING ASSIGNMENTS

1. Using the cues in this speech, write a biography of this candidate that he might include in a campaign brochure. Include (inventing where you need to) details such as where he went to college, family background, marital status, sexual orientation, race, age, party affiliation, disability status, and so on. Once you have written this biography, rewrite it from his opponent's perspective. What details did you change? Where did you use some of the strategies that the speaker employed to tear down his opponent's image?

2. Choose three pretty but empty phrases from this speech. Then, find three comparable phrases in the e. e. cummings poem in this section. Compare the effect of these phrases in each piece. In which piece did the phrases sound more hollow? Justify your answer, discussing the devices used to create (or hide) this effect.

3. Find a recent political speech in print version. (Be sure you get a copy of the text of the whole speech, or most of it. Avoid a reporter's second-hand discussion about what the politician said.) How many of the meaningless tricks that you located in this piece can you find in the actual speech? Were they effective tricks on first reading? Why or why not? Justify your answer.

NEXT TO OF COURSE GOD AMERICA I

e.e. cummings

Edward Estlin Cummings (1894–1962) was born in Cambridge, Massachusetts and educated at Harvard. As an ambulance driver during World War I, he was seized on a mistaken charge and held for three months in a French detention camp. (The experience is described in his novel, *The Enormous Room* [1922]). After the war, he returned to Paris to study painting and to write poetry. Later he resettled in New York City. From his first book of poems, *Tulips and Chimneys* (1923) to his death, cummings constantly experimented with language and typography. Yet for all the idiosyncrasies and playfulness of his poems, cummings wrote about traditional matters. He unremittingly defended the ideals of love and individualism; at the same time, he satirized materialism, pomp, and conventionality.

In the following poem, "next to of course god america i," the poet turns the traditional sonnet form into a satire on the rhetoric and attitudes of patriotism.

"next to of course god america i
love you land of the pilgrims' and so forth oh
say can you see by the dawn's early my
country 'tis of centuries come and go
5 and are no more what of it we should worry
in every language even deafanddumb
thy sons acclaim your glorious name by gorry
by jingo by gee by gosh by gum
why talk of beauty what could be more beaut-
10 iful than these heroic happy dead
who rushed like lions to the roaring slaughter
they did not stop to think they died instead
then shall the voice of liberty be mute?"
He spoke. And drank rapidly a glass of water

QUESTIONS FOR DISCUSSION

1. What is the situation in which this speech seems to be given? How can you tell?
2. Read the poem aloud. Was it smooth and easy reading? Explain. Where do you hesitate, and why?
3. What is the speaker saying in this speech? What is the poet saying in this poem?
4. What is the message of "and so forth" in line 2? What does it say about the speaker?
5. How many clichés can you find here? How many are "patriotic"?
6. Why does the last line of the poem (after the speech has been given) sound awkward? What is the standard word order here? What does this subtle awkwardness reflect about the speaker?
7. How does the speaker describe death during the war? How would you feel if your boyfriend, father, or son were killed—and his death were described this way?
8. Do you think the poet would agree with the speaker in this speech, about how patriotic it is to die for your country? Why or why not?

WRITING ASSIGNMENTS

1. Find a copy of the material that your school sent you when you first contacted them about enrolling. Choose a passage of several short paragraphs that describe the school, and rewrite it in the style of the speech given in this poem. See how many clichés and confusing sentences you can pack into your rewritten edition of your school's promotional material. Then swap your rewritten version with a classmate—see if you can identify exactly what the original passage was that your classmate has rewritten.
2. Review the article "How to Detect Propaganda" at the beginning of this section. Identify one example of each of the seven common devices the article describes. Explain how the example you have chosen matches the description in the article.
3. Find political speeches from a recent campaign, either local or national. (One good source is the periodical *Vital Speeches*, which includes speeches given by members of Congress). Select one and identify all the euphemisms and clichéd phrasing that you can. What effect does the intended audience for each piece seem to have on the amount of euphemism you find? Were there some euphemisms that seemed appropriate and tactful?
4. Find articles from different news sources that discuss the same recent catastrophe—an airline crash, a highway pileup, an earthquake, or something that resulted in many deaths. Do the same as for question 3—that is, identify all the euphemisms and clichés you can in each article. Then compare and contrast your findings—how many euphemisms did you find in each source? What effect does the intended audience for each piece seem to have on the amount of euphemism you find? Were there some euphemisms that seemed appropriate and tactful?

DEHUMANIZING PEOPLE AND EUPHEMIZING WAR

Haig A. Bosmajian

The following essay was inspired by "Politics and the English Language." Haig Bosmajian examines some of the indefensible language that came out of Nazi Germany 60 years ago—language that helped remove the moral obstacles to the extermination of millions of people. He then makes some comparisons with the rhetoric and "jokes" that came out of Ronald Reagan's presidency. Bosmajian concludes that things have not changed much since Orwell warned against those who use words to defend the indefensible. Although Mr. Reagan is out of office and the Cold War is over, this essay serves as a reminder that in our dangerous world, language is still the mightier weapon—the one that precedes the bullet.

Haig Bosmajian is a professor of speech communication at the University of Washington in Seattle and a recipient of the George Orwell Award, presented by the National Council of Teachers of English, for his book *The Language of Oppression*. This essay first appeared in the *Christian Century*, in December 1984.

1   In his definitive work *The Destruction of the European Jews* (Quadrangle, 1961), Raul Hilberg presents some insights that are as relevant to the United States today as they were to Nazi Germany a half-century ago. If we believe that we must remember the tragedies of history so that we will not repeat them, we ought to pay special attention to Hilberg's assertion that

> in a Western society, destructive activity is not just a technocratic phenomenon. The problems arising in a destructive process are not only administrative but also psychological. A Christian is commanded to choose good and to reject evil. The greater his destructive task, therefore, the more potent are the moral obstacles in his way. These obstacles must be removed—the internal conflict must somehow be resolved. One of the principal means through which the perpetrator will attempt to

clear his conscience is by clothing his victim in a mantle of evil, by portraying the victim as an object that must be destroyed.

2   Hilberg's observations apply equally to today's nuclear age, when destroying one's "enemy" carries with it the possibility that one may kill most of humankind and devastate the earth in the process. To remove the moral obstacles to such a course, leaders, both political and religious, euphemize killing and the weapons of destruction and dehumanize the potential victims in order to justify their extermination.

3   In his novel *1984* and in his famous essay "Politics and the English Language," George Orwell warns against those who use words to defend the indefensible. He contends that our language "becomes ugly and inaccurate because our thoughts are foolish, but the slovenliness of our language makes it easier for us to have foolish thoughts." Some ugly and foolish thoughts expressed in slovenly language were put forth by President Ronald Reagan when, during a 1982 conference with some eastern Caribbean leaders, he called Marxism a "virus"; when, in 1983, he labeled the Soviet Union an "evil empire," telling the assembled National Association of Evangelicals in Orlando, Florida, that communism "is the focus of evil in the modern world" and that "we are enjoined by Scripture and the Lord Jesus to oppose it with all our might"; and when, while conferring in 1984 with 19 conservative and religious leaders, he vowed to fight the "communist cancer."

4   When the president takes us into a metaphoric world where his language invites extermination of the "enemy," he clothes the "victim in a mantle of evil, by portraying [him or her] as an object that must be destroyed" (*The Destruction of the European Jews*). A virus, a cancer, and an evil empire all invite destruction and extermination.

5   When the persecution of the Jews began in Nazi Germany a half-century ago, Jews were labeled a "disease" or "parasites"; Hitler talked of the "Jewish bacilli" and the "demon of Communism." This metaphoric language was essential for dehumanizing the "enemy." Defining people as microorganisms and as subhuman made it easier to justify their extermination. As Richard Grunberger points out in *Twelve-Year Reich: A Social History of Nazi Germany* (Holt, Rinehart & Winston, 1971), "the incessant official demonization of the Jew gradually modified the consciousness even of naturally humane people," so that the populace became indifferent to Jewish suffering, "not because it occurred in war time and under conditions of secrecy, but because Jews were astronomically remote and not real people."

6   We cannot, therefore, dismiss Reagan's language as mere political hyperbole. Linguistically, the president's metaphors for defining the "enemy" are frightfully similar to the Nazis' dehumanizing terms for Jews, communists and other "un-Germans." To some, the metaphors may appear to be harmless stylistic devices used by government officials to emphasize a point of view or an argument; they may appear as oratorical ornaments. However, such metaphoric language is

more than ornament, affecting people's conceptual systems and thought processes, influencing how they perceive others, and determining their political views and behavior.

7   Unfortunately, dehumanizing metaphors carry some plausibility, for they allow the expression of aggressive sentiments and attitudes. Belligerent metaphors' functions and effects can readily be understood when one compares their use to that of Reagan's "aggressive" jokes. When during the microphone testing episode in August 1984, the president declared, "My fellow Americans, I'm pleased to tell you today that I've signed legislation that will outlaw Russia forever. We begin bombing in five minutes," this "joke" allowed him to express in an acceptable way the unacceptable view that millions of human beings—Russian children, women and men—ought to be killed and their nation destroyed. The metaphors and jokes permit the speaker to imply brutally hostile sentiments and thoughts which, if stated directly, would be considered coarse and inhumane.

8   When Ronald Reagan was asked whether homosexuals should be barred from public office in the United States, he replied jokingly that they should certainly "be barred from the department of beaches and parks." He was, of course, "just kidding." When he stated that "we [were] told four years ago that 17 million people went to bed hungry every night. Well, that was probably true. They were all on a diet," he was, of course, "just kidding." The metaphors and jokes allow audiences to cheer language that, at another level, expresses destructive aggression against the "enemies": Marxists, homosexuals, the hungry poor.

9   Dehumanizing metaphors are more than just figures of speech; they affect our thoughts and behavior. "The trouble with metaphors is that they have a strong pull on our fancy. Then tend to run away with us. Then we find that our thinking is directed, not by the force of the argument at hand, but by the interest in the image in our mind," says philosopher Monroe Beardsley (*Thinking Straight* [Prentice-Hall, 1965]). The images of Russia as the evil empire and of communism as a virus and a cancer encourage us to take severe measures against them. Such language invites hostility and aggression, not coexistence and compromise.

10   The barriers created by using words that denigrate and dehumanize others are clearly illustrated by the January 1984 "Man of the Year" issue of *Time* magazine. On the cover, Reagan and Andropov stand back to back. The first paragraph of the lead article begins "In the beginning were the words," the second paragraph, "After the words, the walkouts." Using dehumanizing language not only affects our perceptions of the "enemy"; it also affects the "enemy's" perceptions of us. As Seweryn Bialer states, "Among the Soviet elites, who have spent much of their lives manipulating the nuances of ideology, words are taken very seriously. . . . For Soviet leaders and high officials President Reagan's decision to use bellicose language was and is a political fact that amounts to a policy pronouncement" (*New York Review of Books* [February

16, 1984]). In our nuclear age, such misunderstandings may threaten our survival. "The destruction of the Jews was no accident," asserts Hilberg. "When in the early days of 1933 the first civil servant wrote the first definition of a 'non-Aryan' into a civil service ordinance the fate of European Jewry was sealed." Similarly, the destruction of humankind would be no accident; the virus-cancer-evil empire view of reality, coupled with the admonition that Scripture and Jesus Christ authorize us to destroy those so characterized, are but an initial part of a definitional process leading to destruction.

11   Our nation has, of course, always contained people who, needing to denigrate and dehumanize others, have relied on racist and sexist language. Unchallenged, such language has, among other things, given the denigrators power, helping them to keep the subjugated in their place and influencing people's perceptions of those dehumanizingly defined. The power to subjugate that comes with the power to define others is well illustrated not only by the Nazis' characterization of the Jews as bacilli and parasites, but also by the American colonist's and settler's redefinition of the "American Indians." When Columbus arrived in America the native population of what was to become the United States was 1 million; by the late 19th century that population was down to 250,000! To defend the indefensible, the invaders defined the victims as savages, heathens and barbarians. As the New Mexico Supreme Court judges said in an 1896 court opinion, "The idea that a handful of wild, half-naked, thieving, plundering, murdering savages should be dignified with the soverign attributes of nations, enter into solemn treaties . . . is unsuited to the intelligence and justice of this age, or the natural rights of mankind" (United States v. Lucero, 1 N. M. 422, 1896). When such language becomes institutionalized, when it is spoken by judges, religious leaders or presidents, it receives the imprimatur of authorities who have the power and influence to impose their metaphors. In the heat of a political discussion, it is one thing for a private citizen to declare that Marxism is a virus and a cancer that must be destroyed. It is an entirely different thing when the president of the United
12 States uses the same dehumanizing language in public discourse.

Not only is destroying other human beings rationalized and justified through metaphorizing them into creatures, into microorganisms needing to be eradicated, but moral obstacles are also overcome by euphemizing the weapons of destruction and the pain, suffering and death that their use would bring. The brutality and inhumanity of our policies and practices are hidden behind euphemisms. During the Vietnam war, when government officials talked of "regrettable by-products," they meant civilians killed by mistake; "pacification" meant the forcible evacuation of Vietnamese from their huts, the rounding up of all males, the shooting of those who resisted, the slaughtering of domesticated animals and the burning of dwellings; "incursion" meant another invasion of another country; creating a "sanitized belt" meant forcibly removing all the inhabitants of the area being "sanitized," cutting down the trees, bulldozing the land and erecting "defensive positions" with machine guns, mortars and mines.

"By-products," "pacification," "sanitized belts"—such language hides the truth that human beings are dying and families are being destroyed.

13   This past August [1984], Reagan's national security adviser, Robert McFarlane, neutralized and euphemized the horror and inhumanity of war by declaring that America must remain prepared for "low-intensity conflict." In comments prepared for delivery to the Commonwealth Club in San Francisco, McFarlane said, "The use of force can never be our preference or our only choice. It cannot yet be discarded, however, as an instrument of policy. . . . We must be prepared to deal with low-intensity conflict in whatever form it takes." His examples of low-intensity conflicts included the Soviet Union's "risk-taking in Angola, Ethiopia" and other nations. "Rational and resolute management of Western power in the face of Soviet pressure will deter major war," McFarlane concluded (the *Seattle Times,* August 4).

14   "Low-intensity conflicts," "risk-taking," "management of power," "instrument of policy": such language suggests an encounter group dealing with personal problems or a union-management negotiation. One hardly senses that war and killing are being discussed. The destruction of human life has been euphemized through using abstractions. Discussing the language of war, Aldous Huxley focused on the word "force": "The attempt to secure justice, peace and democracy by 'force' seems reasonable enough until we realize, first, that this noncommittal word stands, in the circumstances of our age, for activities which can hardly fail to result in social chaos; and second, that the consequences of social chaos are injustice, chronic warfare and tyranny" (*The Olive Tree* [Harper & Row, 1937]). Huxley's prenuclear concept of the social chaos resulting from using force pales when compared to the probable consequences of a nuclear war.

15   Pentagon documents refer to fighting a nuclear war "over a protracted period" and argue that American nuclear forces "must prevail and be able to force the Soviet Union to seek earliest termination on terms favorable to the United States." The Federal Emergency Management Agency, responsible for civil defense preparations, tells us that "the United States could survive a nuclear attack and then go on to recovery within a relatively few years."

16   What is a "protracted period"? "Protracted" means prolonged, dragged out; does that mean that nuclear weapons would be fired as long as someone were left alive to push the buttons, long after major cities had been destroyed and millions of humans killed? What does it mean to "prevail"? The *American Heritage Dictionary* tells us that it is "to triumph or win a victory." After a protracted nuclear war, it might be difficult to determine who had triumphed amid the massive death and destruction.

17   To say that the "United States could survive a nuclear attack" is ambiguous. "The United States" is an abstraction; in this context, "survive" is an abstraction. Asserting that "the United States could survive" is not the same as saying that its people and other living creatures could survive. What will survive? The military weapons still to be fired by programmed computers? To say that the

"United States could survive" is so ambiguous as to be meaningless, and yet the language gives the impression that life would go on as usual after a nuclear war.

18   Acronyms are still another means used to hide the horrors and the weapons of war. Functioning as euphemisms, they make unpleasant or embarrassing things appear tolerable. This becomes especially evident when we consider some of our everyday acronyms: at one time cancer was the "Big C"; children have "to do a BM"; while "syphilis" may be difficult to utter, "VD" is less of a problem; the "SOB" may hand out a lot of "BS"; "BO" is to be dreaded; and of course we have our "F—" word.

19   Nuclear weapons are called ABMs, SLCMs, MIRVs, and other letters of the alphabet. One reason that "the question of universal death grows stale," Robert Scheer has written, is that the arguments are couched in "terms that pointedly mute just what it is these bombs will do, which is, to start with, to kill the people one loves and nearly everyone else as well." If we seriously are considering using those SLCMs and MIRVs, knowing that they will lead to the killing of the people we love, and if we are willing to consider the possibility of "prevailing" in a "protracted period" of mutual destruction, then how much easier it is to consider exterminating an enemy defined as a cancer, virus or demon.

20   Our political and religious leaders, as well as ordinary citizens, must be persuaded to refrain from dehumanizing people into viruses and cancers residing in an evil empire which Scripture admonishes us to destroy. The euphemisms of war must be exposed for what they are—words and phrases that fool us into accepting the unacceptable. Dehumanizing the "enemy" and euphemizing the weapons of war and war itself is a deadly combination that, unfortunately, has historically been successful in defending the indefensible.

21   A half-century after the Nazis began their persecution of the Jews, a process demanding, in Hilberg's words, that "moral obstacles must be removed—the internal conflicts must somehow be resolved," an American launch-control officer at an Intercontinental Ballistics Missile base, cited in David Barash and Judith Lipton's *Stop Nuclear War* (Grove, 1982), indicated that "we have two tasks: The first is not to let people go off their rockers. That's the negative side. The positive side is to ensure that people act without moral compunction."

TOPICAL CONSIDERATIONS

1. In one sentence summarize Bosmajian's thesis as best as you can.

2. What parallel does the author see between the labeling of Jews as "disease," "parasites," and "bacilli" by the Nazis and the reference to the Soviet Union as an "evil empire" and Communism as "the focus of evil in the world" by President Ronald Reagan?

3. Many people found President Reagan's joke in paragraph 7 funny. Why didn't Bosmajian find this funny? Did you? Why or why not?

4. How do people gain power by using dehumanizing language?

RHETORICAL CONSIDERATIONS

1. What examples of euphemizing the weapons of war and destruction does Bosmajian give?

2. Does Bosmajian end his essay on an optimistic or pessimistic note? Read both the introduction and conclusion before you answer.

WRITING ASSIGNMENTS

1. In paragraph 9, Bosmajian writes: "The images of Russia as the evil empire and of communism as a virus and a cancer encourage us to take severe measures against them. Such language invites hostility and aggression, not coexistence and compromise." Write a paper in which you agree or disagree with this statement.

2. Fashion a list of denigrating labels you have heard in reference to a particular group. Then write an essay explaining how these images may have contributed to the subjugation of that group.

3. Looking back to the Persian Gulf War, do you recall any use of dehumanizing language in reference to Iraqis or other Arabic peoples? If so, what examples can you offer? (You might want to consult past issues of newspapers and magazines.) Do you think such language helped to justify our efforts in the war? Explain.

4. Now consider any denigrating language Iraqis and pro-Iraqi people used to characterize the United States and its allies in the Persian Gulf War. What dehumanizing labels can you offer? How might these have helped nationalize and justify the Iraqi's war against us?

5. Research the words that are used by various contemporary "hate groups": the Ku Klux Klan, white supremacists, and skinheads. Who are their victims? How are they dehumanized? What kinds of labels are used, and how do those labels dehumanize? What kinds of action do they advocate? How does the way they describe the action euphemize, or cover up, what they want to do?

6. Examine several contemporary news stories about conflicts between different ethnic groups—say, African-American and white race relations in the United States, the "ethnic cleansing" conflict in the former Yugoslavia, or tribal conflicts in Africa. Do you find that Bosmajian's observations can be applied to all of these conflicts? Do you think that the process of "dehumanizing people and euphemizing war" is inevitable any time two different groups of people disagree?

Wars, Wimps and Women: Talking Gender and Thinking War

Carol Cohn

After spending a year immersed in the world of defense intellectuals, Carol Cohn discovered that much of the theorizing about conventional and nuclear warfare is conducted in an odd kind of "gender discourse" where human characteristics are polarized according to male and female. According to the codes, *male* is abstract and cool, whereas *female* is concrete and emotional. While her subject matter might seem better suited for the chapter "Language and Sexism," Cohn's analysis points an Orwellian finger at a chilling political practice—one that helped us through the Persian Gulf War.

Carol Cohn is a Senior Research Scholar at the Center for Psychological Studies in the Nuclear Age, an affiliate of the Harvard Medical School. This article first appeared in the collection *Gendering War Talk* (1993), edited by Miriam Cooke and Angela Woollacott.

1   I start with a true story, told to me by a white male physicist:

Several colleagues and I were working on modeling counterforce attacks, trying to get realistic estimates of the number of immediate fatalities that would result from different deployments.[1] At one point, we remodeled a particular attack, using slightly different assumptions, and found that instead of there being thirty-six million immediate fatalities, there would only be thirty million. And everybody was sitting around nodding, saying, "Oh yeah, that's great, only thirty million," when all of a sudden, I *heard* what we were saying. And I blurted out, "Wait, I've just *heard* how we're talking—*Only* thirty million! *Only* thirty million human beings killed instantly?" Silence fell upon the room. Nobody said a word. They didn't even look at me. It was awful. I felt like a woman.

2   The physicist added that henceforth he was careful to never blurt out anything like that again.

3   During the early years of the Reagan presidency, in the era of the Evil Empire, the cold war, and loose talk in Washington about the possibility of fighting and "prevailing" in a nuclear war, I went off to do participant observation
in a community of North American nuclear defense intellectuals and security
affairs analysts—a community virtually entirely composed of white men. They
work in universities, think tanks, and as advisers to government. They theorize
about nuclear deterrence and arms control, and nuclear and conventional war
fighting, about how to best translate military might into political power; in
short, they create the discourse that underwrites American national security
policy. . . . One thing that is clear is that the body of language and thinking
they have generated filters out to the military, politicians, and the public, and
increasingly shapes how we talk and think about war. This was amply evident
during the Gulf War: Gulf War "news," as generated by the military briefers,
reported by newscasters, and analyzed by the television networks' resident security experts, was marked by its use of the professional language of defense
analysis, nearly to the exclusion of other ways of speaking.

4   My goal has been to understand something about how defense intellectuals
think, and why they think that way. Despite the parsimonious appeal of ascrib-
ing the nuclear arms race to "missile envy,"[2] I felt certain that masculinity was
not a sufficient explanation of why men think about war in the ways that they
do. Indeed, I found many ways to understand what these men were doing that
had little or nothing to do with gender.[3] But ultimately, the physicist's story
and others like it made confronting the role of gender unavoidable. Thus, in
this paper I will explore gender discourse, and its role in shaping nuclear and
national security discourse. . . .

5   When I talk about "gender discourse," I am talking not only about words or
language but about a system of meanings, of ways of thinking, images and
words that first shape how we experience, understand, and represent ourselves as men and woman, but that also do more than that; they shape many
other aspects of our lives and culture. In this symbolic system, human characteristics are dichotomized, divided into pairs of polar opposites that are supposedly mutually exclusive: mind is opposed to body; culture to nature;
thought to feeling; logic to intuition; objectivity to subjectivity; aggression to
passivity; confrontation to accommodation; abstraction to particularity; public
to private; political to personal, ad nauseam. In each case, the first term of the
"opposites" is associated with male, the second with female. And in each case,
our society values the first over the second. . . .

6   As gender discourse assigns gender to human characteristics, we can think
of the discourse as something we are positioned *by*. If I say, for example, that a
corporation should stop dumping toxic waste because it is damaging the cre-
ations of mother earth, (i.e., articulating a valuing and sentimental vision of
nature), I am speaking in a manner associated with women, and our cultural
discourse of gender positions me as female. As such I am then associated with
the whole constellation of traits—irrational, emotional, subjective, and so

forth—and I am in the devalued position. If, on the other hand, I say the corporation should stop dumping toxic wastes because I have calculated that it is causing $8.215 billion of damage to eight nonrenewable resources, which should be seen as equivalent to lowering the GDP by 0.15 percent per annum, (i.e., using a rational, calculative mode of thought), the discourse positions me as masculine—rational, objective, logical, and so forth—the dominant, valued position. . . .

7   Let us now return to the physicist who felt like a woman: what happened when he "blurted out" his sudden awareness of the "only thirty million" dead people? First, he was transgressing a code of professional conduct. In the civilian defense intellectuals' world, when you are in professional settings you do not discuss the bloody reality behind the calculations. It is not required that you be completely unaware of them in your outside life, or that you have no feelings about them, but it is required that you do not bring them to the foreground in the context of professional activities. There is a general awareness that you *could not* do your work if you did; in addition, most defense intellectuals believe that emotion and description of human reality distort the process required to think well about nuclear weapons and warfare.

8   So the physicist violated a behavioral norm, in and of itself a difficult thing to do because it threatens your relationships to and your standing with your colleagues.

9   But even worse than that, he demonstrated some of the characteristics on the "female" side of the dichotomies—in his "blurting" he was impulsive, uncontrolled, emotional, concrete, and attentive to human bodies, at the very least. Thus, he marked himself not only as unprofessional but as feminine, and this, in turn, was doubly threatening. It was not only a threat to his own sense of self as masculine, his gender identity, it also identified him with a devalued status—of a woman—or put him in the devalued or subordinate position in the discourse.

10   Thus, both in statement, "I felt like a woman," and his subsequent silence in that and other settings are completely understandable. To have the strength of character and courage to transgress the strictures of both professional and gender codes *and* to associate yourself with a lower status is very difficult. . . .

11   What is it that cannot be spoken? First, any words that express an emotional awareness of the desperate human reality behind the sanitized abstractions of death and destruction—as in the physicist's sudden vision of thirty million rotting corpses. Similarly, weapons' effects may be spoken of only in the most clinical and abstract terms, leaving no room to imagine a seven-year-old boy with his flesh melting away from his bones or a toddler with her skin hanging down in strips. Voicing concern about the number of casualties in the enemy's armed forces, imagining the suffering of the killed and wounded young men, is out of bounds. (Within the military itself, it is permissible, even desirable, to attempt to minimize immediate civilian casualties if it is possible to do so without compromising military objectives, but as we learned in the Persian Gulf War, this is only an extremely limited enterprise; the planning

and precision of military targeting does not admit of consideration of the cost in human lives of such actions as destroying power systems, or water and sewer systems, or highways and food distribution systems.)[4] Psychological effects—on the soldiers fighting the war or on the citizens injured, or fearing for their own safety, or living through tremendous deprivation, or helplessly watching their babies die from diarrhea due to the lack of clean water—all of these are not to be talked about.

12   But it is not only particular subjects that are out of bounds. It is also tone of voice that counts. A speaking style that is identified as cool, dispassionate, and distanced is required. One that vibrates with the intensity of emotion almost always disqualifies the speaker, who is heard to sound like "a hysterical housewife."

13   What gets left out, then, is the emotional, the concrete, the particular, the human bodies and their vulnerability, human lives and their subjectivity—all of which are marked as feminine in the binary dichotomies of gender discourse. In other words, gender discourse informs and shapes nuclear and national security discourse, and in so doing creates silences and absences. It keeps thing out of the room, unsaid, and keeps them ignored if they manage to get in. As such, it degrades our ability to think *well* and *fully* about nuclear weapons and national security, and shapes and limits the possible outcomes of our deliberations.

14   What becomes clear, then, is that defense intellectuals' standards of what constitutes "good thinking" about weapons and security have not simply evolved out of trial and error; it is not that the history of nuclear discourse has been filled with exploration of other ideas, concerns, interests, information, questions, feelings, meanings and stances which were then found to create distorted or poor thought. It is that these options have been *preempted* by gender discourse, and by the feelings evoked by living up to or transgressing gender codes.

15   To borrow a term from defense intellectuals, you might say that gender discourse becomes a "preemptive deterrent" to certain kinds of thought.

16   Let me give you another example of what I mean—another story, this one my own experience.

17   One Saturday morning I, two other women, and about fifty-five men gathered to play a war game designed by the RAND Corporation.[5] Our "controllers" (the people running the game) first divided us up into three sets of teams; there would be three simultaneous games being played, each pitting a Red Team against a Blue Team (I leave the reader to figure out which color represents which country). All three women were put onto the same team, a Red Team.

18   The teams were then placed in different rooms so that we had no way of communicating with each other, except through our military actions (or lack of them) or by sending demands and responses to those demands via the controllers. There was no way to negotiate or to take actions other than military ones. (This was supposed to simulate reality.) The controllers then presented

us with maps and pages covered with numbers representing each side's forces. We were also given a "scenario," a situation of escalating tensions and military conflicts, starting in the Middle East and spreading up Central Europe. We were to decide what to do, the controllers would go back and forth between the two teams to relate the other team's actions, and periodically the controllers themselves would add something that would rachet up the conflict— an announcement of an "intercepted intelligence report" from the other side, the authenticity of which we had no way of judging. . . .

19   Gradually our game escalated to nuclear war. The Blue Team used tactical nuclear weapons against our troops, but our Red Team decided, initially at least, against nuclear retaliation. When the game ended (at the end of the allotted time) our Red Team had "lost the war" (meaning that we had political control over less territory than we had started with, although our homeland had remained completely unviolated and our civilian population safe).

20   In the debriefing afterwards, all six teams returned to one room and reported on their games. Since we had had absolutely no way to know why the other team had taken any of its actions, we now had the opportunity to find out what they had been thinking. A member of the team that had played against us said, "Well, when he took his troops out of Afghanistan, I knew he was weak and I could push him around. And then, when we nuked him and he didn't nuke us back, I knew he was just such a wimp, I could take him for everything he's got and I nuked him again. He just wimped out."

21   There are many different possible comments to make at this point. I will restrict myself to a couple. First, when the man from the Blue Team called me a wimp (which is what it felt like for each of us on the Red Team—a personal accusation), I felt silenced. My reality, the careful reasoning that had gone into my strategic and tactical choices, the intelligence, the politics, the morality— all of it just disappeared, completely invalidated. I could not explain the reasons for my actions, could not protest, "Wait, you idiot, I didn't do it because I was weak, I did it because it made *sense* to do it that way, given my understandings of strategy and tactics, history and politics, my goals and my values." The protestation would be met with knowing sneers. In this discourse, the coding of an act as wimpish is hegemonic. Its emotional heat and resonance is like a bath of sulfuric acid: it erases everything else.

22   "Acting like a wimp" is an *interpretation* of a person's acts (or, in national security discourse, a country's acts, an important distinction I will return to later). As with any other interpretation, it is a selection of one among many possible different ways to understand something—once the selection is made, the other possibilities recede into invisibility. In national security discourse, "acting like a wimp," being insufficiently masculine, is one of the most readily available interpretive codes. (You do not need to do participant observation in a community of defense intellectuals to know this—just look at the "geopolitical analyses" in the media and on Capitol Hill of the way in which George Bush's military intervention in Panama and the Persian Gulf War finally allowed him to beat the "wimp factor.") You learn that someone is being a wimp if he perceives an international crisis as very dangerous and urges caution; if

he thinks it might not be important to have just as many weapons that are just as big as the other guy's; if he suggests that an attack should not necessarily be answered by an even more destructive counterattack; or, until recently, if he suggested that making unilateral arms reductions might be useful for our own security.[6] All of these are "wimping out." . . .

23   "Wimp" is, of course, not the only gendered pejorative used in the national security community; "pussy" is another popular epithet, conjoining the imagery of harmless domesticated (read demasculinized) pets with contemptuous reference to women's genitals. In an informal setting, an analyst worrying about the other side's casualties, for example, might be asked, "What kind of pussy are you, anyway?" It need not happen more than once or twice before everyone gets the message; they quickly learn not to raise the issue in their discussions. Attention to and care for the living, suffering, and dying of human beings (in this case, soldiers and their families and friends) is again banished from the discourse through the expedient means of gender-bashing. . . .

24   Other words are also used to impugn someone's masculinity and, in the process, to delegitimate his position and avoid thinking seriously about it. "Those Krauts are a bunch of limp-dicked wimps" was the way one U.S. defense intellectual dismissed the West German politicians who were concerned about popular opposition to Euromissile deployments.[7] I have heard our NATO allies referred to as "the Euro-fags" when they disagreed with American policy on such issues as the Contra War or the bombing of Libya. Labeling them "fags" is an effective strategy; it immediately dismisses and trivializes their opposition to U.S. policy by coding it as due to inadequate masculinity. . . .

25   "Fag" imagery is not, of course, confined to the professional community of security analysts; it also appears in popular "political" discourse. The Gulf War was replete with examples. American derision of Saddam Hussein included bumper stickers that read "Saddam, Bend Over." American soldiers reported that the "U.S.A." stenciled on their uniforms stood for "Up Saddam's Ass." A widely reprinted cartoon, surely one of the most multiply offensive that came out of the war, depicted Saddam bowing down in the Islamic posture of prayer, with a huge U.S. missile, approximately five times the size of the prostrate figure, about to penetrate his upraised bottom. Over and over, defeat for the Iraqis was portrayed as humiliating anal penetration by the more powerful and manly United States. . . .

26   In the face of this equation, genuine political discourse disappears. One more example: After Iraq invaded Kuwait and President Bush hastily sent U.S. forces to Saudi Arabia, there was a period in which the Bush administration struggled to find a convincing political justification for U.S. military involvement and the security affairs community debated the political merit of U.S. intervention.[8] Then Bush set the deadline, January 16, high noon at the OK Corral, and as the day approached conversations changed. More of these centered on the question compellingly articulated by one defense intellectual as "Does George Bush have the stones for war?"[9] This, too, is utterly extraordinary. This was a time when crucial political questions abounded: Can the

sanctions work if given more time? Just what vital interests does the United States actually have at stake? What would be the goals of military interven- tion? Could they be accomplished by other means? Is the difference between what sanctions might accomplish and what military violence might accomplish worth the greater cost in human suffering, human lives, even dollars? What will the long-term effects on the people of the region be? On the ecology? Given the apparent successes of Gorbachev's last-minute diplomacy and Hus- sein's series of nearly daily small concessions, can and should Bush put off the deadline? Does he have the strength to let another leader play a major role in solving the problem? Does he have the political flexibility to not fight, or is he hell-bent on war at all costs? And so on, ad infinitum. All of these disappear in the sulfuric acid test of the size of Mr. Bush's private parts. . . . [10]

27   Understanding national security discourse's gendered positions may cast some light on a frequently debated issue. Many people notice that the worlds of war making and national security have been created by and are still "manned" by men, and ask whether it might not make a big difference if more women played a role. Unfortunately, my first answer is "not much," at least if we are talking about relatively small numbers of women entering the world of defense experts and national security elites as it is presently constituted. Quite apart from whether you believe that women are (biologically or culturally) less aggressive than men, every person who enters this world is also participating in a gendered discourse in which she or he must adopt the masculine position in order to be successful. This means that it is extremely difficult for anyone, female *or male,* to express concerns or ideas marked as "feminine" and still maintain his or her legitimacy.

28   Another difficulty in realizing the potential benefits of recruiting more women in the profession: the assumption that they would make a difference is to some degree predicated on the idea that "the feminine" is absent from the discourse, and that adding it would lead to more balanced thinking. However, the problem is not that the "female" position is totally absent from the dis- course: parts of it, at least, albeit in a degraded and undeveloped form, are al- ready present, named, delegitimated, and silenced, all in one fell swoop. The inclusion and delegitimation of ideas marked as "feminine" acts as a more powerful censor than the total absence of "feminine" ideas would be.

29   So it is not simply the presence of women that would make a difference. In- stead, it is the commitment and ability to develop, explore, rethink, and revalue those ways of thinking that get silenced and devalued that would make a difference. For that to happen, men, too, would have to be central partici- pants. . . .

30   Finally, I would like to briefly explore a phenomenon I call the "unitary masculine actor problem" in national security discourse. During the Persian Gulf War, many feminists probably noticed that both the military briefers and George Bush himself frequently used the singular masculine pronoun "he" when referring to Iraq and Iraq's army. Someone not listening carefully could simply assume that "he" referred to Saddam Hussein. Sometimes it did; much of the time it simply reflected the defense community's characteristic

habit of calling opponents "he" or "the other guy."[11] A battalion commander, for example, was quoted as saying "Saddam knows where we are and we know where he is. We will move a lot now to keep him off guard."[12] In these sentences, "he" and "him" appear to refer to Saddam Hussein. But, of course, the American forces had *no idea* where Saddam Hussein himself was; the singular masculine pronouns are actually being used to refer to the Iraqi military.

31   This linguistic move, frequently heard in discussions within the security affairs and defense communities, turns a complex state and set of forces into a singular male opponent. In fact, discussions that purport to be serious explorations of the strategy and tactics of war can have a tone which sounds more like the story of a sporting match, a fistfight, or a personal vendetta.

> I would want to suck him out into the desert as far as I could, and then pound him to death.[13]

> Once we had taken out his eyes, we did what could be best described as the "Hail Mary play" in football.[14]

> If the adversary decides to embark on a very high roll, because he's frightened that something even worse is in the works, does grabbing him by the scruff of the neck and slapping him up the side of the head, does that make him behave better or is it plausible that it makes him behave even worse?[15]

32   Most defense intellectuals would claim that using "he" is just a convenient shorthand, without significant import or effects. I believe, however, that the effects of this usage are many and the implications far-reaching. Here I will sketch just a few, starting first with the usage throughout defense discourse generally, and then coming back to the Gulf War in particular.

33   The use of "he" distorts the analyst's understanding of the opposing state and the conflict in which they are engaged. When the analyst refers to the opposing state as "he" or "the other guy," the image evoked is that of a person, a unitary actor; yet states are not people. Nor are they unitary and unified. They comprise complex, multifaceted governmental and military apparatuses, each with opposing forces within it, each, in turn, with its own internal institutional dynamics, its own varied needs in relation to domestic politics, and so on. In other words, if the state is referred to and pictured as a unitary actor, what becomes unavailable to the analyst and policy-maker is a series of much more complex truths that might enable him to imagine many more policy options, many more ways to interact with that state. . . .

34   That tension between personalization and abstraction was striking in Gulf War discourse. In the Gulf War, not only was "he" frequently used to refer to the Iraqi military, but so was "Saddam," as in "Saddam really took a pounding today," or "Our goal remains the same: to liberate Kuwait by forcing Saddam Hussein out."[16] The personalization is obvious: in this locution, the U.S. armed forces are not destroying a nation, killing people; instead, they (or George) are giving Saddam a good pounding, or bodily removing him from where he does not belong. Our emotional response is to get fired up about a bully getting his comeuppance.

35   Yet this personalization, this conflation of Iraq and Iraqi forces with Saddam himself, also abstracts: it functions to substitute in the mind's eye the abstraction of an implacably, impeccably evil enemy for the particular human beings, the men, women, and children being pounded, burned, torn, and eviscerated. A cartoon image of Saddam being ejected from Kuwait preempts the image of the blackened, charred, decomposing bodies of nineteen-year-old boys tossed in ditches by the side of the road, and the other concrete images of the acts of violence that constitute "forcing Hussein [sic] out of Kuwait."[17] Paradoxical as it may seem, in personalizing the Iraqi army as Saddam, the individual human beings in Iraq were abstracted out of existence.[18]

36   In summary, I have been exploring the way in which defense intellectuals talk to each other—the comments they make to each other, the particular usages that appear in their informal conversations or their lectures. In addition, I have occasionally left the professional community to draw upon public talk about the Gulf War. My analysis does *not* lead me to conclude that "national security thinking is masculine"—that is, a separate, and different, discussion. Instead, I have tried to show that national security discourse is gendered, and that it matters. Gender discourse is interwoven through national security discourse. It sets fixed boundaries, and in so doing, it skews what is discussed and how it is thought about. It shapes expectations of other nations' actions, and in so doing it affects both our interpretations of international events and conceptions of how the United States should respond. . . .

NOTES

1. A "counterforce attack" refers to an attack in which the targets are the opponent's weapons systems, command and control centers, and military leadership. It is in contrast to what is known as a "countervalue attack," which is the abstractly benign term for *targeting* and incinerating cities—what the United States did to Hiroshima, except that the bombs used today would be several hundred times more powerful. It is also known in the business, a bit more colorfully, as an "all-out city-busting exchange." Despite this careful targeting distinction, one need not be too astute to notice that many of the ports, airports, and command posts destroyed in a counter*force* attack are, in fact, in cities or metropolitan areas, which would be destroyed along with the "real targets," the weapons systems. But this does not appear to make the distinction any less meaningful to war planners, although it is, in all likelihood, less than meaningful to the victims.

2. The term is Helen Caldicott's, from her book *Missile Envy: The Arms Race and Nuclear War* (New York: William Morrow, 1984).

3. I have addressed some of these factors in: "Sex and Death in the Rational World of Defense Intellectuals," *Signs: Journal of Women in Culture and Society* 12, no. 4 (Summer 1987): 687–718; "Emasculating America's Linguistic Deterrent," in *Rocking the Ship of State: Towards a Feminist Peace Politics,* ed. Adrienne Harris and Ynestra King (Boulder, Colo.: Westview Press, 1989); and *Deconstructing National Security Discourse and Reconstructing Security* (working title, book manuscript).

4. While both the military and the news media presented the picture of a "surgically clean" war in which only military targets were destroyed, the reality was signifi-

cantly bloodier; it involved the mass slaughter of Iraqi soldiers, as well as the death and suffering of large numbers of noncombatant men, women, and children. Although it is not possible to know the numbers of casualties with certainty, one analyst in the Census Bureau, Beth Osborne Daponte, has estimated that 40,000 Iraqi soldiers and 13,000 civilians were killed in direct military conflict, that 30,000 civilians died during Shiite and Kurdish rebellions, and that 70,000 civilians have died from health problems caused by the destruction of water and power plants (Edmund L. Andrews, "Census Bureau to Dismiss Analyst Who Estimated Iraqi Casualties," *New York Times,* March 7, 1992, A7). Other estimates are significantly higher. Greenpeace estimates that as many as 243,000 Iraqi civilians died due to war-related causes (Ray Wilkinson, "Back from the Living Dead," *Newsweek,* January 20, 1992, 28). Another estimate places Iraqi troop casualties at 70,000 and estimates that over 100,000 children have died from the delayed effects of the war (Peter Rothenberg, "The Invisible Dead," *Lies of Our Times* [March 1992]: 7). For recent, detailed reports on civilian casualties, see *Health and Welfare in Iraq after the Gulf Crisis* (International Study Team/Commission on Civilian Casualties, Human Rights Program, Harvard Law School, October 1991), and *Needless Deaths in the Gulf War* (Middle East Watch, 1992). For a useful corrective to the myth of the Gulf War as a war of surgical strikes and precision-guided weaponry, see Paul F. Walker and Eric Stambler, "The Surgical Myth of the Gulf War," *Boston Globe,* April 16, 1991; and " . . . And the Dirty Little Weapons," *Bulletin of the Atomic Scientists* (May 1991): 21–24.

5. The RAND Corporation is a think tank that is a U.S. Air Force subcontractor. In the 1950s many of the most important nuclear strategists did their work under RAND auspices, including Bernard Brodie, Albert Wohlstetter, Herman Kahn, and Thomas Schelling.

6. In the context of the nuclear arms race and the cold war, even though a defense analyst might acknowledge that some American weapon systems served no useful strategic function (such as the Titan missiles during the 1980s), there was still consensus that they should not be unilaterally cut. Such a cut was seen to be bad because it was throwing away a potential bargaining chip in future arms control negotiations, or because making unilateral cuts was viewed as a sign of weakness and lack of resolve. It is only outside that context of hostile superpower competition, and, in fact, after the dissolution of the Soviet threat, that President Bush has responded to Gorbachev's unilateral cuts with some (minor) American unilateral cuts. For a description and critical assessment of the arguments against unilateral cuts, see William Rose, *US Unilateral Arms Control Initiatives: When Do They Work?* (New York: Greenwood Press, 1988). For an analysis of the logic and utility of bargaining chips, see Robert J. Bresler and Robert C. Gray, "The Bargaining Chip and SALT," *Political Science Quarterly* 92, no. 1 (Spring 1977): 65–88.

7. Cohn, unattributed interview, Cambridge, Mass., July 15, 1991.

8. The Bush White House tried out a succession of revolving justifications in an attempt to find one that would garner popular support for U.S. military action, including: we must respond to the rape of Kuwait; we must not let Iraqi aggression be rewarded; we must defend Saudi Arabia; we cannot stand by while "vital U.S. interests" are threatened; we must establish a "new world order"; we must keep down the price of oil at U.S. gas pumps; we must protect American jobs; and finally, the winner, the only one that elicited any real support from the American public, we must destroy Iraq's incipient nuclear weapons capability. What was perhaps most surprising about

this was the extent to which it was publicly discussed and accepted as George Bush's need to find a message that "worked" rather than to actually have a genuine, meaningful explanation. For an account of Bush's decision making about the Gulf War, see Bob Woodward, *The Commanders* (New York: Simon and Schuster, 1991).

9. Cohn, unattributed interview, Cambridge, Mass., July 20, 1991.

10. Within the context of our society's dominant gender discourse, this equation of masculinity and strength with the willingness to use armed force seems quite "natural" and not particularly noteworthy. Hannah Arendt is one political thinker who makes the arbitrariness of that connection visible: she reframes our thinking about "strength," and finds strength in *refraining* from using one's armed forces (Hannah Arendt, *On Violence* [New York: Harcourt, Brace, Jovanovich, 1969]).

11. For a revealing exploration of the convention in strategic, military, and political writings of redescribing armies as a single "embodied combatant," see Elaine Scarry, *The Body in Pain: The Making and Unmaking of the World* (New York: Oxford University Press, 1984): 70–72.

12. Chris Hedges, "War is Vivid in the Gun Sights of the Sniper," *New York Times,* February 3, 1991, A1.

13. General Norman Schwarzkopf, National Public Radio broadcast, February 8, 1991.

14. General Norman Schwarzkopf, CENTCOM News Briefing, Riyadh, Saudi Arabia, February 27, 1991, p. 2.

15. Transcript of a strategic studies specialist's lecture on NATO and the Warsaw Pact (summer institute on Regional Conflict and Global Security: The Nuclear Dimension, Madison, Wisconsin, June 29, 1987).

16. Defense Secretary Dick Cheney, "Excerpts from Briefing at Pentagon by Cheney and Powell," *New York Times,* January 24, 1991, A 11.

17. Scarry explains that when an army is described as a single "embodied combatant," injury, (as in Saddam's "pounding"), may be referred to but is "no longer recognizable or interpretable." It is not only that Americans might be happy to imagine Saddam being pounded; we also on some level know that it is not really happening, and thus need not feel the pain of the wounded. We "respond to the injury . . . as an imaginary wound in an imaginary body, despite the fact that that imaginary body is itself made up of thousands of real human bodies" (Scarry, *Body in Pain,* p. 72).

18. For a further exploration of the disappearance of human bodies from Gulf War discourse, see Hugh Gusterson, "Nuclear War, the Gulf War, and the Disappearing Body" (unpublished paper, 1991). I have addressed other aspects of Gulf War discourse in "The Language of the Gulf War," *Center Review* 5, no. 2 (Fall 1991); "Decoding Military Newspeak," *Ms.,* March/April 1991, p. 81; and "Language, Gender, and the Gulf War" (unpublished paper prepared for Harvard University Center for Literary and Cultural Studies, April 10, 1991).

TOPICAL CONSIDERATIONS

1. What does Cohn mean in paragraph 3 when she writes that the language of war "filters out" from military specialists to the general public? What does the metaphor of filtering describe? What example does she provide in the same paragraph?

2. What does Cohn mean by the phrase "gender discourse" in paragraph 5 and by the statement that "human characteristics are dichotomized"?

3. What does the physicist mean when he says he "felt like a woman" (paragraph 1)? What does feeling like a woman really mean? What does Cohn say about this in paragraphs 7–10? How does she judge the physicist's response to what he said and how people responded?

4. Cohn states in paragraph 13 that "gender discourse informs and shapes nuclear and national security discourse." How does it do that?

5. What effects does gender discourse have on language used to discuss military decisions? In your experience, has gender discourse ever affected a decision about your life—say, as you took the Scholastic Achievement Test (SAT)? Was anything about the SAT similar to what Cohn describes as typically male ways of thinking about something?

6. What kind of war game does Cohn play, beginning with paragraph 16? What kinds of restraints are placed on the players—what may they do and not do? How would you respond to these restrictions? What are they meant to demonstrate? Have you ever played games with similar rules?

7. What was the object of the game—that is, what would it take to win this game? How satisfied did Cohn feel about her team's status as "loser" before and after the debriefing session?

8. What is the difference between men and the "masculine position," and women and "the feminine position" in paragraphs 27–29? In your own opinion, will the problem of short-circuited military thinking be resolved by recruiting more women into the armed forces or by adding the feminine discourse?

9. In paragraphs 30–35, what is the "unitary masculine actor problem"? Can you think of examples of similar events from your own experience—say, when the president of your college or university was blamed for raising tuition?

RHETORICAL CONSIDERATIONS

1. What did you first think when you read Cohn's opening sentence identifying the physicist as a "white male"? What did you discover she meant as you read further? What purpose do you think she may have in mind when she uses this term, rather than leaving the physicist's racial and gender identity unspecified?

2. Can you reverse the opening anecdote about the white male physicist in terms of gender? That is, can you imagine a woman saying "I felt like a man" and having it mean roughly the same kind of thing? What would "feeling like a man" entail?

3. Beginning with paragraph 16 Cohn recalls her war-game experience with the RAND Corporation. What function does that story play in this otherwise analytic piece of writing? How does it help you to understand that gender discourse is not about men and women, but about male and female?

4. How do you respond to the words "wimp," "pussy," and "fag" in paragraphs 22–25? Do you think that such terminology is an effective insult? Have you ever heard this kind of language being used to control someone's behavior? If

so, what were the circumstances? How did the person labeled with such terms respond?

5. In paragraph 26, Cohn complains about journalistic references to "the size of [ex-president] Bush's private parts" as a way of discussing strategy. What problems do you think she has with these references? Have you ever heard praise for achievement in terms of male genitalia? Can you suggest acceptable substitutes—perhaps some using references to female genitalia?

6. Why do you think Cohn uses so many lengthy, fact-filled footnotes? When did you read them—or did you read them at all? What effect did your use of the footnotes have on your understanding of the piece?

WRITING ASSIGNMENTS

1. Describe an incident from your experience in which you "felt like a woman" in the way that Cohn explores that term in her article. What happened? How did you feel about the experience? How did you respond to or resolve the problem? How did your understanding of that experience make you feel about being a man, or about being a woman?

2. Review this chapter's first article, "How to Detect Propaganda" by the Institute for Propaganda Analysis. Is the gendered discourse Carol Cohn describes a form of propaganda? Why or why not? Be sure to set down a solid explanation of what propaganda is and is not before you evaluate gendered discourse.

3. Collect at least three samples of political cartoons on a single issue: a specific military conflict, a current news event, trends in the economy, or other topic. (Political cartoons usually appear in the Op-Ed, or opinions and editorials, section of daily newspapers; some Sunday papers and news weeklies run a "week's best" compendium of cartoons.) Then, using Carol Cohn's ideas about gendered discourse, discuss the way each cartoon uses ideas about maleness or femaleness to communicate ideas. What postures, attitudes, or even stereotypes does the cartoon use to convey its message? What makes it "funny"?

4. Using a library's microforms collection of news media, research and compare news coverage of two military conflicts that are at least 25 years apart. Collect a handful of similar articles about each one—for example, a pair of articles providing an overview of the conflict, a pair discussing a specific military action, and a pair summing up the conflict at the end. Do you find that the language about war has changed? Do you find that the graphics (photographs, charts, maps) supplied with the news articles have changed?

WHEN WORDS GO TO WAR

Bella English

Every war produces its own lingo. The Persian Gulf War was no exception, for it gave rise to some peculiar military/political expressions that rapidly found their way into general usage. What characterized "Gulf-speak" was its sometimes colorful, sometimes bloodless, sometimes tortuous circumlocution. It began flowing like crude oil in August of 1990 when Iraqi forces under Saddam Hussein were "invited" into Kuwait by "young revolutionaries" asking for reinforcement of a new "popular army." Hundreds of U.S. citizens caught in the invasion became, in Hussein's words, "guests" of Iraq. The war began mid-January 1991 with the first of some 100,000 Allied "sorties." So did the now familiar "marvels of militarisms, euphemisms and acronyms," as Bella English recalls. "Hostilities" ended six weeks later with a 100-hour ground war, "the mother of all battles."

The article below gives a review of some of the choice parlance that emerged from the war. It is interesting to note that while the Allied phrasemakers went to great lengths to avoid all mention of flesh and blood, the rhetoric out of Baghdad was full of fire and brimstone and a lot of smoke. This article first appeared in the author's column in the *Boston Globe* on February 27, 1991, the day the war ended.

1   The Persian Gulf War has added several words to our lexicon. People who heretofore thought a "sortie" was a party now know it's a combat mission. Those of us who never heard of Riyadh before now speak of it with great familiarity, as if it were Washington. And who will ever forget what a Scud is?

2   Pentagonese has also reared its ugly head. That's English as a Second Language, popularized by Alexander Haig, who became known for such gems as: "longstanding in time," "We must use careful caution" and "I'll have to caveat my response, senator."[1]

3   The daily military briefings out of Riyadh are marvels of militarisms, euphemisms and acronyms. "Today, our troops executed BDAs in the KTO."

---

[1]Alexander Haig was the one-time commander of NATO forces in Europe and for a short time later secretary of state under President Ronald Reagan. (Ed.)

Translation: Allied forces did bomb damage assessments in the Kuwaiti Theater of Operations, or, in simple English, surveyed how badly we bombed 'em.

4   Of course, it goes against the military grain to speak in simple English. I mean, why use one word when 10 will do? And heaven forbid you should call something by its real name. In this most sanitized of wars, we mustn't admit that blood—American and Arab—is being spilled.

5   That's why body bags have become "human remains pouches." Refrigerated trucks, sort of mobile morgues, are stationed at "collection points." The bombing of civilian areas such as schools, hospitals and homes, has become "collateral damage." You're never "killed in action," but you're KIA, as if that's kinder and gentler. Although allied soldiers who have been captured are still POWs, captured Iraqis have become EPWs, or Enemy Prisoners of War. And when military commanders speak of NBCs, they're not talking about the network; they're talking about nuclear, biological and chemical weapons.

6   We "engage" the enemy instead of creaming him. There is a "weapons delivery" instead of a blanket bombing. Tanks are "neutralized" instead of being blown to kingdom come. The aim of the war is "assertive disarmament." To achieve that goal, the allied forces have used "discriminate deterrence," or precision bombing.

7   Thanks to the war, the world now knows that a "berm" is a sand wall, and that a "new world order" is around the corner. (Winston Churchill George Bush ain't.) We revel in the success of American weapons such as the Patriot and Cruise missiles and scoff at the decidedly inferior Scud. It doesn't take a five-star general to figure out why our weapons are so prettily named, while their weapons have such homely monikers, such as the Soviet-built Scud (rhymes with dud) and the Chinese-built Silkworm, named after one of the lowest forms of life. We gave them these nicknames.

8   And who will ever forget the dreadful noun-turned-verb: attrited? As in, "There are a number of combat forces on the ground being attrited by our troops." Or, killed.

9   While the American side—full of spokesmen and speechwriters—has hidden behind bleached and starched words, Saddam Hussein has employed the opposite tactic to win the hearts and souls of his countrymen. "Apocalypse Now" could be the name of his verbal strategy. Or, as a friend of mine calls it, "Baghdad's Best B.S."

10   "We have prepared ourselves for burning the bodies of the corrupt and evil invaders, and our revenge will be devastating and ruthless," Saddam said in a recent commentary. "We will not hesitate and we will seek to turn the ground war . . . into a hellfire that will sear their scoundrels. Their cohorts will tumble into the great crater of death."

11   "Treachery" is big with Saddam Hussein. "The treacherous committed treachery. The despicable Bush and his treasonous agent Fahd, and all those who supported them in committing crimes, shame and aggression, committed the treachery. Those cowards who have perfected the acts of treachery, treason and vileness, committed treachery after they departed from every path of

virtue, goodness and humanity. They have committed treachery and launched their ground offensive."

12   Someone get this man a thesaurus, please.

13   Saddam promised to make allied troops "swim in their own blood" and pledged to fight "the mother of battles" just before the ground war began, which prompted Tom Brokaw to label him "the father of all con men."

14   Although both sides are claiming God as their chief aide de camp, Saddam is responsible for the oxymoron "holy war." (But we must take credit for the equally absurd "friendly fire.")

15   As Saddam recently stated: "In the name of god, the merciful, the compassionate, our armed forces have performed their holy war duty of refusing to comply with the logic of evil, imposition and aggression. They have been engaged in an epic, valiant battle that will be recorded by history in letters of light."

16   If all else fails, Saddam, there's a job for you in America. Writing for the *National Enquirer.*

TOPICAL CONSIDERATIONS

1. What was your first response to English's essay? Were you aware of the special nature of military language, especially that which came out of the Persian Gulf War? Did this essay change your attitude toward "Pentagonese"? Or, did it confirm your beliefs? Explain.

2. In your own words, what is Bella English arguing for or against? Where in the essay does she state her position? Do you agree with her position?

3. In paragraph 4, the author refers to "this most sanitized of wars." In what ways, linguistically and journalistically, was the Persian Gulf War "sanitized"? Are her examples convincing? Can you think of other "sanitized" Persian Gulf War expressions? From your knowledge of history, do you think the language describing this war was more "sanitized" than that which covered the Vietnam War? World War II? You and classmates might want to form research groups covering the different wars.

4. From what the author says about Gulf War language, what would you guess was her moral or political stand on the war? Explain your answer.

5. What might have been the effect on the American public if during daily briefings a Pentagon spokesperson used desanitized language: "Today 27 Iraqi tanks were blown to kingdom come, 300 Iraqi civilians were killed when we blanket-bombed Baghdad, and 10 U.S. soldiers were killed in action," and so on?

6. What might have been the effect on the American public had our political and military leaders used the kind of rhetoric of Saddam Hussein to win the hearts and souls of Americans: "Today 500 evil and corrupt invaders of Kuwait are swimming in their own blood because of the epic, valiant battle efforts of our glorious armed forces," and so forth? Could you imagine such rhetoric inspiring the American military? the American public? Politics aside, which "tactic" seems more appealing and effective—ours or Hussein's? Explain.

7. The author observes that although allied soldiers captured by Iraqis were "still POWs, captured Iraqis" became "EPWs or Enemy Prisoners of War." Politically speaking, why the distinction? Why not call captured Iraqi soldiers POWs, too?

8. In paragraph 14, the author says that both sides claimed "God as their chief aide de camp." Looking back to the days of the war, do you recall America making such claims? If so, how did such a claim serve Allied purposes? How did such a claim serve Iraqi purposes?

9. The author characterizes "holy war" and "friendly fire" as "equally absurd" oxymorons. What's an oxymoron? How are these two expressions oxymoronic? Do you find these "equally absurd"? Explain. Can you offer a more satisfying alternative for "friendly fire"?

RHETORICAL CONSIDERATIONS

1. Is there any indication in this article of the author's political stand on the Persian Gulf War? In other words, can you tell if she was for or against it? Explain with evidence from the essay.

2. Do you think the author offers balanced criticism of Allied and Iraqi "Gulfspeak"? Explain.

3. In paragraph 5, English writes that KIA is "kinder and gentler" than "killed in action." Why the particular word choice, "kinder and gentler"? What is the original source of these words? What connection is she making between that source and the essay's thesis? How does this word choice provide an ironic commentary on the Persian Gulf War specifically?

4. Explain the tone and impact of the final paragraph. Do you find this an effective conclusion? Does it follow logically from what preceded it? Given the strong public support for the war, do you think it was politically wise of English to end the essay with a poke at Hussein rather than the American military?

WRITING ASSIGNMENTS

1. This essay makes the point that military jargon in general is employed to avoid addressing issues in human terms. With a specific reference to the Persian Gulf War, write a paper in which you defend the military's use of "Pentagonese." In your discussion, consider how such carefully chosen language served public and military morale, Allied security, and the war efforts. In short, argue that sometimes it is politically necessary to sugarcoat the truth.

2. Write an essay arguing just the opposite—that is, how sanitized military jargon only served to cover up the real horrors of the Persian Gulf War and, thus, sustain public support.

3. Using strictly military language, write a parody of an everyday activity or chore such as washing the car, walking the dog, studying for an exam, doing the laundry. Use some of the examples from this essay and other militaristic language you have heard.

4. Even though the Persian Gulf War began and ended within the first two months of 1991, like other wars it produced its own peculiar terms that found their way into general use. Try to make a list of such terms that are still being used. Write a

paper in which you discuss these terms—their original military meanings, how they have slipped into general use, how they have even been adopted by certain professions.

5. Using newspaper indexes and a library's microforms collections, collect some examples of in-depth reporting on the United States' military action in Vietnam between 1964 and 1973. Does any terminology there seem to repeat the kind of sanitizing that Bella English complains about in Gulf War journalism? Does the wording from this earlier war disturb you, or has it become part of everyday language?

6. If possible, briefly review historical accounts of the Vietnam War, either in textbooks that include some discussion of it or in books and articles focusing solely on the Vietnam War. Do the authors criticize the terminology you've found in the journalism, or do they use it without comment? How does a historian's awareness of this language help to shape your understanding of the events he or she is describing?

ELEVEN WAYS OF LOOKING AT THE GULF WAR

Arthur Asa Berger

For many reasons the Persian Gulf War was a phenomenon. The extent and speed of deployment of personnel and equipment, the technological sophistication, its brief duration, the extent of destruction, the relatively low U.S. casualties—these were unparalleled in military and political history. Also, the war was a major media event. So it is not surprising that in addition to some choice linguistic expressions, the war also produced some fascinating metaphors to make sense of the phenomenon. In this piece Arthur Asa Berger reviews eleven different ways various experts and media commentators viewed the Gulf War— for example, as a video game, a chess game, and a medical procedure, to name a few. While focusing on the same historic event, each metaphor renders a distinct and different interpretation of the war, thus raising a provocative question about the role of language in shaping the world and our perceptions of it. In other words, as language is used to justify, rationalize, or understand an event, doesn't that language in some measure shape the event?

Arthur Asa Berger is Professor of broadcast communication arts at San Francisco State University. He has written many books on communication and popular culture, including *Political Culture and Public Opinion* (1991) and, most recently, *An Anatomy of Humor* (1993). This article first appeared in the summer 1994 edition of *Et cetera*.

1   It was General "Stormin' Norman" Schwartzkopf, who said that "war is the most complex thing in the world." And the Gulf war was, in many respects, an incredible achievement. The military transported the equivalent of a good sized city to the Gulf, our government formed a coalition of people who hadn't, in the past, been too friendly toward one another, and strategists planned a brilliant military campaign.

2   But "complex things" tend to cause problems to many people. We have a need, it seems, to make sense of complex things by simplifying them. We use metaphors or schemas to comprehend, as best we can, complex matters.

3   Through the media, assorted experts, and a variety of commentators, we have made sense of the incredible events in the Gulf in at least eleven different ways.

4   In Kurosawa's classic film, *Rashomon,* a bandit subdues a man (ties him up) and then rapes his wife in front of him. That much is sure. Afterwards, the man is killed, but whether he killed himself, was killed by the bandit, or died by accident is difficult to ascertain. This is because everyone involved in the episode tells a different story, including the dead man, whose spirit is channeled by a medium who goes into a trance. I use the concept of *The Rashomon Phenomenon* to describe the process by which "experts" and others gave their opinions on various aspects of the crisis. We had professors, retired generals, think tankers, and diplomats (and many others) discussing the situation and, as often as not, disagreeing with one another. The crisis was like *Rashomon:* you could never know who to believe.

THE WAR AS A VIDEO GAME

5   Some of the visual images shown on television encouraged some persons to describe the crisis and war as a video game. We saw "smart bombs" being aimed at the doorways or ventilating shafts of bunkers and planes zapping Iraqi targets with incredible precision. Because we saw little in the way of Iraqi casualties, the war took on the appearance of a somewhat surrealistic video game. The war also led to a spurt in the popularity of video games which simulated war in the Mideast.

THE GULF WAR AS ARABIAN NIGHTS

6   We can also see the crisis and war as a kind of fairy tale. It is possible to apply the notions of Vladimir Propp, an early student of fairy tales, to the war. He suggested most fairy tales have certain common attributes—a hero is sent on a mission, he has magic weapons given to him by a donor figure, he fights with a villain, and so on. Propp's book, *Morphology of a Folktale,* lists 31 different functions—actions done by heroes, villains, and secondary characters. Most of these functions can be applied to the Gulf crisis. But at the end of the fairy tale, the hero usually weds a princess and ascends the throne. What does this suggest for George, the hero of this tale?

KIGMYISM

7   Kigmies were fantastic creatures created by Al Capp for his *Li'l Abner* cartoon strip. They loved to be kicked. Might we see the tactics of the Iraqi Army as a kind of Kigmyism, spread wide? Unfortunately, this attitude may have led to the

the massacre of unknown thousands of Iraqi soldiers, in a slaughter that we didn't see or know about until after the war. There may also be something of the reverse Kigmy personality in the Iraqis; they kicked (murdered, tortured) those weaker than they were and were Kigmies for those more powerful than they were.

THE CRISIS AS A CHESS GAME

8 In this metaphor, the players (George Bush and the coalition, Saddam Hussein and his followers), moved pawns around and countered one another in something very similar to a game of chess. Saddam didn't use his Queen (poison gas) and was ultimately defeated by players with a better command of the game. Some people have suggested that Saddam and the Iraqi army wasn't in the same league as the coalition and never could have won. The only question was how many pawns he might have captured.

PSYCHO-SADDAM-ANALYSIS

9 Various psychologists, psychiatrists and other experts analyzed Saddam's personality and the frequency with which he blinked his eyelids at certain interviews. He was, some said, a sociopath. Others suggested a serial killer. His rhetoric suggested megalomania. Semioticians analyzed his facial expressions and tried to guess what his smiles meant. Was he cracking up or, for some reason, in good humor. Elements of pyromania also can be discerned.

FRANKENSTEINSADDAM

10 This is a variation of Psycho-Saddam-analysis. Here we see Saddam as a monster figure from horror movies, perhaps a reincarnation of Adolph Hitler, killing masses of people and hiding out in various bombproof bunkers.

THE GULF CRISIS AND WAR AS A MEDIA EVENT

11 The war wasn't planned as a media event, but in a sense it turned into one. When the war started, lots of people were "glued" to their television sets and, to indicate how important the event was, commercials were canceled. Because there was so little actual footage, much of the media's war turned out to be discussion and analysis, in which experts played political and military *Rashomonism.*

THE WAR AS A MEDICAL PROCEDURE

12 The term "surgical strikes" suggest this medical analogy. Saddam and his cohorts are, so to speak, cancers that have to be cut out so the patient, the Middle East, can be cured. It helps to dehumanize an enemy, so you don't feel
normal emotions about the death of human beings. Saddam and the Iraqis
might also be seen as pathological tubers that were rooted out by our "wart
hogs."

ARMAGEDDON

13 Fundamentalists see Saddam as an anti-Christ and the war in the Gulf as Ar-
mageddon, signaling the Second Coming. Orthodox rabbis, on the other hand,
argue that God "hardened" Saddam's heart (the same way God hardened
Pharoah's heart) so he wouldn't withdraw his army and therefore it could be
destroyed. The fact that the war ended on Purim also calls to mind the mirac-
ulous salvation of the Jews from Haman.

THE MALEVOLENT JACK-IN-THE-BOX

14 Here we see Saddam as an evil Jack-in-the-Box who has escaped from confinement (that is, Iraq) and has to be "put back in his box." This also is a
metaphor for learning about limits. Certain conspiracy theorists argue that
Saddam was encouraged to spring out of his box by the American ambassador,
who seemed to suggest that Saddam's invading Kuwait would not be seen by
us as a big deal. We were, of course, looking for an opportunity to put Saddam
back in his box and when he invaded Kuwait, he gave us the opening we were
looking for.

15 Finally, it may be argued that my own somewhat *comedic perspective* represents a way human beings have of coping with horrors beyond our capacity
to understand and deal with.

16 The ways of dealing with the crisis in the Gulf discussed above were suggested by the words people spoke, images shown on television, and material
appearing in newspapers and magazines. We needed to make sense of a phenomenon that was evolving before us, that bewildered us, and that had all the
elements of a tragic drama. It will take time for the full story to be told and for
us to find better ways of making sense of this historic event.

TOPICAL CONSIDERATIONS

1. In his description of the film *Rashomon*, what event is retold in a number of different ways? What is left ambiguous by the differences in the way various people
   remember and retell the event? Why does Berger call descriptions of the Gulf

War an example of the *Rashomon* phenomenon? Can you formulate a definition for this term?

2. In paragraph 12, Berger says that comparing the war to medicine "helps to dehumanize the enemy." How many of his other eleven ways also dehumanize the enemy? How do these examples of dehumanization work? That is, what device allows readers to avoid thinking about human pain?

3. At the end of the article, Berger refers to his "own somewhat comedic perspective." What does this term mean? Where has Berger supplied funny quips that are not, strictly speaking, necessary to convey the different schemas through which we look at the Gulf War?

4. According to Berger, can simplified metaphors or schemas for war (or other horrifying realities) be avoided? Does Berger think it would be desirable to avoid such simplifications? In your own opinion, would it be desirable to avoid such simplifications? Why or why not? Justify your answer.

5. Examine the article "How to Detect Propaganda" again. Do you think that Berger would agree that his metaphors and schemas qualify as propaganda? Why or why not?

RHETORICAL CONSIDERATIONS

1. In his description of the film *Rashomon*, Berger includes the detail of a dead man speaking through a spirit medium. Since mediumship is not widely accepted as an authoritative source of reliable information, what is the effect of this detail in Berger's description of the *Rashomon* phenomenon? How does this part of the analogy imply that the experts describing the war are less than reliable?

2. Which of Berger's comparisons rely on fictional stories to make sense of the Gulf War? Which rely on toys or games? Why do you think Berger uses so many comparisons from childhood to describe the way that the Gulf War has been presented? How do these analogies help us to cope "with horrors beyond our capacity to understand"?

3. Berger suggests that his eleven ways simply a complex subject by dehumanizing. Yet six of his examples refer to Saddam Hussein specifically, and several more allude to him. In your opinion, are these personal references also examples of dehumanization? Why or why not?

4. Try to describe the tone of this article. Did you find humor in it? If so, how does this affect Berger's attitude toward the Gulf War and the reporting about it? Cite specific evidence for your answer.

WRITING ASSIGNMENTS

1. Can you think of other instances in which writers use simplified metaphors or schemas to comprehend complex matters? How about the language used to describe a romantic relationship, a rock concert, or your first year of college to a friend who has no direct experience of it? Using Berger's format and style, come up with at least five possible ways to describe an experience from your daily life. What information is captured in each example? What is left out?

2. Find news coverage of an event or issue with a clear conflict. For example, pro-life/pro-choice clashes around abortion; congressional debates about welfare or the minimum wage; or even a local student issue at your college. Select one or two fairly extensive discussions of each side's views. Then, without taking sides yourself, see how many instances of the *Rashomon* phenomenon you can find. How does each instance work? Are any instances unfair or misleading? Why?

3. Select one of the case study essays on "War Speak." Using Berger's assumptions about how we try to cope with horrifying events, write a letter to one of the authors explaining why the problem he or she describes cannot be entirely avoided. In your letter, refer to Berger's description of *Rashomon*, assuming that the author is unfamiliar with the film.

5 LANGUAGE AND CULTURAL AND ETHNIC IDENTITY

" I STILL DON'T THINK WE'VE QUITE GOT IT, SIR...."

Ours is a nation of immigrants—of people with different racial origins, ethnic identities, religions, and languages. It is a nation whose motto *e pluribus unum* ("one out of many") bespeaks the pride in its multicultural and multilingual heritage. It is a nation whose union is predicated on like-minded moral values, political and economic self-interest, and, of course, a common language. This chapter focuses on issues inherent in American assimilation—the identity conflicts of minorities torn between two cultures and two tongues.

It might come as a surprise to some that English is not the official language of America. Nowhere in the Constitution is there such a provision. The Founders were apparently more concerned with establishing a common political philosophy than a common tongue. For the next 200 years, the new republic swelled with immigrants from every country on earth to become the "great melting pot" of cultures. But, of late, the melting pot has overheated with controversy. A growing number of Americans feel that the common tongue needs protection from non-English speakers. In 1981, a constitutional amendment proposed to make English the official language of the nation. Although it never passed, that proposal formed the bases of resolutions adopted by 23 states limiting government documents and public discourse to English. Another 20 states are considering similar measures.

At stake in the controversy are competing American traditions of multicultural tolerance and a quest for unity through a common language. Proponents of the English-only movement argue that bilingualism creates cultural division and hinders new immigrants' abilities to assimilate. They fear that bilingual education could turn the country into another Yugoslavia, where different culture never find common ground and dissolve into warring factions. Opponents contend that such legislation is nationalistic, racist, and xenophobic. They argue that such legislation not only inflames prejudice against immigrants but violates their civil rights.

WHAT LANGUAGE IS AMERICAN?

We open the debate with "Bilingualism in America: English Should Be the *Only* Language" written by perhaps the most prominent English-only proponent, the late S. I. Hayakawa. A professional linguist and senator from California, Hayakawa founded U. S. English, a national organization dedicated to making English the official language. His essay argues that bilingual education programs are not only costly and confusing, but they fail to help non–English-speaking children become part of mainstream society. Only by communicating in a common tongue, he maintains, can racial isolation, bigotry, and hostility be reduced. In direct opposition to Hayakawa's U. S. English campaigns is "Viva Bilingualism" by James Fallows who contends that the

English-only fears are founded on wrong assumptions about people and language. He says that there is no need to declare English as the official language, because "it already is that—and no one knows better than the immigrants and their children." The debate over official English is not just about language, of course, but about national and cultural identity. The next essay explores the confusion and hardships suffered by a nonnative speaker growing up in a world of two languages and two cultures. "Aria: A Memoir of a Bilingual Childhood" is a poignant personal narrative by Mexican American Richard Rodriguez who abandoned his family language the day he entered grammar school. Though the process of assimilation was painful, Rodriguez recounts the joy of understanding and being understood in the public tongue.

WHAT DO AMERICANS CALL THEMSELVES?

The next cluster of essays focuses on what Americans call themselves—what labels they use to designate their race and ethnic origins. In "Coloring Lessons" David Updike comes face to face with the prejudice inherent in the standard divisions of "black" and "white" Americans. That realization comes to him through the eyes of his 4-year-old son who is biracial. Racial awareness is the heart of the matter in the next piece also. In "African and American," Ellen Goodman explores the reasons that blacks today have turned from the name that distinguished them by color—"black"—to one that distinguished them by ancestry—"African American." As John Yemma says in the next piece, "Ethnic awareness is a great thing." And while his own mixture of Italian, German, and French does not mark him as a "what's-happening-now ethnic group," his surname and complexion have led to mistaken identities. As Yemma amusingly explains in "Innocent and Presumed Ethnic," people feel compelled to place each other into ethnic pigeonholes.

The section closes with the poem, "Theme for English B," by Langston Hughes—a poem that lyrically reflects all of the issues of identity addressed by the essays in this chapter. It also makes subtle political statements about the power of the racial majority.

CASE STUDY: BLACK ENGLISH

Our case studies focus on black English (or Ebonics) and, by extension, cultural identity for black Americans. "From Africa to the New World and into the Space Age" was written by well-known African American linguist Geneva Smitherman. She sketches the historical development of black English, pointing out some technical influences of West African languages, and exploring its historical and cultural importance. As Smitherman points out, black English creates opposing pressures for many black Americans. On one side, she says, is the urge for racial solidarity maintained by the exercise of black English. On the other side is the reality of having to survive socially and economically in mainstream America, which demands that standard "white" English be spoken. But to Rachel L. Jones, who is also black, there is no dilemma or ambivalence. She has outright rejected black English. In "What's Wrong with Black English," she argues that black Americans who reject standard "white" English or who hang on to black idioms shackle themselves. They're just not going to make it in America where "good" English, she says, is right, not white.

BILINGUALISM IN AMERICA: ENGLISH SHOULD BE THE *ONLY* LANGUAGE

S. I. Hayakawa

The question of whether America should have an official language is highly controversial. On one side is the fear that the English-only movement is motivated by racism and xenophobia. Hispanic opponents, especially, feel that laws forbidding the use of Spanish on voting ballots, in marriage ceremonies, and in the classroom would only further violate their civil liberties. On the other side, English-only proponents insist that linguistic diversions in countries such as Canada and Belgium have only led to unrest. Furthermore, they argue that laws providing bilingual education, such as in California, produced chaos and provide little inducement for non-English speakers to move into mainstream America.

Leading the fight to make English the nation's official language was the late Samuel Ichiye Hayakawa, one-time U.S. senator from California and professor of linguistics. Born to Japanese parents in Vancouver, British Columbia, Hayakawa served as honorary chairman of U.S. English, a Washington, D.C.-based public-interest organization working to establish English as this nation's sole official language. In the essay below, Hayakawa explains his reasoning. A pioneer on semantics, he authored several books including *Language in Thought and Action* (1941/1990), *Our Language and Our World* (1959), and *Symbol, Status, and Personality* (1963). This article originally appeared in *USA Today*, in July of 1989, by which time English had been made the official language in 17 states.

1   During the dark days of World War II, Chinese immigrants in California wore badges proclaiming their original nationality so they would not be mistaken for Japanese. In fact, these two immigrant groups long had been at odds with each other. However, as new English-speaking generations came along, the Chinese and Japanese began to communicate with one another. They found they had much in common and began to socialize. Today, they get together and form Asian-American societies.

2   Such are the amicable results of sharing the English language. English unites us as Americans—immigrants and native-born alike. Communicating with each other in a single, common tongue encourages trust, while reducing racial hostility and bigotry.

3   My appreciation of English has led me to devote my retirement years to championing it. Several years ago, I helped to establish U.S. English, a Washington, D.C.-based public interest group that seeks an amendment to the U.S. Constitution declaring English our official language, regardless of what other languages we may use unofficially.

4   As an immigrant to this nation, I am keenly aware of the things that bind us as Americans and unite us as a single people. Foremost among these unifying forces is the common language we share. While it is certainly true that our love of freedom and devotion to democratic principles help to unite and give us a mutual purpose, it is English, our common language, that enables us to discuss our views and allows us to maintain a well-informed electorate, the cornerstone of democratic government.

5   Because we are a nation of immigrants, we do not share the characteristics of race, religion, ethnicity, or native language which form the common bonds of society in other countries. However, by agreeing to learn and use a single, universally spoken language, we have been able to forge a unified people from an incredibly diverse population.

6   Although our 200-year history should be enough to convince any skeptic of the powerful unifying effects of a common language, some still advocate the official recognition of other languages. They argue that a knowledge of English is not part of the formula for responsible citizenship in this country.

7   Some contemporary political leaders, like the former mayor of Miami, Maurice Ferre, maintain that "Language is not necessary to the system. Nowhere does our Constitution say that English is our language." He also told the *Tampa Tribune* that, "Within ten years there will not be a single word of English spoken [in Miami]—English is not Miami's official language—[and] one day residents will have to learn Spanish or leave."

8   The U.S. Department of Education also reported that countless speakers at a conference on bilingual education "expounded at length on the need for and eventually of, a multilingual, multicultural United States of America with a national language policy citing English and Spanish as the two 'legal languages.'"

9   As a former resident of California, I am completely familiar with a system that uses two official languages, and I would not advise any nation to move in

such a direction unless forced to do so. While it is true that India functions with ten official languages, I haven't heard anyone suggest that it functions particularly well because of its multilingualism. In fact, most Indians will concede that the situation is a chaotic mess which has led to countless problems in the government's efforts to manage the nation's business. Out of necessity, English still is used extensively in India as a common language.

10   Belgium is another clear example of the diverse effects of two officially recognized languages in the same nation. Linguistic differences between Dutch- and French-speaking citizens have resulted in chronic political instability. Consequently, in the aftermath of the most recent government collapse, legislators are working on a plan to turn over most of its powers and responsibilities to the various regions, a clear recognition of the diverse effects of linguistic separateness.

11   There are other problems. Bilingualism is a costly and confusing bureaucratic nightmare. The Canadian government has estimated its bilingual costs to be nearly $400,000,000 per year. It is almost certain that these expenses will increase as a result of a massive expansion of bilingual services approved by the Canadian Parliament in 1988. In the United States, which has ten times the population of Canada, the cost of similar bilingual services easily would be in the billions.

12   We first should consider how politically infeasible it is that our nation ever could recognize Spanish as a second official language without opening the floodgates for official recognition of the more than 100 languages spoken in this country. How long would it take, under such an arrangement, before the United States started to make India look like a model of efficiency?

13   Even if we can agree that multilingualism would be a mistake, some would suggest that official recognition of English is not needed. After all, our nation has existed for over 200 years without this, and English as our common language has continued to flourish.

14   I could agree with this sentiment had government continued to adhere to its time-honored practice of operating in English and encouraging newcomers to learn the language. However, this is not the case. Over the last few decades, government has been edging slowly towards policies that place other languages on a par with English.

15   In reaction to the cultural consciousness movement of the 1960s and 1970s, government has been increasingly reluctant to press immigrants to learn the English language, lest it be accused of "cultural imperialism." Rather than insisting that it is the immigrant's duty to learn the language of this country, the government has acted instead as if it has a duty to accommodate an immigrant in his native language.

16   A prime example of this can be found in the continuing debate over Federal and state policies relating to bilingual education. At times, these have come dangerously close to making the main goal of this program the maintenance of the immigrant child's native language, rather than the early acquisition of English.

17   As a former U.S. senator from California, where we spend more on bilingual education programs than any other state, I am very familiar with both the
rhetoric and reality that lie behind the current debate on bilingual education.
My experience has convinced me that many of these programs are short-
changing immigrant children in their quest to learn English.

18   To set the record straight from the start, I do not oppose bilingual education *if it is truly bilingual.* Employing a child's native language to teach him (or
her) English is entirely appropriate. What is not appropriate is continuing to
use the children of Hispanic and other immigrant groups as guinea pigs in an
unproven program that fails to teach English efficiently and perpetuates their
dependency on their native language.

19   Under the dominant method of bilingual education used throughout this
country, non-English-speaking students are taught all academic subjects such
as math, science, and history exclusively in their native language. English is
taught as a separate subject. The problem with this method is that there is no
objective way to measure whether a child has learned enough English to be
placed in classes where academic instruction is entirely in English. As a result,
some children have been kept in native language classes for six years.

20   Some bilingual education advocates, who are more concerned with maintaining the child's use of their native language, may not see any problem with
such a situation. However, those who feel that the most important goal of this
program is to get children functioning quickly in English appropriately are
alarmed.

21   In the Newhall School District in California, some Hispanic parents are
raising their voices in criticism of its bilingual education program, which relies
on native language instruction. Their children complain of systematically being segregated from their English-speaking peers. Now in high school, these
students cite the failure of the program to teach them English first as the reason for being years behind their classmates.

22   Even more alarming is the Berkeley (Calif.) Unified School District, where
educators have recognized that all-native-language instruction would be an inadequate response to the needs of their non-English-speaking pupils. Challenged by a student body that spoke more than four different languages and
by budgetary constraints, teachers and administrators responded with innovative language programs that utilized many methods of teaching English. That
school district is now in court answering charges that the education they provided was inadequate because it did not provide transitional bilingual education for every non-English speaker. What was introduced 20 years ago as an
experimental project has become—despite inconclusive research evidence—
the only acceptable method of teaching for bilingual education advocates.

23   When one considers the nearly 50 percent dropout rate among Hispanic
students (the largest group receiving this type of instruction), one wonders
about their ability to function in the English-speaking mainstream of this
country. The school system may have succeeded wonderfully in maintaining

their native language, but if it failed to help them to master the English language fully, what is the benefit?

ALTERNATIVES

24 If this method of bilingual education is not the answer, are we forced to return to the old, discredited, sink-or-swim approach? No, we are not, since, as shown in Berkeley and other school districts, there are a number of alternative methods that have been proven effective, while avoiding the problems of all-native-language instruction.

25   Sheltered English and English as a Second Language (ESL) are just two programs that have helped to get children quickly proficient in English. Yet, political recognition of the viability of alternate methods has been slow in coming. In 1988, we witnessed the first crack in the monolithic hold that native language instruction has had on bilingual education funds at the Federal level. In its reauthorization of Federal bilingual education, Congress voted to increase the percentage of funds available for alternate methods from four to 25 percent of the total. This is a great breakthrough, but we should not be satisfied until 100 percent of the funds are available for any program that effectively and quickly can get children functioning in English, regardless of the amount of native language instruction it uses.

26   My goal as a student of language and a former educator is to see all students succeed academically, no matter what language is spoken in their homes. I want to see immigrant students finish their high school education and be able to compete for college scholarships. To help achieve this goal, instruction in English should start as early as possible. Students should be moved into English mainstream classes in one or, at the very most, two years. They should not continue to be segregated year after year from their English-speaking peers.

27   Another highly visible shift in Federal policy that I feel demonstrates quite clearly the eroding support of government for our common language is the requirement for bilingual voting ballots. Little evidence ever has been presented to show the need for ballots in other languages. Even prominent Hispanic organizations acknowledge that more than 90 percent of native-born Hispanics currently are fluent in English and more than half of that population is English monolingual.

28   Furthermore, if the proponents of bilingual ballots are correct when they claim that the absence of native language ballots prevents non-English-speaking citizens from exercising their right to vote, then current requirements are clearly unfair because they provide assistance to certain groups of voters while ignoring others. Under current Federal law, native language ballots are required only for certain groups: those speaking Spanish, Asian, or Native American languages. European or African immigrants are not provided ballots

in their native language, even in jurisdictions covered by the Voting Rights Act.

29   As sensitive as Americans have been to racism, especially since the days of the Civil Rights Movement, no one seems to have noticed the profound racism expressed in the amendment that created the "bilingual ballot." Brown people, like Mexicans and Puerto Ricans; red people, like American Indians; and yellow people, like the Japanese and Chinese, are assumed not to be smart enough to learn English. No provision is made, however, for non-English-speaking French-Canadians in Maine or Vermont, or Yiddish-speaking Hassidic Jews in Brooklyn, who are white and thus presumed to be able to learn English without difficulty.

30   Voters in San Francisco encountered ballots in Spanish and Chinese for the first time in the elections of 1980, much to their surprise, since authorizing legislation had been passed by Congress with almost no debate, roll-call vote, or public discussion. Naturalized Americans, who had taken the trouble to learn English to become citizens, were especially angry and remain so. While native language ballots may be a convenience to some voters, the use of English ballots does not deprive citizens of their right to vote. Under current voting law, non-English-speaking voters are permitted to bring a friend or family member to the polls to assist them in casting their ballots. Absentee ballots could provide another method that would allow a voter to receive this help at home.

31   Congress should be looking for other methods to create greater access to the ballot box for the currently small number of citizens who cannot understand an English ballot, without resorting to the expense of requiring ballots in foreign languages. We cannot continue to overlook the message we are sending to immigrants about the connection between English language ability and citizenship when we print ballots in other languages. The ballot is the primary symbol of civic duty. When we tell immigrants that they should learn English—yet offer them full voting participation in their native language—I fear our actions will speak louder than our words.

32   If we are to prevent the expansion of policies such as these, moving us further along the multilingual path, we need to make a strong statement that our political leaders will understand. We must let them know that we do not choose to reside in a "Tower of Babel." Making English our nation's official language *by law* will send the proper signal to newcomers about the importance of learning English and provide the necessary guidance to legislators to preserve our traditional policy of a common language.

TOPICAL CONSIDERATIONS

1. Why does Hayakawa feel it is particularly important for a nation of immigrants to communicate in a single, common tongue? Do you agree with him? Why or why not?

2. What is Hayakawa's assessment of countries that recognize two or more official languages? From what you know of multilingual countries, do you tend to agree or disagree with his assessment?

3. According to the author, how has the cultural consciousness of the 1960s and 1970s led to policies that place other languages on a par with English?

4. Has this essay changed your mind on the issue of English as an official language of the United States? In other words, do you now feel that it is an immigrant's duty to learn English? Or do you agree with advocates of bilingualism that insisting an immigrant learn English is a form of "cultural imperialism"?

5. How does Hayakawa define bilingual education? What does he feel is its biggest flaw? Drawing from your own experience, do you agree with him? Explain your answer.

6. Why does Hayakawa claim that there is "profound racism" in the amendment creating the bilingual ballot? Why do you agree or disagree with this statement?

7. What alternatives to current bilingual education does Hayakawa suggest? Do these alternatives sound reasonable to you?

8. Now that you have read this essay, how would you describe Hayakawa's political leaning? What specific opinions, attitudes, statements, and so on can you single out to support your answer?

RHETORICAL CONSIDERATIONS

1. Did the opening paragraph capture your attention? Did it make you want to read on? Explain your answer. What standard introductory technique is exemplified here?

2. Early in the essay Hayakawa quotes opinions of multilingual advocates. What is his purpose in doing this? Do you think he gives these advocates fair representation? Would you have offered them more voice or less?

3. What aspects of his personal background does Hayakawa use to support his opinions? Do you think these references add to his credibility? Explain your answer.

4. Hayakawa uses India and Belgium as examples of countries having difficulties with more than one official language. What do you make of these examples? Are they well developed? Are they convincing?

5. How does Hayakawa define bilingual education? Is it a good definition in your estimation? Would you have liked some elaboration?

6. What do you make of the name "U.S. English"? Does it sound like a good choice for a group seeking an amendment to the U.S. Constitution declaring English our official language? Explain.

7. Try to determine the audience Hayakawa was writing for. In addition to the level of his discussion, take into consideration his vocabulary and writing style. Did you find the piece easy to follow, or was it difficult in places? Explain.

8. Was the concluding paragraph satisfying to you? Why or why not? How do you evaluate the reference to the "Tower of Babel"? Is it effective?

WRITING ASSIGNMENTS

1. Write an essay supporting an amendment to the U.S. Constitution making English the official language.

2. Write an essay opposing an amendment to the U.S. Constitution making English the official language.

3. A national language is the language of public discourse, control, and power. Do you think that English instruction for minority children should be left to chance or be approached through early and intensive instruction in school? Write a paper in which you explore your thoughts on this question. Consider in your discussion the effects of home language and culture on pride.

4. One argument against bilingual education is that language-minority children cannot be separated from language-majority speakers if they are to have the maximum opportunity for second-language learning and for integration into the life of the school and community. Write a paper in which you take a stand for or against this argument.

5. One argument for bilingual education is that mother-tongue instruction makes possible the recognition and perpetuation of the values of the mother country. Furthermore, immigrant children maintain a pride and identity in their home culture. Write a paper in which you explore your feelings on this probilingual stand.

6. Another argument against bilingual education is that most proponent demands come not from migrant children but from their parents and immigrant organizations with a vested interest in holding back the assimilation of the children. Write a paper in which you explore your own views on this argument.

7. Contact some local schools and ask what bilingual programs they have. If possible, interview some teachers familiar with the programs and write a report evaluating the effectiveness of such programs.

8. Write an interior monologue of a 7-year-old non–English-speaking child entering an all-English kindergarten.

9. Take another look at Maxine Hong Kingston's "The Language of Silence" (page 43). Now try writing a dialogue between Ms. Kingston and Mr. Hayakawa on the subject of bilingual education.

VIVA BILINGUALISM

James Fallows

In 1981, the late Republican Senator from California, S. I. Hayakawa, proposed a constitutional amendment stating that English should be made the official language of the United States. Known as the English Languages Amendment (ELA), the resolution forbade the federal government or any state from making or enforcing any law that required the use of any language other than English. Among other restrictions, the ELA meant that voting ballots could be printed only in English; that bilingual education would be limited to "transitional status"; and that standards for measuring English-language proficiency for prospective citizens would be tightened.

Although no action was ever taken on the proposed amendment, the ELA reopened the debate on naming English as the official language. With mounting support from the advocacy group U.S. English, the English-only movement led 23 states to pass resolutions making English their official language. Another 20 are considering similar measures.

In August 1996, the issue once again entered the federal arena when the House voted to declare English the official language of the United States government. Dubbed the "English Empowerment Act of 1996," the bill would put an end to the current practice of printing some publications and documents in languages other than English to help those for whom English is a second language. Although the measure is still pending in the Senate, the Federal government has once again been thrust into a debate that pits America's traditions of cultural diversity against unity of language.

In the essay below James Fallows offers some arguments against the English-only movement and some of the fears that inspired it. Drawing from his own experience while living in Japan, Fallows sees nothing wrong with bilingualism. On the contrary, he claims that individuals and America as a whole stand to benefit from bilingualism. James Fallows is the Washington editor of the *Atlantic*. This article first appeared in *The New Republic* in 1986.

1 In his classic work of crackpot anthropology, *The Japanese Brain*, Dr. Tadanobu Tsunoda told his Japanese readers not to feel bad about their difficulties learning other languages, especially English. "Isn't it remarkable," he

said (I am paraphrasing), "that whenever you meet someone who speaks English really well, he turns out to be a drip?"

2   The Japanese have their own reasons for seeking such reassurance. Their students learn English exactly the way Americans (used to) learn Latin: through long, boring analyses of antique written passages. Not surprisingly, most of them feel about as comfortable making English conversation as I would if Julius Caesar strolled up for a chat. The few Japanese who do speak good English have generally lived overseas—and to that extent have become less Japanese and, by local standards, more like drips.

3   Still, for all the peculiar Japaneseness of his sentiment, the spirit of Dr. Tsunoda is alive in America today. It is reflected in the general disdain for bilingualism and bilingual education, and in campaigns like the one on California's ballot last week, sponsored by the group called U.S. English, to declare that English is America's "official" language.

4   Yes, yes, everyone needs to learn English. America doesn't want to become Quebec. We have enough other forces pulling us apart that we don't want linguistic divisions too. But is there any reason to get so worked up about today's Spanish-speaking immigrants, even if they keep learning Spanish while in school? I will confess that I once shared U.S. English-type fears about Spanish language separatism. But having spent a long time reporting among immigrants and seeing how much their children wanted to learn English, I'm not worried anymore. And, having been out of the country most of this year, I've come to think that the whole American language scare rests on two bogus and amazingly parochial assumptions.

5   The first is a view of bilingualism as a kind of polygamy. That is, according to Western standards it just doesn't work to have two wives. The partners in a marriage require a certain exclusive commitment from each other. If a man gives it to one wife, there's not enough left over to give to someone else. Similarly with language: there's only so much room in a person's brain, and if he speaks one language—let us say Spanish—really well, he'll be all filled up and won't learn English. And if his brain were not a problem, his heart would be, since he can be truly loyal to only one language. I'm burlesquing the argument a little, but not much. Why would anyone worry about students taking "maintenance" course in Spanish, if not for the fear that Spanish would somehow use up the mental and emotional space English should fill?

6   In the American context, it's easy to see why people might feel this way. Ninety-nine percent of all Americans can happily live their lives speaking and thinking about no language but English. Foreign-language education has been falling off, and except in unusual circumstances—wars, mainly—it has never had much practical reinforcement anyway. When we come across people in the United States who obviously know a foreign language, the main signal is usually that their English is so poor.

7   But suppose that mastering a second language is less like having two wives than like having two children. Maybe there's not really a limit in the brain or heart, and spreading attention among several languages—like

spreading love among several children—may actually enrich everyone involved. Without going through all the linguistic arguments showing that bilingualism is possible and natural (one impressive recent summary was *Mirr˘r of Language* by Kenji Hakuta, published this year) I will merely say that after about five seconds of talking with someone who really is bilingual, the two-child, rather than two-wife, view comes to make much more sense.

8   Everyone has heard about the Scandinavians and Swiss, who grow up in a big swirl of languages and can talk easily to anyone they meet. Their example may seem too high-toned to be persuasive in connection with today's Spanish-speaking immigrants, so consider the more down-to-earth illustrations of multilingualism to be found all over Asia.

9   Seven years ago, the government of Singapore launched a "Speak Mandarin!" campaign, designed to supplant various southern Chinese dialects with Mandarin. (This is roughly similar to a "Speak Like Prince Charles!" campaign being launched in West Virginia.) Since then, competence in Mandarin has gone up—and so has the mastery of English. At the beginning of the Speak Mandarin campaign, the pass rate for O-level (high school) exams in English was 41 percent. Now it's 61 percent. During the same period, the O-level pass rate for Mandarin went from 84 percent to 92 percent. The children managed to get better at both languages at once.

10   Just north of Singapore is Malaysia, another one-time British colony whose main political problem is managing relations among three distinct ethnic groups: Malays, Chinese, and Indians. Each of the groups speaks a different language at home—Malay for the Malays, Cantonese or Hokkien for the Chinese, Tamil for the Indians. But if you put any two Malaysians together in a room, it's almost certain that they'll be able to speak to each other, in either Malay or English, since most people are bilingual and many speak three or more languages. (The Chinese generally speak one or two Chinese dialects, plus English and/or Malay. The Indians speak English or Malay on top of Tamil, and many or most Malays speak English.) Neither Tamil nor the Chinese dialects travel well outside the ethnic group, and Malay doesn't travel anywhere else but Indonesia, so most Malaysians have a strong incentive to learn another language.

11   I should emphasize that I'm talking about people who in no way fit modern America's idea of a rarefied intellectual elite. They are wizened Chinese shopkeepers, unschooled Indian night guards, grubby Malay food hawkers, in addition to more polished characters who've traveled around the world. Yet somehow they all find room in their brains for more than one language at a time. Is it so implausible that Americans can do the same?

12 The second antibilingual assumption, rarely stated but clearly there, is that English is some kind of fragile blossom, about to be blown apart by harsh blasts from the Spanish-speaking world. Come on! Never before in world history has a language been as dominant as English is now. In every corner of the world, people realize that their chances to play on the big stage—to make money, have choices, travel—depend on learning English. They don't always

succeed, but more and more of them try. In Malaysia, in South China, even in linguophobic Japan, my family's main problem as we travel has been coping with people who spring from behind almost every lamppost and tofu stand, eager to practice the English they've picked up from the shortwave radio. Malaysia ships out tens of thousands of young people each year for studies in the United States, Australia, and England. Guess what language they have to learn before they go.

13   It may seem that modern America shamelessly coddles its immigrants, with all those Spanish-speaking street signs and TV broadcasts and "maintenance" courses, which together reduce the incentive to learn English. Well, I've spent most of this year in a position similar to the immigrants', and it's not as comfortable or satisfactory as it may look. Japan makes many more accommodations to the English language than America does to Spanish. Tokyo has four English-language daily newspapers—more than most American cities—plus several magazines. The major train and subway routes have English signs, most big-city restaurants have English menus, all major hotels have English-speaking staff. Students applying for university admission must pass tests in (written) English. Most shopkeepers, policemen, and passersby can make sense of written-down English messages. Even the Shinkansen, or bullet train, makes its announcements in both Japanese and English—which is comparable to the Eastern shuttle giving each "Please have your fares ready" message in Spanish as well as English. The nighttime TV news broadcasts now come in a bilingual version—you push a button on your set to switch from Japanese to English. It is as if the "CBS Evening News" could be simultaneously heard in Spanish.

14   Does all of this reduce the incentive to learn Japanese, or the feeling of being left out if you don't? Hah! Even though Japanese society is vastly more permeated by English than American society is by Spanish, each day brings ten thousand reminders of what you're missing if you don't know the language. You can't read the mainstream newspapers, can't follow most shows on TV, can't communicate above the "please-give-me-a-ticket-to-Kyoto" level. Without learning the language, you could never hope to win a place as anything but a fringe figure. Some adults nonetheless live out a ghettoized, English-only existence, because Japanese is no cinch, but foreign children raised in Japan pick up the language as the only way to participate.

15 The incentives for America's newcomers to learn English are never stronger. How are an immigrant's children going to go to any college, get any kind of white-collar job, live anything but a straitened, ghetto existence unless they speak English? What are the SATs, Bruce Springsteen songs, and the David Letterman show going to be in Spanish—or Korean, or Tagalog? If Malaysians and rural Chinese can see that English is their route to a wider world, are Guatemalans and Cubans who've made it to America so much more obtuse? And if they keep up their Spanish at the same time, even through the dreaded "maintenance" courses, why don't we count that as a good thing? It's good for

them, in making their lives richer and their minds more flexible, and it's good for the country, in enlarging its ability to deal with the rest of the world.

16   The adult immigrants themselves don't usually succeed in learning English, any more than my wife and I have become fluent in Japanese. But that has been true of America's immigrants for two hundred years. (The main exception were the Eastern European Jewish immigrants of the early twentieth century, who moved into English faster than Italians, Germans, Poles, or today's Latin Americans.) The Cubans' and Mexicans' children are the ones who learn, as previous immigrants' children have. When someone can find large numbers of children who are being raised in America but don't see English as a necessity, then I'll start to worry.

17   We don't want to become Quebec—and we're not about to. Quebec, Belgium, Sri Lanka, and other places with language problems have old, settled groups who've lived alongside each other, in mutual dislike, for many years—not new groups of immigrants continually being absorbed. We don't need to declare English our official language, because it already is that—as no one knows better than the immigrants and their children. Anywhere else in the world, people would laugh at the idea that English is in any way imperiled. Let's calm down and enjoy the joke too.

TOPICAL CONSIDERATIONS

1. According to Fallows, what are the positive aspects of being bilingual? Do you agree that the United States should continue to allow for bilingual ballots, signs, newspapers, and schools? Explain your answer.

2. In his essay, S. I. Hayakawa pointed to Belgium and Canada as countries where bilingualism has caused "chronic instability" and costly and confusing bureaucratic problems. How does Fallows address these arguments in his own piece? Did you find his position compelling? Why or why not?

3. Fallows says he has come to believe that the "whole American language scare rests on two bogus and amazingly parochial assumptions." What are the two assumptions? Do you agree that these are important issues in the debate about bilingualism in America?

4. Fallows cites Asia as a place hospitable to bilingualism by necessity. Do you think that concessions to language minorities in America such as bilingual ballots, court translators, health-care workers, and so on, encourage or discourage social separation? Would you resent voting ballots being printed in two or more languages? How about street signs? Explain.

5. Fallows notes that some adults in Japan manage to survive without learning the language, living out a "ghettoized, English-only existence." In light of its growing multiculturalism, how has America been ghettoized by language? Do you see this as problematic? Explain.

6. In his concluding paragraph, Fallows emphasizes the difference between the United States, with its new groups of immigrants who are continually "absorbed," and Belgium, Canada, and other places with their different language

groups who live side by side in mutual dislike. In your observation, are immigrants being "absorbed," into American life? Is such assimilation (of cultural as well as language differences) a desirable goal? Why or why not?

7. "When someone can find large numbers of children who are being raised in America but don't see English as a necessity, then I'll start to worry." Explain this potential worry of Fallows. Do you agree that children are important indicators of cultural participation? Explain.

RHETORICAL CONSIDERATIONS

1. Reread Fallows piece, noting those arguments that are based on his own personal experience. Do you feel that these arguments strengthen his overall conclusion? Why or why not?

2. Examine Fallow's analogy of language as wife and language as children (paragraphs 5–7). Does this analogy work well in the piece? Are the arguments based on these analogies (which lead to the conclusion that all people can "find room in their brains for more than one language at a time") relevant to the opposition view, as set forth by S. I. Hayakawa? Why or why not?

3. Does Fallows successfully address the opposing view in his article? Can you think of any significant counterarguments that he does not face? If so, what are they?

4. Describe Fallows's tone. Is it a successful choice for this piece? Explain.

5. Reread the article, looking for places where Fallows uses humor in his arguments. Is his use of humor successful? Does it strengthen his final conclusion in any way? Why or why not?

WRITING ASSIGNMENTS

1. Write an essay in which you argue about whether concessions to language minority groups such as bilingual education, ballots, health workers, court translators, and so on, encourage or discourage separatism and social disunity. You may base your argument on your own experience, library research, or field work in which you enter bilingual communities and workplaces and conduct interviews.

2. Have you ever been in a place where you did not speak the language? Write an essay reflecting on your experience there. In what ways did your lack of knowledge affect your experience? How does this experience help to shape your views regarding the debate about bilingualism in the United States.

3. Write an essay in which you consider the reasons why Japan offers the aid it does to persons who don't speak Japanese. Are the English-only speakers in Japan comparable to those non-English-speaking residents of the United States? If not, is the difference relevant to the argument? Why or why not?

4. Write a research paper in which you gather information about bilingualism in your state. What is the demographic profile of your state's foreign language population? How does your state provide for such nonnative speakers in terms of education and social policy?

5. How would you vote if there were a resolution to make your community officially bilingually—say, English and Spanish? Write a paper explaining the reasoning behind your vote.

6. Write a research paper based on a city that is known to be bilingual or to have bilingual sections: Santa Fe, Los Angeles, New York City, Quebec. What is the status of bilingual education in that city? How has the question been dealt with? If there is a form of bilingual education, how does it work? You might use relevant newspapers or books about the locale in question to focus your research.

ARIA: A MEMOIR OF A BILINGUAL CHILDHOOD

Richard Rodriguez

During the 1960s the concept of bilingual education arose in an effort to liberalize society's attitude toward non–English-speaking people and at the same time to preserve family language and culture. Supported largely by Hispanic Americans, bilingual education had two major goals: to instruct children in subjects taught in their family language while they mastered English and to encourage children to continue speaking their family language at home. What follows is the poignant memoir of a man who gives up his family language when he enters grammar school and the English-speaking world. It is also a persuasive argument against some precepts of bilingual theories. Richard Rodriguez was born of Spanish-speaking Mexican Americans in 1944 in San Francisco. He has degrees from Stanford, Columbia, and the University of California at Berkeley. In addition to teaching college English, Rodriguez has written several articles for the *American Scholar, Change,* the *Saturday Review,* and other magazines. He is also author of the collection of autobiographical essays, *Hunger of Memory* (1982), from which this piece comes.

1   I remember, to start with, that day in Sacramento, in a California now nearly thirty years past, when I first entered a classroom—able to understand about fifty stray English words. The third of four children, I had been preceded by my older brother and sister to a neighborhood Roman Catholic school. But neither of them had revealed very much about their classroom experiences. They left each morning and returned each afternoon, always together, speaking Spanish as they climbed the five steps to the porch. And their mysterious books, wrapped in brown shopping-bag paper, remained on the table next to the door, closed firmly behind them.

2   An accident of geography sent me to a school where all my classmates were white and many were the children of doctors and lawyers and business executives. On that first day of school, my classmates must certainly have been uneasy to find themselves apart from their families, in the first institution of their lives. But I was astonished. I was fated to be the "problem student" in class.

3   The nun said, in a friendly but oddly impersonal voice: "Boys and girls, this is Richard Rodriguez." (I heard her sound it out: *Rich-heard Road-ree-guess.*) It was the first time I had heard anyone say my name in English. "Richard,"

the nun repeated more slowly, writing my name down in her book. Quickly I turned to see my mother's face dissolve in a watery blur behind the pebbled-glass door.

4 · Now, many years later, I hear of something called "bilingual education"—a scheme proposed in the late 1960s by Hispanic-American social activists, later endorsed by a congressional vote. It is a program that seeks to permit non-English-speaking children (many from lower class homes) to use their "family language" as the language of school. Such, at least, is the aim its supporters announce. I hear them, and am forced to say no: It is not possible for a child, any child, ever to use his family's language in school. Not to understand this is to misunderstand the public uses of schooling and to trivialize the nature of intimate life.

5   Memory teaches me what I know of these matters. The boy reminds the adult. I was a bilingual child, but of a certain kind: "socially disadvantaged," the son of working-class parents, both Mexican immigrants.

6   In the early years of my boyhood, my parents coped very well in America. My father had steady work. My mother managed at home. They were no-body's victims. When we moved to a house many blocks from the Mexican-American section of town, they were not intimidated by those two or three neighbors who initially tried to make us unwelcome. ("Keep your brats away from my sidewalk!") But despite all they achieved, or perhaps because they had so much to achieve, they lacked any deep feeling of ease, of belonging in public. They regarded the people at work or in crowds as being very distant from us. Those were the others, *los gringos*. That term was interchangeable in their speech with another, even more telling: *los americanos*.

7   I grew up in a house where the only regular guests were my relations. On a certain day, enormous families of relatives would visit us, and there would be so many people that the noise and the bodies would spill out to the backyard and onto the front porch. Then for weeks no one would come. (If the doorbell rang, it was usually a salesman.) Our house stood apart—gaudy yellow in a row of white bungalows. We were the people with the noisy dog, the people who raised chickens. We were the foreigners on the block. A few neighbors would smile and wave at us. We waved back. But until I was seven years old, I did not know the name of the old couple living next door or the names of the kids living across the street.

8   In public, my father and mother spoke a hesitant, accented, and not always grammatical English. And then they would have to strain, their bodies tense, to catch the sense of what was rapidly said by *los gringos*. At home, they re-turned to Spanish. The language of their Mexican past sounded in counter-point to the English spoken in public. The words would come quickly, with ease. Conveyed through those sounds was the pleasing, soothing, consoling re-minder that one was at home.

9   During those years when I was first learning to speak, my mother and fa-ther addressed me only in Spanish; in Spanish I learned to reply. By contrast,

English (*inglés*) was the language I came to associate with gringos, rarely heard in the house. I learned my first words of English overhearing my parents speaking to strangers. At six years of age, I knew just enough words for my mother to trust me on errands to stores one block away—but no more.

10   I was then a listening child, careful to hear the very different sounds of Spanish and English. Wide-eyed with hearing, I'd listen to sounds more than to words. First, there were English (gringo) sounds. So many words still were unknown to me that when the butcher or the lady at the drugstore said something, exotic polysyllabic sounds would bloom in the midst of their sentences. Often the speech of people in public seemed to me very loud, booming with confidence. The man behind the counter would literally ask, "What can I do for you?" But by being so firm and clear, the sound of his voice said that he was a gringo; he belonged in public society. There were also the high, nasal notes of middle-class American speech—which I rarely am conscious of hearing today because I hear them so often, but could not stop hearing when I was a boy. Crowds at Safeway or at bus stops were noisy with the birdlike sounds of *los gringos*. I'd move away from them all—all the chirping chatter above me.

11   My own sounds I was unable to hear, but I knew that I spoke English poorly. My words could not extend to form complete thoughts. And the words I did speak I didn't know well enough to make distinct sounds. (Listeners would usually lower their heads to hear better what I was trying to say.) But it was one thing for *me* to speak English with difficulty; it was more troubling to hear my parents speaking in public: their high-whining vowels and guttural consonants; their sentences that got stuck with "eh" and "ah" sounds; the confused syntax; the hesitant rhythm of sounds so different from the way gringos spoke. I'd notice, moreover, that my parents' voices were softer than those of gringos we would meet.

12   I am tempted to say now that none of this mattered. (In adulthood I am embarrassed by childhood fears.) And, in a way, it didn't matter very much that my parents could not speak English with ease. Their linguistic difficulties had no serious consequences. My mother and father made themselves understood at the country hospital clinic and at government offices. And yet, in another way, it mattered very much. It was unsettling to hear my parents struggle with English. Hearing them, I'd grow nervous, and my clutching trust in their protection and power would be weakened.

13   There were many times like the night at a brightly lit gasoline station (a blaring white memory) when I stood uneasily hearing my father talk to a teenage attendant. I do not recall what they were saying, but I cannot forget the sounds my father made as he spoke. At one point his words slid together to form one long word—sounds as confused as the threads of blue and green oil in the puddle next to my shoes. His voice rushed through what he had left to say. Toward the end, he reached falsetto notes, appealing to his listener's understanding. I looked away at the lights of passing automobiles. I tried not to hear any more. But I heard only too well the attendant's reply, his calm, easy tones. Shortly afterward, headed for home, I shivered when my father put his

hand on my shoulder. The very first chance that I got, I evaded his grasp and ran on ahead into the dark, skipping with feigned boyish exuberance.

14   But then there was Spanish: *español,* the language rarely heard away from the house; *español,* the language which seemed to me therefore a private language, my family's language. To hear its sounds was to feel myself specially recognized as one of the family, apart from *los otros.* A simple remark, an inconsequential comment could convey that assurance. My parents would say something to me and I would feel embraced by the sounds of their words. Those sounds said: *I am speaking with ease in Spanish. I am addressing you in words I never use with los gringos. I recognize you as someone special, close, like no one outside. You belong with us. In the family. Ricardo.*

15   At the age of six, well past the time when most middle-class children no longer notice the difference between sounds uttered at home and words spoken in public, I had a different experience. I lived in a world compounded of sounds. I was a child longer than most. I lived in a magical world, surrounded by sounds both pleasing and fearful. I shared with my family a language enchantingly private—different from that used in the city around us.

16   Just opening or closing the screen door behind me was an important experience. I'd rarely leave home all alone or without feeling reluctance. Walking down the sidewalk, under the canopy of tall trees, I'd warily notice the (suddenly) silent neighborhood kids who stood warily watching me. Nervously, I'd arrive at the grocery store to hear there the sounds of the gringo, reminding me that in this so-big world I was a foreigner. But if leaving home was never routine, neither was coming back. Walking toward our house, climbing the steps from the sidewalk, in summer when the front door was open, I'd hear voices beyond the screen door talking in Spanish. For a second or two I'd stay, linger there listening. Smiling, I'd hear my mother call out, saying in Spanish, "Is that you, Richard?" Those were her words, but all the while her sounds would assure me: *You are home now. Come closer inside. With us. "Sí,"* I'd reply.

17   Once more inside the house, I would resume my place in the family. The sounds would grow harder to hear. Once more at home, I would grow less conscious of them. It required, however, no more than the blurt of the doorbell to alert me all over again to listen to sounds. The house would turn instantly quiet while my mother went to the door. I'd hear her hard English sounds. I'd wait to hear her voice turn to soft-sounding Spanish, which assured me, as surely as did the clicking tongue of the lock on the door, that the stranger was gone.

18   Plainly it is not healthy to hear such sounds so often. It is not healthy to distinguish public from private sounds so easily. I remained cloistered by sounds, timid and shy in public, too dependent on the voices at home. And yet I was a very happy child when I was at home. I remember many nights when my father would come back from work, and I'd hear him call out to my mother in Spanish, sounding relieved. In Spanish, his voice would sound the light and free notes that he never could manage in English. Some nights I'd jump up just hearing his voice. My brother and I would come running into the room

where he was with our mother. Our laughing (so deep was the pleasure!) became screaming. Like others who feel the pain of public alienation, we transformed the knowledge of our public separateness into a consoling reminder of our intimacy. Excited, our voices joined in a celebration of sounds. *We are speaking now the way we never speak out in public—we are together,* the sounds told me. Some nights no one seemed willing to loosen the hold that sounds had on us. At dinner we invented new words that sounded Spanish, but made sense only to us. We pieced together new words by taking, say, an English verb and giving it Spanish endings. My mother's instructions at bedtime would be lacquered with mock-urgent tones. Or a word like *sí*, sounded in several notes, would convey added measures of feeling. Tongues lingered around the edges of words, especially fat vowels, and we happily sounded that military drum roll, the twirling roar of the Spanish *r*. Family language, my family's sounds: the voices of my parents and sisters and brother. Their voices insisting: *You belong here. We are family members. Related. Special to one another. Listen!* Voices singing and sighing, rising and straining, then surging, teeming with pleasure which burst syllables into fragments of laughter. At times it seemed there was steady quiet only when, from another room, the rustling whispers of my parents faded and I edged closer to sleep.

19 Supporters of bilingual education imply today that students like me miss a great deal by not being taught in their family's language. What they seem not to recognize is that, as a socially disadvantaged child, I regarded Spanish as a private language. It was a ghetto language that deepened and strengthened my feeling of public separateness. What I needed to learn in school was that I had the right, and the obligation, to speak the public language. The odd truth is that my first-grade classmates could have become bilingual, in the conventional sense of the word, more easily than I. Had they been taught early (as upper-middle-class children often are taught) a "second language" like Spanish or French, they could have regarded it simply as another public language. In my case, such bilingualism could not have been so quickly achieved. What I did not believe was that I could speak a single public language.

20   Without question, it would have pleased me to have heard my teachers address me in Spanish when I entered the classroom. I would have felt much less afraid. I would have imagined that my instructors were somehow "related" to me; I would indeed have heard their Spanish as my family's language. I would have trusted them and responded with ease. But I would have delayed—postponed for how long?—having to learn the language of public society. I would have evaded—and for how long?—learning the great lesson of school: that I had a public identity.

21   Fortunately, my teachers were unsentimental about their responsibility. What they understood was that I needed to speak public English. So their voices would search me out, asking me questions. Each time I heard them I'd look up in surprise to see a nun's face frowning at me. I'd mumble, not really meaning to answer. The nun would persist. "Richard, stand up. Don't look at the floor. Speak up. Speak to the entire class, not just to me!" But I couldn't

believe English could be my language to use. (In part, I did not want to believe it.) I continued to mumble. I resisted the teacher's demands. (Did I
somehow suspect that once I learned this public language my family life
would be changed?) Silent, waiting for the bell to sound, I remained dazed,
diffident, afraid.

22   Because I wrongly imagined that English was intrinsically a public language
and Spanish was intrinsically private, I easily noted the difference between
classroom language and the language at home. At school, words were directed
to a general audience of listeners. ("Boys and girls . . .") Words were meaning-
fully ordered. And the point was not self-expression alone, but to make oneself
understood by many others. The teacher quizzed: "Boys and girls, why do we
use that word in this sentence? Could we think of a better word to use there?
Would the sentence change its meaning if the words were differently
arranged? Isn't there a better way of saying much the same thing?" (I couldn't
say. I wouldn't try to say.)

23   Three months passed. Five. A half year. Unsmiling, ever watchful, my
teachers noted my silence. They began to connect my behavior with the slow
progress my brother and sisters were making. Until, one Saturday morning,
three nuns arrived at the house to talk to our parents. Stiffly they sat on the
blue living-room sofa. From the doorway of another room, spying on the visitors, I noted the incongruity, the clash of two worlds, the faces and voices of
school intruding upon the familiar setting of home. I overheard one voice gen-
tly wondering, "Do your children speak only Spanish at home, Mrs. Rodriguez?" While another voice added, "That Richard especially seems so timid
and shy."

24   *That Rich-heard!*

25   With great tact, the visitors continued, "Is it possible for you and your husband to encourage your children to practice their English when they are
home?" Of course my parents complied. What would they not do for their
children's well-being? And how could they question the Church's authority
which those women represented? In an instant they agreed to give up the language (the sounds) which had revealed and accentuated our family's closeness.
The moment after the visitors left, the change was observed. "*Ahora,* speak to
us only *en inglés,*" my father and mother told us.

26   At first, it seemed a kind of game. After dinner each night, the family gathered together to practice "our" English. It was still then *inglés,* a language foreign to us, so we felt drawn to it as strangers. Laughing, we would try to define
words we could not pronounce. We played with strange English sounds, often
overanglicizing our pronunciations. And we filled the smiling gaps of our sentences with familiar Spanish sounds. But that was cheating, somebody
shouted, and everyone laughed.

27   In school, meanwhile, like my brother and sisters, I was required to attend
a daily tutoring session. I needed a full year of this special work. I also needed
my teachers to keep my attention from straying in class by calling out, "*Rich-
heard*"—their English voices slowly loosening the ties to my other name, with
its three notes, *Ri-car-do.* Most of all, I needed to hear my mother and father

speak to me in a moment of seriousness in "broken"—suddenly heartbreaking—English. This scene was inevitable. One Saturday morning I entered the kitchen where my parents were talking, but I did not realize that they were talking in Spanish until, the moment they saw me, their voices changed and they began speaking English. The gringo sounds they uttered startled me. Pushed me away. In that moment of trivial misunderstanding and profound insight, I felt my throat twisted by unsounded grief. I simply turned and left the room. But I had no place to escape to where I could grieve in Spanish. My brother and sisters were speaking English in another part of the house.

28   Again and again in the days following, as I grew increasingly angry, I was obliged to hear my mother and father encouraging me: "Speak to us *en inglés.*" Only then did I determine to learn classroom English. Thus, sometime afterward it happened: one day in school, I raised my hand to volunteer an answer to a question. I spoke out in a loud voice and I did not think it remarkable when the entire class understood. That day I moved very far from being the disadvantaged child I had been only days earlier. Taken hold at last was the belief, the calming assurance, that I *belonged* in public.

29   Shortly after, I stopped hearing the high, troubling sounds of *los gringos.* A more and more confident speaker of English, I didn't listen to how strangers sounded when they talked to me. With so many English-speaking people around me, I no longer heard American accents. Conversations quickened. Listening to persons whose voices sounded eccentrically pitched, I might note their sounds for a few seconds, but then I'd concentrate on what they were saying. Now when I heard someone's tone of voice—angry or questioning or sarcastic or happy or sad—I didn't distinguish it from the words it expressed. Sound and word were thus tightly wedded. At the end of each day I was often bemused, and always relieved, to realize how "soundless," though crowded with words, my day in public had been. An eight-year-old boy, I finally came to accept what had been technically true since my birth: I was an American citizen.

30   But diminished by then was the special feeling of closeness at home. Gone was the desperate, urgent, intense feeling of being at home among those with whom I felt intimate. Our family remained a loving family, but one greatly changed. We were no longer so close, no longer bound tightly together by the knowledge of our separateness from *los gringos.* Neither my older brother nor my sisters rushed home after school any more. Nor did I. When I arrived home, often there would be neighborhood kids in the house. Or the house would be empty of sounds.

31   Following the dramatic Americanization of their children, even my parents grew more publicly confident—especially my mother. First she learned the names of all the people on the block. Then she decided we needed to have a telephone in our house. My father, for his part, continued to use the word gringo, but it was no longer charged with bitterness or distrust. Stripped of any emotional content, the word simply became a name for those Americans not of Hispanic descent. Hearing him, sometimes, I wasn't sure if he was pronouncing the Spanish word *gringo,* or saying gringo in English.

32   There was a new silence at home. As we children learned more and more English, we shared fewer and fewer words with our parents. Sentences needed to be spoken slowly when one of us addressed our mother or father. Often the parent wouldn't understand. The child would need to repeat himself. Still the parent misunderstood. The young voice, frustrated, would end up saying, "Never mind"—the subject was closed. Dinners would be noisy with the clinking of knives and forks against dishes. My mother would smile softly between her remarks; my father, at the other end of the table, would chew and chew his food while he stared over the heads of his children.

33   My mother! My father! After English became my primary language, I no longer knew what words to use in addressing my parents. The old Spanish words (those tender accents of sound) I had earlier used—*mamá* and *papá*—I couldn't use any more. They would have been all-too-painful reminders of how much had changed in my life. On the other hand, the words I heard neighborhood kids call their parents seemed equally unsatisfactory. "Mother" and "father," "ma," "papa," "pa," "dad," "pop" (how I hated the all-American sound of that last word)—all these I felt were unsuitable terms of address for *my* parents. As a result, I never used them at home. Whenever I'd speak to my parents, I would try to get their attention by looking at them. In public conversations, I'd refer to them as my "parents" or my "mother" and "father."

34   My mother and father, for their part, responded differently, as their children spoke to them less. My mother grew restless, seemed troubled and anxious at the scarceness of words exchanged in the house. She would question me about my day when I came home from school. She smiled at my small talk. She pried at the edges of my sentences to get me to say something more. ("What . . . ?") She'd join conversations she overheard, but her intrusions often stopped her children's talking. By contrast, my father seemed to grow reconciled to the new quiet. Though his English somewhat improved, he tended more and more to retire into silence. At dinner he spoke very little. One night his children and even his wife helplessly giggled at his garbled English pronunciation of the Catholic "Grace Before Meals." Thereafter he made his wife recite the prayer at the start of each meal, even on formal occasions when there were guests in the house.

35   Hers became the public voice of the family. On official business it was she, not my father, who would usually talk to strangers on the phone or in stores. We children grew so accustomed to his silence that years later we would routinely refer to his "shyness." (My mother often tried to explain: both of his parents died when he was eight. He was raised by an uncle who treated him as little more than a menial servant. He was never encouraged to speak. He grew up alone—a man of few words.) But I realized my father was not shy whenever I'd watch him speaking Spanish with relatives. Using Spanish, he was quickly effusive. Especially when talking with other men, his voice would spark, flicker, flare alive with varied sounds. In Spanish he expressed ideas and feelings he rarely revealed when speaking English. With firm Spanish sounds he conveyed a confidence and authority that English would never allow him.

36   The silence at home, however, was not simply the result of fewer words passing between parents and children. More profound for me was the silence created by my inattention to sounds. At about the time I no longer bothered to listen with care to the sounds of English in public, I grew careless about listening to the sounds made by the family when they spoke. Most of the time I would hear someone speaking at home and didn't distinguish his sounds from the words people uttered in public. I didn't even pay much attention to my parents' accented and ungrammatical speech—at least not at home. Only when I was with them in public would I become alert to their accents. But even then their sounds caused me less and less concern. For I was growing increasingly confident of my own public identity.

37   I would have been happier about my public success had I not recalled, sometimes, what it had been like earlier, when my family conveyed its intimacy through a set of conveniently private sounds. Sometimes in public, hearing a stranger, I'd hark back to my lost past. A Mexican farm worker approached me one day downtown. He wanted directions to some place. *"Hijito, . . ."* he said. And his voice stirred old longings. Another time I was standing beside my mother in the visiting room of a Carmelite convent, before the dense screen which rendered the nuns shadowy figures. I heard several of them speaking Spanish in their busy, singsong, overlapping voices, assuring my mother that, yes, yes, we were remembered, all our family was remembered, in their prayers. Those voices echoed faraway family sounds. Another day a dark-faced old woman touched my shoulder lightly to steady herself as she boarded a bus. She murmured something to me I couldn't quite comprehend. Her Spanish voice came near, like the face of a never-before-seen relative in the instant before I was kissed. That voice, like so many of the Spanish voices I'd hear in public, recalled the golden age of my childhood.

38   Bilingual educators say today that children lose a degree of "individuality" by becoming assimilated into public society. (Bilingual schooling is a program popularized in the seventies, that decade when middle-class "ethnics" began to resist the process of assimilation—the "American melting pot.") But the bilingualists oversimplify when they scorn the value and necessity of assimilation. They do not seem to realize that a person is individualized in two ways. So they do not realize that, while one suffers a diminished sense of *private* individuality by being assimilated into public society, such assimilation makes possible the achievement of *public* individuality.

39   Simplistically again, the bilingualists insist that a student should be reminded of his difference from others in mass society, of his "heritage." But they equate mere separateness with individuality. The fact is that only in private—with intimates—is separateness from the crowd a prerequisite for individuality; an intimate "tells" me that I am unique, unlike all others, apart from the crowd. In public, by contrast, full individuality is achieved, paradoxically, by those who are able to consider themselves members of the crowd. Thus it happened for me. Only when I was able to think of myself as an American, no longer an alien in gringo society, could I seek the rights and opportunities necessary for full public individuality. The social and political advantages I enjoy

as a man began on the day I came to believe that my name is indeed *Rich-heard Road-ree-guess.* It is true that my public society today is often imper-sonal; in fact, my public society is usually mass society. But despite the anonymity of the crowd, and despite the fact that the individuality I achieve in public is often tenuous—because it depends on my being one in a crowd—I celebrate the day I acquired my new name. Those middle-class ethnics who scorn assimilation seem to me filled with decadent self-pity, obsessed by the burden of public life. Dangerously, they romanticize public separateness and trivialize the dilemma of those who are truly socially disadvantaged.

40   If I rehearse here the changes in my private life after my Americanization, it is finally to emphasize a public gain. The loss implies the gain. The house I returned to each afternoon was quiet. Intimate sounds no longer greeted me at the door. Inside there were other noises. The telephone rang. Neighbor-hood kids ran past the door of the bedroom where I was reading my school-books—covered with brown shopping-bag paper. Once I learned the public language, it would never again be easy for me to hear intimate family voices. More and more of my day was spent hearing words, not sounds. But that may only be a way of saying that on the day I raised my hand in class and spoke loudly to an entire roomful of faces, my childhood started to end.

TOPICAL CONSIDERATIONS

1. Summarize Rodriguez's argument in this essay.

2. In what ways did Rodriguez as a child feel separate from American culture?

3. How did the author as a young child react to the English language? What was his early impression of the sounds of it? The sounds of native English speakers? Of his parents trying to speak it?

4. What does the author mean by his statement in paragraph 18: "It is not healthy to distinguish public from private sounds so easily"?

5. In paragraph 27, the author recalls from his childhood a "moment of trivial mis-understanding and profound insight." Explain the significance of that moment. How was it a turning point for him?

6. What changes did the Rodriguez family undergo with the Americanization of young Rodriguez and his siblings?

RHETORICAL CONSIDERATIONS

1. Where does Rodriguez place the thesis statement of his essay? How effective is its placement?

2. Rodriguez alternates between straight memoir and argument throughout this piece. Comment on the effectiveness of such alternations. Do they add or detract from the writing?

3. In paragraph 17, Rodriguez refers to "the clicking tongue of the lock on the door." Explain the appropriateness of this metaphor. Find other examples of figu-rative language in the essay.

WRITING ASSIGNMENTS

1. After reading this essay, what are your thoughts about bilingualism? Should bilingualism be encouraged or discouraged?

2. Write a paper in which you speculate on the consequences of "anglicizing" all non–English-speaking children in American schools.

3. Write an essay in which you argue in favor of bilingual education in public school systems. Consider, as an example, a school system in which Spanish, Chinese, or Vietnamese is used interchangeably with English.

4. Write a personal account of the problems you had, if any, assimilating the language environment of your school.

5. Write a paper in which you compare Rodriguez's approach to the subject of bilingualism with that of S. I. Hayakawa. Why would the former choose to write his piece mostly in the first person? Why did Hayakawa choose to write his mostly in the third person? Which was more convincing? Which had more emotional appeal? Explain your answers.

COLORING LESSONS

David Updike

What term do you use to designate your race? Do you use color references—white, black, or red? Or the geographical origins of your ancestors—Asia, Africa, European, Latin America? Everyone has a color, but the choice of terms can be misleading. In this piece, the author, who is white, observes his 4-year-old son trying to make sense of his own biracial identity. Is he brown or black? Are others white or pink? For David Updike, the experience raises questions about the unexamined choice of the terms "black" and "white" and the cultural assumptions attached to them. Though he does not suggest abandoning the terms, he challenges us to be aware of their social "meaning" and to try on occasion not to use them.

David Updike teaches English at Roxbury Community College in Boston. This piece first appeared in the *New York Times* in July 1994.

1   It was the big annual fair at Shady Hill, a private school nestled away in one of our city's finer neighborhoods. Though October, it was warm and the ash gray clouds were giving way to soft, swelling shapes of blue. There were lots of kids already, their parents working the various concessions—apple bobbing and doughnut biting, water-balloon throwing at a heckling buffoon—all ploys to harvest money for the school's scholarship fund.

2   It seemed like the perfect event to bring an almost-4-year-old to, but my son, Wesley, was dragging on my arm, nervously surveying the scene. Getting tired of pulling him, disappointed that he was not having more fun, I stopped finally, kneeled down and asked him what was the matter.

3   He hesitated, looked around, chewing on his sleeve. "Too many pink people," he said softly. I laughed, but Wesley failed to see the humor of it and kept peering out through the thickening throng. "Too many pink people," he repeated. But along with my laugh came a twinge of nervousness—the parent's realization that our apprehensions are not entirely unfounded and that racial awareness comes even to 3-year-olds. I suspected, half wished, that his

state of unhappiness had less to do with too many "pink" people than with too many people.

4   And we had taught him to use "pink" in the first place, in preference to the more common adjective used for people of my complexion. For my wife, we had opted for "brown" because that's the color she actually is: Wesley was learning his colors, after all, and it seemed silly and misleading to be describing people by colors they clearly are not.

5   The issue had arisen at his first day care—predominantly African-American—from which he had returned one day and asked whether he really was "gray." We told him no, he wasn't gray, more brown, but a lighter, pinker shade than his mother.

6   A few months later he came home from his new day care, this time predominantly European-American, and asked, "Mommy, are we brown?"

7   "Yes," she said. "Why?"

8   "Melissa said we're b_ _ _ _ ."

9   "She did?"

10   "Yeah."

11   The whole question caused me to wonder what these two words, b_ _ _ _ and w_ _ _ _—so frequently used and so heavily laden with historical and social baggage—actually mean. I looked in a dictionary: the lighter of the two, I learned, is "the color of pure snow . . . reflecting nearly all the rays of sunlight, or a similar light. . . ."

12   The other means "lacking hue and brightness; absorbing light without reflecting any of the rays composing it . . . gloomy, pessimistic or dismal . . . without any moral light or goodness."

13   I am not the color of pure snow, and my wife and son reflect a good deal of light; they seem much closer in the spectrum to brown, "a dark shade with a yellowish or reddish hue." In any event, perhaps my problem with the two words is that they are, in the spectrum and in people's minds, absolutes and polar opposites, absorbing light or reflecting it but admitting no shades in between except gray—the pallor of the recently departed on the mortuary slab, blood drained from their earthly vessel.

14   All of which is likely to raise the hackles ("hairs on a dog's neck that bristle when the dog is ready to fight") of the anti-politically-correct thought police, who are fed up with all this precious talk about what we should call one another. They resist African-American—too many syllables, so hard to say—though they seem to be comfortable with Italian-American.

15   Let me enrage them further by suggesting that w_ _ _ _ may also have outlived its usefulness in describing people, and that we should take up European-American, instead, in keeping with the now-accepted Native, Asian- and African-American. Or maybe just plain "pink" will do, the color even the palest of us turn when push comes to shove and we reveal our humanity—when angry, say, or while laughing or having sex or lying in the sun, trying to turn brown.

16   W_ _ _ _ and b_ _ _ _ are colors no one really is, monolithic and redolent with historical innuendo and social shading, and the words encourage those of

us who use them   everyone   to continue to think in binary terms, like computers. I am not suggesting the terms be abandoned, tossed onto the scrap heap of language with other discarded words—just that they are used too easily and often and should be traded in, occasionally, for words that admit that issues of race and ethnicity are more complicated than these monosyllables imply. Try not saying them, once or twice, and see how it feels. And if you are teaching a child his or her colors, you might want to adopt a vocabulary that holds true for skin tones and for crayons.

17   But at the fair, things were improving slowly. I had, with misgivings, pointed out to Wesley that I am "pink," like some of his cousins and grandparents and uncles and aunts and school friends, and that it's not nice to say there are "too many" of us.

18   We walked around, mulling all this over, and I bought us a doughnut. We went into a gym and looked at old sports equipment, and I fought the temptation to buy something. We went outside again into the soft yellow sunlight and found happiness at a wading pool where, using fishing poles with magnets dangling from the lines, you could catch plastic fish with paper-clip noses. He caught a few and we traded them for prizes he then clutched tightly in his small, strong hands.

19   But he was still tired, and when I suggested we go home, he nodded and started to suck his thumb. I picked him up and carried him, and as we approached the gate he triumphantly called my attention to a "brown boy" with a baseball hat, who was just then coming in.

20   Again, his observation elicited in me a vague discomfort, and I wondered if we couldn't get away from all this altogether. But how?

21   "Wesley," I finally offered. "Do you have to call him 'brown boy'? Why don't you just say, 'That tall boy' or 'the boy with the blue hat' or 'the boy in the green sweatshirt'?" He mulled over my suggestion, but then rejected it.

22   "No," he said firmly. "He's brown."

TOPICAL CONSIDERATIONS

1. What was your first impression of 3-year-old Wesley's meaning when he announces in paragraph 3 that he sees "too many pink people"? Did you think he was describing race, or something else entirely?

2. Why does Updike say that he and his wife use "pink" and "brown" to refer to skin color?

3. What connotations of the words "black" and "white" does Updike reject in paragraphs 11–13? Beyond literal inaccuracy in these color terms, what cultural implications does he reject?

4. In paragraphs 14–16, how does Updike respond to cultural critics who resent the ongoing, acrimonious discussion about how to describe people of various ethnicities and skin tones?

5. What choice does Wesley make at the end of the article about identifying another child? Why is Updike uncomfortable? What do you think little Wesley's choice has taught his father?

RHETORICAL CONSIDERATIONS

1. What effect does the setting of a private school fair have on this essay? How would the essay be changed if Updike omitted information about the fair, and about his son's participation in exploring the words used for race?

2. This essay changes its tone at several points. If you have trouble identifying tone, try looking for instances where Updike uses these four: tender; philosophical; analytical and angry; wistful. Then, identify words, phrases, and images that help to create the tone. Also identify phrases that signal a transition from one tone to another.

3. Why do you think Updike never uses the word "black" and "white," substituting a first initial followed by blanks for the whole word? Where else have you seen this convention used for presenting words? How effective a strategy do you think it is?

4. If Updike could wave a magic wand and get the world to conform to the views that he is trying to teach his son, what words do you think he would use to describe race, ethnicity, and culture? Do you think this change would be completely satisfactory, or do you think some kinds of issues would still require traditional words? Review paragraphs 15 and 16 before you respond.

5. What color are you? What terms have you used to describe yourself? What terms do friends and family use? What terms do outsiders use? Do you enjoy the color terms that have been used to describe you? Would you change any of these words? Would you add any?

WRITING ASSIGNMENTS

1. Pretend you are Wesley Updike, grown up to your present age. Thinking back to your father's teachings about race, ethnicity, and color (as they are presented in this article), write a letter to your father. Explain why you do or do not appreciate the lessons he tried to teach you.

2. Take Updike up on his suggestion in paragraph 16: avoid using the terms "black" and "white" for a whole day (or any other terms designating ethnicity, rather than literal skin color). Rewrite a passage from a textbook or a newspaper article substituting appropriate crayon-color names. Then, write an essay describing how or whether this changed your perspectives and feelings about race.

3. People of African descent have been referred to as African, Afrikan, Negro, colored, Afro-American, African-American, Aframerican, black, and Black (among other terms). Using an unabridged dictionary (and other resources in African-American history), write a paper discussing the history of these words. Why was one term preferred over another at a given time? What prompted changes?

   Or, explore self-designation terms for Latino/Chicano people; people of Asian descent; people of Native American descent; "cripples" (see Nancy Mairs's article, page 355); African people who live in Africa, or who live in America; or other groups.

4. Examine some articles from the debate that Updike refers to at the beginning of paragraph 14 involving the "anti-politically-correct thought police." You might want to use such terms as "cultural studies" or "ethnicity" as you begin searching news and journal databases and indexes. Find two articles that take opposing sides on a name for a particular ethnic or minority group, and evaluate the arguments each author presents.

5. Compare and contrast the father–son relationship in this essay with the student–teacher relationship in "Theme for English B" by Langston Hughes. What are the differences between the relationships? What are the similarities?

AFRICAN AND AMERICAN

Ellen Goodman

For generations the accepted racial designation was "Negro," whereas "black" was considered racist. Then, in the 1960s, civil rights activist Stokely Carmichael proclaimed the "Doctrine of Black Power," and almost immediately "Negro" was out. Today, many black Americans are moving away from the color-coding "black" and to "African American," paralleling "Mexican American," "Native American," and "Italian American." Although there is still some confusion, the decision of a people to rename itself has profound cultural significance. In the essay below, Ellen Goodman explores the reasons for and the implications of choosing "a name that looks backward in order to move forward." Goodman is a widely syndicated, Pulitzer Prize–winning columnist. Collections of her columns have been published in *At Large* (1983), *Keeping in Touch* (1985), and *Making Sense* (1989), from which this article is taken.

1   I cannot trace my roots very deep. I run out of names and places quickly. Of my eight great-grandparents, only two were born in America. The others, whose names I do not know, came from all over Europe, mostly from towns that were German one year, Polish the next, Russian the third.

2   Some were kicked out of those towns, still others chose to emigrate. They came and married each other—sometimes against their families' wishes—and begat. They became Americans. To trace my ancestry back through even such a short history to one set of ancestors in one town in one country would mean cutting out the others the way Alex Haley did when he chose Kunta Kinte from his lexicon of forebears.

3   Like most third- and fourth-generation Americans, then, I am a genetic melting pot, the product of nationalities that spent centuries trying to murder each other. If there is an ethnicity that makes any sense at all it has been expanded from a country to an entire continent. European American.

4   It is from this personal vantage point that I witness the movement of some of my countrymen and women to name themselves after a different mother continent: Africa.

5   Twenty years ago, the civil-rights leadership told its followers to drop the names that white Americans had given them. They were no longer colored, no longer Negro, but black. Black and proud, black and powerful, black and beautiful.

6   Now there is an impulse to turn from a name that promoted unity on the basis of color to a name that promotes unity on the basis of origin. To turn from a title that describes people in contrast to others, whites, to a title that describes people in connection to their own ancestry. African American.

7   "We are not just former slaves living in the United States," says Ramona Edelin, the head of the National Urbin Coalition, who raised the issue at a recent meeting of leaders, "We are African Americans."

8   "To be called African American has cultural integrity; it puts us in our proper historical context," says Jesse Jackson, speaking for himself and others who have urged the use of a title that until now has been mainly used by academics.

9   At first, as an American who regards her ties to the mother continent Europe with great distance, I regarded the phrase *African American* with great skepticism. After all, what is in a name? Does this one promise to be more precise? If *black* is a word used to describe a huge range of skin color that rarely resembles ebony, then African is a word that covers countries as different as Ethiopia and Kenya. It covers cultures as diverse as the Kikuyu and the Bakuba.

10   Does this name promise unity? How do you find unity identifying with Africans when Africans themselves, like Europeans and Asians, are often in deadly conflict with each other? When the Americans in question may trace their strongest roots to the Caribbean, or may indeed trace much of their genetic heritage to Europe?

11   Does this name make some symbolic point? Trace back 100,000 years and all humans are descendants of a single African "Eve." Go forward far enough from the mother country to the mother continent and we are people of the mother earth.

12   But that line of reasoning is far too abstract, too starry-eyed. The question, it seems to me now, isn't whether this name change makes genetic or ethnic sense, but whether it makes emotional sense. And it does.

13   A change of name is a serious business. A name is identity, a handle on consciousness, a public and collective description of who you are. It may be especially important for those who still carry the surnames of slaveholders.

14   The name *black* emerged out of confrontational politics of the civil-rights movement. But now the toughest battles are not against segregation but against violence and drugs, the destruction of family and community and culture. Today among the leadership you hear less talk of rights and more of values.

15   In this context of change, African American sounds right. It's a name that resonates of cultural history, a name that reflects the real desire to teach children that "I am Somebody." A name that reaches back past slavery and out past the limits of an embattled city block for that lesson.

16   "Who are we if we don't acknowledge our motherland?" asks Ramona Edelin. "We are really adrift if we are just former slaves." She adds, "When a child in a ghetto calls himself African American, immediately he's international. You've taken him from the ghetto and put him on the globe."

17   The black leadership of today has turned inward, toward internal healing, toward self-help. It is a fitting impulse to choose a name that looks backward in order to move forward.

TOPICAL CONSIDERATIONS

1. Goodman states at the opening of her article that she cannot trace her roots very far back. How far back can you trace your own ancestry? Has your knowledge of your family history (or the lack of it) been important in shaping your identity and sense of place in the world? Explain your answer.

2. Goodman offers three different types of reasons for taking a name: genetic, ethnic, and emotional. Which does she decide is the most important reason, and why?

3. What are some of the political issues, as Goodman outlines them, surrounding the move from the names "Negro" and "colored" to "black," and from "black" to the name "African-American"? Why does Goodman come to the conclusion that "African-American sounds right"? Do you agree?

4. How does Goodman's position as a white American woman shape her essay? Think about ways in which her identity and experience as a European American differs from that of African Americans. Would you have read the essay differently if it had been written by an African American? Explain your answer.

RHETORICAL CONSIDERATIONS

1. Describe ways in which Goodman's style is both personal and journalistic in tone. As a reader, do you find this shifting tone effective in promoting her argument? Why or why not?

2. Goodman uses very short choppy paragraphs in this essay. How does this rhetorical choice affect your reading of the piece?

3. In paragraphs 12–15, Goodman sets out arguments against the change to the name African-American. Why does she so carefully present the opposing view? How does she use the opposition's viewpoint to strengthen her own position?

4. Is Goodman's argument strengthened by her final decision to follow the *emotional* reasoning that leads her to the conclusion that the name African-American is right? Why or why not?

WRITING ASSIGNMENTS

1. Goodman defends the use of African-American for what she calls "emotional" reasons. Write a brief essay that either defends or rejects the name for social or historical reasons.

2. Write a paper in which you discuss your own ethnic heritage and the name that accompanies it. Defend or reject that name based on your experiences of how it has affected your life and your social positioning in the United States.

3. Write a paper in which you address the question, "What is an American?" In this paper, consider Goodman's statement that most third- and fourth-generation Americans are "genetic melting pot[s]." How does the concept of American as a

melting pot shape the identities of American citizens from different ethnic and racial backgrounds? Is there something—shared experience, location or, simply, name—that makes us all "American"?

4. Goodman states that the name "black emerged out of confrontational politics of the civil-rights movement." Write a research paper in which you examine these confrontational politics. What were they? Who were the major players? What was the reasoning behind the name "black," and how is it related to the politics and changing racial ideologies of the time?

INNOCENT AND PRESUMED ETHNIC

John Yemma

Today a new level of ethnic awareness enhances the American cultural experience for all. Like so many of us, the author of this piece, John Yemma, loves ethnic foods and music and "generally enjoy[s] splashing around in the full, glorious pool of pluralism." Yet he has profited in an additional and unique way. Because of the spelling of his last name he has, over the years, been taken for a member of a variety of ethnic groups, often in welcome but sometimes with suspicion. Whether or not you can identify with Mr. Yemma, his own presumed-ethnic experience reflects society's compulsion to pigeonhole people according to ethnicity.

John Yemma is a professional journalist who writes for the *Boston Globe* where this piece originally appeared in August 1994.

1 Ethnic awareness is a great thing. It has enhanced the self-esteem of millions of Americans and rescued our nation from slow death by Cheez Whiz and wingtips. It has put color in our workplace, salsa in our diet, soul in our music and has made America a warmer, healthier, vastly more interesting place than the white-bread Levittown it might otherwise have become.

2 Personally and professionally, I'm an ethnophile. I appreciate Afropop, Los Lobos and ZZ Top. I put Vietnamese hot sauce on burritos, adore sushi, love falafel and generally enjoy splashing around in the full, glorious pool of pluralism.

3 I am not, however, from a major, what's-happening-now ethnic group. I know no folk dances, have never tricked out my car with purple running lights and don't sport a culturally significant hairstyle. When I was a kid, our family spoke English, drove a Ford, played touch football and never experienced discrimination that I've been told about.

4 Which is why I'm a little amused to have spent much of my adult life PE— Presumed Ethnic.

5 My first brush with PE status came when I was in high school in Texas. Late in my senior year a guidance counselor summoned me to her office with good news: I had been awarded a scholarship from the LULAC organization.

6 This was wonderful, I said, but isn't LULAC a Latin-American group?

7 "Yes, it is," said the counselor.

8   "I don't know if I can take it," I said. "I'm not Latin American."

9   The counselor leaned over and lowered her voice. Clearly, she had seen this sort of thing before: an earnest young man trying to pass as an Anglo.

10   "John," she said, "don't be afraid to acknowledge your heritage."

11   I wanted the scholarship money, but I really didn't qualify. My dark complexion and vowel-ending name made me seem like the promising young Latino I wasn't. (I finally convinced the counselor and she found me a Rotary Club scholarship instead.)

12   Over the years, I have inadvertently, or very nearly, benefited from being PE any number of times. For one thing, I know I have been thought of as an ethnic by companies and organizations that enjoy the idea of diversity but are too polite to ask. For another, I have developed great sympathy for the challenges faced by legitimately ethnic colleagues.

13   A career in journalism, mostly in the field of foreign news, has helped familiarize me with most ethnic issues and helped me understand the need for self-affirmation that comes from hanging with a group. While I accept that for others, however, I myself believe that the group isn't as important as the individual. OK, I know that is passe and I'm not here to try to sell you on the idea, but I'm hard wired to believe this and can't change.

14   For most people, it's not enough that I feel like I'm just me. It doesn't explain things or allow for easy assumptions about my putative beliefs and prejudices. I must be covering up or trying to pass. Or—greatest of all sins—deeply in denial.

15   As a foreign editor, I've received a number of complaints from readers who have decided that my name betrays vicious biases and secret sympathies. This is especially true when it comes to the Middle East. Lately, though, fresh groups of ready-to-be-offended people have emerged from the Balkans and Central Asia, areas that enjoy histories of intolerance and suspicion every bit as rich as the Middle East. On a number of occasions I've been told that some innocent error or omission in a news story clearly reflects my Armenian, Turkish, Serb, Croat, Polish, Arab and/or Jewish biases.

16   But I'm not complaining. I have the kind of coloration that probably prevented me from becoming a kidnap victim in Beirut and has minimized the kind of casual anti-Americanism that one runs into in places like Mexico City or Paris. Also, you get to meet nice people when you're PE.

17   The hotel clerks in Cairo became fast friends after telling me my name sounded like the Arabic word for mother.

18   After I'd written some articles from Tokyo, a kindly Japanese reader phoned to ask if I was Japanese-American. My wife thought this, too, when she first heard my name, before we met face to face.

19   I have gotten hearty *shaloms* in West Jerusalem and *salaam-aleikums* in East Jerusalem.

20   And not long ago I got a call from the Kenyan embassy in Washington. A diplomat was on his way to Boston and said he very much wanted to come see me. He would be most welcome, I said.

21   "Ah, my friend," he responded in a rich, resonant East African voice. "It will be *my* pleasure to meet a Yemma."

22   When he walked in my office a few days later, I immediately sensed his disappointment. Until that moment, he confessed, he thought I might have had roots in his country. It turns out there is a tribe in northern Kenya with the name Yemma.

23   I intend to find them one day.

24   For the record, I was born in the United States. My father's parents were born in Italy; my mother is of German-French descent. The family name was modestly changed at Ellis Island: Y instead of I. Go figure.

25   So, the only Yemmas that exist are in the United States. This makes my name exclusively and precisely American. And that's what I am.

26   I wonder if that will ever be enough.

TOPICAL CONSIDERATIONS

1. In paragraphs 1–3, how does Yemma say he feels about American ethnic diversity?

2. Why did Yemma reject a college scholarship? How would you have responded to such a mistaken offer? Would you have taken the scholarship? Why or why not.

3. How does Yemma say he has benefitted from mistakes about his ethnic identity (paragraphs 12–13 and 16)? How does Yemma say he has been harmed by the same mistakes (paragraphs 14–15)?

4. A diplomat tells Yemma of a tribe bearing his last name in Kenya; yet Yemma says that "the only Yemmas that exist are in the United States." Why does he make this claim? How does his explanation show that his name is "exclusively and precisely American"?

5. The author is a staff writer for the *Boston Globe;* he says he grew up in Texas, and that he is not from a "major, what's-happening-now ethnic group." Would his Italian-German-French ancestry be considered "ethnic" in other regions of America? Why or why not?

RHETORICAL CONSIDERATIONS

1. What kinds of cultural contrasts does Yemma list to "Cheez Whiz and wingtips," and "white-bread Levittown"? What kinds of metaphors does he use for people and their attitudes? How effective do you think these contrasts are?

2. What are the connotations of Yemma's title, "Innocent and Presumed Ethnic," and his abbreviation "PE"? What other phrases do these terms remind you of? How do they help create a specific tone for this article?

3. In paragraphs 14 and 26, Yemma expresses doubt that his own individual talents are "enough." What does he mean by this? Why doesn't he explain what "enough" means? Do you think this helps or harms his efforts to gain reader sympathy?

4. This article is written as a series of personal anecdotes, rather than as an analytic or philosophical argument. If it were not an anecdotal piece, what would a good thesis sentence be? How would the effect and tone of the article be different?

5. Yemma has been mistaken for Latino, Armenian, Turkish, Serb, Croat, Polish, Arab, Jewish, Japanese, and Kenyan. Why do you think he lists such an extensive catalog of mistaken identities? How would his article have been different if this laundry list of ethnicities had been omitted?

6. Why do you think Yemma waits so long to reveal the truth about his own ethnicity? What effect would it have had on the article if he had begun with the statement "I am of Italian-German-French descent"? What did you imagine Yemma looked like as you read through the article? Why did you imagine him the way you did?

WRITING ASSIGNMENTS

1. Make a list of your classmates' first and last names. Then, try to match ethnicities with the names. How many times were your guesses accurate? Did your opinion of the individuals change once you found out something about their ethnicity that their names did not reveal? If so, why?

2. Are you a member of a "major, what's-happening-now ethnic group"? Or (a different question) are you "ethnic"? Why or why not? What features or qualities help you determine the answer to this question?

3. In your opinion, what is the difference between ethnicity (as Yemma discusses it here) and race (as Updike discusses it)? How or why are the two related to culture? Using an unabridged dictionary and other sociological resources, discuss the differences and similarities among the three terms. Where do they overlap? How or why could these overlaps create confusion?

4. If John Yemma were equal parts Italian, German, French, and Latino, would he be entitled to take the LULAC scholarship that his guidance counselor initially offered him? In your opinion, why or why not?

5. Research the history of name changes at Ellis Island in New York City, or at other entry points into the United States. Why were these changes made? Do you think these changes were appropriate? Justify your answer. How did the people whose names were changed feel about their new names? Can any of your family's members recall name changes?

THEME FOR ENGLISH B

Langston Hughes

Langston Hughes (1902–1967) was a remarkably prolific and celebrated writer. In addition to his autobiography, *The Big Sea* (1940), Hughes published 17 books of poetry, two novels, seven short story collections, and 26 plays. By the time he graduated from Lincoln University (Pennsylvania) in 1926, he had established himself as the best poet of the Harlem Renaissance. He also wrote a column for the *New York Post*. Much of his life was devoted to the promotion of black art, music, and history.

Unlike other African American writers who wrote about more universal themes and, thus, broadened their audiences to include whites, Hughes wrote about black experience and racial themes. The poem below, taken from his collection *Montage from a Dream Deferred*, is written from the point of view of a black college student faced with a universal writing assignment. Like some of the essays in this chapter, the poem raises the conflicts inherent in being a member of an ethnic and racial minority group in a country that celebrates universality. As you read this poem, consider how your own college experience requires you to cross racial, cultural, and class boundaries.

The instructor said,

> *Go home and write*
> *a page tonight.*
> *And let that page come out of you—*
> 5 *Then, it will be true.*

I wonder if it's that simple?
I am twenty-two, colored, born in Winston-Salem.
I went to school there, then Durham, then here
to this college on the hill above Harlem.
10 I am the only colored student in my class.
The steps from the hill lead down into Harlem,
through a park, then I cross St. Nicholas,
Eighth Avenue, Seventh, and I come to the Y,
the Harlem Branch Y, where I take the elevator
15 up to my room, sit down, and write this page:

It's not easy to know what is true for you or me
at twenty-two, my age. But I guess I'm what

I feel and see and hear, Harlem, I hear you:
hear you, hear me—we two—you, me, talk on this page.
20 (I hear New York, too.) Me—who?

Well, I like to eat, sleep, drink, and be in love.
I like to work, read, learn, and understand life.
I like a pipe for a Christmas present,
or records—Bessie, bop, or Bach.
25 I guess being colored doesn't make me *not* like
the same things others folks like who are other races.
So will my page be colored that I write?

Being me, it will not be white.
But it will be
30 a part of you, instructor.
You are white—
yet a part of me, as I am a part of you.

That's American.
Sometimes perhaps you don't want to be a part of me.
35 Nor do I often want to be a part of you.
But we are, that's true!
As I learn from you,
I guess you learn from me—
Although you're older—and white—
40 and somewhat more free.

This is my page for English B.

QUESTIONS FOR DISCUSSION

1. What do the italics in lines 2–5 indicate? Who is talking? How specific is the directive "let the page come out of you"? If you had to write an essay based only on these directions, how would you respond?

2. The speaker in this poem says he is what he feels, sees, and hears. What concrete evidence of these sensations does he supply in stanzas 2 and 4? How can he "be" these things?

3. How is the third stanza of the poem different from stanzas 2 and 4? What question does the speaker ask? To whom or what does he refer each time he uses the pronoun "you"? What does he seem to be asking the instructor, whom he knows will be reading this essay very soon?

4. When does the speaker first mention racial difference between himself and the instructor? How does the speaker express the differences between himself and the instructor—what language does he use? Does he use language that is mostly about color, or mostly about culture?

5. What is the speaker's tone as he discusses racial difference? How does he feel about the instructor? Does the speaker express any reasons for which he thinks the instructor might dislike his essay?

6. In line 10 of "Theme for English B," Hughes writes "I am the only colored student in my class." If you have ever been in a similar situation—the only one of a particular group in a larger group—how did you feel? If not, how did you perceive the person in the minority—did he or she stand out or catch your attention in some way?

WRITING ASSIGNMENTS

1. Have you ever had to write a personal experience paper for a teacher whom you believed didn't like something about you? If so, how did you respond; did you write what you felt? Did you change something about the essay? Did you criticize the teacher's prejudices? If possible, take the comments that a teacher has written on such a paper and write a response to that teacher.

2. Select another essay from this textbook in which the names people call themselves influence the way others perceive them. For instance, you might look at David Updike's "Coloring Lessons," or at Nancy Mairs's "On Being a Cripple." Then, contrast and compare the attitudes of the speaker with the attitudes that Langston Hughes's speaker shows here.

FROM AFRICA TO THE NEW WORLD AND INTO THE SPACE AGE

Geneva Smitherman

Beyond name identification, Geneva Smitherman explains, most African Americans have a common tongue. More than 80 percent, she claims, communicate in black English on occasion. "It has allowed blacks to create a culture of survival in an alien land, and as a by-product has served to enrich the language of all Americans." In the selection below, Smitherman describes some of the features and roots of black English (also known as Ebonics), while exploring its cultural and social significance to so many Americans.

Geneva Smitherman is a professor of black studies and linguistics at Wayne State University. She is the author of *Talkin and Testifyin: The Language of Black America* (1986), from which this essay is taken.

1 "What it is! What it is!"

2 "That cat name Shaft is a bad mother—" "Hush yo mouf!"

3 "Can't nobody never do nothin in Mr. Smith class."

4 "Least my momma don't buy her furniture from the Good Will!"

5 "I come here today to testify what the Lord done did for me."

6 "It bees dat way sometime."

7 What it is! What is it? It is the voice of Black America, variously labeled Black English, Black Dialect, Black Idiom, or recently, Ebonics. Black writer Claude Brown, author of *Manchild in the Promised Land,* called it the "language of soul." White writer Norman Mailer named it the "language of hip." Some folk, like black poet Nikki Giovanni, refer to it as just plain "black talk."

8   Before about 1959 (when the first study was done to change black speech patterns), Black English had been primarily the interest of university academics, particularly the historical linguists and cultural anthropologists. In recent years, though, the issue has become a very hot controversy, and there have been articles on Black Dialect in the national press as well as in the educational research literature. We have had pronouncements on black speech from the NAACP and the Black Panthers, from highly publicized scholars of the Arthur Jensen–William Shockley bent, from executives of national corporations such as Greyhound, and from housewives and community folk. I mean, really, it seem like everybody and they momma done had something to say on the subject!

9   Now, concern over the speech of blacks and educational programs to bring about dialect change have been generated by two major forces. The first major force was the social change movements (or upheavals—depending on where you comin from) of the sixties, spearheaded by the 1954 Supreme Court school desegregation decision, followed by the 1955 refusal of black Rosa Parks to move to the back of the bus, and the emergence of Martin Luther King, Jr., and the civil rights thrust, followed by black power and the black cultural consciousness movement. The second major force was embodied in White America's attempt to deal with this newly released black energy by the implementation of poverty programs, educational and linguistic remediation projects, sociolinguistic research programs, and various other up-from-the-ghetto and "Great Society" efforts. As we all know, these two forces have not acted in concert. While blacks were shouting "I'm black and I'm proud," Anglos were admonishing them to "be like us" and enter the mainstream. While you had black orators, creative artists, and yes, even scholars rappin in the Black Thang, educators (some of them black, to be sure) were preaching the Gospel that Black English speakers must learn to talk like White English speakers in order to "make it."

10   Much that you hear nowadays about Black Dialect tends to be general and to focus on global concerns over social policy and political matters, with insufficient attention to elements of the language itself and the historical background and sociocultural development of that language (aside from the special academics mentioned earlier). That has been unfortunate because we need much more knowledge about the language and the way it functions in the communication system of blacks. Therefore, let us get off this global trip and get down to the nitty-gritty of answering the questions, just what *is* Black English, where did it come from and what are the implications for black-white interaction and teaching black children?

11   In a nutshell: Black Dialect is an Africanized form of English reflecting Black America's linguistic-cultural African heritage and the conditions of servitude, oppression and life in America. Black Language is Euro-American speech with an Afro-American meaning, nuance, tone, and gesture. The Black Idiom is used by 80 to 90 percent of American blacks, at least some of the

time. It has allowed blacks to create a culture of survival in an alien land, and as a by-product has served to enrich the language of all Americans.

12   Think of black speech as having two dimensions: language and style. Though we will separate the two for purposes of analysis, they are often overlapping. This is an important point, frequently overlooked in discussions of Black English. Consider two examples. Nina Simone sing: "It bees dat way sometime." Here the language aspect is the use of the verb *be* to indicate a recurring event or habitual condition, rather than a one-time-only occurrence. But the total expression—"It bees dat way sometime"—also reflects Black English style, for the statement suggests a point of view, a way of looking at life, and a method of adapting to life's realities. To live by the philosophy of "It bees dat way sometime" is to come to grips with the changes that life bees putting us through, and to accept the changes and bad times as a constant, ever-present reality.

13   Reverend Jesse Jackson preach: "Africa would if Africa could. America could if America would. But Africa cain't and America ain't." Now here Reverend Jesse is using the language of Black Dialect when he says "ain't" and when he pronounces *can't* as "cain't." But the total expression, using black rhythmic speech, is the more powerful because the Reb has plugged into the style of Black Dialect. the statement thus depends for full communication on what black poet Eugene Redmond calls "songified" pattern and on an Afro-American cultural belief set. That belief holds that White America has always failed blacks and will continue to do so; and that going back to Africa or getting any help from African countries is neither feasible nor realistic because newly emerging African nations must grapple first with problems of independence (economic and otherwise) inherited from centuries of European colonization.

14   These two very eloquent examples of Black English illustrate that the beauty and power of the idiom lies in its succinctness: saying the same thing in standard written English has taken more than ten times as many words. Black English, then, is a language mixture, adapted to the conditions of slavery and discrimination, a combination of language and style interwoven with and inextricable from Afro-American culture.

15   Where did this black language and style come from? To answer this question, we have to begin at least as far back as 1619 when a Dutch vessel landed in Jamestown with a cargo of twenty Africans. The arrival of this slaveship marked the beginning of slavery in Colonial America. What kind of language did these and immediately succeeding generations of slaves speak? Was it Ibo, Yoruba, Hausa, some other West African language, Pidgin English? We know that these "new Negroes" (as they were often described in Colonial America) did not jump fresh off the boat doing the Bump and speaking White English! Yet we don't have any tape or phono recordings, nor any other actual direct speech samples of early Black American English. Thus we have to rely on reconstructions of black talk based on indirect evidence, such as representations

of Black Dialect in White and Black American literature, written reproductions of the dialect in journals, letters, and diaries by whites, and generalized commentary about slave speech, usually also from whites. Another important source of evidence is based on analogies of Black American speech characteristics with those of other English-based pidgins and creoles found in the Caribbean and in parts of Africa. Language systems such as Jamaican Creole or Nigerian Pidgin English are still in active use today and provide a kind of linguistic mirror image of Black American (Pidgin and Creole) English in its early stages of development.

16   What this image suggests is as follows. African slaves in America initially developed a pidgin, a language of transaction, that was used in communication between themselves and whites. Over the years, the pidgin gradually became widespread among slaves and evolved into a creole. Developed without benefit of any formal instruction (not even a language lab!), this lingo involved the substitution of English for West African words, but within the same basic structure and idiom that characterized West African language patterns. For example, West African languages allow for the construction of sentences without a form of the verb *to be.* Thus we get a typical African-English Pidgin sentence such as "He tell me he God," used by Tituba, a slave from the island of Barbados in the British West Indies, and recorded by Justice Hathorne at the Salem witch trial in 1692. In Tituba's *he God* statement, the words are English, but the grammar or structure is West African. Such sentence patterns, without any form of the verb *be,* can frequently be heard in virtually any modern-day black community.

17   Now, as anyone learning a foreign tongue knows, the vocabulary of the new language is fairly easy to master; to some extent, sounds are also. But syntactical structure and idiomatic rules require considerable time and practice to master. Moreover, the one item of a language that remains relatively rigid and fixed over time is its structure. The formation of this Black American English Pidgin demonstrates, then, simply what any learner of a new language does. They[1] attempt to fit the words and sounds of the new language into the basic idiomatic mold and structure of their native tongue. For example, when I used to teach English to foreign students at the university, I once had a German student render Patrick Henry's famous motto as "Give me the liberty or the death." He was generalizing from the German rule which dictates that definite articles must accompany nouns. Similarly, when I used to teach high school Latin, I'd get native English speakers (whites) who would insist on using the apostrophe rather than the proper case ending to indicate possession, producing, for instance, *agricola's filia* (or sometimes even worse, *agricolae's*

---

[1]In traditional usage, this sentence would have begun with the masculine pronoun "he," since it refers to "any learner," which is singular. However, due to the public's increased awareness of sexist uses of the English language, plural pronouns have now become acceptable substitutes for the masculine singular. I will continue to follow this procedure throughout, along with using "his or her." For an excellent set of guidelines for avoiding sexist language use, see "Guideline for Nonsexist Use of Language in NCTE Publications," National Council of Teachers of English.

filia) for the *farmer's daughter*. And then there is the typical error of the English speaker learning French who forms the compound *paille-chapeau* on the model of *straw hat*.

18   Below are a few of the West African language rules that were grafted onto early Black English, and which still operate in Black English today.

Grammar and Structure Rule in West African Languages	**Black English**
Repetition of noun subject with pronoun	My father, he work there.
Question patterns without *do*	What it come to?
Same form of noun singular and plural	for one boy; five boy

Grammar and Structure Rule in West African Languages	**Black English**
No tense indicated in verb; emphasis on manner or character of action	I know it good when he ask me
Same verb form for all subjects	I know; you know; he know; we know; they know

Sound Rule in West African Languages	**Black English**
No consonant pairs	*jus* (for *just*); *men* (for *mend*)
Few long vowels or two-part vowels (diphthongs)	*rat* or *raht* (for *right*); *tahm* (for *time*)
No /r/ sound	*mow* (for *more*)
No /th/ sound	Black English speaker substitutes /d/ or /f/ for /th/; thus *souf* (for *south*) and *dis* (for *this*)

19   The slave's application of his or her intuitive knowledge of West African rules to English helped bridge the communications gap between slave and master. However, the slaves also had the problem of communicating with each other. It was the practice of slavers to mix up Africans from different tribes, so in any slave community there would be various tribal languages such as Ibo, Yoruba, Hausa. Even though these African language systems shared general structural commonalities, still they differed in vocabulary. Thus the same English-African language mixture that was used between slave and master had

also to be used between slave and slave. All this notwithstanding, it is only logical to assume that the newly arrived Africans were, for a time at least, bilingual, having command of both their native African tongue and the English
pidgin as well. However, there was no opportunity to speak and thus reinforce
their native language, and as new generations of slaves were born in the New
World, the native African speech was heard and used less and less, and the
English pidgin and creole varieties more and more. Needless to say, didn't nobody sit down and decide, consciously and deliberately, that this was the way it
was gon be—languages, pidgins, creoles, dialects was all like Topsy: they jes
grew.

20   Unfortunately, we have little empirical record of this growth in what we
may call its incubation period, that is, for the period from the arrival of the
first slaves in 1619 up until the Revolutionary War in 1776. In point of fact, not
until 1771 do we get an actual recorded sample of Black American speech
from a black. (Slightly before this time, there are a few recorded instances of
whites trying to speak "Negro" in addressing both slaves and Indians.) In the
comedy *Trial of Atticus Before Justice Beau, for a Rape,* written in 1771, a
Massachusetts Negro named Caesar is given a bit part in the play—two short
lines—in what he says:

> Yesa, Master, he tell me that Atticus he went to bus [kiss] 'em one day, and a shilde
> [child] cry, and so he let 'em alone . . . Cause, Master, I bus him myself.

Though scant, this speech sample is striking for its parallel to modern-day
black speech forms. For example, note the lack of *-s* on the verb in *he tell* and
the repetition of the subject in *Atticus he.* Contemporary Black English examples are found in sentences like "The teacher, he say I can't go" and "My
brother, he know how to fix it."

21   As mentioned, if we broaden our scope to encompass African slaves in
English-speaking communities outside the United States, we can pick up
some additional cogent examples of early Black Dialect that parallel the structure of many sentences heard in contemporary Black America. For instance,
there is the seventeenth-century statement of Tituba, "He tell me he God,"
which was alluded to earlier, and there is a 1718 representation of black speech
from the colony of Surinam in South America: "Me bella well" (I am very well).
Both sentences parallel contemporary Black English structures like *My
momma do that all the time* (no *-s* on verb *do*), and *They rowdy* (no form of
verb *to be* in the sentence). Toby, a Barbadian slave in 1715, used plural forms
like "There lives white mans, white womans, negree mans, negree womans . . ."
These forms are similar to today's Black English plurals in phrases like *five
womens* and *these mens.* A possible explanation for the derivation of this kind
of plural is the process of "hypercorrection." That is, in trying to appropriate
White English without the aid of specified grammatical rules (or teachers to
teach the rules), the African speaker took the initiative and made some rather
sensible deductions and analogies about English speech forms. Thus, if in En-

glish an -s is used to indicate the plural, then logically you should put an -s on all words in the plural—we have *one boy, two boys,* and *one book, two books,* so why not *one man, two mans* (or *two mens*), and *one child, two childrens?* Another kind of hypercorrection is in the use of -s in certain verb forms. Not being exactly sure where the -s goes, the speaker chooses the -s with many subject-verb combinations (just to make sure!). Since English requires us to say *he does,* why not *I does?* (And is it *he do* and *they does,* or *he does,* and *they do?*)

22   Though hypercorrection accounts for a small number of Black Dialect patterns, Black English's main structural components are, of course, the adaptations based on African language rules. The historical development we are reconstructing here is the continuity of Africanisms in Black English throughout time and space. We can possibly get a firmer grasp of the total historic picture by considering just one aspect of Black English structure from the early days to the present and from within as well as outside of the United States. Note, then, the following summary illustration of "zero copula" in Black English (that is, sentence patterns with no form of the verb *to be*).

He tell me he God. *Barbados,* 1692

Me bella well (I am very well.) *Surinam,* 1718

Me massa name Cunney Tomsee. (My master's name is Colonel Thompson.) *U.S.,* 1776

Me den very grad. (I am then very glad.) *U.S.,* 1784

You da deble. (You are the devil.) *U.S.,* 1792

He worse than ebber now. *U.S.,* 1821

What dis in heah? (What is this in here?) *U.S.,* 1859

But what de matter with Jasper? (But what is the matter with Jasper?) *U.S.,* 1882

Don't kere, he somethin' t'other wif dis here Draftin' Bo'd. (I don't care, he is something or other [signifying person of authority] with this Draft Board.) *U.S.,* 1926

'E mean tid' dat. (He is mean to do that.) *Gullah Creole, from the Sea Islands, U.S.,* 1949

Di kaafi kuol. (The coffee is cold.) *Jamaica,* 1966

They some rowdy kids. *U.S.,* 1968

A siki. (He sick.) *Surinam,* 1972

This my mother. *U.S.,* 1975

23   It is true that a number of early Black American English forms have survived until the present day, but it is also true that the distance between contemporary Black and White American English is not as great as it once was. And certainly it is not as great as the distance between, say, contemporary Jamaican Creole English and the English of White America and Britain. How

have time and circumstance affected the African element in Black American English? The answer to this question lies in the impact of mainstream American language and culture on Black America, and in the sheer fact of the smaller ratio of blacks to whites in this country (as compared to overwhelmingly huge black populations in the Caribbean and in Africa). With such close linguistic-cultural contact, the influence of the majority culture and language on its minorities is powerful indeed, and there is great pressure on the minorities to assimilate and adopt the culture and language of the majority.

24   In the early period of American history, the African experience was very immediate and real to the slaves and many yearned to escape back to Africa. As time progressed, though, the African slave became rather firmly entrenched in the New World, and hopes of returning to the motherland began to seem more like unattainable fantasies. Having thus resigned themselves to a future in the New World, many slaves began to take on what Langston Hughes has termed the "ways of white folks"—their religion, culture, customs, and, of course, language. At the same time, though, there were strong resistance movements against enslavement and the oppressive ways of white folks. Thus, from the very beginning, we have the "push-pull" syndrome in Black America, that is, *pushing* toward White American culture while simultaneously *pulling* away from it. (W. E. B. DuBois used the term "double consciousness" to refer to this ambivalence among blacks.) A striking example of the phenomenon is the case of the ex-slave Absalom Jones, founder of one of the first separate black church movements within white Protestant denominations. Jones took on the white man's religion, and proceeded to practice it. (The "push.") Yet when he attempted to pray in a white church in Philadelphia in 1787, an usher pulled him from his knees and ousted him from the church. Thereupon, Jones, along with another ex-slave, Richard Allen, established the African Methodist Episcopal Church. (The "pull.")

25   The "push-pull" momentum is evidenced in the historical development of Black English in the push toward Americanization of Black English counterbalanced by the pull of retaining its Africanization. We may use the term "de-creolization" to refer to the push toward Americanizing of the language. As slaves became more American and less African, the Black English Creole also became less Africanized. It began to be leveled out in the direction of White English and to lose its distinctive African structural features—that is, the Black English Creole became de-creolized. This process was undoubtedly quite intense and extensive during the Abolitionist period and certainly following Emancipation. It was a primary tactic of Abolitionists (and, traditionally, all fighters for the black cause) to prove blacks equal to whites and therefore worthy of freedom and equality. How could blacks claim American equality if they were not speaking American lingo? Ay, but here we come to the rub or the pull. For blacks have never really been viewed or treated as equals, thus their rejection of White American culture and English—and hence today the process of de-creolization remains unfinished (not to mention

various undercurrent and sporadic efforts at re-creolization, such as that among writers, artists, and black intellectuals of the 1960s, who deliberately wrote and rapped in the Black Idiom and sought to preserve its distinctiveness in the literature of the period).

26   The dynamics of push-pull can help to illuminate the complex sociolinguistic situation that continues to exist in Black America. That is, while some blacks speak very Black English, there are others who speak very White English, and still others who are competent in both linguistic systems. Historically, black speech has been demanded of those who wish to retain close affinities with the black community, and intrusions of White English are likely to be frowned upon and any black users thereof promptly ostracized by the group. Talkin proper (trying to sound white) just ain considered cool. On the other hand, White America has insisted upon White English as the price of admission into its economic and social mainstream. Moreover, there is a psychological factor operating here: people tend to feel more comfortable when they can relax and rap within the linguistic framework that has been the dialect of their nurture, childhood, identity, and style. Hence, even when there is no compelling social pressure to use Black English, there may be an inner compulsion to "talk black."

27   Let us return to history for a minute to gain a broader understanding of these dynamics. Slaves continued to be imported into America at least up to 1808 when the African slave trade was outlawed by federal legislation. In a sense, we can extend the date even further since the Slave Trade Act was not rigidly enforced. (As late as 1858, just three years before the Civil War, over 400 slaves were brought direct from Africa to Georgia.) This constant influx of slaves made the black community one where there were always numbers of slaves who could speak no English at all. Some idea of the linguistic situation in Black America can be gleaned from newspaper advertisements about runaway slaves. These ads generally cited the slave's degree of competence in English as a method of identification. Judging from the advertisements, there were, linguistically speaking, three groups of African slaves in Colonial times.

28   The recent arrivals ("new" Negroes) knew practically no English at all. An ad in the *New York Evening Post* in 1774 read: "Ran away . . . a new Negro Fellow named Prince, he can't scarce speak a Word of English."

29   Then there were slaves who were not born in the U.S. but had been here some time and were still in the process of learning English; some of these were referred to as speakers of either "bad" English or only "tolerable" English. In 1760 the *North-Carolina Gazette* ran this ad: "Ran away from the Subscriber, living near Salisbury, North Carolina . . . a negro fellow named JACK, African born . . . came from Pennsylvania about two years since . . . He is about 30 years of age, and about 5 feet high, speaks bad English."

30   Those slaves who had successfully mastered English, most of whom, according to the ads, had been born and brought up in America, were referred to as speakers of "good" or "exceptional" English. In 1734 this ad appeared in

the Philadelphia *American Weekly Mercury:* "Run away . . . a Negro Man named *Jo Cuffy,* about 20 Years of age . . . ; he's *Pennsylvania* born and speaks good *English.*"

31   Recall that not all blacks in early America were slaves; many either were freed by their masters or bought themselves out of servitude. An important mark of the free person of color, and thus a survival necessity for runaway slaves, was linguistic competence in White English. Moreover, early black writers such as Phillis Wheatley, Jupiter Hammon, Frederick Douglass, and others wrote in the current White English dialect of their respective times. Clearly, from these very early years, there seemed to be one variety of English prevalent among unlettered blacks and those still bound to the plantation way of life, and another variety, quite like that of whites, used and acquired by those few blacks who were literate and free, as well as by those who were more closely associated with Ole Massa. Furthermore, it is highly probable that the black speakers of White English, because of proximity and necessity, commanded the Black English Creole as well. In Beverly Tucker's 1836 novel, *The Partisan Leader,* this white Southerner distinguished two types of slave speech: field and house. Tucker asserted that the dialect of the house slave was highly similar to that of Ole Massa. Moreover, in the novel, the house slave Tom switches from the dialect acquired from his master to field speech to mislead Yankee invaders.

32   In short, there was a social pattern in early Black America where status— and even survival as a freeman—depended to a great extent on competence in White English (the "push"). Yet, then as now, the linguistic situation was complicated by other forces—the oppression and slavery associated with White English speakers, and the simple fact that there were more black speakers of Black English than black speakers of White English. Hence, both circumstance and psychology would propel blacks toward Black English (the "pull") and require that any black speaker of White English be fluent in Black English as well ("push" and "pull").

33   Our look at the history of black English would be incomplete without attention to the special case of Gullah Creole. This dialect, also known as Geechee speech, is spoken by rural and urban blacks who live in the areas along the Atlantic coastal region of South Carolina and Georgia. While some Geechees inhabit the Sea Islands along the coast, many also live around Charleston and Beaufort. Most of the ancestors of these blacks were brought direct from Nigeria, Liberia, Gambia, Sierra Leone, and other places in West Africa where Ibo, Yoruba, Mandingo, Wolof, and other West African languages were and still are spoken. Today, Gullah people form a special Black American community because they have retained considerable African language and cultural patterns. Even the names Gullah and Geechee are African in origin—they refer to languages and tribes in Liberia. For decades, these people have lived in physical and cultural isolation from both mainstream Black and White America, and they bear living witness to the language and way of life that other

American blacks have long since lost. (However, the African purity of the Geechee community has recently been threatened by the advent of American tourism attempting to capitalize on the "exotic, Old World charm" of the folk. Hotels, night spots, and other modern-day conveniences and tourist attractions are being constructed on the Sea Islands, thereby uprooting large numbers of blacks and disrupting their traditional African way of life.)

34   Despite a twentieth-century white writer's reference to Gullah speech as a "slovenly" approximation of English, issuing forth from "clumsy, jungle tongues and thick lips," anybody knowledgeable about African-English language mixtures can readily discern the systematic African element in Gullah Creole. In black linguist Lorenzo Turner's fifteen-year study of this dialect, he found not only fundamental African survivals in sound and syntax, but nearly 6,000 West African words used in personal names and nicknames, in songs and stories, as well as in everyday conversation. It is important for our understanding of Black English to recognize that black speech outside of Geechee areas was undoubtedly once highly similar to Gullah and is now simply at a later stage in the de-creolization process. For example, both Gullah and non-Gullah blacks still use the West African pattern of introducing the subject and repeating it with a personal pronoun. Thus, the Gullah speaker says, "De man an his wif hang to de tree, they lik to pieces." (The man and his wife hanging to the tree, they were licked to pieces.) The non-Gullah speaker handles the subject in the same way: "Yesterday, the whole family, they move to the West Side." On the other hand, only Gullah blacks still use the West African pattern of placing the adjective after the noun: "day clean broad." Other speakers of Black English follow the same pattern as White English speakers: "broad daylight."

35   We can say, then, that contemporary Black English looks back to an African linguistic tradition which was modified on American soil. While historical records and documents reveal a good deal about the development and change of this Africanized English, there is much that the records don't tell us. As a former slave said, "Everything I tells you am the truth, but they's plenty I can't tell you."

TOPICAL CONSIDERATIONS

1. Smitherman says that concern over the speech of blacks and the educational programs to bring about dialect change have been generated by two major forces. What are those forces, and how would you characterize the conflict between them?

2. In paragraph 10, Smitherman poses the questions, "just what *is* Black English, where did it come from?" Summarize her basic arguments about the origins and content of black English.

3. Smitherman makes distinctions between the dimensions of black speech. What are these distinctions and what effect do they have on the dialect? How do these dimensions help to differentiate black and white English?

4. In terms of the history of black English, Smitherman says (paragraph 15) that we have to "rely on reconstructions of black talk based on indirect evidence, such as representations of Black Dialect in White and Black American literature" and other sources. How reliable and valid do you suppose these representations are? Explain your answer.

5. Beginning in paragraph 17, Smitherman goes into a detailed description of the learning process of the syntactical and idiomatic structures of a new language. Have you ever studied a foreign language and experienced the kinds of errors Smitherman cites?

6. Reread Smitherman's article, looking for at least five instances of structural components of black English that have been adapted from African language rules.

7. What is the "push-pull" syndrome in black America? How does this phenomenon relate to the development of black English?

8. How does the history of slavery in this country bear on the development of black English? For example, why has the process of "de-creolization," according to Smitherman, remained unfinished today?

RHETORICAL CONSIDERATIONS

1. Smitherman begins her essay with examples of black dialect, then slips in and out of black English to the end. Does such movement serve to strengthen her essay? How does her own fluency in both black and white English affect your reading of this piece? Explain your answer.

2. How is this essay organized? Is the material in the essay organized effectively? Explain.

3. Does Smitherman give sufficient evidence for her claims? Point to specific instances in the text where evidence either is used well or is scanty. Explain your choices.

4. Smitherman's arguments are based on linguistics, sociology, cultural studies, and history. Is she successful in making connections between all of these fields in her argument regarding the development of black English? Why or why not? Be sure to make specific references to the text.

WRITING ASSIGNMENTS

1. Look ahead to the next essay, "What's Wrong with Black English" by Rachel L. Jones. Write a dialogue between Jones and Smitherman on the subject of black English and its importance to black people. (You might pay special attention to Smitherman's description of the push-pull syndrome in black America and its effect on language use.)

2. Write an essay in which you take a position in the debate regarding black English. Is it necessary that black English speakers learn to talk like white English speakers in order to "make it"?

3. Write a short research paper in which you examine the differences between the terms *pidgin*, *creole*, and *dialect*, especially with regard to black English language development.

WHAT'S WRONG WITH BLACK ENGLISH

Rachel L. Jones

"Toni Morrison, Alice Walker and James Baldwin did not achieve their eloquence, grace and stature by using only black English in their writing." So argues Rachel L. Jones, a black woman who maintains that black English is an unacceptable medium of communication in American society at large and a handicap to its users. Though she stands in opposition to black writers and, perhaps, some black friends, her essay is a persuasive argument drawn from personal experience and cogent insights. When she wrote this essay, which appeared in the "My Turn" column of *Newsweek* in December 1982, Jones was a sophomore at Southern Illinois University.

1   William Labov, a noted linguist, once said about the use of black English, "It is the goal of most black Americans to acquire full control of the standard language without giving up their own culture." He also suggested that there are certain advantages to having two ways to express one's feelings. I wonder if the good doctor might also consider the goals of those black Americans who have full control of standard English but who are every now and then troubled by that colorful, grammar-to-the-winds patois that is black English. Case in point—me.

2   I'm a 21-year-old black born to a family that would probably be considered lower-middle class—which in my mind is a polite way of describing a condition only slightly better than poverty. Let's just say we rarely if ever did the winter-vacation thing in the Caribbean. I've often had to defend my humble beginnings to a most unlikely group of people for an even less likely reason. Because of the way I talk, some of my black peers look at me sideways and ask, "Why do you talk like you're white?"

3   The first time it happened to me I was nine years old. Cornered in the school bathroom by the class bully and her sidekick, I was offered the opportunity to swallow a few of my teeth unless I satisfactorily explained why I always got good grades, why I talked "proper" or "white." I had no ready answer for her, save the fact that my mother had from the time I was old enough to talk stressed the importance of reading and learning, or that L. Frank Baum and Ray Bradbury were my closest companions. I read all my older brothers'

and sisters' literature textbooks more faithfully than they did, and even light-weights like the Bobbsey Twins and Trixie Belden were allowed into my book-ish inner circle. I don't remember exactly what I told those girls, but I some-how talked my way out of a beating.

4   I was reminded once again of my "white pipes" problem while apartment hunting in Evanston, Illinois, last winter. I doggedly made out lists of available places and called all around. I would immediately be invited over—and imme-diately turned down. The thinly concealed looks of shock when the front door opened clued me in, along with the flustered instances of "just getting off the phone with the girl who was ahead of you and she wants the rooms." When I finally found a place to live, my roommate stirred up old memories when she remarked a few months later, "You know, I was surprised when I first saw you. You sounded white over the phone." Tell me another one, sister.

5   I should've asked her a question I've wanted an answer to for years: how does one "talk white"? The silly side of me pictures a rabid white foam spew-ing forth when I speak. I don't use Valley Girl jargon, so that's not what's meant in my case. Actually, I've pretty much deduced what people mean when they say that to me, and the implications are really frightening.

6   It means that I'm articulate and well-versed. It means that I can talk as freely about John Steinbeck as I can about Rick James. It means that "ain't" and "he be" are not staples of my vocabulary and are only used around family and friends. (It is almost Jekyll and Hyde-ish the way I can slip out of acade-mic abstractions into a long, lean, double-negative-filled dialogue, but I've come to terms with that aspect of my personality.) As a child, I found it hard to believe that's what people meant by "talking proper"; that would've meant that good grades and standard English were equated with white skin, and that went against everything I'd ever been taught. Running into the same type of mentality as an adult has confirmed the depressing reality that for many blacks, standard English is not only unfamiliar, it is socially unacceptable.

7   James Baldwin once defended black English by saying it had added "vitality to the language," and even went so far as to label it a language in its own right, saying, "Language [i.e., black English] is a political instrument" and a "vivid and crucial key to identity." But did Malcolm X urge blacks to take power in this country "any way y'all can"? Did Martin Luther King Jr. say to blacks, "I has been to the mountaintop, and I done seed the Promised Land"? Toni Morrison, Alice Walker and James Baldwin did not achieve their eloquence, grace and stature by using only black English in their writing. Andrew Young, Tom Bradley and Barbara Jordan did not acquire political power by saying, "Y'all crazy if you ain't gon vote for me." They all have full command of stan-dard English, and I don't think that knowledge takes away from their black-ness or commitment to black people.

8   I know from experience that it's important for black people, stripped of cul-ture and heritage, to have something they can point to and say, "This is ours, *we* can comprehend it, *we* alone can speak it with a soulful flourish." I'd be ly-ing if I said that the rhythms of my people caught up in "some serious rap"

don't sound natural and right to me sometimes. But how heartwarming is it for those same brothers when they hit the pavement searching for employment? Studies have proven that the use of ethnic dialects decreases power in the marketplace. "I be" is acceptable on the corner, but not with the boss.

9   Am I letting capitalistic, European-oriented thinking fog the issue? Am I selling out blacks to an ideal of assimilating, being as much like whites as possible? I have not formed a personal political ideology, but I do know this: it hurts me to hear black children use black English, knowing that they will be at yet another disadvantage in an educational system already full of stumbling blocks. It hurts me to sit in lecture halls and hear fellow black students complain that the professor "be tripping dem out using big words dey can't understand." And what hurts most is to be stripped of my own blackness simply because I know my way around the English language.

10   I would have to disagree with Labov in one respect. My goal is no so much to acquire full control of both standard and black English, but to one day see more black people less dependent on a dialect that excludes them from full participation in the world we live in. I don't think I talk white, I think I talk right.

TOPICAL CONSIDERATIONS

1. How does Rachel Jones view James Baldwin's stand on black English? What is the point of her references to Malcolm X, Martin Luther King, Jr., and other notable black political figures and writers in paragraph 7?

2. Jones says that James Baldwin, Toni Morrison, and Alice Walker "did not achieve their eloquence, grace and stature by using only black English in their writing." Does she mean that black English lacks these qualities, that without standard English these writers would have failed? Explain.

3. What is Jones's argument against linguist William Labov?

4. Compare Jones's views of language in the essay above with those of S. I. Hayakawa in the first selection of this chapter. What language values do they share? How do they differ?

5. What does Jones mean by "talking white"? Does the expression mean the same as talking "standard English"? And what is so "frightening" about the implications of those charges?

6. Does the author like anything about black English? What does she find wrong with the practice of it?

RHETORICAL CONSIDERATIONS

1. Does the title of this essay clearly indicate the author's position?

2. Where does the author give a clear thesis statement in her essay?

3. What is the advantage of opening the essay with a statement by William Labov? How does Jones use the statement? Where else in the essay does she refer to Labov and for what effect?

4. What audience would not like this essay? How does she address that disapproval?

5. What is the thrust of the concluding comments in Jones's essay?

WRITING ASSIGNMENTS

1. Jones claims that "for many blacks, standard English is not only unfamiliar, it is socially unacceptable" (paragraph 6). Do you agree with this assertion? Do the black people you know seem unfamiliar with standard English? Do any resist using standard English? Write a paper in which you support or refute Jones's claim.

2. If you are black, would you classify your English as standard or black? Given Jones's opinion here and Geneva Smitherman's in the last essay, write a paper in which you discuss your language and identity. IF you speak black English, where and when do you use it? How is it part of your identity? Do you switch back and forth to standard English? If you speak standard English exclusively, do you feel that you've abandoned your black culture, heritage, and identity? Explain.

3. Write an imaginary dialogue between Rachel Jones and Geneva Smitherman on the subject of black English. You can take as your focus the importance of "talking proper" in making one's way in school, business, profession, and society.

4. You have read various essays in this book on the importance of standards, on language and prejudice, and on the virtues and drawbacks of bilingualism. Synthesize these varied issues into a defense of or attack on the practice of black English.

5. Jones remarks that studies have shown "that the use of ethnic dialects decreases power in the marketplace." If you were a recruiter for a business would an applicant speaking in an ethnic dialect influence your decision to hire? In a paper explain your answer.

6. Do students have a right to their own nonstandard language? Does any group? What would happen if different segments of our society spoke a "private" language? Write a paper in which you explore these questions.

7. In December 1996, the school board in Oakland, California called for measures to train teachers in Ebonics in effort to help students who use Ebonics to master standard English. That decision stirred up a national debate between those who supported the decision and those, like Ms. Jones, who argued that Ebonics is a substandard dialect that only convinces its young users that they are not capable of mastering standard English. Using your library, do some research into that Ebonics debate. In a paper, explore the arguments on each side, measuring them against what Jones says in her article. Where do you stand on the issue? Did the debate make you see black English in a different light? Explain your stand on the issue.

6 SLURS, STEREOTYPES, SWEARS, AND FREE SPEECH

Wasserman/Boston Globe

This chapter explores various forms of offensive language and the controversies surrounding efforts to curb them. Broadly speaking, offensive language is that which denigrates people because of gender, race, ethnicity, class, sexual preference, age, or disability. It also includes obscene or sexually explicit language. Common to all offensive language is its intent: to put down those who are different from us or less fortunate than we are. Whether a racial slur, a sexist statement, or a demeaning stereotype, most people agree that such language is obvious and ugly. And most would agree that using it habitually perpetuates damning and subjugating attitudes toward its victims. However, not everyone agrees that the solution is to curb its use. While noble in intent, efforts to squelch hate talk, to some, shake one of the very pillars of Jeffersonian democracy—the principle of free speech.

WHAT'S POLITICALLY CORRECT?

In fact, no other language issue has generated more debate or has had a more polarizing effect on our society than the efforts of some to change American English—efforts that have become known as *political correctness.* According to William Safire, the term made its first major appearance in 1975 in a statement by Karen DeCrow, then president of the National Organization for Women, as an assertion of NOW's liberal or progressive activities. Picking up momentum from the feminist movement, the term became attached to the celebration of America's rapidly growing multicultural society in general and in particular to efforts aimed at making people more sensitive to built-in language prejudices against racial and ethnic minorities. By the late 1980s, the new sensitivity grew to encompass language biases based on gender as well as sexual orientation, age, class, and physical disability. But around 1990 *politically correct,* abbreviated to *p.c.,* turned into a controversial expression, especially for conservatives who turned the term into a battle cry against the regimentation in language and thoughts by liberals. Not only had the term become synonymous with tyranny—*a la* Orwellian word-and-thought police—but it became a springboard for parody. P.C. critics accuse proponents of squelching free expression while creating such awkward terms as "Chinaperson"; banning words such as "burly," "lady," and "Eskimos"; and generally robbing English of its vitality—all in the name of gender and race neutrality.

The first two essays in this chapter clearly capture much of the conflict and furor surrounding the issue. The first piece is taken from the introduction to one of the most popular and successful "politically correct" language handbooks, Rosalie Maggio's *The Dictionary of Bias-Free Usage.* Examining how English subtly perpetuates prejudice, Maggio offers some simple guidelines for avoiding offensive stereotypes and exclusionary expressions. In direct opposition is literary critic and journalist Michiko Kakutani who vehemently condemns such language-laundering efforts. Directly attacking the consciousness-raising efforts of Rosalie Maggio, Kakutani's "The Word Police" argues that all the fuss about semantics draws attention away from the real problems of prejudice and injustice in our society. But more than that, she is disturbed by the dark Orwellian implications of "P.C. police" hunting down users of "inappropriate" language and replacing it with a lot of "feel-good" doublespeak.

WHAT DO WE CALL OTHERS?

The next seven essays look at the kinds of discriminatory language—names, slurs, stereotypes, and other verbal bullets—that have been leveled at specific groups of people in our society.

If Americans were asked to name the most offensive and unacceptable racial/ethnic epithet in the English language it would probably be "nigger." No other word condenses racial prejudice so powerfully. And, yet, as Gloria Naylor explains in "Nigger: The Meaning of a Word," she grew up hearing it used positively by other black Americans, even as a term of endearment. But when a white boy hurled the term at her in insult, the word suddenly turned bad. Context had become everything. As the title of the next piece suggests, Thomas Friedmann's "Heard Any Good Jews Lately?" explores the prejudicial language used against the Jews—in particular, some common slurs and denigrating stereotypes portrayed in anti-Jewish jokes. But there is an even grimmer side to the discussion, for Friedmann traces these familiar abuses to this century's supremely horrifying example of language prejudice: the Nazi campaign to bend the mind of a whole country as prelude to mass murder.

In the next essay, Charles F. Berlitz takes a clear, objective look at the origin of familiar ethnic and racial slurs in "The Etymology of the International Insult." Surprising as it may be, some terms were once far from insulting, the author explains. However, their sting is no less painful to the victims. Furthermore, given the pluralistic makeup of our society, we might no longer be able to afford them. "Defining the 'American Indian': A Case Study in the Language of Suppression" also takes a historical look at language prejudice used against a single people. Here, Dr. Haig Bosmajian examines the language that helped suppress the Native Americans. His analysis is a warning of the danger for us all, no matter what our ethnic or racial heritage.

In her essay cited above, Gloria Naylor raises the issue of "reclaiming" language—that is, blacks using the word "nigger" in an affectionate context, thus rendering the racial insult impotent. In a sense Nancy Mairs also reclaims language when she decides to call herself a "cripple" instead of the politically correct "handicapped," "disabled," or "differently abled." That is, she reclaims the less euphemistic term not to soften its bite but to wear it as a badge of tough honesty. Recently the same practice of reclaiming language has been seen in the gay community. In the next essay, "Queer," Lillian Faderman discusses how a homophobic slur is now spoken with pride by some lesbians and gays.

Jennifer A. Coleman extends the issue of prejudicial language to those who are overweight. In "Discrimination at Large," she argues that people who would never even think of making an ethnic or racial slur feel no such reluctance when it comes to making fun of fat people. And, yet, she argues that the contempt for fat people is taught, even condoned by mainstream America. And the jokes are as wrong and damaging as any racial slur.

Rounding off this cluster is Nobel Prize lauriate Wole Soyinka's poem "Telephone Conversation," which illustrates unabashed racial discrimination in action.

WHAT'S DIRTY LANGUAGE?

Dirty language has moved from the outer fringe to our culture's mainstream: in movies and television, in rock and rap music, in comedy clubs, and everyday talk. Many seem to enjoy it; others hate it. Bans have been proposed on everything from dictionaries and record albums to off-Broadway plays. Yet, despite public outcry, obscene language has been and will continue to be part of our culture. In the first selection in this cluster, "Mind Your Tongue, Young Man" Sandra Flahive Maurer recalls an experience illustrating that we've become indifferent to swearing in everyday language. In "What 'Dirty Words' Really Mean," noted psychologist Dr. Joyce Brothers examines the hidden motivations behind the use of dirty language, and its consequences. As she explains, obscenities mask the fears, anxieties, and ignorance of those who use them while dehumanizing the targeted.

CASE STUDY: FREEDOM OF SPEECH?

One of the most difficult challenges to higher education has to do with the First Amendment. Does the right to freedom of expression prevent universities from curbing certain forms of speech on campus—namely, racist, sexist, and other offensive discourse? This question is the focus of the two pieces that conclude this chapter. In "Regulating Racist Speech on Campus," Charles R. Lawrence argues that allowing people to demean other members of a college community violates student victims' rights to education. Taking the opposing side in "Free Speech on Campus," Nat Hentoff says that censorship of the language of hate threatens the very nature of a university and the spirit of academic freedom while making the forces of hate more dangerous.

Bias-Free Language: Some Guidelines

Rosalie Maggio

The growing reality of America's multiculturalism has produced a heightened sensitivity to language offensive to members of minority groups. In response, a number of bias-free language guides have been written—guides that caution against terms that might offend not only racial and ethnic groups but women, gays, senior citizens, the handicapped, animal lovers, and the overweight. One of the most successful guides is Rosalie Maggio's *The Dictionary of Bias-Free Usage: A Guide to Nondiscriminatory Language* (1991). In the following excerpt from that guide's introduction, the author discusses how to evaluate and recognize language bias, and why it should be avoided.

Rosalie Maggio is also the author of *The Nonsexist Word Finder* (1987), *How to Say It: Words, Phrases, Sentences, and Paragraphs for Every Situation* (1990), and *The Music Box Christmas* (1990). She has edited numerous college textbooks, and published hundreds of stories and articles in educational publications and children's magazines. She has won several literary honors and awards for her children's fiction and research on women's issues.

1   Language both reflects and shapes society. The textbook on American government that consistently uses male pronouns for the president, even when not referring to a specific individual (e.g., "a president may cast his veto"), reflects the fact that all our presidents have so far been men. But it also shapes a society in which the idea of a female president somehow "doesn't sound right."

2   Culture shapes language and then language shapes culture. "Contrary to the assumption that language merely reflects social patterns such as sex-role stereotypes, research in linguistics and social psychology has shown that these are in fact facilitated and reinforced by language" (Marlis Hellinger, in *Language and Power*, ed., Cheris Kramarae et al.).

3   Biased language can also, says Sanford Berman, "powerfully harm people, as amply demonstrated by bigots' and tyrants' deliberate attempts to linguistically dehumanize and demean groups they intend to exploit, oppress, or exterminate. Calling Asians 'gooks' made it easier to kill them. Calling blacks 'niggers' made it simpler to enslave and brutalize them. Calling Native Americans 'primitives' and 'savages' made it okay to conquer and despoil them. And to talk of 'fishermen,' 'councilmen,' and 'longshoremen' is to clearly exclude and discourage women from those pursuits, to diminish and degrade them."

4   The question is asked: Isn't it silly to get upset about language when there are so many more important issues that need our attention?

5   First, it's to be hoped that there are enough of us working on issues large and small that the work will all get done—someday. Second, the interconnections between the way we think, speak, and act are beyond dispute. Language goes hand-in-hand with social change—both shaping it and reflecting it. Sexual harassment was not a term anyone used twenty years ago; today we have laws against it. How could we have the law without the language; how could we have the language without the law? In fact, the judicial system is a good argument for the importance of "mere words"; the legal profession devotes great energy to the precise interpretation of words—often with far-reaching and significant consequences.

6   On August 21, 1990, in the midst of the Iraqi offensive, front-page headlines told the big story: President Bush had used the word *hostages* for the first time. Up to that time, *detainee* had been used. The difference between two very similar words was of possible life-and-death proportions. In another situation—also said to be life-and-death by some people—the difference between *fetal tissue* and *unborn baby* (in referring to the very same thing) is arguably the most debated issue in the country. So, yes, words have power and deserve our attention.

7   Some people are like George Crabbe's friend: "Habit with him was all the test of truth, / it must be right: I've done it from my youth." They have come of age using *handicapped, black-and-white, leper, mankind,* and pseudo-generic *he*; these terms must therefore be correct. And yet if there's one thing consistent about language it is that language is constantly changing; when the *Random House Dictionary of the English Language: 2nd Edition* was published in 1988, it contained 50,000 new entries, most of them words that had come into use since 1966. There were also 75,000 new definitions. (Incidentally, *RHD-II* asks its readers to "use gender-neutral terms wherever possible" and it never uses *mankind* in definitions where *people* is meant, nor does it ever refer to anyone of unknown gender as *he*.) However, few supporters of bias-free language are asking for changes; it is rather a matter of choice—which of the many acceptable words available to us will we use?

8   A high school student who felt that nonsexist language did demand some changes said, "But you don't understand! You're trying to change the English language, which has been around a lot longer than women have!"

9   One reviewer of the first edition commented, "There's no fun in limiting how you say a thing." Perhaps not. Yet few people complain about looking up

a point of grammar or usage or checking the dictionary for a correct spelling. Most writers are very fussy about finding the precise best word, the exact rhythmic vehicle for their ideas. Whether or not these limits "spoil their fun" is an individual judgment. However, most of us accept that saying or writing the first thing that comes to mind is not often the way we want to be remembered. So if we have to think a little, if we have to search for the unbiased word, the inclusive phrase, it is not any more effort than we expend on proper grammar, spelling, and style.

10   Other people fear "losing" words, as though there weren't more where those came from. We are limited only by our imaginations; vague, inaccurate, and disrespectful words can be thrown overboard with no loss to society and no impoverishment of the language.

11   Others are tired of having to "watch what they say." But what they perhaps mean is that they're tired of being sensitive to others' requests. From childhood onward, we all learn to "watch what we say": we don't swear around our parents; we don't bring up certain topics around certain people; we speak differently to friend, boss, cleric, English teacher, lover, radio interviewer, child. Most of us are actually quite skilled at picking and choosing appropriate words; it seems odd that we are too "tired" to call people what they want to be called.

12   The greatest objection to bias-free language is that it will lead us to absurdities. Critics have posited something utterly ridiculous, cleverly demonstrated how silly it is, and then accounted themselves victorious in the battle against linguistic massacre. For example: "So I suppose now we're going to say: He/she ain't heavy, Father/Sister; he/she's my brother/sister." "I suppose next it will be 'ottoperson'." Cases have been built up against the mythic "woperson," "personipulate," and "personhole cover" (none of which has ever been advocated by any reputable sociolinguist). No grist appears too ridiculous for these mills. And, yes, they grind exceedingly small. Using a particular to condemn a universal is a fault in logic. But then ridicule, it is said, is the first and last argument of fools.

13   One of the most rewarding—and, for many people, the most unexpected— side effects of breaking away from traditional, biased language is a dramatic improvement in writing style. By replacing fuzzy, overgeneralized, cliché-ridden words with explicit, active words and by giving concrete examples and anecdotes instead of one-word-fits-all descriptions you can express yourself more dynamically, convincingly, and memorably.

14   "If those who have studied the art of writing are in accord on any one point, it is on this: the surest way to arouse and hold the attention of the reader is by being specific, definite, and concrete" (Strunk and White, *The Elements of Style*). Writers who talk about *brotherhood* or *spinsters* or *right-hand men* miss a chance to spark their writing with fresh descriptions; they leave their readers as uninspired as they are. Unthinking writing is also less informative. Why use the unrevealing *adman* when we could choose instead a precise, descriptive, inclusive word like *advertising executive, copywriter, account executive, ad writer,* or *media buyer?*

15   The word *manmade,* which seems so indispensable to us, doesn't actually say very much. Does it mean artificial? handmade? synthetic? fabricated? machine-made? custom-made? simulated? plastic? imitation? contrived?

16   Communication is—or ought to be—a two-way street. A speaker who uses *man* to mean *human being* while the audience hears it as *adult male* is an example of communication gone awry.

17   Bias-free language is logical, accurate, and realistic. Biased language is not. How logical is it to speak of the "discovery" of America, a land already inhabited by millions of people? Where is the accuracy in writing "Dear Sir" to a woman? Where is the realism in the full-page automobile advertisement that says in bold letters, "A good driver is a product of his environment," when more women than men influence car-buying decisions? Or how successful is the ad for a dot-matrix printer that says, "In 3,000 years, man's need to present his ideas hasn't changed. But his tools have," when many of these printers are bought and used by women, who also have ideas they need to present? And when we use stereotypes to talk about people ("isn't that just like a welfare mother/Indian/girl/old man"), our speech and writing will be inaccurate and unrealistic most of the time.

DEFINITION OF TERMS

Bias/Bias-Free

18   Biased language communicates inaccurately about what it means to be male or female; black or white; young or old; straight, gay, or bi; rich or poor; from one ethnic group or another; disabled or temporarily able-bodied; or to hold a particular belief system. It reflects the same bias found in racism, sexism, ageism, handicappism, classism, ethnocentrism, anti-Semitism, homophobia, and other forms of discrimination.

19   Bias occurs in the language in several ways.

1. Leaving out individuals or groups. "Employees are welcome to bring their wives and children" leaves out those employees who might want to bring husbands, friends, or same-sex partners. "We are all immigrants in this country" leaves out Native Americans, who were here well before the first immigrants.

2. Making unwarranted assumptions. To address a sales letter about a new diaper to the mother assumes that the father won't be diapering the baby. To write "Anyone can use this fire safety ladder" assumes that all members of the household are able-bodied.

3. Calling individuals and groups by names or labels that they do not choose for themselves (e.g., *Gypsy, office girl, Eskimo, pygmy, Bushman, the elderly, colored man*) or terms that are derogatory (*fairy, libber, savage, bum, old goat*).

4. Stereotypical treatment that implies that all lesbians/Chinese/women/people with disabilities/teenagers are alike.

5. Unequal treatment of various groups in the same material.

6. Unnecessary mention of membership in a particular group. In a land of supposedly equal opportunity, of what importance is a person's race, sex, age, sexual orientation, disability, or creed? As soon as we mention one of these characteristics—without a good reason for doing so—we enter an area mined by
potential linguistic disasters. Although there may be instances in which a person's sex, for example, is germane ("A recent study showed that female patients do not object to being cared for by male nurses"), most of the time it is
not. Nor is mentioning a person's race, sexual orientation, disability, age, or belief system usually germane.

20   Bias can be overt or subtle. Jean Gaddy Wilson (in Brooks and Pinson,
Working with Words) says, "Following one simple rule of writing or speaking
will eliminate most biases. Ask yourself: Would you say the same thing about
an affluent, white man?"

Inclusive/Exclusive

21 Inclusive language includes everyone; exclusive language excludes some people. The following quotation is inclusive: "The greatest revolution of our generation is the discovery that human beings, by changing the inner attitudes of
their minds, can change the outer aspects of their lives" (William James). It is
clear that James is speaking of all of us.

22   Examples of sex-exclusive writing fill most quotation books: "Man is the
measure of all things" (Protagoras). "The People, though we think of a great
entity when we use the word, means nothing more than so many millions of
individual men" (James Bryce). "Man is nature's sole mistake." (W S Gilbert).

Sexist/Nonsexist

23 Sexist language promotes and maintains attitudes that stereotype people according to gender while assuming that the male is the norm—the significant
gender. Nonsexist language treats all people equally and either does not refer
to a person's sex at all when it is irrelevant or refers to men and women in
symmetrical ways.

24   "A society in which women are taught anything but the management of a
family, the care of men, and the creation of the future generation is a society
which is on the way out" (L. Ron Hubbard). "Behind every successful man is a
woman—with nothing to wear" (L. Grant Glickman). "Nothing makes a man
and wife feel closer, these days, than a joint tax return" (Gil Stern). These quotations display various characteristics of sexist writing: (1) stereotyping an entire sex by what might be appropriate for some of it; (2) assuming male superiority; (3) using unparallel terms (*man and wife* should be either *wife and
husband/husband and wife* or *woman and man/man and woman*).

25   The following quotations clearly refer to all people: "It's really hard to be
roommates with people if your suitcases are much better than theirs" (J. D.

Salinger). "If people don't want to come out to the ball park, nobody's going to stop them" (Yogi Berra). "If men and women of capacity refuse to take part in politics and government, they condemn themselves, as well as the people, to the punishment of living under bad government" (Senator Sam J. Ervin). "I studied the lives of great men and famous women, and I found that the men and women who got to the top were those who did the jobs they had in hand, with everything they had of energy and enthusiasm and hard work" (Harry S. Truman).

Gender-Free/Gender-Fair/Gender-Specific

26 Gender-free terms do not indicate sex and can be used for either women/girls or men/boys (e.g., *teacher, bureaucrat, employee, hiker, operations manager, child, clerk, sales rep, hospital patient, student, grandparent, chief executive officer*).

27   Writing or speech that is gender-fair involves the symmetrical use of gender-specific words (e.g., *Ms. Leinwohl/Mr. Kelly, councilwoman/council-man, young man/young woman*) and promotes fairness to both sexes in the larger context. To ensure gender-fairness, ask yourself often: Would I wrote the same thing in the same way about a person of the opposite sex? Would I mind if this were said of me?

28   If you are describing the behavior of children on the playground, to be gender-fair you will refer to girls and boys an approximately equal number of times, and you will carefully observe what the children do, and not just assume that only the boys will climb to the top of the jungle gym and that only the girls will play quiet games.

29   Researchers studying the same baby described its cries as "anger" when they were told it was a boy and as "fear" when they were told it was a girl (cited in Cheris Kramarae, *The Voices and Words of Women and Men*). We are all victims of our unconscious and most deeply held biases.

30   Gender-specific words (for example, *alderwoman, businessman, altar girl*) are neither good nor bad in themselves. However, they need to be used gender-fairly; terms for women and terms for men should be used an approximately equal number of times in contexts that do not discriminate against either of them. One problem with gender-specific words is that they identify and even emphasize a person's sex when it is not necessary (and is sometimes even objectionable) to do so. Another problem is that they are so seldom used gender-fairly.

31   Although gender-free terms are generally preferable, sometimes gender-neutral language obscures the reality of women's or men's oppression. *Battered spouse* implies that men and women are equally battered; this is far from true. *Parent* is too often taken to mean *mother* and obscures the fact that more and more fathers are very much involved in parenting; it is better here to use

the gender-specific *fathers and mothers* or *mothers and fathers* than the gender-neutral *parents*.

Generic/Pseudogeneric

32 A generic is an all-purpose word that includes everybody (e.g., *workers, people, voters, civilians, elementary school students*). Generic pronouns include: *we, you, they*.

33   A pseudogeneric is a word that is used as though it included all people, but that in reality does not. *Mankind, forefathers, brotherhood,* and *alumni* are not generic because they leave out women. When used about Americans, *immigrants* leaves out all those who were here long before the first immigrants. "What a christian thing to do!" uses *christian* as a pseudogeneric for *kind* or *good-hearted* and leaves out all kind, good-hearted people who are not Christians.

34   Although some speakers and writers say that when they use *man* or *mankind* they mean everybody, their listeners and readers do not perceive the word that way and these terms are thus pseudogenerics. The pronoun *he* when used to mean *he and she* is another pseudogeneric.

35   Certain generic nouns are often assumed to refer only to men, for example, *politicians, physicians, lawyers, voters, legislators, clergy, farmers, colonists, immigrants, slaves, pioneers, settlers, members of the armed forces, judges, taxpayers.* References to "settlers, their wives, and children," or "those clergy permitted to have wives" are pseudogeneric.

36   In historical context it is particularly damaging for young people to read about settlers and explorers and pioneers as though they were all white men. Our language should describe the accomplishments of the human race in terms of all those who contributed to them.

SEX AND GENDER

37 An understanding of the difference between sex and gender is critical to the use bias-free language.

38   Sex is biological: people with male genitals are male, and people with female genitals are female.

39   Gender is cultural: our notions of "masculine" tell us how we expect men to behave and our notions of "feminine" tell us how we expect women to behave. Words like *womanly/manly, tomboy/sissy, unfeminine/unmasculine* have nothing to do with the person's sex; they are culturally acquired, subjective concepts about character traits and expected behaviors that vary from one place to another, from one individual to another.

40   It is biologically impossible for a woman to be a sperm donor. It may be culturally unusual for a man to be a secretary, but it is not biologically impossible. To say "the secretary . . . she" assumes all secretaries are women and is sexist because the issue is gender, not sex. Gender describes an individual's personal, legal, and social status without reference to genetic sex; gender is a subjective cultural attitude. Sex is an objective biological fact. Gender varies according to the culture. Sex is a constant.

41   The difference between sex and gender is important because much sexist language arises from cultural determinations of what a woman or man "ought" to be. Once a society decides, for example, that to be a man means to hide one's emotions, bring home a paycheck, and be able to discuss football standings while to be a woman means to be soft-spoken, love shopping, babies, and recipes, and "never have anything to wear," much of the population becomes a contradiction in terms—unmanly men and unwomanly women. Crying, nagging, gossiping, and shrieking are assumed to be women's lot; rough-housing, drinking beer, telling dirty jokes, and being unable to find one's socks and keys are laid at men's collective door. Lists of stereotypes appear silly because very few people fit them. The best way to ensure unbiased writing and speaking is to describe people as individuals, not as members of a set.

Gender Role Words

42 Certain sex-linked words depend for their meanings on cultural stereotypes: *feminine/masculine, manly/womanly, boyish/girlish, husbandly/wifely, fatherly/motherly, unfeminine/unmasculine, unmanly/unwomanly,* etc. What a person understands by these words will vary from culture to culture and even within a culture. Because the words depend for their meanings on interpretations of stereotypical behavior or characteristics, they may be grossly inaccurate when applied to individuals. Somewhere, sometime, men and women have said, thought, or done everything the other sex has said, thought, or done except for a very few sex-linked biological activities (e.g., only women can give birth or nurse a baby, only a man can donate sperm or impregnate a woman). To describe a woman as unwomanly is a contradiction in terms; if a woman is doing it, saying it, wearing it, thinking it, it must be—by definition—womanly.

43   F. Scott Fitzgerald did not use "feminine" to describe the unforgettable Daisy in *The Great Gatsby*. He wrote instead, "She laughed again, as if she said something very witty, and held my hand for a moment, looking up into my face, promising that there was no one in the world she so much wanted to see. That was a way she had." Daisy's charm did not belong to Woman; it was uniquely hers. Replacing vague sex-linked descriptors with thoughtful words that describe an individual instead of a member of a set can lead to language that touches people's minds and hearts.

NAMING

44 Naming is power, which is why the issue of naming is one of the most important in bias-free language.

Self-Definition

45 People decide what they want to be called. The correct names for individuals and groups are always those by which they refer to themselves. This "tradition" is not always unchallenged. Haig Bosmajian (*The Language of Oppression*) says, "It isn't strange that those persons who insist on defining themselves, who insist on this elemental privilege of self-naming, self-definition, and self-identity encounter vigorous resistance. Predictably, the resistance usually comes from the oppressor or would-be oppressor and is a result of the fact that he or she does not want to relinquish the power which comes from the ability to define others."

46 Dr. Ian Hancock uses the term *exonym* for a name applied to a group by outsiders. For example, Romani peoples object to being called by the exonym *Gypsies*. They do not call themselves Gypsies. Among the many other exonyms are: the elderly, colored people, homosexuals, pagans, adolescents, Eskimos, pygmies, savages. The test for an exonym is whether people describe themselves as "redmen," "illegal aliens," "holy rollers," etc., or whether only outsiders describe them that way.

47 There is a very small but visible element today demanding that gay men "give back" the word *gay* a good example of denying people the right to name themselves. A late-night radio caller said several times that gay men had "stolen" this word from "our" language. It was not clear what language gay men spoke.

48 A woman nicknamed "Betty" early in life had always preferred her full name, "Elizabeth." On her fortieth birthday, she reverted to Elizabeth. An acquaintance who heard about the change said sharply, "I'll call her Betty if I like!"

49 We can call them Betty if we like, but it's arrogant, insensitive, and uninformed: the only rule we have in this area says we call people what they want to be called.

"Insider/Outsider" Rule

50 A related rule says that insiders may describe themselves in ways that outsiders may not. "Crip" appears in *The Disability Rag*; this does not mean that the word is available to anyone who wants to use it. "Big Fag" is printed on a gay man's T-shirt. He may use that expression; a non-gay may not so label him.

One junior-high student yells to another, "Hey, nigger!" This would be highly offensive and inflammatory if the speaker were not African American. A group of women talk about "going out with the girls," but a co-worker should not refer to them as "girls." When questioned about just such a situation, Miss Manners replied that "people are allowed more leeway in what they call themselves than in what they call others."

"People First" Rule

51 Haim Ginott taught us that labels are disabling; intuitively most of us recognize this and resist being labeled. The disability movement originated the "people first" rule, which says we don't call someone a "diabetic" but rather "a person with diabetes." Saying someone is "an AIDS victim" reduces the person to a disease, a label, a statistic; use instead "a person with/who has/living with AIDS." The 1990 Americans with Disabilities Act is a good example of correct wording. Name the person as a person first, and let qualifiers (age, sex, disability, race) follow, but (and this is crucial) only if they are relevant. Readers of a magazine aimed at an older audience were asked what they wanted to be called (elderly? senior citizens? seniors? golden agers?). They rejected all the terms; one said, "How about 'people'?" When high school students rejected labels like kids, teens, teenagers, youth, adolescents, and juveniles, and were asked in exasperation just what they would like to be called, they said, "Could we just be people?"

Women as Separate People

52 One of the most sexist maneuvers in the language has been the identification of women by their connections to husband, son, or father—often even after he is dead. Women are commonly identified as someone's widow while men are never referred to as anyone's widower. Marie Marvingt, a Frenchwoman who lived around the turn of the century, was an inventor, adventurer, stunt woman, superathlete, aviator, and all-around scholar. She chose to be affianced to neither man (as a wife) nor God (as a religious), but it was not long before an uneasy male press found her a fit partner. She is still known today by the revealing label "the Fiancée of Danger." If a connection is relevant, make it mutual. Instead of "Frieda, his wife of seventeen years," write "Frieda and Eric, married for seventeen years."

53   It is difficult for some people to watch women doing unconventional things with their names. For years the etiquette books were able to tell us precisely how to address a single woman, a married woman, a divorced woman, or a widowed woman (there was no similar etiquette on men because they have al-

ways been just men and we have never had a code to signal their marital status). But now some women are Ms. and some are Mrs., some are married but keeping their birth names, others are hyphenating their last name with their husband's, and still others have constructed new names for themselves. Some women—including African American women who were denied this right earlier in our history—take great pride in using their husband's name. All these forms are correct. The same rule of self-definition applies here: call the woman what she wants to be called.

TOPICAL CONSIDERATIONS

1. Maggio begins her article with a discussion of the ways language has real effects on people's attitudes and actions. What are some of the examples she supplies? How does language create desirable or undesirable consequences?

2. What are the four excuses people make to avoid using unbiased language? How does Maggio counter those excuses? What additional counterargument does she supply in defense of nonbiased language?

3. What main idea links all the different ways in which bias can occur (see paragraph 18)? Does biased language refer to individuals or to groups of people? Would the following statement be an example of biased (or stereotyped) language? "Mary is wearing her hair in a French braid today, so she'll no doubt wear it that way tomorrow."

4. What are the categories Maggio specifically names as subject to biased language? Can you supply additional categories?

5. Maggio uses the term *symmetrical* several times (e.g., paragraphs 23 and 27). What does this term mean? Does Maggio want to encourage or discourage the use of symmetrical language? Does symmetry refer only to gender bias, or can it refer to other kinds of bias too?

6. What is the difference between gender-free, gender-fair, and gender-specific language in paragraphs 26 through 31? What examples does Maggio supply for each one? When is each kind of nonbiased language appropriate?

7. How can the principles of gender-free, gender-fair, and gender-specific language be applied to language that is biased about handicap, religion, race, age, or other group characteristics? Supply one example for each principle and include a phrase that contains biased language and a revision resolving the problem.

8. What does Maggio mean by a "generic" word? a "pseudogeneric" word? How might pseudogeneric references harm people?

9. What is an *exonym?* Are exonyms ever appropriate, according to Maggio's discussion? Did you recognize all the words Maggio lists in paragraph 46 as exonyms? Can you supply substitutes for all the exonyms? If not, what problems did you encounter? Can you supply examples of other exonyms from your own experience?

10. Why do you think Maggio considers *naming* "one of the most important [issues] in bias-free language" (paragraph 44)? What is so important about the ability to

choose a name? What do you think the woman in paragraph 48 is communicating by choosing to be called Elizabeth? Why do you think Maggio links this announcement to the woman's fortieth birthday celebration?

RHETORICAL CONSIDERATIONS

1. What did the high school student in paragraph 8 really mean to say? Why do you think Maggio includes this statement? What point is she trying to make? Do you think that this student was male or female? Would it make a difference? Why doesn't Maggio specify?

2. Which parts of this essay struck you as being the strongest? Which seemed to be the weakest? What would you say was the difference—the strength of the writing? the attitude? the tone? the number of examples? the quality of examples? Or was it a combination?

WRITING ASSIGNMENTS

1. In your experience, has anyone called you, or a member of a group to which you belong, a name you found offensive? How did that incident make you feel? Has anyone ever revealed to new friends a nickname or a middle name that you have but dislike? What was your response? Write a paper based on your answer.

2. Locate a short piece of journalism in a contemporary newspaper. Select an article discussing one or more of the groups that Maggio says have suffered from biased language. First, rewrite it to reflect as many biases as you can think of. Then, discuss what strategies the author used to avoid the kinds of bias you have written in.

3. Locate an article in a contemporary newspaper that you think displays one or more of the biases Maggio describes. In a letter to the editor (no more than 500 words), persuade the newspaper editors to avoid such biased language in future articles. Remember that your writing will be more effective if you write in a calm, reasonable tone, use specific examples, and explain clearly the benefits of unbiased language.

4. Look back at Susanne K. Langer's essay "Language and Thought" (page 5). How is Maggio's understanding of biased language, and the harm it can create, based on an understanding of language as "symbol" (as Langer uses that term)? What are the distinguishing features of language as symbol that biased language uses? Pay special attention to Maggio's treatment of naming, since Langer claims that "names are the essence of language" (in Langer's paragraph 19).

5. How would you go about designing an advertising campaign for the magazine that Maggio says is "aimed at an older audience"? What words would you use to avoid offensive labeling and to avoid the vagueness of the broadly generic noun "people" (which is the same term the high school students ask to be designated by)?

THE WORD POLICE

Michiko Kakutani

Not everybody applauds the efforts of those hoping to rid the language of offensive terms. To detractors, all such linguistic sensitivity is no more than a symptom of political correctness—a kind of be-sensitive-or-else campaign. They complain that unlike standard dictionaries, which are meant to help people use words, the so-called cautionary guides *warn* people against using them. Such is the complaint of Michiko Kakutani, who specifically targets Rosalie Maggio's *The Bias-Free Word Finder* as an example of the menace of hypersensitivity. She complains that in the name of the "politics of inclusion," proponents hunt down users of "inappropriate" language like the thought police from George Orwell's *1984*. And, claims Kakutani, they fill the English language with sloppy, pious euphemisms.

Michiko Kakutani is a staff writer for the *New York Times*, where this article first appeared in January 1993.

1   This month's inaugural festivities, with their celebration, in Maya Angelou's words, of "humankind"—"the Asian, the Hispanic, the Jew/ The African, the Native American, the Sioux,/ The Catholic, the Muslim, the French, the Greek/ The Irish, the Rabbi, the Priest, the Sheik,/ The Gay, the Straight, the Preacher,/ The privileged, the homeless, the Teacher"—constituted a kind of official embrace of multiculturalism and a new politics of inclusion.

2   The mood of political correctness, however, has already made firm inroads into popular culture. Washington boasts a store called Politically Correct that sells pro-whale, anti-meat, ban-the-bomb T-shirts, bumper stickers and buttons, as well as a local cable television show called "Politically Correct Cooking" that features interviews in the kitchen with representatives from groups like People for the Ethical Treatment of Animals.

3   The Coppertone suntan lotion people are planning to give their longtime cover girl, Little Miss (Ms?) Coppertone, a male equivalent, Little Mr. Coppertone. And even Superman (Super-person?) is rumored to be returning this spring, reincarnated as four ethnically diverse clones: an African-American, an Asian, a Caucasian and a Latino.

4   Nowhere is this P.C. mood more striking than in the increasingly noisy debate over language that has moved from university campuses to the country at

large—a development that both underscores Americans' puritanical zeal for reform and their unwavering faith in the talismanic power of words.

5   Certainly no decent person can quarrel with the underlying impulse behind political correctness: a vision of a more just, inclusive society in which racism, sexism and prejudice of all sorts have been erased. But the methods and fervor of the self-appointed language police can lead to a rigid orthodoxy—and unintentional self-parody—opening the movement to the scorn of conservative opponents and the mockery of cartoonists and late-night television hosts.

6   It's hard to imagine women earning points for political correctness by saying "ovarimony" instead of "testimony"—as one participant at the recent Modern Language Association convention was overheard to suggest. It's equally hard to imagine people wanting to flaunt their lack of prejudice by giving up such words and phrases as "bull market," "kaiser roll," "Lazy Susan," and "charley horse."

7   Several books on bias-free language have already appeared, and the 1991 edition of the Random House *Webster's College Dictionary* boasts an appendix titled "Avoiding Sexist Language." The dictionary also includes such linguistic mutations as "womyn" (women, "used as an alternative spelling to avoid the suggestion of sexism perceived in the sequence m-e-n") and "waitron" (a gender-blind term for waiter or waitress).

8   Many of these dictionaries and guides not only warn the reader against offensive racial and sexual slurs, but also try to establish and enforce a whole new set of usage rules. Take, for instance, *The Bias-Free Word Finder: A Dictionary of Nondiscriminatory Language* by Rosalie Maggio (Beacon Press)—a volume often indistinguishable, in its meticulous solemnity, from the tongue-in-cheek *Official Politically Correct Dictionary and Handbook* put out last year by Henry Beard and Christopher Cerf (Villard Books). Ms. Maggio's book supplies the reader intent on using kinder, gentler language with writing guidelines as well as a detailed listing of more than 5,000 "biased words and phrases."

9   Whom are these guidelines for? Somehow one has a tough time picturing them replacing *Fowler's Modern English Usage* in the classroom, or being adopted by the average man (sorry, individual) in the street.

10   The "pseudogeneric 'he,'" we learn from Ms. Maggio, is to be avoided like the plague, as is the use of the word "man" to refer to humanity. "Fellow," "king," "lord" and "master" are bad because they're "male-oriented words," and "king," "lord" and "master" are especially bad because they're also "hierarchical, dominator society terms." The politically correct lion becomes the "monarch of the jungle," new-age children play "someone on the top of the heap," and the "Mona Lisa" goes down in history as Leonardo's "acme of perfection."

11   As for the word "black," Ms. Maggio says it should be excised from terms with a negative spin: she recommends substituting words like "mouse" for "black eye," "ostracize" for "blackball," "payola" for "blackmail" and "outcast" for "black sheep." Clearly, some of these substitutions work better than oth-

ers: somehow the "sinister humor" of Kurt Vonnegut or "Saturday Night Live" doesn't quite make it; nor does the "denouncing" of the Hollywood 10.

12   For the dedicated user of politically correct language, all these rules can make for some messy moral dilemmas. Whereas "battered wife" is a gender-biased term, the gender-free term "battered spouse," Ms. Maggio notes, incorrectly implies "that men and women are equally battered."

13   On one hand, say Francine Wattman Frank and Paula A. Treichler in their book *Language, Gender, and Professional Writing* (Modern Language Association), "he or she" is an appropriate construction for talking about an individual (like a jockey, say) who belongs to a profession that's predominantly male—it's a way of emphasizing "that such occupations are not barred to women or that women's concerns need to be kept in mind." On the other hand, they add, using masculine pronouns rhetorically can underscore ongoing male dominance in those fields, implying the need for change.

14   And what about the speech codes adopted by some universities in recent years? Although they were designed to prohibit students from uttering sexist and racist slurs, they would extend, by logic, to blacks who want to use the word "nigger" to strip the term of its racist connotations, or homosexuals who want to use the word "queer" to reclaim it from bigots.

15   In her book, Ms. Maggio recommends applying bias-free usage retroactively: she suggests paraphrasing politically incorrect quotations, or replacing "the sexist words or phrases with ellipsis dots and/or bracketed substitutes," or using "sic" "to show that the sexist words come from the original quotation and to call attention to the fact that they are incorrect."

16   Which leads the skeptical reader of *The Bias-Free Word Finder* to wonder whether *All the King's Men* should be retitled *All The Ruler's People; Pet Sematary, Animal Companion Graves; Birdman of Alcatraz, Birdperson of Alcatraz,* and *The Iceman Cometh, The Ice Route Driver Cometh?*

17   Will making such changes remove the prejudice in people's minds? Should we really spend time trying to come up with non-male-based alternatives to "Midas touch," "Achilles' heel," and "Montezuma's revenge"? Will tossing out Santa Claus—whom Ms. Maggio accuses of reinforcing "the cultural male-as-norm system"—in favor of Belfana, his Italian female alter ego, truly help banish sexism? Can the avoidance of "violent expressions and metaphors" like "kill two birds with one stone," "sock it to 'em" or "kick an idea around" actually promote a more harmonious world?

18   The point isn't that the excesses of the word police are comical. The point is that their intolerance (in the name of tolerance) has disturbing implications. In the first place, getting upset by phrases like "bullish on America" or "the City of Brotherly Love" tends to distract attention from the real problems of prejudice and injustice that exist in society at large, turning them into mere questions of semantics. Indeed, the emphasis currently put on politically correct usage has uncanny parallels with the academic movement of deconstruction—a method of textual analysis that focuses on language and linguistic pyrotechnics—which has become firmly established on university campuses.

19   In both cases, attention is focused on surfaces, on words and metaphors; in both cases, signs and symbols are accorded more importance than content. Hence, the attempt by some radical advocates to remove *The Adventures of Huckleberry Finn* from curriculums on the grounds that Twain's use of the word "nigger" makes the book a racist text—never mind the fact that this American classic (written in 1884) depicts the spiritual kinship achieved between a white boy and a runaway slave, never mind the fact that the "nigger" Jim emerges as the novel's most honorable, decent character.

20   Ironically enough, the P.C. movement's obsession with language is accompanied by a strange Orwellian willingness to warp the meaning of words by placing them under a high-powered ideological lens. For instance, the "Dictionary of Cautionary Words and Phrases"—a pamphlet issued by the University of Missouri's Multicultural Management Program to help turn "today's journalists into tomorrow's multicultural newsroom managers"—warns that using the word "articulate" to describe members of a minority group can suggest the opposite, "that 'those people' are not considered well educated, articulate and the like."

21   The pamphlet patronizes minority groups, by cautioning the reader against using the words "lazy" and "burly" to describe any member of such groups; and it issues a similar warning against using words like "gorgeous" and "petite" to describe women.

22   As euphemism proliferates with the rise of political correctness, there is a spread of the sort of sloppy, abstract language that Orwell said is "designed to make lies sound truthful and murder respectable, and to give an appearance of solidity to pure wind." "Fat" becomes "big boned" or "differently sized"; "stupid" becomes "exceptional"; "stoned" becomes "chemically inconvenienced."

23   Wait a minute here! Aren't such phrases eerily reminiscent of the euphemisms coined by the Government during Vietnam and Watergate? Remember how the military used to speak of "pacification," or how President Richard M. Nixon's press secretary, Ronald L. Ziegler, tried to get away with calling a lie an "inoperative statement"?

24   Calling the homeless "the underhoused" doesn't give them a place to live; calling the poor "the economically marginalized" doesn't help them pay the bills. Rather, by playing down their plight, such language might even make it easier to shrug off the seriousness of their situation.

25   Instead of allowing free discussion and debate to occur, many gung-ho advocates of politically correct language seem to think that simple suppression of a word or concept will magically make the problem disappear. In the *Bias-Free Word Finder,* Ms. Maggio entreats the reader not to perpetuate the negative stereotype of Eve. "Be extremely cautious in referring to the biblical Eve," she writes; "this story has profoundly contributed to negative attitudes toward women throughout history, largely because of misogynistic and patriarchal interpretations that labeled her evil, inferior, and seductive."

26   The story of Bluebeard, the rake (whoops!—the libertine) who killed his seven wives, she says, is also to be avoided, as is the biblical story of Jezebel. Of Jesus Christ, Ms. Maggio writes: "There have been few individuals in history as completely androgynous as Christ, and it does his message a disservice to overinsist on his maleness." She doesn't give the reader any hints on how this might be accomplished; presumably, one is supposed to avoid describing him as the Son of God.

27   Of course the P.C. police aren't the only ones who want to proscribe what people should say or give them guidelines for how they may use an idea; Jesse Helms and his supporters are up to exactly the same thing when they propose to patrol the boundaries of the permissible in art. In each case, the would-be censor aspires to suppress what he or she finds distasteful—all, of course, in the name of the public good.

28   In the case of the politically correct, the prohibition of certain words, phrases and ideas is advanced in the cause of building a brave new world free of racism and hate, but this vision of harmony clashes with the very ideals of diversity and inclusion that the multi-cultural movement holds dear, and it's purchased at the cost of freedom of expression and freedom of speech.

29   In fact, the utopian world envisioned by the language police would be bought at the expense of the ideals of individualism and democracy articulated in "The Gettysburg Address." "Fourscore and seven years ago our forefathers brought forth on this continent a new nation, conceived in liberty and dedicated to the proposition that all men are created equal."

30   Of course, the P.C. police have already found Lincoln's words hopelessly "phallocentric." No doubt they would rewrite the passage: "Fourscore and seven years ago our foremothers and forefathers brought forth on this continent a new nation, formulated with liberty, and dedicated to the proposition that all humankind is created equal."

TOPICAL CONSIDERATIONS

1. What kinds of people are mentioned in the lines of Maya Angelou's inauguration poem? What do these people symbolize, according to Kakutani? How many of these groups are represented in your classroom right now?

2. What specific substitutions of words does Kakutani complain about in paragraph 10? Can you supply the "biased" term that the "politically correct" phrase has replaced in the second half of the paragraph?

3. What are the three "messy moral dilemmas" Kakutani points out in paragraphs 12–14? Why does she tag the examples she cites as dilemmas? Why does she object to following politically correct guidelines in each case?

4. What is wrong, according to Kakutani in paragraphs 15 and 16, with Maggio's recommendation that unbiased language be applied retroactively? Rewrite one or two of the titles using Maggio's suggestions as quoted by Kakutani in paragraph 15—that is, use ellipses, brackets, and so on. How well do these suggestions work?

5. What examples of euphemism does Kakutani provide in paragraphs 22–24? What objections does she raise about these euphemisms? Why does she compare the new politically correct terms with terms from Watergate?

RHETORICAL CONSIDERATIONS

1. Describe the tone in Kakutani's first three paragraphs of the article. Do you think this piece is going to be serious, playful, or sarcastic? What evidence did you base your response on?

2. How do you think Kakutani would answer her own rhetorical question in paragraph 9? Why does she use a question there, rather than a declarative sentence such as "These guidelines do not seem to be useful to anyone"? Why does she think Maggio's book has no audience?

3. Why do you think Kakutani replaces the phrase "unbiased language" with the word "euphemism" in paragraph 22? What is the difference between the two terms? Do both make the same assumptions about the way language shapes our experiences? Does Kakutani use the word euphemism fairly?

4. Look closely at the wording of Kakutani's first sentence in paragraph 22. Why doesn't she say outright that political correctness *causes* "sloppy, abstract language"? What do you think Maggio would say about the cause-and-effect relationship of political correctness and language?

5. Kakutani interrupts herself twice to insert a "correction"—to substitute a politically correct term for an incorrect term she has inadvertently let slip. These appear in paragraphs 9 and 26. What's going on here—didn't she have enough time to edit her article?

6. Why do you think Kakutani entitles her article "The Word Police"? What does that title mean? What connections does it imply between the police and reformers promoting politically correct language? What attitudes does Kakutani seem to have toward both groups?

WRITING ASSIGNMENTS

1. Compare the views about language of Rosalie Maggio in "Bias-Free Language" and Kakutani in this article. What powers does each author believe language has? What power does language not have? Cite specific evidence from each author for your comparison.

2. Despite Kakutani's attack on Maggio's book, she agrees with at least some of Maggio's underlying assumptions—for example, about language and power, about the need to end prejudice, and other points. Identify and discuss at least three assumptions or values that both authors would agree on; then, discuss why they believe that different actions are appropriate.

3. Examine some samples of your own writing from earlier in the term, or from previous terms. Where have you struggled with politically correct language use? Have you always been successful in using it? What substitutions or changes did you try that, on rereading, seem less than satisfactory?

4. Identify a national or major city newspaper or news journal that is marketed for a group that sometimes uses biased language. Select an article you think is of spe-

cial interest to that group. (For example, you might examine the African American newspaper *The Chicago Defender* for coverage of the Rodney King beating in 1991 or the arrest of O.J. Simpson for the murder of his ex-wife Nicole Brown Simpson and her friend Ronald Goldman in 1994; or *The Disability Rag* for coverage of legislation benefiting Americans with disabilities; or *Off Our Backs* for coverage of antigay and antilesbian legislation in Colorado.) Then, select a major news source that is marketed for a general audience and find an article of similar length on the same event or issue. Compare the two articles. How did you feel about the issue after reading one? After reading the other? What differences do you see in the way language is used? What assumptions does each make about its readers' values and concerns? Do you think that the language each one uses makes a difference in the feeling you get about the issue? Or does the difference in tone have more to do with what is emphasized in the report rather than with what language is used to convey information?

"NIGGER": THE MEANING OF A WORD

Gloria Naylor

Context can be everything when it comes to the meaning of a word, even a word recognized as an ugly epithet. As Gloria Naylor explains, when she was a little girl, the word "nigger" was spoken comfortably in front of her by relatives and family friends. She had heard it dozens of times, viewing it as a term of endearment. But she really didn't "hear" the term until it was "spit out" of the mouth of a white boy in her third-grade class.

Gloria Naylor, a native of New York City, is an accomplished writer whose first novel *The Women of Brewster Place* (1982) won an American Book Award. She is also the author of *Linden Hills* (1985), *Mama Day* (1988), and *Bailey's Cafe* (1992). This essay first appeared in the *New York Times,* in February 1986.

1   Language is the subject. It is the written form with which I've managed to keep the wolf away from the door and, in diaries, to keep my sanity. In spite of this, I consider the written word inferior to the spoken, and much of the frustration experienced by novelists is the awareness that whatever we manage to capture in even the most transcendent passages falls far short of the richness of life. Dialogue achieves its power in the dynamics of a fleeting moment of sight, sound, smell and touch.

2   I'm not going to enter the debate here about whether it is language that shapes reality or vice versa. That battle is doomed to be waged whenever we seek intermittent reprieve from the chicken and egg dispute. I will simply take the position that the spoken word, like the written word, amounts to a nonsensical arrangement of sounds or letters without a consensus that assigns "meaning." And building from the meanings of what we hear, we order reality. Words themselves are innocuous; it is the consensus that gives them true power.

3   I remember the first time I heard the word nigger. In my third-grade class, our math tests were being passed down the rows, and as I handed the papers to a little boy in back of me, I remarked that once again he had received a much lower mark than I did. He snatched his test from me and spit out that word. Had he called me a nymphomaniac or a necrophiliac, I couldn't have been more puzzled. I didn't know what a nigger was, but I knew that whatever it meant, it was something he shouldn't have called me. This was verified when I raised my hand, and in a loud voice repeated what he had said and watched the teacher scold him for using a "bad" word. I was later to go home and ask the inevitable question that every black parent must face—"Mommy, what does 'nigger' mean?"

4   And what exactly did it mean? Thinking back, I realize that this could not have been the first time the word was used in my presence. I was part of a large extended family that had migrated from the rural South after World War II and formed a close-knit network that gravitated around my maternal grandparents. Their ground-floor apartment in one of the buildings they owned in Harlem was a weekend mecca for my immediate family, along with countless aunts, uncles and cousins who brought along assorted friends. It was a bustling and open house with assorted neighbors and tenants popping in and out to exchange bits of gossip, pick up an old quarrel or referee the ongoing checkers game in which my grandmother cheated shamelessly. They were all there to let down their hair and put up their feet after a week of labor in the factories, laundries and shipyards of New York.

5   Amid the clamor, which could reach deafening proportions—two or three conversations going on simultaneously, punctuated by the sound of a baby's crying somewhere in the back rooms or out on the street—there was still a rigid set of rules about what was said and how. Older children were sent out of the living room when it was time to get into the juicy details about "you-know-who" up on the third floor who had gone and gotten herself "p-r-e-g-n-a-n-t!" But my parents, knowing that I could spell well beyond my years, always demanded that I follow the others out to play. Beyond sexual misconduct and death, everything else was considered harmless for our young ears. And so among the anecdotes of the triumphs and disappointments in the various workings of their lives, the word nigger was used in my presence, but it was set within contexts and inflections that caused it to register in my mind as something else.

6   In the singular, the word was always applied to a man who had distinguished himself in some situation that brought their approval for his strength, intelligence or drive:

7   "Did Johnny *really* do that?"

8   "I'm telling you, that nigger pulled in $6,000 of overtime last year. Said he got enough for a down payment on a house."

9   When used with a possessive adjective by a woman—"my nigger"—it became a term of endearment for husband or boyfriend. But it could be more than just a term applied to a man. In their mouths it became the pure essence of

manhood—a disembodied force that channeled their past history of struggle and present survival against the odds into a victorious statement of being: "Yeah, that old foreman found out quick enough—you don't mess with a nigger."

10   In the plural, it became a description of some group within the community that have overstepped the bounds of decency as my family defined it: Parents who neglected their children, a drunken couple who fought in public, people who simply refused to look for work, those with excessively dirty mouths or unkempt households were all "trifling niggers." This particular circle could forgive hard times, unemployment, the occasional bout of depression—they had gone through all of that themselves—but the unforgivable sin was a lack of self-respect.

11   A woman could never be a "nigger" in the singular, with its connotation of confirming worth. The noun girl was its closet equivalent in that sense, but only when used in direct address and regardless of the gender doing the addressing. "Girl" was a token of respect for a woman. The one-syllable word was drawn out to sound like three in recognition of the extra ounce of wit, nerve or daring that the woman had shown in the situation under discussion.

12   "G-i-r-l, stop. You mean you said that to his face?"

13   But if the word was used in a third-person reference or shortened so that it almost snapped out of the mouth, it always involved some element of communal disapproval. And age became an important factor in these exchanges. It was only between individuals of the same generation, or from an older person to a younger (but never the other way around), that "girl" would be considered a compliment.

14   I don't agree with the argument that use of the word nigger at this social stratum of the black community was an internalization of racism. The dynamics were the exact opposite: the people in my grandmother's living room took a word that whites used to signify worthlessness or degradation and rendered it impotent. Gathering there together, they transformed "nigger" to signify the varied and complex human beings they knew themselves to be. If the word was to disappear totally from the mouths of even the most liberal of white society, no one in that room was naïve enough to believe it would disappear from white minds. Meeting the word head-on, they proved it had absolutely nothing to do with the way they were determined to live their lives.

15   So there must have been dozens of times that the "nigger" was spoken in front of me before I reached the third grade. But I didn't "hear" it until it was said by a small pair of lips that had already learned it could be a way to humiliate me. That was the word I went home and asked my mother about. And since she knew that I had to grow up in America, she took me in her lap and explained.

TOPICAL CONSIDERATIONS

1. Does Naylor think that written or spoken words are more powerful? Why? What does she mean when she says that it is "consensus that gives [words] true power"?

2. What did Naylor do as a response to hearing the word "nigger"? In your judgment, were her actions appropriate and effective ways of handling the situation?

3. List four different meanings that Naylor says she has heard adults apply to the word "nigger." How are these four meanings different from what she believed the boy in her class meant? Are all four meanings positive?

4. Why can't a woman be referred to as a "nigger"? What other term is used for a woman that achieves meaning similar to the term "nigger" for a man?

5. Does Naylor approve of her family and friends' use of the word "nigger"? Why or why not? Does she approve of white people using the word? Why or why not?

6. What does Naylor mean when, after a lengthy discussion of her previous knowledge of the word "nigger," she says that she "didn't 'hear' it" until the boy in the third grade used it? Why does she place the word "hear" in quotation marks?

RHETORICAL CONSIDERATIONS

1. Naylor relates in some detail the circumstances surrounding the first time she heard the word "nigger." Why does she paint such an elaborate picture? Why doesn't she simply list her age and the fact that she heard it used as an insult? What do you think prompted the boy to use this word?

2. In your opinion, what alternative courses of action might Naylor have taken when the boy called her a "nigger"? What might have been the consequences of such different choices?

3. Why does Naylor compare the word "nigger" specifically to "nymphomaniac" and "necrophiliac"? Why these words? How are they similar? How different? (Look them up in your dictionary if you are not sure what they mean.)

4. Do you think the boy in Naylor's class was African American or white? How can you tell? Why do you think Naylor doesn't supply this crucial bit of information?

5. In paragraphs 4 and 5, Naylor provides a detailed discussion of her extended family: where they lived, how they were related, what kind of atmosphere these people generated, and what kinds of discussion children were permitted to eavesdrop on. How is this information related to the subject of Naylor's essay, the meaning of the word "nigger"?

6. At the end of paragraph 3, and again at the end of the article, Naylor tells us that she asked her mother for an explanation. She does say in the final mention that her mother complied with this request. But she doesn't supply her mother's words. What do you think her mother said? Why do you think Naylor doesn't include the explanation here?

WRITING ASSIGNMENTS

1. When did you first become aware of the word "nigger," or of some other powerfully charged, negative label for a group of people? When did you first become aware of racism? Were your recognitions gradual, or can you trace your recognition to a specific time and place? What did you do to try to understand the word or the problem? Write up your answers in a paper.

2. How does Naylor's discussion about the way the word "nigger" has been transformed confirm Rosalie Maggio's observation in her article, "Bias-Free Lan-

guage," that "naming is power"? Name at least two specific principles of bias-free language Maggio describes that Naylor seems to agree with. Write up your answers in a paper.

3. With classmates, brainstorm as many derogatory terms for racial and ethnic minorities you can think of. Select one of these terms and examine the following resources: an unabridged dictionary, a dictionary of American slang, an encyclopedia. What did you find out from each about the term's primary meaning and its connotations? about its origins and history? Prepare a report on your findings for classmates.

4. Research the problem of colleges' and universities' efforts to restrict "hate speech," including racial slurs, on campuses over the past several years. Locate discussions that give examples of more than one school's efforts. What rules have schools made? What are the consequences of violating those rules? Are there any legal problems with these rules? What is your school's policy?

HEARD ANY GOOD JEWS LATELY?

Thomas Friedmann

Perhaps no people in history have been more maligned by prejudice than the Jews. The abuse they have suffered extends back thousands of years. Here, fiction writer Thomas Friedmann discusses the terrible kinds of language abuse Jews have been subjected to. The special lesson of this essay is just how dangerously manipulative the language of prejudice can be, for in Nazi Germany not long ago it began with words and ended with crematoria.

1   The horrors of mass murder can be made bearable if the intended victim is made to appear an object that deserves extermination. The Nazis understood this. Thus, while their bureaucrats searched for the means by which the wholesale destruction of Europe's Jews could be carried out, their propagandists primed the populace to accept psychologically the annihilation of those Jews. In their manipulation of language to justify the "Final Solution," the Nazis resorted to terminology that had been utilized earlier to render Jews subhuman. Martin Luther, urging the expulsion of Jews, had written about them as "a plague and a pestilence." In 1895, three and a half centuries after Luther, a deputy in the German *Reichstag* made clear that Luther's characterization had not been forgotten. He described Jews as "parasites" and "cholera germs." Hitler's propagandists preserved the tradition. They continued to disseminate the notion that Jews were a lower species of life, designating them "vermin," "lice," and "bacilli."

2   Then, in an act that might be considered almost poetic were it not so horrifying and grotesque, the Nazi administrative apparatus captured the spirit of the metaphor its propagandists had devised. It contacted the chemical industries of the *Reich*, specifically the firms that specialized in "combating vermin." Simply, it requested that these manufacturers of insecticides produce another delousing agent, one a bit stronger than the product used for household ticks and flies, but one that would be used for essentially the same purpose. The companies complied. Thus was *Zyklon B* created. The gas, used in a milder form for occasionally fumigating the disease-ridden barracks where other victims were penned, killed millions of men, women, and children. Obscenely clinging to the metaphor they had accepted, the Nazis herded their

Jewish victims into gas chambers of death that were disguised as "showers" and "disinfectant centers."

3   What the bureaucrats accomplished, the propagandists had made psychologically possible. How could anyone object when, with the whiff of invisible gas from the crackling blue crystals of *Zyklon B*, millions of Jews were exterminated? Is not extermination the deserved fate of all vermin?

4   But that was Nazi Germany, people tend to say. The mass murder of so many people was an aberration, an accident of history. That artificial, created language that made it possible for participants to accept the horror of the Holocaust would not have the power again. Surely, that manufactured imagery, that inhuman metaphor, no matter how traditional, can never again conceal that these are Jews that are being threatened, not subhuman creatures. Call them by their name—Jew—and you could never forget that they are people. Certainly the name is an affirmation. *Jew,* by way of Middle English *Giv,* Old French *juiu,* Latin *Judæus,* and Hebrew *Yehudi,* derives from Judah, the foremost of the Twelve Tribes of Israel. Its name means "praised," its emblem is the lion, it has borne a line of kings. Surely the name itself can withstand the ravages of prejudice!

5   But the King's English has not retained the proud heritage of the name. Eric Partridge, in *A Dictionary of Slang and Unconventional English*, lists *Jew* as a verb meaning "to drive a hard bargain," or "to overreach or cheat." In addition, *Jew* as prefix yields to *Jew-down,* meaning to haggle unfairly, *Jew-bail,* meaning "worthless bail," *Jew-balance,* a name for the hammerhead shark, *Jew-food,* mockingly ham, the food forbidden to Jews, *Jews' harp,* whose French origin has nothing to do with Jews but whose sound was picked up by English dramatists to mean Jew and hence an instrument of lesser value, and finally, two astounding phrases, *worth a Jew's eye* and *a Jüdische compliment* or *a Jew's compliment.* As with the slur *sheeny,* which is probably a perversion of the flattering *shaine* (Yiddish) or *schön* (German), meaning "beautiful," both of these apparent phrases of flattery are, in fact, derogatory. To receive *a Jew's compliment* is apparently to be blessed with the misfortune of having "a large penis but little money." The great worth of *a Jew's eye* exists because that was the organ removed when a Jew failed to pay his levy or tax. Another source suggests that it was the teeth that would be threatened with removal. Because Jews invariably paid up, the expression became popular, as in, "If a Jew is willing to pay that much for his teeth, imagine the worth of a Jew's eye."

6   *Jew* also figures in the acronym JAP, applied to certain young women. A JAP, Jewish American Princess, is meant to describe a pampered, snobbish, money-conscious female who is princess in her parents' household. *Jew* is also a pejorative when used in *Jewess.* Why is there no *Protestantess?* Feminists find it doubly offensive, since the *-ess* generally reduces the worth of the noun, as in *poetess.* And, when accounting is dubbed *Jewish engineering,* a cash register a *Jewish piano,* and a dollar bill the *Jewish flag,* the term *Jew* is unmistakably being used as an insult. One thinks of the Greeks for whom any-

one not Greek was a foreigner and hence primitive and uncivilized, a barbarian. Imagine the Jew whose very name is a negative term. Naming himself, he excludes himself from mankind.

7   Only the use of *Indian* comes to mind in this context. As *Jew*, *Indian* is often found as a damning prefix in such compounds as *Indian-cholera, Indian giver,* and *Indian tobacco,* this last the name given to a poisonous North American plant. And while the negative use of *Indian* is at least partially mitigated by positive (*Indian summer*) and neutral uses (*Indian pipe, Indian bread*), no balance exists for *Jew.*

8   Given the derision attached to *Jew* itself, one can imagine the multiplied power of the slur in the slang versions of *Jew: Jew-boy, geese, kike, mockie,* and *sheeny. Sheeny,* incidentally, is thought by some sources to have come from "shiny," a comment on the brilliantined hair of many young British Jews. The coinage of *kike,* the most familiar of these slurs, is attributed by some writers, rather gleefully perhaps and without documentation, to Jews. According to Ernest Von Den Haag, German Jewish immigrants, the earlier arrivals to the United States, were the ones who formulated *kike* to identify their Eastern-European brethren, whom they considered their inferiors. The term is thought to have been derived from *-ki* or *-ky,* the final syllable of many Polish and Russian names. More plausible seems Leo Rosten's suggestion that *kike* comes from "kikel," the Yiddish word for circle. This was the mark with which Jewish immigrants would sign their names when they could not write, preferring it to the commonly used *X* which they thought resembled a cross. Whatever the origin of the term, there is no question that it is a pejorative. At Queen Victoria's court Prime Minister Disraeli wryly defined the name. "A kike," he said, "is a Jewish gentleman who has just left the room."

9   In addition to these opprobations, American English has accepted a great many Yiddish words which are used as insults. A partial list would include: *gonif* (thief), *gunsel* (catamite), *dreck* (feces, junk), *kibbitzer* (irritating bystander), and a host of *sch* words: *schnook, schmuck, schlep, schlock, schmaltzy, schlemiel, schlamazel, schwantz, schnorrer,* and possibly *shyster* (by way of *schiess*—shit). While such easy adoption of foreign words might be considered a sign of the pluralistic nature of the English language and a source of its astonishing variety, the terms cannot help but remind users of their source. Were they not, after all, insults applied by Jews to other Jews in their own tongue?

10   A few words, finally, about Jewish jokes or more precisely, jokes about Jews. One of the more bizarre aspects of Nazi propaganda was its utilization of toys, games, and jokes. German children played with "Jews Get Out," a board game produced by Fabricus Co., and their elders had the opportunity to laugh at caricatures of Jews. A typical one shows a hooknosed Jew in the form of a snake, being crushed under the boot of a National Social German Workers' Party (Nazi) member. Other cartoons, particularly political appeals, contained messages about the acquisitive nature of Jews, and hence, their exploitation of Germans. Below is an update indicating that jokes with a similar message have

been reinvented in this country. Note that each of the jokes reproduced below is American, containing either an American locale or an American idiom. These are "Made in USA," not imported and translated.

> QUESTION: How was the Grand Canyon formed?
> ANSWER: A Jew lost a nickel in a crack.
> QUESTION: Why do Jews have big noses?
> ANSWER: Air is free.
> QUESTION: Why are few Jews in jail?
> ANSWER: Crime doesn't pay.

11   The message in each case is clear. What is the basic nature of Jews? They are money-hungry creatures with no moral restraints who will go to great lengths for financial gain. Just jokes, right? Professor Harvey Mindess, who organized the International Conference on Human at Antioch College, suggested that jokes are good, that laughter "lets out a little of the devil inside all of us." What about the great big devil jokes let in, allowing people to make subtle distinctions between "them" and "us," using laughter as the great divider? Jokes about Jews, about any ethnic group, communicate negative stereotypes that become just a little bit more credible with each telling.

12   A rather self-deprecating joke Israelis tell about themselves points out the increasingly secular nature of their country. The anecdote is about the immigrant Israeli mother who wanted her son to learn Yiddish so he would remember that he was Jewish. But the typical news commentator fails to see the distinction the joke makes. Israel is inevitably "the Jewish State," her neighbors "Arab countries." Why not "Moslem countries"? Why not the "Hebrew State"?

13   And it is similarly good for a laugh when the Mary Tyler Moore character in the film *Ordinary People* responds with a raised eyebrow and an unhappy face upon being informed that her son is not only seeing a psychiatrist but that this psychiatrist is named *Berger.* One of *those* people, of course. Even when they change their names, thanks to Archie Bunker their secret identities as Jews can be penetrated. It's all in the first name, Archie has explained. "They" may be named Smith or Jones, but one knows who they really are when their first names are Moe, and Iz, and Ben, unmistakably Jewish first names, right, Abe Lincoln? Oh yes, those Jewish lawyers, they're not always such smart Ginsbergs!

14   Personally, Archie, I have suffered from reverse discrimination. To this day, it is my first name that draws questions from Jew and Gentile alike. "Tom? What kind of a name is that for a Jewish boy?" And the little jokes go on with their work. Like maggots and earthworms they grind the ground in the quiet, preparing the soil for another little seed of prejudice.

TOPICAL CONSIDERATIONS

   1. According to the essay, how was it possible that the Nazi bureaucrats were able to justify mass extermination?
   2. Does the author ever suggest why the Jews have, throughout history, suffered so much discrimination? What do you think are some of the reasons for such prejudice?

3. Have you ever heard anti-Semitic comments from people? If so, did those who made them speak from personal experiences with Jewish people? Or were they just following stereotyping habits?

4. Friedmann, in paragraph 7, makes the point that *Jew*, like *Indian*, has been used as a negative prefix. Can you think of other races or ethnic groups whose names are used in such pejorative ways?

5. What is Friedmann's point in paragraph 9 in discussing some of the Yiddish words that English has adopted? Why is it not a compliment to Jewishness that English has accepted so many Yiddish terms?

6. Friedmann cites some Jewish jokes "made in USA." What specific images do these portray of Jews? What portraits of the people in question do Polish jokes paint? Italian jokes? Swedish jokes? Iraqi jokes? Catholic jokes? What are the stereotypes? (Heard any good Armenians lately?)

7. In paragraph 6 Friedmann says that the suffix *-ess* reduces the worth of the noun to which it is attached. Do you agree? How does the suffix do that? Can you think of any exceptions?

RHETORICAL CONSIDERATIONS

1. Locate Friedmann's thesis statement in this essay. How effectively does the essay build from it?

2. How well do Friedmann's final comments round off the essay?

3. In paragraph 2 Friedmann refers to what the Nazis did to the Jews as "an act that might be considered almost poetic were it not so horrifying and grotesque." How does he mean the term *poetic* here?

4. Discuss the title of this essay. Why the pun on the word *news*? What is the tone here? Is it appropriate for the essay?

5. Earlier in the text you read more about euphemisms—pleasant terms for disturbing or unpleasant realities. What euphemisms did Hitler's propagandists use in dealing with the Jews? How effective were they, given the Nazi intentions? What is the language message here?

6. Cite passages in which Friedmann uses ironic detachment for rhetorical purposes.

7. For Friedmann, who does Archie Bunker represent?

WRITING ASSIGNMENT

1. In a paper discuss some of the prejudicial terms and formulas you have encountered about Jews. What negative stereotyping qualities do they create?

2. Some comedians build a career on ethnic jokes, many of which are about Jews—and often they are Jewish comedians: Jackie Mason, Joan Rivers, Alan King, Mel Brooks, and so on. Write a paper on how television comics create humor from Jewish stereotypes. How harmless are the jokes, in fact?

THE ETYMOLOGY OF THE INTERNATIONAL INSULT

Charles F. Berlitz

Previous essays in this book have shown that language has the power to slant the way we see the world, to prejudice the way we think. Perhaps no aspect of language is more slanted and prejudiced than that of ethnic, racial, and religious insults. In this essay, Charles F. Berlitz, founder of the internationally known Berlitz School of Languages, takes a look at international insults. Instead of exploring moral issues, he objectively examines these insults' origins, some of which are surprisingly inoffensive.

1 "What is a kike?" Disraeli once asked a small group of fellow politicians. Then, as his audience shifted nervously, Queen Victoria's great Jewish Prime Minister supplied the answer himself. "A kike," he observed, "is a Jewish gentlemen who has just left the room."

2   The word kike is thought to have derived from the ending -*ki* or -*ky* found in many names borne by the Jews of Eastern Europe. Or, as Leo Rosten suggests, it may come from *kikel*, Yiddish for a circle, the preferred mark for name signing by Jewish immigrants who could not write. This was used instead of an *X*, which resembles a cross. Kikel was not originally pejorative, but has become so through use.

3   Yid, another word for Jew has a distinguished historic origin, coming from the German *Jude* (through the Russian *zhid*). *Jude* itself derives from the tribe of Judah, a most honorable and ancient appellation. The vulgar and opprobrious word "Sheeny" for Jew is a real inversion, as it derives from *shaine* (Yiddish) or *schön* (German), meaning "beautiful." How could beautiful be an insult? The answer is that it all depends on the manner, tone or facial expression or sneer (as our own Vice President[1] has trenchantly observed) with which something is said. The opprobrious Mexican word for an American—*gringo*, for example, is essentially simply a sound echo of a song the American troops used to sing when the Americans were invading Mexico—"Green Grow the Lilacs." Therefore the Mexicans began to call the Americans something equivalent to "los green-grows" which became Hispanized to *gringo*. But from this innocent beginning to the unfriendly emphasis with which many Mexicans say

---

[1] A reference to Spiro Agnew, who served as Vice President to Richard Nixon. (Ed.)

gringo today there is a world of difference—almost a call to arms, with unforgettable memories of past real or fancied wrongs, including "lost" Texas and California.[2]

4   The pejorative American word for Mexicans, Puerto Ricans, Cubans and other Spanish-speaking nationals is simply *spik,* excerpted from the useful expression "No esspick Englitch." Italians, whether in America or abroad, have been given other more picturesque appellations. *Wop,* an all-time pejorative favorite, is curiously not insulting at all by origin, as it means, in Neapolitan dialect, "handsome," "strong" or "good looking." Among the young Italian immigrants some of the stronger and more active—sometimes to the point of combat—were called *guappi,* from which the first syllable, "wop," attained an "immediate insult" status for all Italians.

5   "Guinea" comes from the days of the slave trade and is derived from the African word for West Africa. This "guinea" is the same word as the British unit of 21 shillings, somehow connected with African gold profits as well as New Guinea, which resembled Africa to its discoverers. Dark or swarthy Italians and sometimes Portuguese were called *Guineas* and this apparently spread to Italians of light complexion as well.

6   One of the epithets for Negroes has a curious and tragic historic origin, the memory of which is still haunting us. The word is *"coons."* It comes from *baracoes* (the o gives a nasal *n* sound in Portuguese), and refers to the slave pens or barracks (*"baracoons"*) in which the victims of the slave trade were kept while awaiting transshipment. Their descendants, in their present emphasizing of the term "black" over "Negro," may be in the process of upgrading the very word "black," so often used pejoratively, as in "black-hearted," "black day," "black arts," "black hand," etc. Even some African languages use "black" in a negative sense. In Hausa "to have a black stomach" means to be angry or unhappy.

7   The sub-Sahara African peoples, incidentally, do not think that they are black (which they are not, anyway). They consider themselves a healthy and attractive "people color," while whites to them look rather unhealthy and somewhat frightening. In any case, the efforts of African Americans to dignify the word "black" may eventually represent a semantic as well as a socio-racial triumph.

8   A common type of national insult is that of referring to nationalities by their food habits. Thus "Frogs" for the French and "Krauts" for the Germans are easily understandable, reflecting on the French addiction to *cuisses de grenouilles* (literally "thighs of frogs") and that of the Germans for various kinds of cabbage, hot or cold. The French call the Italians *"les macaronis"* while the German insult word for Italians is *Katzenfresser* (Cateaters), an unjust accusation considering the hordes of cats among the Roman ruins fed by individual cat lovers—unless they are fattening them up? The insult word for

---

[2]Other linguists theorize the term "gringo" derives from the seventeenth-century Spanish *griego* for Greek," a term used widely in Latin America, not just Mexico. (Ed.)

an English person is "limey," referring to the limes distributed to seafaring Englishmen as an antiscurvy precaution in the days of sailing ships and long periods at sea.

9   At least one of these food descriptive appellations has attained a permanent status in English. The word "Eskimo" is not an Eskimo word at all but an Algonquin word unit meaning "eaters-of-flesh." The Eskimos naturally do not call themselves this in their own language but, with simple directness, use the word *Inuit*—"the men" or "the people."

10   Why is it an insult to call Chinese "Chinks"? Chink is most probably a contraction of the first syllables of *Chung-Kuo-Ren*—"Middle Country Person." In Chinese there is no special word for China, as the Chinese, being racially somewhat snobbish themselves (although *not* effete, according to recent reports), have for thousands of years considered their land to be the center or middle of the world. The key character for China is therefore the word *chung* or "middle" which, added to *kuo*, becomes "middle country" or "middle kingdom"—the complete Chinese expression for "China" being *Chung Hwa Min Kuo* ("Middle Flowery People's Country"). No matter how inoffensive the origin of "Chink" is, however, it is no longer advisable for everyday or anyday use now.

11   Jap, an insulting diminutive that figured in the . . . [1968] national U.S. election (though its use in the expression "fat Jap" was apparently meant to have an endearing quality by our Vice President) is a simple contraction of "Japan," which derives from the Chinese word for "sun." In fact the words "Jap" and "Nip" both mean the same thing. "Jap" comes from Chinese and "Nip" from Japanese in the following fashion: *Jihpen* means "sun origin" in Chinese, while *Ni-hon* (Nippon) gives a like meaning in Japanese, both indicating that Japan was where the sun rose. Europeans were first in contact with China, and so originally chose the Chinese name for Japan instead of the Japanese one.

12   The Chinese "insult" words for whites are based on the observations that they are too white and therefore look like ghosts or devils, *fan kuei* (ocean ghosts), or that their features are too sharp instead of being pleasantly flat, and that they have enormous noses, hence *ta-bee-tsu* (great-nosed ones). Differences in facial physiognomy have been fully reciprocated by whites in referring to Asians as "Slants" or "Slopes."

13   Greeks in ancient times had an insult word for foreigners too, but one based on the sound of their language. This word is still with us, though its original meaning has changed. The ancient Greeks divided the world into Greeks and "Barbarians"—the latter word coming from a description of the ridiculous language the stranger was speaking. To the Greeks it sounded like the "baa-baa" of a sheep—hence "Barbarians"!

14   The black peoples of South Africa are not today referred to as Negro or Black but as Bantu—not in itself an insult but having somewhat the same effect when you are the lowest man on the totem pole. But the word means simply "the men," *ntu* signifying "man" and *ba* being the plural prefix. This may have come from an early encounter with explorers or missionaries when Cen-

tral or South Africans on being asked by whites who they were may have replied simply "men"—with the implied though probably unspoken follow-up questions, "And who are you?"

15   The basic and ancient idea that one's group are the only people—at least the only friendly or non-dangerous ones—is found among many tribes throughout the world. The Navajo Indians call themselves *Diné*—"the people"—and qualify other tribes generally as "the enemy." Therefore an Indian tribe to the north would simply be called "the northern enemy," one to the east "the eastern enemy," etc., and that would be the *only* name used for them. These ancient customs, sanctified by time, of considering people who differ in color, customs, physical characteristics and habits—and by enlargement all strangers—as potential enemies is something mankind can no longer afford, even linguistically. Will man ever be able to rise above using insult as a weapon? It may not be possible to love your neighbor, but by understanding him one may be able eventually to tolerate him. Meanwhile, if you stop calling him names, he too may eventually learn to dislike *you* less.

TOPICAL CONSIDERATIONS

1. Knowing how racial and ethnic insults originate, do you find that you can more easily accept them?

2. In the first paragraph, Berlitz quotes Disraeli. What do you think was the meaning of Disraeli's definition of *kike*?

3. Berlitz gives etymological meanings of the following words: *Jude, wop, schön, guappi,* and *Chung-Kuo-Ren.* What similarities do the meanings of these words have?

4. Explain the relationship between national insults and national eating habits. Can you think of others not mentioned by Berlitz?

5. Why do so many tribal peoples refer to themselves as "the people"? What does that say about people's habits of insulting others of different ethnic or racial origins?

6. What does Berlitz mean in the last paragraph when he warns that even linguistically, humanity can no longer afford to consider different races and customs as enemies?

RHETORICAL CONSIDERATIONS

1. Berlitz begins this essay with an anecdote. How effective is it? What is the relationship of the anecdote to the rest of the essay?

2. For the most part, Berlitz is objective in his discussion. Can you find instances where he expresses his attitude toward the use of international insults?

3. Berlitz reserves his thesis statement for the final paragraph. Is this an effective strategy? Explain your answer.

4. How would you describe the tone of this essay? Is it appropriate for the subject matter?

WRITING ASSIGNMENTS

1. Write an essay discussing racial and national insults as forms of violence in language.

2. Everyone has been exposed to ethnic and racial insults. Write an essay discussing how the media—movies, television, books, even music—contribute to the growth of prejudicial language.

3. Write an essay answering the question posed at the end of Berlitz's essay: "Will man ever be able to rise above using insult as a weapon?"

4. If you have ever been directly victimized by national or racial insults, describe your experience. What effect did the insults have on you?

5. Choose a racial, national, or religious insult and define it as best you can. How is it insulting? What is its origin?

6. Select a racial or ethnic group in America that has experienced (or continues to experience) prejudice. (You may use one of the groups Berlitz identifies.) List a handful of insulting terms about that group. Consult library resources to determine when the terms originated, and what they originally meant. If the terms have changed meaning, when and how did they change? Can you determine a reason for the changes? By whom were these terms originally used? Who uses them now?

7. Using biographical resources, report on the life of Charles Berlitz and the principles on which he founded the language study method that now bears his name. How did his programs meet a need that he perceived in language training? What philosophies did he hold about cultural difference? How did his study of language help shape those philosophies? What events in his life seem to have influenced his ideas?

DEFINING THE "AMERICAN INDIAN": A CASE STUDY IN THE LANGUAGE OF SUPPRESSION

Haig A. Bosmajian

This chapter began with the proposition that language can be employed to suppress people. Several essays thus far have documented language that has been used against various ethnic and racial groups. Native Americans have, since the colonization of this continent, suffered dehumanization through religious, cultural, and legal redefinition. This excerpt looks back at the linguistic suppression of these people who were conveniently perceived as "savages" and "miscreants" unworthy of ballots or property.

1   One of the first important acts of an oppressor is to redefine the oppressed victims he intends to jail or eradicate so that they will be looked upon as creatures warranting suppression and in some cases separation and annihilation. I say "creatures" because the redefinition usually implies a dehumanization of the individual. The Nazis redefined the Jews as "bacilli," "parasites," "disease," and "demon."[1] The language of white racism has for centuries attempted to "keep the nigger in his place."[2] Our sexist language has allowed men to define who and what a woman is.[3] The labels "traitors," "queers," "pinkos," "saboteurs," and "obscene degenerates" have all been used to attack students protesting the war in Vietnam and the economic and political injustices in this country.[4] One obviously does not listen to, much less talk to, traitors and outlaws, sensualists and queers. One only punishes them or, as Spiro

[1]See Haig A. Bosmajian, "The Magic Word in Nazi Persuasion," *ETC.*, 23 (March 1966), 9–23; Werner Betz, "The National-Socialist Vocabulary," *The Third Reich* (London: Weidenfeld and Nicolson, 1955); Heinz Paechter, *Nazi-Deutsch* (New York: Frederick Ungar, 1944).
[2]See Simon Podair, "Language and Prejudice," *Phylon Review*, 17 (1956), 390–394; Haig A. Bosmajian, "The Language of White Racism," *College English*, 31 (December 1969), 263–272.
[3]See Haig A. Bosmajian, "The Language of Sexism," *ETC.*, 29 (September 1972), 305–313.
[4]See Haig A. Bosmajian, "The Protest Generation and Its Critics." *Discourse: A Review of the Liberal Arts*, 9 (Autumn 1966), 464–469.

Agnew suggested in one of his 1970 campaign speeches, indicates that there are some dissenters who should be separated "from our society with no more regret than we should feel over discarding rotten apples from a barrel."[5]

2   Through the use of the language of suppression the human animal can seemingly justify the unjustifiable, make palatable the unpalatable, and make decent the indecent. Just as our thoughts affect our language, so does our language affect our thoughts and eventually our action and behavior. As George Orwell observed in his famous essay "Politics and the English Language," our language becomes ugly and inaccurate because our thoughts are foolish and then "the slovenliness of our language makes it easier for us to have foolish thoughts." Orwell maintained that "the decadence of our language is probably curable" and that "silly words and expressions have often disappeared, not through any evolutionary process but owing to the conscious action of a minority."[6] This then is our task: to identify the decadence in our language, the silly words and expressions which have been used to justify oppression of varying degrees. . . .

3   A case study of this inhumane use of language and of the linguistic dehumanization process is provided in the manner in which the European invaders of the New World redefined the occupants of what is now called North America and the manner in which white Americans have perpetuated through language the suppression of the "Indians" into the twentieth century. This essay will focus on and examine (1) the natural-religious redefinition of the "Indians"; (2) the political-cultural redefinition of the "Indians"; and (3) the legal redefinition of the "Indians."

THE NATURAL-RELIGIOUS REDEFINITION

4   The "de-civilization," the dehumanization and redefinition of the Indian, began with the arrival of Columbus in the New World. The various peoples in the New World, even though the differences between them were as great as between Italians and Irish or Finns and Portuguese, were all dubbed "Indians," and then "American Indians."[7] Having renamed the inhabitants, the invaders then proceeded to enslave, torture, and kill them, justifying this inhumanity by defining these inhabitants as "savages" and "barbarians." The Europeans' plundering and killing of the Indians in the West Indies outraged a Spanish Dominican missionary, Bartolome de las Casas, who provided the following account of the conquest of the Arawaks and Caribs in his *Brief Relation of the Destruction of the Indies:*

---

[5]*The New York Times,* October 31, 1969, p. 25.

[6]"Politics and the English Language," in C. Muscatine and M. Griffith. *The Borzoi College Reader,* 2nd ed. (New York: Alfred A. Knopf, 1971), p. 88.

[7]Peter Farb, *Man's Rise to Civilization as Shown by the Indians of North America from Primeval Times to the Coming of the Industrial State* (New York: E. P. Dutton and Company, 1968), p. xx.

> They [the Spaniards] came with their Horsemen well armed with Sword and Launce, making most cruel havocks and slaughters. . . . Overrunning Cities and Villages, where they spared no sex nor age; neither would their cruelty pity Women with childe, whose bellies they would rip up, taking out the Infant to hew it in pieces. . . . The children they would take by the feet and dash their innocent heads against the rocks, and when they were fallen into the water, with a strange and cruel derision they would call on them to swim. . . . They erected certain Gallowses. . . . upon every one of which they would hang thirteen persons, blasphemously affirming that they did it in honor of our Redeemer and his Apostles, and then putting fire under them, they burnt the poor wretches alive. Those whom their pity did think to spare, they would send away with their hands cut off, and so hanging by the skin.[8]

After the arrival of the Spaniards, "whole Arawak villages disappeared through slavery, disease, and warfare, as well as by flight into the mountains. As a result, the native population of Haiti, for example, declined from an estimated 200,000 in 1492 to a mere 29,000 only twenty-two years later."[9]

5   The Spaniards were followed by the English who brought with them their ideas of their white supremacy. In his *The Indian Heritage of America*, Alvin M. Josephy, Jr., observes that "in the early years of the sixteenth century educated whites, steeped in the theological teaching of Europe, argued learnedly about whether or not Indians were humans with souls, whether they, too, derived from Adam and Eve (and were therefore sinful like the rest of mankind), or whether they were a previously subhuman species."[10] Uncivilized and satanic as the Indian may have been, according to the European invaders, he could be saved; but if he could not be saved then he would be destroyed. As Roy H. Pearce has put it, "Convinced thus of his divine right to Indian lands, the Puritan discovered in the Indians themselves evidence of a Satanic opposition to the very principle of divinity."[11] However, continues Pearce, the Indian "also was a man who had to be brought to the civilized responsibilities of Christian manhood, a wild man to be improved along with wild lands, a creature who had to be made into a Puritan if he was to be saved. Save him, and you saved one of Satan's victims. Destroy him, and you destroy one of Satan's partisans."[12] Indians who resisted Puritan invasions of their lands were dubbed "heathens," the "heathen" definition and status in turn justifying the mass killing of Indians who refused to give up their lands to the white invaders: "when the Pequots resisted the migration of settlers into the Connecticut Valley in 1637, a party of Puritans surrounded the Pequot village and set fire to it. . . . Cotton Mather was grateful to the Lord that 'on this day we have sent six hundred heathen souls to hell.'"[13]

---

[8]Alvin M. Josephy, Jr., *The Indian Heritage of America* (New York: Bantam Books, Inc., 1969), p. 286.
[9]Farb, p. 243.
[10]Josephy, p. 4.
[11]Roy H. Pearce, *The Savages of America* (Baltimore: The John Hopkins Press, 1965), p. 21.
[12]Pearce, pp. 21–22.
[13]Farb, p. 247.

6   The European invaders, having defined themselves as culturally superior to the inhabitants they found in the New World, proceeded to their "manifest destiny" and subsequently to the massive killing of the "savages." "This sense of superiority over the Indians," write L. L. Knowles and K. Prewitt in *Institutional Racism in America,* "which was fostered by the religious ideology they carried to the new land, found its expression in the self-proclaimed mission to civilize and Christianize—a mission which was to find its ultimate expression in ideas of a 'manifest destiny' and a 'white man's burden.'"[14] But the Christianizing and "civilizing" process did not succeed and "thus began an extended process of genocide, giving rise to such aphorisms as " 'The only good Indian is a dead Indian.' . . . Since Indians were capable of reaching only the state of 'savage,' they should not be allowed to impede the forward (westward, to be exact) progress of white civilization. The Church quickly acquiesced in this redefinition of the situation."[15]

THE POLITICAL-CULTURAL REDEFINITION

7   If the Indians were not defined as outright "savages" or "barbarians," they were labeled "natives," and as Arnold Toynbee has observed in Volume One of *A Study of History,* "when we Westerners call people 'Natives' we implicitly take the cultural colour out of our perceptions of them. We see them as trees walking, or as wild animals infesting the country in which we happen to come across them. In fact, we see them as part of the local flora and fauna, and not as men of like passions with ourselves; and, seeing them thus as something infrahuman, we feel entitled to treat them as though they did not possess ordinary human rights."[16] Once the Indian was labeled "native" by the white invaders, the latter had in effect established the basis for domesticating or exterminating the former.

8   In 1787, at the Constitutional Convention, it had to be decided what inhabitants of the total population in the newly formed United States should be counted in determining how many representatives each state would have in Congress. The Founding Father decided: "Representatives and direct taxes shall be apportioned among the several states . . . according to their respective numbers, which shall be determined by adding to the whole number of free persons, including those bound to service for a term of years, and excluding

---

[14]Louis L. Knowles and Kenneth Prewitt, eds., *Institutional Racism in America* (Englewood Cliffs, N.J.: Prentice-Hall, Inc., 1969), p. 7.

[15]Knowles and Prewitt, p. 8.

[16]*A Study of History* (London: Oxford University Press, 1935), I, p. 152. For further discussion of the connotation of "natives," see Volume II of *A Study of History,* pp. 574–580.

Indians not taxed, three fifths of all other persons." The enslaved black came out three fifths of a person and the Indian came out a nonentity.

9   When the Indians had been defined as "savages" with no future, the final result, as Pearce states, "was an image of the Indian out of society and out of history."[17] Once the Indians were successfully defined as governmental nonentities, no more justification was needed to drive them off their lands and to force them into migration and eventual death. In the nineteenth century, even the "civilized Indians" found themselves being systematically deprived of life and property. . . .

10   While the state and the church as institutions have defined the Indians into subjugation, there has been in operation the use of a suppressive language by society at large which has perpetuated the dehumanization of the Indian. Our language includes various phrases and words which relegate the Indian to an inferior status: "The only good Indian is a dead Indian"; "Give it back to the Indians"; "drunken Indians," "dumb Indians," and "Redskins." Writings and speeches include references to the "Indian problem" in the same manner that references have been made by white Americans to the "Negro problem" and by the Nazis to the "Jewish problem." There was no "Jewish problem" in Germany until the Nazis created the myth; there was no "Negro problem" until white Americans created the myth; similarly, the "Indian problem" has been created in such a way that the oppressed, not the oppressor, evolve as "the problem."

THE LEGAL REDEFINITION

11 As the list of negative "racial characteristics" of the "Indian race" grew longer and longer over the years, the redefinition of the individual Indian became easier and easier. He was trapped by the racial definitions, stereotypes, and myths. No matter how intelligent, how "civilized" the Indian became, he or she was still an Indian. Even the one who managed to become a citizen (prior to 1924) could not discard his or her "Indian-ness" sufficiently to participate in white society. The language of the law was used to reinforce the redefinition of the oppressed into non-persons and this language of suppression, as law, became governmentally institutionalized, and in effect legitimatized. One of the most blatant examples of the use of the racial characteristic argument appears in an 1897 Minnesota Supreme Court decision dealing with the indictment of one Edward Wise for selling intoxicating liquors to an Indian who had severed all his relations with his tribe and had through the provision of the "Land in Severality Act" of February 8, 1887, become a citizen of the United States.[18]

---

[17]Pearce, p. 135.
[18]*State v. Wise*, 72 N. W. 843 (1897).

Wise was indicted for violating a statute which provided that "whosoever sells . . . any spiritous liquors or wines to any Indian in this state shall on conviction thereof be punished. . . ." In finding against Wise, the Minnesota Supreme court emphasized the weaknesses of the "Indian race" and the fact that as a race Indians were not as "civilized" as the whites:

> . . . in view of the nature and manifest purpose of this statute and the well-known conditions which induce its enactment, there is no warrant for limiting it by excluding from its operation sales of intoxicating liquors to any person of Indian blood, even though he may have become a citizen of the United States, by compliance with the act of congress. The statute is a police regulation. It was enacted in view of the well-known social condition, habits, and tendencies of Indians as a race. While there are doubtless notable individual exceptions to the rule, yet it is a well-known fact that Indians as a race are not as highly civilized as the whites; that they are less subject to moral restraint, more liable to acquire an inordinate appetite for intoxicating liquors, and also more liable to be dangerous to themselves and others when intoxicated.[19]

The Minnesota statute, said the Court, applied to and included "all Indians as a race, without reference to their political status. . . . The difference in condition between Indians as a race and the white race constituted a sufficient basis of classification."[20] Under the Court's reasoning, the individual Indian could not control his or her identity. Like it or not, the individual Indian was defined by the Court's language, by the "well-known fact" that "Indians as a race are not as highly civilized as whites," that Indians are "less subject to moral restraint." Like it or not, the individual Indian was identified in terms of the "characteristics" of the "Indians as a race," whether he or she had those characteristics or not, whether he or she was a citizen of the United States or not.

12   Twenty years later, Minnesota denied voting rights to Indians on the basis of their not being "civilized." . . .[21]

13   The state of Arizona, the state with the largest Indian population, until 1948 did not allow Indians the right to vote. Article 7 of Arizona's Constitution concerning the qualifications of voters placed the Indians in that state in the same category as traitors and felons, the same category as persons not of sound mind and the insane; Article 7 provided, in part: "No person under guardianship, *non compos mentis* or insane shall be qualified to vote in any election or shall any person convicted of treason or felony, be qualified to vote at any election unless restored to civil rights." In 1928, the Arizona Supreme Court decided in *Porter v. Hall* that Arizona Indians did not have the right to vote since they were within the specific provisions of Article 7 denying suf-

---

[19]*In re Liquor Election in Beltrami County,* 989.
[20]*In re Liquor Election in Beltrami County,* 989.
[21]*In re Liquor Election in Beltrami County,* 990.

frage to "persons under guardianship";[22] the Arizona Supreme Court said that " . . . so long as the federal government insists that, notwithstanding their citizenship, their responsibility under our law differs from that of the ordinary citizen, and that they are, or may be, regulated by that government, by virtue of its guardianship, in any manner different from that which may be used in the regulation of white citizens, they are, within the meaning of our constitutional provision, 'persons under guardianship,' and not entitled to vote."[23] In defining the Indians of Arizona as it did in the above decision, the Arizona Supreme Court denied suffrage rights to the Indians even though four years earlier, on June 2, 1924, all non-citizen Indians born within the territorial limits of the United States were made citizens thereof by an Act of Congress. After devoting a paragraph to defining "insanity" and "*non compos mentis*," the Arizona Supreme Court followed with a definition and discussion of "persons under guardianship," the category into which the Indians were placed:

> Broadly speaking, persons under guardianship may be defined as those who, because of some peculiarity of status, defect of age, understanding or self-control, are considered incapable of managing their own affairs, and who therefore have some other person lawfully invested with the power and charged with the duty of taking care of their persons or managing their property, or both. It will be seen from the foregoing definitions that there is one common quality found in each: The person falling within any one of the classes is to some extent and for some reason considered by the law as incapable of managing his own affairs as a normal person, and needing some special care from the state.[24]

14 In 1948, however, the Porter decision was overruled in the case of *Harrison v. Laveen*,[25] thus allowing Indians in Arizona the right to vote. In the 1948 decision, the Supreme Court of Arizona stated that the designation of "persons under guardianship" as it appeared in Article 7 did not apply to Indians. As to the argument that the Indians generally fell into that group of people "incapable of managing their own affairs," the Court said in 1948 that "to ascribe to all Indians residing on reservations the quality of being 'incapable of handling their own affairs in an ordinary manner' would be a grave injustice, for amongst them are educated persons as fully capable of handling their affairs as their white neighbors."[26] Finally, four and a half centuries after Columbus "discovered" "America," almost all the descendants of the original occupants of this land were allowed by the descendants of the invaders to participate, through the vote, in effecting some control (however small) over their destiny

---

[22]*Porter v. Hall*, 271 P. 411 (1928).
[23]*Porter v. Hall*, 419.
[24]*Porter v. Hall*, 416.
[25]*Harrison v. Laveen*, 196 P. 2d 456 (1948).
[26]*Harrison v. Laveen*, 463.

in their own land. Almost all of the "red natives" of the land finally were recognized legally as being as fully capable of handling their affairs as "their white neighbors." . . .

TOPICAL CONSIDERATIONS

1. What is the basis for Bosmajian's claim that once "the Indian was labeled 'native' by the white invaders, the latter had in effect established the basis for domesticating or exterminating the former" (paragraph 7)?

2. Explain how Bosmajian uses the authority and arguments of George Orwell.

3. Specifically, how were American Indians legally redefined? What justifications were used by the governments and courts? Do legal problems still exist for Native Americans?

RHETORICAL CONSIDERATIONS

1. Analyze the first paragraph. Which sentence states the basic theme? What is the effect of concluding the paragraph with a quotation from Spiro Agnew?

2. How do the following words suit the purpose and effect of this essay: *de-civilization, dehumanization, oppressors, white invaders?* Can you find others?

3. In the first sentence of paragraph 11, how do the quotation marks around *racial characteristics* and *Indian race* further the author's argument?

WRITING ASSIGNMENTS

1. It has been said that television and movies are guilty of projecting stereotypes of minorities. Describe some stereotypes of Native Americans.

2. We have read essays about how language dehumanizes African Americans, Native Americans, and women. Can you think of other groups—ethnic, religious, racial, political, or other—that have also suffered linguistic oppression? Write an essay based on what you have read or experienced.

3. Select one of Bosmajian's quoted passages in this article. Find the quote in its original context—in the original book, article, or law brief in which it appeared. How did Bosmajian's citation system help (or hinder) you in locating the source material? Next, examine the quote and the context in which it appears; read at least three pages before and three pages following the location of the quote. Does this material add anything to the knowledge of the subject that you obtained from Bosmajian's article? In your opinion, does Bosmajian use his sources fairly? Why do you think Bosmajian selected this specific passage to quote, rather than some other passage in the immediate vicinity? That is, why do you think this quote is (or isn't) especially useful for his purposes?

4. The scope of Bosmajian's article is all Native American tribes and nations living within what is now referred to as the United States. Examine the redefinition and its effects over at least two hundred years for just one tribe or nation. In what specific ways was this tribe redefined, and by whom? What effects did that redefinition have? In your opinion, how important was redefinition in the historical experience of this group with the U.S. government?

ON BEING A CRIPPLE

Nancy Mairs

Given a choice, what might a person with a physical disability or limitation choose to be called? Disabled? Handicapped? Crippled? Common thinking is that a term that masks the limitation, denies it, or normalizes it would be preferred. For Nancy Mairs, a professed lover of language, this is not so. Rejecting euphemisms that only widen the gap between word and reality, the author proclaims that crippled is what she is and *crippled* is the term she chooses.

At the age of 29 Nancy Mairs (born 1943) was diagnosed with multiple sclerosis. Yet in spite of the crippling effect of the disease, she has been an active and productive person. She has taught women's studies and writing at the University of Arizona and UCLA. She is also a freelance writer and author of several books including a collection of poetry, *All the Rooms of the Yellow House,* and several nonfiction works including *Carnal Acts* and, most recently, *Voice Lessons.* This essay originally appeared in *Plaintext* in 1986.

> *To escape is nothing. Not to escape is nothing.*
>
> —LOUISE BOGAN

1   The other day I was thinking of writing an essay on being a cripple. I was thinking hard in one of the stalls of the women's room in my office building, as I was shoving my shirt into my jeans and tugging up my zipper. Preoccupied, I flushed, picked up my book bag, took my cane down from the hook, and unlatched the door. So many movements unbalanced me, and as I pulled the door open I fell over backward, landing fully clothed on the toilet seat with my legs splayed in front of me: the old beetle-on-its-back routine. Saturday afternoon, the building deserted, I was free to laugh aloud as I wriggled back to my feet, my voice bouncing off the yellowish tiles from all directions. Had anyone been there with me, I'd have been still and faint and hot with chagrin. I decided that it was high time to write the essay.

2   First, the manner of semantics. I am a cripple. I choose this word to name me. I choose from among several possibilities, the most common of which are "handicapped" and "disabled." I made the choice a number of years ago, without thinking, unaware of my motives for doing so. Even now, I'm not sure what those motives are, but I recognize that they are complex and not entirely flattering. People—crippled or not—wince at the word "cripple," as they do

not at "handicapped" or "disabled." Perhaps I want them to wince. I want them to see me as a tough customer, one to whom the fates/gods/viruses have not been kind, but who can face the brutal truth of her existence squarely. As a cripple, I swagger.

3   But, to be fair to myself, a certain amount of honesty underlies my choice. "Cripple" seems to me a clean word, straightforward and precise. It has an honorable history, have made its first appearance in the Lindisfarne Gospel in the tenth century. As a lover of words, I like the accuracy with which it describes my condition: I have lost the full use of my limbs. "Disabled," by contrast, suggests any incapacity, physical or mental. And I certainly don't like "handicapped," which implies that I have deliberately been put at a disadvantage, by whom I can imagine (my God is not a Handicapper General), in order to equalize chances in the great race of life. These words seem to me to be moving away from my condition, to be widening the gap between word and reality. Most remote is the recently coined euphemism "differently abled," which partakes of the same semantic hopefulness that transformed countries from "undeveloped" to "underdeveloped," then to "less developed," and finally to "developing" nations. People have continued to starve in those countries during the shift. Some realities do not obey the dictates of language.

4   Mine is one of them. Whatever you call me, I remain crippled. But I don't care what you call me, so long as it isn't "differently abled," which strikes me as pure verbal garbage designed, by its ability to describe anyone, to describe no one. I subscribe to George Orwell's thesis that "the slovenliness of our language makes it easier for us to have foolish thoughts." And I refuse to participate in the degeneration of the language to the extent that I deny that I have lost anything in the course of this calamitous disease; I refuse to pretend that the only differences between you and me are the various ordinary ones that distinguish any one person from another. But call me "disabled" or "handicapped" if you like. I have long since grown accustomed to them; and if they are vague, at least they hint at the truth. Moreover, I use them myself. Society is no readier to accept crippledness than to accept death, war, sex, sweat, or wrinkles. I would never refer to another person as a cripple. It is the word I use to name only myself.

TOPICAL CONSIDERATIONS

  1. Where is Mairs in the episode with which this article opens? How does she respond to falling over? How would her response have been different if the day of the week was different, and why? Can you recall a situation where you have been alone and been able to correct an embarrassing slip or mishap? How would your response have been different if you had been surrounded by people, or unable to correct the problem?

  2. Why does Mairs say she prefers the harshness of the word "cripple"? What image does this allow her to project to other people, whether or not they are crippled? Why does she want people to wince when they hear her self-description?

3. In paragraph 3, why does Mairs explicitly reject the terms "disabled," "handicapped," and "differently abled"? If you are disabled, which term do you prefer? If you are able-bodied, which term do your disabled friends (if you have any) prefer? Which term would you prefer if you were disabled?

4. What does Mairs mean when she says that she refuses to "deny that [she has] lost anything in the course of this calamitous disease"? What does she not want to deny? Why is the choice of language so important to her, especially when it focuses on loss and calamity?

5. Mairs compares crippledness to "death, war, sex, sweat, or wrinkles." What does being a cripple have in common with these five other terms? Make a list of alternate terms for these words, and then discuss why society seems to have so many other ways to describe death, war, and so on.

RHETORICAL CONSIDERATIONS

1. What rhetorical purpose does the location of the opening incident have for establishing Mairs's position? Look carefully at the building she is in, and the activities she is thinking about. What do these say about the work she does?

2. Who is the audience for this article and how can you tell? For instance, what terms does Mairs use for disabled and able-bodied people? Do you know (or can you find out) how the terms differ inside and outside the disabled community?

3. Mairs seems especially enraged at the term "differently abled" as a substitute for "crippled." What are the connotations of "semantic hopefulness" and "verbal garbage" as she argues against this offensive term? How does this description show that Mairs finds the term condescending and ignorant?

4. The tone in Mairs's article seems angry, although she only directly attacks one misleading phrase as unacceptable. Review her article carefully for material that seems angry. What or whom is Mairs angry at? Why doesn't she make direct statements about her anger? Do you think this is an effective strategy for this article? Why or why not? Justify your answer.

5. How is disabled status similar to being a "brown" person in a sea of "pink" ones (to use Updike's terminology)? How is it different? Does being disabled make a person a member of an ethnic culture? Why or why not?

WRITING ASSIGNMENTS

1. Imagine that you are interested in dating an able-bodied person (if you are disabled), or a disabled person (if you are able-bodied). What issues would you encounter? For instance, what would this person need to know about you (or vice versa) medically and emotionally—and in some cases, mentally? How comfortable would you feel talking about the disability? What special benefits or limitations do you think this mixed relationship would lead to in the kinds of places you would go on dates?

2. Using library resources, a telephone directory, and your campus accessibility offices, find out what newsletters, social groups, or independent living centers are available in your home town, or in your school's community. Write a report to the

mayor, the campus coordinator, or an op-ed newspaper column assessing the adequacy of support services, accessibility, and groups in your town.

3. Invite one of your school's academic advisers or support services staff members to your class for a presentation about your school's offerings for disabled students and its accessibility features. Based on this presentation, research the changes that have been made on other campuses around the country. You may wish to research a specific accessibility issue, such as American Sign Language interpretation or wheelchair ramping, for your report.

4. Find out more about the Americans with Disabilities Act (the ADA) passed in early 1990s by the U.S. Federal government. What are the provisions of the act? Why was it necessary? What steps have businesses, schools, and other public facilities taken to meet the ADA's requirements?

QUEER

Lillian Faderman

There was a time when the word *queer* was a slur against homosexuals and lesbians. But similar to African Americans who in the 1960s learned that it was possible to take a one-time taboo word, *black,* and reclaim it with pride, many gays and lesbians have taken back the enemy's prime insult, *queer,* and "valorized it," as Lillian Faderman explains below. While not all gays and lesbians easily embrace the old taboo label, some have realized the political power that is inherent in renaming oneself.

Lillian Faderman is a professor of English at California State University, Fresno, and the author of numerous articles and books on women's relationships including *Surpassing the Love of Men* (1981) and *Odd Girls and Twilight Lovers: A History of Lesbian Life in Twentieth Century America* (1991). This article first appeared in the *Boston Globe,* in 1991.

1   When I was in elementary school in East Los Angeles during the late 1940s, playground lore had it that Thursday was queer day. I had no idea what "queer" meant, but I knew it was something you did not want to be. I was 16 when I had my first relationship with another female, who told me that in the Midwestern elementary school she had attended, Friday was queer day, and that what we had just done together made me a queer. I think that was the only time, until a couple of years ago, that I had heard that word used by a lesbian, though I did hear drag queens use it when they were camping it up in the gay bars of the 1950s and 1960s: "Hello, Miss Thing, Hello, Duchess Ding-a-Ling, Hello, all you queers."

2   However, most of us gays and lesbians hated that word, not only because "queer" was the term straight people were most likely to hurl at us as an insult for our sexuality, but also because it had nonsexual connotations—weird, eccentric, suspicious—that were disturbing to us in our desire to fit in and to be just like heterosexuals in all ways but what we did in bed. In fact, long before the word "queer" became a pejorative for "homosexual," it meant bad things. In Old German (whence it eventually evolved into English) *quer* denoted "oblique," "perverse," "odd." Its meanings deteriorated in English. In the 1600s, for example, a "queer mort" was a syphilitic harlot. A 1796 "Dictionary of the Vulgar Tongue" lists 23 uses of the word "queer," all of them negative,

but none of them denoting a person who loves the same sex. In the 19th century, "queer bub" was bad liquor," a "queer chant" was a false name or address. To "shove the queer" meant to pass counterfeit money.

3   According to Eric Partridge, the slang lexicographer, it was not until 1910 in the United States and 1915 in the British Empire that the term queer was first used to refer to "sexually degenerate men or boys." Hugh Rawson in "Wicked Words" traces the word back a bit earlier. He cites an ad placed in a 1902 issue of "The Blue Book," a directory of the red-light district of New Orleans, that seems to suggest (though ambiguously) a homosexual definition of the word: The ad copy says of Diana and Norma, "Their names have become known on both continents, because everything goes as it will, and those that cannot be satisfied there must surely be of a queer nature."

4   It's possible, also, that the term had some early, less hostile, usage among homosexuals themselves, perhaps as a code word (like "gay") that few heterosexuals would have understood. For example, in Gertrude Stein's 1903 manuscript about lesbian relationships, "QED," Helen invites Adele to meet Jane Fairfield by saying, "She is queer and will interest you and you are queer and will interest her. Oh! I don't want to listen to your protests, you are queer and interesting even if you don't know it and you like queer and interesting people even if you think you don't." Yet such uses of the term were apparently rare. In Farmer and Henley's 1909 "Dictionary of Slang . . . Past and Present," "queer" continued to have many negative definitions, but not one of them referred to homosexuality. As late as 1927, a novel by Fredrick Niven was entitled "Queer Fellows," but the eponymous characters were hoboes, not gay men.

5   By the time I came on the gay and lesbian scene in the 1950s, the term was interchangeable with other homophobic words such as "fairy" and "bulldyke." It even had a variety of forms, all expressing hostility: "eerquay" in Pig Latin, "queervert" in place of "invert," "Timesqueer" to mean a "queer of Times Square," etc. The word was certainly "queered" for us homosexuals. Linguistics researcher Julia Penelope, in a 1970 article for American Speech, said that the gays and lesbians she interviewed all knew the term but felt it was only used by heterosexuals to express their disdain for homosexuals. However, pejoratives were beginning by then to be put to interesting use. African-Americans had already adopted the term "black," perhaps because it had once been the worst thing that could be said about a person of color in America to insult him or her. They knew that to coin slogans such as "Black is Beautiful" would defuse that word, take all its power to hurt and turn it around to make it heal.

6   Lesbians understood the same thing to be true about the word "dyke" by the early 1970s, when young lesbians began to prefer calling themselves "dyke" to any other label. "Dyke" became synonymous for them with a brave, beautiful, powerful modern "Amazon." Harry Hay, the founder in the 1950s of the first national gay organization in America, the Mattachine Society, began using the term "fairy" publicly in 1970 to say that he and his friends were

not only different from heterosexuals but more spiritual, more artistic and much nicer. He formed another organization, which he called Radical Faeries in 1978. But "queer" remained a politically incorrect term in the gay and lesbian subculture.

7   For some gays and lesbians, it remains politically incorrect today. When the rather conservative national gay and lesbian news magazine, *The Advocate,* first used the term in a positive manner in late 1990, the Letters to the Editor section was filled with protests and many threatened to cancel their subscriptions. My middle aged lesbian friends tell me, "It will always be an insult to me," and "It's a put-down: Queer as a three-dollar bill. False currency. Like you don't ring true." But many younger gays and lesbians have embraced the term "queer" in self-description that not only valorizes it but also says to straights who might still want to use that word derogatorily, "In your face!"

8   Young gay and lesbian culture has become suffused with it in the last year or two. The crossover lesbian rock group 2 NICE GIRLS flash the term in many of their lyrics. . . .

9   In April 1990, a New York group of young gays and lesbians who felt that homosexual rights were not advancing quickly enough designed some radical militant tactics that hark back to the 1960s and 1970s and began to call themselves Queer Nation. The idea caught on quickly. There are now enclaves of Queer Nation all over the country. Yoav Shernock of Los Angeles Queer Nation explains that "queer" is an ideal term because it includes "faggots," "fairies," "lezzies," "dykes." It's an umbrella term for both men and women (as the term "gay" once was but ceased to be in the 1970s when many lesbian-feminists wanted to break away from all men, including homosexual men, and form their own women's culture). But it does more than bring gay men and lesbians together, Shernock observes. "Gay" used to be an empowering term 20 years ago. But now it means middle-class white men who want to assimilate. It hasn't included blacks or poor people or women. The word "queer" helps set up a new community that "gay" has excluded.

10   It is a fighting word, a rallying cry to battle and a warning to heterosexuals of the new homosexual militancy. Shernock, explains of the term "queer": "It's a word of pride. It tells people that we're opposed to assimilating. Those who believe that they're just like anyone else except for who they sleep with aren't queer. They're gay. Being queer is more than who you sleep with. We don't want to fit into the straight world like gays do. We just want to make our own safe space. Sure, the dictionary says that 'queer' means deviating from the normal. We do—we're exceptional. We're fabulous—we're queer."

TOPICAL CONSIDERATIONS

1. Why, according to the author, was *queer* a particularly hateful word to gays and lesbians? How do any gays or lesbians you know feel about this term?

2. Why won't some conservative gays and lesbians accept the word *queer?*

3. Do you still hear the word *queer* used? If so, is it used pejoratively against gay men? against lesbians? Have you heard it used with pride by gays and lesbians? Do you think that the word is, in fact, becoming defused? Do you suppose gays and lesbians who speak with pride of being *queer* hope that straight society will accept the term as being neutral as it has accepted *gay?*

4. Faderman draws a parallel between blacks reclaiming *black* and gays and lesbians reclaiming *queer*—that is, taking a harmful word and turning "it around to make it heal." Do you think the parallel is legitimate? That is, do you think that the one-time slur, *black,* was equivalent to *queer* in its power to hurt? Do you think that queer will be as successful in its turnaround?

5. Why does Faderman say that *queer* is preferred to *gay* as an umbrella term for homosexual men and women? Do you agree with the explanation? Do you agree that gay excludes some people? Explain your answer in terms of your own observations.

6. As shown throughout this text, language is a powerful political tool for raising consciousness. Did Faderman's discussion here in any way raise your consciousness regarding lesbians and gays? Explain your answer.

RHETORICAL CONSIDERATIONS

1. In paragraphs 2 and 3, Faderman briefly discusses the etymology of the word *queer.* How does that historical glimpse add to her discussion and to the credibility of her argument?

2. While this is not strictly a personal essay, Faderman does occasionally measure the history of homophobic terms according to her own past experience. How do these personal accounts add to the discussion?

3. Can you tell from the writing that the author is a professor of English? Comment on the style of the writing, the vocabulary, allusions, secondary sources, references, and so forth.

4. Discuss the impact of the final Shernock quotation. Did it succinctly summarize the author's points? Did the tone of the passage help convey the message of the words?

WRITING ASSIGNMENTS

1. As best you can, try to trace the history of the word *gay.* When did it first connote sexual behavior? Was this connotation exclusively homosexual? Was it ever a "code" used by gays? About when did the term begin to lose its pejorative sense? Use etymological and slang dictionaries.

2. Faderman describes the effort of lesbians in the 1970s to defuse the term *dyke.* Using etymological and slang dictionaries, try to trace the word from its earliest usages to the present usage.

3. Faderman claims that *gay* is a term that fails to include blacks, poor people, and women. Do some research on this claim. That is, using library resources and, if possible, interviews, try to determine if the term is widely perceived as meaning white, middle-class, and male.

4. If you are gay or lesbian, and/or if you know gays and lesbians, write a paper discussing whether the efforts of Queer Nation members and others to defuse *queer* may be successful.

5. Faderman cites signs of militant pride among lesbians who embrace the term *queer*. Examine samples of lesbian rock music and, as best you can, try to evaluate the degree and kinds of militancy you find. Is it subtle or in-your-face aggressive? What messages of pride can you demonstrate? Write a paper based on your findings.

DISCRIMINATION AT LARGE

Jennifer A. Coleman

"Fat is the last preserve for unexamined bigotry," argues Jennifer A. Coleman. People who would otherwise be sensitive to language, gestures, and actions that insult people on the basis of their race, ethnicity, gender, sexual orientation, and religion have no qualms about making fat jokes. As Coleman explains below, she has suffered far more prejudice and offense for her weight than her gender. Part of the problem is that our culture lampoons fat people—and wrongly. Jennifer Coleman is a lawyer in Buffalo, New York. Her article first appeared in *Newsweek* in August 1993.

1 Fat is the last preserve for unexamined bigotry. Fat people are lampooned without remorse or apology on television, by newspaper columnists, in cartoons, you name it. The overweight are viewed as suffering from moral turpitude and villainy, and since we are at fault for our condition, no tolerance is due. All fat people are "outed" by their appearance.

2 Weight-motivated assaults occur daily and are committed by people who would die before uttering anti-gay slogans or racial epithets. Yet these same people don't hesitate to scream "move your fat ass" when we cross in front of them.

3 Since the time I first ventured out to play with the neighborhood kids, I was told over and over that I was lazy and disgusting. Strangers, adults, classmates offered gratuitous comments with such frequency and urgency that I started to believe them. Much later I needed to prove that it wasn't so. I began a regimen of swimming, cycling and jogging that put all but the most compulsive to shame. I ate only cottage cheese, brown rice, fake butter and steamed everything. I really believed I could infiltrate the ranks of the nonfat and thereby establish my worth.

4 I would prove that I was not just a slob, a blimp, a pig. I would finally escape the unsolicited remarks of strangers ranging from the "polite"—"You would really be pretty if you lost weight"—to the hostile ("Lose weight, you fat slob"). Of course, sometimes more subtle commentary sufficed: oinking, mooing, staring, laughing and pointing. Simulating a foghorn was also popular.

5   My acute exercise phase had many positive points. I was mingling with my obsessively athletic peers. My pulse was as low as anyone's, my cholesterol levels in the basement, my respiration barely detectable. I could swap stats from my last physical with anyone. Except for weight. No matter how hard I tried to run, swim or cycle away from it, my weight found me. Oh sure, I lost weight (never enough) and it inevitably tracked me down and adhered to me more tenaciously than ever. I lived and breathed "Eat to win." "Feel the burn." But in the end I was fit and still fat.

6   I learned that by societal, moral, ethical, soap-operatical, vegetable, political definition, it was impossible to be both fit and fat. Along the way to that knowledge, what I got for my trouble was to be hit with objects from moving cars because I dared to ride my bike in public, and to be mocked by diners at outdoor cafés who trumpeted like a herd of elephants as I jogged by. Incredibly, it was not uncommon for one of them to shout: "Lose some weight, you pig." Go figure.

7   It was confusing for awhile. How was it I was still lazy, weak, despised, a slug and a cow if I exercised every waking minute? This confusion persisted until I finally realized: it didn't matter what I did. I was and always would be the object of sport, derision, antipathy and hostility so long as I stayed in my body. I immediately signed up for a body transplant. I am still waiting for a donor.

8   Until then, I am more settled because I have learned the hard way what thin people have known for years. There simply are some things that fat people must never do. Like: riding a bike ("Hey, lady, where's the seat?"), eating in a public place ("No dessert for me, I don't want to look like her"). And the most unforgivable crime: wearing a bathing suit in public ("Whale on the beach!").

9   Things are less confusing now that I know that the nonfat are superior to me, regardless of their personal habits, health, personalities, cholesterol levels or the time they log on the couch. And, as obviously superior to me as they are, it is their destiny to remark on my inferiority regardless of who I'm with, whether they know me, whether it hurts my feelings. I finally understand that the thin have a divine mandate to steal self-esteem from fat people, who have no right to it in the first place.

10   Fat people aren't really jolly. Sometimes we act that way so you will leave us alone. We pay a price for this. But at least we get to hang on to what self-respect we smuggled out of grade school and adolescence.

11   Hating fat people is not inborn; it has to be nurtured and developed. Fortunately, it's taught from the moment most of us are able to walk and speak. We learn it through Saturday-morning cartoons, prime-time TV and movies. Have you ever seen a fat person in a movie who wasn't evil, disgusting, pathetic or lampooned? Santa Claus doesn't count.

12   Kids catch on early to be sensitive to the feelings of gay, black, disabled, elderly and speech-impaired people. At the same time, they learn that fat people are fair game. That we are always available for their personal amusement.

13   **Never thin enough:** The media, legal system, parents, teachers and peers respond to most types of intolerance with outrage and protest. Kids hear that employers can be sued for discriminating, that political careers can be destroyed and baseball owners can lose their teams as a consequence of racism, sexism or almost any other "ism."

14   But the fat kid is taught that she deserves to be mocked. She is not OK. Only if she loses weight will she be OK. Other kids see the response and incorporate the message. Small wonder some (usually girls) get it into their heads that they can never be thin enough.

15   I know a lot about prejudice, even though I am a white, middle-class, professional woman. The worst discrimination I have suffered because of my gender is nothing compared to what I experience daily because of my weight. I am sick of it. The jokes and attitudes are as wrong and damaging as any racial or ethnic slur. The passive acceptance of this inexcusable behavior is sometimes worse than the initial assault. Some offensive remarks can be excused as the shortcomings of jackasses. But the tacit acceptance of their conduct by mainstream America tells the fat person that the intolerance is understandable and acceptable. Well it isn't.

TOPICAL CONSIDERATIONS

1. What does Coleman mean when she says that "fat is the last preserve for unexamined bigotry"? Where does Coleman compare the treatment of fat people to the treatment of other groups?

2. Whom did Coleman at first blame for her size? What made her place the blame where she did?

3. Identify two measures Coleman took to end being a fat person. How successful were they? Be sure to think about Coleman's own standards of success, as well as those of other people around her.

4. Have you ever gone on a diet-and-exercise regimen like the one Coleman describes? What were the results of your efforts?

5. What kinds of animals has Coleman been compared to in paragraphs 6–8? What does each comparison imply? Why does she find these comparisons offensive?

6. Does Coleman mean what she says in paragraph 9—that thin people are "obviously superior" to her, for example? How does this paragraph illustrate her ability to act "jolly," mentioned in paragraph 10?

7. How do people learn prejudice against fat people in the first place? List at least two ways Coleman names in paragraphs 11–13.

8. What does Coleman think about the relative amounts of damage that various kinds of prejudice create? Which ones are worse?

RHETORICAL CONSIDERATIONS

1. Coleman uses strong language to identify the problems she is having: *bigotry, assault,* and *hatred,* along with *inexcusable behavior, offensive remarks, prejudice and insult.* Why do you think she uses strong language? How would you respond if she toned down her language?

2. Identify three instances in which Coleman uses sarcasm. Do you think it is effective?

3. What audience do you think Coleman has in mind for her article? Where do you find specific evidence to support your decision about her audience?

4. Why does Coleman use the female pronoun when she writes that "the fat kid is taught that she deserves to be mocked," in paragraph 14? Is she doing a feminist switch on the generic *he*? What evidence do you find that Coleman believes fat to be a feminist issue?

5. In your experience, are women more concerned about their body image than men are?

6. Do you think that Coleman would agree with Diane White in her article "Euphemisms for the Fat of the Land" (page 176)? Does Coleman use any euphemisms in her article? Compare the tone of the two articles.

7. In your opinion, is Coleman being overly sensitive to the comments she has heard? Do you think she had a reason to be overly sensitive?

WRITING ASSIGNMENTS

1. Design and administer a poll to determine how your peers feel about weight and body image generally. You might ask questions such as: Have you ever gone on a diet? for how long? Was it successful? On a scale of 1 (most satisfied) to 5 (least satisfied), rate how happy you are about your weight right now. Do you hope to lose or gain weight in the future? (You may think up additional questions.) Analyze your findings. Were more men than women concerned about weight? Were there differences between people of different racial or ethnic groups or of different ages?

2. Think of another group that suffers from discrimination, but whose problems are not commonly mentioned as worthy of concern or widespread media attention. For example, you might discuss the problems of athletes ("jocks"), engineering and computer students ("nerds"), people with unusual pastimes or vocations (men who have chosen dance as a profession, women who play football, people who keep snakes as pets, or whatever). Write a letter to the editor of your local newspaper explaining what problems these people experience, along with why and how others should avoid inadvertent or deliberate insult to them.

3. In your school's library, research current findings on anorexia, bulimia, and eating disorders. What do researchers believe causes these disorders? Who suffers from them? How can these disorders be controlled?

4. Using back issues of newspapers in library microforms departments, collect samples of advertisements, including photographs or realistic images of women over the past 100 years. Try to collect one from each decade. Make sure all portray as much of the woman's body as possible, and try to keep products advertised roughly analogous. (For example, don't mix and match sexy perfume ads with ads for laundry products.) What kinds of changes, if any, have taken place over the course of the century? What conclusions can you draw about changes in socially accepted ideals for "the perfect body"?

Telephone Conversation

Wole Soyinka

Born in Nigeria in 1934 and educated at Leeds University in England, Wole Soyinka is an outspoken social critic and celebrated poet and playwright. By the mid-1960s he had written several plays including *The Swamp Dwellers, The Lion and the Jewel,* and *The Strong Breed.* He is also the author of two novels, three volumes of poetry and twelve other plays. A social reformer who, during the 1960s, was imprisoned by the Nigerian government for his political activities, Soyinka often wrote about the clash between colonial and tribal values, at the center of which was a deep concern for human suffering and social justice. In 1986 he was awarded the Nobel Prize for literature. His latest book is *The Open Sore of a Continent: A Personal Narrative of the Nigerian Crisis* (1996).

Like any good poem, "Telephone Conversation" manages to find large meaning in small events. In this case, the poet telescopes an otherwise banal exchange between two people—in this case a prospective renter and a landlady. The only problem is that the renter is black and the landlady is bigoted. In the brief and somewhat amusing interlude, we are reminded of how the smallest daily social interaction can raise fundamental questions about identity—especially for people of color.

1   The price seemed reasonable, location
    Indifferent. The landlady swore she lived
    Off premises. Nothing remained
    But self-confession. "Madam," I warned,
5 "I hate a wasted journey—I am African."
    Silence. Silenced transmission of
    Pressurized good-breeding. Voice, when it came,
    Lipstick coated, long gold-rolled
    Cigarette-holder pipped. Caught I was, foully.
10 "HOW DARK?" . . . I had not misheard. . . . "ARE YOU LIGHT
    OR VERY DARK?" Button B. Button A. Stench
    Of rancid breath of public hide-and-speak.
    Red booth. Red pillar-box. Red double-tiered

Omnibus squelching tar. It *was* real! Shamed
15 By ill-mannered silence, surrender
Pushed dumbfoundment to beg simplification.
Considerate she was, varying the emphasis—
"ARE YOU DARK? OR VERY LIGHT?" Revelation came.
"You mean—like plain or milk chocolate?"
20 Her assent was clinical, crushing in its light
Impersonality. Rapidly, wave-length adjusted,
I chose. "West African sepia"—and as afterthought,
"Down in my passport." Silence for spectroscopic
Flight of fancy, till truthfulness changed her accent
25 Hard on the mouthpiece. "WHAT'S THAT?" conceding
"DON'T KNOW WHAT THAT IS." "Like brunette."
"THAT'S DARK, ISN'T IT?" "Not altogether.
Facially, I am brunette, but madam, you should see
The rest of me. Palm of my hand, soles of my feet
30 Are a peroxide blonde. Friction, caused—
Foolishly madam—by sitting down, has turned
My bottom raven black—One moment madam!"—
      sensing
Her receiver rearing on the thunderclap
About my ears—"Madam," I pleaded, "wouldn't
      you rather
35 See for yourself?"

QUESTIONS FOR DISCUSSION

1. Why does the speaker in this poem choose to tell the landlady he is African? How might his journey to see the apartment have been wasted if he did not tell her this detail? What details about the poem helped you respond?

2. What questions does the landlady ask the speaker? What is she implying about the conditions under which she would be willing to rent the speaker the apartment? What would make the speaker a desirable tenant, according to the landlady?

3. How dark does the speaker say he is? What are the connotations of each of his choices? Do you think he is deliberately choosing language that is confusing or unfamiliar to the landlady? If so, why?

4. How does the speaker describe the colors of the palms of his hands and soles of his feet? What color is his bottom? How is the last line of the poem a deliberate insult? In effect, what is the speaker telling the landlady she is welcome to do?

5. What visual images does the speaker use in lines 7–9 to characterize the landlady's tone of voice? How do these images help to characterize the landlady, even though she remains invisible on the other end of the telephone wire?

6. How do you think the speaker feels in the five minutes following the end of this telephone conversation? What victories, if any, has he won? Why might he feel sad or angry?

WRITING ASSIGNMENTS

1. Have you ever been asked inappropriate questions that had nothing to do with qualifications for a job, an apartment, or something else you were trying to get? Write a personal narrative or a poem about such an incident, explaining what you did and how you felt about the questions. Do you have any snappy comebacks now that you couldn't think of (or didn't dare use) at the time?

2. Rewrite the ending of this poem, in prose or in poetry, so that the speaker tells the landlady exactly what he thinks about her questions. What do you think he would say? How would the landlady respond?

3. Take one of the other personal narrators in this section (for example, Nancy Mairs), and imagine that he or she is having a similar conversation with a landlady. What objections might a landlady or landlord raise to such a person as a prospective tenant? How do you think the author you have chosen would respond?

MIND YOUR TONGUE, YOUNG MAN

Sandra Flahive Maurer

Profanity has infused American popular culture. Rock lyrics resonate with it; movie scripts, even those rated PG, seem obligated to swear; radio talk-show hosts cuss all the time; and late-night TV is streaked with blue language. Eavesdrop at any public gathering and you're bound to hear foul language in the most casual of conversations. In a comic yet disturbing vignette, the author of this piece observes "[t]here is a concern about profanity, yet we're swearing much more." And while nobody seems to be doing much about it, the author raises the question that maybe something should be done. What do you think? Should we clean up our act? Can we?

Sandra Flahive Maurer is director of college relations at Grand View College, Des Moines, Iowa. Her essay appeared in the "My Turn" column of *Newsweek* in October 1994.

1   It was one of those days filled with the little vexations of life. In the morning, insult was added to injury when I got a speeding ticket after having root canal. At work, the computer fouled me up by going down. By noon, the banana I'd brought for lunch had turned black and squishy, and finally, as I sped for home at the end of the day, the needle on the car's fuel indicator shook convulsively in its demand for a thirst-quenching gulp of gas.

2   Although I don't remember that I uttered any profanities upon encountering the day's irritations, in all likelihood I did. Like most people, I've never been known to have a lily-white mouth.

3   On that particular evening, I was eager to get home because I was giving a dinner party. However, my main concern was that I couldn't make it without first obliging the car's needs. I whipped off the freeway and headed for the nearest convenience store, only to find all eight pumps taken.

4   "Damn," I remember exclaiming as I impatiently waited my turn. But I soon found myself using another expletive when a cheeky woman in a Volvo tried to nudge ahead of me and cheat me of my already established territorial rights.

5   Eventually I was able to sidle up to a pump and fill the tank. Then I darted inside to pay—only to have to wait in line for the privilege of forking over money. As I stood, swearing under my breath about another delay in my life, I was only vaguely aware of a young man in front of me. He had plunked a Pepsi on the counter and was reaching into his pocket for money.

6   "Ninety-four cents, please," declared the middle-aged clerk. "Oh, and I'll take this pack of cigarettes, too," the young man stated matter-of-factly, as he pitched his selection on the counter.

7   "ID," countered the clerk, in a tone that suggested he had made this request many times before. The casual command caused me to focus on the person ahead of me. He was extremely slight with delicate features and a face as smooth as a baby's heel. I silently agreed with the clerk's decision to question his age. He could have been 21—or he could have been 15. It was impossible to tell.

8   "ID," said the clerk a second time, after the customer failed to respond with anything but a surly look.

9   Apparently the question about his age was more than he could stand, and upon being asked twice, the young man burst forth with a string of verbal garbage. "Goddam it! I don't have any f— — — ing identification with me. I don't haul the f— — — ing thing everywhere I go!" To which the clerk calmly remarked, "Then, it will be 94 cents for the Pepsi. No ID, no cigarettes."

10   With that rejection, the angry young man spewed a stream of obscenities that have become part of today's vocabulary. "I just ain't got my f— — — ing ID with me today. I told you."

11   I'd been observing the exchange more out of a sense of indifference than anything. All I wanted was to pay for my gas and get on my way. But my indifference vanished when the clerk, reacting to the profanity, suddenly reached across the counter with both arms, grabbed the fellow by the collar and literally plucked him off the floor. With fire in his eyes and passion in his voice, he growled, "That is enough! You watch what you say in here, do you understand? There's a lady present!" Then he shoved the guy away with obvious contempt.

12   The foulmouthed offender was stunned. So was I! Instinctively, I looked around to see where the "lady" was. I glanced up and down the nearby aisles and peered high into the corners where mirrors reveal all activity in the store. I had an image of some little old woman in a housedress, shuffling along in sturdy orthopedic shoes, her white hair done up in a bun, her purse dangling from her arm. I didn't see her anywhere.

13   All I saw in the mirror was the reflection of the two combatants—and my own. The obvious hit me hard. *I* was the "lady." I was flabbergasted by the clerk's stern admonition on my behalf. No one had tried to protect me from offensive language before.

14   With considerable speed the astonished young man paid for his drink and scurried from the store. I did likewise, still so startled by the clerk's actions that I didn't respond to his gallantry.

15   It was only after I began driving from the convenience store that I realized the significance of the episode. Profanity seems to be one of those problems about which almost everyone agrees something should be done. Yet few of us ever do anything about it. On the contrary, most of us contribute, if not to its proliferation, at least to its continuation, by swearing ourselves or making no attempt to curb it in others.

16   I recalled with guilt all the less-than-delicate language that had rolled off my tongue through the years—when I was mad, when I was glad, when I was trying to be dramatic and, yes, even when I had to wait in line for a few seconds. But nothing as crass as what I'd just heard.

17   And now, in an act of omission myself, I had failed to respond. Why hadn't *I* told the culprit to knock it off when the first raunchy words foamed out of his mouth? Why hadn't I given so much as a second's thought to rebuking him about his language? It's so familiar that it passes unnoticed, just runs off our backs. At the very least, why hadn't I thanked the clerk for taking a stand against offensive language in his store?

18   Recently I read a newspaper article that stated although Americans do have a concern about all the unbridled profanity around us every day, the reality is that we are swearing more, hearing it less.

19   Unfortunately, there must be some truth to the story—as shown by my experience in the convenience store. Granted it seems only natural that someone might be in shock after being subjected to a string of raw expressions while waiting to pay for gas. What surprises me is how much more astonished I was by the store clerk's gallant intervention and stand against vulgarity in his establishment than by the cussing of an angry young punk denied a pack of cigarettes.

TOPICAL CONSIDERATIONS

1. What kind of a day was Maurer having when the experience she relates took place? How serious are the incidents that she describes in paragraphs 1–5? Do you think that all of these things really happened, or has she taken some creative liberties? Have you ever had a day like this?

2. Why did the young man in the store use profanity to the clerk? Do you think that language was justified? Why or why not? Have you ever made a similar response?

3. What does the store clerk do when the young man swears? Do you think the store clerk was justified in his actions? Explain.

4. What surprises Maurer about the clerk's response? What surprises her about her own response? Why does Maurer reflect on her own use of foul language?

5. Maurer says that Americans don't like profanity, but they use it (and listen to it) with indifference. Do you agree? Explain your answer. Can you think of other kinds of behavior that people say they don't like but that they practice or ignore? Why do you think this is so?

RHETORICAL CONSIDERATIONS

1. In paragraphs 6–10, what specific words and descriptions does Maurer use to show that her sympathies lie with the clerk rather than the young man? Explain how these terms reflect her sympathies.

2. What do you think the thesis for this article is? Is it implied, or is it fully stated within the piece? In your opinion, how effective is Maurer's placement of the thesis?

3. Why does Maurer use personal narrative to discuss the prevalence of foul language? How effective is her use of this anecdote? Does she convince you that profanity is indeed on the rise? If not, what kind of evidence would you find convincing?

4. In your opinion, would the young man's language have been inappropriate if he were telling his friends about his experience at the convenience store? Would Maurer have been wrong to repeat the young man's language? In your opinion, is it possible to use curse words and still be "polite"? If so, when?

5. What kind of solution does Maurer offer to the problem she describes? If she were to make a more direct statement about her solution, what do you think she would say? How effective a piece of writing would an article focused on a solution be?

6. In "The Word Police," Michiko Kakutani takes an opposing view—that we should not try to curb the language that other people use. What do you think she would say to Maurer about the incident in the convenience store? Do you think that Kakutani would agree with some of Maurer's sympathies? Why or why not? Justify your answer.

WRITING ASSIGNMENTS

1. Do you think that the use of profanity has increased? Give examples from your personal life, from television and other media, and from your friends' and family's observations to support your response.

2. Adults sometimes censor their language when children are present; men or women sometimes curtail their language when the other gender is present. Do you think this a double standard? Why or why not? Justify your answer.

3. Maurer claims that Americans are (or should) be concerned about the growing problem of cursing. Does the prevalence of cursing vary from one ethnic group, religion, special interest group, age group (or other cultural group) to another? List the different cultural groups with which you associate (age, race, disability status, etc.), and then describe the different levels of profanity used among the groups. How does each group express itself using profanity? How does each group respond to the use of profanity? Are there accepted profanities in one group that another group would find offensive or incomprehensible? Why do you think this is so? Justify your answer.

4. Using government documents or local or national newspaper indexes, find out what laws or statutes are currently in effect for your community concerning the use of profanity. Are any of these laws outmoded? Are any regularly ignored? Are any enforced selectively?

What "Dirty Words" Really Mean

Dr. Joyce Brothers

> Dr. Joyce Brothers, a psychologist famous as an author and television personality, here offers her perspective on obscene language. Brothers admits that a defiant outpouring of blue language can be healthy. But probing further into the motivations behind dirty words, she finds that the use of obscenity indicates unhealthy phobias.
>
> Dr. Joyce Brothers is the author of several self-help books including *What Every Woman Ought to Know About Love and Marriage* (1985), *What Every Woman Should Know About Men* (1987), *Dr. Joyce Brothers' the Successful Woman* (1988), and *Widowhood* (1990).

1 We were talking, a group of us at a party, about a new book remarkable for its ferocious obscenity. "I couldn't read it," someone said. "All those dirty words." At that, an indignant young woman fixed the speaker with a withering glance and announced, "There are no dirty words—only dirty minds."

2 This extreme position, accepting any kind of language, however gross or violent, is not uncommon today. Individuals who pride themselves on their sophistication often feel it's important to be shockproof. ("I'm so enlightened, so aware, nothing fazes me.") Such an attitude betrays a misunderstanding of the nature of obscenity and, more seriously, of its emotional meaning. There have always been "dirty" words—and probably there always will be.

3 Of course, the words themselves change from one generation to another. In the Victorian period, a respectable woman would have hesitated to call a leg a *leg* ("limb" being both more refined and less aggressive). It was only a generation ago that Clark Gable, as Rhett Butler in the movie version of *Gone with the Wind,* created a sensation by declaring that he didn't give a *damn.* And Norman Mailer became notorious during the Forties for his free use of earthy terms denoting sexual intercourse.

WHAT MAKES A WORD DIRTY

4 What gives dirty words their shock power? Partly convention. We are startled by language that violates our sense of what may and may not be said. More important is the fact that such words are connected with emotions and experiences that both frighten and fascinate. "Hell" and "damn" have lost a good

deal of their force as religion becomes a less potent influence in daily life. But sex, in spite of the much-heralded sexual revolution, remains a subject highly charged with emotion, and most dirty language which retains its power to disturb is sex-related.

5   One source of dirty talk about sex is simple awkwardness. There are situations in which the common coarse term is the easiest way to describe certain parts of the anatomy, certain physical functions. Any doctor knows that men or women with genital or excretory problems are often at a loss for words to explain the trouble. Even if the patient is familiar with medical terminology, he may feel self-conscious using it. (Can he pronounce the word correctly? Will he sound pretentious?) And lovers, understandably, may feel that such terms as "sexual intercourse" and "copulation" are a cold, impersonal way to describe the sex act.

6   Furthermore, there exists in most people a deep ambivalence about sex, a confusion that may express itself in deliberately ugly language. The fact that, as the poet Yeats says, "Love has pitched his mansion in the place of excrement" still muddles our feelings about sex. On an unconscious level, we may feel there is something dirty, something soiling about physical union. Semen and the lubricating fluids of the vagina are at one level regarded as if they were body wastes—when in fact they are nothing of the sort. For most, the sex drive is strong enough to overcome any squeamishness, but there remains a lingering unease.

OBSCENITY IS MEANT TO INSULT

7   This ambivalence turns the obscene word for intercourse into an insult, the thrust of the insult being directed at the person who receives the sexual attention. ("————you.") Although we no longer consider women passive participants in the sex act, much of the vehemence of obscenity has been directed against the female and her sexual role, as if being the receiver of semen was somehow humiliating.

8   Ultimately, dirty words are ugly not because they refer to sex but because they imply a narrow, mechanical master-and-victim concept of sexuality. Prohibiting the use of such words will not change basic attitudes that give rise to them. They lose their power only when we are able to see sex as neither exploitation nor salvation but a human, often imperfect, activity bringing a man and woman together in a loving way.

WORDS DON'T ALWAYS MEAN WHAT THEY SAY

9   Of course some kinds of obscenity are only superficially sexual. The real emotional meaning of a dirty word can't be understood apart from the situation in which it occurs. A child's occasional filthy language is probably a kind of testing and self-assertion; he says the unspeakable to get a rise out of his parents.

(And they would do well not to overreact.) A normally "refined" woman may at times need the release of profanity. (She's been driving in a rainstorm, say, hears the thump-thump of a flat tire—and pulling over to the side of the road, finds the spare is flat too.) In a wildly frustrating situation, there's something healthy about the defiant outpouring of gutter language; it's more positive than helpless weeping. Women who have serious responsibilities thrust upon them—supporting a whole family, running a business—are more likely to use dirty words than women with simpler lives. Few people would judge them harshly for that. And among some young people, the use of profanity is so constant as to be meaningless—like everything else, dirty words wear out with overuse.

10   Dirty words are often used by teenagers in telling off-color stories and this can be considered part of their sex education. As their bodies grow and change, both boys and girls wonder and worry. To keep from being overwhelmed by these fears, they turn them into jokes or dirty-word stories. By telling and retelling off-color stories, they gain a little information, more misinformation and a lot of reassurance. They learn that they aren't the only ones in the group disturbed about their future roles in courtship and marriage. Using dirty words and stories to laugh at sexual doubts and fears, may diminish their importance and make them less frightening.

11   Most of us are disturbed, though, when a bright, attractive young woman punctuates her every sentence with a four-letter word. Other women view such language as a threat to conventional notions of femininity. Men sense it as an implicit challenge. ("I have just as much right as any man to say what I feel like saying.") It's not surprising that college campuses, the scene of so many rebellions, are also centers of an almost total language freedom, with "nice" girls using words which were once the prerogative of truckdrivers. This phenomenon is a predictable reaction to the easing of social and sexual restraints on women, such restrictions having always been more severe for women than for men. (Psychologist Philip Zimbardo reports that among agitated mental patients, it's women who use the most obscene language. "The psychological controls we put on women are so tight that when they break through, they really let go.")

OBSCENITY VENTS FEARS

12 Obscene language serves as a tension-releaser for men too. And men cut off from women—in prison, during wartime, on submarines—are likely to employ an unusual amount of obscenity, partly to vent the fears about homosexual impulses aroused by such highly charged, intimate situations.

13   So far I've been talking about occasional, casual obscenity. But anyone who seems obsessed with the use of dirty words is not simply giving vent to healthy self-expression. The repeated, compulsive use of obscene language is a sign of psychological disturbance. The child who constantly assaults a parent with abusive language, the adolescent preoccupied with dirty words, the man or

woman unable to become sexually aroused without a tirade of filthy language, the man who delights in muttering obscenities at female passersby—these people are using language in an aggressive, hostile way, expressing their own inner confusion.

THE PROFANITY OF RACIAL EPITHETS

14 Inner confusion also generates another large class of dirty words. These have nothing to do with bathroom or bedroom, but they are obscene in that they too are dehumanizing and distorting. Derogatory epithets applied to persons of different race, religion or culture are as hostile as sexual slurs. Like other kinds of obscenity, they stem from fear and ambivalence. An insecure individual easily feels threatened by differences in appearance and behavior; his instinctive defense, often, is foul language.

15 Such name-calling is not limited to ethnic groups. Calling policemen "pigs," men "male chauvinists" and feminists "bra burners" is using aggressive, deliberately insulting language to deny the individual uniqueness of another person.

16 Fortunately, this type of obscenity is being slowly drained of its power. One way to render it impotent is for the group in question to use the supposedly derogatory term for themselves. So, blacks may refer to themselves ironically as "niggers," policemen call themselves "pigs" and men laughingly speak of themselves as "male chauvinists." Or a group may adopt a term originally derisive and insist on its usage, a term which acknowledges differentness—with pride. Mexican-Americans, for example, now often refer to themselves as Chicanos.

17 Even a TV program like *All in the Family* may help reduce fears and prejudices simply by airing them. Archie Bunker is funny because week after week his fears and misconceptions about minority groups are shown to be unrealistic and unreasonable, and we laugh at his narrow view of the world.

DIRTY WORDS MASK FEAR

18 Ethnic, sexual or whatever, all forms of obscenity, as psychologist Renatus Hartogs observes, "have one thing in common: they are the mask of fear. They camouflage a reality too unbearable without the release obtained through the therapeutic four-letter word. . . . Because the mask hides our fears from ourselves, the obscene person rarely knows just what he is masking. The freedom he gains through his vernacular is illusory."

19 The real argument against the use of dirty words, then, is not that they shock or disturb the listener but that they are a limiting, self-deceiving form of expression that reveals insecurity rather than unconventionality. There is nothing *more* conventional than dirty words.

TOPICAL CONSIDERATIONS

1. Explain some of the reasons people use obscene language.

2. In Dr. Brothers's analysis, what *does* make a word dirty? Do you agree or disagree?

3. Comment on the statement that "ambivalence turns the obscene word for intercourse into an insult" (paragraph 7). What "ambivalence" does the author mean?

4. What is particularly healthy about the occasional "defiant outpouring of gutter language" (paragraph 9)?

5. Is the use of obscene language really part of a teenager's sex education? If it was for you, how did your peers, parents, and teachers react?

6. Do women use obscene language more than men do? Why or why not?

7. How does Dr. Brothers relate the use of sexual and excremental obscenities to racial and ethnic epithets? Would she agree with Bosmajian's claim (see "Defining the 'American Indian,'" page 347) that white people hold on to their epithets and clichés because they want linguistic power over others?

RHETORICAL CONSIDERATIONS

1. Is the general organization of this essay clear and logical? Do the section titles reflect a logical progression from point to point? Are the transitions smooth?

2. The subject matter of obscene language is potentially sensational, but the tone and style of this essay are not. How does Dr. Brothers manage to maintain a serious and intelligent tone?

3. Dr. Brothers does not spell out the obscene words she refers to. Why do you think she refrains? Does it work for or against her candid discussion?

4. Does Dr. Brothers offer the reader ample supporting data? Or does she rely on her authority as a psychologist?

WRITING ASSIGNMENTS

1. Other than bathroom and bedroom obscenities and racial epithets, can you think of any words that strike you as obscene? Why do they offend you? Why does this make them obscene?

2. Do obscenities really mask fears? Do you believe that people who swear often realize what they are actually implying about themselves and others?

3. Why would intelligent adults use obscenity to indicate sophistication? What does such use suggest about the power of certain words?

4. Decide on a list of about five common "dirty words." Then use the *Oxford English Dictionary (OED)* to look up the etymology of each word you have chosen. When do you find these words were first used? Did they originally mean the same things they mean now or have meanings changed? If meanings have changed, what connections do you see between old meanings and those that we understand the words to have today? Does knowing the word's original meaning help you feel more comfortable using the word?

5. Using indexes and data bases in your library, locate articles by psychologists in professional journals that address questions about taboo or obscene language.

Find at least one additional article that appeared within the last ten years; and find two articles that first appeared at least thirty years ago. Do you find that opinions have changed about the use of dirty words? Do psychologists from previous decades have different ideas about the meaning or function of dirty words? If so, what disagreements or differences can you find between psychologists today and those from several decades ago, based on your sample selection of articles?

REGULATING RACIST SPEECH ON CAMPUS

Charles R. Lawrence III

The last few years have seen a disturbing rise in racist and sexist language on college campuses. Some administrations have dealt with the problem by outright banning of such offensive language on the grounds that racial slurs are violent verbal assaults that interfere with students' rights to an education. Others fear that putting sanctions on racist speech violates the First Amendment guarantee of free expression. In the following essay, a professor of law argues for the restricting of free speech by appealing to the U.S. Supreme Court's landmark decision in the case of *Brown* v. *Board of Education.*

Charles R. Lawrence teaches law at Stanford University and the University of California at Los Angeles. He is the author of many articles on law and coauthor of the book, *The Bakke Case: The Politics of Inequality* (1979). A longer version of this article appeared in the February 1990 issue of *Duke Law.*

1   I have spent the better part of my life as a dissenter. As a high-school student, I was threatened with suspension for my refusal to participate in a civil-defense drill, and I have been a conspicuous consumer of my First Amendment liberties ever since. There are very strong reasons for protecting even racist speech. Perhaps the most important of these is that such protection reinforces our society's commitment to tolerance as a value, and that by protecting bad speech from government regulation, we will be forced to combat it as a community.

2   But I also have a deeply felt apprehension about the resurgence of racial violence and the corresponding rise in the incidence of verbal and symbolic assault and harassment to which blacks and other traditionally subjugated and excluded groups are subjected. I am troubled by the way the debate has been

framed in response to the recent surge of racist incidents on college and university campuses and in response to some universities' attempts to regulate harassing speech. The problem has been framed as one in which the liberty of free speech is in conflict with the elimination of racism. I believe this has placed the bigot on the moral high ground and fanned the rising flames of racism.

3   Above all, I am troubled that we have not listened to the real victims, that we have shown so little understanding of their injury, and that we have abandoned those whose race, gender, or sexual preference continues to make them second-class citizens. It seems to me a very sad irony that the first instinct of civil libertarians has been to challenge even the smallest, most narrowly framed efforts by universities to provide black and other minority students with the protection the Constitution guarantees them.

4   The landmark case of *Brown v. Board of Education* is not a case that we normally think of as a case about speech. But *Brown* can be broadly read as articulating the principle of equal citizenship. *Brown* held that segregated schools were inherently unequal because of the *message* that segregation conveyed—that black children were an untouchable caste, unfit to go to school with white children. If we understand the necessity of eliminating the system of signs and symbols that signal the inferiority of blacks, then we should hesitate before proclaiming that all racist speech that stops short of physical violence must be defended.

5   University officials who have formulated policies to respond to incidents of racial harassment have been characterized in the press as "thought police," but such policies generally do nothing more than impose sanctions against intentional face-to-face insults. When racist speech takes the form of face-to-face insults, catcalls, or other assaultive speech aimed at an individual or small group of persons, it falls directly within the "fighting words" exception to First Amendment protection. The Supreme Court has held that words which "by their very utterance inflict injury or tend to incite an immediate breach of the peace" are not protected by the First Amendment.

6   If the purpose of the First Amendment is to foster the greatest amount of speech, racial insults disserve that purpose. Assaultive racist speech functions as a preemptive strike. The invective is experienced as a blow, not as a proffered idea, and once the blow is struck, it is unlikely that a dialogue will follow. Racial insults are particularly undeserving of First Amendment protection because the perpetrator's intention is not to discover truth or initiate dialogue but to injure the victim. In most situations, members of minority groups realize that they are likely to lose if they respond to epithets by fighting and are forced to remain silent and submissive.

7   Courts have held that offensive speech may not be regulated in public forums such as streets where the listener may avoid the speech by moving on, but the regulation of otherwise protected speech has been permitted when the speech invades the privacy of the unwilling listener's home or when the

unwilling listener cannot avoid the speech. Racist posters, fliers, and graffiti in dormitories, bathrooms, and other common living spaces would seem to clearly fall within the reasoning of these cases. Minority students should not be required to remain in their rooms in order to avoid racial assault. Minimally, they should find a safe haven in their dorms and in all other common rooms that are a part of their daily routine.

8   I would also argue that the university's responsibility for insuring that these students receive an equal educational opportunity provides a compelling justification for regulations that insure them safe passage in all common areas. A minority student should not have to risk becoming the target of racially assaulting speech every time he or she chooses to walk across campus. Regulating vilifying speech that cannot be anticipated or avoided would not preclude announced speeches and rallies—situations that would give minority-group members and their allies the chance to organize counter-demonstrations or avoid the speech altogether.

9   The most commonly advanced argument against the regulation of racist speech proceeds something like this: we recognize that minority groups suffer pain and injury as the result of racist speech, but we must allow this hate mongering for the benefit of society as a whole. Freedom of speech is the lifeblood of our democratic system. It is especially important for minorities because often it is their only vehicle for rallying support for the redress of their grievances. It will be impossible to formulate a prohibition so precise that it will prevent the racist speech you want to suppress without catching in the same net all kinds of speech that it would be unconscionable for a democratic society to suppress.

10 Whenever we make such arguments, we are striking a balance on the one hand between our concern for the continued free flow of ideas and the democratic process dependent on that flow, and, on the other, our desire to further the cause of equality. There can be no meaningful discussion of how we should reconcile our commitment to equality and our commitment to free speech until it is acknowledged that there is real harm inflicted by racist speech and that this harm is far from trivial.

11 To engage in a debate about the First Amendment and racist speech without a full understanding of the nature and extent of that harm is to risk making the First Amendment an instrument of domination rather than a vehicle of liberation. We have not known the experience of victimization by racist, misogynist, and homophobic speech, nor do we equally share the burden of the societal harm it inflicts. We are often quick to say that we have heard the cry of the victims when we have not.

12 The *Brown* case is again instructive because it speaks directly to the psychic injury inflicted by racist speech by noting that the symbolic message of segregation affected "the hearts and minds" of Negro children "in a way unlikely ever to be undone." Racial epithets and harassment often cause deep emotional scarring and feelings of anxiety and fear that pervade every aspect of a victim's life.

13   *Brown* also recognized that black children did not have an equal opportunity to learn and participate in the school community if they bore the additional burden of being subjected to the humiliation and psychic assault contained in the message of segregation. University students bear an analogous burden when they are forced to live and work in an environment where at any moment they may be subjected to denigrating verbal harassment and assault. The same injury was addressed by the Supreme Court when it held that sexual harassment that creates a hostile or abusive work environment violates the ban on sex discrimination in employment of Title VII of the Civil Rights Act of 1964.

14   Carefully drafted university regulations would bar the use of words as assault weapons and leave unregulated even the most heinous of ideas when those ideas are presented at times and places and in manners that provide an opportunity for reasoned rebuttal or escape from immediate injury. The history of the development of the right to free speech has been one of carefully evaluating the importance of free expression and its effects on other important societal interests. We have drawn the line between protected and unprotected speech before without dire results. (Courts have, for example, exempted from the protection of the First Amendment obscene speech and speech that disseminates official secrets, that defames or libels another person, or that is used to form a conspiracy or monopoly.)

15   Blacks and other people of color are skeptical about the argument that even the most injurious speech must remain unregulated because, in an unregulated marketplace of ideas, the best ones will rise to the top and gain acceptance. Our experience tells us quite the opposite. We have seen too many good liberal politicians shy away from the issues that might brand them as being too closely allied with us.

16   Whenever we decide that racist speech must be tolerated because of the importance of maintaining societal tolerance for all unpopular speech, we are asking blacks and other subordinated groups to bear the burden for the good of all. We must be careful that the ease with which we strike the balance against the regulation of racist speech is in no way influenced by the fact that the cost will be borne by others. We must be certain that those who will pay that price are fairly represented in our deliberations and that they are heard.

17   At the core of the argument that we should resist all government regulation of speech is the ideal that the best cure for bad speech is good, that ideas that affirm equality and the worth of all individuals will ultimately prevail. This is an empty ideal unless those of us who would fight racism are vigilant and unequivocal in that fight. We must look for ways to offer assistance and support to students whose speech and political participation are chilled in a climate of racial harassment.

18   Civil rights lawyers might consider suing on behalf of blacks whose right to an equal education is denied by a university's failure to insure a nondiscriminatory educational climate or conditions of employment. We must embark upon the development of a First Amendment jurisprudence grounded in the

reality of our history and our contemporary experience. We must think hard about how best to launch legal attacks against the most indefensible forms of hate speech. Good lawyers can create exceptions and narrow interpretations that limit the harm of hate speech without opening the floodgates of censorship.

19   Everyone concerned with these issues must find ways to engage actively in actions that resist and counter the racist ideas that we would have the First Amendment protect. If we fail in this, the victims of hate speech must rightly assume that we are on the oppressors' side.

TOPICAL CONSIDERATIONS

1. What reasons does Lawrence offer for protecting racist speech from governmental restrictions? Do you agree? How else can a community fight such speech?

2. According to the author, how in the debate over racist language does the fight against racism conflict with the fight for free speech? What fundamental problem does Lawrence have with this conflict? Are his reasons convincing to you? Why or why not?

3. According to the author, how can the case of *Brown v. Board of Education* be interpreted to cover protection of victims of racist speech?

4. Why, according to Lawrence, is racist speech "undeserving of First Amendment protection" (paragraph 6)? Do you agree? If not, why not? If so, can you think of any circumstances when racist speech should be protected?

5. What legal measures does Lawrence suggest for the protection of African American students against hate speech?

6. Has this article affected your thinking on the subject of free speech and censorship? Has it changed your mind about the use of racially or sexually abusive language? Explain your answer.

7. Have you ever been the victim of abusive speech—speech that victimized you because of your race, gender, religion, ethnicity, or sexual preference? If so, do you agree with Lawrence's argument about the "psychic injury" (paragraph 12) such speech can cause? Did you experience such injury? Explain your answer.

8. Is there any racial tension on your campus? If so, do you see a link between racial tension and racist speech? What suggestions would you make to school officials to deal with such tension? Do you think that banning hate speech might lessen racial tension and violence? How about in society at large? Explain your reasoning.

RHETORICAL CONSIDERATIONS

1. Where in the essay do you get a clear focus on Lawrence's line of argument? What are the first signals that he sends to clue the reader? Can you point to a thesis statement?

2. Lawrence opens his essay saying that he has a long history as a "dissenter." What would you say is his strategy here? What kinds of assumptions does he make of his

audience? What does his refusing to participate in a civil-defense drill have to do with the essay's central issues?

3. How convincingly does Lawrence argue that racist speech should not be protected by the First Amendment? What is the logic of his argument? What evidence does he offer as support?

4. Select one of Lawrence's arguments that you think is especially strong or especially weak, and explain why you regard it so.

5. Consider the author's voice in this essay. What sense do you get of Charles R. Lawrence III as an individual? In a paragraph, try to characterize him. Take into consideration his stand here as well as the style and tone of his writing.

WRITING ASSIGNMENTS

1. As Lawrence points out, many university officials—as well as legal scholars—view the outlawing of hate speech as contrary to the democratic spirit of pluralism and tolerance. Write a paper in which you argue that hate speech should be protected if we are to remain a legitimate democracy. In your discussion, explain just where you would draw the line on the protection, if at all.

2. Taking the opposite stand from above, and using some of your own ideas, write a paper in which you argue that racist (and/or sexist) speech should be outlawed because it can only contribute to the victimization of people and the already tense social conditions in America. In your discussion, explain just what kinds of hate speech you would want to see banned, and why. Also explain why you think such speech could be controlled by regulation.

3. Suppose that a leader of a known hate group were invited to your campus, someone certain to speak in inflammatory racist language. Would you defend that person's right to address the student body? Why or why not? Should that person be protected under the First Amendment? Would you attend? Why or why not?

4. What if a condition of acceptance to your school was signing an agreement that you would refrain from using racist, sexist, or otherwise abusive language on campus—an agreement that could lead to suspension. Weighing the social benefits against the restrictions on freedom of expression, write a paper in which you explain why you would or would not sign the agreement.

FREE SPEECH ON CAMPUS

Nat Hentoff

Taking the opposing stand, First Amendment expert Nat Hentoff argues
that instituting sanctions on hate speech seriously mocks the pluralistic
nature of a university and academic freedom and inquiry. He warns that
preventing or punishing offensive language could lead to Orwellian
nightmares. Nat Hentoff is a staff writer for the *New Yorker* and the *Village Voice,* as well as a columnist for the *Washington Post.* Much of his
writing focuses on the subject of freedom of expression including his
book *The First Freedom: The Tumultuous History of Free Speech in
America* (1989). He is also author of *American Heroes: In and Out of
School* (1987), *Boston Boy: A Memoir* (1988), and *Free Speech for
Me—But Not for Thee: How the American Left and Right Relentlessly
Censor Each Other* (1992). This article first appeared in the May 1989
issue of the *Progressive.*

1   A flier distributed at the University of Michigan some months ago proclaimed
that blacks "don't belong in classrooms, they belong hanging from trees."

2   At other campuses around the country, manifestations of racism are becoming commonplace. At Yale, a swastika and the words WHITE POWER! were
painted on the building housing the University's Afro-American Cultural Center. At Temple University, a White Students Union has been formed with
some 130 members.

3   Swastikas are not directed only at black students. The Nazi symbol has
been spray-painted on the Jewish Student Union at Memphis State University.
And on a number of campuses, women have been singled out as targets of
wounding and sometimes frightening speech. At the law school of the State
University of New York at Buffalo, several women students have received
anonymous letters characterized by one professor as venomously sexist.

4   These and many more such signs of the resurgence of bigotry and know-
nothingism throughout the society—as well as on campus—have to do solely
with speech, including symbolic speech. There have also been physical assaults on black students and on black, white, and Asian women students, but
the way to deal with physical attacks is clear: call the police and file a criminal
complaint. What is to be done, however, about speech alone—however disgusting, inflammatory, and rawly divisive that speech may be?

5   At more and more colleges, administrators—with the enthusiastic support
of black students, women students, and liberal students—have been answer-

ing that question by preventing or punishing speech. In public universities, this is a clear violation of the First Amendment. In private colleges and universities, suppression of speech mocks the secular religion of academic freedom and free inquiry.

6   The Student Press Law Center in Washington, D.C.—a vital source of legal support for student editors around the country—reports, for example, that at the University of Kansas, the student host and producer of a radio news program was forbidden by school officials from interviewing a leader of the Ku Klux Klan. So much for free inquiry on that campus.

7   In Madison, Wisconsin, the *Capital Times* ran a story in January about Chancellor Sheila Kaplan of the University of Wisconsin branch at Parkside, who ordered her campus to be scoured of "some anonymously placed white supremacist hate literature." Sounding like the legendary Mayor Frank ("I am the law") Hague of Jersey City, who booted "bad speech" out of town, Chancellor Kaplan said, "This institution is not a lamppost standing on the street corner. It doesn't belong to everyone."

8   Who decides what speech can be heard or read by everyone? Why, the Chancellor, of course. That's what George III used to say, too.

9   University of Wisconsin political science professor Carol Tebben thinks otherwise. She believes university administrators "are getting confused when they are acting as censors and trying to protect students from bad ideas. I don't think students need to be protected from bad ideas. I think they can determine for themselves what ideas are bad."

10   After all, if students are to be "protected" from bad ideas, how are they going to learn to identify and cope with them? Sending such ideas underground simply makes them stronger and more dangerous.

11   Professor Tebben's conviction that free speech means just that has become a decidedly minority view on many campuses. At the University of Buffalo Law School, the faculty unanimously adopted a "Statement Regarding Intellectual Freedom, Tolerance, and Political Harassment." Its title implies support of intellectual freedom, but the statement warned students that once they enter "this legal community," their right to free speech must become tempered "by the responsibility to promote equality and justice."

12   Accordingly, swift condemnation will befall anyone who engages in "remarks directed at another's race, sex, religion, national origin, age, or sex preference." Also forbidden are "other remarks based on prejudice and group stereotype."

13   This ukase is so broad that enforcement has to be alarmingly subjective. Yet the University of Buffalo Law School provides no due-process procedures for a student booked for making any of these prohibited remarks. Conceivably, a student caught playing a Lenny Bruce, Richard Pryor, or Sam Kinison album in his room could be tried for aggravated insensitivity by association.

14   When I looked into this wholesale cleansing of bad speech at Buffalo, I found it had encountered scant opposition. One protestor was David Gerald

Jay, a graduate of the law school and a cooperating attorney for the New York Civil Liberties Union. Said the appalled graduate: "Content-based prohibitions constitute prior restraint and should not be tolerated."

15   You would think that the law professors and administration at this public university might have known that. But hardly any professors dissented, and among the students only members of the conservative Federalist Society spoke up for free speech. The fifty-strong chapter of the National Lawyers Guild was on the other side. After all, it was more important to go on record as vigorously opposing racism and sexism than to expose oneself to charges of insensitivity to these malignancies.

16   The pressures to have the "right" attitude—as proved by having the "right" language in and out of class   can be stifling. A student who opposed affirmative action, for instance, can be branded a racist.

17   At the University of California at Los Angeles, the student newspaper ran an editorial cartoon satirizing affirmative action. (A student stops a rooster on campus and asks how the rooster got into UCLA. "Affirmative action," is the answer.) After outraged complaints from various minority groups, the editor was suspended for violating a publication policy against running "articles that perpetuate derogatory or cultural stereotypes." The art director was also suspended.

18   When the opinion editor of the student newspaper at California State University at Northridge wrote an article asserting that the sanctions against the editor and art director at UCLA amounted to censorship, he was suspended too.

19   At New York University Law School, a student was so disturbed by the pall of orthodoxy at that prestigious institution that he wrote to the school newspaper even though, as he said, he expected his letter to make him a pariah among his fellow students.

20   Barry Endick described the atmosphere at NYU created by "a host of watchdog committees and a generally hostile classroom reception regarding any student comment right of center." This "can be arguably viewed as symptomatic of a prevailing spirit of academic and social intolerance of . . . any idea which is not 'politically correct.'"

21   He went on to say something that might well be posted on campus bulletin boards around the country, though it would probably be torn down at many of them: "We ought to examine why students, so anxious to wield the Fourteenth Amendment, give short shrift to the First. Yes, Virginia, there are racist assholes. And you know what, the Constitution protects them, too."

22   Not when they engage in violence or vandalism. But when they speak or write, racist assholes fall right into this Oliver Wendell Holmes definition—highly unpopular among bigots, liberals, radicals, feminists, sexists, and college administrators: "If there is any principle of the Constitution that more imperatively calls for attachment than any other, it is the principle of free thought—not free only for those who agree with us, but freedom for the thought we hate."

23   The language sounds like a pietistic Sunday sermon, but if it ever falls wholly into disuse, neither this publication nor any other journal of opinion—right or left—will survive.

24 Sometimes, college presidents and administrators sound as if they fully understand what Holmes was saying. Last year, for example, when the *Daily Pennsylvanian*—speaking for many at the University of Pennsylvania—urged that a speaking invitation to Louis Farrakhan be withdrawn, University President Sheldon Hackney disagreed.

25   "Open expression," said Hackney, "is the fundamental principle of a university." Yet consider what the same Sheldon Hackney did to the free-speech rights of a teacher at his own university. If any story distills the essence of the current decline of free speech on college campuses, it is the Ballad of Murray Dolfman.

26   For twenty-two years, Dolfman, a practicing lawyer in Philadelphia, had been a part-time lecturer in the Legal Studies Department of the University of Pennsylvania's Wharton School. For twenty-two years, no complaint had ever been made against him; indeed his student course evaluations had been outstanding. Each year students competed to get into his class.

27   On a November afternoon in 1984, Dolfman was lecturing about personal-service contracts. His style somewhat resembles that of Professor Charles Kingsfield in *The Paper Chase*. Dolfman insists that students he calls on be prepared—or suffer the consequences. He treats all students this way—regardless of race, creed, or sex.

28   This day, Dolfman was pointing out that no one can be forced to work against his or her will—even if a contract has been signed. A court may prevent the resister from working for someone else so long as the contract is in effect but, Dolfman said, there can "be nothing that smacks of involuntary servitude."

29   Where does this concept come from? Dolfman looked around the room. Finally, a cautious hand was raised: "The Constitution?"

30   "Where in the Constitution?" No hands. "The Thirteenth Amendment," said the teacher. So, what does *it* say? The students were looking everywhere but at Dolfman.

31   "We will lose our liberties," Dolfman often told his classes, "if we don't know what they are."

32   On this occasion, he told them that he and other Jews, as ex-slaves, spoke at Passover of the time when they were slaves under the Pharaohs so that they would remember every year what it was like not to be free.

33   "We have ex-slaves here," Dolfman continued, "who should know about the Thirteenth Amendment." He asked black students in the class if they could tell him what was in that amendment.

34   "I wanted them to really think about it," Dolfman told me recently, "and know its history. You're better equipped to fight racism if you know all about those post–Civil War amendments and civil rights laws."

35   The Thirteenth Amendment provides that "neither slavery nor involuntary servitude . . . shall exist within the United States."

36   The black students in his class did not know what was in that amendment, and Dolfman had them read it aloud. Later, they complained to university officials that they had been hurt and humiliated by having been referred to as ex-slaves. Moreover, they said, they had no reason to be grateful for a constitutional amendment which gave them rights which should never have been denied them—and gave them precious little else. They had not made these points in class, although Dolfman—unlike Professor Kingsfield—encourages rebuttal.

37   Informed of the complaint, Dolfman told the black students he had intended no offense, and he apologized if they had been offended.

38   That would not do—either for the black students or for the administration. Furthermore, there were mounting black-Jewish tensions on campus, and someone had to be sacrificed. Who better than a part-time Jewish teacher with no contract and no union? He was sentenced by—George Orwell would have loved this—the Committee on Academic Freedom and Responsibility.

39   On his way to the stocks, Dolfman told President Sheldon Hackney that if a part-time instructor "can be punished on this kind of charge, a tenured professor can eventually be booted out, then a dean, and then a president."

40   Hackney was unmoved. Dolfman was banished from the campus for what came to be a year. But first he was forced to make a public apology to the entire university and then he was compelled to attend a "sensitivity and racial awareness" session. Sort of like a Vietnamese reeducation camp.

41   A few conservative professors objected to the stigmatization of Murray Dolfman. I know of no student dissent. Indeed, those students most concerned with making the campus more "sensitive" to diversity exulted in Dolfman's humiliation. So did most liberals on the faculty.

42   If my children were still of college age and wanted to attend the University of Pennsylvania, I would tell them this story. But where else could I encourage them to go?

TOPICAL CONSIDERATIONS

1. In your own words, summarize the argument Nat Hentoff is making here. What would you say his purpose is in the essay?

2. How are college and university administrators dealing with the recent rise in incidents of verbal abuse on American campuses? What is Hentoff's reaction to their handling of such problems?

3. With regard to the First Amendment, Hentoff distinguishes between physical assaults and those that are verbal and/or symbolic. What distinctions does he make? How does Charles R. Lawrence III, in the previous essay, distinguish between the two? Explain the different interpretations of the two authors.

4. If a leader of the Ku Klux Klan was barred from speaking at your school, would you protest? How about a member of the American Nazi party? The PLO? What about Louis Farrakhan? Explain your reasons.

5. In paragraph 9, the author quotes Professor Carol Tebben who states, "I don't think students need to be protected from bad ideas." Do you agree with Professor Tebben? Do you feel that students can "determine for themselves what ideas are bad"? What constitutes a *bad idea* to you? Can you imagine any *bad ideas* that you feel should be censored? What would they be, and under what circumstances?

6. Hentoff argues that many people who concur with sanctions on free speech do so to avoid being considered sexist or racist. Does this describe people you know? Do you think a person who opposes sexism and racism can still support freedom of speech? Or, do you think it's racist and sexist to be opposed to sanctions on racist and sexist speech? Explain your answers.

7. What problems does Hentoff have with University of Buffalo Law School's "Statement Regarding Intellectual Freedom, Tolerance, and Political Harassment"? What explanation does he offer for the wide acceptance of and "scant opposition" to that "ukase"? What are your feelings about such a Statement?

8. Would Hentoff agree that "sticks and stones will break my bones, but names will never hurt me"? Would Charles R. Lawrence III? Would you?

9. In paragraph 17, Hentoff cites the case of the UCLA student newspaper that ran an editorial cartoon satirizing affirmative action. From Hentoff's description, does the cartoon sound offensive to you? As described, how might it have been offensive to minority students? Do you think the administration was morally and legally justified in suspending the editor and art director? If this happened on your campus, how would you react? Explain why.

10. What do you make of the Dolfman case that Hentoff discusses in the last half of the essay? From what we're told, do you think that Dolfman was insensitive to the black students in his class? Do you think the black students were justified in their complaints? Do you think the administration was right in suspending Dolfman? Explain your answers.

RHETORICAL CONSIDERATIONS

1. Consider the title of this essay. What different meanings can it have? How does it forecast Hentoff's position in the essay? Do you think it's an effective title?

2. Where in the essay does Hentoff's line of argument begin to take focus? Is his line of argument carried clearly throughout the essay? Where does he state his thesis?

3. Consider the case of the editorial cartoon in the UCLA student newspaper (paragraphs 17 and 18). What about the cartoon does Hentoff want you to believe? Is his description of it satisfying to you? Would you prefer to actually see it before passing judgment on its offensiveness? Suppose you learned that Hentoff left out some particularly offensive details in the cartoon, say, a racist caricature of the rooster, how would that affect the impact of his argument?

4. Find two or three of Hentoff's sentences that you find particularly effective as examples of persuasive writing, then explain why they are effective.

5. Explain the meaning of the aside reference to George Orwell in paragraph 38. How is it an appropriate remark?

6. What do you make of the conclusion of this essay? What is the strategy of ending it with the question he asks? What is Hentoff's message here? Is his conclusion consistent with the development of his argument?

WRITING ASSIGNMENTS

1. In paragraph 10, Hentoff claims, "Sending such [bad] ideas underground simply makes them stronger and more dangerous." Explore this claim in a paper in which you try to imagine how certain "bad ideas" could become stronger and more dangerous were they censored.

2. Suppose your school had such a "Statement" as that at the University of Buffalo Law School (paragraph 11). Weighing the social benefits against the restrictions to the freedom of speech, would you be willing to sign a pledge of allegiance to it? Write a paper in which you explain your decision.

3. Where does *offensive* language end and *racist* and *sexist* language begin? Write a paper in which you try to determine these distinctions. Give clear examples to support your arguments.

4. Take another look at Charles Lawrence's essay. Which of the two arguments on the free speech issue seems the most persuasive? Explain exactly why you feel that way. Try to support your answer with specific evidence from each of the essays.

5. Write a letter to Nat Hentoff arguing that hate speech—racist, sexist, and otherwise—should be regulated because it can only contribute to the already tense social conditions in America.

7 LANGUAGE, GENDER, AND SEXISM

DAVE

D uring the last 30 years, the feminist movement in America has stirred up its share of linguistic controversy. Many people in the movement have made the claim—and rightfully so—that our language prejudices its users against women by perpetuating cultural assumptions that make *male* the norm and *female* the deviation. Others claim that men and women talk differently, that their choice of words and style of expression are distinct because of social conditioning—that is, because boys and girls are brought up learning two very different conversational patterns. This chapter explores the way language and gender are intertwined with social values—how language is sexist and, thus, denigrates and oppresses women *and* men.

HOW DOES ENGLISH PREJUDICE US AGAINST WOMEN AND MEN?

The first five essays focus on how language can create and reinforce gender prejudices. The first essay, "Sexism in English: A 1990s Update" by Alleen Pace Nilsen, grew out of a study of how metaphors, slang, general usages, and definitions in American English reveal society's attitudes toward males and females. In spite of the good efforts to rid English of its prejudice, the real challenge is to rid people's minds of sexism. Taking the opposing view is the late vice-president, Spiro T. Agnew who sees no repression of women reflected in the language. As suggested by the title of Agnew's essay, "English Anyone?" he argues that degenderized English is both foolish and awkward. Instead of gender equality, he claims, all that degenderizing English will accomplish is a setback in fluency.

While Jack Rosenthal agrees that degenderizing English is a good thing, we may only be scratching the surface, he says in the next essay, "Gender Benders." If we are going to rid English of sexual bias against women we will first have to alter some basic values in our culture—values he calls "hidden gender," as they lie deep within the language.

Thus far, the selections in this chapter have considered how the language works against women. But what about men? What about sexist expressions that exclude, prejudge, and prescribe how males should behave? These are questions not often raised in protests against sexism, but they are serious questions at the heart of Professor Eugene R. August's protest in "Real Men Don't: Anti-Male Bias in English."

HOW DO MEN AND WOMEN TALK?

Since the feminist movement began, a growing number of scholars have attempted to prove that there are important differences in the way men and women use English. Apparently motivating the researchers is the desire to demonstrate that such language/gender differences can be attributed either to discriminatory kinds of socialization or genetic disposition. In the first piece in this cluster, "Sex Differences," linguist Ronald Macaulay says that while some differences in expression reflect social and cultural conditioning, most other claims of male and female English are based on foolish myths and age-old stereotypes. Social and cultural conditioning are clearly the root cause of the different conversational styles between men and women. So says bestselling sociolinguist Deborah Tannen in the next piece. "'I'll Explain It to You': Lecturing and Listening" is a lively explanation of why men and women are sometimes not equals in conversation—and why conversation between them is fraught with difficulty when men dominate, and women let them. While people might think that the world of computer communication would be a gender-neutral zone— one where men don't have to talk tough and women can feel empowered—it really isn't. On the contrary, men and women type a different language on line. So says journalist Nathan Cobb who explores gender "Netiquette" in the next piece, "Gender Wars in Cyberspace."

The next selection is a famous short story by Ernest Hemingway, "Hills Like White Elephants." While the story is quite short and consists mostly of dialogue, it brilliantly captures not only the plight of the two lovers, their different personalities, and value systems, but also some basic differences in language style and expression reflective of the observations on gender discussed in the preceding essays.

CASE STUDIES ON SEXISM IN THE BIBLE

Perhaps the most male-dominated tradition cited by feminists is the language of organized religion. From the beginning of the feminist movement, the challenge to patriarchal language has exploded into controversy involving nothing less than the nature of God, man, and woman. This cluster's four selections demonstrate some of the controversy, at the center of which lies the language of the Bible. Not only were the Scriptures written by men, but the language is male-dominated. Written in parable form, the first essay, "Is God Purple?" dramatically illustrates how the fundamental assumption that God is male has worked against females for millennia. In an attempt to reflect the controversy over biblical language and its profound ramifications, two versions of the story of the creation of man and woman from Genesis are included. The first is from the Revised Standard Version of the Bible; the second, from *An Inclusive Language Lectionary,* which, since the early 1980s, has been publishing a nonsexist—or "inclusive-language"—version of selected biblical passages. In the final essay, "Don't Rewrite the Bible," Michael Golden admits that it's impossible to determine God's gender. Nonetheless, he argues vehemently that the issue is not sexism but religious revisionism. Leave God and tradition alone, he insists.

SEXISM IN ENGLISH: A 1990s UPDATE

Alleen Pace Nilsen

More than 25 years ago, Alleen Pace Nilsen began the laborious but rewarding task of learning what the English language could tell her about
sexism. She started by reading a desk dictionary, noting every entry
that revealed something about the way men and women are viewed in
our society. Underpinning this study was the conviction that the "language a culture uses is telltale evidence of the values and beliefs of
that culture." In this updated report on her research, Nilsen notes
changes that have occurred in the language over the past two
decades—changes that reflect conscious decisions to eliminate sexism
embedded in language.

Alleen Pace Nilsen is an English professor and assistant vice-president
for academics affairs at Arizona State University.

1   Twenty years ago I embarked on a study of the sexism inherent in American English. I had just returned to Ann Arbor, Michigan, after living for two years (1967–69) in Kabul, Afghanistan, where I had begun to look critically at the role society assigned to women. The Afghan version of the *chaderi* prescribed for Moslem women was particularly confining. Afghan jokes and folklore were blatantly sexist, such as this proverb: "If you see an old man, sit down and take a lesson; if you see an old woman, throw a stone."

2   But it wasn't only the native culture that made me question women's roles, it was also the American community.

3   Most of the American women were like myself—wives and mothers whose husbands were either career diplomats, employees of USAID, or college pro-fessors who had been recruited to work on various contract teams. We were suddenly bereft of our traditional roles: some of us became alcoholics, others

got very good at bridge, while still others searched desperately for ways to contribute either to our families or to the Afghans. The local economy provided few jobs for women and certainly none for foreigners; we were isolated from former friends and the social goals we had grown up with.

4   When I returned in the fall of 1969 to the University of Michigan in Ann Arbor, I was surprised to find that many other women were also questioning the expectations they had grown up with. In the spring of 1970, a women's conference was announced. I hired a babysitter and attended, but I returned home more troubled than ever. The militancy of these women frightened me. Since I wasn't ready for a revolution, I decided I would have my own feminist movement. I would study the English language and see what it could tell me about sexism. I started reading a desk dictionary and making notecards on every entry that seemed to tell something about male and female. I soon had a dog-eared dictionary, along with a collection of notecards filling two shoe boxes.

5   Ironically, I started reading the dictionary because I wanted to avoid getting involved in social issues, but what happened was that my notecards brought me right back to looking at society. Language and society are as intertwined as a chicken and an egg. The language a culture uses is telltale evidence of the values and beliefs of that culture. And because there is a lag in how fast a language changes—new words can easily be introduced, but it takes a long time for old words and usages to disappear—a careful look at English will reveal the attitudes that our ancestors held and that we as a culture are therefore predisposed to hold. My notecards revealed three main points. Friends have offered the opinion that I didn't need to read the dictionary to learn such obvious facts. Nevertheless, it was interesting to have linguistic evidence of sociological observations.

WOMEN ARE SEXY; MEN ARE SUCCESSFUL

6   First, in American culture a woman is valued for the attractiveness and sexiness of her body, while a man is valued for his physical strength and accomplishments. A woman is sexy. A man is successful.

7   A persuasive piece of evidence supporting this view are the eponyms—words that have come from someone's name—found in English. I had a two-and-a-half-inch stack of cards taken from men's names but less than a half-inch stack from women's names, and most of those came from Greek mythology. In the words that came into American English since we separated from Britain, there are many eponyms based on the names of famous American men: *Bartlett pear, boysenberry, diesel engine, Franklin stove, Ferris wheel, Gatling gun, mason jar, sideburns, sousaphone, Schick test,* and *Winchester rifle.* The only common eponyms taken from American women's names are *Alice blue* (after Alice Roosevelt Longworth), *bloomers* (after Amelia Jenks Bloomer), and *Mae West jacket* (after the buxom actress). Two

out of the three feminine eponyms relate closely to a woman's physical anatomy, while the masculine eponyms (except for *sideburns* after General Burnsides) have nothing to do with the namesake's body but, instead, honor the man for an accomplishment of some kind.

8   Although in Greek mythology women played a bigger role than they did in the biblical stories of the Judeo-Christian cultures and so the names of goddesses are accepted parts of the language in such place names as Pomona from the goddess of fruit and Athens from Athena and in such common words as *cereal* from Ceres, *psychology* from Psyche, and *arachnoid* from Arachne, the same tendency to think of women in relation to sexuality is seen in the eponyms *aphrodisiac* from Aphrodite, the Greek name for the goddess of love and beauty, and *veneral disease* from Venus, the Roman name for Aphrodite.

9   Another interesting word from Greek mythology is *Amazon.* According to Greek folk etymology, the *a* means "without" as in *atypical* or *amoral,* while *mazon* comes from *mazos* meaning "breast" as still seen in *mastectomy.* In the Greek legend, Amazon women cut off their right breasts so that they could better shoot their bows. Apparently, the storytellers had a feeling that for women to play the active, "masculine" role the Amazons adopted for themselves, they had to trade in part of their femininity.

10   This preoccupation with women's breasts is not limited to ancient stories. As a volunteer for the University of Wisconsin's *Dictionary of American Regional English (DARE),* I read a western trapper's diary from the 1930s. I was to make notes of any unusual usages or language patterns. My most interesting finding was that the trapper referred to a range of mountains as *The Teats,* a metaphor based on the similarity between the shapes of the mountains and women's breasts. Because today we use the French wording, *The Grand Tetons,* the metaphor isn't as obvious, but I wrote to mapmakers and found the following listings: *Nippletop* and *Little Nipple Top* near Mount Marcy in the Adirondacks; *Nipple Mountain* in Archuleta County, Colorado; *Nipple Peak* in Coke County, Texas; *Nipple Butte* in Pennington, South Dakota; *Squaw Peak* in Placer County, California (and many other locations); *Maiden's Peak* and *Squaw Tit* (they're the same mountain) in the Cascade Range in Oregon; *Mary's Nipple* near Salt Lake City, Utah; and *Jane Russell Peaks* near Stark, New Hampshire.

11   Except for the movie star Jane Russell, the women being referred to are anonymous—it's only a sexual part of their body that is mentioned. When topographical features are named after men, it's probably not going to be to draw attention to a sexual part of their bodies but instead to honor individuals for an accomplishment. For example, no one thinks of a part of the male body when hearing a reference to Pike's Peak, Colorado, or Jackson Hole, Wyoming.

12   Going back to what I learned from my dictionary cards, I was surprised to realize how many pairs of words we have in which the feminine word has acquired sexual connotations while the masculine word retains a serious businesslike aura. For example, a *callboy* is the person who calls actors when it is

time for them to go on stage, but a *callgirl* is a prostitute. Compare *sir* and *madam*. *Sir* is a term of respect, while *madam* has acquired the specialized meaning of a brothel manager. Something similar has happened to *master* and *mistress*. Would you rather have a painting by an *old master* or an *old mistress?*

13   It's because the word *woman* had sexual connotations, as in "She's his woman," that people began avoiding its use, hence such terminology as *ladies' room, lady of the house,* and *girls' school* or *school for young ladies.* Feminists, who ask that people use the term *woman* rather than *girl* or *lady,* are rejecting the idea that *woman* is primarily a sexual term. They have been at least partially successful in that today *woman* is commonly used to communicate gender without intending implications about sexuality.

14   I found two hundred pairs of words with masculine and feminine forms, e.g., *heir-heiress, hero-heroine, steward-stewardess, usher-usherette.* In nearly all such pairs, the masculine word is considered the base, with some kind of a feminine suffix being added. The masculine form is the one from which compounds are made, e.g., from *king-queen* comes *kingdom* but no *queendom,* from *sportsman-sportslady* comes *sportsmanship* but not *sportsladyship.* There is one—and only one—semantic area in which the masculine word is not the base or more powerful word. This is in the area dealing with sex and marriage. When someone refers to a *virgin,* a listener will probably think of a female, unless the speaker specifies *male* or uses a masculine pronoun. The same is true for *prostitute.*

15   In relation to marriage, there is much linguistic evidence showing that weddings are more important to women than to men. A woman cherishes the wedding and is considered a bride for a whole year, but a man is referred to as a groom only on the day of the wedding. The word *bride* appears in *bridal attendant, bridal gown, bridesmaid, bridal shower,* and even *bridegroom. Groom* comes from the Middle English *grom,* meaning "man," and in the sense is seldom used outside of the wedding. With most pairs of male/female words, people habitually put the masculine word first, *Mr. and Mrs., his and hers, boys and girls, men and women, kings and queens, brothers and sisters, guys and dolls,* and *host and hostess,* but it is the *bride and groom* who are talked about, not the *groom and bride.*

16   The importance of marriage to a woman is also shown by the fact that when a marriage ends in death, the woman gets the title of *widow.* A man gets the derived title of *widower.* This term is not used in other phrases or contexts, but *widow* is seen in *widowhood, widow's peak,* and *widow's walk.* A *widow* in a card game is an extra hand of cards, while in typesetting it is an extra line of type.

17   How changing cultural ideas bring changes to language is clearly visible in this semantic area. The feminist movement has caused the differences between the sexes to be downplayed, and since I did my dictionary study two decades ago, the word *singles* has largely replaced such sex specific and value-laden terms as *bachelor, old maid, spinster, divorcee, widow,* and *widower.*

And in 1970 I wrote that when a man is called *a professional* he is thought to be a doctor or a lawyer, but when people hear a woman referred to as *a professional* they are likely to think of a prostitute. That's not as true today because so many women have become doctors and lawyers that it's no longer incongruous to think of women in those professional roles.

18   Another change that has taken place is in wedding announcements. They used to be sent out from the bride's parents and did not even give the name of the groom's parents. Today, most couples choose to list either all or none of the parents' names. Also it is now much more likely that both the bride and groom's picture will be in the newspaper, while a decade ago only the bride's picture was published on the "Women's" or the "Society" page. Even the traditional wording of the wedding ceremony is being changed. Many officials now pronounce the couple "husband and wife" instead of the old "man and wife," and they ask the bride if she promises to "love, honor, and cherish," instead of "to love, honor, and obey."

WOMEN ARE PASSIVE; MEN ARE ACTIVE

19 The wording of the wedding ceremony also relates to the second point that my cards showed, which is that women are expected to play a passive or weak role while men play an active or strong role. In the traditional ceremony, the official asks, "Who gives the bride away?" and the father answers, "I do." Some fathers answer, "Her mother and I do," but that doesn't solve the problem inherent in the question. The idea that a bride is something to be handed over from one man to another bothers people because it goes back to the days when a man's servants, his children, and his wife were all considered to be his property. They were known by his name because they belonged to him, and he was responsible for their actions and their debts.

20   The grammar used in talking or writing about weddings as well as other sexual relationships shows the expectation of men playing the active role. Men *wed* women while women *become* brides of men. A man *possesses* a woman; he *deflowers* her; he *performs;* he *scores*; he *takes away* her virginity. Although a woman can *seduce* a man, she cannot offer him her virginity. When talking about virginity, the only way to make the woman the actor in the sentence is to say that "She lost her virginity," but people lose things by accident rather than by purposeful actions, and so she's only the grammatical, not the real-life, actor.

21   The reason that women tried to bring the term *Ms.* into the language to replace *Miss* and *Mrs.* relates to this point. Married women resent being identified only under their husband's names. For example, when Susan Glascoe did something newsworthy, she would be identified in the newspaper only as Mrs. John Glascoe. The dictionary cards showed what appeared to be an attitude on the part of the editors that it was almost indecent to let a respectable woman's name march unaccompanied across the pages of a dictionary.

Women were listed with male names whether or not the male contributed to the woman's reason for being in the dictionary or in his own right was as famous as the woman. For example, Charlotte Brontë was identified as Mrs. Arthur B. Nicholls, Amelia Earhart as Mrs. George Palmer Putnam, Helen Hayes as Mrs. Charles MacArthur, Jenny Lind as Mme. Otto Goldschmit, Cornelia Otis Skinner as the daughter of Otis, Harriet Beecher Stowe as the sister of Henry Ward Beecher, and Edith Sitwell as the sister of Osbert and Sacheverell. A very small number of women got into the dictionary without the benefit of a masculine escort. They were rebels and crusaders: temperance leaders Frances Elizabeth Caroline Willard and Carry Nation, women's rights leaders Carrie Chapman Catt and Elizabeth Cady Stanton, birth control educator Margaret Sanger, religious leader Mary Baker Eddy, and slaves Harriet Tubman and Phillis Wheatley.

22   Etiquette books used to teach that if a woman had *Mrs.* in front of her name, then the husband's name should follow because *Mrs.* is an abbreviated form of *Mistress* and a woman couldn't be a mistress of herself. As with many arguments about "correct" language usage, this isn't very logical because *Miss* is also an abbreviation of *Mistress.* Feminists hoped to simplify matters by introducing *Ms.* as an alternative to both *Mrs.* and *Miss,* but what happened is that *Ms.* largely replaced *Miss,* to become a catch-all business title for women. Many married women still prefer the title *Mrs.,* and some resent being addressed with the term *Ms.* As one frustrated newspaper reporter complained, "Before I can write about a woman, I have to know not only her marital status but also her political philosophy." The result of such complications may contribute to the demise of titles, which are already being ignored by many computer programmers who find it more efficient to simply use names, for example in a business letter: "Dear Joan Garcia," instead of "Dear Mrs. Joan Garcia," "Dear Ms. Garcia," or "Dear Mrs. Louis Garcia."

23   The titles given to royalty provide an example of how males can be disadvantaged by the assumption that they are always to play the more powerful role. In British royalty, when a male holds a title, his wife is automatically given the feminine equivalent. But the reverse is not true. For example, a *count* is a high political officer with a *countess* being his wife. The same is true for a *duke* and a *duchess* and a *king* and a *queen.* But when a female holds the royal title, the man she marries does not automatically acquire the matching title. For example, Queen Elizabeth's husband has the title of *prince* rather than *king,* but if Prince Charles should become king while he is still married to Lady or Princess Diana, she will be known as the queen. The reasoning appears to be that since masculine words are stronger, they are reserved for true heirs and withheld from males coming into the royal family by marriage. If Prince Phillip were called *King Phillip,* it would be much easier for British subjects to forget where the true power lies.

24   The names that people give their children show the hopes and dreams they have for them, and when we look at the differences between male and female names in a culture, we can see the cumulative expectations of that culture. In

our culture girls often have names taken from small, aesthetically pleasing items, e.g., *Ruby, Jewel,* and *Pearl. Esther* and *Stella* mean "star," *Ada* means "ornament," and *Vanessa* means "butterfly." Boys are more likely to be given names with meanings of power and strength, e.g., *Neil* means "champion," *Martin* is from Mars, the God of War, *Raymond* means "wise protection," *Harold* means "chief of the army," *Ira* means "vigilant," *Rex* means "king," and *Richard* means "strong king."

25   We see similar differences in food metaphors. Food is a passive substance just sitting there waiting to be eaten. Many people have recognized this and so no longer feel comfortable describing women as "delectable morsels." However, when I was a teenager, it was considered a compliment to refer to a girl (we didn't call anyone a *woman* until she was middle-aged) as a *cute tomato,* a *peach,* a *dish,* a *cookie, honey, sugar,* or *sweetie-pie.* When being affectionate, women will occasionally call a man *honey* or *sweetie,* but in general, food metaphors are used much less often with men than with women. If a man is called a *fruit,* his masculinity is being questioned. But it's perfectly acceptable to use a food metaphor if the food is heavier and more substantive than that used for women. For example pin-up pictures of women have long been known as *cheesecake,* but when Burt Reynolds posed for a nude centerfold the picture was immediately dubbed *beefcake,* c.f., *a hunk of meat.* That such sexual references to men have come into the language is another reflection of how society is beginning to lessen the differences between their attitudes toward men and women.

26   Something similar to the *fruit* metaphor happens with references to plants. We insult a man by calling him a *pansy,* but it wasn't considered particularly insulting to talk about a girl being a *wallflower,* a *clinging vine,* or a *shrinking violet,* or to give girls such names as *Ivy, Rose, Lily, Iris, Daisy, Camellia, Heather,* and *Flora.* A plant metaphor can be used with a man if the plant is big and strong, for example, Andrew Jackson's nickname of *Old Hickory.* Also, the phrases *blooming idiots* and *budding geniuses* can be used with either sex, but notice how they are based on the most active thing a plant can do which is to bloom or bud.

27   Animal metaphors also illustrate the different expectations for males and females. Men are referred to as *studs, bucks,* and *wolves* while women are referred to with such metaphors as *kitten, bunny, beaver, bird, chick,* and *lamb.* In the 1950s we said that boys went *tomcatting,* but today it's just *catting around* and both boys and girls do it. When the term *foxy,* meaning that someone was sexy, first became popular it was used only for girls, but now someone of either sex can be described as *a fox.* Some animal metaphors that are used predominantly with men have negative connotations based on the size and/or strength of the animals, e.g., *beast, bullheaded, jackass, rat, loanshark,* and *vulture.* Negative metaphors used with women are based on smaller animals, e.g., *social butterfly, mousy, catty,* and *vixen.* The feminine terms connote action, but not the same kind of large scale action as with the masculine terms.

WOMEN ARE CONNECTED WITH NEGATIVE CONNOTATIONS; MEN WITH POSITIVE CONNOTATIONS

28 The final point that my notecards illustrated was how many positive connotations are associated with the concept of masculine, while there are either trivial or negative connotations connected with the corresponding feminine concept. An example from the animal metaphors makes a good illustration. The word *shrew* taken from the name of a small but especially vicious animal was defined in my dictionary as "an ill-tempered scolding woman," but the word *shrewd* taken from the same root was defined as "marked by clever, discerning awareness" and was illustrated with the phrase "a shrewd businessman."

29   Early in life, children are conditioned to the superiority of the masculine role. As child psychologists point out, little girls have much more freedom to experiment with sex roles than do little boys. If a little girl acts like a *tomboy,* most parents have mixed feelings, being at least partially proud. But if their little boy acts like a *sissy* (derived from *sister*), they call a psychologist. It's perfectly acceptable for a little girl to sleep in the crib that was purchased for her brother, to wear his hand-me-down jeans and shirts, and to ride the bicycle that he has outgrown. But few parents would put a boy baby in a white and gold crib decorated with frills and lace, and virtually no parents would have their little boy wear his sister's hand-me-down dresses, nor would they have their son ride a girl's pink bicycle with a flower-bedecked basket. The proper names given to girls and boys show this same attitude. Girls can have "boy" names—*Cris, Craig, Jo, Kelly, Shawn, Teri, Toni,* and *Sam*—but it doesn't work the other way around. A couple of generations ago, *Beverley, Frances, Hazel, Marion,* and *Shirley* were common boys' names. As parents gave these names to more and more girls, they fell into disuse for males, and some older men who have these names prefer to go by their initials or by such abbreviated forms as *Haze* or *Shirl.*

30   When a little girl is told to *be a lady,* she is being told to sit with her knees together and to be quiet and dainty. But when a little boy is told to *be a man* he is being told to be noble, strong, and virtuous—to have all the qualities that the speaker looks on as desirable. The concept of manliness has such positive connotations that it used to be a compliment to call someone a *he-man,* to say that he was doubly a man. Today many people are more ambivalent about this term and respond to it much as they do to the word *macho.* But calling someone a *manly man* or a *virile man* is nearly always meant as a compliment. *Virile* comes from the Indo-European *vir* meaning "man," which is also the basis of *virtuous.* Contrast the positive connotations of both *virile* and *virtuous* with the negative connotations of *hysterical.* The Greeks took this latter word from their name for *uterus* (as still seen in *hysterectomy*). They thought that women were the only ones who experienced uncontrolled emotional outbursts, and so the condition must have something to do with a part of the body that only women have.

31   Differences in the connotations between positive male and negative female connotations can be seen in several pairs of words that differ denotatively only in the matter of sex. *Bachelor* as compared to *spinster* or *old maid* has such positive connotations that women try to adopt them by using the term *bachelor-girl* or *bachelorette*. *Old maid* is so negative that it's the basis for metaphors: pretentious and fussy old men are called *old maids,* as are the leftover kernels of unpopped popcorn, and the last card in a popular children's game.

32   *Patron* and *matron* (Middle English for *father* and *mother*) have such different levels of prestige that women try to borrow the more positive masculine connotations with the word *patroness,* literally "female father." Such a peculiar term came about because of the high prestige attached to *patron* in such phrases as *a patron of the arts* or *a patron saint. Matron* is more apt to be used in talking about a woman in charge of a jail or a public restroom.

33   When men are doing jobs that women often do, we apparently try to pay the men extra by giving them fancy titles, for example, a male cook is more likely to be called a *chef* while a male seamstress will get the title of *tailor.* The armed forces have a special problem in that they recruit under such slogans as "The Marine Corps builds men!" and "Join the Army! Become a Man." Once the recruits are enlisted, they find themselves doing much of the work that has been traditionally thought of as "women's work." The solution to getting the work done and not insulting anyone's masculinity was to change the titles as shown below:

waitress	orderly
nurse	medic or corpsman
secretary	clerk-typist
assistant	adjutant
dishwasher or kitchen helper	KP (kitchen police)

34   Compare *brave* and *squaw.* Early settlers in America truly admired Indian men and hence named them with a word that carried connotations of youth, vigor, and courage. But they used the Algonquin's name for "woman" and over the years it developed almost opposite connotations to those of *brave. Wizard* and *witch* contrast almost as much. The masculine *wizard* implies skill and wisdom combined with magic, while the feminine *witch* implies evil intentions combined with magic. Part of the unattractiveness of both *witch* and *squaw* is that they have been used so often to refer to old women, something with which our culture is particularly uncomfortable, just as the Afghans were. Imagine my surprise when I ran across the phrases *grandfatherly advice* and *old wives' tales* and realized that the underlying implication is the same as the Afghan proverb about old men being worth listening to while old women talk only foolishness.

35   Other terms that show how negatively we view old women as compared to young women are *old nag* as compared to *filly, old crow* or *old bat* as compared to *bird,* and of being *catty* as compared to being *kittenish.* There is no matching set of metaphors for men. The chicken metaphor tells the whole story of a woman's life. In her youth she is a *chick.* Then she marries and begins *feathering her nest.* Soon she begins feeling *cooped up,* so she goes to *hen parties* where she *cackles* with her friends. Then she has her *brood,* begins to *henpeck* her husband, and finally turns into an *old biddy.*

36   I embarked on my study of the dictionary not with the intention of prescribing language change but simply to see what the language would tell me about sexism. Nevertheless I have been both surprised and pleased as I've watched the changes that have occurred over the past two decades. I'm one of those linguists who believes that new language customs will cause a new generation of speakers to grow up with different expectations. This is why I'm happy about people's efforts to use inclusive language, to say *he or she* or *they* when speaking about individuals whose names they do not know. I'm glad that leading publishers have developed guidelines to help writers use language that is fair to both sexes, and I'm glad that most newspapers and magazines list women by their own names instead of only by their husbands' names and that educated and thoughtful people no longer begin their business letters with "Dear Sir" or "Gentlemen," but instead use a memo form or begin with such salutations as "Dear Colleagues," "Dear Reader," or "Dear Committee Members." I'm also glad that such words as *poetess, authoress, conductress,* and *aviatrix* now sound quaint and old-fashioned and that *chairman* is giving way to *chair* or *head, mailman* to *mail carrier, clergyman* to *clergy,* and *stewardess* to *flight attendant.* I was also pleased when the National Oceanic and Atmospheric Administration bowed to feminist complaints and in the late 1970s began to alternate men's and women's names for hurricanes. However, I wasn't so pleased to discover that the change did not immediately erase sexist thoughts from everyone's mind, as shown by a headline about Hurricane David in a 1979 New York tabloid, "David Rapes Virgin Islands." More recently a similar metaphor appeared in a headline in the *Arizona Republic* about Hurricane Charlie, "Charlie Quits Carolinas, Flirts with Virginia."

37   What these incidents show is that sexism is not something existing independently in American English or in the particular dictionary that I happened to read. Rather, it exists in people's minds. Language is like an X ray in providing visible evidence of invisible thoughts. The best thing about people being interested in and discussing sexist language is that as they make conscious decisions about what pronouns they will use, what jokes they will tell or laugh at, how they will write their names, or how they will begin their letters, they are forced to think about the underlying issue of sexism. This is good because as a problem that begins in people's assumptions and expectations, it's a problem that will be solved only when a great many people have given it a great deal of thought.

TOPICAL CONSIDERATIONS

1. What led Nilsen to undertake her study of the relationship between sexist language and a society's behavior? Briefly summarize her findings in your own words.

2. Nilsen reaches the conclusion that "language and society are as intertwined as a chicken and an egg" (paragraph 5). Do you agree with her? Why or why not? Cite some examples from your own native or ancestral language to support your position.

3. What support does Nilsen offer for her assertion that American English reflects an American culture that values women for their physical appearance and expects them to be passive, while it values men for their achievements and expects them to be active?

4. What effect has the feminist movement had on American language, according to Nilsen? Were you aware of this effect before you read this article? If so, what particular effects can you attribute to the feminist movement?

5. Does Nilsen simply cite examples of loaded language, or does she argue for social change? Support your answer.

6. In the final paragraph, Nilsen refers to language with a simile ("like an X ray"). What does she mean by that comparison?

RHETORICAL CONSIDERATIONS

1. How does Nilsen develop her essay? Do you find this method of development persuasive? Why or why not?

2. What is Nilsen's main argument? Does she convince you? Why or why not?

3. What is the tone of Nilsen's essay? How does she create this tone?

4. Select a section that you feel is particularly useful in making Nilsen's point. What is it about this section that you find effective?

WRITING ASSIGNMENTS

1. Choose a classmate to act as your partner. With that person, create a number of flash cards containing words or expressions Nilsen cites as having implications about society's expectations for males or females. Working independently, ask several people to respond to the flash cards. Meet with your partner to discuss your findings. Make a list of the similarities and differences you encountered.

2. Select two issues of the same magazine, one from twenty years ago and one from the last six months. Briefly describe any differences you note in the language used to refer to women and men in articles or advertising, then and now.

3. Write a letter from Jack Rosenthal ("Gender Benders") to Nilsen, expressing Rosenthal's response to Nilsen's essay. Be sure to take Rosenthal's stated views into consideration in crafting your letter.

ENGLISH ANYONE?

Spiro T. Agnew

As shown in Alleen Pace Nilsen's essay, some formerly sexist terms have found gender-free substitutes that are part of today's general usage. Not everyone, however, has welcomed the changes. Some, in fact, argue that degenderized English is not only ludicrous but grammatically inexcusable. One such person was Spiro T. Agnew, a former governor of Maryland and U.S. vice-president. In the essay below, Agnew argues that the only thing feminists will accomplish by eliminating so-called sexist language is inhibiting fluency.

During his term of office under Richard Nixon (1969–1973), Agnew became known for his colorful speeches attacking dissidents and the news media. On October 10, 1973, he resigned his post after being charged with accepting bribes while governor and vice-president. He was also convicted of income tax evasion. In 1976 he published a novel, *The Canfield Decision.* This article was first published in *Conservative Digest,* in May 1989. Agnew died in 1996.

1   Americans have good reason to be concerned about today's shocking misuses of the English language, not just in the schools, but also in the greater community. There is a laissez-faire attitude about the increasing debasement of spoken and written English. Much careless usage of the language has come about in recent years—partly because of the feminist movement but more often because no one seems to care. Quite a few prestigious publications are guilty of sloppy editing. The tendency today is to allow mistakes to become so commonplace that they are eventually accepted as the norm and incorporated into the established grammar and vocabulary.

2   An example of a formerly incorrect practice that now has been purged of error is the current use of the word "unique." The definitions of "unique" for most of my lifetime were "exclusive, unmatched, distinctive or particular." In a phrase, "one of a kind." Now, however, the word has been corrupted to include "unusual, uncommon or rare."

3   This came about from acceptance of the frequent incorrect usage of "unique," so that in some circumstances a word that meant "one of a kind" was reduced to meaning only "unusual." I say, "in some circumstances" because the dictionaries still include, "exclusive, unmatched, distinctive, and particular" as definitions of "unique." So now, when the word "unique" is em-

ployed, we must guess what the user intends. Does he mean "one of a kind" or simply "unusual"? In the second case, the use of the adjective "very" is correct; in the first, it is not. Here the acceptance of the vernacular has weakened the language and made it imprecise.

4   The most irritating and inexcusable errors are those in simple grammar, especially where there was an opportunity for editing, as in television commercials, commentaries, or newspaper columns. You have undoubtedly heard or read: "Sears is having their sale." Or, "Everyone to their own opinion." Or, "A large number of participants were gathered." In the first instance, the error cannot be explained away. Either do it the British way, "Sears are having their sale," or our way, "Sears is having its sale." But, please, no more singular verbs and plural pronouns. In the second example, the feminists have intimidated us to abandon the long-accepted use of, "Everyone to his own opinion," because of their adamant refusal to accept the masculine pronoun to include any human. *If* we must yield to such petulance, it should be, "All to their own opinions" or, "Everyone may have a different opinion." Yet why must we bastardize the language to accommodate carping and insecurity of this type? In the last example above, it is plain editorial carelessness not to see that the singular "number," not the plural "participants," governs the verb usage.

5   And while we are on the subject of bruised female egos, can there be anyone more sophomoric than the insistence on eliminating words like "mankind" or any other use of "man" to mean in the broader sense, "human"? The use of "person" to replace "man" can become very awkward, as witness: "garbage person," or "snowperson." Should one want to get really ludicrous, how about "horsepersonship" or "personhole cover"?

6   The June 6, 1988, edition of the *South China Morning Post* reported that, upon the urging of the Broadcasting Corporation Director-General, who lamented that her sex is not a sub-species of men, Radio New Zealand has banned 151 "sexist" words. It is reported that these words include: manhole, snowman, bridesmaid, masterpiece, fatherland, landlord, heroine, master of ceremonies, mother nature, and one-man show. The lady states that "girl" should not be used because "females over the age of 16 are women." She goes on to say, "Nonsexist language may threaten some people but we cannot afford to be held back by such rigid thinkers." As an admitted "rigid thinker" on this subject, I would venture that this woman's attitude demonstrates an even greater lack of flexibility. I am a strong advocate for eliminating discrimination against women, but how is this accomplished by inhibiting the fluency maintained over hundreds of years?

7   Where a singular subject is to include both sexes, it is indisputable that the political and journalistic sectors of our society have yielded to the pressure to abandon the masculine pronouns. Consider the following television commercial: "The first time I meet a prospective customer, I ask them to sit down with me." To avoid the masculine pronoun "him," the ad agency has sloppily used the sexless plural, "them." Some say we should amend "them" to be both singular and plural. Others would like to coin a new sexless pronoun that can answer

both purposes. I contend that the proper use of "his" in such instances does nothing to demean women or affect their rights, and that we should abandon these ridiculous squabbles over semantics and get on with important matters such as fairer compensation and more job opportunities for women.

8   Errors made during spontaneous debate or adlibbed remarks are not the subjects of this complaint, although these would be less frequent if edited writings were more correct. We all make mistakes in conversation. What I am complaining about are the repeated grammatical errors in books, magazines, newspapers, prepared discourses by television commentators, television and radio advertisements—in short, any place where the opportunity for editing was available. I call upon the print media, who are all too ready to [sic] to death the improper utterances of those they dislike, to locate and correct the [sics] within their own organizations.

9   The communication of thoughts is essential to the pursuit of excellence, and a pure, exact language is equally important to the communication of thoughts. Contaminating influences can come from such varied sources as "bureaucratese" and "street language." To learn through the communication of ideas, we must understand each other—perfectly. This mandates care in the way we express ourselves. If our ideas are worthwhile, we should express them in a worthwhile way. Only then will our lagging pursuit of excellence become "hot pursuit."

TOPICAL CONSIDERATIONS

1. Take another look at Nilsen's "Sexism in English: A 1990's Update." The main argument is that discrimination against women is deeply rooted in our language. Summarize Agnew's main argument here. According to him, what bearing does language have on the issues of discrimination against women? Where do you stand on the issue? Do you feel that traditional male-centered usages (e.g., *snow-man* and all-inclusive masculine pronouns) have any bearing on the discrimination against women?

2. Do you think that the feminist movement has been responsible in any way for what Agnew sees as "the increasing debasement of spoken and written English"? Can you give any examples of nonsexist language changes that you consider "debasement" of English? Or do you think that the nonsexist changes are good for women and the language?

3. How do you use the word *unique*? Does it only mean "one of a kind," or can it include "unusual"? Do you or people you know ever use *unique* with the intensifier *very*—for example, she's a "very unique" person? What's your feeling about Agnew's statement that the usage of *unique* to include " 'unusual, uncommon or rare' " is an example of linguistic corruption?

4. In paragraph 4, Agnew says that he finds "most irritating and inexcusable" those errors in "simple grammar." Have you ever been irritated by someone or some ad's misuse of language? If so, what kinds of bad usage get to you? If not, do you think this essay (or others in this collection) have made you more sensitive to language usage? Do you think today's students are concerned much with "language

debasement"? Or can they not be bothered? Do you or your friends ever correct another's grammar or usage? Do you ever knowingly use ungrammatical expressions, say, for effect or to avoid sounding too awkward or "proper"?

5. Agnew finds nothing "more sophomoric than the insistence of eliminating words like 'mankind' or any any other use of 'man' to mean . . . 'human.'" (See paragraph 5.) What does Nilsen say about this particular issue? What are your own feelings about avoiding such male-centered terms? Do you use *human* and *humankind* for *man* and *mankind?* Do your friends? your parents? your instructors? Do you find such avoidance "sophomoric"?

6. In paragraph 6, Agnew says that he is "a strong advocate for eliminating discrimination against women." From what you've read here, do you agree with his self-assessment. If not, explain. If so, explain how Agnew's defense of women can be independent of his defense of language. In what sense does he claim to be an advocate of women?

7. Do you and your friends avoid using masculine pronouns? If so, has this essay bolstered your attitude that one can maintain traditional usage and still not be discriminatory toward women?

8. Throughout, Agnew argues that it is the feminists who have insisted on removing sexist usages from English. Does such a stand make a woman a feminist? Can a woman resent sexist language and not be a "feminist"? Would you consider men who avoid sexist language feminists? Explain.

RHETORICAL CONSIDERATIONS

1. Agnew asks, in paragraph 4, "why must we bastardize the language to accommodate carping and insecurity" of feminists. Consider the particular language he chose here. Using a dictionary, discuss the implications of the word *bastardize.* Why this word instead of *change* or even the less neutral *debase?* What is the meaning of *carping?* What are the implications of its use here? What kind of "insecurity" is implied by Agnew here? Do you think that women who call for the desexualizing of English are insecure in any way? Now consider *petulance* and *bruised female egos.* Given these terms, what portrait does Agnew's language paint of the women who call for nonsexist language changes? Do you think this is a fair assessment of such women?

2. In paragraph 6, Agnew writes: "The lady states that 'girl'" should not be used because 'females over the age of 16 are women.'" How would the Broadcasting Corporation Director-General respond to his use of *lady* here? What is the tone of this phrasing?

3. And speaking of bruised egos, do you think the word *sophomoric* is an insult to sophomores? or *bastard* to children born out of wedlock? Explain.

WRITING ASSIGNMENTS

1. In a journal, make note of all the examples of sexist language you hear this week. Try to determine what is sexist about them—that is, how women are denigrated by their usage. Are some more blatant than others? Which seem more subtle, more rigidly part of traditional usage? What nonsexist alternatives can you come up with?

2. Write a response to Spiro Agnew in which you argue that good grammar and fluency need not be sacrificed for linguistic equality. In other words, point out to him that age-old usage and terminology has been detrimental to women, that language habits have subtle ways of affecting attitudes of users.

3. In paragraph 6, Agnew lists ten words that the Broadcasting Corporation Director-General banned from Radio New Zealand. In your own words, explain how each is sexist. Try to come up with nonsexist alternatives.

4. As mentioned in the headnote, Mr. Agnew was a conservative Republican who served in the Nixon administration. Had you not known that, you might still have guessed his political stand from reading this piece. Go through this essay again and try to determine the features that underscore his conservative voice. Consider his attitudes toward language and women as well as his writing style and phraseology.

GENDER BENDERS

Jack Rosenthal

Before we can rid the English language of sexism we might have to consider some deeply embedded values in our culture—values we all share; values that Jack Rosenthal calls Hidden Gender; values that surface when most people, if asked, will say chicken soup is feminine and beef soup is masculine. Purging English of sexist terms, though worthwhile, says the author, may be little more than a superficial effort.

Jack Rosenthal is editor of the *New York Times* editorial page and a contributor to the "On Language" column in that paper's Sunday *Magazine* where this article first appeared in 1986.

1 Chicken soup and beef soup. Which is masculine and which is feminine? In English, neither chicken nor beef nor soup has formal gender. Yet most people find the question easy to answer: chicken soup is feminine and beef soup is masculine, and that unanimity demonstrates how vast is the task of stamping out sexist words. That effort, while constructive, remains superficial; deep within language lurks the powerful force of Hidden Gender.

2   Many languages use formal gender to categorize nouns and pronouns as masculine, feminine, and neuter. There's not much logic in these categories. "In German," Mark Twain once write, "a young lady has no sex, while a turnip has. Think what overwrought reverence that shows for the turnip and what callous disrespect for the girl." A Spanish butterfly is aptly feminine: *la mariposa*. A French butterfly is masculine, but at least the word sounds delicate: *le papillon*. A German butterfly is, as an old linguistic's joke observes, masculine and sounds it: *der Schmetterling*.

3   Beyond formal gender, societies observe a ceremonial gender. A nation is a "she." So is a ship, an invention, an engine. Think of "Star Trek": one can just hear Scotty down in the engine room calling Captain Kirk: "I canna' get her into warp drive, Capt'n!"

4   Women's liberation has brought a new turn toward neutering language—using firefighter instead of fireman and generalizing with "they" instead of "he." This process, generally positive, can be carried to extremes. When someone once denounced *yeoman* as sexist and urged *yeoperson* instead, the *Times* groaned in an editorial, fearing the ultimate absurdity—*woperson*. Nonsense, several letter writers promptly responded. The ultimate absurdity, they observed, would be *woperdaughter.*

5   Hidden Gender, compared with such questions of surface gender, rolls beneath the language like the tide. The chicken soup/beef soup question is just one illustration. Consider some variations on the idea, which began as a children's game and has been elaborated by Roger W. Shuy and other sociologists at Georgetown University.

6   Which of the following is masculine and which is feminine:

Ford and Chevrolet

Chocolate and vanilla

Salt and pepper

Pink and purple

7   From English speakers, the answers usually come back the same, regardless of age, race, class, region—or sex. Some people see no gender at all in any of the terms. But those who do usually say that Ford, chocolate, pepper and purple are masculine.

8   The consensus is not limited to these pairs. You can get the same predictability by making up other combinations—coffee and tea, shoes and boots, skis and skates, plane and train.

9   Why does almost everybody label chicken soup feminine? One obvious explanation is that beef connotes cattle—big, solid, stolid animals. Chickens are small, frail, agile. Why does almost everybody label Chevrolet feminine? Perhaps for reasons of sound. Ford ends in a tough, blunt consonant, almost as masculine-sounding as *Mack truck*. By comparison, Chevro-lay seems graceful and flexible.

10   Why do so many people label vanilla feminine? Sound is probably part of it, but so also is color and character. Chocolate, being darker and with a more pronounced taste, is masculine in this pairing. Likewise for pepper and purple.

11   Consider the attributes associated with masculine: solid, blunt, more pronounced, and those associated with feminine: frail, graceful, light. They do not arise from the words themselves but from the pairings. What the game exposes is that Hidden Gender is relative.

12   In assigning gender to one word or the other, we expose attributes so deeply embedded in our culture that most of us, male or female, macho or feminist, share them. We turn values into gender and gender into communication.

13   Try playing the game with single words instead of pairs. When you ask people the gender of fork, you'll get blank looks. Hidden Gender only shows up when people are asked to give relative importance to two words.

14   Which is masculine and which is feminine: knife or fork? Usually, the answer is that fork is feminine. But why? There's nothing inherently feminine about the word fork. The answer is obvious when you try a different pair. Which is masculine and which is feminine: fork or spoon?

15   Purging language of sexist terms is worth doing for its own sake, but the superficiality of the effort should also be recognized. Whether one refers to

ocean liners or God as "she" is a cosmetic matter. Hidden Gender endures, and the only way to alter it is to alter the culture on which it feeds.

TOPICAL CONSIDERATIONS

1. In your own words, try to explain the phenomenon of hidden gender. Had you ever thought about the concept before? Did the author open your mind to aspects of language you hadn't considered? Do you think this essay might in some ways change your attitudes toward language and gender prejudice? If so, how?

2. Looking back over the essay, do you think Rosenthal is opposed to sexist language? Is he arguing in favor of eliminating gender prejudice? What evidence can you cite to support your answers?

3. What might Alleen Pace Nilsen say about hidden gender? Does Rosenthal's thesis support her efforts to eliminate sexist language, undercut them, or neither? What would Nilsen say to Rosenthal's final statement: "Whether one refers to ocean liners or God as 'she' is a cosmetic matter"?

4. What might Spiro Agnew have said about hidden gender? Do you think he would have considered it damaging to women? Might he have regarded the phenomenon as confirmation of his stand against neutering English? Explain your thoughts.

5. In paragraph 11, Rosenthal lists attributes associated with masculine—*solid, blunt, more pronounced;* and feminine—*frail, graceful, light.* Do you agree with these associations? Would you have chosen any different terms? Explain your answer.

6. Do you think the results of the hidden gender game would be different were players asked to determine which object is "male" and which is "female"? Do you think *masculine* and *feminine* are already loaded with values? Explain your answer.

7. Rosenthal says that there is nothing inherently feminine about the word *fork* when paired with *knife,* but with *spoon,* he says, it's a different story. In this pairing, which is masculine and which feminine? Try to explain your answers. What principle(s) did you use? Can you think of other pairings that use the same principles?

8. Consider Rosenthal's last line in the essay: "Hidden Gender endures, and the only way to alter it is to alter the culture on which it feeds." What kinds of cultural alterations might he be talking about? Is he calling for such alterations? What, if any, alterations would you want to see made? What are the chances of altering our culture so as to rid the language of hidden gender?

RHETORICAL CONSIDERATIONS

1. Does the opening question capture your attention? How and why? How does this technique affect your response to what follows in the essay?

2. At what point in the essay do you know the author's focus? What technique did he use to clarify it for you?

3. Which part of this essay did you find most interesting? Which part was least interesting?

4. From paragraph 3 to the end the author shifts his approach and directly addresses the reader. Try to explain the strategy here—that is, how the author attempts to engage the reader and how effective the strategy is. Is this a strategy you might employ in your writing?

5. Is the final statement satisfying to you?

6. What do you remember best about this essay?

WRITING ASSIGNMENTS

1. If hidden gender is so deep and powerful a force in language, is it worth the effort to purge the language of sexism? Or, is that effort simply "cosmetic" surgery as Rosenthal suggests? Write out your own thoughts in an essay. In your discussion try to determine whether we have two separate or related issues in hidden gender and sexist language.

2. Try the hidden gender game on your friends. Show them the list in paragraph 6 and ask them to determine the genders. Then ask them to explain their answers. (You might even try a list of your own.) In a paper discuss the results and what you learned about hidden gender.

LIFE AS A FEMALE GENTLEMAN

Lani Guinier

Lani Guinier, a graduate of Yale Law School, is a prominent civil rights attorney. In 1993 she was nominated, though ultimately rejected, for the job of assistant attorney general for civil rights. She is also black. In this essay her anecdotes from law school and her brief time in the political arena demonstrate how the white, male ruling elite felt empowered to treat her as invisible and to distort her ideas at will. But more than that, she raises the issue of how race and gender can make a person vulnerable to redefinition and invisibility. This essay originally appeared in the *Boston Globe* in January 1994.

1   In 1984, I returned to Yale Law School to participate on a panel of mainly black alumni reminiscing about the 30 years since Brown vs. Board of Education. It was a panel sponsored by the current black students who were eager to hear the voices of those who came before them. Each of us on the panel spoke for 10 minutes in a room adorned by the traditional portraits of larger-than-life white men. It was the same classroom in which, 10 years earlier, I had sat for "Business Units," the name Yale gave to "corporations," with a white male professor who addressed all of us, male and female, as gentlemen.

2   Every morning, at 10 minutes after the hour, he would enter the classroom and greet the upturned faces: "Good morning, gentlemen." He described this ritual the first day. He had been teaching for many years; he was a creature of habit. He readily acknowledged the presence of a few "ladies" by then in attendance, but admonished those of us born into that other gender not to feel excluded by his greeting. We, too, in his mind, were simply gentlemen.

3   In his view, "gentlemen" was an asexual term, one reserved for reference to those who shared a certain civilized view of the world and who exhibited a similarly civilized demeanor. By his lights, the greeting was a form of honorific. It was evocative of the traditional values of men, in particular men of good breeding, who possess neither a race nor a gender. If we were not already, law school would certainly teach us how to be gentlemen. That lesson was at the heart of becoming a professional.

4   Now back in the familiar classroom preparing to address a race- and gender-mixed audience, I felt the weight of the presence of those stern gentlemen's portraits. For me, this was still not a safe place.

5   Yet, all the men on the panel reminded us how they felt to return "home," with fondly revealed stories about their three years in law school. Anecdotes about their time as law students, mostly funny and a touch self-congratulatory, abounded. These three black men may not have felt safe, either, but they each introduced their talks with brief yet loving recollections of their experiences. Even the so-called "black radical" among us waxed nostalgic and personal with proud detail about his encounters as the law school troublemaker.

6   It was my turn. No empowering memories found my voice. I had no personal anecdotes for the profound sense of alienation and isolation that caught in my throat every time I opened my mouth. Nothing resonated there for a black woman, even after my 10 years as an impassioned civil rights attorney. Instead, I promptly began my formal remarks, trying as hard as I could to find my voice in a room in which those portraits spoke louder than I ever could. I spoke slowly, carefully and never once admitted, except by my presence on the podium, that I had ever been at this school or in that room before. I summoned as much authority as I could to be heard over the sounds of silence erupting from those giant images of gentlemen hanging on the wall and from my own ever-present memory of slowly disappearing each morning and becoming a gentlemen of Business Units I.

7   Immediately after my presentation, the other black woman on the panel rose to speak. She, too, did not introduce herself with personal experiences or warm reminiscences about her past association with the law school, but, like me, remained upright and, I thought, dignified. Afterwards she and I huddled to talk about how different the law school we had experienced was from the one recollected by our male colleagues.

8   We were the minority within a minority whose existence, even physical presence, had been swallowed up within the traditions associated with educating *gentlemen.* Even from our places up front at the podium, those portraits were like some attic jury reminding us that silence about what we knew was the price of our presence.

9   Years and career options intervened. I joined the academy along with other women, including women of color. The memory receded of the time when larger-than-life gentlemen imposed such heavy silences on women. Then, in the spring of 1993, I was nominated to be assistant attorney general for civil rights, and those law student memories assumed contemporary urgency. Once again, a larger-than-life jury commanded silence.

10   This time, I was explicitly admonished not to speak, as a courtesy to the Senate prior to confirmation hearings. I could not explain misconceptions contained in ideas attributed to me because I was not allowed to speak for myself or even to be myself. This time, the jury spoke in a way more personal, more overtly hostile and more public than I had known before. This experience was much worse than my transformation from black woman to gentleman as a law student. Yet that law student experience proved an important reference point. The academy had prepared me well for the feeling of being cast outside the mainstream, even as I was welcomed within it.

11   Unlike many male colleagues whose breeding, status and gender assured them traditional presumptions of respectability both inside the academy and beyond, I never became my resume. Instead, as the assistant attorney general for civil rights-designate, I was defined entirely by my opponents and those in the media who took control over my image. Like the female gentleman of Business Units I, I had fallen down a rabbit hole, only this time it was in Washington.

12   In this "wonderland," the distortions were so great, even my own mother could not recognize me in the images the media produced. Things got curiouser and curiouser. I was like Alice, her size changing every 10 minutes, facing the Caterpillar, who demanded to know just who she was:

13   "I-I hardly know, sir, just at present—at least I know who I was when I got up this morning, but I think I must have been changed several times since then.'

14   "What do you mean by that?' said the Caterpillar sternly. 'Explain yourself.'

15   "'I cannot explain myself, I'm afraid, sir,' said Alice, 'because I'm not myself, you see.'"

16   Identified by my ideas—or more precisely by caricatures of them—I came to represent America's worst fears about race. Sentences, words, even phrases separated by paragraphs in my "controversial" law review articles were served up to demonstrate I was outside the mainstream of polite society.

17   I became a cartoon character, Clinton's "quota queen." It didn't matter that I never advocated quotas. It did not matter that I am a professor of law, gainfully employed, with life tenure. Like the welfare queen, quota queen was a racial stereotype and an easy headline looking for a person. And, like Alice, I walked into the looking glass of manipulated images from which my real ideas were never allowed to emerge.

18   Through my law review articles, I had spoken about the problems of a democracy in which people of color have a vote but no voice. I had written about people like Milagros Robledo, a Latino voter in Philadelphia. Following a recent absentee voting scandal, Mr. Robledo lamented that he knows now what his vote means: "It means a lot to politicians. It means nothing to me."

19   As a civil rights lawyer, I challenged electoral systems in which voters were alienated from actively participating in the process of self-government. As a law professor, I promoted alternative, race-neutral remedies to empower all voters and to make elected officials more accountable to all their constituents. I had followed the trails blazed by James Madison, an author of the Constitution, and traversed by Nikolas Bowie, my then 4-year-old son, both of whom taught me about democracy. I sought consensus, positive-sum solutions to the dilemma—identified two centuries before by Madison—of a self-interested majority that fails to rule on behalf of all the people. In those situations where 51 percent of the voters were excluding the other 49 percent on the basis of their race, their gender, or their ideas, I questioned whether 51 percent of the people should enjoy 100 percent of the power.

20   As Madison reminded us, if the majority in a racially mixed society does not

represent the interests of the whole, but instead single-mindedly pursues its own special interests, then majority rule can become majority tyranny. And in playing "Sesame Street" games, Nikolas had provided the insight that children often "take turns." Politics could be different if adults learned how to do the same. Winners would not win everything, and losers would not be permanently excluded. They could take turns.

21   Yet, while I remained silent, those who opposed my nomination had a platform from which to speak, defining the parameters of conversation and debate. Like the gentlemen's portraits featured prominently along the walls of my law school experience, even the self-proclaimed radicals among my conservative critics enjoyed the larger-than-life status of neutral observers.

22   I did not get a hearing, but I did not lose my voice for long. In the many intervening years since law school, I had gained the confidence to question directly speech that silences rather than enlightens. I had been forewarned by those law student memories of larger-than-life gentlemen's portraits dominating the debate.

23   I began to comprehend what W. E. B. Du Bois eloquently described at the dawn of this century as the twoness, the double identity of being black and American. For me, there was a threeness because I was also a woman.

24 Living as an outsider "within the veil," I, like Du Bois, saw myself revealed through the eyes of others. Yet, like Alice through the looking glass, the experience eventually became a gift. As Du Bois would say, it was the gift of second sight.

25   At the twilight of the century, many of us who are not white or male still live "within the veil." We, too, may experience Du Bois' peculiar sensation of measuring one's soul by the tape of others. But, drawing on the multiple consciousness of second-sighted outsiders, we have found within our own voice a source of information and legitimacy.

26   Yes, I didn't get a hearing. Nor as a female gentleman law student did I speak out. But as a result of conferences like the one in Boston Thursday, organized by women of color in the academy, some of us are working to ensure that other voices are heard. And by insisting on our ability to speak out about our ideas, we can spark the debate that we have so often been denied.

27   But when we speak, despite our experience, we need not speak from anger: for we are women with a gift, not a grievance. Real democracy is strengthened by including those who were left out. Our gift then is to turn silence into insight and to make a chorus of many voices contending. As Supreme Court Justice Potter Stewart wrote in 1967, our government reflects "the strongly felt American tradition that the public interest is composed of many diverse interests, [which] . . . in the long run . . . can best be expressed by a medley of component voices."

28   "Gifted with second sight," we can share our stories so the rest of the world gains from our knowledge and experience. Remember, though, that our stories are not monolithic. Nor are they monotone or monologue. They are part

of a dynamic conversation, in which there is a space for everyone to have her say. As Nikki Giovanni writes, the purpose of leadership is to speak until the people gain a voice.

29 And if we persist in telling our own stories in our own voices, eventually we will be heard over the thunderous silence of the gentlemen and their larger-than-life portraits. Like Alice in Wonderland, our stories will become classics in their own right, because we shall speak until all the people gain a voice.

TOPICAL CONSIDERATIONS

1. Returning to Yale to participate in a panel discussion, Guinier speaks of being in a "familiar classroom" that is at the same time "not a safe place" for her (paragraph 4). Explain why she feels uneasy in such a well-known place. How does her treatment as a student there contribute to this feeling of uneasiness?

2. How might Guinier respond to Eugene R. August's claims about the use of prejudicial language that "omits males from certain kinds of considerations" within society ("Real Men Don't: Anti-Male Bias in English")? Cite specific passages from Guinier's essay to support your answer. Who builds the stronger case for his or her ideas about sexist language, Guinier or August? Why?

3. Throughout her career, Guinier was reminded of the "heavy silences [imposed] on women" by "larger-than-life gentlemen" (paragraph 9). Discuss the effect these attempts at silencing had on her view of possibilities for women within American society.

RHETORICAL CONSIDERATIONS

1. What does Guinier mean by referring to herself as a "female gentleman"?

2. Consider the professor's tone (paragraphs 2–3) in addressing Guinier's law class. How do you think he expects to be perceived by his student audience? Do you think he is perceived as he expects to be? Why or why not?

3. Guinier uses historical and literary allusions in her essay. Do you think they provide effective support for her argument? Why or why not?

WRITING ASSIGNMENTS

1. Lani Guinier writes about her experience of feeling "cast outside the mainstream, even as I was welcomed within it" (paragraph 10). Think about or read about another individual or group that has experienced cultural exclusion. Write an editorial such as you might send to a large metropolitan newspaper (e.g., the *New York Times* or the *Chicago Tribune*) expressing your feelings about the chosen group's treatment. Then write an editorial for a small-town weekly newspaper in which you express your feelings. How do the two pieces differ in tone or choice of language?

2. Assume that you have been invited to conduct a two-day seminar on sexist language for university professors such as Guinier's former law teacher. What would you say to them? What sorts of activities would you plan for inclusion in the semi-

nar? What assignments would you make? How would you evaluate the participants' learning?

3. A recent issue of the *African American Review* (Volume 30, Number 2, pp. 197–204) contains an interview with Lani Guinier, conducted by Lise Funderburg. Read Funderburg's interview in light of Guinier's "Life as a Female Gentleman." In a short essay, compare the two, focusing on such aspects as content, tone, and audience. Do you see any changes in Guinier's point of view?

REAL MEN DON'T: ANTI-MALE BIAS IN ENGLISH

Eugene R. August

For years we have heard cries of protest against the way English is prejudicial against women. But what about sexist language against men? What about the way English usage excludes, restricts, even dangerously dehumanizes males? This is not a language issue we've heard much about or even given much thought to. But Professor Eugene R. August has devoted considerable time and effort to studying this reverse sexism. In the following essay, he breaks new ground in an insightful examination of how our language subtly victimizes males as it does females.

August, who teaches English and is Chair of Humanities at the University of Dayton, has become a pioneer in the emerging field of men's studies. He is author of *Men's Studies: A Selected and Annotated Interdisciplinary Bibliography* (1985). This essay has been updated for this edition.

1   Despite numerous studies of sex bias in language during the past three decades, only rarely has anti-male bias been examined. In part, this neglect occurs because many of these studies have been based upon assumptions that, at best, are questionable and, at worst, exhibit their own sex bias. Whether explicitly or implicitly, many of these studies reduce human history to a tale of male oppressors and female victims or rebels. In this view of things, all societies become *patriarchal societies,* a familiar term used to suggest that for centuries males have conspired to exploit and demean females. Accordingly, it is alleged in many of these studies that men control language and that they use it to define women and women's roles as inferior.

2   Despite the popularity of such a view, it has received scant support from leading social scientists, including one of the giants of modern anthropology, Margaret Mead. Anticipating current ideology, Mead in *Male and Female* firmly rejected the notion of a "male conspiracy to keep women in their place," arguing instead that

> the historical trend that listed women among the abused minorities . . . lingers on to obscure the issue and gives apparent point to the contention that this is a man-made world in which women have always been abused and must always fight for their rights.

It takes considerable effort on the part of both men and women to reorient our-selves to thinking—when we think basically—that this is a world not made by men alone, in which women are unwilling and helpless dupes and fools or else powerful schemers hiding their power under their ruffled petticoats, but a world made by mankind for human beings of both sexes. (298, 299–300)

The model described by Mead and other social scientists shows a world in which women and men have lived together throughout history in a symbiotic relationship, often mutually agreeing upon the definition of gender roles and the distribution of various powers and duties.

3   More importantly for the subject of bias in speech and writing, women—as well as men—have shaped language. As Walter J. Ong reminds us,

Women talk and think as much as men do, and with few exceptions we all . . . learn to talk and think in the first instance largely from women, usually and predomi-nantly our mothers. Our first tongue is called our "mother tongue" in English and in many other languages. . . . There are no father tongues. . . . (36)

Feminists such as Dorothy Dinnerstein agree: "There seems no reason to doubt that the baby-tending sex contributed at least equally with the history-making one to the most fundamental of all human inventions: language" (22). The idea that language is "man made," as Dale Spender and others argue, fits ideology better than the evidence.

4   During the past thirty years, anti-male bias in English has been greatly fos-tered by *misandry*, hatred of men, that is the acceptable sexism of the media, the educational world, and the entertainment industry. A related term is *an-drophobia*, an irrational fear and loathing of males. "There has been a verita-ble blitzkrieg on the male gender," note Robert Moore and Douglas Gillette, "what amounts to an outright demonization of men and a slander against mas-culinity" (156). This misandry has given rise to a language of anti-male hatred that excludes, restricts, and denigrates men and masculinity.

5   Much of this misandry is the work of what Christina Hoff Sommers calls *gender feminists* (19–25). Distinguished from *equity feminists*, who seek legal and social equality between the sexes, gender feminists see themselves en-gaged in a crusade against a sex and gender system constructed by powerful males. This system, which they label *patriarchy*, allegedly oppresses females and privileges males. Gender feminism owes much to Marxist theory of class warfare and is often fueled by a lesbian separatist agenda (Spender ch.4). It caricatures males as inherently evil, a class of privileged oppressors who hate and fear women. Among the tools of patriarchy's oppression are fatherhood, the two-parent family, and language. In Adrienne Rich's oft-quoted remark: "*This is the oppressors' language*" (qtd. in Spender 178).

6   Gender feminist misandry, distortions of patriarchy, and views of language have all been challenged, mostly by equity feminists and men's rights advo-cates. Still, gender feminism remains perhaps the most influential ideology of our time. Its impact on nearly all aspects of life, including language, continues to be immense.

7   In modern English, three kinds of anti-male language are evident: first, gender-exclusive usage that omits males from certain kinds of consideration; second, gender-restrictive language that attempts to restrict males to an accepted gender role, some aspects of which may be outmoded, burdensome, or destructive; and third, negative stereotypes of males.

8   Gender feminists insist upon gender-inclusive language and seek to eradicate terms such as *man* and *he* used generically for humans of both sexes. Yet gender feminism fosters its own forms of gender-exclusive usage for political purposes. The Ms. Foundation, for example, resolutely refuses to alter its *Take Our Daughters to Work Day* to *Take Our Children to Work Day,* lest boys be invited. Gender feminist groups lobbied successfully in Congress for a *Violence Against Women Act,* even though American males are almost twice as likely as females to be victims of violent crimes (even when rape is included in the tally) and three times more likely to be victims of murder (Farrell *Myth* 32). A woman who kills her male partner can plead the *Battered Woman's Syndrome;* a man who kills (or even defends himself against) a violent female partner cannot plead the *Battered Man's Syndrome.*

9   In the U.S. media, which is heavily influenced by gender feminism, language routinely excludes males as victims. Male victims are simply not news; women (and children) victims are. If men suffer harm, media language is gender-neutral: "Fifteen miners were killed in a West Virginia mine explosion today." If women are victims, the language becomes gender-specific: "Two women were among the fifteen miners killed in a West Virginia mine explosion today."

10   In academia and the media, there is an almost complete ban on discussing the victims of domestic violence, sexual harassment, and rape in gender-inclusive terms.

11   Every responsible study of domestic violence from the 1970s to the present has reported significant numbers of violent women and battered men (see, e.g., Straus 40–41), but gender feminists steadfastly deny the existence of abusive women and abused men. The slogan for a national campaign against domestic violence reads: "Domestic violence is the one thing that hurts women and their children the most. . . ." Not only does the slogan erase all hint of battered men, but it also proclaims that children belong exclusively to mothers ("women and *their* children"). Similarly, the term *wife and child abuse* conceals the existence of an estimated 282,000 husbands who are battered annually (O'Reilly 23).

12   Although males have already won court cases of sexual harassment against female bosses, *sexual harassment* is still widely defined as "harassment of women by men."

13   The term *rape* is a favorite with misandrists, who insist that rape is a crime committed *only* by males in which *only* females are victims. "Crime knows no gender," writes a reporter: "Yet, there is one crime that only women are prey to: rape" (Mougey). A college brochure defines *rape* as "*the* universal crime against women." Such statements ignore entirely the millions of boys and men who are raped each year, many of them (but by no means all) in so-

called "correctional facilities." The belief that a male cannot be raped by a female is still widespread, despite evidence to the contrary (e.g., Sarrel, Struckman-Johnson).

14   The word *rape* is often used as a brush to tar all males. In *Against Our Will* Susan Brownmiller writes: "From prehistoric times to the present, I believe, rape . . . is nothing more or less than a conscious process of intimidation by which *all men* keep *all women* in a state of fear" (15; italics in original). Making the point explicitly, Marilyn French states, "All men are rapists and that's all they are" (Jennes 33). Given this kind of smear tactic, *rape* is often stretched into a vague "accordion term" or used metaphorically. To provide "evidence" of an epidemic of rape on college campuses, Mary Koss expanded the term *rape* so broadly that 73% of the women whom Koss defined as rape victims did not agree that they had been raped (Sommers 213–14). Used metaphorically, *rape* means anything that one wishes to blame on males alone. Ecofeminist Andreé Collard's *Rape of the Wild: Man's Violence Against Animals and the Earth* suggests that only males do harm to the environment. Such usage trivializes the word *rape* and the suffering of genuine rape victims.

15   Unlike gender-exclusive language, gender-restrictive language is usually applied to males only, often to keep them within the confines of a socially prescribed gender role. When considering gender-restrictive language, one must keep in mind that—as Ruth E. Hartley has pointed out—the masculine gender role is enforced earlier and more harshly than the feminine role is (235). In addition, because the boy is often raised primarily by females in the virtual absence of close adult males, his grasp of what is required of him to be a man is often unsure. Likewise, prescriptions for male behavior are usually given in the negative, leading to the "Real Men Don't" syndrome, a process that further confuses the boy. Such circumstances leave many males extremely vulnerable to language that questions their masculinity.

16   Furthermore, during the past twenty years an increasing number of men and women have been arguing that aspects of our society's masculine gender role are emotionally constrictive, unnecessarily stressful, and potentially lethal. Rejecting "the myth of masculine privilege," psychologist Herb Goldberg reports in *The Hazards of Being Male* that "every critical statistic in the area of longevity [early death], disease, suicide, crime, accidents, childhood emotional disorders, alcoholism, and drug addiction shows a disproportionately higher male rate" (5). But changes in the masculine role are so disturbing to so many people that the male who attempts to break out of familiar gender patterns often finds himself facing hostile opposition which can be readily and powerfully expressed in a formidable array of sex-biased terms.

17   To see how the process works, let us begin early in the male life cycle. A boy quickly learns that, while it is usually acceptable for girls to be *tomboys*, God forbid that he should be a *sissy*. In *Sexual Signatures: On Being a Man or a Woman*, John Money and Patricia Tucker note:

> The current feminine stereotype in our culture is flexible enough to let a girl behave "boyishly" if she wants to without bringing her femininity into question, but

any boy who exhibits "girlish" behavior is promptly suspected of being queer. There isn't even a word corresponding to "tomboy" to describe such a boy. "Sissy" perhaps comes closest, or "artistic" and "sensitive," but unlike "tomboy," such terms are burdened with unfavorable connotations. (72)

Lacking a favorable or even neutral term to describe the boy who is quiet, gentle, and emotional, the English language has long had a rich vocabulary to insult and ridicule such boys—*mama's boy, mollycoddle, milksop, muff, lightweight, twit, softy, cream-puff, pantywaist, weakling, weenie, Miss Nancy,* and so on. The currently popular *wimp* and *wuss* can be used to insult males from childhood right into adulthood.

18   Discussion of words such as *sissy* as insults have been often one-sided: most commentators are content to argue that the female, not the male, is being insulted by such usage. "The implicit sexism" in such terms, writes one commentator, "disparages the woman, not the man" (Sorrels 87). Such arguments are typical of gender feminist special pleading. A boy who has been called a *sissy* knows that *he* has been insulted, not his sister. The object of ridicule in such expressions is not the feminine but the male who cannot differentiate himself from the feminine. Ong argues in *Fighting for Life* that most societies place heavy pressure on males to differentiate themselves from females because the prevailing environment of human society is feminine (70–71). In English-speaking societies, terms such as *sissy* and *weak sister,* which have been used by both females and males, are not insults to females but ridicule of males who have allegedly failed to differentiate themselves from the feminine.

19   Being *all boy* carries penalties, however: for one thing, it means being less lovable. As the nursery rhyme tells children, little girls are made of "sugar and spice and all that's nice," while little boys are made of "frogs and snails and puppy-dogs' tails." Or, as an American version of the rhyme puts it:

> Girls are dandy,
> Made of candy—
> That's what little girls are made of.
> Boys are rotten,
> Made of cotton—
> That's what little boys are made of.
> (Baring-Gould 176)

When not enjoined to *be all boy,* our young lad will be urged to *be a big boy, be a brave soldier,* and (the ultimate appeal) *be a man.* These expressions almost invariably mean that the boy is about to suffer something painful or humiliating. The variant—*take it like a man*—provides the clue. As Paul Theroux defines it, *be a man* means: "Be stupid, be unfeeling, obedient and soldierly, and stop thinking."

20   Following our boy further along the life cycle, we discover that in school he will find himself in a cruel bind: girls his age will be biologically and socially more mature than he is, at least until around age eighteen. Until then, any ineptness in his social role will be castigated by a host of terms that are reserved

almost entirely for males. "For all practical purposes," John Gordon remarks, "the word 'turkey' (or whatever the equivalent is now) can be translated as 'a boy spurned by influential girls'" (141). The equivalents of *turkey* are many: *jerk, nerd, clod, klutz, schmuck, dummy, goon, dork, reject, retard, square, dweeb, jackass, meathead, geek, zero, goofball, drip*, and numerous others, including many obscene terms. A Michigan high school decided to do away with a scheduled "Nerd Day" after a fourteen-year-old male student, who apparently had been so harassed as a nerd by other students, committed suicide ("'Nerd' day"). In this case, the ability of language to devastate the emotionally vulnerable young male is powerfully and pathetically dramatized.

21   As our boy grows, he faces threats and taunts if he does not take risks or endure pain to prove his manhood. *Coward*, for example, is a word applied almost exclusively to males in our society, as are its numerous variants—*chicken, chicken-shit, yellow, yellow-bellied, lily-livered, weak-kneed, spineless, squirrelly, fraidy cat, gutless wonder, weakling, butterfly, jellyfish*, and so on. If our young man walks away from a stupid quarrel or prefers to settle differences more rationally than with a swift jab to the jaw, the English language is richly supplied with these and other expressions to call his masculinity into question.

22   Chief among the other expressions that question masculinity is a lengthy list of homophobic terms such as *queer, pansy, fag, faggot, queen, queeny, pervert, bugger, deviant, fairy, tinkerbell, puss, priss, flamer, feller, sweet, precious, fruit, twinkie, sodomite*, and numerous others, many obscene. For many people, *gay* is an all-purpose word of ridicule and condemnation. Although homosexuals are being insulted by these terms, the target is often the heterosexual male who fails or refuses to live up to someone else's idea of masculinity. In "Homophobia Among Men" Gregory K. Lehne explains, "Homophobia is used as a technique of social control by homosexist individuals to enforce the norms of male sex-role behavior. . . . [H]omosexuality is not the real threat, the real threat is change in the male sex-role" (77).

23   Nowhere is this threat more apparent than in challenges to our society's male-only military obligation. When a young man and a young woman reach the age of eighteen, both may register to vote; only the young man is required by law to register for military service. For the next decade at least, he must stand ready to be called into military service and even into combat duty in wars, "police actions," "peace-keeping missions," and "rescue missions," often initiated by legally dubious means. Should he resist this obligation, he may be called a *draft dodger, deserter, peacenik, traitor, shirker, slacker, malingerer*, and similar terms. Should he declare himself a conscientious objector, he may be labeled a *conchy* or any of the variants of *coward*.

24   In his relationships with women, he will find that the age of equality has not yet arrived. Usually, he will be expected to take the initiative, do the driving, pick up the tab, and in general show a deferential respect for women that is a left-over from the chivalric code. Should he behave in an *ungentlemanly* fashion, a host of words—which are applied almost always to males alone—can be used to tell him so: *louse, rat, creep, sleaze, scum, stain, worm, fink, heel,*

beast, fascist, stinker, animal, savage, bounder, cad, wolf, gigolo, womanizer, Don Juan, pig, rotter, boor, and so on.

25   In sexual matters he will usually be expected to take the initiative and to *perform.* If he does not, he will be labeled *impotent.* While it is sexist to call a woman *frigid,* it is acceptable to call a man *impotent.* Metaphorically, *impotent* can be used to demean any male whose efforts in any area are deemed inadequate. Even if our young man succeeds at his sexual performance, the sex manuals are ready to warn him that if he reaches orgasm before a specified time, he is guilty of *premature ejaculation.*

26   When our young man marries, he will be required by law and social custom to support his wife and children. Should he not succeed as breadwinner or should he relax in his efforts, the language offers numerous terms to revile him: *loser, dead beat, bum, freeloader, leech, parasite, goldbrick, sponge, mooch, scrounger, ne'er-do-well, good for nothing,* and so on. If he does not meet child support payments, he will be labeled a *deadbeat dad*—even if he is disabled, unemployed, or broke. If women in our society hate being regarded as sex objects, men have been regarded as success objects, that is, judged by their ability to provide a standard of living. The title of a recent book—*How to Marry a Winner*—reveals immediately that the intended audience is female (Collier).

27   When he becomes a father, our young man will discover that he is a second-class parent, as the traditional interchangeability of *mother* and *parent* indicates. The law has been particularly obtuse in recognizing fathers as parents, as evidenced by the awarding of child custody to mothers in 90% of divorce cases. In one case a father's petition for custody of his four-year-old son was denied because, as the family court judge said, "Fathers don't make good mothers" (qtd. in Levine 21). The judge apparently never considered whether *fathers* make good *parents.*

28   And so it goes throughout our young man's life: if he deviates from society's gender role norm, he will be penalized and he will hear about it.

29   The final form of anti-male bias to be considered here is negative stereotyping. Sometimes this stereotyping is indirectly embedded in the language, sometimes it resides in misandric assumptions about males that shape responses to seemingly neutral words, and sometimes it is overtly created for political reasons. It is one thing to say that some aspects of the traditional masculine gender role are limiting and hurtful; it is quite another to denounce males in general as evil or to portray them in wholesale fashion as oppressors and exploiters. In *The New Male* Goldberg writes, "Men may very well be the last remaining subgroup in our society that can be blatantly, negatively and vilely stereotyped with little objection or resistance" (103). With the ascendancy of gender feminism, such sexist stereotyping is not only familiar but fashionable.

30   In English, crime and evil are usually attributed to the male. Nearly all the words for law-breakers suggest males rather than females. These words include *murderer, swindler, crook, criminal, burglar, thief, gangster, mobster, hood, hitman, killer, pickpocket, mugger,* and *terrorist.* For whatever reasons,

English usage conveys a subtle suggestion that males are to be regarded as guilty in matters of law-breaking.

31   This hint of male guilt extends to a term like *suspect*. When the suspect is unknown, he or she is usually presumed to be a he. For example, even before a definite suspect had been identified, the perpetrator of a series of Atlanta child murders was popularly known as *The Man*. When a male and female are suspected of a crime, the male is usually presumed the guilty party. In a notorious murder case, when two suspects—Debra Brown and Alton Coleman—were apprehended, police discovered *Brown's* fingerprint in a victim's car and interpreted this as evidence of *Coleman's* guilt. As the Associated Press reported:

> Authorities say for the first time they have evidence linking Alton Coleman with the death of an Indianapolis man. A fingerprint found in the car of Eugene Scott has been identified as that of Debra Brown, Coleman's companion. . . ." ("Police")

Nowhere does the article suggest that Brown's fingerprint found in the victim's car linked Brown with the death: the male suspect was presumed the guilty party, while the female was only a "traveling companion." Even after Brown had been convicted of two murders, the Associated Press was still describing her as "the accused accomplice of convicted killer Alton Coleman" ("Indiana").

32   In some cases, this presumption of male guilt extends to crimes in which males are not the principal offenders. As noted earlier, a term such as *wife and child abuse* ignores battered husbands, but it does more: it suggests that males alone abuse children. In reality most child abuse is committed by mothers (Straus 71). Despite this fact, a study of child abuse bears the title *Sins of the Fathers* (Inglis).

33   Not only crimes but vices of all sorts have been typically attributed to males. As Muriel R. Schulz points out, "The synonyms for inebriate . . . seem to be coded primarily 'male': for example, *boozer, drunkard, tippler, toper, swiller, tosspot, guzzler, barfly, drunk, lush, boozehound, souse, tank, stew, rummy,* and *bum*" (126). Likewise, someone may be *drunk as a lord* but never *drunk as a lady*.

34   Sex bias or sexism itself is widely held to be a male-only fault. When sexism is defined as "contempt for women"—as if there were no such thing as contempt for men—the definition of sexism is itself sexist (Bardwick 34).

35   Part of the reason for this masculinization of evil may be that in the Western world the source of evil has long been depicted in male terms. In the Bible, the Evil One is consistently referred to as *he*, whether the reference is to the serpent in the Garden of Eden, Satan as Adversary in Job, Lucifer and Beelzebub in the gospels, Jesus' tempter in the desert, or the dragon in Revelations. Beelzebub, incidentally, is often translated as *lord of the flies*, a term designating the demon as masculine. So masculine is the word devil that the female prefix is needed, as in *she-devil*, to make a feminine noun of it. The masculinization of evil is so unconsciously accepted that writers often attest to it even while attempting to deny it, as in this passage:

> From the very beginning, the Judeo-Christian tradition has linked women and evil. When second-century theologians struggled to explain the Devil's origins, they surmised that Satan and his various devils had once been angels. (Gerzon 224)

If the Judeo-Christian tradition has linked women and evil so closely, why is the writer using the masculine pronoun *his* to refer to Satan, the source of evil according to that tradition? Critics of sex-bias in religious language seldom notice or mention its masculinization of evil: of those objecting to God the Father as sexist, no one—to my knowledge—has suggested that designating Satan as the Father of Lies is equally sexist. Few theologians talk about Satan and her legions.

36   The tendency to blame nearly everything on men has climaxed in recent times with the popularity of such terms as *patriarchy, patriarchal society,* and *male-dominated society.* More political than descriptive, these terms are rapidly becoming meaningless, used as all-purpose smear words to conjure up images of male oppressors and female victims. They are a linguistic sleight of hand which obscures the point that, as Mead has observed (299–300), societies are largely created by both sexes for both sexes. By using a swift reference to *patriarchal structures* or *patriarchal attitudes,* a writer can absolve females of all blame for society's flaws while fixing the onus solely on males. The give-away of this ploy can be detected when *patriarchy* and its related terms are never used in a positive or neutral context, but are always used to assign blame to males alone.

37   Wholesale denunciations of males as oppressors, exploiters, rapists, Nazis, and slave-drivers have become all too familiar during the past three decades. Too often the academic community, rather than opposing this sexism, has been encouraging it. All too many scholars and teachers have hopped on the male-bashing bandwagon to disseminate what John Gordon calls "the myth of the monstrous male." With increasing frequency, this academically fashionable misandry can also be heard echoing from our students. "A white upper-middle-class straight male should seriously consider another college," declares a midwestern college student in *The New York Times Selective Guide to Colleges.* "You [the white male] are the bane of the world. . . . Ten generations of social ills can and will be strapped upon your shoulders" (qtd. in Fiske 12). It would be comforting to dismiss this student's compound of misinformation, misandry, sexism, racism, and self-righteousness as an extreme example, but similar yahooisms go unchallenged almost everywhere in modern academia.

38   Surely it is time for men and women of good will to confront the misandry that prevails on most campuses. For teachers and writers, the first task is to recognize and condemn forms of anti-male bias in language, whether they are used to exclude males from equal consideration with females, to reinforce restrictive aspects of the masculine gender role, or to stereotype males callously. For whether males are told that fathers don't make good mothers, that real men don't cry, or that all men are rapists, the results are potentially dangerous: like any other group, males can be subtly shaped into what society keeps telling them they are. In *Why Men Are the Way They Are* Warren Farrell puts

the matter succinctly: "The more we make men the enemy, the more they will have to behave like the enemy" (357).

WORKS CITED

Bardwick, Judith. *In Transition: How Feminism, Sexual Liberation, and the Search for Self-Fulfillment Have Altered Our Lives.* New York: Holt, 1979.

Baring-Gould, William S., and Ceil Baring-Gould. *The Annotated Mother Goose: Nursery Rhymes Old and New, Arranged and Explained.* New York: Clarkson N. Potter, 1962.

Brownmiller, Susan. *Against Our Will: Men, Women and Rape.* New York: Simon, 1975.

Collier, Phyllis K. *How to Marry a Winner.* Englewood Cliffs, NJ: Prentice, 1982.

Dinnerstein, Dorothy. *The Mermaid and the Minotaur: Sexual Arrangements and Human Malaise.* New York: Harper, 1976.

Farrell, Warren. *The Myth of Male Power: Why Men Are the Disposable Sex.* New York: Simon, 1993.

———. *Why Men Are the Way They Are: The Male-Female Dynamic.* New York: McGraw-Hill, 1986.

Fiske, Edward B. *The New York Times Selective Guide to Colleges.* New York: New York Times Books, 1982.

Gerzon, Mark. *A Choice of Heroes: The Changing Faces of American Manhood.* Boston: Houghton, 1982.

Goldberg, Herb. *The Hazards of Being Male: Surviving the Myth of Masculine Privilege.* Rev. ed. New York: NAL, 1987.

———. *The New Male: From Self-Destruction to Self-Care.* New York: NAL, 1980.

Gordon, John. *The Myth of the Monstrous Male, and Other Feminist Fables.* New York: Playboy P, 1982.

Hartley, Ruth E. "Sex-Role Pressures and the Socialization of the Male Child." *The Forty-Nine Percent Majority: The Male Sex Role.* Eds. Deborah S. David and Robert Brannon. Reading, MA: Addison-Wesley, 1976. 235–44.

"Indiana jury finds Brown guilty of murder, molesting." *Dayton Daily News* 18 May 1986: 7A.

Inglis, Ruth. *Sins of the Fathers: A Study of the Physical and Emotional Abuse of Children.* New York: St. Martin's, 1978.

Jennes, Gail. "All Men Are Rapists." *People* 20 Feb. 1978: 33–4.

Lehne, Gregory K. "Homophobia Among Men." *The Forty-Nine Percent Majority: The Male Sex Role.* Eds. Deborah S. David and Robert Brannon. Reading, MA: Addison-Wesley, 1976. 66–88.

Levine, James A. *Who Will Raise the Children? New Options for Fathers (and Mothers).* Philadelphia: Lippincott, 1976.

Mead, Margaret. *Male and Female: A Study of the Sexes in a Changing World.* New York: Morrow, 1949, 1967.

Money, John, and Patricia Tucker. *Sexual Signatures: On Being a Man or a Woman.* Boston: Little, 1975.

Moore, Robert, and Douglas Gillette. *King Warrior Magician Lover: Rediscovering the Archetypes of the Mature Masculine.* New York: HarperCollins, 1990.

Mougey, Kate. "Rape: An act of confiscation." *Kettering-Oakwood [OH] Times* 4 Feb. 1981: 1b.

" 'Nerd' day gets a boot after suicide." *Dayton Daily News* 24 Jan. 1986: 38.

Ong, Walter J. *Fighting for Life: Contest, Sexuality, and Consciousness*. Ithaca, NY: Cornell UP, 1981.

O'Reilly, Jane, et al. "Wife-Beating: The Silent Crime." *Time* 5 Sept. 1983: 23–4, 26.

"Police: Print links Coleman, death." *Dayton Daily News* 31 Aug. 1984: 26.

Sarrel, Philip M., and William H. Masters. "Sexual Molestation of Men by Women." *Archives of Sexual Behavior* 11 (1982): 117–31.

Schulz, Muriel R. "Is the English Language Anybody's Enemy?" *Speaking of Words: A Language Reader*. Eds. James MacKillop and Donna Woolfolk Cross. 3rd ed. New York: Holt, 1986. 125–27.

Sommers, Christina Hoff. *Who Stole Feminism? How Women Have Betrayed Women*. New York: Simon, 1994.

Sorrels, Bobbye D. *The Nonsexist Communicator: Solving the Problems of Gender and Awkwardness in Modern English*. Englewood Cliffs, NJ: Prentice, 1983.

Spender, Dale. *Man Made Language*. London: Routledge, 1980.

Straus, Murray A., Richard J. Gelles, and Suzanne K. Steinmetz. *Behind Closed Doors: Violence in the American Family*. Garden City, New York: Doubleday, 1981.

Struckman-Johnson, Cindy. "Forced Sex on Dates: It Happens to Men, Too." *Journal of Sex Research* 24 (1988): 234–41.

Theroux, Paul. "The Male Myth." *New York Times Magazine* 27 Nov. 1983: 116.

TOPICAL CONSIDERATIONS

1. In the opening paragraph August says that the lack of studies of anti-male sex bias in language exhibits, in part, a "form of sex bias" itself. What does he mean by this? Do you agree with him?

2. August says that people should be aware of how English "denigrates and stereotypes males." What are the three kinds of anti-male usage to which he refers? Are these familiar categories to you? Do you agree that they are denigrating to males?

3. How, according to August, is the term *rape* used as "a brush to tar all males" (paragraph 14)? Do you agree? Do you automatically associate the term with male perpetrators? Explain your answer.

4. In paragraph 16 August says that "gender-restrictive language" is "emotionally constrictive" for males. How is that so? Do you agree? What is his point regarding the term "tomboy"?

5. In paragraph 20 August lists examples of terms young people use to label social outcasts. Do you agree that such insults are reserved almost exclusively for males? Do you agree that they can cause emotional damage?

6. How does the language condemn men for being liberated from old chivalric codes with respect to treatment of women?

7. How does male-stereotyping language demonstrate homophobia, according to the author? Do you think this is true regarding female homosexuality? In other words, is the language as condemnatory of lesbians as it is of gay men? What terms have you heard for lesbian? Are these as numerous and as denigrating as are those for gay men?

8. Do you agree that our language subtly conveys the message that "crime and evil are usually attributed to the male"?

9. Do you agree that the term "sexism" is in itself sexist (paragraph 34)?

RHETORICAL CONSIDERATIONS

1. How effective is August's reference to Margaret Mead in paragraph 2? Does the fact that Meads' observation was originally written in 1949 have any bearing on its credibility? Does it seem dated, or timeless?

2. Where does August give his thesis statement?

3. How thorough and convincing are August's use of examples to support his argument throughout the essay? Can you find places where more examples would have helped strengthen his point?

4. How effective is the Farrell quotation at the end of the essay? How well does it summarize a main theme of the essay?

WRITING ASSIGNMENTS

1. What are your feelings about how language has built-in anti-male prejudices? Write a paper in which you explore your reactions to some of the arguments in this essay. Has this essay made you aware of anti-male bias or the extent of it in English? Has it changed your attitudes at all?

2. If you are a male, write a paper in which you discuss the various pressures you've felt to conform to constrictive male models of behavior. If you are a female, write a paper discussing your own preconceptions of male behavior.

3. In the essay, August talks about polling his students on words for law-breakers and finding that most students made male associations with the terms. Try conducting a poll of your own on such terms, then write up the results and your interpretation.

4. Alleen Pace Nilsen ("Sexism in English: A 1990s Update") argues that the English language is strongly biased against women. How might she react to August's arguments? Write a dialogue between Nilsen and August. Try to capture areas in which they would agree or disagree.

Sex Differences

Ronald Macaulay

Contrary to popular belief, men and women do not speak different forms of English. Nor are there innate or genetic differences in the way males and females acquire or use language. So argues Ronald Macaulay, a professor of linguistics and an expert on language acquisition. While social background can generate some differences in the way the sexes speak, it is pure myth and stereotyping that sex differences show up in language patterns. Males do not, for instance, instinctively gravitate to coarse language nor are females preternaturally drawn to the language of nurturing.

Ronald Macaulay is professor of linguistics at Pitzer College. He is the author of *Generally Speaking: How Children Learn Language* (1980), *Locating Dialect in Discourse: The Language of Honest Men and Bonnie Lasses in Ayr* (1991), and, most recently, *The Social Art: Language and Its Uses* (1994), from which this essay is taken.

I think the English women speak awfy nice. The little girls are very feminine just because they've a nice voice. But the same voice in an Englishman—nae really. I think the voice lets the men down but it flatters the girls.
ABERDEEN HOUSEWIFE

1   More nonsense has been produced on the subject of sex differences than on any linguistic topic, with the possible exception of spelling. Perhaps this is appropriate. The relations between the sexes have generally been considered a fit topic for comedy. In his book *Language: Its Nature, Development and Origin*, Otto Jespersen has a chapter entitled "The Woman" in which he manages to include every stereotype about women that was current at the time. It is almost unfair to quote directly but even in the 1920s Jespersen should have known better, particularly since he lived in Denmark where women have traditionally shown an independent spirit. Here are a few examples:

There can be no doubt that women exercise a great and universal influence on linguistic development through their instinctive shrinking from coarse and gross expressions and their preference for refined and (in certain spheres) veiled and indirect expressions.

Men will certainly with great justice object that there is a danger of the language becoming languid and insipid if we are always to content ourselves with women's expressions.

Women move preferably in the central field of language, avoiding everything that is out of the way or bizarre, while men will often either coin new words or expressions or take up old-fashioned ones, if by that means they are enabled, or think they are enabled, to find a more adequate or precise expression for their thoughts. Woman as a rule follows the main road of language, where man is often inclined to turn aside into a narrow footpath or even to strike out a new path for himself. . . .

   Those who want to learn a foreign language will therefore always do well at the first stage to read many ladies' novels, because they will there continually meet with just those everyday words and combinations which the foreigner is above all in need of, what may be termed the indispensable small-change of a language.

Woman is linguistically quicker than man: quicker to learn, quicker to hear, and quicker to answer. A man is slower: he hesitates, he chews the cud to make sure of the taste of words, and thereby comes to discover similarities with and differences from other words, both in sound and in sense, thus preparing himself for the appropriate use of the fittest noun or adjective.

The superior readiness of speech of women is a concomitant of the fact that their vocabulary is smaller and more central than that of men.

2   Such stereotypes are often reinforced by works of fiction. Since little information about prosodic features or paralinguistic features is contained in the normal writing system, novelists frequently try to indicate the tone of voice by descriptive verbs and adjectives to introduce dialogue. An examination of several novels revealed an interesting difference between the expression used to introduce men's or women's speech:

MEN	WOMEN
said firmly	said quietly
said bluntly	asked innocently
said coldly	echoed obediently
said smugly	said loyally
urged	offered humbly
burst forth	whispered
demanded aggressively	asked mildly
said challengingly	agreed placidly
cried furiously	smiled complacently
exclaimed contemptuously	fumbled on
cried portentously	implored
grumbled	pleaded

The surprising part is that the two lists are totally distinct. No doubt the novelists intended to be realistic in describing two very different styles of speech but, in doing so, they also reinforce the stereotypes of men and women.

3   In the past twenty years the question of sex differences in language has been a growth industry as scholars have attempted to claim and to counter claims that there are or are not important differences in the ways in which males and females use language. It would, of course, be surprising if there were not. Both men and women will use the forms of language, registers, and styles appropriate to the activities in which they are engaged. To the extent that these activities differ between males and females, it is to be expected that their language will differ. This much is obvious. There is no need to look for a genetic basis for such differences. It is also obvious that those in a position of power often expect to be treated with deference by those over whom they have power. To the extent that in Western industrialized societies men have more often been in positions of power over women rather than the reverse, it is hardly surprising if women are sometimes found to have used deferential language. There have also been certain violent activities, such as fighting or contact sports, that until recently have been exclusively a male province, and there are forms of language appropriate to them that may have been less common among women.

4   Even in making such banal statements, one must qualify them by reference to "Western industrialized societies" or by limiting them to a single section of the community. For example, it is probably true that in Britain until World War I middle-class women were less likely to swear in public than middle-class men, but working-class women were less inhibited. (G. K. Chesterton reported that in an argument with a fishwife he could not compete in obscenities with her but triumphed in the end by calling her "An adverb! A preposition! A pronoun!")

5   In sociolinguistic studies of complex communities such as Glasgow, New York, and Norwich, it has been shown that women in the lower middle class are likely to be closer in their speech to the women in the class immediately above them than are the men, who are likely to be closer to the men in the class immediately below them. It has been suggested that this is because lower-class speech is associated with toughness and virility and the men in the lower middle class choose to identify with this image rather than with the less "masculine" speech of the upper-class men. It may not be unimportant that in these studies the interviewers were all men.

6   There seems, however, to be a deep-seated desire to find essential differences between the speech of men and women that can either be attributed to some discriminatory kind of socialization or, even better, to genetic disposition. This can be seen in many references to sex differences in language development. Popular belief and scholarly opinion has generally maintained that girls are more advanced in language development than boys at the same age. Jespersen, for example, claimed that girls learned to talk earlier and more quickly than boys, and that the speech of girls is more correct than that of boys.

7   For about fifty years after Jespersen this view was maintained in the scholarly literature on children's development. In 1954 Professor Dorothea McCarthy published an article summarizing what was known about children's language development at that time. Her conclusion about sex differences is:

> One of the most consistent findings to emerge from the mass of data accumulated on language development in American white children seems to be a slight difference in favor of girls in nearly all aspects of language that have been studied.

8   What McCarthy actually found, however, was that the differences were not large enough to be statistically significant. Although psychologists are normally very careful not to make claims about differences that could be the result of chance (that is, are not statistically significant), McCarthy was so convinced that girls were more advanced in their speech that she chose to interpret the evidence the way she did. In a survey of the literature up till 1975, I found that none of the studies provided convincing evidence of consistent sex differences in language development. I concluded that the burden of proof remained with those who wished to claim otherwise. To the best of my knowledge, the situation has not changed since then.

9   What I did find were many examples of preconceived notions of sex differences from the assertion that girls have an innate tendency toward sedentary pursuits to claims that it is easier and more satisfying for the girl baby to imitate the mother's speech than it is for the boy baby to imitate the father's. One example will illustrate the kind of attitude:

> The little girl, showing in her domestic play the over-riding absorption in personal relationships through which she will later fulfill her role of wife, mother and "expressive" leader of the family . . . learns language early in order to communicate. The kind of communication in which she is chiefly interested at this stage concerns the nurturant routines which are the stuff of family life. Sharing and talking about them as she copies and "helps" her mother about the house must enhance the mutual identification of mother and child, which in turn . . . will reinforce imitation of the mother's speech and promote further acquisition of language, at first oriented toward domestic and interpersonal affairs but later adapted to other uses as well. Her intellectual performance is relatively predictable because it is rooted in this early communication, which enables her (environment permitting) to display her inherited potential at an early age.

This is contrasted with the interests of boys:

> Their preoccupation with the working of mechanical things is less interesting to most mothers and fathers are much less available.

As a result the boy's language development is slower:

> His language, less fluent and personal and later to appear than the girl's, develops along more analytic lines and may, in favourable circumstances, provide the groundwork for later intellectual achievement which could not have been foreseen in his first few years.

Girls, of course, are more predictable:

> The girl, meanwhile, is acquiring the intimate knowledge of human reactions which we call feminine intuition. Perhaps because human reactions are less regular than those of inanimate objects, however, she is less likely to develop the strictly logical habits of thought that intelligent boys acquire, and if gifted may well come to prefer the subtler disciplines of the humanities to the intellectual rigour of science.

I am not sure whether the writer considered himself a scientist, but if his writing is an example of intellectual rigor, then give me the subtlety of the humanities any day. What makes his statement all the more incredible is that it comes after describing a longitudinal study of children that showed no important sex differences in language development.

10   One of the problems with attempting to demonstrate differences in language development is that measures of linguistic proficiency, particularly for young children, are extremely crude instruments. Thus it is not surprising that samples of linguistic behaviour will reveal occasional differences between subgroups of the sample. Such sex differences that have shown up on tests are much smaller than those that have been shown to relate to social background. The fact that most studies show no sex differences and that many of the findings of small differences have been contradicted in other studies should be sufficient warning against drawing conclusions about the linguistic superiority of either sex.

11   There are some differences between males and females that do not depend upon unreliable tests of language development. Boys are much more likely to suffer from speech disorders, such as stuttering, than girls. Adult males on average have deeper voices than adult females because the vibrating part of the vocal cords is about a third longer in men. However, there may be social influences on this physiological difference. It has been claimed that in the United States women may speak as if they were smaller than they are (that is, with higher-pitched voices) and men as if they were bigger than they are (that is, with lower-pitched voices). The "Oxford voice" common among Oxford fellows (all male) at one time was remarkably high pitched, and other social groups have adopted characteristic pitch levels that are not totally "natural."

12   It was reported that once during a debate in the French parliament when a delegate pointed out that there were differences between men and women, another delegate shouted out *Vive la difference*! It is not necessary to believe that men and women are the same to be skeptical about claims as to the differences in the way men and women speak. The desire to emphasize the differences seems to be widespread. Jespersen's chapter remains as a warning signal to all who venture into this murky area that one's prejudices may show through. Jesperson obviously believed (and no doubt so did many of his readers) that what he was saying was self-evident. However, he ends the chapter by observing that "great social changes are going on in our times which may eventually modify even the linguistic relations of the two sexes." Eventually,

even scholars following in Jespersen's footsteps may come to see that men and women are simply people and that what they have in common is more important than *la difference*, at least as far as their use of language is concerned.

13   It is, however, disturbing to find in a work published in 1991 the following passage by a distinguished and respected scholar:

> [I]t is clear why, as sociolinguists have often observed, women are more disposed to adopt the legitimate language (or the legitimate pronunciation): since they are both inclined towards docility with regard to the dominant usages both by the sexual division of labour, which makes them specialize in the sphere of consumption, and by the logic of marriage, which is their main if not their only avenue of social advancement and through which they circulate upwards, women are predisposed to accept, from school onwards, the new demands of the market in symbolic goods.

It is a salutary reminder that progress is often an illusion.

TOPICAL CONSIDERATIONS

1. Why does Macaulay refer to much of the work done on sex differences as "nonsense"?

2. Macaulay charges that fiction often reinforces sexual stereotypes, as novelists attempt to introduce men's or women's speech. Are there any problems with the examples he cites? Support your answer.

3. What examples does Macaulay give to indicate how society influences male or female speech patterns?

4. Since Macaulay sees so many flaws in Jespersen's findings, why does he devote such a large portion of his article to discussing and even quoting Jespersen?

5. Does Macaulay feel that a lessening of sexist language indicates that society has made significant progress in the way it views the sexes?

RHETORICAL CONSIDERATIONS

1. Compare and contrast the techniques Macaulay uses to develop his essay with those used by Alleen Pace Nilsen ("Sexism in English: A 1990s Update").

2. Macaulay wrote his essay for a scholarly audience. In your opinion, is the language used in the essay more like that of a class lecture, a textbook, a radio talk, a professional journal, or a conference presentation? Why?

WRITING ASSIGNMENTS

1. Macaulay gives a list of expressions authors use to introduce women's and men's speech, and discusses how such expressions perpetuate sexual stereotypes. Ernest Hemingway made a conscious effort to omit such qualifiers, yet his works have traditionally been viewed as expressions of extreme machismo. Discuss Hemingway's "Hills Like White Elephants" as either bias-free or bias-ridden, based on its use of stereotypical language.

2. Keep a journal of the expressions writers you encounter use to introduce male and female characters' speech. What conclusions can you draw?

3. Watch a television program with a story line (a situation comedy, a drama, a full-length movie, etc.). Write a brief critique of the program, based on its presentation of linguistic sex differences.

4. Discuss Nathan Cobb's "Gender Wars in Cyberspace" as one of the following: a rebuttal to Otto Jespersen, as quoted by Macaulay, or a rebuttal to Macaulay. Support your position with quotes from or specific references to both essays.

"I'LL EXPLAIN IT TO YOU": LECTURING AND LISTENING

Deborah Tannen

It is easy to assume that because English belongs to those who use it, men and women speak the same language. That may not be the case. There is strong evidence that male and female conversational patterns differ significantly. In fact, using fascinating examples from her own studies, sociolinguist Deborah Tannen shows that men and women use language in essentially different ways based on gender and cultural conditioning. From early childhood, girls use speech to seek confirmation and reinforce intimacy, whereas boys use it to protect their independence and negotiate group status. Carrying these styles into adulthood, men end up lecturing while women nod warmly and are bored. Is there hope for the sexes? Yes, says the author: by understanding each other's gender style, and by learning to use it on occasion to find a common language.

Deborah Tannen is professor of linguistics at Georgetown University and author of the widely acclaimed *That's Not What I Meant!* (1986). The article here comes from her most recent and bestselling book, *You Just Don't Understand: Women and Men in Conversation* (1990).

1

At a reception following the publication of one of my books, I noticed a publicist listening attentively to the producer of a popular radio show. He was telling her how the studio had come to be built where it was, and why he would have preferred another site. What caught my attention was the length of time he was speaking while she was listening. He was delivering a monologue that could only be called a lecture, giving her detailed information about the radio reception at the two sites, the architecture of the station, and so on. I later asked the publicist if she had been interested in the information the producer had given her. "Oh, yes," she answered. But then she thought a moment and said, "Well, maybe he did go on a bit." The next day she told me, "I was thinking about what you asked. I couldn't have cared less about what he was saying. It's just that I'm so used to listening to men go on about things I don't

443

care about, I didn't even realize how bored I was until you made me think about it."

2   I was chatting with a man I had just met at a party. In our conversation, it emerged that he had been posted in Greece with the RAF during 1944 and 1945. Since I had lived in Greece for several years, I asked him about his experiences: What had Greece been like then? How had the Greek villagers treated the British soldiers? What had it been *like* to be a British soldier in wartime Greece? I also offered information about how Greece had changed, what it is like now. He did not pick up on my remarks about contemporary Greece, and his replies to my questions quickly changed from accounts of his own experiences, which I found riveting, to facts about Greek history, which interested me in principle but in the actual telling left me profoundly bored. The more impersonal his talk became, the more I felt oppressed by it, pinned involuntarily in the listener position.

3   At a showing of Judy Chicago's jointly created art work *The Dinner Party*, I was struck by a couple standing in front of one of the displays: The man was earnestly explaining to the woman the meaning of symbols in the tapestry before them, pointing as he spoke. I might not have noticed this unremarkable scene, except that *The Dinner Party* was radically feminist in conception, intended to reflect women's experiences and sensibilities.

4   While taking a walk in my neighborhood on an early summer evening at twilight, I stopped to chat with a neighbor who was walking his dogs. As we stood, I noticed that the large expanse of yard in front of which we were standing was aglitter with the intermittent flickering of fireflies. I called attention to the sight, remarking on how magical it looked. "It's like the Fourth of July," I said. He agreed, and then told me he had read that the lights of fireflies are mating signals. He then explained to me details of how these signals work—for example, groups of fireflies fly at different elevations and could be seen to cluster in different parts of the yard.

5   In all these examples, the men had information to impart and they were imparting it. On the surface, there is nothing surprising or strange about that. What is strange is that there are so many situations in which men have factual information requiring lengthy explanations to impart to women, and so few in which women have comparable information to impart to men.

6   The changing times have altered many aspects of relations between women and men. Now it is unlikely, at least in many circles, for a man to say, "I am better than you because I am a man and you are a woman." But women who do not find men making such statements are nonetheless often frustrated in their dealings with them. One situation that frustrates many women is a conversation that has mysteriously turned into a lecture, with the man delivering the lecture to the woman, who has become an appreciative audience.

7   Once again, the alignment in which women and men find themselves arrayed is asymmetrical. The lecturer is framed as superior in status and expertise, cast in the role of teacher, and the listener is cast in the role of student. If

women and men took turns giving and receiving lectures, there would be nothing disturbing about it. What is disturbing is the imbalance. Women and men fall into this unequal pattern so often because of the differences in their interactional habits. Since women seek to build rapport, they are inclined to play down their expertise rather than display it. Since men value the position of center stage and the feeling of knowing more, they seek opportunities to gather and disseminate factual information.

8   If men often seem to hold forth because they have the expertise, women are often frustrated and surprised to find that when they have the expertise, they don't necessarily get the floor.

FIRST ME, THEN ME

9   I was at a dinner with faculty members from other departments in my university. To my right was a woman. As the dinner began, we introduced ourselves. After we told each other what departments we were in and what subjects we taught, she asked what my research was about. We talked about my research for a little while. Then I asked her about her research and she told me about it. Finally, we discussed the ways that our research overlapped. Later, as tends to happen at dinners, we branched out to others at the table. I asked a man across the table from me what department he was in and what he did. During the next half hour, I learned a lot about his job, his research, and his background. Shortly before the dinner ended there was a lull, and he asked me what I did. When I said I was a linguist, he became excited and told me about a research project he had conducted that was related to neurolinguistics. He was still telling me about his research when we all got up to leave the table.

10   This man and woman were my colleagues in academia. What happens when I talk to people at parties and social events, not fellow researchers? My experience is that if I mention the kind of work I do to women, they usually ask me about it. When I tell them about conversational style or gender differences, they offer their own experiences to support the patterns I describe. This is very pleasant for me. It puts me at center stage without my having to grab the spotlight myself, and I frequently gather anecdotes I can use in the future. But when I announce my line of work to men, many give me a lecture on language—for example, about how people, especially teenagers, misuse language nowadays. Others challenge me, for example questioning me about my research methods. Many others change the subject to something they know more about.

11   Of course not all men respond in this way, but over the years I have encountered many men, and very few women, who do. It is not that speaking in this way is *the* male way of dong things, but that it *a* male way. There are women who adopt such styles, but they are perceived as speaking like men.

IF YOU'VE GOT IT, FLAUNT IT—OR HIDE IT

12 I have been observing this constellation in interaction for more than a dozen years. I did not, however, have any understanding of *why* this happens until fairly recently, when I developed the framework of status and connection. An experimental study that was pivotal in my thinking shows that expertise does not ensure women a place at center stage in conversation with men.

13   Psychologist H. M. Leet-Pellegrini set out to discover whether gender or expertise determined who would behave in what she terms a "dominant" way—for example, by taking more, interrupting, and controlling the topic. She set up pairs of women, pairs of men, and mixed pairs, and asked them to discuss the effects of television violence on children. In some cases, she made one of the partners an expert by providing relevant factual information and time to read and assimilate it before the videotaped discussion. One might expect that the conversationalist who was the expert would talk more, interrupt more, and spend less time supporting the conversational partner who knew less about the subject. But it wasn't so simple. On the average, those who had expertise did talk more, but men experts talked more than women experts.

14   Expertise also had a different effect on women and men with regard to supportive behavior. Leet-Pellegrini expected that the one who did not have expertise would spend more time offering agreement and support to the one who did. This turned out to be true—*except* in cases where a woman was the expert and her nonexpert partner was a man. In this situation, the women experts showed support—saying things like "Yeah" and "That's right"—far *more* than the nonexpert men they were talking to. Observers often rated the male nonexpert as more dominant than the female expert. In other words, the women in this experiment not only didn't wield their expertise as power, but tried to play it down and make up for it through extra assenting behavior. They acted as if their expertise were something to hide.

15   And perhaps it was. When the word *expert* was spoken in these experimental conversations, in all cases but one it was the man in the conversation who used it, saying something like "So, you're the expert." Evidence of the woman's superior knowledge sparked resentment, not respect.

16   Furthermore, when an expert man talked to an uninformed woman, he took a controlling role in structuring the conversation in the beginning *and* the end. But when an expert man talked to an uninformed man, he dominated in the beginning but not always in the end. In other words, having expertise was enough to keep a man in the controlling position if he was talking to a woman, but not if he was talking to a man. Apparently, when a woman surmised that the man she was talking to had more information on the subject than she did, she simply accepted the reactive role. But another man, despite a lack of information, might still give the expert a run for his money and possibly gain the upper hand by the end.

17   Reading these results, I suddenly understood what happens to me when I talk to women and men about language. I am assuming that my acknowledged expertise will mean I am automatically accorded authority in the conversation, and with women that is generally the case. But when I talk to men, revealing that I have acknowledged expertise in this area often invites challenges. I *might* maintain my position if I defend myself successfully against the challenges, but if I don't, I may lose ground.

18   One interpretation of the Leet-Pellegrini study is that women are getting a bum deal. They don't get credit when it's due. And in a way, this is true. But the reason is not—as it seems to many women—that men are bums who seek to deny women authority. The Leet-Pellegrini study shows that many men are inclined to jockey for status, and challenge the authority of others, when they are talking to men too. If this is so, then challenging a woman's authority as they would challenge a man's could be a sign of respect and equal treatment, rather than lack of respect and discrimination. In cases where this is so, the inequality of the treatment results not simply from the men's behavior alone but from the differences in men's and women's styles: Most women lack experience in defending themselves against challenges, which they misinterpret as personal attacks on their credibility.

19   Even when talking to men who are happy to see them in positions of status, women may have a hard time getting their due because of differences in men's and women's interactional goals. Just as boys in high school are not inclined to repeat information about popular girls because it doesn't get them what they want, women in conversation are not inclined to display their knowledge because it doesn't get them what they are after. Leet-Pellegrini suggests that the men in this study were playing a game of "Have I won?" while the women were playing a game of "Have I been sufficiently helpful?" I am inclined to put this another way: The game women play is "Do you like me?" whereas the men play "Do you respect me?" If men, in seeking respect, are less liked by women, this is an unsought side effect, as is the effect that women, in seeking to be liked, may lose respect. When a woman has a conversation with a man, her efforts to emphasize their similarities and avoid showing off can easily be interpreted, through the lens of status, as relegating her to a one-down position, making her appear either incompetent or insecure.

A SUBTLE DEFERENCE

20 Elizabeth Aries, a professor of psychology at Amherst College, set out to show that highly intelligent, highly educated young women are no longer submissive in conversations with male peers. And indeed she found that the college women did talk more than the college men in small groups she set up. But what they said was different. The men tended to set the agenda by offering

opinions, suggestions, and information. The women tended to react, offering agreement or disagreement. Furthermore, she found that body language was as different as ever: The men sat with their legs stretched out, while the women gathered themselves in. Noting that research has found that speakers using the open-bodied position are more likely to persuade their listeners, Aries points out that talking more may not ensure that women will be heard.

21   In another study, Aries found that men in all-male discussion groups spent a lot of time at the beginning finding out "who was best informed about movies, books, current events, politics, and travel" as a means of "sizing up the competition" and negotiating "where they stood in relation to each other." This glimpse of how men talk when there are no women present gives an inkling of why displaying knowledge and expertise is something that men find more worth doing than women. What the women in Aries's study spent time doing was "gaining a closeness through more intimate self-revelation."

22   It is crucial to bear in mind that both the women and the men in these studies were establishing camaraderie, and both were concerned with their relationships to each other. But different aspects of their relationships were of primary concern: their place in a hierarchical order for the men, and their place in a network of intimate connections for the women. The consequence of these disparate concerns was very different ways of speaking.

23   Thomas Fox is an English professor who was intrigued by the differences between women and men in his freshman writing classes. What he observed corresponds almost precisely to the experimental findings of Aries and Leet-Pellegrini. Fox's method of teaching writing included having all the students read their essays to each other in class and talk to each other in small groups. He also had them write papers reflecting on the essays and the discussion groups. He alone, as the teacher, read these analytical papers.

24   To exemplify the two styles he found typical of women and men, Fox chose a woman, Ms. M, and a man, Mr. H. In her speaking as well as her writing, Ms. M held back what she knew, appearing uninformed and uninterested, be-cause she feared offending her classmates. Mr. H spoke and wrote with au-thority and apparent confidence because he was eager to persuade his peers. She did not worry about persuading; he did not worry about offending.

25   In his analytical paper, the young man described his own behavior in the mixed-gender group discussions as if he were describing the young men in Leet-Pellegrini's and Aries's studies:

> In my sub-group I am the leader. I begin every discussion by stating my opinions as facts. The other two members of the sub-group tend to sit back and agree with me. . . . I need people to agree with me.

Fox comments that Mr. H reveals "a sense of self, one that acts to change him-self and other people, that seems entirely distinct from Ms. M's sense of self, dependent on and related to others."

26   Calling Ms. M's sense of self "dependent" suggests a negative view of her way of being in the world—and, I think, a view more typical of men. This view

reflects the assumption that the alternative to independence is dependence. If this is indeed a male view, it may explain why so many men are cautious about becoming intimately involved with others: It makes sense to avoid humiliating dependence by insisting on independence. But there is another alternative: *inter*dependence.

27   The main difference between these alternatives is symmetry. Dependence is an asymmetrical involvement: One person needs the other, but not vice versa, so the needy person is one-down. Interdependence is symmetrical: Both parties rely on each other, so neither is one-up or one-down. Moreover, Mr. H's sense of self is also dependent on others. He requires others to listen, agree, and allow him to take the lead by stating his opinions first.

28   Looked at this way, the woman and man in this group are both dependent on each other. Their differing goals are complementary, although neither understands the reasons for the other's behavior. This would be a fine arrangement, except that their differing goals result in alignments that enhance his authority and undercut hers.

DIFFERENT INTERPRETATIONS—AND MISINTERPRETATIONS

29 Fox also describes differences in the way male and female students in his classes interpreted a story they read. These differences also reflect assumptions about the interdependence or independence of individuals. Fox's students wrote their responses to "The Birthmark" by Nathaniel Hawthorne. In the story, a woman's husband becomes obsessed with a birthmark on her face. Suffering from her husband's revulsion at the sight of her, the wife becomes obsessed with it too and, in a reversal of her initial impulse, agrees to undergo a treatment he has devised to remove the birthmark—a treatment that succeeds in removing the mark, but kills her in the process.

30   Ms. M interpreted the wife's complicity as a natural response to the demand of a loved one: The woman went along with her husband's lethal schemes to remove the birthmark because she wanted to please and be appealing to him. Mr. H blamed the woman's insecurity and vanity for her fate, and he blamed her for voluntarily submitting to her husband's authority. Fox points out that he saw her as individually responsible for her actions, just as he saw himself as individually responsible for his own actions. To him, the issue was independence: The weak wife voluntarily took a submissive role. To Ms. M, the issue was interdependence: The woman was inextricably bound up with her husband, so her behavior could not be separated from his.

31   Fox observes that Mr. H saw the writing of the woman in the class as spontaneous—they wrote whatever popped into their heads. Nothing could be farther from Ms. M's experience as she described it: When she knew her peers would see her writing, she censored everything that popped into her head. In contrast, when she was writing something that only her professor would read, she expressed firm and articulate opinions.

32   There is a striking but paradoxical complementarity to Ms. M's and Mr. H's styles, when they are taken together. He needs someone to listen and agree. She listens and agrees. But in another sense, their dovetailing purposes are at cross-purposes. He misinterprets her agreement, intended in a spirit of connection, as a reflection of status and power: He thinks she is "indecisive" and "insecure." Her reasons for refraining from behaving as he does—firmly stating opinions as facts—have nothing to do with her attitudes toward her knowledge, as he thinks they do, but rather result from her attitudes toward her relationships with her peers.

33   These experimental studies by Leet-Pellegrini and Aries, and the observations by Fox, all indicate that, typically, men are more comfortable than women in giving information and opinions and speaking in an authoritative way to a group, whereas women are more comfortable than men in supporting others. . . .

LISTENER AS UNDERLING

34   Clearly men are not always talking and women are not always listening. I have asked men whether they ever find themselves in the position of listening to another man giving them a lecture, and how they feel about it. They tell me that this does happen. They may find themselves talking to someone who presses information on them so insistently that they give in and listen. They say they don't mind too much, however, if the information is interesting. They can store it away for future use, like remembering a joke to tell others later. Factual information is of less interest to women because it is of less use to them. They are unlikely to try to pass on the gift of information, more likely to give the gift of being a good audience.

35   Men as well as women sometimes find themselves on the receiving end of a lecture they would as soon not hear. But men tell me that it is most likely to happen if the other man is in a position of higher status. They know they have to listen to lectures from fathers and bosses.

36   That men can find themselves in the position of unwilling listener is attested to by a short opinion piece in which A. R. Gurney bemoans being frequently "cornered by some self-styled expert who harangues me with his considered opinion on an interminable agenda of topics." He claims that this tendency bespeaks a peculiarly American inability to "converse"—that is, engage in a balanced give-and-take—and cites as support the French observer of American customs Alexis de Tocqueville, who wrote, "An American . . . speaks to you as if he was addressing a meeting." Gurney credits his own appreciation of conversing to his father, who "was a master at eliciting and responding enthusiastically to the views of others, though this resiliency didn't always extend to his children. Indeed, now I think about it, he spoke to us many times as if he were addressing a meeting."

37   It is not surprising that Gurney's father lectured his children. The act of

giving information by definition frames one in a position of higher status, while the act of listening frames one as lower. Children instinctively sense this—as do most men. But when women listen to men, they are not thinking in terms of status. Unfortunately, their attempts to reinforce connections and establish rapport, when interpreted through the lens of status, can be misinterpreted as casting them in a subordinate position—and are likely to be taken that way by many men.

WHAT'S SO FUNNY?

38 The economy of exchanging jokes for laughter is a parallel one. In her study of college students' discussion groups, Aries found that the students in all-male groups spent a lot of time telling about times they had played jokes on others, and laughing about it. She refers to a study in which Barbara Miller Newman found that high school boys who were not "quick and clever" became the targets of jokes. Practical joking—playing a joke *on* someone—is clearly a matter of being one-up: in the know and in control. It is less obvious, but no less true, that *telling* jokes can also be a way of negotiating status.

39   Many women (certainly not all) laugh at jokes but do not later remember them. Since they are not driven to seek and hold center stage in a group, they do not need a store of jokes to whip out for this purpose. A woman I will call Bernice prided herself on her sense of humor. At a cocktail party, she met a man to whom she was drawn because he seemed at first to share this trait. He made many funny remarks, which she spontaneously laughed at. But when she made funny remarks, he seemed not to hear. What had happened to his sense of humor? Though telling jokes and laughing at them are both reflections of a sense of humor, they are very different social activities. Making others laugh gives you a fleeting power over them: As linguist Wallace Chafe points out, at the moment of laughter, a person is temporarily disabled. The man Bernice met was comfortable only when he was making her laugh, not the other way around. When Bernice laughed at his jokes, she thought she was engaging in a symmetrical activity. But he was engaging in an asymmetrical one.

40   A man told me that sometime around tenth grade he realized that he preferred the company of women to the company of men. He found that his female friends were more supportive and less competitive, whereas his male friends seemed to spend all their time joking. Considering joking an asymmetrical activity makes it clearer why it would fit in with a style he perceived as competitive. . . .

MUTUAL ACCUSATIONS

41 Considering these dynamics, it is not surprising that many women complain that their partners don't listen to them. But men make the same

complaint about women, although less frequently. The accusation "You're not listening" often really means "You don't understand what I said in the way that I meant it," or "I'm not getting the response I wanted." Being listened to can become a metaphor for being understood and being valued.

42   In my earlier work I emphasized that women may get the impression men aren't listening to them even when the men really are. This happens because men have different habitual ways of showing they're listening. As anthropologists Maltz and Borker explain, women are more inclined to ask questions. They also give more listening responses—little words like *mhm*, *uh-uh*, and *yeah*—sprinkled throughout someone else's talk, providing a running feedback loop. And they respond more positively and enthusiastically, for example by agreeing and laughing.

43   All this behavior is doing the work of listening. It also creates rapport-talk by emphasizing connection and encouraging more talk. The corresponding strategies of men—giving fewer listener responses, making statements rather than asking questions, and challenging rather than agreeing—can be understood as moves in a contest by incipient speakers rather than audience members.

44   Not only do women give more listening signals, according to Maltz and Borker, but the signals they give have different meanings for men and women, consistent with the speaker/audience alignment. Women use "yeah" to mean "I'm with you, I follow," whereas men tend to say "yeah" only when they agree. The opportunity for misunderstanding is clear. When a man is confronted with a woman who has been saying "yeah," "yeah," "yeah," and then turns out not to agree, he may conclude that she has been insincere, or that she was agreeing without really listening. When a woman is confronted with a man who does *not* say "yeah"—or much of anything else—she may conclude that *he* hasn't been listening. The men's style is more literally focused on the message level of talk, while the women's is focused on the relationship or metamessage level.

45   To a man who expects a listener to be quietly attentive, a woman giving a stream of feedback and support will seem to be talking too much for a listener. To a woman who expects a listener to be active and enthusiastic in showing interest, attention, and support, a man who listens silently will seem not to be listening at all, but rather to have checked out of the conversation, taken his listening marbles, and gone mentally home.

46   Because of these patterns, women may get the impression that men aren't listening when they really are. But I have come to understand, more recently, that it is also true that men listen to women less frequently than women listen to men, because the act of listening has different meanings for them. Some men really *don't* want to listen at length because they feel it frames them as subordinate. Many women do want to listen, but they expect it to be reciprocal—I listen to you now; you listen to me later. They become frustrated when they do the listening now and now and now, and later never comes.

MUTUAL DISSATISFACTION

47 If women are dissatisfied with always being in the listening position, the dissatisfaction may be mutual. That a woman feels she has been assigned the role of silently listening audience does not mean that a man feels he has consigned her to that role—or that he necessarily likes the rigid alignment either.

48   During the time I was working on this book, I found myself at a book party filled with people I hardly knew. I struck up a conversation with a charming young man who turned out to be a painter. I asked him about his work and, in response to his answer, asked whether there has been a return in contemporary art to figurative painting. In response to my question, he told me a lot about the history of art   so much that when he finished and said, "That was a long answer to your question," I had long since forgotten that I had asked a question, let alone what it was. I had not minded this monologue—I had been interested in it—but I realized, with something of a jolt, that I had just experienced the dynamic that I had been writing about.

49   I decided to risk offending my congenial new acquaintance in order to learn something about his point of view. This was, after all, a book party, so I might rely on his indulgence if I broke the rules of decorum in the interest of writing a book. I asked whether he often found himself talking at length while someone else listened. He thought for a moment and said yes, he did, because he liked to explore ideas in detail. I asked if it happened equally with women and men. He thought again and said, "No, I have more trouble with men." I asked what he meant by trouble. He said, "Men interrupt. *They* want to explain to *me*."

50   Finally, having found this young man disarmingly willing to talk about the conversation we had just had and his own style, I asked which he preferred: that a woman listen silently and supportively, or that she offer opinions and ideas of her own. He said he thought he liked it better if she volunteered information, making the interchange more interesting.

51   When men begin to lecture other men, the listeners are experienced at trying to sidetrack the lecture, or match it, or derail it. In this system, making authoritative pronouncements may be a way to begin an *exchange* of information. But women are not used to responding in that way. They see little choice but to listen attentively and wait for their turn to be allotted to them rather than seizing it for themselves. If this is the case, the man may be as bored and frustrated as the woman when his attempt to begin an exchange of information ends in his giving a lecture. From his point of view, she is passively soaking up information, so she must not have any to speak of. One of the reasons men's talk to women frequently turns into lecturing is *because* women listen attentively and do not interrupt with challenges, sidetracks, or matching information.

52   In the conversations with male and female colleagues that I recounted at the outset of this chapter, this difference may have been crucial. When I talked to the woman, we each told about our own research in response to the other's encouragement. When I talked to the man, I encouraged him to talk about his work, and he obliged, but he did not encourage me to talk about

mine. This may mean that he did not want to hear about it—but it also may not. In her study of college students' discussion groups, Aries found that women who did a lot of talking began to feel uncomfortable; they backed off and frequently drew out quieter members of the group. This is perfectly in keeping with women's desire to keep things balanced, so everyone is on an equal footing. Women expect their conversational partners to encourage them to hold forth. Men who do not typically encourage quieter members to speak up, assume that anyone who has something to say will volunteer it. The men may be equally disappointed in a conversational partner who turns out to have nothing to say.

53   Similarly, men can be as bored by women's topics as women can be by men's. While I was wishing the former RAFer would tell me about his personal experiences in Greece, he was probably wondering why I was boring him with mine and marveling at my ignorance of the history of a country I had lived in. Perhaps he would have considered our conversation a success if I had challenged or topped his interpretation of Greek history rather than listening dumbly to it. When men, upon hearing the kind of work I do, challenge me about my research method, they are inviting me to give them information and show them my expertise—something I don't like to do outside of the classroom or lecture hall, but something they themselves would likely be pleased to be provoked to do.

54   The publicist who listened attentively to information about a radio station explained to me that she wanted to be nice to the manager, to smooth the way for placing her clients on his station. But men who want to ingratiate themselves with women are more likely to try to charm them by offering interesting information than by listening attentively to whatever information the women have to impart. I recall a luncheon preceding a talk I delivered to a college alumni association. My gracious host kept me entertained before my speech by regaling me with information about computers, which I politely showed interest in, while inwardly screaming from boredom and a sense of being weighed down by irrelevant information that I knew I would never remember. Yet I am sure he thought he was being interesting, and it is likely that at least some male guests would have thought that he was. I do not wish to imply that all women hosts have entertained me in the perfect way. I recall a speaking engagement before which I was taken to lunch by a group of women. They were so attentive to my expertise that they plied me with questions, prompting me to exhaust myself by giving my lecture over lunch before the formal lecture began. In comparison to this, perhaps the man who lectured to me about computers was trying to give me a rest.

55   The imbalance by which men often find themselves in the role of lecturer, and women often find themselves in the role of audience, is not the creation of only one member of an interaction. It is not something that men do to women. Neither is it something that women culpably "allow" or "ask for." The imbalance is created by the difference between women's and men's habitual styles. . . .

HOPE FOR THE FUTURE

56 What is the hope for the future? Must we play out our assigned parts to the closing act? Although we tend to fall back on habitual ways of talking, repeating old refrains and familiar lines, habits can be broken. Women and men both can gain by understanding the other gender's style, and by learning to use it on occasion.

57   Women who find themselves unwillingly cast as the listener should practice propelling themselves out of that position rather than waiting patiently for the lecture to end. Perhaps they need to give up the belief that they must wait for the floor to be handed to them. If they have something to say on a subject, they might push themselves to volunteer it. If they are bored with a subject, they can exercise some influence on the conversation and change the topic to something they would rather discuss.

58   If women are relieved to learn that they don't always have to listen, there may be some relief for men in learning that they don't always have to have interesting information on the tips of their tongues if they want to impress a woman or entertain her. A journalist once interviewed me for an article about how to strike up conversations. She told me that another expert she had interviewed, a man, had suggested that one should come up with an interesting piece of information. I found this amusing, as it seemed to typify a man's idea of a good conversationalist, but not a woman's. How much easier men might find the task of conversation if they realized that all they have to do is listen. As a woman who wrote a letter to the editor of *Psychology Today* put it, "When I find a guy who asks, 'How was your day?' and really wants to know, I'm in heaven."

TOPICAL CONSIDERATIONS

1. Explain the lecturer-listener relationship described in the opening paragraphs. How does Tannen explain this asymmetry in conversations? Is this pattern typical of male-female conversations in your experience—or of your family, or your peers?

2. According to the Leet-Pellegrini study, what typical role patterns evolve in conversations when women are the experts and men the nonexperts? And when men are the experts and women the nonexperts? How does Tannen explain these different reactions?

3. Does Tannen's explanation of why men challenge women's authority (paragraphs 18 and 19) seem valid to you? Or, do you think Tannen lets men off the hook too easily?

4. Imagine you are Ms. M's academic adviser. Would you advise her to maintain or to change her current style of speaking and writing in class. What about Mr. H.?

5. According to the author, what happens when men find themselves being lectured to in a conversation with another man? Does Tannen's analysis ring true to your experience? Explain.

6. Why are men more interested in telling jokes, according to this article? in playing practical jokes? Do you agree? Do you know of exceptions?

7. Tannen closes her piece with advice on how to break old conversational habits: how to talk more if you are a listener, and how to listen more if you are a talker. Do you find her advice helpful? oversimplified? too optimistic? too unrealistic? What obstacles might someone encounter in trying to break old conversational habits?

8. Try a class experiment. Break into two groups: one half to hold discussion about a topic of interest, the other half to observe the discussion group to see if the lecturer-listener patterns emerge or not. What do you make of the results?

RHETORICAL CONSIDERATIONS

1. This piece opens with four anecdotes. What point are they making? Are the anecdotes effective? Are there subtle differences, or did you find them repetitious?

2. Do you find the section headings—such as "First Me, Then Me"—helpful in structuring the essay? Did you find them informative, funny, silly, or distracting? What might these headings suggest about the audience Tannen's writing is intended for?

3. One reviewer credited Deborah Tannen with a "sharp eye for telling episode and revealing detail" and praised her for "entertaining vignettes of everyday life." Do you agree? Which examples did you find most compelling or interesting?

4. Try to evaluate Tannen's use of outside authorities. How well do they support her views about how men and women converse? Do these references fit into her discussion smoothly, or are they intrusive? Does she ever disagree with the authorities she cites or interpret information differently?

5. Do you think that the pattern of summary and analysis is overused in this essay?

6. What standard techniques does Tannen use in the conclusion of her essay?

WRITING ASSIGNMENTS

1. Many people interested in gender and language complain that communication breaks down because men attempt to dominate women. Tannen maintains that the effect of dominance "is not always the result of an intention to dominate" but the result of the fact that males and females have distinctly different conversational styles based on gender and cultural conditioning. She says that as early as childhood boys learn to use speech as a way of getting attention and establishing status in a group; girls, to the contrary, use speech to confirm and maintain intimacy. Write a paper in which you support or refute Tannen's stand.

2. If you tend to be a lecturer, take the role of listener in a conversation. Or, if you tend to be a listener, experiment by being more outgoing and forceful in a conversation. Did you have difficulties adapting to a different role? Were you able to maintain it? Did you like the change, or were you uncomfortable? Did anybody notice the difference in you? Write a paper describing your experience. As Tannen does, use the summary-and-analysis approach in your discussion.

3. Write a paper explaining why you do or do not think the conversational patterns described by Tannen apply to you. Use some specific details to support your position.

4. Using audio- or videotape, record a conversation in which a group of men and women talk. Write a paper analyzing the conversational patterns you see emerging. Does what you see support or contradict Tannen's views?

5. Write a dialogue between a man and woman in which you employ some of the gender patterns Tannen discusses here. Then write the same dialogue so that the two speakers are conversationally equal.

6. Do you think that understanding gender patterns in conversation will change the way women and men talk to each other? Do you think such changes are necessary and healthy? Or do you think that some men and women have a need for the established patterns, sexist or not? Write a paper in which you explore these questions.

GENDER WARS IN CYBERSPACE

Nathan Cobb

It might be said that cyberspace is the final frontier of gender language. While people are mastering the etiquette of nonsexist communication in the classroom, office, and nightclub, a curious phenomenon has reared its head on the Internet. In the piece below, Nathan Cobb describes how the computer exchanges between men and women demonstrate a curious throwback patterning—insult and aggression on the part of males and conciliation and passivity on the part of females.

Nathan Cobb is a writer for the *Boston Globe* where this essay first appeared in March 1995.

1 Consider the Yo alert.

2 Yo?

3 Yo. Subscribers to ECHO, a small online service based in Manhattan, use the greeting to signify important messages when they converse with one another via computer. But there's a difference between those who Yo and those who don't.

4 "What we've found is that men tend to 'Yo' a lot more than women," says Stacy Horn, who founded ECHO five years ago. "And they're much more likely to 'Yo' strangers. Women simply do not 'Yo' strangers."

5 But wait. Isn't cyberspace supposed to be gender neutral, a place where women can feel empowered and men don't think they have to flex their pecs? Aren't the Internet and its commercial online siblings supposed to go beyond the notion that men are men and women are women, washing away this pre-Infobahn concept with rivers of sexless text? "Online, we don't know gender," declares Newton-based Internet analyst Daniel Dern.

6 A growing group of people beg to differ, no small number of them women. They contend not only that there are differences between male and female 'Netiquette—a k a online manners—but also differences in the overall conversational styles used by men and women who "talk" via computer.

7 "Although a lot of people have said that online communication removes cues about gender, age and background, that's not true," argues Laurel Sutton, a graduate student in linguistics at the University of California at Berkeley who has studied online discourse. "Everything that you communicate about

yourself when you communicate face-to-face comes through when you communicate online. So men talk like men and women talk like women."

STILL A MAN'S CYBERWORLD

8   Statistically speaking, of course, it's still a man's cyberworld out there. Among the major online services, CompuServe estimates that 83 percent of its users are men, while America Online pegs its male subscribers at 84 percent. Prodigy claims a 60/40 male/female ratio among users. Nobody keeps figures for the Internet, the vast web of interconnected computer networks that is owned and operated by no single entity, but estimates of female participation run from 10 to 35 percent. Indeed, most of the computer culture is male-dominated.

9   If you don't think there's a shortage of women online, listen to the dialogue one recent evening inside an America Online "chat" room known as the Romance Connection, a kind of digital dating bar. When the lone female in the room departed—assuming she really was female—after entertaining the other 22 members of the group with a bit of softcore titillation, there was an awkward pause.

10   "What are we going to do now?" one participant typed.

11   "Who wants to play the naked female?" someone else asked.

12   "Not me," came a response.

13   "Not me, either," came another.

14   "Well, if you can't fake it, don't volunteer," offered the first.

15   Most women who go online quickly learn that many such chat areas and certain Internet newsgroups—places where cyberians sharing similar interests can post messages to one another—are spots where testosterone-based lifeforms are likely to harass them, inquiring about their measurements and sexual preferences as if they've phoned 1–900-DIALSEX. "It's like walking into a real bad '70s disco," says David Fox, the author of *Love Bytes*, a new book about online dating. "The fact that people can be anonymous is a major factor. I mean, a 13-year-old can go around living his teen-age fantasy of picking up women."

16   As a result, many women adopt gender-neutral screen names, switching from, say, Victoria to VBG, Nova to Vanity, and Marcia to Just Being Me. "This way, if some jerk comes along you can always say you're a man," says Pleiades (real name: Phyllis), whose screen handle refers to the seven daughters of Atlas and Pleione but is apparently enough to throw off pursuers.

17   Almost everyone also agrees that men "flame" more than women, meaning they are more prone to firing off missives that are intended as insults or provocations. "For men, the ideal of the Internet is that it should be this exchange of conflicting views," says Susan Herring, a linguistics professor at University of Texas at Arlington who has written extensively about women's participation on computer networks. "But women are made uncomfortable by flaming. As

little girls, women are taught to be nice. Little boys are taught to disagree and argue and even fight."

18   A recent case in point: Entering a debate on smoking in restaurants that was taking place in a newsgroup on the Internet, a user named Colleen politely staked out her position as a question. "Why is it necessary to smoke inside a restaurant?" she asked. In reply, a user named Peter instantly flamed. He announced he would not pay good money to eat if he couldn't smoke at the same time. "You people are complete and utter morons!" he declared.

19   "Women come online more to build relationships, to talk about issues," contends Susan William DeFife, the founding partner of Women's Leadership Connection (WLC), an online service linked to Prodigy.

20   Ask Rebecca Shnur of Easton, Pa., a WLC subscriber who effusively likens being online to an "all-night college bull session. It's been a long time since I've talked like this with women," she says.

21   Men tend to be less concerned about making permanent connections. "I think they're much more willing to just jump online and see where it goes," says DeFife. "And, of course, to flame."

22   If men tend to be flamers, do women tend to be flamees? Nancy Tamosaitis, a New York author who has written several books about the online world, thinks they do. "By expressing any kind of strong opinion, women tend to get flamed a lot more than men do," Tamosaitis says. "There's a real strong culture on Internet. Men feel they own it. It's like an old boys' club. They don't want women or newcomers, especially female newcomers."

23   When Tamosaitis is flamed, she points out, it's almost always by a man. "I can count the flames I've gotten from women on the fingers of both hands," she says. "And men seem to bring it to a personal level. A woman will say, 'You're out of place!' A man will say, 'You're ugly!'"

CONFRONTATION WORKS

24   But women who seek a softer, gentler information superhighway may find themselves sending messages into the wind. Says Sherry Terkle, an MIT professor and an authoritative voice on the subject of sociology and technology: "If you send out an online message that's inclusive, that includes many points of view, or that's conciliatory, you may get no response. And women are more likely to make that kind of communication, whereupon no message comes back.

25   "But if you make a controversial statement, maybe even an exaggeration, you're more likely to get responses. So the medium pushes people toward a controversial style. It rewards the quick jab. It encourages a kind of confrontational style, which men are more comfortable with."

26   When Susan Herring, the University of Texas linguist, disseminated an electronic questionnaire on 'Netiquette, even some of the online comments

about the survey itself took on male/female styles. "I hope this doesn't sound terribly rude, but a survey is one of the last things I want to see in my mailbox," apologized one woman in declining to respond. A man who also had better things to do was less polite. "What bothers me most," he declared, "are abuses of networking such as yours: unsolicited, lengthy and intrusive postings designed to further others' research by wasting my time."

WOMEN ARE "LURKERS"

27 Meanwhile, research shows that women who go online tend to send fewer messages per capita than do men and that their messages are shorter. There is also a widespread belief that more women than men are "lurkers": people who go online to read other people's messages rather than to participate. "It's the same way you find many women sitting in physics class and acting like wallpaper," Terkle says, referring to male-dominated science classrooms. "They're just not comfortable because it matters who's in charge. It matters who seems to be in a position of power."

28 Even Michael O'Brien, an Internet magazine columnist who is by no means convinced that there is much difference between the online sexes ("I see fewer differences on the Internet than in everyday life"), allows that women "usually come across as the voice of reason. You almost never see a female counterflame. Men flame back and forth. Usually women just shut up and go away."

29 In her best-selling 1990 book, *You Just Don't Understand: Women & Men in Conversation,* Georgetown University linguist Deborah Tannen described men as being comfortable with the language of confrontation and women comfortable with consensus. A self-described e-mail junkie, Tannen sees much of the same behavior online. "Actually, I would say that the differences that typify men's and women's [offline] style actually get *exaggerated* online," she says. "I subscribe to very few universals, but one I believe in is that men are more likely to use opposition, or fighting, or even warlike images. Women are not as likely to do that. They're more likely to take things as a nasty attack."

30 Tannen recalls coming across a seemingly angry online message written by a male graduate student that concluded with the command to "get your hands off my Cyberspace!"

31 "I had an exchange with the fellow about it because it struck me, a woman, as being fairly hostile and inappropriate," Tannen recalls. "But then I realized I was overinterpreting the hostility of what to him was a fairly ritualized and almost playful statement."

32 Nancy Rhine wishes more women would adopt this type of playfulness in cyberspace. Slightly more than a year ago, Rhine founded Women's Wire, a minuscule online service (1,500 subscribers compared to, say, America Online's 2 million), because she believed women weren't participating enough

online. Between 90 and 95 percent of her subscribers are female, she says, and she contends that Women's Wire is a more polite and less flame-filled place than other services.

33   "But there's a pro and con to that," she concedes "On the one hand, this is a very comfortable environment. On the other hand, I sometimes wish there were more characters posting things that were thought-provoking and stimulating.

34   "Women are conditioned to be nice, to be the caretakers, and that's the way it feels online here," Rhine says. "But I'd like to see us take more risks. I'd like to see women be more outrageous online."

TOPICAL CONSIDERATIONS

1. What is the "Yo alert"? Is it used equally by men and women?
2. What are the bases of what Cobb discusses as the differences between men and women online?
3. Do linguists who study the Internet believe there are differences in the ways women and men express themselves online? Explain your answer.

RHETORICAL CONSIDERATIONS

1. Who is Cobb's audience? Explain your answer.
2. What tone does Cobb adopt in setting the context for his article? Cite details to support your answer.

WRITING ASSIGNMENTS

1. If possible, sign on to the Internet. Discuss evidence you find to support or refute Cobb's assertions about women's and men's language online and its implications for gender power relations.
2. You are a member of a campus group pledged to defend gender equity. Write a letter to the editor of your campus newspaper, defending or rejecting the use of tuition-based funds to expand campus access to the Internet. Base your argument on the findings relayed in Cobb's article.
3. With a group of four to five classroom colleagues, compose your own 'Netiquette. Come to consensus on the number and content of the rules themselves, as well as the penalties you will invoke for their violation. Present your new rules to the class.

HILLS LIKE WHITE ELEPHANTS

Ernest Hemingway

Ernest Hemingway (1898–1961), short story writer and novelist, began his career as a reporter. During World War I he was an ambulance driver in France and Italy where he was wounded in combat. He returned to civilian life and moved to Paris as a newspaper correspondent. While living there he established himself as a writer of fiction, turning out several books including what might be his best novel, *The Sun Also Rises* (1926), which won him instant acclaim. He went on to write several others including *A Farewell to Arms* (1929), *For Whom the Bell Tolls* (1940), and *The Old Man and The Sea* (1952), which was awarded a Pulitzer Prize. In 1954 he received the Nobel Prize for literature. Hemingway often wrote about the experience of danger—war, hunting, bullfighting—experiences that were the test of courage, honor, and what he called "grace under pressure." His writing is distinguished by hard-edged realism, irony, stylistic simplicity, and powerful dialogue. In 1961, fearing his own physical and mental demise, Hemingway killed himself with a shotgun.

Hemingway's stories almost always express courage in the face of death and disillusionment. And at the center of many of his stories are the struggles of men and women in love. The story below is no different. The reader doesn't know the names or histories of the two people, or even if they are married. The reader knows only what is overheard— that there is a struggle in progress. Remarkably, the story is nearly all dialogue, and very realistic dialogue at that. It brilliantly captures the language styles and patterns of male manipulation and female acquiescence.

1 The hills across the valley of the Ebro were long and white. On this side there was no shade and no trees and the station was between two lines of rails in the sun. Close against the side of the station there was the warm shadow of the building and a curtain, made of strings of bamboo beads, hung across the open door into the bar, to keep out flies. The American and the girl with him sat at a

table in the shade, outside the building. It was very hot and the express from Barcelona would come in forty minutes. It stopped at this junction for two minutes and went on to Madrid.

2   "What should we drink?" the girl asked. She had taken off her hat and put it on the table.

3   "It's pretty hot," the man said.

4   "Let's drink beer."

5   "Dos cervezas," the man said into the curtain.

6   "Big ones?" a woman asked from the doorway.

7   "Yes. Two big ones."

8   The woman brought two glasses of beer and two felt pads. She put the felt pads and the beer glasses on the table and looked at the man and the girl. The girl was looking off to the line of hills. They were white in the sun and the country was brown and dry.

9   "They look like white elephants," she said.

10   "I've never seen one," the man drank his beer.

11   "No, you wouldn't have."

12   "I might have," the man said. "Just because you say I wouldn't have doesn't prove anything."

13   The girl looked at the bead curtain. "They've painted something on it," she said. "What does it say?"

14   "Anis del Toro. It's a drink."

15   "Could we try it?"

16   The man called "Listen" through the curtain. The woman came out from the bar.

17   "Four reales."

18   "We want two Anis del Toro."

19   "With water?"

20   "Do you want it with water?"

21   "I don't know," the girl said. "Is it good with water?"

22   "It's all right."

23   "You want them with water?" asked the woman.

24   "Yes, with water."

25   "It tastes like licorice," the girl said and put the glass down.

26   "That's the way with everything."

27   "Yes," said the girl. "Everything tastes of licorice. Especially all the things you've waited so long for, like absinthe."

28   "Oh, cut it out."

29   "You started it," the girl said. "I was being amused, I was having a fine time."

30   "Well, let's try and have a fine time."

31   "All right. I was trying. I said the mountains looked like white elephants. Wasn't that bright?"

32   "That was bright."

33   "I wanted to try this new drink. That's all we do, isn't it—look at things and try new drinks?"

34   "I guess so."

35   The girl looked across at the hills.

36   "They're lovely hills," she said. "They don't really look like white elephants. I just meant the coloring of their skin through the trees."

37   "Should we have another drink?"

38   "All right."

39   The warm wind blew the bead curtain against the table.

40   "The beer's nice and cool," the man said.

41   "It's lovely," the girl said.

42   "It's really an awfully simple operation, Jig," the man said. "It's not really an operation at all."

43   The girl looked at the ground the table legs rested on.

44   "I know you wouldn't mind it, Jig. It's really not anything. It's just to let the air in."

45   The girl did not say anything.

46   "I'll go with you and I'll stay with you all the time. They just let the air in and then it's all perfectly natural."

47   "Then what will we do afterward?"

48   "We'll be fine afterward. Just like we were before."

49   "What makes you think so?"

50   "That's the only thing that bothers us. It's the only thing that's made us unhappy."

51   The girl looked at the bead curtain, put her hand out and took hold of two of the strings of beads.

52   "And you think then we'll be all right and be happy."

53   "I know we will. You don't have to be afraid. I've known lots of people that have done it."

54   "So have I," said the girl. "And afterward they were all so happy."

55   "Well," the man said, "if you don't want to you don't have to. I wouldn't have you do it if you didn't want to. But I know it's perfectly simple."

56   "And you really want to?"

57   "I think it's the best thing to do. But I don't want you to do it if you don't really want to."

58   "And if I do it you'll be happy and things will be like they were and you'll love me?"

59   "I love you now. You know I love you."

60   "I know. But if I do it, then it will be nice again if I say things are like white elephants, and you'll like it?"

61   "I'll love it. I love it now but I just can't think about it. You know how I get when I worry."

62   "If I do it you won't ever worry?"

63   "I won't worry about that because it's perfectly simple."

64   "Then I'll do it. Because I don't care about me."

65   "What do you mean?"

66   "I don't care about me."

67   "Well, I care about you."

68   "Oh, yes. But I don't care about me. And I'll do it and then everything will be fine."

69   "I don't want you to do it if you feel that way."

70   The girl stood up and walked to the end of the station. Across, on the other side, were fields of grain and trees along the banks of the Ebro. Far away, beyond the river, were mountains. The shadow of a cloud moved across the field of grain and she saw the river through the trees.

71   "And we could have all this," she said. "And we could have everything and every day we make it more impossible."

72   "What did you say?"

73   "I said we could have everything."

74   "We can have everything."

75   "No, we can't."

76   "We can have the whole world."

77   "No, we can't."

78   "We can go everywhere."

79   "No, we can't. It isn't ours any more."

80   "It's ours."

81   "No, it isn't. And once they take it away, you never get it back."

82   "But they haven't taken it away."

83   "We'll wait and see."

84   "Come on back in the shade," he said. "You mustn't feel that way."

85   "I don't feel any way," the girl said. "I just know things."

86   "I don't want you to do anything that you don't want to do——"

87   "Nor that isn't good for me," she said. "I know. Could we have another beer?"

88   "All right. But you've got to realize——"

89   "I realize," the girl said. "Can't we maybe stop talking?"

90   They sat down at the table and the girl looked across at the hills on the dry side of the valley and the man looked at her and at the table.

91   "You've got to realize," he said, "that I don't want you to do it if you don't want to. I'm perfectly willing to go through with it if it means anything to you."

92   "Doesn't it mean anything to you? We could get along."

93   "Of course it does. But I don't want anybody but you. I don't want any one else. And I know it's perfectly simple."

94   "Yes, you know it's perfectly simple."

95   "It's all right for you to say that, but I do know it."

96   "Would you do something for me now?"

97   "I'd do anything for you."

98   "Would you please please please please please please please stop talking?"

99   He did not say anything but looked at the bags against the wall of the station. There were labels on them from all the hotels where they had spent nights.

100   "But I don't want you to," he said, "I don't care anything about it."

101   "I'll scream," the girl said.

102   The woman came out through the curtains with two glasses of beer and put them down on the damp felt pads. "The train comes in five minutes," she said.

103   "What did she say?" asked the girl.

104   "That the train comes in five minutes."

105   The girl smiled brightly at the woman, to thank her.

106   "I'd better take the bags over to the other side of the station," the man said. She smiled at him.

107   "All right. Then come back and we'll finish the beer."

108   He picked up the two heavy bags and carried them around the station to the other tracks. He looked up the tracks but could not see the train. Coming back, he walked through the barroom, where people waiting for the train were drinking. He drank an Anis at the bar and looked at the people.They were all waiting reasonably for the train. He went out through the bead curtain. She was sitting at the table and smiled at him. "Do you feel better?" he asked.

109   "I feel fine," she said. "There's nothing wrong with me. I feel fine."

QUESTIONS FOR DISCUSSION

1. What key issue does this story revolve around? How does the title relate to the issue? Specifically, how does it relate to the woman's dilemma? What does the likening of the hills to white elephants say about the woman's view of things? What does the man's reaction (paragraph 10) say about him?

2. Give a brief character sketch of the man in this story. How does his dialogue and action reveal his personality?

3. Give a brief character sketch of the woman. How does her dialogue and action reveal her personality? What, for example, do you make of the fact that her opening statement in the story is a question? What does that say about her? What about the other questions she asks?

4. Are the characters sympathetic? Explain. Are they compatible with each other? How would you describe the nature of their relationship?

5. In her essay "I'll Explain It to You": Lecturing and Listening," Deborah Tannen describes an asymmetry in the way men and women communicate—that is, men dominate and women submit. Do you see any such patterning in this story? If so, explain.

6. The two characters here are defined with a minimum of information. That is, we know nothing of their history, education, social class, means of support, or aspirations. We don't even know their names, or if they are married. Is this lack of biographical data necessary for the success of the story? Explain.

7. Find examples where the woman's language is metaphorical or ironic. Can you find similar examples of the man's language?

8. Although Hemingway gives minimal description to the setting, how does it help mirror the condition of the two characters? Consider, for instance, the contrast between the brown and dry country on one side of the station and the "fields of grain and trees along the banks of the Ebro." Also, consider the fact that they are sitting at a station between tracks leading in opposite directions.

9. Explain the meaning of the man's statement in paragraph 44: "I know you wouldn't mind it, Jig. It's really not anything. It's just to let the air in."

10. What is suggested by the fact that the male is identified as "the American" and "the man" and the female as "the girl"? How do these distinctions slant the reader's regard for the two characters?

11. In paragraphs 91–95 the pronoun *it* is used nine times. Try to determine what "it" refers to in each instance.

12. Most of this story is dialogue, and the narrative is almost entirely objective, like stage directions in a play. Almost, except for a single adverb in the narrative. What is it? Explain its meaning. What does it reveal about the characters?

13. What do you make of the final statement, "I feel fine"?

WRITING ASSIGNMENTS

1. Nearly all friction turns on the conflict between what the main character wants and the obstacles to the fulfillment of those wants. What does Jig want? What does the man want? Write a paper describing how they are at odds.

2. Write a dialogue between the two characters that might take place a year later.

3. Write a paper describing how the conversation in this story fits the male/female conversation patterns as described by Deborah Tannen.

IS GOD PURPLE?

Mary Jo Meadow

What follows is a complaint against the way religious language and traditions have discriminated against women. Cleverly framed as a parable, ''Is God Purple?'' examines how the male-dominated language of Scriptures helped create and perpetuate the inequality of the sexes. As illustrated, so ancient and deeply seated are these biases that we fail to see the central irony: that although all people are created equal in the eyes of God, such is not the case in the eyes of men—and, unfortunately, many women. Mary Jo Meadow is Professor of Psychology and Director of Religious Studies at Mankato State University.

1 In the beginning, when God made heaven and earth, God made two different kinds of people: purple people and green people. The holy books say that God made people in the image of God: purple and green. Purple people and green people were really quite a bit alike. The biggest difference was that green people gave birth to new people, and purple people had larger and stronger bodies. Outside that, they were about the same.

2   As time passed, things did not go as well for the green people as they did for the purple. The greens were often incapacitated with bearing children, and the purples used their greater strength to take control of running things. Some said that purple people were jealous because green people could make new people. Others thought it was just because people tend to use whatever power they have to get themselves into positions of advantage. In a rough world where physical strength easily won out, the purples could dominate the greens.

3   As different languages developed, a peculiar thing happened in many of them. People had come to think of purple people as being really human, and to consider green people something lesser made to serve purple people. So the languages used the word purple-person to stand for all people. They made a different word—one that meant partner or counterpart of purple people—that was used when only green people were referred to. When both green

people and purple people were referred to together, they used the word purple-person. These words reflected how they felt about the value of purple persons and green persons. When these languages talked about God, most of them called God purple. After all, God was the most important person there was, so it certainly would not do to think of God as anything but purple. Calling God purple then made purpleness even more valuable than greenness. Language affects people that way.

4   Religions usually had control of education and most of them refused to let green people study; they thought that learning was for purple people only, and that green people should take care of the routine things of life so purples would be free to study and run the world. Later, people would say that since green people hadn't made significant contributions to culture, that proved they were really not as capable as purple people. Living this way—with purple people running the world and making all the decisions, and with the word purple-person standing for a fully human person and for God—green people and purple people became even more fully convinced that purples were more valuable. That's how people are: they tend to think that people who have the most power and whose names are used the most are more important than other people. It got so bad that green people were often treated pretty much like animals. They could be beaten and abused by purple people without anyone seeing anything wrong with it. Some people didn't even think that green people were really persons.

5   One day God decided to become a person, too. God came as a purple person—probably that was the only way God could get people to listen. Nobody thought that green people could say anything worth listening to. The purple-person-God was very kind to green people; some purples thought this God was too kind to greens and was making a mistake. But the purple-person-God treated greens as though they were real people, listening to them, and wanting to be with them—to actually share ideas with them, not just using them to wait on all the purple people. Since the purple people who kept the records of God's visit seldom counted green people at meetings, we don't know all the things that green people did with the purple-person-God.

6   After God left, a new religion grew up around God's visit. The purple people and green people both shared important positions in this religion at first, but pretty soon the purple people wound up in charge. An important purple person named Paul said some good things—once Paul even said that in God there isn't any distinction between purple persons and green persons. But Paul also passed on a lot of the old ideas that green people were really less than purple people—that they should be kept in their lowly place.

7   In this new religion, God was always referred to as a purple person. All of God was called purple—not only God as a human purple person, but also God high away in heaven. Some important purple persons—like Jerome, Augustine, and Chrysostom—seemed rather afraid of green persons and said that, because they are weaker and more sinful than purple persons, they drag down

purple people. They thought a very few green people could rise above their greenness and be worthy of friendship with purple people—but, of course, most could not. Sine these purple persons said they spoke with God's authority, everybody believed them.

8   Finally purple people got so confused about green people that they discussed it at a big meeting called a church council. They wanted to decide whether green people really have souls like purple people. Of course, only purple people were allowed to go to such an important meeting. The purple people had a hard time of it, and the vote was very close, but they did say that green people have souls. Since the purple people said so, that made it so. Still, they didn't treat green people any differently. The purple people kept on making all the decisions—even those about green people—and the green people kept on serving the purple people so the purples could fully develop themselves. Nobody—not even the greens—thought that maybe a green person should also be developed. Later, people would say that since green people had not developed themselves over the centuries, it proved that they didn't really have a knack for it.

9   Over all this time, people weren't really aware that they thought less of green people than purple people, but you could tell by the way different people were treated. Most purple people had green people attached to them who left their own lives, gave up their names and identity, and followed the purples around taking care of their daily needs to leave the purple people free for important things. Nobody did this for green people. When green people did get jobs of their own, they were paid less than purples—only about half as much—as though their work was not as valuable. Many jobs and types of education were forbidden them, and they hardly ever got into decision-making places—especially important ones like church and government. Over time, some people realized this could not be how God wanted things. They explained that when the word purple person means human being, it makes people consider purpleness superior. And when God is called a purple person, it makes purple persons seem more godly than green persons. People aren't aware they think this way—and would even deny it—but they keep on treating green people as less valuable—so they must think they are.

10   Many purple persons don't want to hear this. When people have an advantage, they don't want to lose it and they twist things all around to keep them the same. People are like that. Some purple people said that green people are envious. Others said that they don't understand that God wants different, but equal, roles for purple and green people. One purple person said it might be okay to think of God as both green and purple, except that it wouldn't reflect God's purple majesty properly. A purple religious leader named Paul very carefully explained that since God was a purple person when visiting the earth, it meant that green people couldn't reflect the image of God as well as purple people, and so they couldn't be leaders in the religion. This shows how the way we use language affects our thinking about greenness and purpleness.

11   Some green people are also against change. They believe so strongly in their own inferiority that they wouldn't feel safe with a God who wasn't purple—and they don't want green persons as religious leaders because they think green people need the guidance and leadership of purple people. That's another thing about people: when they take their own inferiority for granted, they are terrified at the thought of becoming more responsible for themselves and their lives. In another place where people were either black or white, and the whites were considered better than blacks, many black people had wanted to stay under the care of whites until they finally realized how much it was destroying them.

12   Many people who are against change have said silly things. They said the family would fall apart, or immorality would be widespread, or disease would run wild, or even that green people would take over the world if anything changed. Scholars who study how people and families work try to explain how silly these fears are, but when people are scared they usually can't listen to reason. Others say that change would mess up religion, or would disturb people's faith, or make it impossible to worship. Some even said that, since God is a purple person, it is right to keep green people down. Others said that green people have the better part; they can practice humility and service—very important religious ideals.

13   The green people who are trying to make things better see the issue as one of justice, as it had been for black people. These green people say—as black people had said—that separate but equal never really works. They point out that the religion lets only purple people make big decisions and allows only purple people to do the very holy things. They also note that if green people really had the better part, at least some of the purples would have been fighting for it—and no purple people seem to want to do the things green people are expected to do. It would be sad if people's faith were hurt because we stopped calling God purple or started treating green people equally, but the religion says that people are supposed to be treated justly. The way green people have been treated is really a big sin of the religion—just as it was a big sin not to try to get justice for black people when white people enslaved them and considered them inferior.

14   And that's where things stand today. We are left with questions to think about. Are green people really meant to serve purple people? Are green people not able to reflect God's image as well as purple people? Are purple people the "real" people with green people only a tag-on idea? Are green people really treated fairly in their religion when purple people make all the decisions and do the holy things, when the religion uses the word purple person to refer to all people, and when it calls God a purple person? Finally, is God really purple?

TOPICAL CONSIDERATIONS

1. According to Meadow's parable of creation, what initially distinguished green and purple people? How, in time, did things begin to go wrong for the greens? Do you

think the author's explanation of the roots of male domination and female subjugation even though it is simplified, rings true?

2. How did languages work for purple people and against green people? What English words reflect this observation? Can you think of any foreign equivalents? Do you know if the antifemale bias is as evident in other languages as it is in English? Do you know of any languages where it is less evident?

3. In what ways did religions discriminate against greens? Can you think of specific examples of Meadow's claims?

4. According to Meadow, why did God decide to become a purple person instead of a green one? How does Meadow portray the purple-person-God? What does her comment about the record-keeping of the purple-person-God's visit say about religion?

5. In paragraph 9, the author says that eventually "some people realized this could not be how God wanted things." Historically speaking, who might these people be? Would you share their view?

6. How, according to Meadow, did language affect green people in terms of religious leadership? What specifically is the author's complaint? Do you agree that language has had such an effect?

7. Meadow says that "green people are also against change." How does she explain herself? Do you agree with her assessment? Do you know such "green" people who are so convinced of their own inferiority that they don't feel safe with anything but a "purple" God? Who else might not "want green persons as religious leaders"?

8. Does Meadow's portrayal of the evolution and nature of sexism in a parable form make the issues more or less convincing? Did you learn anything? Have your attitudes about language and/or sexism been affected any? Explain your answer.

RHETORICAL CONSIDERATIONS

1. How effective is the title of Meadow's essay? How does it summarize the core issue? Does the author answer the title question? How?

2. Why do you think Meadow chose the colors purple and green to represent the sexes? What do these colors traditionally represent or symbolize? What associations do you make with them?

3. Find some examples of the author's use of irony in the essay.

4. Toward the end of the essay, Meadow makes an analogy between her green and purple people and the blacks and whites of our society. How effective is this comparison? Does it make her message more convincing?

WRITING ASSIGNMENTS

1. Mary Joe Meadow raises a familiar complaint—that most organized religions still refuse to allow women to take leadership roles despite the liberation from male domination of other social institutions. Write a paper in which you explore your

own feelings about women as religious leaders. Do you think women should be given the opportunity to be priests, ministers, and rabbis?

2. In paragraph 3, the author expresses a complaint that Alleen Pace Nilsen also expressed: that languages use words for *male* that stand for all people—in English, for example, *man, men,* and *mankind.* Write an essay in which you attempt to analyze how the frequent generic use of these terms might have subtly prejudiced you (or people you know) against women. Do you think of men as "real people" and women as "only a tag-on"?

3. Write a color parable in which you illustrate just the converse complaint of Meadow—that is, that religion, history and language have forced males to conform to certain damaging roles. (You might first consider reading the August essay, "Real Men Don't: Anti-Male Bias in English.")

4. This article raises the argument that there should be a nonsexist translation of the Scriptures. Write a paper in which you explore your own thoughts on this. Do you think that there should be a nonsexist translation of the Bible? Do you think that a full, nonbiased translation of the Bible along the lines of the Lectionary (presented later in this chapter) would be widely accepted? Why or why not? Explain your reasons.

THE CREATION OF MAN AND WOMAN (GEN. 1:26–2:9, 15–18, 21–25)

Revised Standard Version of the Bible

One of the most surprising challenges to male-dominated traditions is coming from organized religion, where issues of sexism are being confronted, in part, in matters of language. Yet, as Mary Jo Meadow suggests, the challenge to patriarchal language traditions has not really been felt where it would count the most: in the Bible. In 1980 a committee appointed by the National Council of Churches prepared *An Inclusive Language Lectionary,* which contains readings from the Old Testament in language that is bias-free, "inclusive" of males and females equally. By the third installment, a storm of controversy arose—a controversy that had as much to do with language as with the nature of man, woman, and God. What follows are two versions of the story of the creation of man and woman. The first is in the language of the Revised Standard Version of the Bible; the second is in the language of *An Inclusive Language Lectionary.* The writing assignments that follow ask you to express your own opinions of the issues.

1 ²⁶Then God said, "Let us make man in our image, after our likeness; and let them have dominion over the fish of the sea, and over the birds of the air, and over the cattle, and over all the earth, and over every creeping thing that creeps upon the earth." ²⁷So God created man in his own image, in the image of God he created him; male and female he created them. ²⁸And God blessed them, and God said to them, "Be fruitful and multiply, and fill the earth and subdue it; and have dominion over the fish of the sea and over the birds of the air and over every living thing that moves upon the earth." ²⁹And God said, "Behold, I have given you every plant yielding seed which is upon the face of all the earth, and every tree with seed in its fruit; you shall have them for food. ³⁰And to every beast of the earth, and to every bird of the air, and to everything that creeps on the earth, everything that has the breath of life, I have given every green plant for food." And it was so. ³¹And God saw everything

that he had made, and behold, it was very good. And there was evening and there was morning, a sixth day.

2 ²:¹Thus the heavens and the earth were finished, and all the host of them. ²And on the seventh day God finished his work which he had done, and he rested on the seventh day from all his work which he had done. ³So God blessed the seventh day and hallowed it, because on it God rested from all his work which he had done in creation.

3 ⁴These are the generations of the heavens and the earth when they were created.

4 In the day that the LORD God made the earth and the heavens, ⁵when no plant of the field was yet in the earth and no herb of the field had yet sprung up—for the LORD God had not caused it to rain upon the earth, and there was no man to till the ground; ⁶but a mist went up from the earth and watered the whole face of the ground—⁷then the LORD God formed man of dust from the ground, and breathed into his nostrils the breath of life; and man became a living being. ⁸And the LORD God planted a garden in Eden, in the east; and there he put the man whom he had formed. ⁹And out of the ground the LORD God made to grow every tree that is pleasant to the sight and good for food, the tree of life also in the midst of the garden, and the tree of the knowledge of good and evil. . . .

5 ¹⁵The LORD God took the man and put him in the garden of Eden to till it and keep it. ¹⁶And the LORD God commanded the man, saying, "You may freely eat of every tree of the garden; ¹⁷but of the tree of the knowledge of good and evil you shall not eat, for in the day that you eat of it you shall die."

6 ¹⁸Then the LORD God said, "It is not good that the man should be alone; I will make him a helper fit for him." . . . ²¹So the LORD God caused a deep sleep to fall upon the man, and while he slept took one of his ribs and closed up its place with flesh; ²²and the rib which the LORD God had taken from the man he made into a woman and brought her to the man. ²³Then the man said,

"This at last is bone of my bones and flesh of my flesh; she shall be called Woman, because she was taken out of Man."

7 ²⁴Therefore a man leaves his father and his mother and cleaves to his wife, and they become one flesh. ²⁵And the man and his wife were both naked, and were not ashamed.

GOD CREATES HUMANKIND (GEN. 1:26–2:9, 15–18, 21–25)

An Inclusive Language Lectionary

1   ²⁶Then God said, "Let us make humankind in our image, after our likeness; and let them have dominion over the fish of the sea, and over the birds of the air, and over the cattle, and over all the earth, and over every creeping thing that creeps upon the earth." ²⁷So God created humankind in God's own image, in the image of God was the human being created; male and female God created them. ²⁸And God blessed them, and God said to them. "Be fruitful and multiply, and fill the earth and subdue it; and have dominion over the fish of the sea and over the birds of the air and over every living thing that moves upon the earth." ²⁹And God said, "Behold, I have given you every plant yielding seed which is upon the face of all the earth, and every tree with seed in its fruit; you shall have them for food. ³⁰And to every beast of the earth, and to every bird of the air, and to everything that creeps on the earth, everything that has the breath of life, I have given every green plant for food." And it was so. ³¹And God saw everything that was made, and behold, it was very good. And there was evening and there was morning, a sixth day.

2   ²:¹Thus the heavens and the earth were finished, and all the host of them. ²And on the seventh day God finished the work which God had done, and on the seventh day rested from all the work which God had done. ³So God blessed the seventh day and hallowed it, because on it God rested from all the work which God had done in creation.

3   ⁴In the day that God the SOVEREIGN ONE made the earth and the heavens, ⁵when no plant of the field was yet in the earth and no herb of the field had yet sprung up—for the SOVEREIGN ONE had not caused it to rain upon the earth, and there was no one to till the ground; ⁶but a mist went up from the earth and watered the whole face of the ground—⁷then God the SOVEREIGN ONE formed a human creature[1] of dust from the ground, and breathed into the creature's nostrils the breath of life; and the human creature became a living

---

[1]Life begins with the creation of *ha-adam*, in v. 7. This Hebrew word does not refer to a particular person, but to a human creature from the earth. The creation of sexuality of male and female, man and woman—does not occur until vs. 21–24.

being. ⁸And God the SOVEREIGN ONE planted a garden in Eden, in the east; and there God put the human being whom God had formed. ⁹And out of the ground God the SOVEREIGN ONE made to grow every tree that is pleasant to the sight and good for food, the tree of life also in the midst of the garden, and the tree of the knowledge of good and evil. . . .

4   ¹⁵God the SOVEREIGN ONE took and placed the human being in the garden of Eden to till it and keep it. ¹⁶And God the SOVEREIGN ONE commanded the human being, saying, "You may freely eat of every tree of the garden; ¹⁷but of the tree of the knowledge of good and evil you shall not eat, for in the day that you eat of it you shall die."

5   ¹⁸Then God the SOVEREIGN ONE said, "It is not good that the human being should be alone; I will make a companion corresponding to the creature." . . . ²¹So God the SOVEREIGN ONE caused a deep sleep to fall upon the human being, and took a rib out of the sleeping human being and closed up the place with flesh; ²²and God the SOVEREIGN ONE built the rib which God took from the human being into woman and brought her to the man. ²³Then the man said,

> "This at last is bone of my bones and flesh of my flesh; she shall be called Woman, because she was taken out of Man."²

6   ²⁴Therefore a man leaves his father and his mother and cleaves to his wife, and they become one flesh. ²⁵And the man and woman were both naked, and were not ashamed.

WRITING ASSIGNMENTS

1. Write a paper in which you explore your own thoughts on nonsexist translation of the Bible.

2. Compare the two versions of the creation excerpts from Genesis. What do you think of the specific changes made in the *Lectionary*? Consider the effect on both the meaning and sound of the passage.

3. Try your own hand at eliminating sexist language from Scriptures. Select a different passage from the Bible, or one from another religious text, and render it in nonsexist language.

4. Do you think that a full nonsexist translation of the Bible along the lines of the *Lectionary* would be widely accepted? Should such a translation be accepted? Why or why not? Write a paper in which you explore your thoughts on this.

---

²This literary pun on "man" (*ish*) and "woman" (*ishshah*) intends to show relationship rather than biological origin. The relationship is one of equality: "bone of my bones and flesh of my flesh."

DON'T REWRITE
THE BIBLE

Michael Golden

As the title suggests, the piece below represents the other side of the controversy over nonsexist Bible translation. Michael Golden, who teaches at an elementary school in Brooklyn, New York, claims that what the inclusive Language Lectionary Committee has done is not nonsexist, "it is merely absurd." He argues that in the name of female liberation the Bible is being rewritten, not retranslated.

1 In line with our national obsession with obliterating distinctions between men and women for fear of being labeled sexist, the National Council of Churches has recently released the "Inclusive Language Lectionary," a modernized translation of key Bible passages. The council, an organization of major Protestant denominations, apparently feels that masculine references to such eminent authority figures as Jesus Christ and even God offend the sensibilities of its distaff members. Thus the new volume of Bible readings, meant to be used in public worship services, refers to God as "Sovereign One" rather than "Lord"; "King" becomes "Monarch" and "Son of God" becomes "Child of God." Women's lib, it seems, has gone otherworldly; indeed, nothing is sacred in our manic quest for a perfectly egalitarian society.

2 Now, bra burning may be one thing, but before we start tinkering with the Bible we should seriously consider just what we're doing with this semantic sleight of hand. Before I'm called a chauvinist pig and worse, let me state that I'm all for the women's movement and its primary goals—equality of opportunity in the workplace, shared responsibilities in the home, political power, financial independence and so forth. I am fervently against discrimination of any kind to any group. But when the Bible is called sexist and is rewritten, I believe we're going just a bit overboard.

PATERNAL

3 There is, after all, something to be said for tradition, especially when one's fundamental beliefs are at stake. I suppose a case could be made for the sexual neutrality of God; after all, at the risk of sounding sacrilegious, I submit that

we can't really be sure what we're dealing with here. But for whatever histori-cal, cultural, philosophical, psychological or theological reasons one wishes to choose, all the major religions have as their Almighty a paternal figure, whether it be God, Buddha, Allah, Muhammad or Confucius. And I suggest that this state of affairs in no way diminishes the status of women.

4   I cannot, for the life of me, understand why Jesus Christ must have his mas-culinity denied him for the sake of linguistic neutrality. What possibly can be accomplished by calling him (him?) the Child of God instead of Son of God? This may sound blasphemous, but what else is one to make of this bizarre form of heavenly hermaphroditism? Just how far do we go here? What be-comes of all those magnificent Renaissance paintings depicting Jesus Christ with those sinewy muscles and dark beard?

5   By rewriting the Bible we are also opening up a Pandora's box for other tra-ditions and disciplines. Perhaps there will be those who insist that history be rewritten. George Washington will no longer be referred to as the Father of Our Country; that appellation is blatantly sexist. How about Parent of Our Country? Not quite as catchy, but at least there is no paternal bias.

6   In the interest of fairness, of course, this gender genocide can work both ways. What will become of Mother Earth, Mother Nature, Mother Courage and Mother Goose? Certainly these maternal eminences must be neutered as well. Will we be reading to our children Parent Goose stories in the future? Will we arouse the wrath of Progenitor Nature?

7   There are instances where traditions can be changed in order to accommo-date modern, nonsexist views, even when they are only token gestures. The National Weather Service avoided a storm of controversy several years ago when they began giving hurricanes and tropical tempests masculine as well as the traditional feminine names. Thus, we now have Tropical Storm Tommy as well as Hurricane Hilda, and meteorologists can no longer be accused of cast-ing aspersions on the feminine temperament. But when we start looking sky-ward past those ominous clouds and gaze toward the heavens with an eye to eliminating sexual distinctions, then we're headed for trouble.

MATERNAL

8   In our egalitarian philosophy we are terribly afraid to admit that there are dif-ferences between sexes, or races, or nationalities or humans of any group at all. Somehow the possibility that physical or psychological differences of any sort exist strikes that fear that this will be equated with superiority or inferior-ity of certain groups. But the denial that differences exist, whether biological or otherwise, only leads to absurdities; indeed, it is a denial of our own hu-manity. We cannot respect differences among people unless we first admit to them. This is not sexism or racism; it is merely common sense. What the coun-cil has done in its rewriting of the Bible is not progressive or nonsexist; it is merely absurd.

9   Instead of denying that differences occur between men and women, we should celebrate those differences. After all, Mother Earth—er, Ancestor Earth?—would be an awfully dull place if we couldn't distinguish between masculine and feminine characteristics. Different does not mean inferior. As one noted French—uh, Frenchperson—once said, *"Vive la différence!"*

10   And, for God's sake, let's leave the Bible alone!

TOPICAL CONSIDERATIONS

1. What lies at the heart of Golden's argument against rewriting the Bible?

2. Golden prefaces his attack on the Inclusive Language Lectionary Committee by saying that their efforts are part of "our national obsession with obliterating distinctions between men and women for fear of being labeled sexist." Do you believe there is such an "obsession"? What evidence—or lack of evidence—do you find?

3. In paragraph 2, Golden says that he is "all for the women's movement and its primary goals." Do you believe that statement from what he says in the essay? Wouldn't the efforts to desexualize the Bible qualify as a "primary goal" of the women's movement? Golden says that he is also "fervently against discrimination of any kind to any group." Isn't that a contradiction of his stand against the Inclusive Language Lectionary, whose stated intention was the elimination of discrimination in the Bible?

4. In paragraph 4, Golden wonders what the move to sexually neutralize Jesus Christ will have on Renaissance paintings. What is his fear? Do you think it is legitimate?

5. Golden fears that rewriting the Bible will open up a Pandora's box for other traditions and disciplines. Do you think there is a danger of that?

6. Do you find appellations such as Father of Our Country, Mother Earth, Mother Country, and Mother Goose discriminatory or sexist?

7. At the end of the essay Golden says that instead of denying the differences between men and women we should celebrate them. Can we not still celebrate the differences and yet eliminate linguistic bias in the Bible?

8. Many people have proclaimed the sexist, patriarchal nature of the Bible and its tradition. Even Golden admits to it when he says that "all major religions have as their Almighty a paternal figure. . . . "But would not a nonsexist translation of the Bible constitute theological as well as historical revisionism? A changing of the way things were because we didn't like them?

RHETORICAL CONSIDERATIONS

1. How would you define the tone of this essay? Find examples of invectives, irony, allusion, hyperbole. Do you think the author has a sense of humor? If so, where exactly does he display it?

2. Where is Golden's thesis statement in this essay?

3. What is the effect and tone of "women's lib" in paragraph 1?

4. Although the title of the essay is rather specific, Golden digresses to talk about appellations and hurricane names and other nonbiblical matters. Do you think this weakens his essay?

5. Explain the rhetorical purpose and effect of "—er, Ancestor Earth?" and "—uh, Frenchperson," in paragraph 9.

6. Explain the effectiveness of the one-line paragraph that concludes the essay.

WRITING ASSIGNMENTS

1. What do you think of Golden's stand here? Do you agree that the Bible should not be rewritten to remove sexual bias from it? Write a paper in which you express your own thoughts on this.

2. Golden claims that we have a "national obsession with obliterating distinctions between men and women for fear of being labeled sexist." Do you agree with him that America is so obsessed? Do you see evidence of the degenderizing of men and women? Write an essay in which you address these questions.

3. Golden refers to appellations such as "Father of Our Country" and "Mother Nature" as potential victims of the women's liberation movement. What do you think of such terms? Are they sexist? Are you offended by them? What other appellations can you think of? Write a paper answering these questions.

4. Compare the two versions of the Genesis excerpts on previous pages in this text. Or, select a different passage from the Bible and render it in nonsexist language. Now evaluate the differences. Do you consider the new version a retranslation or a rewriting of the original? What besides language has been changed? What has been gained? What has been lost?

8 | DOUBLE TALK, EUPHEMISMS, AND PROFESSIONAL JARGON

RHYMES WITH ORANGE

French diplomat Charles Talleyrand once said that humans were "given the power of speech in order that [they] might conceal [their] thoughts." What Talleyrand didn't mention was the exotic, lively, and often foolish contortions people have engaged in to camouflage the truth. This chapter is dedicated to the language of faking it—euphemisms, jargon, and other double talk. Some of it you've heard, some of it you use, and all of it is currently fashionable in one circle or another.

BUREAUCRATIC DOUBLE TALK

The chapter begins with "Doubts About Doublespeak," in which professional word watcher William Lutz defines different kinds of doublespeak, then reviews some of the latest marvels from the most notorious creators of language designed not to communicate—government bureaucrats.

EUPHEMISMS: SUGARCOATING REALITY

One form of double talk is the euphemism, the topic of the next two essays. In "Euphemisms," Hugh Rawson presents a lively and sardonic exposé of language that goes out of its way to avoid unpleasant realities. As he explains, euphemisms can be negative or positive, and they range from squeamish evasions to status-boosting occupational labels to some truly nasty maskings. A particularly nasty masking of the late 1990s is the subject of Nathan Cobb's *"Talking* DOWN." As companies shrink their work forces, they expand their vocabularies. The buzzword at the top of their evasive lexicon is "downsizing"—a word that strikes fear in the hearts of many.

PROFESSIONAL JARGON: LANGUAGE OF THE TRADES

The next two pieces look at different types of professional jargon—the special lingo of some trades that provides its users with communication shortcuts while baffling outsiders. In "Doctor Talk," novelist, screenwriter, and essayist Diane Johnson discusses the twin languages of medicine—one highly technical, the other a bland, noncommittal patter—both intended to put distance between physician and patient. Moving from doctors to lawyers, the jargon becomes a thick stew of Latinisms, archaic English, and fancy circumlocutions—all intended to keep the spirit of tradition (and, quite possibly, legal fees) aloft as reported by George Gordon Coughlin in "It May Not Be English, But It's Strictly Legal."

CASE STUDY

The chapter closes with a dramatic illustration of nearly every complaint ever aired about double talk, euphemisms, and jargon. In "Little Red Riding Hood Revisited," satirist Russell Baker reconstructs a familiar folk tale, barely recognizable amid all the bureaucratic and professional verbiage. Ultimately this amusing little piece captures the very reason for double talk: to evade both meaning and responsibility.

DOUBTS ABOUT DOUBLESPEAK

William Lutz

It has been said that the only things we cannot change are death and taxes. Well, that's not exactly right. We can call them "terminal living" and "revenue enhancement" to make people feel better about them. And that, in part, is the nature of what William Lutz rails against here: *doublespeak.* It is language intended not to reveal but to conceal, not to communicate but to obfuscate. In this essay, Lutz categorizes four kinds of doublespeak, distinguishing annoying though relatively harmless professional jargon from ruthlessly devious coinages such as "ethnic cleansing," which attempt to mask barbaric acts.

William Lutz is a professor of English at Rutgers University. He is the editor of the *Quarterly Review of Doublespeak* as well as author of *Beyond Nineteen Eighty-Four: Doublespeak in a Post-Orwellian Age* (1989) and *Doublespeak: From Revenue Enhancement to Terminal Living* (1990). This article first appeared in *State Government News,* in July 1993.

1　During the past year, we learned that we can shop at a "unique retail biosphere" instead of a farmers' market, where we can buy items made of "synthetic glass" instead of plastic, or purchase a "high velocity, multipurpose air circulator," or electric fan. A "waste-water conveyance facility" may "exceed the odor threshold" from time to time due to the presence of "regulated human nutrients," but that is not to be confused with a sewage plant that stinks up the neighborhood with sewage sludge. Nor should we confuse a "resource development park" with a dump. Thus does doublespeak continue to spread.

2　　Doublespeak is language which pretends to communicate but doesn't. It is language which makes the bad seem good, the negative seem positive, the unpleasant seem attractive, or at least tolerable. It is language which avoids, shifts or denies responsibility; language which is at variance with its real or purported meaning. It is language which conceals or prevents thought.

3   Doublespeak is all around us. We are asked to check our packages at the desk "for our convenience" when it's not for our convenience at all but for someone else's convenience. We see advertisements for "preowned," "experienced" or "previously distinguished" cars, not used cars and for "genuine imitation leather," "virgin vinyl" or "real counterfeit diamonds." Television offers not reruns but "encore telecasts." There are no slums or ghettos, just the "inner city" or "substandard housing" where the "disadvantaged" or "economically nonaffluent" live and where there might be a problem with "substance abuse." Nonprofit organizations don't make a profit, they have "negative deficits" or experience "revenue excesses." With doublespeak it's not dying but "terminal living" or "negative patient care outcome."

4   There are four kinds of doublespeak. The first kind is the euphemism, a word or phrase designed to avoid a harsh or distasteful reality. Used to mislead or deceive, the euphemism becomes doublespeak. In 1984 the U.S. State Department's annual reports on the status of human rights around the world ceased using the word "killing." Instead the State Department used the phrase "unlawful or arbitrary deprivation of life," thus avoiding the embarrassing situation of government-sanctioned killing in countries supported by the United States.

5   A second kind of doublespeak is jargon, the specialized language of a trade, profession or similar group, such as doctors, lawyers, plumbers or car mechanics. Legitimately used, jargon allows members of a group to communicate with each other clearly, efficiently and quickly. Lawyers and tax accountants speak to each other of an "involuntary conversion" of property, a legal term that means the loss or destruction of property through theft, accident or condemnation. But when lawyers or tax accountants use unfamiliar terms to speak to others, then the jargon becomes doublespeak.

6   In 1978 a commercial 727 crashed on takeoff, killing three passengers, injuring 21 others and destroying the airplane. The insured value of the airplane was greater than its book value, so the airline made a profit of $1.7 million, creating two problems: the airline didn't want to talk about one of its airplanes crashing, yet it had to account for that $1.7 million profit in its annual report to its stockholders. The airline solved both problems by inserting a footnote in its annual report which explained that the $1.7 million was due to "the involuntary conversion of a 727."

7   A third kind of doublespeak is gobbledygook or bureaucratese. Such doublespeak is simply a matter of overwhelming the audience with words—the more the better. Alan Greenspan, a polished practitioner of bureaucratese, once testified before a Senate committee that "it is a tricky problem to find the particular calibration in timing that would be appropriate to stem the acceleration in risk premiums created by falling incomes without prematurely aborting the decline in the inflation-generated risk premiums."

8   The fourth kind of doublespeak is inflated language, which is designed to make the ordinary seem extraordinary, to make everyday things seem impressive, to give an air of importance to people or situations, to make the simple seem complex. Thus do car mechanics become "automotive internists," elevator operators become "members of the vertical transportation corps," grocery store checkout clerks become "career associate scanning professionals," and smelling something becomes "organoleptic analysis."

9   Doublespeak is not the product of careless language or sloppy thinking. Quite the opposite. Doublespeak is language carefully designed and constructed to appear to communicate when in fact it doesn't. It is language designed not to lead but mislead. Thus, it's not a tax increase but "revenue enhancement" or "tax-base broadening." So how can you complain about higher taxes? Those aren't useless, billion dollar pork barrel projects; they're really "congressional projects of national significance," so don't complain about wasteful government spending. That isn't the Mafia in Atlantic City; those are just "members of a career-offender cartel," so don't worry about the influence of organized crime in the city.

10   New doublespeak is created every day. The Environmental Protection Agency once called acid rain "poorly-buffered precipitation" then dropped that term in favor of "atmospheric deposition of anthropogenically-derived acidic substances," but recently decided that acid rain should be called "wet deposition." The Pentagon, which has in the past given us such classic doublespeak as "hexiform rotatable surface compression unit" for steel nut, just published a pamphlet warning soldiers that exposure to nerve gas will lead to "immediate permanent incapacitation." That's almost as good as the Pentagon's official term "servicing the target," meaning to kill the enemy. Meanwhile, the Department of Energy wants to establish a "monitored retrievable storage site," a place once known as a dump for spent nuclear fuel.

11   Bad economic times give rise to lots of new doublespeak designed to avoid some very unpleasant economic realities. As the "contained depression" continues so does the corporate policy of making up even more new terms to avoid the simple, and easily understandable, term "layoff." So it is that corporations "reposition," "restructure," "reshape," or "realign" the company and "reduce duplication" through "release of resources" that involves a "permanent downsizing" or a "payroll adjustment" that results in a number of employees being "involuntarily terminated."

12   Other countries regularly contribute to doublespeak. In Japan, where baldness is called "hair disadvantaged," the economy is undergoing a "severe adjustment process," while in Canada there is an "involuntary downward development" of the work force. For some government agencies in Canada, wastepaper baskets have become "user friendly, space effective, flexible, deskside sortation units." Politicians in Canada may engage in "reality augmentation," but they never lie. As part of their new freedom, the people of Moscow can visit "intimacy salons," or sex shops as they're known in other countries.

When dealing with the bureaucracy in Russia, people know that they should show officials "normal gratitude," or give them a bribe.

13   The worst doublespeak is the doublespeak of death. It is the language, wrote George Orwell in 1946, that is "largely the defense of the indefensible . . . designed to make lies sound truthful and murder respectable, and to give an appearance of solidity to pure wind." In the doublespeak of death, Orwell continued, "defenseless villages are bombarded from the air, the inhabitants driven out into the countryside, the cattle machine-gunned, the huts set on fire with incendiary bullets. This is called pacification. Millions of peasants are robbed of their farms and sent trudging along the roads with no more than they can carry. This is called transfer of population or rectification of frontiers." Today, in a country once called Yugoslavia, this is called "ethnic cleansing."

14   It's easy to laugh off doublespeak. After all, we all know what's going on, so what's the harm? But we don't always know what's going on, and when that happens, doublespeak accomplishes its ends. It alters our perception of reality. It deprives us of the tools we need to develop, advance and preserve our society, our culture, our civilization. It breeds suspicion, cynicism, distrust and, ultimately, hostility. It delivers us into the hands of those who do not have our interests at heart. As Samuel Johnson noted in 18th century England, even the devils in hell do not lie to one another, since the society of hell could not subsist without the truth, any more than any other society.

TOPICAL CONSIDERATIONS

1. What is *doublespeak,* according to Lutz? What is its purpose?
2. Lutz divides doublespeak into four types. What are they? Give some of your own examples of each type. As best you can, rank these four according to which are most offensive or harmful. Explain your choices.
3. In paragraph 4, Lutz classifies *euphemisms* as a form of doublespeak. How does his definition differ from Hugh Rawson's in the next article, "Euphemisms"? In your opinion, are there instances when euphemisms are useful? Explain your answer.
4. Lutz says that "inflated language" is designed to make the ordinary seem extraordinary, as with elevated job titles. In your opinion, is there anything wrong with elevating job titles in this way? Why or why not?
5. In your opinion, is doublespeak as widespread as Lutz claims? Are its effects as serious as he perceives them to be?

RHETORICAL CONSIDERATIONS

1. Examine Lutz's introductory paragraph. How does this paragraph set the tone for the piece? Is it effective?
2. What is the opposing view in this piece? How does Lutz handle it in his argument? Are there counterarguments that Lutz has missed in his essay?

3. Are there any places in the essay where Lutz employs doublespeak in his own writing? If so, what effect does this have on your reading?

4. Consider Lutz's voice in this article. Is he a reliable narrator? Does he provide adequate documentation for his assertions? Cite specific examples from the text to support your answers.

WRITING ASSIGNMENTS

1. Write an essay in which you examine instances of doublespeak in the media, a particular profession, or among your acquaintances. Make a case either for or against its usage.

2. Was there ever a time when doublespeak had an impact on your life? Write a personal narrative reflecting on the effect, positive or negative, that doublespeak has had in your experience. You might consider having been swayed by advertising or political jargon.

3. Lutz defines *doublespeak* as "language which conceals or prevents thought" and "language which pretends to communicate but doesn't." Write an essay describing an experience wherein you used doublespeak. What was your goal in communicating as such? How was doublespeak useful to you in this situation?

4. Over the course of one day, record all the instances of doublespeak you encounter—from ads, TV shows, news articles, films, menus, and so on. (Whenever possible, photocopy or tape these instances.) In a paper, try to classify the different kinds of doublespeak you found, then analyze its different functions and try to determine the effects on the intended audience.

5. Look through a newspaper or magazine for a short and clear discussion of an interesting topic. Then have some fun rewriting the piece entirely in doublespeak.

EUPHEMISMS

Hugh Rawson

Following a recent accident at a nuclear power plant, local officials explained what had happened as an "energetic dissembly." The multibil-
lion dollar nosedive the stock market took in 1987 was not a crash but a
"fourth quarter equity retreat." Economists in the Bush administration,
trying to sugarcoat the anathema of raising taxes, resorted to calling an
inevitable increase "revenue enhancement." When the CIA ordered a
"nondiscernible microbionoculator" it got a poison dart. According to
Saddam Hussein, the hundreds of American citizens taken hostage after
the 1990 Iraqi invasion of Kuwait were "guests hosted by the Baghdad
government." These are euphemisms, or what Hugh Rawson in this sardonic and entertaining essay calls "society's basic *lingua non franca*."
Rawson is the author of *Wicked Words* (1989) and *A Dictionary of Euphemisms and Other Double-talk* (1981), which this essay introduces.

1   Mr. Milquetoast gets up from the table, explaining that he has to go to the *little boys' room* or *see a man about a dog;* a young woman announces that she is
enceinte. A secretary complains that her boss is a pain in the *derriére;* an undertaker (or *mortician*) asks delicately where to ship the *loved one*. These are
euphemisms—mild, agreeable, or roundabout words used in place of coarse,
painful, or offensive ones. The term comes from the Greek *eu*, meaning "well"
or "sounding good," and *phēmē*, "speech."

2   Many euphemisms are so delightfully ridiculous that everyone laughs at
them. (Well, almost everyone: The people who call themselves the National
Selected Morticians usually manage to keep from smiling.) Yet euphemisms
have very serious reasons for being. They conceal the things people fear the
most—death, the dead, the supernatural. They cover up the facts of life—of
sex and reproduction and excretion—which inevitably remind even the most
refined people that they are made of clay, or worse. They are beloved by individuals and institutions (governments, especially) who are anxious to present
only the handsomest possible images of themselves to the world. And they are

embedded so deeply in our language that few of us, even those who pride themselves on being plain-spoken, ever get through a day without using them.

3   The same sophisticates who look down their noses at *little boys' room* and other euphemisms of that ilk will nevertheless say that they are going to the *bathroom* when no bath is intended; that Mary has been *sleeping* around even though she has been getting precious little shut-eye; that John has *passed away* or even *departed* (as if he'd just made the last train to Darien); and that Sam and Janet are *friends*, which sounds a lot better than "illicit lovers."

4   Thus, euphemisms are society's basic *lingua non franca*. As such, they are outward and visible signs of our inward anxieties, conflicts, fears, and shames. They are like radioactive isotopes. By tracing them, it is possible to see what has been (and is) going on in our language, our minds, and our culture.

5   Euphemisms can be divided into two general types—positive and negative. The positive ones inflate and magnify, making the euphemized items seem altogether grander and more important than they really are. The negative euphemisms deflate and diminish. They are defensive in nature, offsetting the power of tabooed terms and otherwise eradicating from the language everything that people prefer not to deal with directly.

6   Positive euphemisms include the many fancy occupational titles, which salve the egos of workers by elevating their job status: *custodian* for janitor (itself a euphemism for caretaker), *counsel* for lawyer, the many kinds of *engineer* (*exterminating engineer, mattress engineer, publicity engineer,* ad infinitum), *help* for servant (itself an old euphemism for slave), *hooker* and *working girl* for whore, and so forth. A common approach is to try to turn one's trade into a profession, usually in imitation of the medical profession. *Beautician* and the aforementioned *mortician* are the classic examples, but the same imitative instinct is responsible for social workers calling welfare recipients *clients*, for football coaches conducting *clinics*, and for undertakers referring to corpses as *cases* or even *patients*.

7   Other kinds of positive euphemisms include personal honorifics such as *colonel*, the *honorable*, and *major*, and the many institutional euphemisms, which convert madhouses into *mental hospitals*, colleges into *universities*, and small business establishments into *emporiums, parlors, salons*, and *shoppes*. The desire to improve one's surroundings also is evident in geographical place names, most prominently in the case of the distinctly nongreen *Greenland* (attributed to an early real estate developer named Eric the Red), but also in the designation of many small burgs as *cities*, and in the names of some cities, such as *Troy*, New York (*neé* Vanderheyden's Ferry; its name-change in 1789 began a fad for adopting classical place names in the United States).

8   Negative, defensive euphemisms are extremely ancient. It was the Greeks, for example, who transformed the Furies into the *Eumenides* (the Kindly Ones). In many cultures, it is forbidden to pronounce the name of God (hence, pious Jews say *Adonai*) or of Satan (giving rise to the *deuce*, the *good*

man, the *great fellow,* the generalized *Devil,* and many other roundabouts). The names of the dead, and of animals that are hunted or feared, may also be euphemized this way. The bear is called *grandfather* by many peoples and the tiger is alluded to as the *striped one.* The common motivation seems to be a confusion between the names of things and the things themselves: The name is viewed as an extension of the thing. Thus, to know the name is to give one power over the thing (as in the Rumpelstiltskin story). But such power may be dangerous: "Speak of the Devil and he appears." For mere mortals, then, the safest policy is to use another name, usually a flattering, euphemistic one, in place of the supernatural being's true name.

9   As strong as—or stronger than—the taboos against names are the taboos against particular words, especially the infamous *four-letter words.* (According to a recent Supreme Court decision, the set of *four-letter words* actually contains some words with as few as three and as many as 12 letters, but the logic of Supreme Court decisions is not always immediately apparent.) These words form part of the vocabulary of practically everyone above the age of six or seven. They are not slang terms, but legitimate Standard English of the oldest stock, and they are euphemized in many ways, typically by conversion into pseudo-Latin (e.g., *copulation defecation, urination*), into slang (*make love, number two, pee*), or into socially acceptable dashes (*f——, s——, p——,* etc.). In the electronic media, the function of the dash is fulfilled by the *bleep* (sometimes pronounced *blip*), which has completed the circle and found its way into print.

10   The taboo against words frequently degenerates into mere prudery. At least—though the defensive principle is the same—the primitive (or *preliterate*) hunter's use of *grandfather* seems to operate on a more elemental level than the excessive modesty that has produced *abdomen* for belly, *afterpart* for ass, *bosom* for breast, *limb* for leg, *white meat* for breast (of a chicken), and so on.

11   When carried too far, which is what always seems to happen, positive and negative euphemisms tend finally to coalesce into an unappetizing mush of elegancies and genteelisms, in which the underlying terms are hardly worth the trouble of euphemizing, e.g., *ablutions* for washing, *bender* for knee, *dentures* for false teeth, *expectorate* for spit, *home* for house, *honorarium* for fee, *ill* for sick, *libation* for drink, *perspire* for sweat, *position* for job, etc., etc., etc.

12   All euphemisms, whether positive or negative, may be used either unconsciously or consciously. Unconscious euphemisms consist mainly of words that were developed as euphemisms, but so long ago that hardly anyone remembers the original motivation. Examples in this category include such now-standard terms as *cemetery* (from the Greek word for "sleeping place," it replaced the more deathly "graveyard"), and the names of various barnyard animals, including the *donkey* (the erstwhile ass), the *sire* (or studhorse), and the *rooster* (for cock, and one of many similar evasions, e.g., *haystack* for hay-

cock, *weather vane* for weathercock, and Louisa May *Alcott,* whose father changed the family name from the nasty-sounding Alcox). Into this category, too, fall such watered-down swear words as *cripes, Jiminy Cricket, gee,* and *gosh,* all designed to avoid taking holy names in vain and now commonly used without much awareness of their original meaning, particularly by youngsters and by those who fill in the balloons in comic strips. Then there are the words for which no honest *Anglo-Saxon* (often a euphemism for "dirty") equivalents exist, e.g., *brassiere,* which has hardly anything to do with the French *bras* (arm) from which it derives, and *toilet,* from the diminutive of *toile* (cloth).

13   Conscious euphemisms constitute a much more complex category, which is hardly surprising, given the ingenuity, not to say the deviousness, of the human mind. This is not to imply that euphemisms cannot be employed more or less honestly as well as knowingly. For example, garbage men are upgraded routinely into *sanitation men,* but to say "Here come the sanitation men" is a comparatively venial sin. The meaning does come across intelligibly, and the listener understands that it is time to get out the garbage cans. By the same token, it is honest enough to offer a woman condolences upon the "loss of her husband," where *loss* stands for death. Not only are amenities preserved: By avoiding the troublesome term, the euphemism actually facilitates social discourse.

14   Conscious euphemisms also lead to social double-thinking, however. They form a kind of code. The euphemism stands for "something else," and everyone pretends that the "something else" doesn't exist. It is the essentially duplicitous nature of euphemisms that makes them so attractive to those people and institutions who have something to hide, who don't want to say what they are thinking, and who find it convenient to lie about what they are doing.

15   It is at this point, when speakers and writers seek not so much to avoid offense as to deceive, that we pass into the universe of dishonest euphemisms, where the conscious elements of circumlocution and double-talk loom large. Here are the murky worlds of the CIA, the FBI, and the military, where murder is translated into *executive action,* an illegal break-in into a *black bag job,* and napalm into *soft* or *selective ordnance.* Here are the Wonderlands in which Alice would feel so much at home: advertising, where small becomes *medium* if not *large,* and politics, where gross errors are passed off as *misspeaking* and lies that won't wash anymore are called *inoperative.* Here, too, are our great industries: the prison business, where solitary confinement cells are disguised as *adjustment centers, quiet cells,* or *seclusion;* the atomic power business, where nuclear accidents become *core rearrangements* or simply *events;* the death business, where *remains* (not bodies) are *interred* (not buried) in *caskets* (not coffins); and, finally, of murder on its largest scale, where people are put into *protective custody* (imprisonment) in *concentration camps* (prison camps) as a first step toward achieving the *Final Solution* (genocide). George Orwell wrote in a famous essay ("Politics and the English Language," 1946) that "political language . . . is designed to make lies sound truthful and murder respectable, and to give an appearance of solidity to pure

wind." His dictum applies equally through the full range of dishonest euphemisms. . . .

16   Euphemisms are in a constant state of flux. New ones are created almost daily. Many of them prove to be nonce terms—one-day wonders that are never repeated. Of those that are ratified through reuse as true euphemisms, some may last for generations, even centuries, while others fade away or develop into unconscious euphemisms, still used, but reflexively, without thought of their checkered origins. The ebb and flow of euphemisms is governed to a large extent by two basic rules: Gresham's Law of Language and the Law of Succession.

17   In monetary theory, where it originated, Gresham's Law can be summarized as "bad money drives out good"—meaning that debased or underweight coins will drive good, full-weight coins out of circulation. (By the by: Though Sir Thomas Gresham, 1519–1579, has gotten all the credit, the effect was noticed and explained by earlier monetary experts, including Nicolaus Koppernick, 1473–1543, who doubled as an astronomer and who is better known as Copernicus.) In the field of language, on the same principle, "bad" meanings or associations of words tend to drive competing "good" meanings out of circulation. Thus, *coition, copulation,* and *intercourse* once were general terms for, respectively, coming together, coupling, and communication, but after the words were drawn into service as euphemisms, their sexual meanings became dominant, so that the other senses are hardly ever encountered nowadays except in very special situations. The same thing happened to *crap* (formerly a general term for chaff, residue, or dregs), *feces* (also dregs, as of wine or salad oil), and *manure* (literally: "to work with the hands").

18   Gresham's Law remains very much in force, of course. Witness what has happened to *gay*, whose homosexual meaning has recently preempted all others. The law is by no means limited to euphemisms, and its application to other words help explain why some euphemisms are formed. Thus, the incorrect and pejorative uses of "Jew" as a verb and adjective caused many people, Jews as well as Gentiles, to shift to *Hebrew* even though that term should, in theory, be reserved for the Jews of ancient times or their language. A similar example is "girl," whose pejorative meanings have recently been brought to the fore, with the result that anxiety-ridden men sometimes fall into the worse error of referring to their *lady* friends.

19   Gresham's Law is the engine that powers the second of the two great euphemistic principles: the Law of Succession. After a euphemism becomes tainted by association with its underlying "bad" word, people will tend to shun it. For example, the seemingly innocent *occupy* was virtually banned by polite society for most of the seventeenth and eighteenth centuries because of its use as a euphemism for engaging in sex. (A man might be said to *occupy* his wife or to go to an *occupying* house.) Once people begin to shun a term, it usually is necessary to develop a new euphemism to replace the one that has failed. Then the second will become tainted and a third will appear. In this way, chains of euphemisms evolve. Thus, "mad" has been euphemized successively

as *crazy, insane, lunatic, mentally deranged,* and just plain *mental.* Then there are the poor and backward nations that have metamorphosed from *underdeveloped* to *developing* to *emergent. (Fledgling* nations never really took hold despite the imprimatur of Eleanor Roosevelt.) A new chain seems to be evolving from the FBI's *black bag job,* which has fallen into sufficient disrepute that agents who condone break-ins are more likely now to talk in terms of *surreptitious entries, technical trespasses, uncontested physical searches,* or *warrantless investigations.*

20   Extraordinary collections of euphemisms have formed around some topics over the years as a result of the continual creation of new terms, and it seems safe to say that the sizes of these collections reflect the strength of the underlying taboos. Nowhere is this more evident than in the case of the *private parts,* male and female, whose Anglo-Saxon names are rarely used in mixed company, except by those who are on intimate terms. Thus, the monumental *Slang and Its Analogues* (J. S. Farmer and W. E. Henley, 1890–94) lists some 650 synonyms for *vagina,* most of them euphemistic, and about half that number for *penis.* (These are just the English synonyms; for *vagina,* for example, Farmer and Henley include perhaps another 900 synonyms in other languages.) Other anatomical parts that have inspired more than their share of euphemisms include the *bosom, bottom, limb,* and *testicles.* All forms of sexual *intercourse* and the subjects of *defecation, urination,* and the *toilet* also are richly euphemistic, as are *menstruation* (well over 100 terms have been noted), all aspects of death and dying, or *passing away,* and disease (it used to be *TB* and the sexual, *social diseases* that were euphemized; now it is cancer, usually referred to in *obituaries,* or death notices, as a *long illness*).

21   The incidence of euphemisms may also reflect society's ambivalent feelings on certain subjects. Alcohol, for example, is responsible for a great many euphemisms: There are 356 synonyms for "drunk"—more than for any other term—in the appendixes to the *Dictionary of American Slang* (Harold Wentworth and Stuart Berg Flexner, 1976). The practice of punishing criminals with death *(capital punishment)* also makes many people uncomfortable, judging from the number of linguistic evasions for it, both in the United States, where the electric chair may be humorously downplayed as a *hot seat,* and in other countries, such as France, where the condemned are introduced to *Madame la guillotine.* Meanwhile, the so-called victimless crime of prostitution has inspired an inordinate number of euphemisms, with some 70 listed in this book under *prostitute* (a sixteenth-century Latinate euphemism for "whore," which itself may have begun life as a euphemism for some now-forgotten word, the Old English *hōre* being cognate with the Latin *cara,* darling). The precarious position of *minorities* (a code term for blacks and/or Hispanics) and other oft-oppressed groups (e.g., homosexuals, servants, women) also is revealed by the variety of terms that have been devised to characterize them.

22   Just as the clustering of euphemisms around a given term or topic appears to reflect the strength of a particular taboo, so the unusual accumulation of

euphemisms around an institution is strongly indicative of interior rot. Thus, the Spanish Inquisition featured an extensive vocabulary of words with double meanings (e.g., *auto da fé* for act of faith, and the *question* for torture). In our own time, the number of euphemisms that have collected around the CIA and its attempts at *assassination*, the FBI and its reliance on break-ins and *informants*, and the prison business and its noncorrectional *correctional facilities*, all tend to confirm one's darker suspicions. This is true, too, of the *Defense* (not War) *Department*, with its *enhanced radiation weapons* (neutron bombs) and its *reconnaissance in force* (search-and-destroy) missions. The military tradition, though, is very old. As long ago as ca. 250 B.C., a Macedonian general, Antigonus Gonatas, parlayed a "retreat" into a *strategic movement to the rear.* And, finally, there is politics, always a fertile source of doubletalk, but especially so during the Watergate period when euphemisms surfaced at a rate that is unlikely (one hopes) ever to be matched again: *Deep Six, expletive deleted, inoperative, sign off,* and *stonewall* are only a few of the highpoints (or lowpoints, depending upon one's perspective) of this remarkably fecund period. . . .

23   The ancient Egyptians called the deadhouse, where bodies were turned into mummies, the *beautiful house,* and the ways of expunging offensive expressions from language have not changed since. Simplest is to make a straight substitution, using a word that has happier connotations than the term one wishes to avoid. Frequently, a legitimate synonym will do. Thus, *agent, speculator,* and *thrifty* have better vibes than "spy," "gambler," and "tight," although the literal meanings, or denotations, of each pair of words are the same. On this level, all the euphemist has to do is select words with care. Other principles may be applied, however, a half dozen of which are basic to creating—and deciphering—euphemisms. They are:

24   *Foreign languages sound finer.* It is permissible for speakers and writers of English to express almost any thought they wish, as long as the more risqué parts of the discussion are rendered in another language, usually French or Latin. The versatility of French (and the influence of French culture) is evident in such diverse fields as love (*affair, amour, liaison*), war (*matériel, personnel, sortie, triage*), women's underwear (*brassiere, chemise, lingerie*), and dining (goat, cow, deer, and other animals with English names when they are alive and kicking are served up on the dinner table as the more palatable *chevron, filet mignon,* and *venison*). *French* itself is a euphemistic prefix word for a variety of "wrong" and/or "sexy" things, such as the *French disease* (syphilis). . . . Latin is almost equally popular as a source of euphemisms, especially for the body's sexual and other functions. Thus, such words as *copulation, fellatio, masturbation, pudendum,* and *urination* are regarded as printable and even broadcastable by people (including United States Supreme Court justices) who become exercised at the sight and sound of their English counterparts. Other languages have contributed. For example, the Dutch *boss*

(master), the Spanish *cojones* (balls), and the Yiddish *tushie* (the ass). Not strictly speaking a foreign language is potty talk, a distinct idiom that has furnished many euphemisms, i.e., *number one, number two, pee, piddle,* and other relics of the nursery, often used by adults when speaking to one another as well as when addressing children.

25   *Bad words are not so bad when abbreviated.* Words that otherwise would create consternation if used in mixed company or in public are acceptable when reduced to their initial letters. Essentially, such abbreviations as *BS* and *SOB* work the same way as the dash in *f——*. Everyone knows what letters have been deleted, but no one is seriously offended because the taboo word has not been paraded in all its glory. Dean Acheson even got away with *snafu* when he was secretary of state, though the acronym did cause some comment among the British, not all of whom felt this to be a very diplomatic way of apologizing for an American—er—*foul up.* This acronym also is noteworthy for spawning a host of picturesque albeit short-lived descendants, including *fubar* (where *bar* stands for Beyond All Recognition), *janfu* (Joint Army-Navy), *tarfu* (Things Are Really), and *tuifu* (The Ultimate In). Abbreviations function as euphemisms in many fields, e.g., the child's *BM*, the advertiser's *BO*, the hypochondriac's *Big C*, and the various shortenings for offbeat sex, such as *AC/DC* for those who swing both ways, *bd* for bondage and discipline, and *S/M*.

26   *Abstractions are not objectionable.* The strength of particular taboos may be dissipated by casting ideas in the most general possible terms; also, abstractions, being quite opaque to the uninformed eye (and meaningless to the untrained ear) make ideal cover-up words. Often, it is only a matter of finding the lowest common denominator. Thus, *it, problem, situation,* and *thing* may refer to anything under the sun: the child who keeps playing with *it* and the girl who is said to be doing *it, problem* days and *problem* drinking; the *situation* at the Three Mile Island, Pennsylvania, nuclear power plant; an economic *thing* (slump, recession, or depression), *our thing* (i.e., the Costa Nostra), or the Watergate *thing* (elaborated by the president himself into the *pre-thing* and the *post-thing*). The American tendency toward abstraction was noted early on by de Tocqueville, who believed that democratic nations as a class were "addicted to generic terms and abstract expressions because these modes of speech enlarge thought and assist the operation of the mind by enabling it to include many objects in a small compass." The dark side of this is that abstractions are inherently fuzzy. As de Tocqueville also noted: "An abstract term is like a box with a false bottom; you may put in what ideas you please, and take them out again without being observed" [*Democracy in America*]. Bureaucrats, engineers, scientists, and those who like to be regarded as scientists, are particularly good at generalizing details out of existence. They have produced such expressions as *aerodynamic personnel decelerator* for parachute, *energy release* for radiation release (as from a nuclear

reactor), *episode* and *event* for disasters of different sorts and sizes, *impact attenuation device* for a crash cushion, and *Vertical Transportation Corps* for a group of elevator operators.

27   *Indirection is better than direction.* Topics and terms that are too touchy to be dealt with openly may be alluded to in a variety of ways, most often by mentioning one aspect of the subject, a circumstance involving it, a related subject, or even by saying what it is not. Thus, people really do come together in an *assembly center* and soldiers do stop fighting when they *break off* contact with *the enemy,* but these are indirect euphemisms for "prison" and "retreat," respectively. *Bite the dust* is a classic of this kind, and the adjective is used advisedly, since the expression appears in Homer's *Iliad,* circa 750 B.C. Many of the common anatomical euphemisms also depend on indirection—the general, locational, it's-somewhere-back-there allusions to the *behind,* the *bottom,* and the *rear,* for example. A special category of anatomical euphemisms are those that conform to the Rule of the Displaced Referent, whereby "unmentionable" parts of the human body are euphemized by referring to nearby "mentionable" parts, e.g., *chest* for breasts; *fanny,* a word of unknown origin whose meaning has not always been restricted to the back end of a person; *tail,* which also has had frontal meanings (in Latin, *penis* means "tail"), and *thigh,* a biblical euphemism for the balls. Quaintest of the indirect euphemisms are those that are prefaced with a negative adjective, telling us what they are not, such as *unnatural, unthinkable,* and *unmentionable.* (The latter also appears as a noun in the plural; some women wear *upper unmentionables* and *lower unmentionables.*) An especially famous negative euphemism is the dread *love that dare not speak its name,* but the phrase was not totally dishonest in the beginning, since it dates to 1894 (from a poem by Oscar Wilde's young *friend,* Alfred, Lord Douglas), when "homosexual" was still so new a word as not to be known to many people, regardless of their *sexual orientation.*

28   *Understatement reduces risks.* Since a euphemism is, by definition, a mild, agreeable, or roundabout word or phrase, it follows logically that its real meaning is always worse than its apparent meaning. But this is not always obvious to the uninitiated, especially in constructions that acknowledge part of the truth while concealing the extent of its grimness. Thus, a nuclear reactor that is said to be *above critical* is actually out of control, *active defense* is attack, *area bombing* is terror bombing, *collateral damage* is civilian damage (as from nuclear bombs), and so on. The soft sell also is basic to such euphemisms as *companion, partner,* and *roommate,* all of which downplay "lover"; to *pro-choice* for pro-abortion, and to *senior citizen* for old person. The danger with understatement is that it may hide the true meaning completely. As a result, euphemists often erect signposts in front of the basic term, e.g., *close personal friend, constant companion, criminal conversation* (a legalism for adultery), *meaningful relationship,* etc. The signposts ensure that even a dullard would get the message.

29   *The longer the euphemism, the better.* As a rule, to which there are very few exceptions (*hit* for murder, for instance), euphemisms are longer than the words they replace. They have more letters, they have more syllables, and frequently, two or more words will be deployed in place of a single one. This is partly because the tabooed Anglo-Saxon words tend to be short and partly because it almost always takes more words to evade an idea than to state it directly and honestly. The effect is seen in euphemisms of every type. Thus, *Middle Eastern* dancing is what better "belly" dancers do; more advertisers agree that *medication* gives faster relief than "medicine"; the writers of financial reports eschew "drop" in favor of *adjustment downward,* and those poor souls who are required to give testimony under oath prefer *at this point in time* to "now." The list is practically endless. . . .

TOPICAL CONSIDERATIONS

1. What is a euphemism? What are some of the "serious" functions of euphemisms, according to Rawson?

2. Rawson divides euphemisms into two basic types. What are they? Give some of your own examples of these types.

3. In paragraph 6, the author writes, "Positive euphemisms include the many fancy occupational titles, which salve the egos of workers by elevating their job status." Is there anything wrong with wanting to elevate one's job status this way? Would you rather be called a *garbage man* or a *sanitation engineer?* A *mortician* or *undertaker?* A *reporter* or *journalist?* A *hairdresser* or *cosmetician?*

4. How do certain conscious euphemisms serve more to deceive than to avoid offense? How can euphemisms lead to self-deception?

5. Rawson says that the homosexual meaning of the word *gay* has preempted all other meanings. In your experience is that so? Do you ever use the word to mean joyous or festive?

6. Rawson says a great number of euphemisms have formed around sexual organs and intercourse. What does so much sexual euphemizing say about our society? Does it suggest contempt? fascination? ambivalence? shame? pride?

7. Rawson lists six principles for creating—and deciphering—euphemisms. See if you can come up with examples of your own for each: (1) foreign languages sound finer; (2) bads words are not so bad when abbreviated; (3) abstractions are not objectionable; (4) indirection is better than direction; (5) understatement reduces risks; and (6) the longer the euphemism, the better.

RHETORICAL CONSIDERATIONS

1. What method does Rawson use to define euphemisms?

2. What is the topic sentence of paragraph 2?

3. Rawson says that few of us go through the day without using euphemisms. Can you spot any in Rawson's own writing? What about the word "vibes" in paragraph 23? Or the word *tight,* which itself is a euphemism for stingy?

WRITING ASSIGNMENTS

1. Rawson says in paragraph 2 that euphemisms "are embedded so deeply in our language that few of us . . . ever get through a day without using them." Consider some of the euphemisms you have used today already. What were they? How were they euphemistic?

2. Euphemisms hide what embarrasses you and cover what you don't want seen. Pretend you are a real estate agent and attempt to write a euphemistic description of a piece of property located next to a swamp—or a one-room apartment above a bar noted for noise and brawls. See how attractive you can make the place sound.

3. As Rawson points out, some of the most colorful euphemisms come from the military establishment. During the Vietnam War, "terminate with extreme prejudice" was an official euphemism for murder. Also, soldiers did not "fight" but rather they "made contact" with enemy forces. Look back to the war in the Persian Gulf and try to come up with some sanitized military language that was in common use. In a paper describe how these samples were used to soften some of the nastier aspects of that conflict.

4. Select a piece of writing—for example, a university catalog, a political speech, a newspaper article, a company's brochure, a travel agency's promotion flyer—and study it, looking for euphemisms. After examining the context in detail, try to analyze the effect of the euphemisms used. How do they represent what is being sold? Do the terms seem accurate? exaggerated? dangerously misleading? Explain your findings and conclusions in a paper.

*T*ALKING DOWN

Nathan Cobb

Paradoxically, today's economy seems to prosper and expand only as the work force shrinks. In order to communicate with and placate an increasingly expendable and devalued work force, a new breed of euphemisms has evolved. Instead of "firing" or "laying off" employees, a company "downsizes." Instead of a "pay cut" an employee experiences "remuneration adjustment." In the satirical piece below, Nathan Cobb offers some definitions of popular "down" terms while exposing the incongruity between language that sounds so crisp, sensible, and upbeat and the grim message.

Nathan Cobb is a writer for the *Boston Globe* where this essay first appeared in May 1996.

1   You don't have to be a weatherman to know which way the wind's blowing, but it doesn't hurt to have a computer. What my computer tells me today is that, as far as the workplace is concerned, "downsizing" has become an official '90s buzzword. If you don't think so, look it up. Or, in this case, call it up: "Downsize" and its various relatives ("downsizing," "downsized," etc.) will turn up in the *Globe* 770 times this year at their current appearance rate. Last year, they appeared 461 times. The year before, 314. The year before that, 257. You get the picture.

2   Everybody's been talkin' the downsize talk in 1996. Pat Buchanan has lamented downsizing, Bob Dole has discovered it, and the *New York Times* has run a series about it that was so long it's surprising any writer would bother to mention the subject again. But, hey, everybody's into downsizing, especially the frightened assembly-line workers, wounded managers, scared clerical personnel, and depressed professionals who are walkin' the downsize walk.

3   What makes downsizing such a buzzword—for the downsizer, as opposed to the downsizee—is that it has a ring of painlessness. It's not like "laid off" or, God forbid, "fired." It's a word that makes the act of doing it sound like little more than trimming the hedges. How could anyone possibly object to being downsized? Memo to *The New Yorker* magazine: Have some cartoonist draw a picture of a guy walking through the front door and cheerfully announcing to his wife, "Honey, I've been downsized!"

4   Clearly, what corporate America will need in the future is more terms like this, more ways to make the shattering of people's lives sound like the tinkling of fine crystal. Feel free to send along your own suggestions, which we'll be

glad to pass along to the next CEO we meet on the Concorde. In the meantime, here are ours, along with the type of explanation that's certain to accompany them:

5 *Geographic realignment.* You've been transferred to the Boise office and you start next week. Hope you and the family enjoy the trip. Incidentally, how *is* the family?

6 *Position modification.* You're no longer a VP. We're moving you to route sales in the Northern Maine district. C'mon now, stop whimpering. Think of it as a fresh start.

7 *Benefits alteration.* We won't be paying your health insurance any longer. Your sick leave's being reduced, too. Meanwhile, do something about that cough. You sound terrible.

8 *Facilities transfiguration.* We're moving you to a smaller office. No, it's not a corner office. No, it doesn't have a sofa. No, your secretary's not going. By the way, what secretary?

9 *Transportation modulation.* We're taking back the company car. But we don't want you to think you've been reduced to taking a cab from now on. Take the subway.

10 *Remuneration adjustment.* We're cutting your pay 20 percent. It's not just you, it's everybody. Even the chairman of the board has to make sacrifices. No, I can't name two of them.

11 *Incentive diminishment.* We're eliminating certain of your perks: your parking space, your key to the executive washroom, your holiday bonus. Merry Christmas!

12 *Occupational retooling.* We'd like to retrain you at our expense. We know you've spent 20 years in human resources, but have you thought about refrigeration maintenance?

13 *Premature leavetaking.* No, we're not asking you to take early retirement. We feel you've got many productive years ahead of you. At another company.

14 *Technological adaptation.* The company is moving toward more effective use of high technology to deal with issues of human resources. In other words, you've been replaced by a computer.

15 *Execubabble comprehension.* We're not sure that you're a team player, but we'd like to help you become one. First you need to learn the new language of the workplace, the new vocabulary of corporate culture. It all started, as you probably know, back in the 1990s with the word "downsize" . . .

TOPICAL CONSIDERATIONS

1. What is "downsizing"? Have you ever experienced this phenomenon; has anyone in your family? How did you feel about the results of downsizing?

2. Cobb lists eleven terms, and then provides translations of each term. What is dishonest about each of the terms? How does the official language obscure the painful reality of the bad news being given to the employee? If you have ever experienced similar events, did you think you were dealt with honestly?

3. Why do you think a supervisor would use the kind of language Cobb describes here? How would you feel if you had to tell a fellow employee of several years that he or she was being fired, or would have his or her benefits cut? Do you think you would use this kind of language or not?

4. What kinds of jobs are downsized? What kinds of benefits and privileges do they have in common before the cuts take place? What kinds of employees has Cobb left out of his discussion?

5. What kinds of responses do the downsizees have to each of the eleven situations that Cobb has described? Sketch a brief rebuttal from each person given the bad news, using the clues that Cobb has used within the scenarios of a supervisor delivering bad news.

RHETORICAL CONSIDERATIONS

1. What is the tone of this article? Does the author endorse the attitudes and euphemistic language used to convey bad news? What do you think is the author's stance? Explain.

2. Who is the "you" in Cobb's eleven examples of euphemistic language? Why would Cobb choose to present this information in a mock dialogue between supervisor and worker? What would be the difference if Cobb had written more objective definitions of these terms? Try rewriting one or two examples without the "you" to see what the difference is.

3. Cobb uses informal patterns for the usual standards of published written English. For instance, he uses incomplete sentences, dropped letters ("talkin'"), and colloquialisms ("C'mon now"). What effect do these informal patterns have on the tone of his article? What kind of relationship does he seem to be trying to establish with his readers?

4. Would you classify Cobb's examples as "doublespeak," as defined by William Lutz ("Doubts About Doublespeak")? Or are they "euphemisms" as defined by Hugh Rawson ("Euphemisms")? What are the differences and similarities (if any) between doublespeak and euphemisms? Where does the language Cobb describes fit within these descriptions?

WRITING ASSIGNMENTS

1. Write three biographies of a hypothetical person who experiences all of the downsizing events described here. Include such details as gender, race, marital status, kind of job held, sexual orientation, disability status, and so on. Write the first biography as a personal journal entry from the point of view of the employee. Write the second biography from the point of view of a supervisor sympathetic to the employee. Write the third biography from the point of view of a supervisor who is unsympathetic to the employee.

2. Come up with a list of terms that describe some of the unpleasant realities of college life. For instance, see if you can coin phrases that a teacher might use to tell a student he or she has failed an exam, or something the registrar might use to remind you to pay a bill. On a separate sheet of paper, write down definitions for each term. Then, swap your first list with a classmate. See how much of the true

meaning you can identify in each other's lists. What strategies did you each use to recast the painful reality as something neutral or even pleasant?

3. Look up articles about economic woes in the past decade. Focus on a specific area, such as insider trading on the stock market, or high unemployment, or the rate of inflation. Select two or three sources from different kinds of news reporting—financial journals, large daily newspapers, and a weekly news magazine. Does each one use a similar number of obscuring words and phrases? Do they use different kinds? What do such words suggest about the audience to which each article is pitched?

DOCTOR TALK

Diane Johnson

Jargon is defined as the language of trades—among specialists it can serve as a shortcut in communications. It is also defined as confused and unintelligible language—used in speaking to nonspecialists it can obscure communication and intimidate the listener. In this essay, Diane Johnson discusses a double dialect of medical doctors: one that is highly jargonistic; the other, bland and noncommittal. Each, Johnson claims, is calculated to put emotional distance between doctor and patient, even though real communication may be a matter of life and death.

Diane Johnson is a professor of English at the University of California at Davis and is married to a professor of medicine. She is the author of several novels including *The Shadow Knows* (1974) and nonfiction books including the collections of essays, *Terrorists and Novelists* (1982) and *Natural Opium: Some Travelers' Tales* (1992), and the biography, *Dashiell Hammet: A Life* (1983). With Stanley Kubrick she wrote the screenplay for "The Shining" (1980) based on the Stephen King novel. Her latest book is *Le Divorce* (1997).

1   In Africa or the Amazon, the witch doctor on your case has a magic language to say his spells in. You listen, trembling, full of hope and dread and mystification; and presently you feel better or die, depending on how things come out. In England and America too, until recent times, doctors talked a magic language, usually Latin, and its mystery was part of your cure. But modern doctors are rather in the situation of modern priests; having lost their magic languages, they run the risk of losing the magic powers too.

2   For us, this means that the doctor may lose his ability to heal us by our faith; and doctors, sensing powerlessness, have been casting about for new languages in which to conceal the nature of our afflictions and the ingredients of cures. They have devised two main dialects, but neither seems quite to serve for every purpose—this is a time of transition and trial for them, marked by various strategies, of which the well-known illegible handwriting on your

prescription is but one. For doctors themselves seem to have lost faith too, in themselves and in the old mysteries and arts. They have been taught to think of themselves as scientists, and so it is first of all to the language of science that they turn, to control and confuse us.

3   Most of the time scientific language can do this perfectly. We are terrified, of course, to learn that we have "prolapse of the mitral valve"—we promise to take our medicine and stay on our diet, even though these words describe a usually innocuous finding in the investigation of an innocent heart murmur. Or we can be lulled into a false sense of security when the doctor avoids a scientific term: "you have a little spot on your lung"—even when what he puts on the chart is "probable bronchogenic carcinoma."

4   With patients, doctors can use either scientific or vernacular speech but with each other they speak Science, a strange argot of Latin terms, new words, and acronyms, that yearly becomes farther removed from everyday speech and is sometimes comprised almost entirely of numbers and letter: "His pO_2 is 45; pCO_2, 40; and pH 7.4." Sometimes it is made up of peculiar verbs originating from the apparatus with which they treat people: "Well, we've bronched him, tubed him, bagged him, cathed him, and PEEPed him," the intern tells the attending physician. ("We've explored his airways with a bronchoscope, inserted an endotrachial tube, provided assisted ventilation with a resuscitation bag, positioned a catheter in his bladder to monitor his urinary output, and used positive end-expiratory pressure to improve oxygenation.") Even when discussing things that can be expressed in ordinary words, doctors will prefer to say "he had a pneumonectomy" to saying "he had a lung removed."

5   One physician remembers being systematically instructed, during the 1950s, in scientific-sounding euphemisms to be used in the presence of patients. If a party of interns were examining an alcoholic patient, the wondering victim might hear them say that he was "suffering from hyper-ingestion of ethynol." In front of a cancer victim they would discuss his "mitosis." But in recent years such discussions are not conducted in front of the patient at all, because, since Sputnik, laymen's understanding of scientific language has itself increased so greatly that widespread ignorance cannot be assumed.

6   Space exploration has had its influence, especially on the *sound* of medical language. A CAT-scanner (computerized axial tomography), *de rigueur* in an up-to-date diagnostic unit, might be something to look at the surface of Mars with. The resonance of physical, rather than biological, science has doubtless been fostered by doctors themselves, who, mindful of the extent to which their science is really luck and art, would like to sound astronomically precise, calculable and exact, even if they cannot be so.

7   Acronyms and abbreviations play the same part in medical language that they do in other walks of modern life: We might be irritated to read on our chart "this SOB patient complained of DOE five days PTA." (It means "this Short of Breath patient complained of Dyspnea On Exertion five days Prior To Admission.") To translate certain syllables, the doctor must have yet more esoteric knowledge. Doctor A, reading Dr. B's note that a patient has TTP, must know whether Doctor B is a hematologist or a chest specialist in order to know

whether the patient has thrombotic thrombocytopenic purpura, or traumatic tension pneumothorax. That pert little word ID means identification to us, but Intradermal to the dermatologist, Inside Diameter to the physiologist, Infective Dose to the bacteriologist; it stands for our inner self, it can mean *idem* (the same), or it can signify a kind of rash.

8   But sometimes doctors must speak vernacular English, and this is apparently difficult for them. People are always being told to discuss their problems with their doctors, which, considering the general inability of doctors to reply except in a given number of reliable phrases, must be some of the worst advice ever given. Most people, trying to talk to the doctor—trying to pry or to wrest meaning from his evasive remarks ("I'd say you're coming along just fine")—have been maddened by the vague and slightly inconsequential nature of statements which, meaning everything to you, ought in themselves to have meaning but do not, are noncommittal, or unengaged, have a slightly rote or rehearsed quality, sometimes a slight inappropriateness in the context ("it's nothing to worry about really"). This is the doctor's alternative dialect, phrases so general and bland as to communicate virtually nothing.

9   This dialect originates from the emotional situation of the doctor. In the way passers-by avert their eyes from the drunk in the gutter or the village idiot, so the doctor must avoid the personality, the individuality, any involvement with the density, of his patients. He must not let himself think and feel with them. This shows in the habit doctors have of calling patients by the name of their diseases: "put the pancreatitis in the other ward and bring the chronic lunger in here." In order to retain objective professional judgment, the doctor has long since learned to withdraw his emotions from the plight of the patient and has replaced his own ability to imagine them and empathize with them with a formula language—the social lie and the understatement—usually delivered with the odd jocularity common to all gloomy professions.

10   "Well, Mrs. Jones, Henry is pretty sick. We're going to run a couple of tests, have a look at that pump of his." ("Henry is in shock. We're taking him to the Radiology Department to put a catheter in his aorta and inject contrast material. If he has what I think he has, he has a forty-two percent chance of surviving.") We might note an apparent difference of style in English and American doctors, with the English inclined to drollery in such situations. One woman I know reported that her London gynecologist said to her, of her hysterectomy, "We're taking out the cradle, but we're leaving in the playpen!" Americans on the other hand often affect tough talk: "Henry is sick as hell."

11   The doctor's *we,* by the way, is of special interest. Medical pronouns are used in special ways that ensure that the doctor is never out alone on any limb. The referents are cleverly vague. The statement "we see a lot of that" designates him as a member of a knowledgeable elite, "we doctors"; while "how are we today" means you, or him and you, if he is trying to pass himself off as a sympathetic alter ego. Rarely does he stand up as an *I.* Rarely does he even permit his name to stand alone as Smith, but affixes syllables before and after—the powerful abbreviation *Dr.* itself, which can even be found on his golf bags or skis; or the letters *M.D.* after, or sometimes the two buttressing his

name from both sides, like bookends: "Dr. Smart Smith, M.D."; in England a little train of other letters may trail behind: F.R.C.P. In America another fashionable suffix has been observed recently: *Inc.* Dr. Smart Smith, M.D., Inc. This stands for Incorporated, and indicates that the doctor has made himself into a corporation, to minimize his income taxes. A matrix of economic terms already evident in the vocabulary of some doctors is expected to become more pervasive as time goes on.

12   We may complain even of how the doctor talks to us; doctors will say, on the other hand, that it is we who do not listen. Very likely this is true. Our ears thunder with hope and dread. We cannot hear the doctor. He says "bone marrow test," we think he says "bow and arrow test." We have all been struck with disbelief, listening to an account by a friend or family member of his trip to the doctor; the cannot cannot possibly have said it was okay to go on smoking, that she doesn't need to lose weight, that he must never eat carrots. This is the case. According to doctors, patients hear themselves. The patient says, "I can't even look at a carrot," and then imagines the doctor has interdicted them. Doctors' sense of our inability to understand things may increase their tendency to talk in simple terms to us, or not to speak at all. Nonetheless, we all hear them talking, saying things they say they never say.

TOPICAL CONSIDERATIONS

1. In paragraph 1, Johnson says that until recently, "doctors talked in a magic language, usually Latin, and its mystery was part of your cure." How was the mystery of Latin part of the cure?

2. According to Johnson, what constitutes current doctor talk now that the profession has lost its magic language?

3. Do you think that doctors today regard themselves less highly than doctors of the past? If a doctor speaks in scientific jargon does that mean he has lost self-esteem?

4. The Birk and Birk essay, "Selection, Slanting, and Charged Language" (page 77) emphasizes the power of word choice in determining judgment on a subject. Discuss the different effects of Johnson's two examples in paragraph 3: "you have a little spot on your lung" versus you have "probable bronchogenic carcinoma." What does Johnson say about doctors who choose the former wording?

5. Is there anything wrong with doctors talking in jargon among themselves? Might it be too impersonal or dehumanizing?

6. In paragraph 8, Johnson says that doctors have difficulty speaking vernacular English. What does she mean by this? Why are such doctors so evasive?

7. Johnson talks about the doctors' *we.* What is the effect of this plural pronoun? Does your own doctor use the doctors' *we?*

RHETORICAL CONSIDERATIONS

1. Johnson begins with her essay with a reference to witch doctors. How effective is this opener? Does she draw a clear parallel between witch doctors and modern medical workers?

2. Judging from the tone of this essay, what would you say Johnson's attitude toward doctors is? Is she suspicious of them? Is she sorry for them? Is she sympathetic?

3. What are the transitions linking paragraphs 1 and 2; what transitions link 3 and 4? What other paragraph transitions does Johnson employ in the essay?

4. Rhetorically speaking, how well does Johnson's final paragraph round off the essay? What is the point of the example in that paragraph of a patient's hearing "bow and arrow test" for "bone marrow test"?

WRITING ASSIGNMENTS

1. We all have been to doctors at some point. If your experience with them exposed you to medical jargon, write a paper about the language you recall. Was it confusing and intimidating? Or was it bland and noncommittal?

2. Write a paper on how you think doctors should talk to their patients about their conditions.

IT MAY NOT BE ENGLISH, BUT IT'S STRICTLY LEGAL

George Gordon Coughlin

There is probably no occupational jargon more confusing and intimidating than that of lawyers. Theirs is the language of the law, of the court, of contracts and legal documents. And no language has been more criticized. In the eighteenth century Jonathan Swift said it was a language "no mortal can understand"; Jeremy Bentham called it "literary garbage." Over the years lawyers have changed, but not their jargon, as George Gordon Coughlin tells us. The question arises about conscious efforts of some lawyers to keep the archaic double talk alive. Is it for the sake of tradition or to keep some people in practice? Coughlin is a practicing attorney. This piece was first published in *Parade* magazine.

1   Charles A. Beardsley, the late president of the American Bar Association, once spoofed his fellow lawyers for their use of high-sounding, nonsensical language. In parody, he said, "Beware of and eschew pompous prolixity."

2   Beardsley then took lawyers to task for the language used in wills. He said:

> And then, if a lawyer were going to draw my will, he would probably start like this: "In the name of God, Amen. I, Charles A. Beardsley, of the City of Oakland, County of Alameda, State of California, being of sound and disposing mind and memory, and not acting under any fraud, duress, or any undue influence of any person, whatsoever, do make, publish, and declare this my last will and testament, in the manner following, that is to say."
>
> And this is all it means: "I, Charles A. Beardsley, make my will as follows."

3   Over the centuries, the most caustic critics of law language and advocates of reform have been the lawyers themselves. Yet legal language remains as far removed from the mainstream of verbal and written communication as the minuet is from the hustle.

4   Four centuries ago, Sir Thomas More was a successful London lawyer before he became Henry VIII's Lord Chancellor. His wit was renowned and apparently unfailing. History tells us that he jested even on the scaffold to which Henry VIII eventually dispatched him. Sir Thomas continually poked fun at his fellow lawyers, calling them "people whose profession is to disguise matters."

5   Jonathan Swift wrote that the language of lawyers was such that "no mortal can understand." The 18th-century philosopher and jurist Jeremy Bentham was more direct. Law talk, he said, was "literary garbage."

6   Garbage or not, lawyers still endlessly grind out documents beginning, "To all to whom these presents come or may come; greeting." And with perfectly straight faces they continue to do business with such word tools as: "Now therefore in consideration of the premises and the representations, warranties, covenants, and undertakings of the parties hereinafter set forth. . . . "

7   Thomas Jefferson was sharply critical of his own profession. He held that from time immemorial lawyers have been devoted to cloudy phrases "which from verbosity . . . are rendered more perplexed and incomprehensible not only to common readers but to lawyers themselves."

8   The only period in American history when plain language was the language of the law was in the early settlement of the Old West. Miners and prospectors made their own law without benefit or hindrance of lawyers. For example: "All persons buying a claim shall have an undisputable [sic] right to the same."

9   Some modern lawyers seem to be restraining their verbiage, but the body of the profession clings as if to a life raft to its stilted phrases: "May it please the court"; "Know all men by these presents"; "Comes now the plaintiff"; "Be it remembered."

10   And be it remembered, also, that the word "witnesseth," often used by lawyers, does not exist—in any dictionary. Do we need any of that in a busy world with crowded court calendars?

11   Consider now redundancies rampant in the simplest transactions: false and untrue; separate and apart; each and every; to have and to hold; warrant and defend; from and after; for and during; force and effect; aid and abet; by and with; cease and desist.

12   The whole bag of esoteric, useless and meaningless words and phrases was inherited along with the law they represent. Archaic legal language has been carefully preserved and elevated almost without alteration to the heights of a sacred trust. Almost from the beginning of recorded law, contracts, writs, deeds, and such were not accepted in court unless framed in stilted, formal words. Wordy language was carefully mummified in law formbooks.

13   Plain people long ago discarded such quaintisms as *thence* and *thereforth*, *theretofore* and *therewith*, but lawyers love such words. And the *here* words march on the scene like an army with banners: *herewith; heretofore; hereby; hereinafter; hereinbefore*.

14   One of the hallmarks of law language is the use of everyday words to express special legal meanings. To most people the phrase "to make a motion" involves some kind of movement. To a lawyer it means "to apply for a court order." When a lawyer delivers legal papers, he "serves" them, yet no food or tennis is involved. In law, "action" has nothing to do with activity. It means "lawsuit."

15   Other examples of common words with special legal meaning: *executed—*

signed and delivered; *instrument*—legal document; *master*—employer, *prayer*—request to a court; *without prejudice*—without loss of legal rights; *specialty*—sealed contract; *plead*—file papers in a lawsuit; *consideration*—essential ingredient of a contract; *said*—mentioned before.

16   Lawyers display a weakness for flexible words with ambiguous meaning or no meaning at all. They often use them just because they are vague. Most flexible words, however, slip unconsciously into the tedious double-talk of the legal document.

17   Consider: *reasonable, substantial, and/or, forthwith*—all flexible words. A "reasonable" length of time to one may be unreasonable to another; ditto, "substantial," and so on.

18   There is a legion of laymen who sincerely believe that lawyers use Latin and French phrases and mix up the English language deliberately in order to baffle the public and make something that is simple appear scholarly and, ergo, worth a hefty fee. Such belief is unfounded. Today there is no intention to confuse. Lawyers simply use the language of the trade.

19   Legal jargon is taught in law schools, and the sad fact is that most graduates can't write clearly because their thought has been obscured by legalese.

20   Foreign-language legal phrases abound. Some are needed because they resist simple translation; also, court papers and proceedings containing such phrases and words are the warp and woof of American law. *Habeas corpus,* for example, refers to an ancient order or writ which commanded that a person (generally a prisoner) be brought before a judge to determine if he is being legally detained. Literally, the Latin translates "you have the body." Since most people concerned with the problem know what *Habeas corpus* means, there's no point in substituting an awkward translation. *Corpus delicti* doesn't translate easily. It means "body of the crime." An *ex post facto* law is a law passed after the occurrence of an act. It would be hard to come up with a simple English equivalent.

21   But there is an abundance of easily transferable foreign legal phrases: *ab initio*—from the beginning; *amicus curiae*—a friend of the court; *causa mortis*—in contemplation of death; *caveat emptor*—let the buyer beware; *caveat venditor*—let the seller beware; *cestui que trust*—the beneficiary of a trust; *certiorari*—review by a court; *et al.*—and others; *ex contracta*—arising out of a contract; *flagrante delicto*—caught in the act; *force majeure*—superior force, Act of God; *laches*—undue delay; *lis pendens*—notice of pending suit; *particeps criminis*—participant in a crime.

22   The most effective route to badly needed reform would seem to be for lawyers and judges with clout to tell the nation's law schools that while love and respect for tradition are noble emotions, they should not obscure the present. Law schools can, if they would, break away from tradition, teach students to cut through the prevailing tangle of words and uncover the bare bones of simple declaratory sentences. What the law school doesn't teach, the law student isn't likely to perpetuate. It's up to the law schools of America to teach lawyers to talk plain English.

TOPICAL CONSIDERATIONS

1. In plain English, what does "beware of and eschew pompous prolixity" mean?

2. What are some of the important substantive differences between the shorter version of Beardsley's will and the longer original. Aren't there some fine legal points left out in the shorter?

3. Coughlin says that lawyers themselves are "the most caustic critics of law language." If so, why does lawyer jargon still flourish? Would you say the fuzziness and verbiage is intentional? What does Coughlin say about this?

4. What special effects are created by legal language that preserves Latin phrases and archaic English words? Is it similar to the magic of the doctor talk that Diane Johnson speaks of in the previous essay?

5. In paragraph 11, Coughlin cites some redundancies. Can you discover any differences in meaning in the pairs cited?

6. How does Coughlin defend the retention of some Latin terms in legal communications?

7. Do you think that law schools will "break from tradition" and teach law students to communicate in simple declaratory English?

RHETORICAL CONSIDERATIONS

1. What is the function of the Beardsley anecdote in paragraph 1? How well does it prepare the reader for what follows?

2. Most of the paragraphs in this essay are of nearly equal length—short. Why do you think the essay was written this way? Is the narrative flow choppy as a result? Could some paragraphs be combined?

3. In paragraph 18, Coughlin declares that lawyers do not intend to confuse people with their jargon. How well does he support this claim?

WRITING ASSIGNMENTS

1. If you have access to a legal document or a contract, examine the language and analyze it in an essay. Was the wording intelligible to you? Or was it vague, prolix, and intimidating? If the latter, attempt to render it in clear, concise English.

2. Write an essay defending legal language on the grounds that it preserves tradition and keeps alive the use of Latin and some quaint English phraseology.

3. If there is a law school in your area, interview instructors or law students. (If not, consult a practicing attorney.) In their lives, what is the value and function of legalese? Would they change it if they could? If not, why not? If so, how might they go about changing it? (You might ask interviewees to respond to Coughlin's closing statement: "What the law school doesn't teach, the law student isn't likely to perpetuate. It's up to the law schools of America to teach lawyers to talk plain English.")

LITTLE RED RIDING HOOD REVISITED

Russell Baker

Russell Baker, who has been writing professionally since 1962, is the Pulitzer Prize–winning columnist of the *New York Times*. His "Observer" column, from which this piece comes, is famous for its humorous, sometimes satirical criticism of social issues, trends, American politics, and current jargon. In this characteristically humorous piece, Baker takes a familiar folk tale and transforms it into modern American double talk just to demonstrate how silly and obfuscating such language is.

Baker is the author of a dozen books including bestselling *Growing Up* (1982), *The Good Times* (1989), and *There's a Country in My Cellar* (1991), his most recent memoirs.

1   In an effort to make the classics accessible to contemporary readers, I am translating them into the modern American language. Here is the translation of "Little Red Riding Hood":

2   Once upon a point in time, a small person named Little Red Riding Hood initiated plans for the preparation, delivery and transportation of foodstuffs to her grandmother, a senior citizen residing at a place of residence in a forest of indeterminate dimension.

3   In the process of implementing this program, her incursion into the forest was in midtransportation process when it attained interface with an alleged perpetrator. This individual, a wolf, made inquiry as to the whereabouts of Little Red Riding Hood's goal as well as inferring that he was desirous of ascertaining the contents of Little Red Riding Hood's foodstuffs basket, and all that.

4   "It would be inappropriate to lie to me," the wolf said, displaying his huge jaw capability. Sensing that he was a mass of repressed hostility intertwined with acute alienation, she indicated.

5   "I see you indicating," the wolf said, "but what I don't see is whatever it is you're indicating at, you dig?"

6   Little Red Riding Hood indicated more fully, making one thing perfectly clear—to wit, that it was to her grandmother's residence and with a consignment of foodstuffs that her mission consisted of taking her to and with.

7   At this point in time the wolf moderated his rhetoric and proceeded to grandmother's residence. The elderly person was then subjected to the disadvantages of total consumption and transferred to residence in the perpetrator's stomach.

8   "That will raise the old woman's consciousness," the wolf said to himself. He was not a bad wolf, but only a victim of an oppressive society, a society that not only denied wolves' rights, but actually boasted of its capacity for keeping the wolf from the door. An interior malaise made itself manifest inside the wolf.

9   "Is that the national malaise I sense within my digestive tract?" wondered the wolf. "Or is it the old person seeking to retaliate for her consumption by telling wolf jokes to my duodenum?" It was time to make a judgment. The time was now, the hour had struck, the body lupine cried out for decision. The wolf was up to the challenge. He took two stomach powders right away and got into bed.

10   The wolf had adopted the abdominal-distress recovery posture when Little Red Riding Hood achieved his presence.

11   "Grandmother," she said, "your ocular implements are of an extraordinary order of magnitude."

12   "The purpose of this enlarged viewing capability," said the wolf, "is to enable your image to register a more precise impression upon my sight systems."

13   "In reference to your ears," said Little Red Riding Hood, "it is noted with the deepest respect that far from being underprivileged, their elongation and enlargement appear to qualify you for unparalleled distinction."

14   "I hear you loud and clear, kid," said the wolf, "but what about these new choppers?"

15   "If it is not inappropriate," said Little Red Riding Hood, "it might be observed that with your new miracle masticating products you may even be able to chew taffy again."

16   This observation was followed by the adoption of an aggressive posture on the part of the wolf and the assertion that it was also possible for him, due to the high efficiency ratio of his jaw, to consume little persons, plus, as he stated, his firm determination to do so at once without delay and with all due process and propriety, notwithstanding the fact that the ingestion of one entire grandmother had already provided twice his daily recommended cholesterol intake.

17   There ensued flight by Little Red Riding accompanied by pursuit in respect to the wolf and a subsequent intervention on the part of a third party, heretofore unnoted in the record.

18   Due to the firmness of the intervention, the wolf's stomach underwent ax-assisted aperture with the result that Red Riding Hood's grandmother was enabled to be removed with only minor discomfort.

19   The wolf's indigestion was immediately alleviated with such effectiveness that he signed a contract with the intervening third party to perform with

grandmother in a television commercial demonstrating the swiftness of this dramatic relief for stomach discontent.

20   "I'm going to be on television," cried grandmother.

21   And they all joined her happily in crying, "What a phenomena!"

TOPICAL CONSIDERATIONS

1. Baker uses many examples of jargon. Select some and try to determine what professions they are drawn from.

2. Cite some examples of repetition and excessive Latinisms.

3. Can you find any political allusions in this rewrite of Little Red Riding Hood?

4. In your own words, state Baker's thesis.

5. The ending of this version is different from that of the original. In what ways is it different? Why do you think Baker made the changes?

RHETORICAL CONSIDERATIONS

1. Discuss the tone of this essay. Does Baker capture the flavor of officialdom?

2. Discuss the satiric import of the first line. For what purpose did Baker select the words "small person," "senior citizen," "delivery and transportation," "a place of residence," and "forest of indeterminate dimension"? What is he poking fun at?

WRITING ASSIGNMENTS

1. Choose another story—such as Jack and the Beanstalk, Hansel and Gretel, Cinderella—and write a modern version using Baker's satiric approach.

2. Find a particularly flagrant example of bad jargon in Baker's piece and write an essay on its failure to communicate.

3. Write a letter to Russel Baker in full-blown jargon telling him how much you liked his modernized version and how much more you got out of it than you would out of the traditional version.

9 | STANDARD AND NONSTANDARD ENGLISH

GRAMMARIAN

In 1850, American poet Walt Whitman predicted that Americans would be "the most fluent people in the world, the most perfect users of words." Nearly a century and a half has passed, yet, to some, those words were far more optimistic than prophetic. Language guardians lament that America will be the death of English. They cry out that our language is rife with slang, bad grammar, neologisms, and bureaucratic double talk; that substandard dialects and the influx of immigrants are corrupting the common tongue; and that high school students have the verbal skills of third graders. At the heart of the outcry is the question of standards: What are they? What should they be? This chapter addresses the questions of standard and nonstandard English and the social issues intricately bound to them.

WHAT'S "GOOD" ENGLISH?

The chapter opens with an amusing and engaging discussion of just what is "good" and "bad" English by Bill Bryson. His essay, "Good English and Bad," serves as an overview to the more pointed discussions that follow, including the debate that rages in the next two essays. John Simon is one of America's famous and formidable language guardians. In "Why Good English Is Good for You," he argues that good English is a serious social and personal issue. Learning to express oneself properly, grammatically, is worth the effort because it not only improves memory and thinking, but it instills pride in expression that could profit careers and social affairs. Going head to head with language conservative John Simon is language liberal Jim Quinn. In "Simonspeak," Quinn attempts to dismantle John Simon's argument by pointing out that new words and diversity in usage are good for English. Furthermore, he argues, the use of some pet illiteracies never hurt the writings of Shakespeare, Dickens, and Austen.

WHAT'S NOT? SLANG AND DIALECTS

Nothing in our language is more nonstandard or more American than slang. In the next piece, "It Ain't No Big Thing," Paul Dickson takes a look at the nature, use, and function of contemporary slang. From his assessment, it is as dynamic a cultural force in this last decade of the twentieth century as it has ever been. Fed by different groups and professions, subcultures and countercultures, musicians and black rappers, slang is far from losing its renegade vitality, especially with television soaking up the latest catch phrase and beaming them to every American living room within seconds.

Surprisingly, television hasn't made a dent in American dialects. So says

Patrick Cooke who investigates some rich and stubborn regional dialects in the next piece—"Are Accents Out? Hey, Dude, Like NEH-oh Way!"

The chapter concludes with an amusing look at a curious new speech pattern that has been sweeping the country, particularly among teenagers and twenty-somethings. As James Gorman describes in "Like, Uptalk?" it consists of a rising intonation at the end of a phrase. While nobody knows exactly where the phenomenon began, you will probably recognize it. You may even be a practitioner. At the least, you should get a few laughs. Like not a bad way to say goodbye?

GOOD ENGLISH AND BAD

Bill Bryson

Over 350 million people in the world speak English, and much of the rest of the world is attempting to. But as Paul Roberts explains in his essay (Chapter 1), the English language, with its various historical influences, is very complex. In fact, deceptively so. Even language authorities will stumble over its idiosyncrasies, as demonstrated below. And the reason is simple: In an effort to establish criteria for *good* English for generations to come, seventeenth-century grammarians wrote rules of English modeled on those of Latin, which, though dead, was considered the most admirable and purest tongue. But as Bill Bryson explains, imposing Latin rules on English is like asking people to play baseball according to the rules of football. They don't go together; likewise, ancient standards of usage don't always describe how the language works today. In this lively and engaging discussion, Bill Bryson explains how the distinction of *good* English from *bad* English is mostly a matter of conditioning and prejudice.

Bill Bryson is an American journalist living in England. He has worked for the *Times* of London and the *Independent* and has written articles for the *New York Times, Esquire, GQ,* and other journals. His books include *A Dictionary of Troublesome Words, The Lost Continent,* and the highly acclaimed *The Mother Tongue* (1990), from which this essay comes.

1   Consider the parts of speech. In Latin, the verb has up to 120 inflections. In English it never has more than five (e.g., *see, sees, saw, seeing, seen*) and often it gets by with just three (*hit, hits, hitting*). Instead of using loads of different verb forms, we use just a few forms but employ them in loads of ways. We need just five inflections to deal with the act of propelling a car—*drive, drives, drove, driving,* and *driven*—yet with these we can express quite complex and subtle variations of tense: "I drive to work every day," "I have been driving since I was sixteen," "I will have driven 20,000 miles by the end of this year." This system, for all its ease of use, makes labeling difficult. According to any textbook, the present tense of the verb *drive* is *drive*. Every junior high school

pupil knows that. Yet if we say, "I used to drive to work but now I don't," we are clearly using the present tense *drive* in a past tense sense. Equally if we say, "I will drive you to work tomorrow," we are using it in a future sense. And if we say, "I would drive if I could afford to," we are using it in a conditional sense. In fact, almost the only form of sentence in which we cannot use the present tense form of *drive* is, yes, the present tense. When we need to indicate an action going on right now, we must use the participial form *driving.* We don't say, "I drive the car now," but rather "I'm driving the car now." Not to put too fine a point on it, the labels are largely meaningless.

2   We seldom stop to think about it, but some of the most basic concepts in English are naggingly difficult to define. What, for instance, is a sentence? Most dictionaries define it broadly as a group of words constituting a full thought and containing, at a minimum, a subject (basically a noun) and predicate (basically a verb). Yet if I inform you that I have just crashed your car and you reply, "What!" or "Where?" or "How!" you have clearly expressed a complete thought, uttered a sentence. But where are the subject and predicate? Where are the noun and verb, not to mention the prepositions, conjunctions, articles, and other components that we normally expect to find in a sentence? To get around this problem, grammarians pretend that such sentences contain words that aren't there. "What!" they would say, really means "What are you telling me—you crashed my car?" while "Where?" is a shorthand rendering of "Where did you crash it?" and "How?" translates as "How on earth did you manage to do that, you old devil you?" or words to that effect. The process is called *ellipsis* and is certainly very nifty. Would that I could do the same with my bank account. Yet the inescapable fact is that it is possible to make such sentences conform to grammatical precepts only by bending the rules. When I was growing up we called that cheating.

3   In English, in short, we possess a language in which the parts of speech are almost entirely notional. A noun is a noun and a verb is a verb largely because the grammarians say they are. In the sentence "I am suffering terribly" *suffering* is a verb, but in "My suffering is terrible," it is a noun. Yet both sentences use precisely the same word to express precisely the same idea. *Quickly* and *sleepily* are adverbs but *sickly* and *deadly* are adjectives. *Breaking* is a present tense participle, but as often as not it is used in a past tense sense ("He was breaking the window when I saw him"). *Broken,* on the other hand, is a past tense participle but as often as not it is employed in a present tense sense ("I think I've just broken my toe") or even future tense sense ("If he wins the next race, he'll have broken the school record"). To deal with all the anomalies, the parts of speech must be so broadly defined as to be almost meaningless. A noun, for example, is generally said to be a word that denotes a person, place, thing, action, or quality. That would seem to cover almost everything, yet clearly most actions are verbs and many words that denote qualities—*brave, foolish, good*—are adjectives.

4   The complexities of English are such that the authorities themselves often stumble. Each of the following, penned by an expert, contains a usage that at least some of his colleagues would consider quite wrong.

"Prestige is one of the few words that has had an experience opposite to that described in 'Worsened Words.'" (H. W. Fowler, *A Dictionary of Modern English Usage,* second edition) It should be "one of the few words that *have* had."

"Each of the variants indicated in boldface type count as an entry." (*The Harper Dictionary of Contemporary Usage*) It should be "each . . . *counts.*"

"It is of interest to speculate about the amount of dislocation to the spelling system that would occur if English dictionaries were either proscribed or (as when Malory or Sir Philip Sidney were writing) did not exist." (Robert Burchfield, *The English Language*) Make it "*was* writing."

"A range of sentences forming statements, commands, questions and exclamations cause us to draw on a more sophisticated battery of orderings and arrangements." (Robert Burchfield, *The English Language*) It should be *causes.*

"The prevalence of incorrect instances of the use of the apostrophe . . . together with the abandonment of it by many business firms . . . suggest that the time is close at hand when this moderately useful device should be abandoned." (Robert Burchfield, *The English Language*) The verb should be *suggests.*

"If a lot of the available dialect data is obsolete or almost so, a lot more of it is far too sparse to support any sort of reliable conclusion." (Robert Claiborne, *Our Marvelous Native Tongue*) *Data* is a plural.

"His system of citing examples of the best authorities, of indicating etymology, and pronunciation, are still followed by lexicographers." (Philip Howard, *The State of the Language*) His system are?

"When his fellowship expired he was offered a rectorship at Boxworth . . . on condition that he married the deceased rector's daughter." (Robert McCrum, et al., *The Story of English*) A misuse of the subjunctive: It should be "on condition that he marry."

5   English grammar is so complex and confusing for the one very simple reason that its rules and terminology are based on Latin—a language with which it has precious little in common. In Latin, to take one example, it is not possible to split an infinitive. So in English, the early authorities decided, it should not be possible to split an infinitive either. But there is no reason why we shouldn't, any more than we should forsake instant coffee and air travel because they weren't available to the Romans. Making English grammar conform to Latin rules is like asking people to play baseball using the rules of football. It is a patent absurdity. But once this insane notion became established grammarians found themselves having to draw up ever more complicated and circular arguments to accommodate the inconsistencies. As Burchfield notes in *The English Language,* one authority. F. Th. Visser, found it necessary to devote 200 pages to discussing just one aspect of the present participle. That is as crazy as it is amazing.

6   The early authorities not only used Latin grammar as their model, but actually went to the almost farcical length of writing English grammars in that language, as with Sir Thomas Smith's *De Recta et Emendata Linguae Anglicae Scriptione Dialogus* (1568), Alexander Gil's *Logonomia Anglica* (1619), and

John Wallis's *Grammatica Linguae Anglicanae* of 1653 (though even he accepted that the grammar of Latin was ill-suited to English). For the longest time it was taken entirely for granted that the classical languages *must* serve as models. Dryden spoke for an age when he boasted that he often translated his sentences into Latin to help him decide how best to express them in English.

7   In 1660, Dryden complained that English had "not so much as a tolerable dictionary or a grammar; so our language is in a manner barbarous." He believed there should be an academy to regulate English usage, and for the next two centuries many others would echo his view. In 1664, The Royal Society for the Advancement of Experimental Philosophy formed a committee "to improve the English tongue," though nothing lasting seems to have come of it. Thirty-three years later in his *Essay Upon Projects*, Daniel Defoe was calling for an academy to oversee the language. In 1712, Jonathan Swift joined the chorus with a *Proposal for Correcting, Improving and Ascertaining the English Tongue.* Some indication of the strength of feeling attached to these matters is given by the fact that in 1780, in the midst of the American Revolution, John Adams wrote to the president of Congress appealing to him to set up an academy for the purpose of "refining, correcting, improving and ascertaining the English language" (a title that closely echoes, not to say plagiarizes, Swift's pamphlet of sixty-eight years before). In 1806, the American Congress considered a bill to institute a national academy and in 1820 an American Academy of Language and Belles Lettres, presided over by John Quincy Adams, was formed, though again without any resounding perpetual benefits to users of the language. And there were many other such proposals and assemblies.

8   The model for all these was the Académie Française, founded by Cardinal Richelieu in 1635. In its youth, the academy was an ambitious motivator of change. In 1762, after many years of work, it published a dictionary that regularized the spellings of some 5,000 words—almost a quarter of the words then in common use. It took the *s* out of words like *estre* and *fenestre*, making them *[ace]tre* and *fen[ace]tre*, and it turned *roy* and *loy* into *roi* and *loi*. In recent decades, however, the academy has been associated with an almost ayatollah-like conservatism. When in December 1988 over 90 percent of French schoolteachers voted in favor of a proposal to introduce the sort of spelling reforms the academy itself had introduced 200 years earlier, the forty venerable members of the academy were, to quote the London *Sunday Times*, "up in apoplectic arms" at the thought of tampering with something as sacred as French spelling. Such is the way of the world. Among the changes the teachers wanted and the academicians did not were the removal of the circumflex on *[ace]tre, fen[ace]tre*, and other such words, and taking the *-x* off plurals such as *bureaux, chevaux*, and *chateaux* and replacing it with an *-s*.

9   Such actions underline the one almost inevitable shortcoming of national academies. However progressive and far-seeing they may be to begin with, they almost always exert over time a depressive effect on change. So it is probably fortunate that the English-speaking world never saddled itself such a body, largely because as many influential users of English were opposed to academies as favored them. Samuel Johnson doubted the prospects of arresting change

and Thomas Jefferson thought it in any case undesirable. In declining an offer to be the first honorary president of the Academy of Language and Belles Lettres, he noted that had such a body been formed in the days of the Anglo-Saxons English would now be unable to describe the modern world. Joseph Priestley, the English scientist, grammarian, and theologian, spoke perhaps most eloquently against the formation of an academy when he said in 1761 that it was "unsuitable to the genius of a free nation. . . . We need make no doubt but that the best forms of speech will, in time, establish themselves by their own superior excellence: and in all controversies, it is better to wait the decisions of time, which are slow and sure, than to take those of synods, which are often hasty and injudicious." [Quoted by Baugh and Cable, page 269]

10   English is often commended by outsiders for its lack of a stultifying authority. Otto Jespersen as long ago as 1905 was praising English for its lack of rigidity, its happy air of casualness. Likening French to the severe and formal gardens of Louis XIV, he contrasted it with English, which he said was "laid out seemingly without any definite plan, and in which you are allowed to walk everywhere according to your own fancy without having to fear a stern keeper enforcing rigorous regulations." [*Growth and Structure of the English Language,* page 16]

11   Without an official academy to guide us, the English-speaking world has long relied on self-appointed authorities such as the brothers H. W. and F. G. Fowler and Sir Ernest Gowers in Britain and Theodore Bernstein and William Safire in America, and of course countless others. These figures write books, give lectures, and otherwise do what they can (i.e., next to nothing) to try to stanch (not staunch) the perceived decline of the language. They point out that there is a useful distinction to be observed between *uninterested* and *disinterested,* between *imply* and *infer, flaunt* and *flout, fortunate* and *fortuitous, forgo* and *forego,* and *discomfort* and *discomfit* (not forgetting *stanch* and *staunch*). They point out that *fulsome,* properly used, is a term of abuse, not praise, that *peruse* actually means to read thoroughly, not glance through, that *data* and *media* are plurals. And from the highest offices in the land they are ignored.

12   In the late 1970s, President Jimmy Carter betrayed a flaw in his linguistic armory when he said: "The government of Iran must realize that it cannot flaunt, with impunity, the expressed will and law of the world community." *Flaunt* means to show off; he meant *flout.* The day after he was elected president in 1988, George Bush told a television reporter he couldn't believe the enormity of what had happened. Had President-elect Bush known that the primary meaning of *enormity* is wickedness or evilness, he would doubtless have selected a more apt term.

13   When this process of change can be seen happening in our lifetimes, it is almost always greeted with cries of despair and alarm. Yet such change is both continuous and inevitable. Few acts are more salutary than looking at the writings of language authorities from recent decades and seeing the usages that heightened their hackles. In 1931, H. W. Fowler was tutting over *racial,* which he called "an ugly word, the strangeness of which is due to our instinctive feel-

ing that the termination -al has no business at the end of a word that is not obviously Latin." (For similar reasons he disliked *television* and *speedometer*.) Other authorities have variously—and sometimes hotly—attacked *enthuse, commentate, emote, prestigious, contact* as a verb, *chair* as a verb, and scores of others. But of course these are nothing more than opinions, and, as is the way with other people's opinions, they are generally ignored.

14   So if there are no officially appointed guardians for the English language, who sets down all those rules that we all know about from childhood—the idea that we must never end a sentence with a preposition or begin one with a conjunction, that we must use *each other* for two things and *one another* for more than two, and that we must never use *hopefully* in an absolute sense, such as "Hopefully it will not rain tomorrow"? The answer, surprisingly often, is that no one does, that when you look into the background of these "rules" there is often little basis for them.

15   Consider the curiously persistent notion that sentences should not end with a preposition. The source of this stricture, and several other equally dubious ones, was one Robert Lowth, an eighteenth-century clergyman and amateur grammarian whose *A Short Introduction to English Grammar,* published in 1762, enjoyed a long and distressingly influential life both in his native England and abroad. It is to Lowth we can trace many a pedant's most treasured notions: the belief that you must say *different from* rather than than *different to* or *different than,* the idea that two negatives make a positive, the rule that you must not say "the heaviest of the two objects," but rather "the heavier," the distinction between *shall* and *will,* and the clearly nonsensical belief that *between* can apply only to two things and *among* to more than two. (By this reasoning, it would not be possible to say that St. Louis is between New York, Los Angeles, and Chicago, but rather that it is among them, which would impart a quite different sense.) Perhaps the most remarkable and curiously enduring of Lowth's many beliefs was the conviction that sentences ought not to end with a preposition. But even he was not didactic about it. He recognized that ending a sentence with a preposition was idiomatic and common in both speech and informal writing. He suggested only that he thought it generally better and more graceful, not crucial, to place the preposition before its relative "in solemn and elevated" writing. Within a hundred years this had been converted from a piece of questionable advice into an immutable rule. In a remarkable outburst of literal-mindedness, nineteenth-century academics took it as read that the very name *pre-position* meant it must come before something—anything.

16   But then this was a period of the most resplendent silliness, when grammarians and scholars seemed to be climbing over one another (or each other; it doesn't really matter) in a mad scramble to come up with fresh absurdities. This was the age when, it was gravely insisted, Shakespeare's *laughable* ought to be changed to *laugh-at-able* and *reliable* should be made into *relionable.* Dozens of seemingly unexceptional words—*lengthy, standpoint, international, colonial, brash*—were attacked with venom because of some supposed etymological deficiency or other. Thomas de Quincey, in between bouts of opium tak-

ing, found time to attack the expression *what on earth.* Some people wrote *mooned* for *lunatic* and *foresayer* for *prophet* on the grounds that the new words were Anglo-Saxon and thus somehow more pure. They roundly castigated those ignoramuses who impurely combined Greek and Latin roots into new words like *petroleum* (Latin *petro* + Greek *oleum*). In doing so, they failed to note that the very word with which they described themselves, *grammarians,* is itself a hybrid made of Greek and Latin roots, as are many other words that have lived unexceptionably in English for centuries. They even attacked *hand-book* as an ugly Germanic compound when it dared to show its face in the nineteenth century, failing to notice that it was a good Old English word that had simply fallen out of use. It is one of the felicities of English that we can take pieces of words from all over and fuse them into new constructions—like *trusteeship,* which consists of a Nordic stem (*trust*), combined with a French affix (*ee*), married to an Old English root (*ship*). Other languages cannot do this. We should be proud of ourselves for our ingenuity and yet even now authorities commonly attack almost any new construction as ugly or barbaric.

17   Today in England you can still find authorities attacking the construction *different than* as a regrettable Americanism, insisting that a sentence such as "How different things appear in Washington than in London" is ungrammatical and should be changed to "How different things appear in Washington from how they appear in London." Yet *different than* has been common in England for centuries and used by such exalted writers as Defoe, Addison, Steele, Dickens, Coleridge, and Thackeray, among others. Other authorities, in both Britain and America, continue to deride the absolute use of *hopefully. The New York Times Manual of Style and Usage* flatly forbids it. Its writers must not say, "Hopefully the sun will come out soon," but rather are instructed to resort to a clumsily passive and periphrastic construction such as "It is to be hoped that the sun will come out soon." The reason? The authorities maintain that *hopefully* in the first sentence is a misplaced modal auxiliary—that it doesn't belong to any other part of the sentence. Yet they raise no objection to dozens of other words being used in precisely the same unattached way—*admittedly, mercifully, happily, curiously,* and so on. The reason *hopefully* is not allowed is because, well, because somebody at the *New York Times* once had a boss who wouldn't allow it because his professor had forbidden it, because *his* father thought it was ugly and inelegant, because *he* had been told so by his uncle who was a man of great learning . . . and so on.

18   Considerations of what makes for good English or bad English are to an uncomfortably large extent matters of prejudice and conditioning. Until the eighteenth century it was correct to say "you was" if you were referring to one person. It sounds odd today, but the logic is impeccable. *Was* is a singular verb and *were* a plural one. Why should *you* take a plural verb when the sense is clearly singular? The answer—surprise, surprise—is that Robert Lowth didn't like it. "I'm hurrying, are I not?" is hopelessly ungrammatical, but "I'm hurrying, aren't I?"—merely a contraction of the same words—is perfect English. *Many* is almost always a plural (as in "Many people were there"), but not when it is followed by *a*, as in "Many a man was there." There's no inherent

reason why these things should be so. They are not defensible in terms of grammar. They are because they are.

19   Nothing illustrates the scope of prejudice in English between than the issue of the split infinitive. Some people feel ridiculously strong about it. When the British Conservative politician Jock Bruce-Gardyne was economic secretary to the Treasury in the early 1980s, he returned unread any departmental correspondence containing a split infinitive. (It should perhaps be pointed out that a split infinitive is one in which an adverb comes between *to* and a verb, as in *to quickly look*.) I can think of two very good reasons for not splitting an infinitive.

1. Because you feel that the rules of English ought to conform to the grammatical precepts of a language that died a thousand years ago.

2. Because you wish to cling to a pointless affectation of usage that is without the support of any recognized authority of the last 200 years, even at the cost of composing sentences that are ambiguous, inelegant, and patently contorted.

20   It is exceedingly difficult to find any authority who condemns the split infinitive—Theodore Bernstein, H. W. Fowler, Ernest Gowers, Eric Partridge, Rudolph Flesch, Wilson Follett, Roy H. Copperud, and others too tedious to enumerate here all agree that there is no logical reason not to split an infinitive. Otto Jespersen even suggests that, strictly speaking, it isn't actually possible to split an infinitive. As he puts it: "'To' . . . is no more an essential part of an infinitive than the definite article is an essential part of a nominative, and no one would think of calling 'the good man' a split nominative." [*Growth and Structure of the English Language,* page 222]

21   Lacking an academy as we do, we might expect dictionaries to take up the banner of defenders of the language, but in recent years they have increasingly shied away from the role. A perennial argument with dictionary makers is whether they should be *prescriptive* (that is, whether they should prescribe how language should be used) or *descriptive* (that is, merely describe how it is used without taking a position). The most notorious example of the descriptive school was the 1961 *Webster's Third New International Dictionary* (popularly called *Webster's Unabridged*), whose editor, Philip Gove, believed that distinctions of usage were elitist and artificial. As a result, usages such as *imply* as a synonym for *infer* and *flout* being used in the sense of *flaunt* were included without comment. The dictionary provoked further antagonism, particularly among members of the U.S. Trademark Association, by refusing to capitalize trademarked words. But what really excited outrage was its remarkable contention that *ain't* was "used orally in most parts of the U.S. by many cultivated speakers."

22   So disgusted was the *New York Times* with the new dictionary that it announced it would not use it but would continue with the 1934 edition, prompting the language authority Bergen Evans to write: "Anyone who solemnly announces in the year 1962 that he will be guided in matters of English usage by a dictionary published in 1934 is talking ignorant and pretentious nonsense," and he pointed out that the issue of the *Times* announcing the decision contained nineteen words condemned by the *Second International*.

23   Since then, other dictionaries have been divided on the matter. *The American Heritage Dictionary,* first published in 1969, instituted a usage panel of distinguished commentators to rule on contentious points of usage, which are discussed, often at some length, in the text. But others have been more equivocal (or prudent or spineless depending on how you view it). The revised *Random House Dictionary of the English Language,* published in 1987, accepts the looser meaning for most words, though often noting that the newer usage is frowned on "by many"—a curiously timid approach that at once acknowledges the existence of expert opinion and yet constantly places it at a distance. Among the looser meanings it accepts are *disinterested* to mean uninterested and *infer* to mean imply. It even accepts the existence of *kudo* as a singular—prompting a reviewer from *Time* magazine to ask if one instance of pathos should now be a patho.

24   It's a fine issue. One of the undoubted virtues of English is that it is a fluid and democratic language in which meanings shift and change in response to the pressures of common usage rather than the dictates of committees. It is a natural process that has been going in for centuries. To interfere with that process is arguably both arrogant and futile, since clearly the weight of usage will push new meanings into currency no matter how many authorities hurl themselves into the path of change.

25   But at the same time, it seems to me, there is a case for resisting change—at least slapdash change. Even the most liberal descriptivist would accept that there must be *some* conventions of usage. We must agree to spell *cat* c-a-t and not e-l-e-p-h-a-n-t, and we must agree that by that word we mean a small furry quadruped that goes *meow* and sits comfortably on one's lap and not a large lumbering beast that grows tusks and is exceedingly difficult to housebreak. In precisely the same way, clarity is generally better served if we agree to observe a distinction between *imply* and *infer, forego* and *forgo, fortuitous* and *fortunate, uninterested* and *disinterested,* and many others. As John Ciardi observed, resistance may in the end prove futile, but at least it tests the changes and makes them prove their worth.

26   Perhaps for our last words on the subject of usage we should turn to the last words of the venerable French grammarian Dominique Bonhours, who proved on his deathbed that a grammarian's work is never done when he turned to those gathered loyally around him and whispered: "I am about to— or I am going to—die; either expression is used."

TOPICAL CONSIDERATIONS

1. How did early grammarians help shape the rules of current usage? According to Bryson, how did they contribute to some of the idiosyncrasies of English rules? Give some examples of rules that do not work.

2. Given all the anomalies in the English language, what is the author suggesting about standards of usage? How does his discussion make you feel about your own lapses in grammar?

3. What, according to Bryson, is the difference between "good English" and "bad English"? What is his basis of distinction? Do you agree with his views?

4. Bryson reports that for centuries grammarians called for the official regulation of English usage. What fundamental attitudes about language did these proposals underscore? What about the attitude of Thomas Jefferson and John Priestly? Where does Bryson stand on the issue of regulation?

5. Do you think Bryson's attitude toward today's guardians of good English will influence your own attitude? Do you think you'll be more or less careful about splitting infinitives or using such expressions as *different from* and *hopefully*?

RHETORICAL CONSIDERATIONS

1. What kind of personality does Bryson project in this essay? In other words, based on his tone, word choice, his style, the examples he chooses, his comments, and so on, how would you describe him?

2. Describe some of the different ways Bryson projects his attitude toward prescriptive grammar.

3. What is the author's strategy in citing some grammatical errors of language authorities? How well do they serve his purpose?

4. What examples of Bryson's sense of humor can you point to? How does his humor contribute to the essay? Is this a strategy you might employ in your writing?

5. What parts of this essay did you find most interesting? most informative? Which parts were not so interesting to you?

6. How would you evaluate Bryson's own use of English? How might Bryson respond to criticism that while defending nonstandard usage, his own writing strictly obeys the rules of traditional usage?

7. What do you make of Bryson's concluding paragraph? Is it satisfying to you? Does it make a point consistent with preceding arguments? Is it consistent with the general tone of the essay? Explain your answers.

WRITING ASSIGNMENTS

1. Do you think that dictionaries should be prescriptive instead of descriptive—that is, should they take a position on the traditional rules of proper grammar, usage, and spelling? Write a letter to Bill Bryson explaining how you feel about this and give three specific reasons.

2. Have you ever been bothered by someone's poor grammar or usage? If so, describe in a brief essay your experience and your feelings. Has this essay affected your attitude at all? Explain.

3. As best you can, try to describe your own English usage. Do you think you speak "good English"? Explain your answer with specific references.

4. If you heard the president or some other official make grammatical and usage errors in an interview, would that affect your view of that person? Would it make him or her seem less deserving of your respect or seem more down-to-earth? Write out your thoughts in an essay, perhaps citing some examples of faulty presidential usage you've found on your own.

WHY GOOD ENGLISH IS GOOD FOR YOU

John Simon

John Simon, who currently reviews theater for *New York* magazine, is a renowned critic of the arts and of the shoddy language of Americans. For years he wrote a regular language column for *Esquire,* from which some essays were published in a 1980 collection about the decline of literacy, *Paradigms Lost.* The essay below, taken from that collection, is not just a wry and incisive look at the way American English is being abused. It is a strong argument in favor of using good English—an effort that improves not only communication but also memory and thinking.

1 What's good English to you that . . . you should grieve for it? What good is correct speech and writing, you may ask, in an age in which hardly anyone seems to know, and no one seems to care? Why shouldn't you just fling bloopers riotously with the throng, and not stick out from the rest like a sore thumb by using the language correctly? Isn't grammar really a thing of the past, and isn't the new idea to communicate in *any* way as long as you can make yourself understood?

2   The usual, basic defense of good English (and here, again, let us not worry about nomenclature—for all I care, you may call it "Standard English," "correct American," or anything else) is that it helps communication, that it is perhaps even a *sine qua non* of mutual understanding. Although this is a crude truth of sorts, it strikes me as, in some ways, both more and less than the truth. Suppose you say, "Everyone in their right mind would cross on the green light" or "Hopefully, it won't rain tomorrow," chances are very good that the person you say this to will understand you, even though you are committing obvious solecisms or creating needless ambiguities. Similarly, if you write in a letter, "The baby has finally ceased its howling" (spelling *its* as *it's*), the recipient will be able to figure out what was meant. But "figuring out" is precisely what a listener or reader should not have to do. There is, of course, the fundamental matter of courtesy to the other person, but it goes beyond that: why waste time on unscrambling simple meaning when there are more complex questions that should receive our undivided attention? If the many cooks had to worry first about which out of a large number of pots had no leak in it, the broth, whether spoiled or not, would take forever to be ready.

3   It is, I repeat, only initially a matter of clarity. It is also a matter of concision. Space today is as limited as time. If you have only a thousand words in which to convey an important message it helps to know that "overcomplicated" is correct and "overly complicated" is incorrect. Never mind the grammatical explanations; the two extra characters and one space between words are reason enough. But what about the more advanced forms of wordmongering that hold sway nowadays? Take redundancy, like the "hopes and aspirations" of Jimmy Carter, quoted by Edwin Newman as having "a deeply profound religious experience"; or elaborate jargon, as when Charles G. Walcutt, a graduate professor of English at CUNY, writes (again as quoted by Newman): "The colleges, trying to remediate increasing numbers of . . . illiterates up to college levels, are being highschoolized"; or just obfuscatory verbiage of the pretentious sort, such as this fragment from a letter I received: "It is my impression that effective inter personal verbal communication depends on prior effective intra-personal verbal communication." What this means is that if you think clearly, you can speak and write clearly—except if you are a "certified speech and language pathologist," like the writer of the letter I quote. (By the way, she adds the letters Ph.D. after her name, though she is not even from Germany, where *Herr* and *Frau Doktor* are in common, not to say vulgar, use.)

4   But except for her ghastly verbiage, our certified language pathologist (whatever that means) is perfectly right: there is a close connection between the ability to think and the ability to use English correctly. After all, we think in words, we conceptualize in words, we work out our problems inwardly with words, and using them correctly is comparable to a craftsman's treating his tools with care, keeping his materials in good shape. Would you trust a weaver who hangs her wet laundry on her loom, or lets her cats bed down in her yarn? The person who does not respect words and their proper relationships cannot have much respect for ideas—very possibly cannot have ideas at all. My quarrel is not so much with minor errors that we all fall into from time to time even if we know better as it is with basic sloppiness or ignorance or defiance of good English.

5   Training yourself to speak and write correctly—and I say "training yourself" because nowadays, unfortunately, you cannot depend on other people or on institutions to give you the proper training, for reasons I shall discuss later—training yourself, then, in language, means developing at the very least two extremely useful faculties: your sense of discipline and your memory. Discipline because is language is with us always, as nothing else is: it follows us much as, in the old morality play, Good Deeds followed Everyman, all the way to the grave; and, if the language is written, even beyond. Let me explain: if you keep an orderly apartment, if you can see to it that your correspondence and bill-paying are attended to regularly, if your diet and wardrobe are maintained with the necessary care—good enough; you are a disciplined person.

6   But the preliminary discipline underlying all others is nevertheless your speech: the words that come out of you almost as frequently and—if you are tidy—as regularly as your breath. I would go so far as to say that, immediately

after your bodily functions, language is first, unless you happen to be an ascetic, an anchorite, or a stylite; but unless you are a sty*lite,* you had better be a sty*list.*

7   Most of us—almost all—must take in and give out language as we do breath, and we had better consider the seriousness of language pollution as second only to air pollution. For the linguistically disciplined, to misuse or mispronounce a word is an unnecessary and unhealthy contribution to the surrounding smog. To have taught ourselves not to do this, or—being human and thus also imperfect—to do it as little as possible, means deriving from every speaking moment the satisfaction we get from a cap that snaps on to a container perfectly, an elevator that stops flush with the landing, a roulette ball that comes to rest exactly on the number on which we have placed our bet. It gives us the pleasure of hearing or seeing our words—because they are abiding by the rules—snapping, sliding, falling precisely into place, expressing with perfect lucidity and symmetry just what we wanted them to express. This is comparable to the satisfaction of the athlete or ballet dancer or pianist finding his body or legs or fingers doing his bidding with unimpeachable accuracy.

8   And if someone now says that "in George Eliot's lesser novels, she is not completely in command" is perfectly comprehensible even if it is ungrammatical, the "she" having no antecedent in the nominative (*Eliot's* is a genitive), I say, "Comprehensible, perhaps, but lopsided," for the civilized and orderly mind does not feel comfortable with that "she"—does not hear that desired and satisfying click of correctness—unless the sentence is restructured as "George Eliot, in her lesser novels, is not . . . " or in some similar way. In fact, the fully literate ear can be thrown by this error in syntax; it may look for the antecedent of that "she" elsewhere than in the preceding possessive case. Be that as it may, playing without rules and winning—in this instance, managing to communicate without using good English—is no more satisfactory than winning in a sport or game by accident or by disregarding the rules: which is really cheating.

9   The second faculty good speech develops is, as I have mentioned before, our memory. Grammar and syntax are partly logical—and to that extent they are also good exercisers and developers of our logical faculty—but they are also partly arbitrary, conventional, irrational. For example, the correct "compared to" and "contrasted with" could, from the logical point of view, just as well be "contrasted to" and "compared with" ("compared with," of course, is correct, but in a different sense from the one that concerns us here, namely, the antithesis of "contrasted with"). And, apropos *different,* logic would have to strain desperately to explain the exclusive correctness of "different from," given the exclusive correctness of "other than," which would seem to justify "different than," jarring though that is to the cultivated ear.

10   But there it is: some things are so because tradition, usage, the best speakers and writers, the grammar books and dictionaries have made them so. There may even exist some hidden historical explanation: something, perhaps,

in the Sanskrit, Greek, Latin, or other origins of a word or construction that you and I may very easily never know. We can, however, memorize; and memorization can be a wonderfully useful thing—surely the Greeks were right to consider Mnemosyne (memory) the mother of the Muses, for without her there would be no art and no science. And what better place to practice one's mnemonic skills than in the study of one's language?

11   There is something particularly useful about speaking correctly and precisely because language is always there as a foundation—or, if you prefer a more fluid image, an undercurrent—beneath what is going on. Now, it seems to me that the great difficulty of life lies in the fact that we must almost always do two things at a time. If, for example, we are walking and conversing, we must keep our mouths as well as feet from stumbling. If we are driving while listening to music, we must not allow the siren song of the cassette to prevent us from watching the road and the speedometer (otherwise the less endearing siren of the police car or the ambulance will follow apace). Well, it is just this sort of bifurcation of attention that care for precise, clear expression fosters in us. By learning early in life to pay attention both to what we are saying and to how we are saying it, we develop the much-needed life skill of doing two things simultaneously.

12   Put another way, we foster our awareness of, and ability to deal with, form and content. If there is any verity that modern criticism has fought for, it is the recognition of the indissolubility of content and form. Criticism won the battle, won it so resoundingly that this oneness has become a contemporary commonplace. And shall the fact that form *is* content be a platitude in all the arts but go unrecognized in the art of self-expression, whether in conversation or correspondence, or whatever form of spoken or written utterance a human being resorts to? Accordingly, you are going to be judged, whether you like it or not, by the correctness of your English as much as by the correctness of your thinking; there are some people to whose ear bad English is as offensive as gibberish, or as your picking your nose in public would be to their eyes and stomachs. The fact that people of linguistic sensibilities may be a dying breed does not mean that they are wholly extinct, and it is best not to take any unnecessary chances.

13   To be sure, if you are a member of a currently favored minority, many of your linguistic failings may be forgiven you—whether rightly or wrongly is not my concern here. But if you cannot change your sex or color to the one that is getting preferential treatment—Bakke case or no Bakke case—you might as well learn good English and profit by it in your career, your social relations, perhaps even in your basic self-confidence. That, if you will, is the ultimate practical application of good English; but now let me tell you about the ultimate impractical one, which strikes me as being possibly even more important.

14   Somewhere in the prose writings of Charles Péguy, who was a very fine poet and prose writer—and, what is perhaps even more remarkable, as good a human being as he was an artist—somewhere in those writings is a passage about

the decline of pride in workmanship among French artisans, which, as you can deduce, set in even before World War I, wherein Péguy was killed. In the passage I refer to, Péguy bemoans the fact that cabinet-makers no longer finish the backs of furniture—the sides that go against the wall—in the same way as they do the exposed sides. What is not seen was just as important to the old artisans as what is seen—it was a moral issue with them. And so, I think, it ought to be with language. Even if no one else notices the niceties, the precision, the impeccable sense of grammar and syntax you deploy in your utterances, you yourself should be aware of them and take pride in them as in pieces of work well done.

15   Now, I realize that there are two possible reactions among you to what I have said up to this point. Some of you will say to yourselves: what utter nonsense! Language is a flexible, changing, living organism that belongs to the people who speak it. It has always been changed according to the ways in which people chose to speak it, and the dictionaries and books on grammar had to, and will have to, adjust themselves to the people and not the other way around. For isn't it the glory of language that it keeps throwing up new inventions as surf tosses out differently polished pebbles and bits of bottle glass onto the shore, and that in this inexhaustible variety, in this refusal to kowtow to dry-as-dust scholars, lies its vitality, its beauty?

16   Others among you, perhaps fewer in number, will say to yourselves: quite so, there is such a thing as Standard English, or purity of speech, or correctness of expression—something worth safeguarding and fostering; but how the devil is one to accomplish that under the prevailing conditions: in a democratic society full of minorities that have their own dialects or linguistic preferences, and in a world in which television, advertising, and other mass media manage daily to corrupt the language a little further? Let me try to answer the first group first, and then come back to the questions of the second.

17   Of course language is, and must be, a living organism to the extent that new inventions, discoveries, ideas enter the scene and clamor rightfully for designations. Political, social, and psychological changes may also affect our mode of expression, and new words or phrases may have to be found to reflect what we might call historical changes. It is also quite natural for slang terms to be invented, become popular, and, in some cases, remain permanently in the language. It is perhaps equally inevitable (though here we are on more speculative ground) for certain words to become obsolescent and obsolete, and drop out of the language. But does that mean that grammar and syntax have to keep changing, that pronunciations and meanings of words must shift, that more complex or elegant forms are obliged to yield to simpler or cruder ones that often are not fully synonymous with them and not capable of expressing certain fine distinctions? Should, for instance, "terrestrial" disappear entirely in favor of "earthly," or are there shades of meaning involved that need to remain available to us? Must we sacrifice "notwithstanding" because we have "in spite of" or "despite"? Need we forfeit "jettison" just because we have "throw over-

board"? And what about "disinterested," which is becoming a synonym for "uninterested," even though that means something else, and though we have no other word for "disinterested"?

18   "Language has *always* changed," say these people, and they might with equal justice say that there has always been war or sickness or insanity. But the truth is that some sicknesses that formerly killed millions have been eliminated, that some so-called insanity can today be treated, and that just because there have always been wars does not mean that someday a cure cannot be found even for that scourge. And if it cannot, it is only by striving to put an absolute end to war, by pretending that it can be licked, that we can at least partly control it. Without such assumptions and efforts, the evil would be so widespread that, given our current weaponry, we would no longer be here to worry about the future of language.

19   But we are here, and having evolved linguistically this far, and having the means—books of grammar, dictionaries, education for all—to arrest unnecessary change, why not endeavor with might and mind to arrest it? Certain cataclysms cannot be prevented: earthquakes and droughts, for example, can scarcely, if at all, be controlled; but we can prevent floods, for which purpose we have invented dams. And dams are precisely what we can construct to prevent floods of ignorance from eroding our language, and, beyond that, to provide irrigation for areas that would otherwise remain linguistically arid.

20   For consider that what some people are pleased to call linguistic evolution was almost always a matter of ignorance prevailing over knowledge. There is no valid reason, for example, for the word *nice* to have changed its meanings so many times—except ignorance of its exact definition. Had the change never occurred, or had it been stopped at any intermediate stage, we would have had just as good a word as we have now and saved some people a heap of confusion along the way. But if *nice* means what it does today—and it has two principal meanings, one of them, as in "nice distinction," alas, obsolescent—let us, for heaven's sake, keep it where it is, now that we have the means with which to hold it there.

21   If, for instance, we lose the accusative case *whom*—and we are in great danger of losing it—our language will be the poorer for it. Obviously, "The man, whom I had never known, was a thief" means something other than "The man who I had never known was a thief." Now, you can object that it would be just as easy in the first instance to use some other construction; but what happens if *this* one is used incorrectly? Ambiguity and confusion. And why should we lose this useful distinction? Just because a million or ten million or a billion people less educated than we are cannot master the difference? Surely it behooves us to try to educate the ignorant up to our level rather than to stultify ourselves down to theirs. Yes, you say, but suppose they refuse to or are unable to learn? In that case, I say, there is a doubly good reason for not going along with them. Ah, you reply, but they are the majority, and we must accept their way or, if the revolution is merely linguistic, lose our

"credibility" (as the current parlance, rather confusingly, has it) or, if the revolution is political, lose our heads. Well, I consider a sufficient number of people to be educable enough to be capable of using *who* and *whom* correctly, and to derive satisfaction from this capability—a sufficient number, I mean, to enable us to preserve *whom,* and not to have to ask "for who the bell tolls."

22   The main problem with education, actually, is not those who need it and cannot get it, but those who should impart it and, for various reasons, do not. In short, the enemies of education are the educators themselves: miseducated, underpaid, overburdened, and intimidated teachers (frightened because, though the pen is supposed to be mightier than the sword, the switchblade is surely more powerful than the ferrule), and professors who— because they are structural linguists, democratic respecters of alleged minority rights, or otherwise misguided folk—believe in the sacrosanct privilege of any culturally underprivileged minority or majority to dictate its ignorance to the rest of the world. For, I submit, an English improvised by slaves and other strangers to the culture—to whom my heart goes out in every human way—under dreadfully deprived conditions can nowise equal an English that the best literary and linguistic talents have, over the centuries, perceptively and painstakingly brought to a high level of excellence.

23   So my answer to the scoffers in this or any audience is, in simplest terms, the following: contrary to popular misconception, language does not belong to the people, or at least not in the sense in which *belong* is usually construed. For things can rightfully belong only to those who invent or earn them. But we do not know who invented language: is it the people who first made up the words for *father* and *mother,* for *I* and *thou,* for *hand* and *foot*; or is it the people who evolved the subtler shadings of language, its poetic variety and suggestiveness, but also its unambiguousness, its accurate and telling details? Those are two very different groups of people and two very different languages, and I, as you must have guessed by now, consider the latter group at least as important as the former. As for *earning* language, it has surely been earned by those who have striven to learn it properly, and here even economic and social circumstances are but an imperfect excuse for bad usage; history is full of examples of people rising from humble origins to learn, against all kinds of odds, to speak and write correctly—even brilliantly.

24   *Belong,* then, should be construed in the sense that parks, national forests, monuments, and public utilities are said to belong to the people: available for properly respectful use but not for defacement and destruction. And all that we propose to teach is how to use and enjoy the gardens of language to their utmost aesthetic and salubrious potential. Still, I must now address myself to the group that, while agreeing with my aims, despairs of finding practical methods for their implementation.

25   True enough, after a certain age speakers not aware of Standard English or not exceptionally gifted will find it hard or impossible to change their ways. Nevertheless, if there were available funds for advanced methods in teaching;

if teachers themselves were better trained and paid, and had smaller classes and more assistants; if, furthermore, college entrance requirements were heightened and the motivation of students accordingly strengthened; if there were no structural linguists and National Councils of Teachers of English filling instructors' heads with notions about "Students' Rights to Their Own Language" (they have every right to it as a *second* language, but none as a *first*); if teachers in all disciplines, including the sciences and social sciences, graded on English usage as well as on specific proficiencies; if aptitude tests for various jobs stressed good English more than they do; and, above all, if parents were better educated and more aware of the need to set a good example to their children, and to encourage them to learn correct usage, the situation could improve enormously.

26   Clearly, to expect all this to come to pass is utopian; some of it, however, is well within the realm of possibility. For example, even if parents do not speak very good English, many of them at least can manage an English that is good enough to correct a very young child's mistakes; in other words, most adults can speak a good enough four-year-old's idiom. They would thus start kids out on the right path; the rest could be done by the schools.

27   But the problem is what to do in the most underprivileged homes: those of blacks, Hispanics, immigrants from various Asian and European countries. This is where day-care centers could come in. If the fathers and mothers could be gainfully employed, their small children would be looked after by day-care centers where—is this asking too much?—good English could be inculcated in them. The difficulty, of course, is what to do about the discrepancy the little ones would note between the speech of the day-care people and that of their parents. Now, it seems to me that small children have a far greater ability to learn things, including languages, than some people give them credit for. Much of it is indeed rote learning, but, where languages are concerned, that is one of the basic learning methods even for adults. There is no reason for not teaching kids another language, to wit, Standard English, and turning this, if desirable, into a game: "At home you speak one way; here we have another language," at which point the instructor can make up names and explanations for Standard English that would appeal to pupils of that particular place, time, and background.

28   At this stage of the game, as well as later on in school, care should be exercised to avoid insulting the language spoken in the youngsters' homes. There must be ways to convey that both home and school languages have their validity and uses and that knowing both enables one to accomplish more in life. This would be hard to achieve if the children's parents were, say, militant blacks of the Geneva Smitherman sort, who execrate Standard English as a weapon of capitalist oppression against the poor of all races, colors, and religions. But, happily, there is evidence that most black, Hispanic, and other non-Standard English-speaking parents want their children to learn correct English so as to get ahead in the world.

29   Yet how do we defend ourselves against the charge that we are old fogeys who cannot emotionally adjust to the new directions an ever-living and changing language must inevitably take? Here I would want to redefine or, at any rate, clarify, what "living and changing" means, and also explain where we old fogeys stand. Misinformed attacks on Old Fogeydom, I have noticed, invariably represent us as people who shudder at a split infinitive and would sooner kill or be killed than tolerate a sentence that ends with a preposition. Actually, despite all my travels through Old Fogeydom, I have yet to meet one inhabitant who would not stick a preposition onto the tail of a sentence; as for splitting infinitives, most of us O.F.'s are perfectly willing to do that, too, but tactfully and sparingly, where it feels right. There is no earthly reason, for example, for saying "to dangerously live," when "to live dangerously" sounds so much better; but it does seem right to say (and write) "What a delight to sweetly breathe in your sleeping lover's breath"; that sounds smoother, indeed sweeter, than to "breathe in sweetly" or "sweetly to breathe in." But infinitives begging to be split are relatively rare; a sensitive ear, a good eye for shades of meaning will alert you whenever the need to split arises; without that ear and eye, you had better stick to the rules.

30   About the sense in which language is, and must be, alive, let me speak while donning another of my several hats—actually it is not a hat but a cap, for there exists in Greenwich Village an inscription on a factory that reads "CRITIC CAPS." So with my drama critic's cap on, let me present you with an analogy. The world theater today is full of directors who wreak havoc on classic plays to demonstrate their own ingenuity, their superiority, as it were, to the author. These directors—aborted playwrights, for the most part—will stage productions of *Hamlet* in which the prince is a woman, a flaming homosexual, or a one-eyed hunchback.

31   Well, it seems to me that the same spirit prevails in our approach to linguistics, with every newfangled, ill-informed, know-nothing construction, definition, pronunciation enshrined by the joint efforts of structural linguists, permissive dictionaries, and allegedly democratic but actually demagogic educators. What really makes a production of, say, *Hamlet* different, and therefore alive, is that the director, while trying to get as faithfully as possible at Shakespeare's meanings, nevertheless ends up stressing things in the play that strike him most forcefully; and the same individuality in production design and performances (the Hamlet of Gielgud versus the Hamlet of Olivier, for instance—what a world of difference!) further differentiates one production from another, and bestows on each its particular vitality. So, too, language remains alive because each speaker (or writer) can and must, *within the framework of accepted grammar, syntax, and pronunciation,* produce a style that is his very own, that is as personal as his posture, way of walking, mode of dress, and so on. It is such stylistic differences that make a person's—or a nation's—language flavorous, pungent, alive, and all this without having to play fast and loose with the existing rules.

32   But to have this, we need, among other things, good teachers and, beyond

them, enlightened educators. I shudder when I read in the *Birmingham* (Alabama) *Post-Herald* of October 6, 1978, an account of a talk given to eight hundred English teachers by Dr. Alan C. Purves, vice-president of the National Council of Teachers of English. Dr. Purves is quoted as saying things like "We are in a situation with respect to reading where . . . ," and culminating in the following truly horrifying sentence: "I am going to suggest that when we go back to the basics, I think what we should be dealing with is our charge to help students to be more proficient in producing meaningful language—language that says what it means." Notice all the deadwood, the tautology, the anacoluthon in the first part of that sentence; but notice especially the absurdity of the latter part, in which the dubious word "meaningful"—a poor relation of "significant"—is thought to require explaining to an audience of English teachers.

33   Given such leadership from the N.C.T.E., the time must be at hand when we shall hear—not just "Don't ask for who the bell rings" (*as not* and *tolls* being, of course, archaic, elitist language), but also "It rings for you and I."

TOPICAL CONSIDERATIONS

1. In your own words, why is good English good for you?

2. Consider the two examples Simon gives in paragraph 2: "Everyone in their right mind would cross on the green light" and "Hopefully, it won't rain tomorrow." If they communicate perfectly well, why haggle over the minor grammatical errors?

3. How does Simon justify so strong a statement as that in paragraph 7: "Language pollution . . . [is] second only to air pollution"? Do you agree? Can you think of circumstances in which bad language might be a threat to health—mental or otherwise?

4. Simon argues that good speech develops memory. How does he explain that? Can you substantiate that from your own experience and practice?

5. What, according to Simon, is "the ultimate practical application of good English"? What is the "ultimate impractical one"?

6. One counterresponse to Simon's call for upholding the standards of correct English is the assertion: "Language is a flexible, changing, living organism that belongs to the people who speak it." (This statement is nearly identical to Bill Bryson's claim in the previous essay.) How does Simon answer that charge? Can the language have rigid standards and still allow natural changes to occur? If so, give examples.

7. Simon singles out the word *nice* as one of the many victims of too much change. What are some of the current meanings of *nice?* Can you think of other words that have suffered too much change? What about the words *awful, terrific, wonderful, fantastic?* What changes have they undergone since their original meanings?

8. Simon claims that "the enemies of education are the educators themselves" (paragraph 22). How does he justify such an assertion? Do you agree, given your own educational experience?

9. According to Simon, who are linguistically "the most underprivileged" children? What suggestions does Simon make for dealing with them?

RHETORICAL CONSIDERATIONS

1. From the tone and attitudes of this essay, what kind of man would you say Simon is? Does he sound "cranky and pedantic" or snobbish and elitist? Or does he sound reasonable and friendly? Cite passages to substantiate your answer.

2. In paragraph 3, Simon makes clear his attitude toward the "certified speech and language pathologist" he quotes. In what ways does he make his feelings known?

3. In paragraph 4, Simon compares a person who does not respect words with a weaver who lets her cat sleep in the yarn and hangs her laundry on her loom. How effective in this analogy?

WRITING ASSIGNMENTS

1. Simon says that "you are going to be judged, whether you like it or not, by the correctness of your English as much as by the correctness of your thinking." Write an essay about an occasion when you judged people on the basis of their English—or an occasion when you were judged on that basis. Describe how their language prejudiced you for or against them—or how such prejudices might have operated for or against you.

2. Simon criticizes parents strongly for not setting good language examples for their children. Write a paper describing the quality of language training in your own home. Did your parents encourage you to learn correct usage? Were they strict with you about it? Do you feel adequately trained in English usage, or handicapped because of your upbringing?

3. This essay by Simon was originally an address to a college audience. Imagine yourself addressing an audience on the same subject: "Why Good English Is Good for You." This time you are addressing not Simon's college students, but a group of people who speak nonstandard, "uneducated" English. Write a speech that they might benefit from, and in language that they would understand and not be repelled by.

Simonspeak

Jim Quinn

In the previous piece, language guardian John Simon argues that American English is being corrupted with neologisms, bad grammar, and fuzzy wording. What follows, as the title suggests, is a direct counterattack on Simon. Like his adversary, Jim Quinn is a journalist and language watcher. Unlike Simon, he argues that language change is not only inevitable but good. The English language is resilient, and new words and diversity in usage only enrich the mother tongue. Point for point, Quinn counters Simon's complaints with reason and historical evidence.

Jim Quinn is the author of several books including two on language, *Word of Mouth* (1971) and *American Tongue and Cheek* (1981), from which this essay comes. He also writes regularly on language for various magazines.

With regard to the question what is to be considered correct and not correct in grammar I must repeat what I have said elsewhere that it is not, of course, my business to decide such questions for Englishmen; the only thing I have had to do is to observe English usage as objectively as I could. But psychological and historical studies often make one realize that much of what is generally considered "bad grammar" is due neither to sheer perversity or ignorance on the part of the speaker or writer, but is ultimately due to the imperfections of the language as such, i.e., as it has been handed down traditionally from generation to generation (or rather from older to younger children), or else in general tendencies common to all mankind—tendencies which in other cases have led to forms or usages which are recognized by everybody as perfectly normal and unobjectionable. This is why the profoundest students of languages are often more tolerant than those who judge everything according to rule-of-thumb logic or to the textbooks of grammar that were the fashion in their own school days.

OTTO JESPERSEN,
"THE SYSTEM OF GRAMMAR"

1   John Simon, like Otto Jespersen, is not a native speaker of English, and still has a trace of a foreign accent. Nothing wrong with that—a European accent impresses lots of people, and makes speech more interesting even to those of us who aren't impressed.

2   And Simon's *writing* is almost always impressive; he has a superb talent for vituperation and insult, and uses it with a kind of communicable glee: whether you agree with him or not, you find yourself enjoying his pleasure in being cruel.

3   So it's worth pointing out in a book about correct English that Simon writes with a trace of a foreign accent, too. In *Esquire* (December 1977), he attacks Paul Owens, a man who dared to disagree in print with Simon's language strictures:

> I wonder, furthermore, whether Owens realizes the implications of a statement like "Except for 'hopefully,' a word I cheerfully misuse because I like the sound of it, I do not recall committing any of the four locutions that [Simon] finds definitive of gibberish." Here's a pretty kettle of fishiness! . . . Even Mr. Owens' arithmetic is off: Once you confess to "hopefully," only three locutions are left for you to be innocent of.

4   What an extraordinary idea that seems to those of us who grew up speaking English! Of course it *is* true—arithmetically—but it's just not the way we talk. Imagine somebody saying:

> Except for Hawaii, I do not recall that any of the forty-nine states is composed entirely of islands.
>
>   Except for Judas, none of the eleven Apostles committed suicide.

5   Simon's mathematically correct misunderstanding of the way the phrase *except for* is used in English demonstrates that Jespersen's disclaimer printed at the beginning of this chapter was not mere false humility. It is difficult to learn idiom. No one would dream of recommending humility to Simon—he's too much fun without it—but he might study English a little more carefully before he makes certain pronouncements: "[The noun] *chair* sounds, at best, like a fossilized metaphor or metonymy not worth preserving; at worst, like a stick of furniture."

6   Simon is attacking the use of the word *chair* for *chairman,* a desexed term that is favored by many people who think that the sex of the person who presides over a meeting is as meaningless in that context as the sex of a person who writes a novel. We have *novelist,* a word for both men and women; it does seem that we could get along without the word *chairwoman* or *chairman* as easily as we get along without *noveler* and *noveless. Chair* seems a perfectly reasonable substitute to me—and I suspect that Simon would admire the metonymy (using one object to represent another—as *the crown* for *the king*), if he would only take the trouble to find out a little more about it. The word *chair* has been a metonymy for *chairman* since the seventeenth century. We all remember that it is the usual word for *chairman* in *The Pickwick Papers*—people cry *Chair! Chair!* at meetings because they want the person in the chair, regardless of the person's sex, to recognize them. *Chair* is not, as Simon says, an invention of sympathizers with equality for women; it is the way people talk at meetings. If all the feminists in America were converted tomorrow to docile helpmeets

and mindless little china dolls—horrible and intolerable as that would be—the word *chair* would still be used for a person who chairs a meeting.

7   Simon is, however, worth more attention than many other pop grammarians if only because he believes that change can be stopped. This position has gone out of fashion with his fellows; they content themselves with announcing that they are fighting rear guard actions, doomed to failure, outnumbered by the unwashed, and reveling in the glory of the fray: lost causism at its most elitist and romantic best, the kind of thing that used to be popular in the movies about the Confederate volunteers, who were all committed to making a great stand for the Old South. The movies managed to concentrate on the last stand, and avoid the fact that it was the last stand of human slavery.

8   All of which is beside the point, at least at present.

9   Simon's attitude is that we are now able to rely on nineteenth-century English, because a number of the great minds of that century settled once and for all every possible question about language. All we have to do is hold on to what is right:

> . . . Ignorant, obfuscatory change, unnecessary change, producing linguistic leveling and flatness, could be stopped in its tracks by concerted effort. The fact that this has not *often* [emphasis added] happened in the past is no excuse for the present. We have acquired a set of fine, useful, previously unavailable tools, culminating in the Oxford English Dictionary and a number of excellent treatises and handbooks on grammar. While, that is, grammar was still concerned with form, not transformation; "transformational grammar," as the new trend calls itself, is indeed one of the aberrations of the academic bureaucracy. . . .

10   It is ironic that Simon should insist that the OED is a weapon against change. Lounsbury found the OED a weapon against pop grammarians like Simon. Let's see who is right. Simon says:

> My point is that things have at last been sufficiently established—classified and codified—and there is neither need nor excuse for changes based on mere ignorance. Just because some people are too thickheaded to grasp, for example, that "anyone" is singular, as the "one" in it plainly denotes, does not mean that the rest of us must put up with "anyone can do as they please. . . . " We cannot and must not let "one" become plural. That way madness lies.

11   The OED says of *their*: "Often used in relation to a singular substantive or pronoun denoting a person, after *each, every, either, neither, no one, every one,* etc. Also so used instead of *his* or *her,* when the gender is inclusive or uncertain." Also *they, them,* in the same way.

12   Among users cited, in a tradition that stretches back to the fourteenth century, are Fielding, Goldsmith, Thackeray, Walter Bagehot, Shaw, Chesterfield, Ruskin, and Richardson.

13   In no case does the OED call this usage an error (let alone madness). It does say the usage is "not favoured by grammarians." But it refers the reader to grammarian Otto Jespersen and his defense of the usage. Jespersen mentions that the usage can be found in Congreve, Defoe, Shelley, Austen, Scott,

George Eliot, Stevenson, Zangwill, and Oliver Wendell Holmes, as well as Swift and Herbert Spencer.

14   Jespersen points out that if you try to put the sentence *Does anybody prevent you?* into another interrogative formula, beginning *Nobody prevents you,* then "you will perceive that *Nobody prevents you, does he?* is too definite, and you will therefore say (as Thackeray does, *The Story of Pendennis,* II, p. 260), *Nobody prevents you, do they?*"

15   All this does not matter to Simon—the OED only matters when it agrees with him:

> There are, however, standard excuses adduced by well-meaning and misguided liberals or ill-meaning and unguidable ignoramuses (some of whom consult and misinterpret the Oxford English Dictionary to bolster their benightedness). Foremost among them is, "But look at Shakespeare [or Dickens, or Hemingway, or any other famous writer] who wrote X instead of the supposedly correct Y. If it's good enough for Shakespeare [or whomever], why not for you and me?

16   Simon's answer is extraordinary.

> Well, Shakespeare wrote in an age when what we call modern English was still in its formative phase. His grammar was good enough for his era; it is not good enough for ours—any more than his politics, medicine, or Latin is. As for more recent writers of distinction, their forte was not necessarily grammar; or at any rate, they could occasionally slip up. . . .

17   We now begin to see what a useful tool the OED is for Simon: he can leaf through it, find whatever agrees with his own prejudices about language, and claim that he is defending the great nineteenth-century traditionalists. If Simon discovers a writer from the distant past who used *anyone* with *they,* as Shakespeare did, then Shakespeare's language is not good enough for us. If he discovers a modern writer who uses the same construction, then the OED is merely noting a "lapse": "Such lapses were duly noted and set down; sometimes with glee, sometimes dispassionately for the record. Yet merely because we cannot match the excellence of the greater writers, we need not duplicate their errors."

18   It now becomes completely impossible to argue with Simon about grammar—everything he likes is right, everything he dislikes is wrong. *De gustibus non est disputandum:* reviewing language is just like reviewing theater.

19   Except—the OED did not proceed by noting down errors of famous writers. It proceeded to study the language by studying the actual usage throughout history. There are, in the opinion of the OED editors, grammatical errors, and they are clearly noted: when Thomas Hardy wrote "Who are you speaking of?" (*Far from the Madding Crowd,* p. 70), the OED called it "a grammatical error," and then changed its mind in 1923, when the *Oxford Shorter Dictionary* noted "*Whom* is no longer current in natural colloquial speech."

20   But the OED does not say that the use of *they* and *their* with singular antecedents is "a grammatical error." The OED does not even say that the use is "considered ungrammatical" (which is the OED's way of warning readers that

though there is nothing wrong with a usage, there are lots of uninformed people—the OED does not, of course, use terms Simon is fond of, like ignoramus—who think otherwise).

21   The OED simply notes the usage as correct.

22   I add from *The Evolution of the English Language*, by George H. McKnight, still more evidence. McKnight notes that Richard Grant White, in *Every-Day English*, complains about the fact that the British often combine *them* and *their* and *they* with singular antecedents, and adds:

> The kinds of "misuse" here condemned in American use, in British use are established not only by long tradition but by current practice. The awkward necessity so often met with in American speech of using the double pronoun "his or her," is obviated by the "misuse" of their. . . .

23   McKnight then gives a long list of quotes illustrating this point: Jane Austen, Thomas De Quincey, Matthew Arnold, Cardinal Newman, James Stephens, Frank Swinnerton, Lord Dunsany, Samuel Butler in *The Way of All Flesh*, and A. E. (Jane Austen, *Mansfield Park:* "nobody put *themselves* out of the way"; James Stephens, *The Crock of Gold:* "everybody has to take *their* chance.")

24   I have spent a long time on this single construction, but I want to be very plain about this. If you go away from this book with none of your cherished opinions about good English changed, at least you must recognize that there is *no* justification for attacking the use of plural pronouns with singular antecedents when the sex is uncertain or mixed. For example, says Bergen Evans:

> Only the word *his* would be used in every soldier carried his own pack, but most people would say *their* rather than *his* in everybody brought their own lunch. And it would be a violation of English idiom to say was he? in nobody was killed, were they? The use of *they* in speaking of a single individual is not a modern deviation from classical English. It is found in the works of many great writers including Malory. . . .

25   And another list, all of which we have heard before.

26   Again, from the OED: "The pronoun referring to *every one* [sometimes written as one word] is often plural: the absence of a singular pronoun of common gender rendering this violation of grammatical concord sometimes *necessary* [my italics for *necessary*]."

27   To Simon, this necessity, this historically correct way of writing and speaking English, is *madness*. But he might as well say using the word *man* instead of *homme* is madness. Plural pronouns with singular antecedents are part of the language, an idiom, as indefensible—and as impossible to justify—as the meaning of words. If Simon prefers to use singular pronouns, and violate this idiom, he is welcome to, of course. Many Europeans who learned English as a second or third language do violate this idiom. We understand what he means. But if he doesn't *like* the idiom—well, nobody asked him to, did they?

28   Here are other examples of unidiomatic construction:

> Miss Oates refers to a conversation "between" three people. Now I realize that in our sadly permissive dictionaries, "between" is becoming acceptable as a synonym

for "among." But do not buy this, good people; the "tween" comes from the Anglo-Saxon "twa" meaning two, and if we start meddling with such palpable etymological sense (who cannot hear the "two" in "tween"?) we become barbarous or trendy, even if we happen to be in the dictionary business.

29   *Between* is discussed at length on pages 43–47 (the *Harper Dictionary* chapter), but the OED, that fine and useful tool, insists that *between* has been "from its earliest appearance, extended to more than two." And the OED further insists that *between* is the only word you can use in certain situations where the relationship is each to each to each: as in a conversation between three people. You may remember, for example, an old-fashioned way of saying something was a secret: "Let's just keep this between you, me, and the fence post." Again, it is okay to violate this rule if you want to—but criticizing Joyce Carol Oates because she follows it, and calling the OED barbarous and trendy, is an overstatement which tends to weaken your standing as an expert, at least a judicious expert.

30   In 1977, Simon went to a meeting of the National Council of Teachers of English, and had a wonderful time criticizing academic jargon: "What would Carlyle and Arnold (to pull two great names out of a hat) have made of 'Developing Language Arts/Communication Skills through Interarts Strategies' . . . in the particular session I audited . . . "

31   Carlyle and Arnold would not, of course, have had an easy time understanding the title of that session. Ironically, they would not have had an easy time understanding John Simon either; it is easy to tell what Carlyle and Arnold would have made of the verb *audit*, because it is defined in the OED as "1. To make an official and systematic examination of (accounts), so as to ascertain their accuracy. 2. To examine, 'hear' (a pupil). rare. [one example listed, in 1805]." And that's all. *Audit* in Simon's sense—"sit in on a session and listen without participating"—is not even listed in the OED Supplement (1972), indicating that it is at the very least an Americanism and, almost certainly, a bit of academic jargon as arcane as any Simon criticized.

32   It's kind of fun to think that Simon, if he's lucky, might eventually be immortalized in the twenty-first-century supplement to the OED as the man who introduced this strange new use of an ancient word to print, and that some equally careless reader of the OED in the future will criticize "ignoramuses" like Simon who can't keep the meaning of simple words straight.

> In the January–February issue of *Harvard Magazine* . . . I find one Josh Rubins writing: "What *have* (emphasis Rubins') surfaced are similes. . . . " Now it is bad enough not to know that "*What* as subject takes the singular verb, whether the complementary noun be singular or plural" (Eric Partridge, *Usage & Abusage*) but ignorance italicized is considerably worse yet.

Depends on what it's ignorance of. From the OED:

> What are your views? (Austen, *Sense and Sensibility*, 147). What have often been censured as Shakespeare's conceits are completely justifiable (Coleridge, *Shakespeare Lectures*, 90). What I want are details (Wilde, *Lord Arthur Saville's Crime*, 20).

From *A Dictionary of Contemporary American Usage* by Bergen and Cornelia Evans:

> The pronoun "what" may be followed by either a singular or a plural verb as in "what appears to be the important points" or "what appear to be the important points."

33 Maybe Rubins is ignorant of Partridge, but familiar with English literature—and a different grammar book. Taking Partridge at his unsupported word is no worse than taking the Evanses at their unsupported word, of course; but when experts disagree, the rest of us should be allowed to choose what sounds best to us.

34 I really can't think that Simon, or Partridge, would want that sentence by Coleridge to read:

> What has often been censured as Shakespeare's conceits is completely justifiable.

35 Finally, Simon, who insists that Shakespeare's grammar is not good enough for us, insists that we should all work ceaselessly to prevent "little horrors" from being embedded in the language:

> Instead of embedding, let's start uprooting. Wouldn't it be nice if half a millennium from now, people could read today's writers without elaborate footnotes and glossaries such as we require to read Shakespeare?

36 First, it would not only be nice—it would be amazing.

37 Second, if Simon is successful in uprooting the word *chair* for "person who chairs a meeting," people will need a glossary to read Dickens—and *Ms.* magazine. If he drives out the ordinary use of *they* with *anyone* and *everyone*, every reader of Shaw and Wilde will have to have help (that way glossaries lie). If he uproots the normal use of *except for*, he will have so changed the way we think in our language that future generations may even need special instruction to understand our mathematics.

38 And third, our grammar and our politics and medicine have about as much chance of being good enough for the twenty-sixth century as Shakespeare's grammar and politics and medicine had of being good enough for ours.

39 I repeat that however much I disagree with him, I like to read John Simon. His command of the language, especially for a nonnative, is almost unparalleled: the written language, that is.

40 It's when Simon comes up against an idiom (like "What are your views?") that he feels he has to go to a grammar book for justification, and the justification can only be as good as the book itself. Sometimes, in the case of Partridge, it is just plain mistaken.

41 It's difficult to talk this way without sounding like a jingoist of the worst kind, but it is a fact that people who learn the language as natives speak it in a different way than people who learn it as students. So—I hope this won't be misunderstood—when Simon begins preaching against the way we talk in English, it would probably be a service to him, and to the integrity of English, if someone would tell him: "Look, Mr. Simon, you're really, like, a good writer, you know? But you're having this trouble understanding when people, like,

talk. So, look, why not go back to, like, Berlitz? Or wherever you learned how to write so good? And take a conversational course this time. And get your head straight."

TOPICAL CONSIDERATIONS

1. Summarize the words of Jespersen that Quinn uses to open his piece. Take another look at Bill Bryson's piece ("Good English and Bad") at the beginning of this chapter and try to determine whether Jespersen is a *descriptive* or *prescriptive* linguist. What about Jim Quinn? What about John Simon? Explain your answers with supporting evidence.

2. Explain Simon's "mathematically correct misunderstanding" of the phrase *except for.* Is Quinn suggesting that Simon's problem is not being a native English speaker, or is he saying something else?

3. Summarize the reasoning behind Quinn's attack of Simon's objection to the use of *chair* for *chairman.* Do you find his reasoning convincing? Enough to change Simon's mind, perhaps? Which term do you use? Do you ever say *chairwoman* or *chairperson?* If more people knew the history of *chair,* do you think they'd be inclined to use it? Explain your answers.

4. Simon complains that we should not let "'one' become plural. That way, madness lies." What do you make of Simon's statement? What strategy does Quinn use to counter him here? With whom do you side?

5. According to Quinn, how does Simon misuse the authority of the OED? How has the OED attempted to avoid value judgments on usage?

6. Take a look at the Simon statement on "uprooting" the "little horrors" in English for posterity's sake (paragraph 35). How does this capture Simon's basic philosophical view of language? If everyone took Simon's advice, what according to Quinn might be the consequences? What are your thoughts here?

7. In your own words, how does Quinn explain Simon's problems with English idioms. Do you think Quinn sounds like a "jingoist"? Explain your answer.

8. Review Quinn's philosophical stand on language and change. How might he respond to Paul Dickson's attitude toward slang ("It Ain't No Big Thing")? How about Spiro Agnew's attitude toward the elimination of sexist terms ("English Anyone?")? How about some of the professional jargon described in Chapter 8?

RHETORICAL CONSIDERATIONS

1. Did you find any parts of this essay humorous? If so, which ones? What did you find funny about them? Did you find any of Quinn's criticism of Simon excessive or cruel? Explain your answer.

2. Who might be "the unwashed" Quinn speaks of in paragraph 7? What images and suggestions does the metaphor call to mind?

3. Consider the author's voice in this piece—his language, style, and tone of this essay. What sense do you get of Jim Quinn as an individual?

4. Evaluate the imaginary advice to Mr. Simon at the end. Did you find it amusing? What do you make of the choice of language and the use of colloquialisms? How about the attitude—do you find it appropriate or condescending? Explain.

WRITING ASSIGNMENTS

1. If you had to choose, with whom would you want to spend an hour—Jim Quinn or John Simon? Why? What kinds of things would you want to talk about? What might you ask him?

2. Write a letter to Mr. Quinn explaining why you agree or disagree with his criticism of John Simon. Use specific details from this essay and/or Simon's to support your stand.

3. Write a letter to Mr. Simon explaining why you agree or disagree with Jim Quinn's criticism of him.

4. Now that you've read Bryson, Simon, and Quinn, write an essay on where you stand. Do you think we need language guardians such as John Simon? Or would we be better off without them?

5. Consider the English language education you got in school. Do you think it was overly prescriptive? Do you think you needed to be drilled so much on the rules of grammar? Were they useful to you as a writer, or were they unnecessary instructions?

IT AIN'T NO BIG THING

Paul Dickson

No debate about language standards would be complete without a look at slang. We all use it, but few of us ever consider where slang comes from, how it functions for social subgroups, and the way it passes in and out of standard speech. What follows is an amusing discussion of contemporary slang—its variety, its origins, its rise and fall.

Paul Dickson is a freelance writer whose articles have appeared in a number of newspapers and magazines including *Esquire, Smithsonian,* and *Playboy.* He has written over twenty books, five of which are on American English including *Slang!* (1990), from which this essay comes. His other books include *Words, Names* and *The Dickson Baseball Dictionary.* It is interesting to note that Mr. Dickson holds the record in the *Guinness Book of World Records* for most synonyms for one word. He was able to find 2,231 different ways of saying *drunk.* Awesome!

"Correct English is the slang of prigs who write histories and essays. And the strongest slang of all is the slang of poets."

GEORGE ELIOT, 1872

1. THE QUICK & DIRTY

1 People seem fascinated by slang, and it is widely beloved, especially in the abstract by people who cringe when it is actually spoken. If you can accept it, you can't get all bent out of shape—and start yelling "double negative"—when someone says that something "ain't no big thing."

2 Slang is. Period. Whether it is in favor or out of favor does not matter. It is renegade language that thumbs its nose at the very people who study and write about it. It is unruly, unrefined, irreverent, and illogical. It can be brutally frank and direct, or deceptively kind and euphemistic. Euphemism is the verbal trick that has been termed the deodorant of language, and slang has given us dozens of terms for drunkenness and insanity that are remarkably gentle.

3   What else is it? This is what amounts to the current conventional wisdom on the subject, or at least this slang watcher's beliefs about the beast.

—That slang is as old as language itself, and that American slang started on the *Mayflower.* Mario Pei, in *The Story of Language,* points out that the slang use of a piece of pottery for the head found in "crackpot" has counterparts in ancient language, including Latin and Sanskrit. He also points out that Shakespeare used the slang of his time, and by doing so gave us such words as *hubbub, fretful, fireworks,* and *dwindle.*

—That it binds and identifies and thrives in groups with a strong sense of novelty and group activity. Farmers produce little slang, but boxers, science fiction fans, surfers, high school students, and actors produce a lot.

—That slang is produced by living languages, and the moment it stops being produced, the language in question is dead. It is also true that slang replenishes standard language. English words as diverse as *snide, hold up, nice* (as in "nice work"), *bogus, strenuous, clumsy,* and *spurious* were regarded as slang not that long ago. Contemporary slang terms such as *sleazy, hassle,* and *gridlock* look like locks on acceptance—as does *lock on* for that matter. Much slang has become so common that when we use it we forget that it is slang: "Pick up the *phone* and find out what time the *movie* starts."

—That it is all but impossible to destroy slang, especially with the argument that it is improper or impolite. For most of the twentieth century there has been a battle waged against the word *ain't.* The anti-ain't-ers never had a chance. When, for example, they criticized the late Dizzy Dean for using the a-word on his radio broadcasts, he all but liquidated their argument by pointing out, "Lots of people who don't say 'ain't' ain't eatin'."

—That America is particularly hospitable to slang, and it tends to be embraced rather than spurned. American slang has been called one of the "successful stories" of English, and one estimate, made in the *Reader's Digest Success with Words,* claims that there are some 35,000 expressions which are, or once were, American slang. There are those, including the author of this book, who suspect that that immense estimate of 35,000 may be on the low side. In terms of the overall language, the number skyrockets when one considers the British, Irish, Scotch, Australian, and Canadian contributions to the pool.

—That it is not that hard to create slang, but it is hard to sustain a "new slang" without a group that continues to speak it. This is exactly what happened to the short-lived Valley Girl (1982–83) and the Citizen's Band radio slang (1975–77). Each of these received tremendous media attention, but a few months after each had peaked, they seemed to live on mostly in yellowing paperback quickies like *The Official CB Slanguage Language Dictionary* and *How to Be a Valley Girl.* If there is a high mortality rate with new slang, it is also true that terms making it through infancy tend to be absorbed as part of the standard language.

—That it often has as much to do with who says something as what they are saying. A simple word like *hot* has many conventional and slang meanings, depending on whether you are talking to a musician, police officer, electrician, florist, radiologist, cook, or basketball player. If a television talk-show guest talks about the Green Room, he's referring to the room in which guests wait to go on camera, regardless of its actual color. On the other hand, to a surfer on a California beach, the Green Room is the sought-for-realm inside the curl of a wave. By extension, at some West Coast colleges, to be doing exceptionally well is to be in the Green Room.

—That slang is often as much defined by context and position (in the sense that cowgirl and girl cow, OK and KO, and breaking ball and ball breaker, all differ) as by the expression itself. The word *say* is not slang unless it is used at the beginning of a sentence, in the sense of "tell me." This is as much true of the contemporary teenager who says, "Say, how much did that cost?" as it is in the line, "Oh, say, can you see, by the dawn's early light."

4   Despite all of this, people still have a tough time defining slang.

2. DEFINITIONS

5   Consider these questions:

- "Hey! No bullshit, but what the hell is slang anyhow?"
- "Could you please define slang?"
- "Can a suitable set of parameters be developed through which slang can be, first, identified and defined, and second, distinguished from conventional English, jargon, dialect, lingo, and argot?"

6   These three questions are, of course, the same question posed three separate ways. But their impact is quite different because of how they are stated. The first version of the question is stated in simple street slang. It is both direct and rude. The second version is phrased in standard, or conventional, English. It is at once forthright and polite. The third question approximates what has been called *bureaucratese* but which is spoken beyond the bureaucracy. It is bloated, indirect, and sleep-inducing. For lack of a better term, it is the jargon of a sizable slice of white-collar America.

7   The three questions only answer themselves to a point. Slang, conventional English, and jargon sound different, and if we speak English we pretty much know which is which. But exactly how does slang distinguish itself from argot, cant, and jargon?

8   The answer is not an easy one. In his monumental *American Language* (*Supplement Two*), H. L. Mencken grappled with it and, without even mentioning jargon, wrote, "The boundaries separating true slang from cant and ar-

got are not easily defined," adding later, "There is a constant movement of words and phrases from one category to another." Mencken's conclusion was that cant and argot belonged to the speech of small and cohesive groups, with cant having the extra characteristic of deceiving and mystifying outsiders. At another point (*The American Language*, 4th edition), he says, "The essence of slang is that it is of general dispersion, but still stands outside the accepted canon of the language."

9   Mencken believed that slang was driven by exuberance and word-making energy. He compared slang's relationship to language to that between dancing and music.

10   What about jargon? The rough distinction that seems to work is that jargon is technical, professional talk which as often as not, like cant, acts as a barrier to keep outsiders from understanding what is going on. But not always. For instance, medical doctors have a polysyllabic, latinate jargon as well as a blunt and sometimes cruel slang. It is one thing to say that one has a *bilateral probital hematoma* (jargon), but quite another to say that you have a shiner, black eye, or mouse (slang).

11   But, by the same token, some slang and some jargon are one and the same; for example, the slang and jargon of truck drivers overlap considerably. Perhaps the simplest definition of jargon was the one made by Mario Pei many years ago in the *Story of Language,* in which he termed it " . . . the special terminology in use in any given walk of life."

12   Finally there is dialect, which appears to be a different manner of speaking the same language with a different but consistent grammar and set of distinct expressions. By this definition the black English that was so widely discussed and debated in the 1970s would qualify as a dialect. By the same token, many of the words used in predominantly black rap music are slang. Rap slang is much more likely to be understood by a nonblack teenager than by a middle-aged black person. One can, in fact, make the case that rap slang and general teenage slang have so much in common, there are only a handful of words and phrases they do not share.

13   So if we can give slang a place, it occupies a perch between conventional English on one hand and the private, in-group cants, jargons, and dialects.

3. I HEARD IT ON TV

14   One final point that should be covered here has to do with the state of slang today. How is it faring in this the last decade of the twentieth century?

15   The simple answer is that it appears as dynamic a force in language as it has ever been during a period of peace and stability. Conflict is a catalyst for the creation of new slang, and English is still digesting terms created during World War II.

16   But there is another factor now in place that over time will rival anything else in history as a dispenser of language.

17   Television has become this great dispenser, soaking up words and phrases from one part of the population and repeating it for all of us to hear. Kids who have never been on a sled know what a luge is, and people who have never sat in a Catskills hotel and listened to a Brooklyn-born comic speak of *shtick* and *schlock*. For a moment we all knew enough CB talk (Ten-four, Good Buddy) and Valley Girl talk (gag me with a spoon) to fake those slangs. This was not because we all drove eighteen-wheelers or hung out in the shopping malls and video parlors of the San Fernando Valley, but because we *heard* it on television.

18   This fact has not been missed by the professional linguists and students of television. Frederick Mish, editorial director at Merriam-Webster Inc. in Springfield, Massachusetts, points out the electronic media has become a major influence on American English, especially when it comes to new words. "It overarches all the other influences and promulgates them. Whether you're talking about a new word or phrase from technology or cookery, it is likely to come to us through television," says Mish. Tom Shales, the *Washington Post* TV critic, has termed television "America's dictionary as well as its mirror."

19   Perhaps the most dramatic case of electronically transmitted slang occurred in the spring of 1989 after a gang of Harlem teenagers entered Central Park and brutally beat and raped a jogger. Within hours of the arrest of the teenagers, the New York police announced that their interrogation had yielded a name for vile rampage and other acts of senseless violence: *wilding*.

20   Although the police pointed out that they had never heard the term before that night, the word *wilding* had spread into every nook and cranny of the English-speaking world within hours. Television, with assists from radio and the wire services, had put the term and its grotesque connotations into the minds of tens of millions.

21   Hearing is the key to all of this. So much is said and written about the visual impact of television, we sometimes forget that it is equally auditory. This was particularly true of both Watergate and Iran-contra—what was spoken and "misspoken"—and America's manned ventures into outer space. The launches, the splashdowns and costly animation were memorable, but so were the voices of the astronauts, the reporters, and even the official NASA spokesmen. For a while we were all saying A-okay and counting backwards 10–9–8–7 . . . Television is a linguistic paradise. You can flip to *Donahue* and hear the latest in sensitive psychological talk, dial up the news and hear the latest in boardroom or diplomatic jargon, screen the new sitcoms for the next catch phrase, and catch a few innings of the ball game to listen for the latest nickname for spit balls (referred to of late as "wet ones"). Most Americans know what they know of police slang from cop shows ranging from *Dragnet* to *Hill Street Blues*. TV westerns of the 1950s invented a slang for the Old West with new terms like *gunslinger* and *bounty hunter.*

22   If this sounds a bit too passive, go to the other extreme and think of the quirky little ways TV talk affects us. Kids who dream of being asked to spell "relief" by their teacher so they can reply, "R-O-L-A-I-D-S," or how they will someday try to tell their kids how they sat back and waited for Hans and Franz, the Teutonic body builders on *Saturday Night Live,* to say "Ve're going

to pump *you* up." If half the teenagers in America are at this moment imitating Hans and Franz, the other half are imitating the Church Lady saying "Isn't that special." Their kids probably won't understand what was so special about it, just like my kids draw a blank when I try to tell them how I loved the Burns and Allen signature—"Say goodnight, Gracie." "Goodnight, Gracie."

23   Television, in fact, creates its own indigenous slang in the form of rallying cries and catch phrases. A case in point is "Where's the beef?" which is gone now but marked the winter of 1984 linguistically as it was repeated over and over by the late Clara Peller in a series of ads for the Wendy's hamburger chain and then became a rejoinder in the presidential debates on television.

24   This kind of thing is nothing new, but the Wendy's commercials are an especially dramatic example of how we mark time with catch words and phrases in the television age. It goes on all the time, and the odds favor a major, new national pet phrase every few years and numbers of minor ones. It will be fresh one moment and a cliché emblazoned across a million tee-shirts the next.

25   Such was the case with the late Gilda Radner's chirpy "Never mind," from *Saturday Night Live* and Steven Martin's "Well, excuuuuuse me." Then John Belushi took the word *no*, extruded it into something that took three seconds to say, and it became his signature.

26   The most obvious impact has come with signature lines uttered by characters, comedians, and advertisers. If there were a Hall of Fame for such phrases, it would be hard to know where to begin. Just for starters, you'd have to consider: "Would you believe?" from Don Adams as Maxwell Smart; McGarrett's "Book 'em," from *Hawaii Five-O*; Flo's endearing "Well, kiss my grits," from *Alice;* Jack Paar's "I kid you not," Mork's "Nano-nano," and the Fonz's "Aaaaaaaay!" There was a bunch from *Laugh-In,* including Artie Johnson's "Verrrrrrry interesting!" And the ubiquitous "Sock it to me!" Then there is "Heeerrrre's Johnny," Tommy Smothers's "Mom always loved you best," and Charlie Brown's "Good grief," which appeared first in the comic strips but needed television to make it a household term.

27   It can be argued that *yucky* was in use before *Sesame Street,* but that show did for that article of slang what *The A-Team* did for *sucker.* And speaking of *Sesame Street,* it can be argued that this was the instrument by which the term *you guys,* as slang for males and females as opposed to males alone (as in *Guys and Dolls*) became popular. Shows like *Star Trek* created their own vocabulary and left a noun in its wake, *Trekkies,* for those who follow the show.

28   This ability to change the way we speak by electronically transmitted buzzwords and catch phrases is not new. Radio had its impact: "the $64 question" is a permanent part of the language, and people over forty shudder nostalgically with a line like "Gotta straighten out that closet one of these days, Molly." But it is television that has really moved the process into high gear and given it "may-jor mo-tion."

29   If we like them because of the way they are said, we remember them because they are our mental souvenirs, and we hang on to them for the same reason the Smithsonian hangs on to Archie Bunker's chair, the Fonz's jacket, and J. R.'s cowboy hat. Our souvenirs can, in fact, be the least funny element

in a show. For all the great, funny lines from M*A*S*H, what we will all recall, even after the reruns have stopped, is the chilling phrase "Incoming wounded." And scores of funny lines from *All in the Family* have been forgotten by people, like me, who can only remember that Archie called his son-in-law "meathead" and his wife "dingbat."

30   The big question is, Where's the magic? Why do so many of these phrases work? It clearly defies full analysis, but it would appear that timing is terribly important. It is doubtful we all would have been running around saying "Where's the beef?" during the Iranian hostage crisis or during the last days of the Vietnam War. It wouldn't have been an appropriate catch phrase at the time or a verbal souvenir to recall a time of crisis.

31   If you listen carefully, you'll be among the first to catch someone who will have the touch and give us not one hot, new line or phrase, but a whole bunch of them. Looking back, it can be argued that the last great television phrase maker was Jackie Gleason, a man with as many signatures as a second mortgage. "To the moon, Alice," "How sweet it is," "One of these days," "And away we go," were all his. He even had words for the times, in the person of *The Honeymooners'* Ralph Kramden, when he got too nervous to talk: "Hommina, hommina."

32   Television itself is never at a loss for words.

TOPICAL CONSIDERATIONS

1. Now that you've read this piece, what things about slang have you learned? Do you feel that you better understand what it is and how it works? Do you have a greater appreciation for it? Do you feel better about using it? Explain your answers.

2. Dickson says that slang has given us "dozens of terms for drunkenness and insanity that are remarkably gentle." See how many "kind and euphemistic" terms for each you can come up with. Now how many "brutally frank and direct" synonyms can you think of?

3. Dickson says that Valley Girl and CB slang were short lived. Does he say why they never caught on? Can you think of any "Val" or CB terms not mentioned in the essay? Any that people still use?

4. From your experience, do you agree that "farmers produce little slang"? Can you think of any? By contrast, Dickson says that high-school students produce a lot of slang. Did you and your friends have a slang of your own? If so, do you agree that it helped bind and identify your group? Did you use slang that high-school students from different parts of the country used? Can you recall where it might have originated—TV, movies, radio, rap, rock music?

5. Do you feel that Dickson helped you distinguish slang from jargon and dialect? What are the differences? Do the distinctions get blurry for you?

6. Dickson says that television has had a profound influence on the dissemination of slang. What are some of the current "pet phrases" from television? What were the sources? Have any achieved tee-shirt status? Which do you think will last long? Which might pass into standard usage? Which will probably die out soon? Explain your last three answers.

7. Dickson gives examples of slang terms and phrases that have come from television past. Can you think of any "mental souvenirs" from television of your youth?

8. Is there anyone on today's television who has the stuff to rival Jackie Gleason— that is, to create "not one hot, new line or phrase, but a whole bunch of them"? If so, who? And what might be the secret?

RHETORICAL CONSIDERATIONS

1. How does Dickson's choice of titles help establish his attitude toward slang?

2. How many different references does Dickson make to language experts and other outside sources? Why do you suppose he cites them? How do these references add to his discussion?

3. How would you define the author's "voice" here? In what different ways does he establish his attitude toward the subject of slang?

WRITING ASSIGNMENTS

1. Dickson makes the point that there is a kind of tribal quality about slang: it gives a group tightness and identity. He also says that students produce a lot of slang. Drawing from your own experience, write a paper in which you explore the function and use of slang by young people.

2. In paragraph 5, Dickson opens with a question written in street slang, standard English and jargon. Try your own hand at "slanguage" by taking a short newspaper editorial and rewriting it in slang. (If necessary, consult a dictionary of slang.) Now do the same piece in "bureaucratese." (You might want to look at some of the pieces in the previous chapters, in particular the Rawson and Lutz articles— pages 491 and 486, respectively.) What differences have you made in the tone, effect and communicability? Which do you prefer, and why?

ARE ACCENTS OUT? HEY, DUDE, LIKE NEH-OH WAY!

Patrick Cooke

Television may be "the great dispenser" of slang, but, according to Patrick Cooke, it hasn't touched American accents. That's rather surprising since for years people were concerned that all the rich and varied regional dialects would be homogenized or flattened to the standard of network news anchors. In this article the author takes a look at some great American accents—how they hang in there, how they change, how they function to identify one group while shunning others. The social implications of dialects is both amusing and disturbing. Some people pay money to reduce their regional dialects to avoid stereotyping and sound more like Peter Jennings or Diane Sawyer. And, yet, dialect studies show that black and white Americans continue to grow further apart linguistically.

Patrick Cooke is a writer living in San Francisco. This article first appeared in the *New York Times Magazine,* in November 1989.

1   I have never much liked the way I talk. In upstate New York, where I was raised, people said things like "Lemme have a HEE-am SEEN-wich" and "You scared the BEE-JEES-us outa me." It had no grace. Nowhere in our local speech was there the hint of a drawl, or any majestic New England tones, or even a trace of down-state Brooklynese—which can sound almost poetic if you are in the right mood. No, up in the lovely glens of New York we went around loudly meowing through our noses, saying "Everything's gist FEE-an-TEE-astic, FEE-ab-ulos!" and scaring the bejesus out of one another.

2   If American mobility and television have conspired to dilute regional accents, as language critics have been insisting for most of this century, word never reached *my* old hometown. Nor, according to linguists of the American Dialect Society, have accents been much corrupted anywhere else. We are not all beginning to sound the same—despite what some people believe.

3   A couple of years ago, the novelist Thomas Williams wrote that "in the last 30 years I've seen the very speech of my own state, New Hampshire, change gradually toward something like Middle Western standard, as though the last generation learned as much of its tongue from Captain Kangaroo and Johnny

Carson as it did from its parents and grandparents." That's probably easy enough to believe these days. The nation is seemingly becoming more homogenized, and if a Big Mac tastes the same in Hollywood, Fla., as it does in Hollywood, Calif., it is not unreasonable to presume that we all sound like Ronald McDonald.

4   But consider this: A few years ago a cargo handler for Pan-American World Airways named Paul Prinzivalli was suspected of having phoned in bomb threats to the airline's offices in Los Angeles. The charge was based on tapes made of the caller, who, officials thought, had a heavy East Coast accent similar to Prinzivalli's. It wasn't until William Labov, a linguist at the University of Pennsylvania, testified that the caller had a Boston accent—and Prinzivalli had a metropolitan New York accent—that the charges were dropped. "I had to fly out there," says Labov, who has spent nearly 30 years listening to gibbering Americans from coastal Massachusetts to the bone-dry Southwest, "and explain to a room full of Californians that not everybody on the East Coast sounds the same."

5   The truth is, say linguists, that various regions of the country are sounding increasingly different from one another. Yes, certain words have vanished—seldom do you hear a worm called a john-jumper any more. But accents? Hardly.

6   Every American has one. New dialects spring up where they are least expected; familiar ones change continually but remain potent enough to define us or betray us. And we are pegged for our origins every time we do something as innocent as order a ham sandwich.

7   Those origins can be traced back to the day the English carried their bags ashore at Jamestown, Va., in 1607, and at Massachusetts 13 years later. The accent they brought along was part Elizabethan London and part rural speech from counties like Yorkshire and Lancashire. Those sounds—particularly the vowels—became the basis for the American English that was spoken in early Colonial settlements such as Boston, New York City and Charleston.

8   Dialects tend to burrow in these "focal areas," as linguists call such cities of influence, and soon more and more of them began to dot the landscape. In fact, America quickly became something of a shattered mirror of focal areas as waves of ethnic groups began grabbing land and building cities—the Dutch in New York, the Irish and Italians in New England, and the Ulster Scots and Germans in the South (where present-day stresses on words like "IN-surance" and "JU-ly" are relics of Germanic constructions).

9   The American English that began to move west during the 19th century came from the Eastern inland parts of the country—people along the Eastern seaboard did not participate in western migration as readily as those further inland, beach-front property being what it is. The dialect of Southern inland regions such as northern Georgia and the western Carolinas spread as far west as Texas, and established a few new focal areas, like Nashville and Little Rock, Ark., along the way. When this dialect collided with the Spanish influence in the Southwest, it then veered north into the Rockies.

10   "At the same time, there were all kinds of Northerners moving west," says Lee Pederson, a linguist at Emory University who has studied both Northern and Southern accents. "The dialect of Chicago, for example, is purely Northern inland. It came from western New England and Hartford, Conn., and became the basis for what you hear now around Cleveland, Detroit and the Great Lakes."

11   By the time prairie schooners came to a halt at the Pacific Ocean in the mid-1800's, the English they carried was a mixture of sundry Eastern dialects, mingled with foreign influences from the immigrants who were picked up en route. It retained little of its Colonial origins. Then, too, these California settlers discovered that not only had a few coastal Northeasterners beaten them around Cape Horn and planted their own brand of Northern accent in San Francisco and Los Angeles, but they also had claimed most of the good beachfront property.

12   Today's state boundaries—and often even city borders—are all but useless for determining who speaks what. Within Boston, for example, where ethnic communities have remained closely knit, you hear differences between the English spoken by the Italian Americans, Irish Americans and Americans who speak Yiddish. Even outside the East Coast, in those provinces thought to speak only dreary, standard American, regional peculiarities persist. In Pittsburgh, the football team is called the "STILL-ers"; in Idaho, the locals call the capital "BOY-see"; in Wisconsin, the big town by the lake is "Muh-WAUK-ee"; in New Mexico, they say "cheat" for sheet, and in Chicago it seems one Daley or another has always been the "Mare.

13   Dialects change with all the speed of a john-jumper, but they do change. It is quite possible that you do not speak precisely the way your grandfather does, although you both grew up on the same street. Linguists used to record those slight generational dissimilarities and then lament the demise of a regional dialect. Starting in the 1960's, however, socio-linguists began wondering why sounds change at all, and whether there might be some clues to social behavior behind the variances.

14   In 1963, for example,William Labov discovered that there were two distinct ways of speaking among year-round residents of Martha's Vineyard off the coast of Massachusetts—though it all sounded Yankee to outsiders. The older residents, who planned to remain on the island, had somehow reinforced their dialect as a way of distancing themselves from the mainlanders, who had begun buying up large portions of the island. The younger residents, who planned to leave the island, spoke more like the mainlanders than the people who had raised them.

15   Just as the islanders perceived outsiders as a threat to local life, so too, it appears, have established groups in the large cities viewed the wave of new ethnic groups—blacks, Hispanics, and Asians—that have flooded into their communities since World War II. Using dialect has been one way of circling the wagons.

16   "Many of the things that people struggle for in this world, particularly jobs and houses, they achieve through their connections within the local commu-

nity," says Labov. Language changes are often a defensive reaction against newcomers who seem to threaten these rights and privileges.

17   Sometimes these changes come in the form of new vocabulary; more often, linguists have learned, it is the vowel sounds that are affected. In the mid-1970s, Labov began studying the Northern dialect region from New England to the Great Lakes. He recorded the range of speech across three generations, and compared his findings with earlier linguistic surveys from the 1940's. He was startled to discover that a wholesale shifting of the short vowel sounds had occurred.

18   The shift essentially worked this way: Imagine that the numbers on the face of a clock are replaced by vowels. Whether because of a defensive reaction to new groups entering the territory or some other unknown factors, the vowel *a* at 1 o'clock begins crowding the vowel *e* at 2 o'clock. That then begins nudging *i* and so on, until the whole face has shifted slightly.

19   Linguists are uncertain why the chain reaction begins at a particular vowel, but in the North—especially in Chicago, Detroit, Cleveland, Buffalo, Rochester and my old hometown—they found that among many speakers the word "John" was now pronounced "Jan." The word "Ann" had become "Ian," and the word "ham" had somehow wandered over into "Lemme have a HEE-am SEEN-wich."

20   Meanwhile, other shifts were discovered elsewhere in the East, but with different sets of vowels pressuring one another. In Philadelphia, "crayon" and "crown" were both said as "crayon"; "bounce" and "balance" both came out as "balance." In the Southern states, "pen" and "pin" had become homophonous. So cramped were other Southern vowels that people had begun to break words like "bed" into two syllables: "BEE-id."

21   Researchers found that these shifts in pronunciation generally behave like a slow-moving virus. Occasionally, though, the speed picks up dramatically. "In 1976 in Eastern Pennsylvania, we found that 5 percent of the kids we studied had merged the words 'caught' and 'cot' so that both were said as 'cot,'" says Labov. "Last year we went back and found that 80 percent are now doing it."

22   As accents continue to evolve, certain regions, principally the North and South, are finding it progressively difficult to understand one another. For example, when Labov's research team played a tape recording of a Chicago speaker to 40 lifelong residents of Birmingham, Ala., the sentence "He hadda wear socks" was interpreted correctly by only two people. The rest guessed that he said "He hadda wear slacks" or maybe it was "sacks." The sentence "When we had the busses with the antennas on the top" sounded for all the world to some Alabamans like "When we had the bosses Whitney antennas on the top."

23   There was another surprising, and disturbing, discovery. In none of these areas have lower-class blacks adopted the regional dialect changes. "One of the things we found, to our astonishment, was how similar black speech is throughout the country," says Labov. The reason, researchers say, is that while white middle-class residents of these areas look to the local community for

their rewards, blacks, long denied those local rewards, view themselves as a national group with national aspirations. The result, says Labov, is that blacks and whites continue to grow further apart in the way each group speaks the language.

24   Some Americans, hoping perhaps to identify with a particular group—or conversely, to not be identified with a group—are desperate to purge any trace of their origins. And who could blame them? We are all instinctively aware of the stereotypes that arise the moment a person begins to speak. When television needs a hick with a heart of gold, it looks southward for a twangy moron like Ernest, the comedian of commercial fame: "Hey, Vern!" When a cold-hearted killer is called for, it's a Brooklynese speaker croaking "youse guys"—a surviving Irish pronunciation that New York City Mayor David Dinkins would like to hear shifted into oblivion.

25   Beverly Inman-Ebel, a speech pathologist in Chattanooga, Tenn., has spent the last seven years teaching Southerners—housewives and beauty queens, businessmen and politicians—how to reduce their regional dialects. "People come to me seeking a voice that doesn't stand out," she says. "When I ask clients whom they admire and would love to sound like, the men say Ronald Reagan and the women say Diane Sawyer."

26   For $75 to $175 an hour, Inman-Ebel helps clients untangle features of the Southern vowel shift, making "ten" and "tin" two separate vowels again. Sounding regional, she says, is increasingly a barrier to success. "One company just sent me three executives for accent reduction," she says. "One of them will become the C.E.O. How they speak is certainly not the only criterion for the promotion, but it is a factor."

27   Still, despite the best efforts of speech pathologists, most of us are pretty much stuck with our accents by the time we reach the age of 13. With that in mind, think of how often you've heard a 16-year-old say, "Hey, dude, like NEH-oh way!" Spooky, isn't it?

28   A couple of years ago, James W. Hartman, a linguist at the University of Kansas, started wondering about these sounds that teenagers make. He had heard Moon Unit Zappa's gag-me-with-a-spoon routine, which parodied the way kids talk in the San Fernando Valley, about 1,500 miles west in Los Angeles County. Why was he hearing something disturbingly similar in the high school halls and shopping malls of Lawrence, Kan.? In Shakespeare's time, a fist fight between two boys might have started with the words "I yuke to pringle with you!" Now, it was something closer to "Yer rilly gonna fill, like, SEH-oh bad in a minute, man." Could English still be on the correct evolutionary path?

29   Hartman first detected this phenomenon in 1983, while doing research for the Dictionary of American Regional English. He noticed that some young people were using certain vowel sounds that were not features of the areas where they grew up.

30   "The most mystifying aspect of all is why some sounds are chosen and others are not," says Hartman of the new accent, which appears to be a mix of var-

ious Northern and Southern dialects. "It's almost as though these kids all sat down at a meeting and agreed that these are the features we're going to use."

31   The "fronted O" sound, for example, which comes out as GEH-oh and NEH-oh, had long been a feature in the Baltimore area, but Hartman observed that something happened when it was picked up by kids in the Los Angeles area, kids who had no connection whatever to Baltimore. They added it to, among other things, a softening of vowels that fall before the letter *l* (words like "sale" were being pronounced "sell").

32   Hartman's research, still in its preliminary stages, has shown that the young people making these new noises appear to be between 16 and 25 years old; they typically come from upwardly mobile families and are college bound. That would make this latest phenomenon more of a social dialect—much like the Boston Brahmin accent—than a regional dialect.

33   In fact, what's most remarkable about the new dialect is how widespread it has become. Strongest in Southern California, where it seems to have started, the dialect apparently traveled across the United States from west to east roughly along Route 70. It is the first American dialect ever to move in that direction, which has prompted the name Sun-Belt Speak. But so far, the engine pumping it through young channels remains something of a mystery.

34   The influence of television has mostly been ruled out, simply because TV has little, if any, effect on an accent. "Peer pressure, school, or anything you have an involvement in affects language—not television," says Donna Christian, director of the research division at the Center for Applied Linguistics in Washington. "What matters is who will judge you or whom you're trying to impress in some way. There's no reason to become more like the television."

35   There's probably nothing to fear from Sun-Belt Speak. It will prove no better at uprooting entrenched regional accidents than Johnny Carson has been. Like any other new dialect that has passed over the continent in the last four centuries, a vowel here or a word there may survive. But in 80 years, these, too, will become but a faint addition to the drawls and quacks we hear around us. Right?

36   "I don't have a clue," says Hartman. "But I will say that since I started looking into this, people have sent me tapes from all over the country, and Sun-Belt Speak is more widespread than I'd first thought. It has appeared in northern Ohio and southern Florida, for example. I wouldn't even be surprised if it showed up soon in a place like, say, upstate New York."

TOPICAL CONSIDERATIONS

1. Before you read this essay, had you given much thought to your accent? Did you even think you spoke with one? How would you describe it? Is it a particular regional dialect, a social one, or a little of each? Does it show any particular ethnic or racial influence? Do you like your accent? Why or why not?

2. Have you ever tried to hide your dialect? If so, what were the circumstances? Have you ever reinforced your dialect so as to shun outsiders? If so, describe the reasons. If not, could you imagine yourself doing so? Under what circumstances?

3. What are the implications in the discovery that blacks throughout the nation do not adopt regional dialect changes? Do these implications ring true to you? Can you think of exceptions? How about the opposite phenomenon—that is, whites picking up black dialect? What have you observed? What do you make of that?

4. Were you surprised to learn that in parts of the country people pay high fees to reduce their accents? Explain your reaction. Could you imagine doing the same? Why or why not?

5. In the preceding piece, "It Ain't No Big Thing," Paul Dickson tells how powerful the influence of television is on the success of slang. According to Cooke how does television influence accents? From your own experience, does that strike you as an accurate assessment? What forces seem to have greatest influence on accents according to experts? Does that jive with your experience?

6. Does Paul Dickson's distinction of dialect from slang agree with what you've read here? How would he classify *john-jumper* and other such terms? Can you think of other expressions that are used only in certain areas?

RHETORICAL CONSIDERATIONS

1. What do you think of the title of Cooke's essay? Does it seem appropriate to the subject matter and the author's attitude?

2. What do you think of the author's technique of opening his essay with statements about his own accent. How does this serve to set the tone and purpose of the piece?

3. What parts of this essay did you find most interesting? Did any part seem to drag for you? If so, where, and what is the difference between the two parts?

4. Did you think the author gave enough examples of dialects? Would you like to have seen more? less?

WRITING ASSIGNMENTS

1. Have you ever been in a situation where you felt self-conscious about the way you speak? Did others shun you because of your accent? Did you feel discriminated against? Did you try to suppress your accent? If so, try to capture in an essay the circumstances, feelings, and reasons for your self-consciousness.

2. Do you like the way you talk? Write an essay in which you describe and evaluate your accent. What do you like about it? What do you not like about it? Have you worked at changing it any? Could you imagine any circumstances that would move you to hire a speech coach to change it? Explain your reasons.

3. Cooke makes the point that people make value judgments about dialects—judgments sometimes created by stereotypes. Are there some accents you just cannot stand? If so, what are they, and why do you not like them? What stereotypes and attitudes might your feelings be rooted in?

4. In paragraphs 17–21, the author talks about shifts in vowels. Have you noticed such shifts in your community? Maybe you can test the vowel shift by polling people on how they pronounce words such as *ham, John, crayon, crown, bounce, pen,* and others. Then run the same test on older people of your community. When

you have gathered your data, write a report on your findings. Look over what Cooke reports about the shift in vowels in parts of the country. What conclusions can you make about your findings?

5. Do you think that a national TV news anchor could be successful if he or she had a strong regional dialect—that is, spoke, say, with a twang or drawl or in Brooklynese? Or, is there an unwritten rule that news people have to speak anchor-talk to maintain ratings? Write a paper in which you explore your thoughts on these questions.

LIKE, UPTALK?

James Gorman

There's a new way of talking. It's subtle, but you've heard it. You may even practice it. It started with teenagers and was quickly adopted by twentysomethings; but like many nonstandard language phenomena, it has moved into the mainstream. And it's beginning to get to people like James Gorman who offers here some humorous insights on *uptalk*— like, its possible origins, significance, and consequences?

James Gorman teaches journalism at New York University. This article first appeared in the *New York Times,* in August 1993.

1   I used to speak in a regular voice. I was able to assert, demand, question. Then I started teaching. At a university? And my students had this rising intonation thing? It was particularly noticeable on telephone messages. "Hello? Professor Gorman? This is Albert? From feature writing?"

2   I had no idea that a change in the "intonation contour" of a sentence, as linguists put it, could be as contagious as the common cold. But before long I noticed a Jekyll-and-Hyde transformation in my own speech. I first heard it when I myself was leaving a message. "This is Jim Gorman? I'm doing an article on Klingon? The language? From *Star Trek*?" I realized then that I was unwittingly, unwillingly speaking uptalk.

3   I was, like, appalled?

4   Rising intonations at the end of a sentence or phrase are not new. In many languages, a "phrase final rise" indicates a question. Some Irish, English and Southern American dialects use rises all the time. Their use at the end of a declarative statement may date back in America to the 17th century.

5   Nonetheless, we are seeing, well, hearing, something different. Uptalk, under various names, has been noted on this newspaper's Op-Ed page and on National Public Radio. Cynthia McLemore, a University of Pennsylvania linguist who knows as much about uptalk as anyone, says the frequency and repetition of rises mark a new phenomenon. And although uptalk has been most common among teen-agers, in particular young women, it seems to be spreading. Says McLemore, "What's going on now in America looks like a dialect shift." In other words, what is happening may be a basic change in the way Americans talk.

6   Nobody knows exactly where uptalk came from. It might have come from California, from Valley Girl talk. It may be an upper-middle-class thing, probably starting with adolescents. But everybody has an idea about what uptalk

means. Some twentysomethings say uptalk is part of their attitude: cool, ironic, uncommitted.

7   I myself was convinced that uptalk was tentative, testing, oversensitive; not feminine so much as wimpy, detumescent. Imagine how it would sound in certain cocksure, authoritative occupations, like police work:

You're under arrest? You have some rights?

Or surgery:

So, first I'll open up your chest?

8   I also thought how some of the great dead white males of the much maligned canon might sound, reintoned:

It was really dark? Like, on the deep? The face of the deep?

Or:

Hi, I'm Ishmael? I'll be your narrator?

Or:

A horse? A horse? My kingdom for a horse?

9   My speculations have some support; there are linguists who see uptalk as being about uncertainty and deference to the listener. But McLemore scoffs at these ideas. People tend to hear what they want to hear, she says. One can, for instance, take a speech pattern common among women and link it to a stereotype of women. (Uncertain? Deferential?)

10   Deborah Tannen—a linguist at Georgetown, who, with her book *You Just Don't Understand: Women and Men in Conversation,* may have overtaken Noam Chomsky and become the best-known linguist in America—contends that broad theorizing about uptalk is downright foolish. Speech patterns are contagious, she says, and they spread the way fads do. "There's a fundamental human impulse to imitate what we hear," she says. "Teen-agers talk this way because other teen-agers talk this way and they want to sound like their peers."

11   That doesn't mean rises have no function. They can be used as a signal that "more is coming," says Mark Aronoff of the State University of New York at Stony Brook. An adolescent might be signaling "I have more to say; don't interrupt me." McLemore says an early study of telephone conversation suggested that rises may be used as a probe of sorts, to see if the hearer is getting what you are saying.

12   A friend of mine (of no formal linguistic expertise) likes this latter interpretation. He insists that the spread of uptalk indicates the lack of shared knowledge in our society. Our society, he contends, has become so fragmented that no one knows anymore whether another person will have a clue as to what he's saying. We need to test the hearer's level of understanding.

13   *Like, suppose I want to talk about Sabicas? Or Charles Barkley? Or nitric oxide? The molecule of the year? For 1992?*

14   By using the questioning tone, I'm trying to see if my conversational partner knows anything at all about flamenco guitar, professional basketball or neurochemistry.

15   McLemore studied intonation in one very particular context. She observed uses of intonation in a Texas sorority, where uptalk was not at all about uncertainty or deference. It was used most commonly by the leaders, the senior officers. Uptalk was a kind of accent, or tag, to highlight new information for listeners: "We're having a bake sale? On the west mall? On Sunday?" When saying something like "Everyone should know that your dues should be in," they used a falling intonation at the end of the sentence.

16   The sorority members' own interpretation of uptalk was that it was a way of being inclusive. McLemore's conclusions are somewhat similar. She says the rises are used to connect phrases, and to connect the speaker to the listener, as a means of "getting the other person involved."

17   Since McLemore did her study, people are constantly calling to her attention other uses of uptalk. It seems to be a common speech pattern in Toronto, where, she says, a radio show called "Ask the Pastors" displays uptalk in spades. She also found that on another radio show the Mayor of Austin, Tex., used rises to mark items in a list. Asked to explain why he should maintain bike paths, he said things like: Austin has a good climate? It's good for bike riding? McLemore also observed a second-grade teacher who used rises freely for commands and statements: "Jason? Back to your chair? Thank you?"

18   I confess to ambivalence about uptalk. When I use it, I judge it to mark a character flaw. On the other hand, there are some ritual utterances that could clearly benefit from a change in pitch contour.

19   *Mea culpa? Mea culpa? Mea maxima culpa?*

20   Or, to reflect the true state of matrimony in our society:

21   *I do?*

22   I do not, however, want the speech pattern to spread to airplane pilots. I don't want to hear: *This is Captain McCormick? Your pilot? We'll be flying to Denver? Our cruising altitude will be, like, 30,000 feet?*

23   McLemore, however, says it seems possible that we will be hearing such an intonation among pilots in the future. After all, it looks as if pilots are getting younger every year. Once commercial airline pilots start using uptalk, McLemore notes, it will mean that a full-blown dialect shift has occurred. Uptalk won't be uptalk anymore. It will be, like, American English?

TOPICAL CONSIDERATIONS

1. How does Gorman define *uptalk?* Are you familiar with the phenomenon? If so, do you or any of your acquaintances speak in uptalk? From your observations, would you agree that uptalk is on the rise? Explain.

2. In his opening paragraph, Gorman differentiates speech functions: assertions, demands, and questions. In your own words, explain each of these functions. How might they be "equalized" with the new shift to uptalk? Is this shift, in your opinion, ultimately damaging to effective communication? Why or why not?

3. According to Gorman, what are the possible origins of uptalk? With what social group does he associate its most common use? Does your experience support his claim?

4. How, according to some, might uptalk serve to reinforce certain stereotypical ideas of female behavior and speech? Does Gorman agree with this association? Do you agree? Explain.

5. What are some other possible explanations for the rise of uptalk? Which theory do you think best explains this "dialect shift"? Use specific examples from the essay in your response.

6. In paragraph 12 Gorman discusses the link between the advent of uptalk and the fragmented nature of contemporary society. Summarize, in your own words, the argument being made here. In what ways do you think our society is becoming more fragmented? Do you agree with this hypothesis regarding the usefulness of uptalk? Explain.

7. In his concluding paragraph, Gorman notes that the adoption of uptalk by mainstream America will signal a "full-blown dialect shift," a shift that will make uptalk just another feature of "American English." Do you think uptalk will ever become part of mainstream American English? Explain your answer.

RHETORICAL CONSIDERATIONS

1. Consider Gorman's introductory paragraph. Is it effective in gaining the reader's interest? Is there any confusion about the subject of the essay? Did the title help? Explain.

2. Given that the phenomenon of uptalk is an oral one, how well does Gorman translate it into the essay? Are you able to "hear" what he is talking about? Do his examples throughout serve as effective "translations"? Explain.

3. Gorman attempts a sort of history and theory of uptalk. Does he provide enough evidence for his claims as to its origins and usage? Point to specific places in the text where his evidence is either adequate or too thin.

4. Gorman changes point of view (person) several times, especially in the second half of the piece. Why does he do this? Is it an effective rhetorical strategy for this particular article? Why or why not?

5. Did you find this piece informative, amusing, or both? or neither? Explain your answer, referring to specific details from the essay.

WRITING ASSIGNMENTS

1. Gorman says that teenagers and "twentysomethings" are the most frequent users of uptalk. Conduct an interview with other students at your school to determine their familiarity and interpretation of uptalk. Write a paper exploring your findings. Try to determine if different demographic groups have different responses. Also, what different theories do your respondents have as to the cause and meaning of uptalk? Try to determine what the differences are, based on respondents' background, gender, race, and so on.

2. Do the above assignment, but interview people about other characteristics of teenage or twentysomething speech, such as the meaning of particular slang terms.

3. Gorman rewrites the openings of classics such as *Moby Dick.* Pick a famous literary work (or famous lines of poetry, drama, or fiction) and "rewrite" it (or them) making strategic use of uptalk.

4. Write a paper in which you question the idea of "standard English." What is standard English? Who determines the standards? What kind of groups or dialects fall outside of this standard, and what are the consequences of this? What are some of the dangers of imposing a language standard on a population as diverse as that of the United States?

5. Write a paper in which you examine the effects of certain dialects on the perceptions of its speakers. How are stereotypes created through the use of dialects? What effects do such stereotypes have on both their objects and those who subscribe to them?

CREDITS

CARTOON CREDITS

Page 1 Sidney Harris

Page 59 Sidney Harris

Page 95 Drawing by Roz Chast. Copyright © The New Yorker Magazine.

Page 183 Drawing by P. Steiner. Copyright © The New Yorker Magazine.

Page 247 Reprinted with special permission of King Features Syndicate.

Page 309 Dan Wasserman/Boston Globe, copyright © 1988. Distributed by the Los Angeles Times Syndicate. Reprinted with permission.

Page 395 David Miller. All rights reserved. Reprinted with permission of Tribune Media Services.

Page 483 Hilary B. Price. All rights reserved. Reprinted with permission of King Features Syndicate.

Page 519 Sidney Harris

TEXT CREDITS

Susanne K. Langer, "Language and Thought," from "The Lord of Creation," *Fortune,* January 1044. Reprinted by permission.

Steven Pinker, "Language Instinct," from *The Language Instinct.* Copyright © 1994 by Steven Pinker. Reprinted by permission of William Morrow & Company, Inc.

Paul Roberts, "A Brief History of English," from *Understanding English.* Copyright © 1958 by Paul Roberts. Copyright renewed. Reprinted by permission of Addison-Wesley Educational Publishers.

Eudora Welty, "Wordstruck." Reprinted by permission of the publishers, from *One Writer's Beginnings* by Eudora Welty. Cambridge, Mass.: Harvard University Press. Copyright © 1983, 1984 by Eudora Welty.

Malcolm X, "Homemade Education," from *The Autobiography of Malcolm X.* Copyright © 1964 by Alex Haley and Malcolm X. Copyright © 1965 by Alex Haley and Betty Shabazz. Reprinted by permission of Random House, Inc.

Johnny Connors, "The Man That Spelt *Knife* Was a Fool." Reprinted from *Gypsies* by Jeremy Sanford and Johnny Connors. Every effort has been made to locate the copyright holder of this selection. A suitable fee for this use has been reserved by the publisher.

Maxine Hong Kingston, "The Language of Silence," from *The Woman Warrior.* Copyright © 1975, 1976 by Maxine Hong Kingston. Reprinted by permission of Alfred A Knopf, Inc.

Edite Cunha Pedrosa, "Talking in the New Land." Excerpt reprinted from *New England Monthly,* August 1990, by permission of the author.

Peter Elbow, "Freewriting," from *Writing Without Teachers*. Copyright © 1975 by Peter Elbow. Used by permission of Oxford University Press, Inc.

William Zinsser, "Simplicity," from *On Writing Well*, 4th ed. Copyright © 1976, 1980, 1985, 1988, 1990. Reprinted by permission of the author.

Kurt Vonnegut, "How to Write with Style." Copyright © 1982 by International Paper Company. Reprinted by permission of International Paper Company.

Newman P. Birk and Genevieve B. Birk, "Selection, Slanting, and Charged Language," from *Understanding and Using Language*, 5th ed. Copyright © 1972 by Macmillan Publishing Company. Reprinted by permission of Macmillan Publishing Company.

Donald M. Murray, "The Maker's Eye: Revising Your Own Manuscript," *The Writer*, October 1973. Copyright © 1973 by Donald M. Murray. Reprinted by permissions of the author and Roberta Pryor, Inc.

Richard Wilbur, "The Writer," from *The Mind Reader*. Copyright © 1971 by Richard Wilbur. Reprinted by permission of Harcourt Brace & Company.

John Leo, "Journalese as a Second Tongue." Copyright © 1984 by Time Inc. Reprinted by permission.

Neil Postman and Steve Powers, "TV News: All the World in Pictures," from *How to Watch TV News*. Copyright © 1992 by Neil Postman and Steve Powers. Used by permission of Viking Penguin, a division of Penguin Books USA, Inc.

Dave Barry, "In Depth, but Shallowly," from *Dave Barry's Bad Habits,* Holt Rinehart and Winston, 1987. Reprinted by permission.

Tom Shachtman, "Dumbing Down: TV Talk-Show Talk," from *The Inarticulate Society: Eloquence and Culture in America*. Reprinted with the permission of The Free Press, a division of Simon and Schuster. Copyright © 1995 by Tom Shachtman.

Charles G. Russell and Paul Many, "Collective Bias," from "How Language Collectives Comprise Journalistic Accuracy," *Et Cetera,* Spring 1994.

Caryl Rivers, "Read All About It! (But Don't Believe It)," from "The Bias of Language, the Bias of Pictures," *The Boston Globe*, May 1996.

Edward S. Herman, "Terrorism: Civilized and Barbaric." Reprinted by permission of the author.

"Two-Headed Monsters," from the *Columbia Journalism Review*. Reprinted by permission.

William Lutz, "With These Words I Can Sell You Anything," from *Doublespeak,* by William Lutz. Copyright © 1989 by Blonde Bear, Inc. Reprinted by permission of HarperCollins Publishers, Inc.

Charles A. O'Neill, "The Language of Advertising." Revised version copyright © 1997 by Charles A. O'Neill. Reprinted by permission of the author.

George F. Will, "Printed Noise." Copyright © 1993, The Washington Post Writers Group. Reprinted with permission.

Diane White, "Euphemisms for the Fat of the Land," *The Boston Globe*, September 8, 1982. Reprinted courtesy of The Boston Globe.

Patricia Volk, "A Word from Our Sponsor," *New York Times Magazine*, August 23, 1987. Reprinted by permission of The New York Times Company.

"How to Detect Propaganda," from Institute for Propaganda Analysis. Every effort has been made to locate the copyright holder of this selection. A suitable fee for this use has been reserved by the publisher.

George Orwell, "Politics and the English Language," from *Shooting an Elephant and Other Essays* by George Orwell. Copyright © 1946 by Sonia Brownell Orwell and renewed 1974 by Sonia Orwell. Reprinted by permission of Harcourt Brace & Company.

Anthony Lewis, "Words Matter," *New York Times Magazine*, May 3, 1995. Reprinted by permission of The New York Times Company.

John Yoakum, "Everyspeech," *New York Times*, November 2, 1994. Reprinted by permission of The New York Times Company.

e. e. cummings, "next to of course god america i," from *Complete Poems: 1904–1962*, edited by George J. Firmage. Copyright © 1926, 1954, © 1991 by the Trustees for the e. e. cummings Trust. Copyright © 1985 by George James Firmage. Reprinted by permission of Liveright Publishing Corporation.

Haig A. Bosmajian, "Dehumanizing People and Euphemizing War," from *The Christian Century*, December 5, 1984. Reprinted by permission.

Carol Cohn, "Wars, Wimps and Women: Talking Gender and Thinking War," from *Gendering War*. Copyright © 1993 Princeton University Press. Reprinted by permission.

Bella English, "When Words Go to War," *The Boston Globe*, February 27, 1992. Reprinted courtesy of The Boston Globe.

Arthur Asa Berger, "Eleven Ways of Looking at the Gulf War," *Et cetera*, Summer 1994. Reprinted by permission of the author.

S. I. Hayakawa, "Bilingualism in America: English Should Be the *Only* Language," *USA Today Magazine*, July, 1989. Copyright © 1989 by the Society for the Advancement of Education.

James Fallows, "Viva Bilingualism," *The New Republic*, November 24, 1986. Reprinted by permission.

Richard Rodriguez, "Aria: A Memoir of a Bilingual Childhood," *The American Scholar*. Copyright © 1980 by Richard Rodriguez. Reprinted by permission of the author.

David Updike, "Coloring Lessons," *New York Times Magazine*, July 31, 1994. Reprinted by permission of The New York Times Company.

Ellen Goodman, "African and American," *The Boston Globe*, 1988. Copyright © 1988 The Boston Globe Newspaper Company/Washington Post Writers Group. Reprinted with permission.

John Yemma, "Innocent and Presumed Ethnic," *The Boston Globe*, 1994. Copyright © 1994 The Boston Globe Newspaper Company/Washington Post Writers Group. Reprinted with permission.

Langston Hughes, "Theme for English B," from *Collected Poems* by Langston Hughes. Copyright © 1994 by the Estate of Langston Hughes. Reprinted by permission of Alfred A Knopf, Inc.

Geneva Smitherman, "From Africa to the New World and into the Space Age," *Talkin and Testifyin*, by Geneva Smitherman, 1986. Reprinted by permission of the Wayne State University Press.

Rachel L. Jones, "What's Wrong with Black English," *Newsweek*, December 27, 1982. Copyright © 1982 by Rachel Jones. Reprinted by permission of the author.

Rosalie Maggio, "Bias-Free Language: Some Guidelines," from *The Dictionary of Bias-Free*

Usage: A Guide to Nondiscriminatory Language by Rosalie Maggio. Copyright © 1991 by Rosalie Maggio. Published by The Oryx Press. Used by permission of Rosalie Maggio and The Oryx Press, (800) 279-6799.

Michiko Kakutani, "The Word Police," *New York Times Magazine,* January 31, 1993. Reprinted by permission of The New York Times Company.

Gloria Naylor, "'Nigger': The Meaning of a Word," *New York Times Magazine,* February 20, 1986. Reprinted by permission of The New York Times Company.

Thomas Friedmann, "Heard Any Good Jews Lately?" from *Speaking of Words* by James MacKillop and Donna Woolfolk Cross, Holt Rineholt and Winston 1982, copyright © Thomas Freedman. Used by permission of the author.

Charles F. Berlitz, "The Etymology of the International Insult." Reprinted from *Penthouse* Magazine. Copyright © 1970. Reprinted by permission of the author and *Penthouse* Magazine.

Haig A. Bosmajian, "Defining the 'American Indian': A Case Study in the Language of Suppression," from *The Speech Teacher,* March 1973. Reprinted by permission of the Speech Communication Association and the author.

Nancy Mairs, "On Being a Cripple." Excerpt from *Plaintext* by Nancy Mairs. Reprinted by permission of The University of Arizona Press.

Lillian Faderman, "Queer," *The Boston Globe,* July 28, 1991. Reprinted by permission of the author.

Jennifer A. Coleman, "Discrimination at Large," from "My Turn," *Newsweek,* August 1993. Copyright © 1993 Newsweek, Inc. All rights reserved. Reprinted by permission.

Wole Soyinka, "Telephone Conversation." Reprinted by permission of the author.

Sandra Flahive Maurer, "Mind Your Tongue, Young Man," *Newsweek.* Copyright © 1993 Newsweek, Inc. All rights reserved. Reprinted by permission.

Dr. Joyce Brothers, "What 'Dirty Words' Really Mean," *Good Housekeeping,* May 1973. Reprinted by permission of the Hearst Corporation.

Charles R. Lawrence III, "Regulating Racist Speech on Campus," *The Chronicle of Higher Education,* October 25, 1989. Reprinted by permission of the author.

Nat Hentoff, "Free Speech on Campus," *The Progressive,* May 1989. Reprinted by permission of the author.

Alleen Pace Nilsen, "Sexism in English: A 1990s Update," in Eschholz, Rose, and Clark, *Language Awareness,* St. Martin's Press, 1994. Reprinted by permission of the author.

Spiro T. Agnew, "English Anyone?" *Conservative Digest,* May 1989. Reprinted by permission.

Jack Rosenthal, "Gender Benders," *New York Times,* August 10, 1986. Reprinted by permission of The New York Times Company.

Lani Guinier, "Life as a Female Gentleman," *The Boston Globe,* January 1994. Reprinted by permission of the C. Sheedy Lit. Agency.

Eugene R. August, "Real Men Don't: Anti-Male Bias in English." Copyright © Eugene R. August. Reprinted by permission.

Ronald Macaulay, "Sex Differences," from *The Social Art: Language and Its Uses.* Copyright © 1996 by Ronald Macaulay. Used by permission of Oxford University Press, Inc.

Deborah Tannen, "'I'll Explain It to You': Lecturing and Listening." Copyright © 1990 Deborah Tannen, Ph.D. Reprinted by permission of William Morrow & Company, Inc.

Nathan Cobb, "Gender Wars in Cyberspace," *The Boston Globe*. Reprinted courtesy of The Boston Globe.

Ernest Hemingway, "Hills Like White Elephants," reprinted with permission of Scribner, a Division of Simon & Schuster, from *Men Without Women* by Ernest Hemingway. Copyright © 1927 Charles Scribner's Sons. Copyright renewed 1955 by Ernest Hemingway.

Mary Jo Meadow, "Is God Purple?" Copyright © 1987 by Mary Jo Meadow. Reprinted by permission from Rosalie Maggio, *The Nonsexist Word Finder*, Oryx Press, 1987.

"The Creation of Man and Woman," excerpted from Genesis in the Revised Standard Version of the Bible, copyright © 1946, 1952, 1971, 1973. Reprinted by permission of the National Council of the Churches of Christ in the U.S.A.

"God Creates Humankind," excerpt from Genesis in *An Inclusive Language Lectionary: Readings for Year A*, Copyright © 1983 by the Division of Education and Ministry of the National Council of the Churches of Christ in the U.S.A., used by permission.

Michael Golden, "Don't Rewrite the Bible," *Newsweek*, November 7, 1983. Copyright © 1983 by Michael Golden. Reprinted by permission of the author.

William Lutz, "Doubts About Doublespeak," *State Government News*, July 1993, Vol. 36, No. 7, pp. 22-24. Copyright © 1993 by The Council of State Governments. Reprinted with permission from *State Government News*.

Hugh Rawson, "Euphemisms," reprinted from *A Dictionary of Euphemisms and Other Doubletalk* by Hugh Rawson. Copyright © 1981 by Hugh Rawson. Used by permission of Crown Publishers, Inc.

Nathan Cobb, *"Talking* DOWN," *The Boston Globe*. Reprinted courtesy of *The Boston Globe*.

Diane Johnson, "Doctor Talk," from Leonard Michaels and Christopher Ricks, eds., *The State of the Language*. Copyright © 1980 The Regents of the University of California. Reprinted by permission of University of California Press.

George Gordon Coughlin, "It May Not Be English, but It's Strictly Legal." Reprinted from *Parade* Magazine, Copyright © 1976, by permission of *Parade* Magazine and the author.

Russell Baker, "Little Red Riding Hood Revisited" *New York Times Magazine*, January 13, 1980. Reprinted by permission of The New York Times Company.

Bill Bryson, "Good English and Bad," excerpt from *The Mother Tongue* by Bill Bryson. Copyright © 1990 by Bill Bryson. Reprinted by permission of William Morrow & Company, Inc.

John Simon, "Why Good English Is Good for You," reprinted from *Paradigms Lost* by John Simon. Copyright © 1976, 1977, 1978, 1979, 1980 by John Simon. Used by permission of Clarkson N. Potter, Inc.

Jim Quinn, "Simonspeak," pp. 30-38, from *American Tongue and Cheek* by Jim Quinn. Copyright © 1981 by Jim Quinn. Reprinted by permission of Pantheon Books, a division of Random House, Inc.

Paul Dickson, "It Ain't No Big Thing," pp. xiii-xxi, from *Slang!* by Paul Dickson. Reprinted by permission of Simon & Schuster, Inc.

Patrick Cooke, "Are Accents Out? Hey Dude, Like NEH-oh Way!" *New York Times Magazine*, November 19, 1989. Reprinted by permission of The New York Times Company.

James Gorman, "Like, Uptalk?" *New York Times Magazine*, August 15, 1993. Reprinted by permission of The New York Times Company.

INDEX OF AUTHORS AND TITLES